Modern Media Literacy:

Generative AI, Social Media, and the News

Tom Hallaq
Kansas State University, USA

Jacob Groshek
Kansas State University, USA

IGI Global
Scientific Publishing
Publishing Tomorrow's Research Today

Vice President of Editorial	Melissa Wagner
Director of Acquisitions	Mikaela Felty
Director of Book Development	Jocelynn Hessler
Production Manager	Mike Brehm
Cover Design	Jose Rosado

Published in the United States of America by
IGI Global Scientific Publishing
701 East Chocolate Avenue
Hershey, PA, 17033, USA
Tel: 717-533-8845
Fax: 717-533-7115
Website: https://www.igi-global.com E-mail: cust@igi-global.com

Library of Congress Cataloging-in-Publication Data

LCCN: 2025008252 (CIP Data Pending)
ISBN13: 9798337308722
Isbn13Softcover: 9798337308739
EISBN13: 9798337308746

British Cataloguing in Publication Data
A Cataloguing in Publication record for this book is available from the British Library.

List of Reviewers

Ann Marie Ade Embry-Riddle, *Aeronautical University, USA*
Julia Bihl, *Université Catholique de Louvain, Belgium*
Francesca Cubeddu, *IRPPS-CNR, Italy*
Basil Osayin Daudu Kogi, *State University, Nigeria*
Meghalee Das, *James Madison University, USA*
Lesley Farmer, *California State University, USA*
Pierre Fastrez, *Université Catholique de Louvain, Belgium*
Janice Fernandes, *University of West London, UK*
Ranita Ganguly, *3D Technologies LLC, USA*
Esther Haineaux, *University of Namur, Belgium*
Marko Haralović, *Zagreb, Croatia*
Abduljalil Hazaea, *Najran University, Saudi Arabia*
Charlotte Im, *University College London, UK*
Lalit Kumar, *Clardentity Learning and Development International, India*
Man Luo, *Bowling Green State University, USA*
Lauren Maher, *Texas Tech University, USA*
Barney McCoy, *University of Nebraska at Lincoln, USA*
Utsav Murari, *Manipal University Jaipur, India*
Hemlata Parmar, *Manipal University, India*
Divya Rajan, *St. Xavier's Catholic College of Engineering, India*

Table of Contents

Detailed Table of Contents

Today, where artificial intelligence (AI) is at the forefront of our world, information literacy has become more relevant, and critical, than ever before. Information literacy is the set of skills and knowledge that allows individuals to "recognize when information is needed and have the ability to locate, evaluate, and use effectively the needed information" (American Library Association, 1989). As AI continues to evolve and become more robust, it is crucial for educators to support learners as they develop and expand their critical thinking skills. By understanding how artificial intelligence works, particularly generative AI, and the limitations it carries, educators can implement strategies that foster both information literacy skills and AI awareness, equipping learners with the skills needed to navigate and leverage these technologies responsibly in an evolving digital landscape.

The emergence of generative AI has transformed the media landscape, making it increasingly difficult to distinguish between real and artificially created content. This chapter explores its influence on media literacy, particularly in the realms of social media and news consumption. It examines developments in language models and deep learning, highlighting concerns such as misinformation, deepfakes, and echo chambers. While these challenges exist, AI also contributes to fact-checking, personalized content, and improved accessibility. Through real-world examples, the chapter emphasizes the need for ethical AI practices and stronger media literacy. It encourages collaboration among experts, educators, policymakers, and media organizations to promote transparency and trust in digital information.

Chapter 11

Climate change intersects many disciplines, and this chapter explores the nexus of the science of climate change with political and mediated interpretations of that science through a literacy course taught at the undergraduate level. It begets discussions of fake news and misinformation in the form of climate skepticism and denialism, which have permeated online and social-media spaces, and those discussions eventually help students develop their critical-dialoguing skills as a logical application of their refined critical-thinking capabilities. Major assessments include student presentations about climate change in connection to countries of their choice and a final synthesis paper, which is a cogent literature review that students compose from content that they have read, watched and/or discussed, looking for relationships around a predetermined theme. This best-practices chapter includes sections that identify lessons learned, and it contains appendices that offer rubrics and assignment exemplars that fulfill the book's objective for "applied learning and curriculum design."

Foreword

"Fasten your seat belts, it's going to be a bumpy night," is a quote from the 1950 film *All About Eve*. I could not help but recall this quote when I began to think about the state of media and media literacy in 2025.

New technology has created a challenge for media literacy education: how do we build on the past while tackling the future—to ensure students are more skeptical about what they consume when anything can be altered to appear authentic? Never before has teaching these new and emerging techs been so important.

Recently, the World Economic Forum identified misinformation and disinformation as a top global risk - they said: "Misinformation and disinformation undermine trust in institutions, including media and government." An April 2025 Global Study found that "Generation Z –those aged 13-28-- appear to be the group most vulnerable to misinformation." The researchers blame the low quality of information these younger consumers encounter day in and day out.

In August 2024, world scientists sounded the alarm: They warned that truth is under attack and highlighted the urgent need for critical thinking and scientific literacy to combat the rising problem.

Students today are the digital generation. They are so-called "digital natives," but most agree they are not all necessarily media literate: they've not all been taught how to think (or view) critically. I know, for example, that K-12 education has not kept up. In 1999, when Rutgers University Professor Robert Kubey and I co-authored a commentary in *Education Week* ("Has Media Literacy Found a Curricular Foothold?"), elements of media literacy could be found in most states' teaching standards. But by 2011, all of those gains had been wiped out by the endorsement of Common Core standards by 43 states. It was that year that colleague Richard Beach and I noted again in *Education Week* ("Why Core Standards Must Embrace Media Literacy") the change and the omissions (Beach & Baker, 2011; Kubey & Baker, 1999).

> *...other than a mention of the need to "evaluate information from multiple oral, visual, or multimodal sources," there is no specific reference in the common*

standards to critical analysis and production of film, television, advertising, radio, news, music, popular culture, video games, media remixes, and so on. Nor is there explicit attention on fostering critical analysis of media messages and representations.

As a media literacy educator who works primarily with K-12 educators, I know that this is a particularly challenging time for all educators. How do they keep up as well as teach media literacy, AI (artificial intelligence), algorithms, disinformation, fake news, social media and critical thinking (just to name a few)? How do they include all of these elements in a classroom where the curriculum is already overcrowded? Will professional development training provide educators with the necessary tools and resources to adequately address the changes?

Those and more important and timely topics are also addressed in this new textbook. It could not come at a more opportune time: educators are seeking advice and recommendations for how to begin to address technologies that are shaping every aspect of our lives. This text provides an excellent starting point.

Frank W. Baker
Media Literacy Clearinghouse, USA

REFERENCES

Beach, R., & Baker, F. W. (2011). *Why core standards must embrace media literacy*. Truth, and Verification.

Kubey, R., & Baker, F. (1999). Has media literacy found a curricular foothold. *Education Week*, *19*(9), 38.

Frank W. Baker is a nationally recognized media literacy consultant and the webmaster of Media Literacy Clearinghouse, a respected media literacy resource Web site. He has worked in television news and as an administrator for instructional television and distance learning in the Orange County (Orlando), Florida, public school system.

Preface

I. INTRODUCTION

Media Consumption Evolution in the Digital Age

The landscape of media influence has experienced dramatic transformations in recent years. In the days of yesteryear, the influence of media was relatively simpler to understand but still very powerful. Today's digital era is filled with mediated messages all around us, making media influence all the more impactful in the lives of everyday people, particularly affecting the lives of immersed youth who know no other world. So, in this world where intelligence can be artificial, news is often fake, and nearly all media is a social experience, how can we best use the media surrounding us to communicate effectively with others? How are we, and our youth, supposed to navigate this brave technological world when we are all, collectively, being bombarded by mediated messages at every turn? With all these influences saturating the modern world, media literacy has become more important than ever.

Since media first emerged, media literacy has been a concern of educators and governments across the globe. According to Wang, et al. (2020), media literacy was first introduced as a concept nearly 100 years ago by British scholars Lewis and Sampson but has been part of understanding how users interact and engage with mediated messages wherever and whenever communication moved beyond inter- (or intra-) personal. To understand the scope of media literacy, it is crucial to examine its foundational definitions. Across the world, the same analytical tools are referred to in different terms, including media education, media competence, cyberliteracy, new literacies, digital literacy, web literacy, and more (Hobbs, 2019). Nevertheless, the most widely accepted definition of media literacy was established during the Aspen Institute conference in 1993, which defined media literacy as a "movement to expand notions of literacy to include the powerful post-print media that dominate our informational landscape," noting that it "helps people understand, produce and negotiate meanings in a culture made up of powerful images, words and sounds" (Aufderheide, p. 1).

Aufderheide's 1993 statement makes it clear that media literacy is not merely referring to how one consumes media but also the ability to produce media and navigate this mediated world full of "powerful images, words and sounds" (Aufderheide, 1993, p. 1). Impacted by artificial intelligence, social media, and news information, media literacy has become an essential skillset for learning, employment, and social interaction. Adapting to new technologies leads to increased information and, consequently, greater empowerment. (Cho et al., 2024). Indeed, in our own work (Groshek & Vogts, 2025) media consumption patterns, particularly in rural areas, are increasingly shaped not just by access but by algorithmic reinforcement of cultural and ideological identities. This adds urgency to media literacy education, which must now further account for how digital infrastructures influence belief formation.

Navigating Truth, Misinformation, and Ethical Concerns

According to media literacy expert Renee Hobbs, "Media literacy is positioned as a way to solve the problem of children and young people, who can be duped or misled by media messages from advertising, news, and Hollywood" (Hobbs, 2019, p.2). Indeed, it is the influence of media on young people that has been of greatest concern, as these youth are often observed imitating the values portrayed in popular culture as viewed through media. One of the great debates surrounding the issue of media literacy centers on the argument of whether media are forms of social control or means of increased freedom of expression and communication (Hobbs, 2019). Understanding the historical, legal, and ethical contexts of consumed media can enlighten media use and allow populations of all ages and geographies to better navigate the often-confusing byways of media messages.

On one hand, arguments for media literacy are designed to prevent young people from misinterpreting media messages; on the other hand, there are arguments for the necessity of using online media to engage young people in their communities and the democratic process. In her book, *Everyday Media Literacy: An Analog Guide for Your Digital Life,* Christian (2023) argues that media literacy is an essential component to civic engagement. She states, "... media literacy is all about being active, engaged and intentional about your media use... This process of participation online and offline is rich, nuanced and dynamic. It's media literacy in action" (p. 276).

To this point, Parry and colleagues (2021) note that "Progress towards resolving these debates and developing a deeper understanding of the role of media use in human behavior requires 'transparent and robust analytical practices', but also confidence that the measures that are adopted to assess use of digital media are valid indicators of actual usage patterns" (p. 1535). Over the years, a number of survey instruments have been developed to measure media literacy levels of both youth and adults, including the Digital Online Media Literacy Assessment (Hallaq, 2016), the General Social Survey (Hargittai, 2005), and the Digital Teaching Competence Questionnaire (COMDID) (La´zaro-Cantabrana, 2018). These instruments have met various levels of success in determining the media literacy levels of the populations they measure. However, media literacy is more than simply a measurement through a survey instrument. It also includes empowering young people and their teachers to not only gain access to the information available but to give them tools to analyze that information and then use it to create effective, impactful, and meaningful mediated messages of their own. Largely due to these still-ongoing debates, the Aspen Institute articulated a working definition for media literacy as the ability to "access, analyze, evaluate and produce communication in a variety of media forms" (Aufderheide, 1993, p. 1).

Shaping Information Dissemination and Public Discourse Through Social Media and AI

Media literacy has often been shaped by the introduction of new media technologies such as the television, the internet, and other technological advances impacting media distribution and access. The introduction of social media brought an increase in fake news, real news, and, most recently, the common availability of artificial intelligence into the media environment. These advances in technology make media literacy ever more necessary. Young people are particularly vulnerable to the influences of media (see Wang et al., 2019; Twenge et al., 2020; cf. Orben and Przybylski, 2019). Yet these technologies also carry the power to influence social change both negatively and positively. Current researchers agree that combining the literacy skills of traditional mass media with the newer introduction of social media creates a more comprehensive media literacy framework for the 21st century (Cho et al., 2024).

II. THE CHALLENGES

Information Overload and Credibility

The contemporary mediated world is saturated with a constant flow of information and knowledge spread across the internet and traditional media. But it is no longer sufficient to have access to information; something actionable must be done with that knowledge. The concepts of a particular topic must be understood along with the capabilities to evaluate the information received (Bender, 2024). Pérez-Escoda et al. (2021) shared that the exponential flood of information all across the world exacerbates the problem of misinformation, leading to the World Health Organization (WHO) declaring an "infodemic" (p. 1). This phenomenon has been brought on, in part, due to the ability of users to also become content creators or producers. Researchers have called on policymakers to make efforts to correct these problems through legislation and regulations while also promoting media literacy among public sectors (Cho et al. 2024 and Pérez-Escoda et al., 2021).

Social Media's Influence on News Narratives

The early 21st-century platform of MySpace is often credited as the beginning of social media. The past twenty years have seen the introduction of hundreds of social media platforms that have come and gone. Regardless of the platform, the movement has captured large audiences worldwide. Ortiz-Ospina (2019) noted, "...in 2019, there were 7.7 billion people worldwide, with at least 3.5 billion online. This means social media platforms were used by one in three people worldwide and more than two-thirds of all Internet users" (p. 1). More and more, news is accessed using social media. Research shows that this type of news access affects the credibility of the news content, causing increased skepticism and decreased news credibility, ultimately leading to the profound risks and opportunities for democratic systems (Karlsen and Aalberg 2023).

AI-Generated Content and Ethics

Introduced to the general public in January 2023 (Roumeliotis and Tselikas, 2023), ChatGPT is one of the most frequently referenced artificial intelligence models, however, AI applications have been in development since the 1960s (Wang, 2020). The first news story written entirely by an algorithm was printed by the LA Times in 2014 (Gentzkow, 2018). Given this fact, Tiernan, et al. (2023) reiterated the importance of considering practical applications of AI and their impact on students and society as a whole in terms of accessing, evaluating, and consuming media. As AI has developed, so have the problems associated with it; for example, the increase in deepfake videos that have emerged in recent elections serves as a blatant reminder of AI's ability to spread misinformation.

As AI content becomes more complex and more commonplace, detecting AI becomes increasingly difficult. In Asia, Google is using AI tools to detect fake news, and automated stories are found in newsrooms from reputable news sources such as the LA Times and BBC (de-Lima-Santos and Ceron, 2021). But young people may not have easy access to these high-tech tools. They need to learn how to evaluate

AI-generated media on their own at some level while still being prepared for a new world filled with AI content. Some researchers suggest that AI is a useful classroom tool that can aid students in learning concepts and gaining critical thinking skills (Bender, 2024).

Among the practical applications of AI are computational thinking, programming abilities, and interpersonal skills that "account for an important part of extension of students' media literacy" (Wang, 2020, p. 1). That same author asserted that media literacy, STEM training and entrepreneurship all "lay a foundation for AI training" (Wang, 2020, p. 1). Even media news outlets are leaning on AI for assistance in their workflows for newsgathering, production, and distribution (Rinehart and Kung, 2022).

Global and Cultural Variations in Media Literacy

While regional and generational understanding of media may differ among participants, researchers in the field of media literacy recognize that social media especially, "can link people across time and space" in a way that brings greater interaction between those linked through these media channels than their spatially closer neighbors (Manca et al., 2021, p. 14) creating a smaller global space through the use of media. However, in many developing countries, limited internet access in some regions magnifies the digital divide created by restricted technology access in rural and impoverished areas.

Education and Policy Gaps

In her landmark white paper report for the Knight Foundation, media literacy researcher Renee Hobbs (2010) importantly noted, "Strategic partnerships between families, schools, non-governmental organizations and libraries can help build a community education movement for digital and media literacy education" (p. 21). The key here is the partnerships between various entities that each contribute to the whole learning of a student. Hobbs goes on to mention that instructional practices required for teaching media literacy are not dependent on specific tools, texts, or technologies, but "They *do* require the presence of educators who have the skills and experience necessary...to support genuine learning" (Hobbs, 2010, p. 24, emphasis in the original). Still, consistency in media education is lacking across the globe and even across individual nations. This lack of foundational framework clearly illustrates the need for stronger structures for media literacy education and its oversight.

III. SEARCHING FOR SOLUTIONS

Developing AI Literacy

As AI continues to intensify as a key societal tool, multiple authors (Chen and Chen, 2023, de-Lima-Santos and Ceron, 2021, Gentzkow, 2018, and Rinehart and Kung, 2022) suggest the need to teach core skills in how to critically engage with AI-generated content whether that engagement comes from the perspective of a content creator or audience member. Because AI is already an integrated tool in many industries, including media providers, it becomes essential for audiences of all ages to be literate in how AI is being used to alter or manipulate public interactions. Teaching students how to identify AI-generated content, understand how AI algorithms work, and evaluate the ethical implications of AI will lead to increased literacy in this area and create young people who are better prepared to face the mediated world. Teaching these skills will improve communication and facilitate understanding of the world.

Strengthening Critical Thinking Skills

In considering the universality of media literacy, some researchers have suggested a differentiation between generalized media literacy skills and those that are more specialized. Specifically, the definitions suggest that universal media literacy applies more across media platforms and less across cultures (Manca et al., 2021). As an example, some media practices apply across X (formerly Twitter), Instagram, Facebook, WhatsApp, etc., while each platform also requires literacies specific to itself, regardless of which culture from which the user hails. At the same time, other literacy skills are influenced within a local context. (Manca et al., 2021)

Hobbs (2010) observed, "Digital and media literacy education activates independent thinking, authentic dialogue, collaboration, reflection, creativity, and social responsibility as applied to the practices of responding to, creating and sharing messages" (p. 24). Teaching strategies such as fact-checking, source evaluation, and identifying logical fallacies aid in developing media-literate students at all levels of education. It is through media literacy education that a healthy skepticism and analytical approaches to digital content are encouraged.

Here, our own recent scholarship has further illuminated the layered complexity of modern media literacy, especially in rural contexts where traditional gatekeeping institutions have eroded, and hybrid media systems—combinations of legacy and digital platforms—have taken root (Groshek & Vogts, 2025). Misinformation is no longer merely encountered; for many, misinformation finds them. This "Misinformation Finds Them" (MFT) paradigm is a powerful evolution of the "News Finds

Me" (NFM) effect, where individuals believe that important news will reach them without effort. However, under MFT, the passive absorption of information is not just biased—it is actively shaped by partisan social circles, algorithmic prioritization, and bonding social capital that reinforces ideological homogeneity, which demands augmented critical thinking skills and redoubled educational efforts to counterbalance.

Enhancing Educational Curricula

Encouraging a constructivist approach to media literacy, Manca et al. (2021) recommended that educators and researchers with an interest in media literacy education consider integrating learning theory along with practice to fully provide media literacy training, especially related to "identity development through social media participation" (p. 13). These same researchers emphasize that social media literacy specifically is more than technical skills but also includes the ability to evaluate media content. Hobbs (2010) wrote that "Digital and media literacy education activates independent thinking, authentic dialogue, collaboration, reflection, creativity, and social responsibility as applied to the practices of responding to, creating and sharing messages" (p. 24).

Media literacy education can impact learning at all levels of education and in all subjects (Hobbs 2010 p. 24). Its influence is broad and powerful inside the classroom and beyond, where AI intersects with career and social life as well. Speaking specifically of social media, Manca et al. (2021) promoted the perspective that "social media supports a range of activities, such as communication and connection" (p. 3). In an educational context, the authors asserted, "... social media literacy as a cognitive process... develops critical thinking skills, supports the development of writing and literacy skills, and can lead to improved cognitive and metacognitive processes," which helps us create and contribute to something bigger than ourselves through social advocacy and community engagement (Manca et al., 2021 p. 3).

Policy and Regulation

Though the various stakeholders in the media literacy sphere continue to disagree on a singular model for success in developing media literacy among their various constituents, a wide range of educators, researchers, and institutions continue to provide guidance on how to achieve this success. Successful strategies also continue to emerge with the development of new technologies and media distribution channels. This is one of the purposes of this edited collection – to provide current information on the developments related to media literacy through innovation, research, and legal and educational policy that will impact the way individuals interact with media to become more media literate.

IV. ORGANIZATION OF THE BOOK

This volume has attempted to capture perspectives from across the globe in an effort to reach a wide audience and inform about how other cultures and governments approach media literacy. Authors hail from global universities and institutions that support media literacy research and practice. An attempt has been made to group chapters addressing similar components of media literacy. Key chapters highlight topics such as:

- The historical context of media literacy and its relevance today
- The impact of social media on society
- The role of YouTubers in shaping Gen Z's perspectives
- AI's influence on news narratives and ethical considerations
- Digital literacy skills for evaluating credibility
- Regional perspectives on media literacy

Although an attempt has been made to provide a broad view of worldwide media literacy, this volume should not be considered the end-all, be-all of media literacy information. It is merely an effort to add to the body of knowledge to move the cause of better media literacy forward for all.

V. CONCLUSION

Channels of media distribution continue to emerge along with the increase in mediated content. There is no escaping it; media is part of our lives if we are to live among one another. The important parts of successfully navigating the mediated world are to have the ability to access media, be aware of its influence, know how to analyze and evaluate the messages, and the ability to create our own media messages. Just like traditional literacy, media literacy has become an essential skill for success in school, work, and social life. Media literacy aids in developing critical thinking skills, which will then lead to improved communication, better intercultural relationships, and greater community engagement.

In an age where information is both abundant and easily manipulated, cultivating AI and media literacy is not merely an educational goal but a civic necessity, ensuring a well-informed and engaged populace for generations to come. As the editors of this volume, we encourage you to engage critically with the media of today's world. Think critically about its impact on your life and the lives of those you influence, and do your part to make this mediated world a better one for those who follow. The consequences of not doing so are not abstract.

Our hybrid media environments are now congealed with distrust in mainstream media and belief in conspiratorial narratives, often co-existing with intense religious and civic identities. Modern media literacy must address not just fact-checking, but also epistemological reorientation. Data reported in this volume show that many citizens see misinformation as a societal threat—but one that affects others, not themselves. This third-person effect contributes to unchecked belief reinforcement and the normalization of radical perspectives.

Incorporating such findings reframes the need for media literacy as not just an educational intervention, but a democratic imperative. Civic engagement cannot thrive where informational self-awareness and media literacy are absent. As misinformation floods the public sphere online and offline, the hybrid media ecosystem becomes not just a venue for content consumption but a battlefield of belief formation.

The AI-Mediation of the Future

In the evolving ecology of media technologies, the intersection of generative AI, social media platforms, and digitally networked publics marks not merely a shift in communication practice but a transformation in how power is distributed, claimed, and contested. Where broadcast once unified messages across wide demographics, platformed media—particularly algorithmic systems optimized for engagement—have introduced what we term a "hybridization of influence," where political participation and persuasion are increasingly shaped by emergent techno-social architectures. This structure is neither neutral nor evenly accessible.

Empirical analysis in this volume and elsewhere shows that algorithmic personalization—especially in short-form video and AI-assisted news recommendations—can entrench ideological echo chambers, a process previously likened to the "systemic filtration of discourse" (Groshek & Engelbert, 2013). Recent developments in generative AI compound this challenge. AI doesn't merely respond to data—it curates narratives and sets agendas. When large language models are fine-tuned on engagement metrics or deployed within content-delivery ecosystems (e.g., TikTok's recommendation engine or Meta's LLaMA integrations), they inherit and amplify platform logics that prioritize emotional intensity over deliberative nuance.

In this context, media literacy must be reimagined not simply as the ability to decode media messages but as an epistemological stance—one that resists technological determinism while interrogating how automated systems recalibrate agency. Here, prior longitudinal analyses of social media data revealed early signals of this shift, where digital participation did not uniformly increase civic engagement, but instead clustered among pre-engaged, elite users. In a similar vein, today's AI-generated media must be scrutinized for who it empowers, especially considering that those empowered may not necessarily be human actors.

Thus, a "computational civic literacy" becomes necessary: an evolved form of media literacy that understands the logic of platforms, the influence of AI prompt architectures, and the ways in which media producers and consumers are mutually shaped by opaque decision systems. With this framework in mind, this volume seeks to center not only media effects but also media ethics and media equity, particularly as they pertain to generational voices navigating a complex terrain of digital influence.

In closing, we, the editors, would like to acknowledge the contributions of the publisher, the authors, and the reviewers who have lent their knowledge and experience to this publication. We sincerely hope it will add something valuable and meaningful to the collection of information and implementation of strategies on this vital topic. As the artist and poet Lucebert once wrote, "alles van waarde is weerloos," meaning that "everything of value is vulnerable." We could not agree more and believe deeply that media literacy is of tremendous value to all generations, but as AI advances with minimal guardrails, it is more vulnerable than ever.

Tom Hallaq
Kansas State University, USA

Jacob Groshek
Kansas State University, USA

REFERENCES

Aufderheide, P. (1993). National leadership conference on media literacy. In *Conference report. Washington, DC: Aspen Institute.*

Chen, A., & Chen, D. O. (2023). Accuracy of chatbots in citing journal articles. *JAMA Network Open*, *6*(8), e2327647–e2327647. DOI: 10.1001/jamanetworkopen.2023.27647 PMID: 37552482

Cho, H., Cannon, J., Lopez, R., & Li, W. (2024). Social media literacy: A conceptual framework. *New Media & Society*, *26*(2), 941–960. DOI: 10.1177/14614448211068530 PMID: 38328341

Christian, S. E. (2023). *Everyday media literacy: an analog guide for your digital life*. Routledge. DOI: 10.4324/9781003247029

de-Lima-Santos, M. F., & Ceron, W. (2021). Artificial intelligence in news media: current perceptions and future outlook. *Journalism and media, 3*(1), 13-26. DOI: 10.3390/journalmedia3010002

Gentzkow, M. (2018). *Media and artificial intelligence*. Toulouse Network for Information Technology Whitepaper.

Groshek, J., & Engelbert, J. (2013). A Cross-National Comparison of Populist Political Movements and Media Uses in the United States and the Netherlands. *New Media & Society, 15*(2), 183–202. DOI: 10.1177/1461444812450685

Groshek, J., & Vogts, T. (2025). *Misinformation Finds Them: Hybrid Media and Radicalization in Rural America*. Peter Lang Publishing.

Hallaq, T. (2016). Evaluating Online Media Literacy in Higher Education: Validity and Reliability of the Digital Online Media Literacy Assessment (DOMLA). *The Journal of Media Literacy Education*, *8*(1), 62–84. DOI: 10.23860/jmle-8-1-5

Hargittai, E. (2005). Survey measures of web-oriented digital literacy. *Social Science Computer Review*, *23*(3), 371–379. https://ssc.sagepub.com/content/23/3/371.short. DOI: 10.1177/0894439305275911

Hobbs, R. (2010). *Digital and Media Literacy: A Plan of Action. A White Paper on the Digital and Media Literacy Recommendations of the Knight Commission on the Information Needs of Communities in a Democracy*. Aspen Institute. 1 Dupont Circle NW Suite 700, Washington, DC 20036.

Hobbs, R. (2019). Media literacy foundations. *The international encyclopedia of media literacy*, 1-19.

Lázaro-Cantabrana, J. L., Gisbert-Cervera, M., & Silva-Quiroz, J. E. (2018). Una rúbrica para evaluar la competencia digital del profesor universitario en el contexto latinoamericano. *Edutec. Revista Electrónica de Tecnología Educativa*, (63), 1–14.

Orben, A., & Przybylski, A. K. (2019). Screens, teens, and psychological well-being: Evidence from three time-use diary studies. *Psychological Science*, *30*(5), 682–696. DOI: 10.1177/0956797619830329 PMID: 30939250

Parry, D. A., Davidson, B. I., Sewall, C. J., Fisher, J. T., Mieczkowski, H., & Quintana, D. S. (2021). A systematic review and meta-analysis of discrepancies between logged and self-reported digital media use. *Nature Human Behaviour*, *5*(11), 1535–1547. DOI: 10.1038/s41562-021-01117-5 PMID: 34002052

Rinehart, A., & Kung, E. (2022). Artificial Intelligence in Local News. *A survey of US newsrooms' AI readiness*.

Roumeliotis, K. I., & Tselikas, N. D. (2023). ChatGPT and open-ai models: A preliminary review. *Future Internet*, *15*(6), 192. DOI: 10.3390/fi15060192

Tiernan, P., Costello, E., Donlon, E., Parysz, M., & Scriney, M. (2023). Information and Media Literacy in the Age of AI: Options for the Future. *Education Sciences*, *13*(9), 906. DOI: 10.3390/educsci13090906

Twenge, J. M., Haidt, J., Joiner, T. E., & Campbell, W. K. (2020). Underestimating digital media harm. *Nature Human Behaviour*, *4*(4), 346–348. DOI: 10.1038/s41562-020-0839-4 PMID: 32303719

Wang, H., Liu, Y., Han, Z., & Wu, J. (2020, Jun). Extension of media literacy from the perspective of artificial intelligence and implementation strategies of artificial intelligence courses in junior high schools. In *2020 International Conference on Artificial Intelligence and Education (ICAIE)* (pp. 63-66). IEEE. DOI: 10.1109/ICAIE50891.2020.00022

Wang, Y., McKee, M., Torbica, A., & Stuckler, D. (2019). Systematic literature review on the spread of health-related misinformation on social media. *Social Science & Medicine*, *240*, 112552. DOI: 10.1016/j.socscimed.2019.112552 PMID: 31561111

Acknowledgements

Without the support and encouragement of my wife, I could not succeed. She is my rock. Thank you, Tammy. I would also like to recognize the examples set by my parents, John H. Hallaq and Janice E. Hallaq. They showed me the value of education throughout life.

- Tom Hallaq

I would like to acknowledge the tremendous support of my wife, Megan Clough Groshek, over the years. Nothing in my life is possible without her.

- Jacob Groshek

In addition to the acknowledgements above, the editors would like to recognize the exceptional contributions and efforts of the chapter authors and reviewers, whose efforts often go unseen. Combined with the peer reviews of each of the published authors, additional reviews were provided by the individuals listed previously. Their work has been invaluable.

The image included as part of the cover design of this publication was generated using artificial intelligence tools. It is presented for illustrative and creative purposes, as a demonstration of AI's design capabilities at the time of printing. The publisher and author make no claim of human authorship or originality in the image.

Section 1

Giving Context to Media Literacy

Chapter 1
Media Literacy:
Some Historical Context

Stephen Price
https://orcid.org/0009-0008-2340-870X
University of Central Missouri, USA

ABSTRACT

This chapter sets the foundation of the book by giving a historical overview of media literacy research and education. The chapter looks back at the 1990s and 2000s and the media literacy scholarship that came out during those periods. In many ways, these texts set the standard for media literacy research, as well as media literacy pedagogy and curriculum development. The chapter continues by looking at where media literacy scholarship is today – the challenges seen in students and in media literacy education itself. Americans have access to more information than any other time in human history, but they are also resistant to facts and opinions that challenge their own thoughts. Although there has been much progress in media education, there is also still an extreme need for it.

INTRODUCTION

I find it hard to believe that almost 30 years have passed since I began studying media literacy. At the time, many of us were very passionate about it and pushed for classes in media literacy and critical thinking about the media we consume every day. Messaris (1994) studied what training was needed versus what was naturally understood when we read media texts. Silverblatt (1995) sought to define the concept of media literacy and develop a framework for becoming more media literate. Zettl (1999) wrote about the role of media aesthetics as a foundational language used in media messages. Hobbs (2007) wrote about the need for media literacy classes in

DOI: 10.4018/979-8-3373-0872-2.ch001

high schools, and Potter (1998) wrote textbooks for college classes. They focused on actual skills and training that lead to a more literate media consumer. In many ways, media literacy scholars got their wish. High schools and colleges now train students to think critically about their media habits and consumption. Production classes now exist in high schools across the country where news shows are produced, websites are designed, films are analyzed, and students are taught how to interpret media messages.

But we still have a long way to go. The media are now vastly different than 30 years ago, when the Internet was in its infancy. Our modern media environment is more saturated with competing media messages than ever, and we must re-evaluate our pedagogical approaches to explore the challenges presented in our current post-truth era. The classes in many schools are electives and not required for everyone. Students in production classes often focus on technical skills and button pushing, not the rationale behind the images and sounds. Students in media literacy classes have trouble seeing past the "theory" to understand how their own habits shape the world around them. We also live in a post-truth environment. Thirty years ago, the problem involved searching to find *any* information. Now, we have the entire world's information literally in our pockets, but we are challenged to dredge through seemingly infinite amounts of bad information to find the good.

Our students are more media savvy than ever. They use cell phones to shoot and edit Tik-Tok videos and post them instantaneously. They have a natural eye for composition and a feel for how to connect with audiences because they've grown up in this environment. McLuhan's (1964) famous line about the technology shaping the message seems to be ever-relevant. Yet, these same students rarely take the time to critically consume the media they seek to produce. The available content clearly resonates with consumers, but is rarely fact-checked. Social media personalities follow. And, personally saddest for me, even though I have students who want to produce broadcast news, they rarely even watch it.

This chapter will look at some historical trends in the way we think about media literacy. It will also provide some of my perspective about our current state of media literacy pedagogy and where we might want to go in the future: how do we teach critical analysis of media to people who are both engulfed by it and unaware of it at the same time? How do we teach production skills to people who grew up with a camera in their hands, yet have trouble differentiating between what they do and what professionals do? I cannot promise definitive answers, but will do my best to illuminate the challenges.

AN INFLUENTIAL PERIOD: 1990S TO THE 2010S

While there are certainly books and articles that emphasize the importance of teaching people how to read television texts and how to interpret the messages consumed through our media, the way we discussed media literacy in an academic setting really took off in the period between the 1990s and the 2010s. My goal here is not to give a comprehensive literature review of media literacy, but to focus on that period that shaped the subject tremendously. For a wonderful history of research leading up to the 1990s, Renee Hobbs and Amy Jensen (2009) wrote a fairly thorough synopsis of the academics that laid the groundwork for the push in the 1990s, titled, *The Past, Present, and Future of Media Literacy Education* in the inaugural edition of the Journal of Media Literacy Education. That journal is still published by the National Association of Media Literacy Educators, or NAMLE.

The National Association of Media Literacy Educators currently defines media literacy as "the ability to access, analyze, evaluate, create, and act using all forms of communication" (namle.org). Media Literacy Now defines it as "the ability to decode media messages (including the systems in which they exist), the ability to assess the influence of those messages on thoughts, feelings, and behaviors, and the ability to create media thoughtfully and conscientiously" (medialiteracynow.org). Those are both comprehensive definitions that hint at curriculum and assessment of learning objectives. My favorite definition of media literacy might still be Livingstone's (2004): "the ability to access, analyze, evaluate, and create messages across a variety of contexts."

The "access" part is easy in today's media environment. "Analyze" and "evaluate" have been critical to media literacy across most definitions. What I like most about Livingstone's definition is that it includes "create." At the time, being "literate" in media didn't inherently include both reading and writing media texts. The push was to create an informed media consumer who wasn't swayed by advertising or manipulated into certain thoughts or opinions. The industry was grappling with lawsuits that acknowledged the actual damage wrought by cigarette ads targeting minors. To many, media literacy is as important as learning to read and write in a foreign language. Advocates like myself felt strongly that students needed to become more critical consumers of media, and that an important part of that included learning basic production skills.

The Media Literacy Now definition goes a bit too far for my taste, although I understand the sentiment. To "create media thoughtfully and conscientiously" is a valiant goal. But I'm not sure one has to reach those lofty ideals to be media literate. Still, all three of these definitions require an ability to read media messages within context and using critical thinking skills. All three of these definitions require some knowledge of production techniques. And all three require the depth that one must be able to "evaluate" the messages.

"Evaluation" means that students need to be taught to understand how the context of the message shapes both the encoding and decoding (Hall, 1980). Evaluating messages means understanding the motives and goals of the encoding. Students must be able to look at the message and understand the intentions of the author, both good and bad. I recall a heated discussion I had with a friend, perhaps around 2005. We were discussing the film *Fahrenheit 911* by Michael Moore (2004), and my friend claimed that the film was biased and one-sided. His argument was that Moore manipulated the situations in the film to express certain opinions without showing the "other side" of those opinions. He continued this argument for a while before I stopped him and said, "What do you think a documentary film is?" Every media message has bias. Humans are inherently biased in their presentation of facts and their arguments about opinions. Knowing this is the first step towards evaluating media messages and becoming media literate.

The second step to media literacy is the ability to write in the medium as well. Students in my Media Aesthetics class learn about Zettl's (2016) "aesthetic fields". Lighting, sounds, compositions, colors, and editing techniques of media texts are analyzed. We watch a clip from Zack Snyder's "Batman v Superman: Dawn of Justice" (2016) film on the first day. I show them the clip at the beginning of class, and then we talk about communication and how visuals are encoded. When I show them the clip a second time, they see elements they've likely never been consciously aware of before. They can talk about how Superman is shown in color because he's seeing the world as nuanced. Batman is mostly black and white because, to him, the world is only right and wrong. The students notice that when Superman floats down to Batman's level and the fight begins, the color disappears from his suit. He's literally and figuratively fighting on Batman's level now. The point of this lesson and my mentioning it here is that media literacy is about analyzing the messages behind the messages. When I tell my students that the film cost almost $250 million to make and brought in $875 million worldwide, they're floored. In their memory, the film wasn't good, and it flopped. We talk about how every single shot is well-planned and every element is intentional. They start to understand the financial reasons why the film was made and how important it is to analyze each shot and scene within all of these contextual elements.

Later in the semester, I put a camera in their hands and they shoot stills and videos to capture aesthetic elements. At that point, they've begun reading media texts in different ways. They're ready to start writing their own media messages. They submit a project on light/shadows, one on color, one on editing, one on composition, and one on depth of field. The class only mentions media literacy as a general foundation for the content, but it is absolutely a class where many students are learning to read and write visual images for the first time. This is a class that answers the calls of 90s media literacy scholars. And, in our Digital Media Production degree program, it is a required and foundational course. Our students are also required to take a course titled "Media Literacy," which focuses on their own personal media consumption habits. Finally, they take a standard Media and Society class in the General Education curriculum. However, as I'll elaborate on later, even inside of the gen ed program, these courses are *options and not requirements for every student.* Graduates of our degree program encounter an amazing amount of theory and practice across their coursework. Many other students leave college without ever having taken a media literacy class.

DEFINING AND THEORIZING ABOUT MEDIA LITERACY

When Messaris (1994) and Silverblatt (1995) first wrote their seminal books on the topic, they were really looking to unlock the keys to media literacy. In his book, *Visual Literacy*, Messaris considers abilities that come naturally to us when we analyze visual images. Depth, for instance, can be determined instinctually by occlusion and linear perspective, but relative size is something that must be taught (p. 56) if it is to be used to interpret the depth cues in images. I was drawn to Messaris's book because of the analysis presented. He covered a number of visual elements, as Zettl did in *Sight, Sound, Motion* (2016) and identified how they could be read by the viewer. I was fascinated to learn the nature of our visual instincts, and that some elements must be learned (or are at least specific to visual messages and require some literacy). *Visual Literacy* advances two goals for learners. The first is to develop an aesthetic appreciation for visual images. The second is to become aware of visual manipulation. For the second, Messaris supports formal training in schools and classes. Returning to the previously mentioned fears about advertising, Messaris and others felt that visual manipulation in ads (specifically ads targeting children, like where the cartoon on the cereal box comes to life and talks to the kids in the ads) was dangerous and that literacy would help combat or mitigate their effects. Awareness of manipulation might prevent someone from enjoying a show's entertainment elements, but it would be replaced by an appreciation for the art itself (p. 136). In the end, Messaris advocates for formal educational training in both analysis and production of visual messages.

Silverblatt (1995) breaks down the definition of media literacy even further. The goals for Silverblatt are more significantly focused on the societal impact of media texts, not just the individual impact of those same texts (pp. 2-3). To him, a media consumer should be aware of how advertisements and news might direct them towards certain ideas or behaviors. Silverblatt focuses on specific production values, how viewers read them, and how they transfer values and messages to the audience. Therefore, to Silverblatt, learning how to interpret and analyze production cues is the foundation of media literacy. Much like Messaris and Zettl (1998), Silverblatt believes that analysis is essential to achieving literacy. Silveblatt takes it one step further, however, by talking about how media shape our society. Pulling from Gerbner and Gross's (1976) Cultivation Theory, Silverblatt says the media shape the way we see the world, so if we have an awareness of the modes of production, we can be more aware of how our worldviews are skewed. Silverblatt's book is, admittedly, one of the texts that led me to study media literacy. To me, it was the noblest of missions to work toward as a media scholar: to create a more informed public and lessen the influence of media on society.

When I was able to shadow Art Silverblatt for a day at Webster University as a grad student, I found myself in awe at his ability to break down complex ideas into simple explanations. He was also able to articulate how production skills lead to media literacy, but that classes must be taught in a manner that bridges that gap for the students. Instead of button pushing, Silverblatt felt that production skills should be taught as communication acts. Each decision leads the viewer in a specific direction, and producers need to be aware of what they intend to communicate to those audiences. Almost all my own research has been connected by a thread of media literacy, and throughout, I tie the production aesthetics to the messages they communicate. Even when I wrote my dissertation on the subtle self-reflexivity in the TV show, *Boston Legal*, I justified it through the lens of media literacy – that a self-reflexive style of production was an acknowledgement that audiences had become more sophisticated viewers, and that in turn, self-reflexivity educated viewers about the modes of production in a way that led to a more literate audience.

THE ROLE OF PRODUCTION EDUCATION IN MEDIA LITERACY (APPLICATION)

Zettl's (1998) article in the *Journal of Communication* expands Silverblatt's book into a workable theoretical framework for media literacy. In the article, Zettl builds on his textbook for studying media aesthetics, *Sight, Sound, Motion* (first published in 1973). He discusses using his five aesthetic fields – "light and color", "2D space", "3D space", "time/motion", and "sound" – as the foundational blocks of any media message. By identifying those building blocks and analyzing the context, the genres, and attempts at influence, as well as the various theoretical perspectives, we can truly and fully analyze a text. The goal for Zettl wasn't merely to analyze texts, although that is a primary goal for media literacy education. Zettl ended the article by advocating for formal training in media literacy for media producers as well. To be an effective encoder of messages, one must be versed in the five aesthetic fields, but one must also understand the cultural context, the theoretical frameworks, and the societal impact of their stories. Much like the definition previously provided by Media Literacy Now, I believe that Zettl felt a desire for media producers to go beyond art and strive to be conscientious communicators.

WHAT SHOULD BE THE FOCUS FOR CURRICULUM?

In 1998, James Potter wrote *Media Literacy*, the first book on the subject that reads like a textbook, one I continue to use to teach my college classes on the subject. The book is a turning point in curriculum development in my mind. Potter doesn't feel the need to justify media literacy as a subject of study. He is also unconcerned about whether production training or textual analysis is the basis for becoming media literate. Instead, his book teaches people how to analyze their own media consumption habits. By considering personal use and then learning about societal issues that have been and continue to be influenced by the media, Potter reflects the subject inward in a way that I've found highly effective in reaching students. Other books, like Richard Campbell's *Media and Culture* (1997), which I also use in a different class, reflect on how media and society intertwine. Campbell does a masterful job of educating readers on how media industries work and how the business and history affect our current landscape. But Potter's book teaches readers to interrogate their own media habits in a way that negates the third-person effect (Davison, 1983). Students reading Potter can't help but look inward and discover the truth of themselves as media consumers, instead of reading about media effects and thinking themselves immune.

Renee Hobbs also wrote a highly effective text for high school students in 2007. In *Reading the Media: Media Literacy in High School English*, Hobbs studies high schools that are teaching students to, in effect, become media literate. She lays out empirical research to make the argument, but then spends ample time in the book discussing how to create an effective course for high school students. I remember chatting with Hobbs at the National Communication Association annual conference when her book was published. She laid out an impressive argument for the types of exercises students should be doing – analyzing advertising, learning about media industries, and defending against the effects of advertising. Today, this type of literacy is essential as teens' self-esteem plummets as their media use increases. As far back as Jean Kilbourne's film, *Killing Us Softly* (1979), advertising's effect on body image has been shown to be detrimental. Hobbs relies heavily on textual analysis to teach media literacy, but like Potter, she encourages students to look inward at their own media consumption patterns.

Twenty years ago, I presented a paper at the National Communication Association that outlined efforts being made towards curriculum. At the time, NCA had 23 goals for communication education efforts in high schools and colleges. Only two of those goals were specific to media literacy. Renee Hobbs's book hadn't been published, but there were already 29 states that had adopted guidelines for media literacy in high schools. The guidelines were mostly based on the two goals NCA had published, but no state had defined a curriculum or assessments for media literacy. It's fair to say that things have changed in the last 20 years. According to medialiteracynow.org, 3/4 of states have specifically addressed goals for media literacy in K-12 education. In 2005, I wrote that "media scholars, legislatures, educators, and the general public will readily agree that media literacy is a good thing…. It is an arduous task, starting with media scholarship that is more practically oriented, and finishing with an educational system that treats visual communication with the same importance it currently places on written communication" (Price, p. 10). In many ways, this task has been accomplished. Schools see great value in media education. Parents acknowledge that media literacy is important. As a parent myself, I try to stay aware of current research about screen time, guided viewing, and other strategies to prevent my children from falling prey to some of the more disastrous media effects. On the other hand, it has never been easier to access media. We have never, in the history of the planet, been bombarded by so many media messages throughout our day. My son is 12 years old and doesn't have a cell phone yet, but I see his similarly aged friends glued to their screens in a way that I can tell impacts their social skills and ability to interact with others. As far as we have come, we still have a long way to go when it comes to media literacy education.

SOME THOUGHTS ON THE CURRENT STATE OF MEDIA LITERACY EDUCATION

There have been many articles discussing the need for media literacy in the current media landscape and political climate. One only has to read the daily news to see attacks on journalism and other concerning trends. NPR and PBS are undergoing massive PR campaigns to combat the threats to their CPB funding. CBS is being sued by the Trump Administration for how it edited a 60 Minutes segment. Because of the highly polarized political environment in America, even the traditional news media are seen to be taking sides and are attacked constantly. While there are many current events, media effects theories, and media literacy issues that could be explored from 2012 to the present, to cover all of them would require too many pages. The research after about 2012 becomes more focused on specific issues, and much of it uses media literacy to validate "why this research is important" and is not necessarily the focus of the research itself. And so, in this chapter, I won't go much beyond reviewing the literature in the period between the 1990s and the 2010s. Although I will explore some of the current challenges that media literacy, as a pedagogical construct, faces.

Lately, I've been disheartened by the way American society interacts with the media. For years, we've collectively taught students to be skeptical of what they consume. We've taught them that all media sources are biased. We've taught them that media effects are almost always negative and that they need to be wary of media consumption. The college students I teach these days have taken all of these lessons to heart, but they've lost sight of the outcomes that were supposed to be associated with the lessons. Instead of consuming news from multiple sources and triangulating the truth through the biases, students tend to reject all sources of news as "too biased." They are beyond skeptical of even mainstream sources of information and instead turn to opinion leaders they trust as their preferred source of news. These opinion leaders are most often found on social media, and they're most often not trained as journalists. Students have been taught that Wikipedia is completely false and that you should reject anything written there. In fact, Wikipedia is generally a broadly reliable source of information, even if some of it is false, and it should always be verified through additional research. For the last 20 years, students have only learned the first half of the concept of media literacy, but have stopped their consideration there. Our polarized political climate and distrust of news sources we don't agree with are partly to be blamed on us, the media literacy advocates. We have done a great job of teaching fear, but a terrible job of teaching actual literacy and discernment between quality information and ideological opinions. We have also stopped short of requiring media literacy courses for all students – they are often still electives. At my university, Media Literacy is a general education requirement, but there are other courses that can satisfy the same "bucket", so students can get a college degree without ever having taken it.

THE MEDIUM IS THE MESSAGE

In 1964, Marshall McLuhan wrote, "the medium is the message" (p. 7). For a time, scholars dismissed this as an overstatement – I can remember professors in graduate school telling me this. In the late 1980s and 1990s, scholars could very firmly put media texts into specific categories: magazines, films, television shows, newspapers, and pop music, for example. Across those media texts, there were obvious differences, but the medium itself could be easily classified and then dismissed. McLuhan seemed less relevant until social media really took hold. Although there are many benefits to the internet age that we went through, and the blazing speed at which information is currently readily available to us, there are drawbacks to the current age of media housed online.

It's difficult to argue that the medium of TikTok, for example, has nothing to do with how the messages are created and received. TikTok's short-form videos have had a detrimental impact on attention spans, expectations for instant gratification, and other effects that we hardly dreamed of in the 90s. Social media encourage the broad and rapid spread of information without verification of anything that is shared. The need for social interaction, especially for validation of our thoughts and ideas, leads to posting just to get "likes" or "shares". Content is increasingly inflammatory. Many platforms are designed that way – Facebook and X (formerly Twitter) recently removed their fact-checking devices in favor of letting people post freely. The medium here *is* the message. Social media may have started as places to connect with old friends and create new communities, but instead, algorithms on many platforms have led to echo chambers where we only see posts from people we interact with more frequently. Assuming we're "liking" posts we agree with, this means we mostly see content we agree with. Instead of being an open forum to discuss ideas, social media have turned into places where we semi-anonymously shout at people who don't agree with our opinions.

THE CHALLENGES OF THE POST-TRUTH ERA

These echo chambers are a feature of a "post-truth" (*Oxford Dictionary*'s 2016 word of the year) society. The internet is filled with so much information and so many opinions that one can seemingly always find information to validate their stance on an issue. Instead of consuming news sources that might challenge their existing opinions, people instead gravitate towards news sources (or opinions) that validate them. Plenty of news sources exist. The problem is, of course, that some sources do a better job of focusing less on opinions and instead report facts. Some sources of information have bigger budgets and more staff members to track down additional quotes and verify their information before they publish. These more legitimate sources of news are being replaced by lesser options because we've continuously told students they can't trust any news sources. If you can't trust any of them, you have to replace them with something. So people tend to still pay attention to those opinion leaders they agree with. Eventually, opinions substitute for actual facts. Or, as is often the case, there aren't actually facts available to agree on, and we're left with conflicting opinions and little willingness to consider anything outside of our own sphere, where we've built up our arguments already and dug in our defenses.

As an example of this, I had a friend who posted on Facebook that there were strong women in the Bible. In the comments section, there were strong opinions expressed with little willingness to even consider other options. Either side of this argument could find bible verses to back up their opinion. Both sides found other sources on the internet that were writing opinions to match their own. This was in part the draw to the internet in its infancy: it was a public forum where anyone could reach out to the masses with any ideas they had. With the internet, we could immediately create information and disseminate it without the need for a printing press or a small fortune to rent cameras and TV studios. A number of reasons exist for why and how we got to where we are today with information illiteracy, but the vast amount of misinformation online and the lack of barriers to accessing it are a large part of it.

If you're reading this book, you probably already know a lot of this. If, like me, you're an educator, you probably encounter these feelings through conversations with people around you as well. I rarely post my political opinions on social media, but occasionally, I'll post something about education or healthcare (I'm a teacher and my wife is a nurse practitioner). However, most of my posts are about opening up your mind to new information, verifying information before tagging it with opinionated outrage and spreading it, and I especially encourage people to seek out information sources that are legitimate and that both confirm and challenge existing opinions. As Hoechsmann, M. & Poyntz, S. (2012) point out, "while the technologies of media use change, so too do the perspectives and practices of the users…" (p. 7). In other words, the medium is the message, and the user is also the medium and the message. Our interactions on social media only reinforce that our opinions are more entrenched now than they were three decades ago when the internet was in its infancy. When we had limited access to information and very limited ability to produce information, we consumed higher-quality information and did it while employing critical thinking skills.

Having grown up in the 1980s, I can remember a time when there were really only three channels on TV, a local newspaper, and a handful of local radio stations. My parents spent a small fortune on a set of *Encyclopedia Britannica* books. I had a local public library and a school library. When it came to news sources, even that was more than we could pay close attention to. But I don't remember my parents questioning the information in the encyclopedias the way we completely discount information on Wikipedia these days. I don't remember my parents watching one news channel and completely discounting the information on the other two. If we missed the 6:00 p.m. newscast, we might even stick around for the world news at 6:30 p.m. Or we might switch over to one of the other channels. Even though my parents had their favorite local news anchors, they certainly didn't think the others were complete liars. Even typing those words seems bizarre. Yet, here we are now – living in a world where we are regularly discounting valid information simply because it challenges our existing opinions on a topic. Discounting valid information simply because it's being shared by someone we disagree with on a regular basis. Discounting valid information simply because the source is someone from the opposite political party. Speaking of politics (it's difficult to write a chapter like this without mentioning politics): both parties and all ends of the political spectrum do this. I've seen it with Democrats and Republicans, and I've seen it with liberals and conservatives. A good indication of your own biases on this is considering whether you read that last sentence and your gut reaction was, "not my fellow party mates" or "not my friends." I'll address this more fully later, but all of us, myself included, need to work on this.

THE CHALLENGES OF TEACHING CRITICAL THINKING SKILLS

In the 1990s, media literacy scholars debated whether critical thinking skills were the foundation for media literacy or whether it was production training. Some, like myself, felt that both were important. It's also likely that many were simply being pragmatic: it has always been more expensive to purchase equipment and teach production skills. By focusing on critical thinking and textual analysis of media messages, media scholars thought that students would be able to see through manipulation. By teaching students about media ownership patterns, legislative regulations, capitalistic motivations, and media effects, we thought that we could create the critical media consumers that Livingstone (2004) desired. I teach a class on media and society, and as the semester proceeds, I can see students in the class begin to question things they took for granted. For instance, they have a basic understanding that state-run media might not be the best system, but they don't ever question the free-market system in America. Weeks into the class, some of them still argue that media consolidation is better for the consumer because it puts more money in the hands of the large conglomerates, which will invest that money into high-quality programming. They completely ignore the fact that these companies still rarely take risks on shows they are afraid won't turn a profit. Instead, these students continue to argue this media version of trickle-down economics. When I point out that the BBC is state-funded (but not state-run), but in a way that prevents the government from attaching strings to the funding, they begin to understand that news in America is really more entertainment than news. After all, news media are driven by ratings and advertising dollars. I ask them why so many reality shows are produced. Their answer is usually, "because they're so popular." There might be some truth to this supposition, but for the most part, reality shows are made in mass because they are simply cheaper to produce. The economics are complex, and as students understand them, they also understand why commercials are designed to catch our attention, create a need, and call to action. They understand why streaming services started producing shows as one continuous storyline broken into pieces (to keep people binge watching), and why the models are now shifting to prevent viewers from paying for a month, binge watching certain shows, and then cancelling the service. They understand that the future of streaming will probably be funded by commercials, just as broadcast TV and cable were. But I don't know that they truly change their behaviors based on that knowledge. Instead, they acquiesce to a system that seems inevitable to them. I encourage them to support quality journalism. I encourage them to look at where they stand on the political spectrum in relation to their news sources and how that might color their understanding of media bias. But after the class ends, I think at least some of them probably dismiss my teachings as "liberal bias in academia" and go back to passively consuming the news and entertainment sources they relied on before the class began.

I find students in my media literacy class to be a bit more informed by the end of the class than those students in the media and society one. In the media literacy class, I use Potter's book and ask the students to keep a media use journal. They report on their media use and how it has changed over the course of the semester. They also complete an audience analysis project, an aesthetic analysis project, and a narrative structure analysis project. Dissecting the texts and their intended audiences, as well as analyzing themselves as members of those audiences, leaves a more lasting impact. They're able to understand that the media affect them as well. Suddenly, the aesthetics and narrative storylines that used to appeal to them become texts to study critically. When they situate themselves as both audience members and social scientists, they can understand how the media actually impacts their lives and not just the lives of others. The third-person effect is powerful. We never want to admit that we can be manipulated so easily. But ironically, realizing that no one is immune is the first step towards becoming more immune. The problem here is that they can reflect inward, but they don't necessarily see beyond the individual impact the media have on the world around them. When taken alongside the media and society class, students could make real progress in terms of fully comprehending the influence of media on their lives and the worlds in which they live – though these classes are both general education courses and unless the student is one of our majors, I don't often get to see their progress after they've completed both. And if they are one of our majors, they're taking production classes concurrently with these classes, and the gains in media literacy are more obviously discerned.

THE IMPORTANCE OF TEACHING MEDIA LITERACY AS PART OF PRODUCTION SKILLS

I also teach media production classes and see students increase their media literacy skills through learning production techniques (Price, 2009). In our introductory course to single-camera video production, students learn to shoot and edit video. I always emphasize storytelling and communicating to the target audience when teaching production, and they begin to understand that they're not just pushing buttons or framing shots randomly. Students in both this class and in my basic audio production course all begin their pre-production planning by first defining their audience and then doing research to understand how their project will best reach that audience.

By connecting their projects to a specific audience and defining a desired outcome or message, students in production classes can gain skills in media literacy. They begin to realize that everything they consume – every single media message – is purposefully targeted and designed. They realize that media production is a two-way street of encoding and decoding messages (Hall, 1980). When they plan, shoot, and edit a scene, they're doing so with intent and with an audience in mind. Many have never even considered this when they watch a TV show – that the writers, directors, and editors were actually thinking about them (as a member of the broader audience) as they created the show. And they especially haven't considered that each and every shot is placed deliberately to tell the story, and that those stories communicate messages, morals, political commentaries, social norms, etc. to the audience.

The problem I face in production classes, with regard to media literacy is that many students get overwhelmed by the button-pushing and have little bandwidth leftover to learn the broader implications of why they're pushing those buttons in the first place. Cameras are complex tools for storytelling. Learning how to expose a shot properly, light a shot, focus a shot, frame a shot, and capture good audio are essential skills and a valuable part of visual storytelling. But those skills are not the messages themselves. A project can look and sound amazing and still fall flat in its message or narrative. Conversely, a project can have a profound message that forces the audience to look deeply at a topic of great importance, but if it looks and sounds like garbage, the audience won't wade through it to get to the deeper meaning. The days of passable filmmaking in documentary films have been replaced by an expectation that everything on our screens should look and sound at least moderately professional. Audiences are a bit more forgiving with non-fiction visual storytelling, but the expectations have definitely risen as cell phone cameras and other technologies have gotten better and more abundant. In order to set themselves up for success, students in production classes often focus on the skills to make their media projects look and sound professional. They assume that if they can do that, the storytelling will follow on its own. Or they take it for granted that they will learn how to incorporate quality storytelling after they learn the production skills. Essentially, students believe that if they produce something that looks good, audiences will automatically find it to be profound and thought-provoking. That assumption most often fails. And as the teacher, I'm most often okay with the reality that most of their projects are not profound and thought-provoking. To grade something harshly just because it isn't a groundbreaking media text seems like too high a bar. I might comment on the connection to the target audience or the goals set forth in pre-production, but I typically only take off points if those things are glossed over in the planning phase, or if the project itself isn't high enough quality. I'm sure that reinforces the notion that as long as it looks and sounds good, it is good, but I don't have the heart to flunk someone simply because they didn't create something that connected deeply with their target audience. Which is probably also why I think the medialiteracynow.org definition to "create media thoughtfully and conscientiously" is too lofty for a definition of media literacy.

MEDIA LITERACY 2.000

In Hoechsmann and Poyntz's (2012) book, *Media Literacies: A Critical Introduction*, the authors use the term "media literacy 2.000", a play on how things changed in the early 2000s in terms of media literacy education. In the time period I alluded to previously, schools were rapidly introducing courses in media literacy to their curriculum, and numerous textbooks were being written. The authors, though, suggest that media literacy needs to be more than just coursework. Because students are constantly inundated with media messages, educators need to develop lessons beyond critical analysis of media texts. Teachers should teach production skills, but as a way to make sense of the media environment that students are also consumers of: "formal media education takes what may appear natural in a media-saturated environment, however, and challenges learners to see through facets of media that may have been uncritically absorbed" (p. 15). In other words, it's great that we teach people in a controlled setting to consume media texts with critical thinking skills, but if they turn around and go home only to passively binge Netflix for the next five hours without employing those same critical thinking skills, their education has failed them.

Hoechsmann and Poyntz argue that the goal of media literacy is "a necessary component of citizenship education that is essential in increasingly semiotic societies" (p. 16). This argument gives us the "why" of media literacy education. On face value, I think most of us agree that media literacy is important – especially in our current polarized political and information environment. But the authors put into words that good citizenship depends on being media literate. A decade ago, even before the 2016 election, there were indications that our post-truth era was beginning.

What I like most about the idea of "Media Literacy 2.000" is its three requirements. The first requirement is to teach critical analysis skills. Many schools are already doing this. The second requirement is to teach production skills. Many schools are also doing this. The third requirement is to combine these two teachings in a way that forces students to apply media literacy skills outside of the classroom, in the media-saturated world they live in. We can't only teach these things in academic isolation.

As mentioned previously, I also teach a class called Media Aesthetics that I patterned off of Zettl's *Sight Sound Motion* (2016) book. Students in the class learn about Zettl's aesthetic fields and then use a DSLR camera to shoot examples of those concepts. We also watch examples of the aesthetic elements in class and discuss the media texts. I try to make the examples relevant to their own media use – we even watch a clip from Disney's *Frozen* to discuss music theory and how songs use progressions to highlight changes in the characters. Sometimes I show clips from *The Godfather* or scenes from other movies they probably haven't seen, but I also just ask them what their favorite movies are, and we bring up clips from those and analyze them. I think this is essential to ensure I'm teaching them in ways that extend outside the classroom. If all I do is use clips from movies they've never seen (even if they are critically acclaimed) and probably never will, I'm encouraging them to think that media literacy is something that only happens inside a classroom.

Revisiting the debate between teaching production skills and teaching critical analysis, I think the answer is both. My own experiences, coupled with the literature and textbooks that argue for both, lead me to believe that students need classes like the Media Aesthetics class. They need to analyze media messages and also turn right around and produce their own messages in order to solidify the concepts in practice. And they need to be doing all of that in the media environment they swim in every day. We should be analyzing and producing TikTok videos. We should be looking at commercials and how they control our consumer behaviors, and then we should be teaching our students how to produce effective commercials. We shouldn't just look at *Citizen Kane*, we should also watch *Riverdale*, *Spiderman: Into the Spiderverse*, and *The Floor is Lava*. Instead of just teaching our students how to produce award-winning films, we should also teach them how cheap reality TV shows are made.

In Finland, media literacy skills are taught beginning in pre-Kindergarten. At every grade level, students have a class in media where they learn to analyze story structures and aesthetic elements. In high school, they take classes in production that emphasize the connections between the class projects and the media they consume on a daily basis. There are even classes in AI literacy already being taught in their schools. "In 2023, Finland was once again ranked at the top of the Media Literacy Index, comparing 47 European and OECD countries" (toolbox.finland.fi). At the university at which I currently teach, we are certainly discussing AI, how we might incorporate it into courses, how to teach students to use it ethically, and how we might leverage it in media production. But there certainly isn't a nationwide push toward AI literacy for students in America. Instead, our reaction is ad-hoc and largely determined by the individual teacher and how they want to address AI education. There are similar serious challenges in media literacy that have arisen in the last 20 years, and there are even more following AI on the horizon. I realize that the rest of this chapter focuses on my limited American-centered worldview, so I want to acknowledge here that Finland is not the only country emphasizing media literacy across its curriculum. Canada and the UK also have educational goals that address media literacy and are doing a remarkable job educating students to be more critical consumers of their television shows, films, games, and other media sources.

Before the 2024 U.S. election, I told students to keep an eye out for "deep fakes," where videos could be made to look and sound like the politician, but saying or doing something that never actually happened. Again, most of you are probably aware, but we used to say that "seeing is believing." When I studied the way that people interacted with media sources on 9-11 (Price, 2006), that phrase kept popping up. Participants in the study who heard about the tragedy from any other source immediately sought out visuals to confirm the news. They didn't believe it was true until they saw visual evidence with their own eyes. Now that technology exists that can easily fake the visual evidence, how do we confirm truth? When I can use AI to create a video where a politician says something absolutely horrible, people are left to their own opinions and ideological beliefs as the only basis for truth. Recently, our president seemed convinced that an image of a hand had "MS-13" tattooed on it, and justified deporting a legal immigrant to the U.S. because of gang affiliations. When he was shown the actual image without the letters superimposed, he claimed that image was fake. When given two sets of viable-looking images, we're left to believe whatever we believed in the first place. We've seen this coming for years, which is why we've taught students that they can't necessarily believe everything they see and read in the news. But we have also done a poor job of teaching them what other sources and approaches they might use to replace or supplement the visual evidence. We've done a poor job of teaching them how to find truth, or at least how to solidify their opinions with facts and opinions from multiple other sources, so they can break free of their echo chambers.

MEDIALITERACYNOW.ORG

There are so many fantastic resources available on the web for media literacy advocates these days. As of today, medialiteracynow.org has over 800 resources for educators across a variety of subjects and grade levels. Their website has a toolkit for educators, and one designed for social media and cell phones in schools. The non-profit tracks a number of legislative efforts to add media literacy to the curriculum in different states. The website has links to contact state legislators in support of the proposed bills. The organization also funds research in media literacy and publishes results on the website. For example, it found that 62% of the adults in one of its surveys had no media literacy training, yet 84% supported a requirement for media literacy education in schools (medialiteracynow.org). That so few adults have been trained in media literacy, even though most support it, is one of the major challenges of our times.

NAMLE.ORG

The National Association for Media Literacy Education also has a website full of information and resources. Although they have fewer direct resources than medialiteracynow.org, namle.org is designed more as a community of educators with whom to share ideas. Members of the community can attend a conference and interact with others who are also passionate about media literacy. They also compile research, like a recent "State of Media Literacy Education Report 2024" that is available for download. This report contains facts from annual surveys – for example, most respondents said media literacy is not a core subject in their school, and educators listed a lack of time and competing requirements as the main reasons media literacy wasn't taught as part of their curriculum. Information like this is essential if we are to continue pushing legislatures to implement media education in K-12 schools. I'm sure that everyone reading this book understands why it is so important to teach media literacy in schools, but many people in America don't place the same value on media literacy as they do on math, science, reading, etc. And that's not to say those things aren't important. And as a father of two, I understand that schools have to make tough choices about what they include in the curriculum and what they exclude. But there are an increasing number of studies like the ones being done on namle.org that highlight why media education is so vital and how exactly we're falling short currently.

Namle.org and medialiteracynow.org can be found easily with a Google search. I have no doubt that there are many other great resources out there on the web. I hardly scratched the surface of what other countries are doing with their media literacy education as well. Finland seems like a great system to model future efforts on. I'm sure there are others that do a great job as well. Being an educator in America, I have my own perspectives and biases about our system and how it compares globally.

Media literacy still underpins everything I do. I continue to lean heavily on Zettl, Silverblatt, Potter, McLuhan, and others who set the foundation for this line of thinking when I make decisions about the courses I teach and how to approach curriculum decisions. I also regularly read and watch the news and engage with others on social media. My friends online know me to advocate for media literacy at every turn. I rarely call out someone's biases or engage in arguments with people. But I do post things like Pete Buttigieg's recent speech to the Harvard Kennedy School's Institute of Politics (https://www.youtube.com/watch?v=qiV7xv24KDI). In that speech, Mr. Buttigieg discusses information literacy and laments that even though we have more information available to us than at any point in human history, we've never been less informed about issues because we live in our echo chambers and we don't interact with others the way we used to – in person and in a cordial, open-minded way. The words I wrote on social media when I posted an excerpt from this talk weren't a chastisement to conservatives. I have many friends on both sides of the aisle, and I understand many of the perspectives out there. I also see a vast amount of misinformation and disinformation out there being spread on social media, and my goal in posting is to help others see that and to challenge them to verify information and search for additional information that may challenge their biases. Holding on to bad information, simply because we agree with it, is one of the biggest challenges in American politics today. Even though we've made vast strides in media literacy, we've gotten worse as a society at verifying information and searching out additional information.

THE CHALLENGES FOR MEDIA EDUCATION MOVING FORWARD

I'm sure there have been other moments in American history when the country was as divided or more polarized than it is currently. Having said that, I can't remember a time during my lifetime when we've dug so deeply into our political ideologies that we won't even listen to other perspectives. Media literacy education is a great way to bring people back together. When my students learn how to look inward into their own media habits, and they understand how media shape their worldviews, they almost always realize that politics and news are way more complicated than they previously assumed. We have great conversations in class about current news events, but the students first have to learn how to search for legitimate information that they both agree with and that they disagree with. I can easily identify some of the challenges; the solutions are much more difficult. They require educators, parents, and politicians to work together to acknowledge the importance of media literacy and to lift those skills to the same level as reading, math, and science.

Young People Don't Watch or Read the News

One of the first challenges I've seen with college students is teaching them what news is and why professional journalists are important. These students, even my students who want to work in the journalism field when they graduate, simply don't watch or read the news. They've never seen a local newscast. They've never read a newspaper unless part of an article showed up in their social media feed. By and large, they don't know the difference between a blog and an actual newspaper. This is a generation that has been told that the media are biased, and they learned that lesson well. This is also a generation that expects everything online to be free. When we discuss professional journalists and how they investigate issues, verify information, and typically seek more than one source, they begin to realize that there's a difference between what Barbara Walters did and what Tomi Lahren did. But they are also unwilling to pay for a subscription to an actual newspaper. They don't choose to watch the local CBS newscast as part of their Paramount+ subscription. Some of them actually stay up-to-date with news and politics by watching late night talk shows (or at least YouTube clips from those talk shows) or Saturday Night Live, but most just see what other people post on social media and rarely dig any deeper than the words posted by their friend or the person they follow. Many of them don't even watch the video clip to go with the words, they just assume the words accurately recap the clip.

As Buttigieg points out in the video previously mentioned, our social media feeds are governed by algorithms. As with TV news bias, this isn't an evil plot. It's simply because social media platforms can't show you everything all at once, so they put in front of you the things they think you want to see (which means you'll interact more with the platform and they can charge more for advertising). But those algorithms often prevent us from seeing different viewpoints. When we get all of our news filtered through these algorithms on social media, it's likely to put us deeper into our echo chambers and solidify our stances on issues so deeply that we think anyone else's perspective is completely brainwashed.

The other thing pushing us further apart is the commercial pressure on news sources. Legitimate news sources try their best to verify sources, produce quality content, and remain impartial. But that rarely attracts viewers/listeners/readers. Instead, American society gravitates toward news sources that cater to ideologies. Fox News is popular, not because it's "fair and balanced" in its reporting, but because its anchors and personalities say sensational things that get their audiences worked up. MSNBC does the exact same thing on the left. When news outlets convince their audiences that they're the only ones to be trusted, then their ratings go up and their advertising money flows in because they have a dedicated audience. But the downside of this is that those viewers are taught not to trust news from any other source. Media literacy advocates like myself don't teach that Fox News or MSNBC are bad sources of news, but that people should watch both, as well as a number of other channels.

When I was growing up, my parents rarely shied away from talking about politics or news in front of the kids. My father worked for the Missouri House of Representatives, and politics just came up naturally over the dinner table. We also watched the news often enough, both local and national. And my parents subscribed to the local newspaper. I was fortunate, but I think growing up in that kind of home environment is still a key to teaching media literacy today. Schools can't do everything, and schools certainly have to be careful not to endorse any one perspective. Parents should be aware of their own media consumption and the habits they pass on to their kids. Parents who don't engage with news sources are inadvertently teaching their kids that news isn't important. Parents who rant about politics from one point of view or another probably aren't setting the best example, but they're at least letting their kids see that news is important, that information has value, and that consuming news helps you make more informed decisions about topics. As kids grow up, they will hopefully challenge their own stances and make up their own minds, so I don't think parents need to worry about swaying their children to one political ideology or away from it. I've seen too many families where children held different beliefs than their parents to think that parents always have a lasting impact on their children's political stances. But I also see students and family members whose parents didn't engage with the news. That lack of caring seems to trickle down to younger generations. It especially seems dangerous when parents don't engage with the news and convince their children that it's because the news is too biased to be trusted. Those children don't just ignore the news; they have contempt for it and actively avoid it.

Production Natives Swimming in Their Media-Saturated Environment

Production skills are an effective way to increase media literacy. When students engage in production, they naturally begin to assess the production values and the messages sent to them through the shows they watch and the media they consume. But what happens when we're trying to teach production skills to students who have grown up shooting YouTube or TikTok videos? Two of the most challenging students I've had in college over the last decade already had some level of success on YouTube. One had over a million followers. They were great students who knew exactly what they wanted to get out of school, but they came to college to learn how to produce higher-quality videos and to become more proficient with a camera. And it was even more difficult to convince them that they needed to worry about things like depth of field and exposure because they had already experienced success without having that knowledge. I'm not saying this to bash them – to be honest, it's hard to argue with their results. But it does highlight the challenge of teaching media literacy to students who grew up producing content with their cell phones or working on the livestream teams in their churches.

The same is true for students who are surrounded by media sources every hour of every day. When we watch television with our children, it takes effort to pause the show to answer their questions about what is happening and why characters are behaving in certain ways. Just the other day, my son asked why the character Nightcrawler on the X-Men cartoon had the ability to teleport. I paused the show, looked at him, and answered with all seriousness, "Because that's the way the character's creators chose to write it into the comics." I think it's a valuable lesson for him to learn that these choices are intentional things done by media creators. He should learn that there are people on both sides of a media text – the producers and the audiences – and that each has a role to play in the stories and messages conveyed. As he played a game on his iPad, he asked why it was so difficult to level up one of the characters he had just unlocked. I said, "Because the game designers want you to get impatient and spend actual money on the game in order to skip ahead." I wasn't being snide. I think it's important for him to learn why games exist and why companies spend time and money to develop them. But it takes effort and patience to teach these lessons. Once I pause the show, he almost regrets that he asked a question because he just wants to keep watching. I almost regret my commitment to media literacy because I just want to keep watching. It would be easier to just say, "Be quiet and watch the show", and honestly, I find myself doing that sometimes. But I have to remind myself that he is inundated by media constantly, and I need to be sure I give him the skills he needs to successfully navigate that world. At 12 years old, I've even started teaching him how to shoot still images with a DSLR camera. I let him shoot at family gatherings, and I try to teach him some basic skills when he seems open to it. My hope is that someday, he will be a media-literate citizen, regardless of the career path he chooses.

REFERENCES

Buttigieg, P. (2024). *A conversation with U.S. secretary of transportation Pete Buttigieg*. [video] Institute of Politics Harvard Kennedy School YouTube. Retrieved March 11, 2025 from https://www.youtube.com/watch?v=qiV7xv24KDI

Campbell, R. (1997). *Media and culture: An introduction to mass communication*. St. Martin's Press.

Davison, W. (1983). The third-person effect in communication. *Public Opinion Quarterly*, *47*(1), 1–15. DOI: 10.1086/268763

Finland Toolbox. *Media literacy and education in Finland*. Retrieved March 11, 2025 from toolbox.finland.fi

Gerbner, G., & Gross, L. (1976). Living with television: The violence profile. *Journal of Communication*, *26*(2), 172–199. DOI: 10.1111/j.1460-2466.1976.tb01397.x PMID: 932235

Hall, S. (1980). Encoding/decoding. In Hall, S., Hobson, D., Lowe, A., & Willis, P. (Eds.), *Culture, Media* (pp. 128–139). Language.

Hobbs, R. (1998). The seven great debates in the media literacy movement. *Journal of Communication*, *48*(1), 6–32. DOI: 10.1111/j.1460-2466.1998.tb02734.x

Hobbs, R. (2007). *Reading the media: Media literacy in high school English*. Teachers College Press.

Hobbs, R., & Jensen, A. (2009). The Past, Present, and Future of Media Literacy Education. *The Journal of Media Literacy Education*, *1*, 1–11. DOI: 10.23860/jmle-1-1-1

Hoechsmann, M., & Poyntz, S. (2012). *Media literacies: A critical introduction*. Blackwell Publishing. DOI: 10.1002/9781444344158

Kilbourne, J., & Jhally, S. (Director). (1979). *Killing us softly: Advertising's image of women* [motion picture]. Media Education Foundation.

Livingstone, S. (2004). Media literacy and the challenge of new information and communication technologies. *Communication Review*, *7*(1), 3–15. DOI: 10.1080/10714420490280152

McLuhan, M. (1994). *Understanding media (original work published in 1964)*. MIT Press. Medialiteracynow.org.

Messaris, P. (1994). *Visual literacy: image, mind, and Reality*. Westview Press, Inc.

Messaris, P. (1998). Visual aspects of media literacy. *Journal of Communication, 48*(1), 70–81. DOI: 10.1111/j.1460-2466.1998.tb02738.x

National Association of Media Literacy Educators. *Resources: Media literacy defined.* namle.org.

Potter, J. (1998). *Media literacy.* Sage Publications, Inc.

Price, S. (2005, Nov). *Learning to read: Working toward a practical model of media literacy.* Paper presented at the annual convention of the National Communication Association, Boston, MA.

Price, S. (2006, Apr). *Images of horror: Exploring the visual memory of 9-11.* Paper presented at the bi-annual conference on Visual Communication: Rhetorics and Technology, Rochester, NY.

Price, S. (2009, Nov). *Media literacy as a foundation for teaching television production.* Discussion Panel at the annual convention of the National Communication Association, Chicago, IL.

Silverblatt, A. (1995). *Medial literacy: Keys to interpreting media messages.* Praeger Publishers.

Zettl, H. (1998). Contextual media aesthetics as the basis for media literacy. *Journal of Communication, 48*(1), 81–95. DOI: 10.1111/j.1460-2466.1998.tb02739.x

Zettl, H. (2016). *Sight, sound, motion* (8th ed.). Wadsworth.

KEY TERMS AND DEFINITIONS

Media Text: A single mediated message. A text can be a TV show, a TV commercial, a magazine, a billboard on the side of the road, a facebook post, etc.

Aesthetics: The visual and aural elements that make up a media text. The way a shot is composed, the colors used in set design or editing, the music used in the background, etc. Aesthetics are the results of conscious decisions on the part of the media producer.

Encoding: The way the media text is produced, using aesthetic elements. Encoding the message implies that the media message is packaged into the text and sent to the audience for them to decode.

Decoding: The way the audience "reads" the media text. This includes the fact that every audience member has a different perspective and likely interprets the messages in slightly different ways. Hall (1980) calls this a "negotiated reading" of the text.

Cultivation Effect: Heavy media users (as defined by Gerbner) think that the world is more like the world they see in the media than it actually is. For example, people who watch crime shows on TV often overestimate the amount of actual crime in the world.

Opinion Leader: The people whose opinions we respect when it comes to news stories and events. These can be people we interact with in-person or online. They can also be TV personalities and others that we only receive one-sided communication from (when we watch TV news, for example).

Post-truth: The idea that there is so much information available that one can find "facts" and opinions to support almost any idea out there.

Third-person Effect: Essentially, Davison's (1983) research showed that people overestimate the effect media have on others and underestimate the effect media has on them.

AI: Artificial intelligence in media generally refers to the ability that computers have to generate images, videos, and audio that never actually existed. Essentially, it can create a video of a person, including a politician or other public figure, that is completely fake and attributes a message to that person in a way that we believe because we are seeing it with our own eyes.

Social Media Algorithms: Computer processes that analyze our previous behavior on social media, such as what type of posts we click on more often, whose posts we comment on more often, or even which advertisements we pause on as we're scrolling through our feeds. After recognizing this behavior, the computers then predict which content we will interact with more and present more of that type of content.

Echo Chamber: When our content is curated by algorithms, we aren't even exposed to people and ideas that differ from our own. It's not that we see things we disagree with. It's that we don't even see them in the first place.

Chapter 2
The Legal Context of News Literacy

Edward L. Carter
https://orcid.org/0009-0000-7509-3940
Brigham Young University, Provo, USA

ABSTRACT

The legal context for news literacy includes international human rights law, regional policymaking and governance, national legislation and regulatory efforts. Additionally, news literacy is enhanced by understanding certain legal concepts, including balancing of interests and logical reasoning using analogies. A fundamental question on which law contributes is the definition of news or journalism. Given the increasing presence of disinformation and misinformation in the marketplace of ideas, the news literate citizen must be able to critically analyze not only the content of news but also the environment—legal and otherwise—in which it exists and with which it interacts. The goal of this chapter is to expand on these and other aspects of the legal context of news literacy.

INTRODUCTION

Five areas of knowledge and skills have been identified as the "core of news literacy": the context in which news is produced, the process of news creation, the content of news, the circulation of news, and factors related to news consumption (Tully et al., 2022, p. 1593). This chapter focuses on the legal framework in which news exists, including the "legal protections and constraints in which content producers within and outside of news organizations operate in global contexts" (Tully et al., 2022, p. 1594). The global context is critical due to the cross-border nature of modern communication technology. The legal and constitutional protections for

DOI: 10.4018/979-8-3373-0872-2.ch002

news in the United States, including those under the First Amendment to the U.S. Constitution, function within a broader global system of international human rights law standards.

The chapter first explores the background and connections among news literacy, law and communication technologies. This exploration includes discussion of the emerging issues relating to regulation of artificial intelligence, social media and online content algorithms. The chapter then examines global standards for news literacy, primarily as reflected in the Sustainable Development Goals (SDGs) and the Convention on the Rights of the Child. After discussing the expectations for public news literacy education under these international legal norms, the chapter turns to the legal context of news literacy within regional and national legal frameworks. One of these frameworks is the European Commission's 2021 effort to establish harmonized rules for artificial intelligence, known as the "Artificial Intelligence Act." The chapter then considers the role of law in defining news, followed by an examination of how the law addresses intent in relation to false information. While the marketplace of ideas metaphor suggests that unintentional falsehoods, or misinformation, can be corrected through the collective rational behavior of citizens, contemporary circumstances have highlighted its limitations in protecting news from the harmful effects of intentional falsehoods or disinformation.

A series of legal doctrines in U.S. constitutional law and international human rights law already distinguish disinformation from misinformation. The difference in legal status between intentional and unintentional falsehoods is embodied in the doctrine of actual malice, which originates from the 1964 U.S. Supreme Court decision in *New York Times Co. v. Sullivan*. A related concept appears in Article 19 of the International Covenant on Civil and Political Rights (ICCPR; United Nations General Assembly, 1976). Following a discussion of these standards, the chapter examines other contributions of legal concepts to the field of news literacy and their role in helping news consumers develop analytical skills. A basic understanding of legal principles, such as the burden of proof, evidentiary rules, and balancing of interests, can enhance the analytical tools available to news consumers. Within the concept of balancing interests, news consumers should understand the values underlying legal protections for news, including the pursuit of truth, the facilitation of democratic decision-making, the provision of a societal safety valve, the oversight of government power, and the promotion of social cohesion and compromise. Discussion of these topics is accompanied by AI-related examples that could be integrated into media literacy curricula.

BACKGROUND OF NEWS LITERACY AND LAW ON GENERATIVE AI, DEEPFAKES AND ALGORITHMS

Scholars and policymakers have long recognized the relationship between news literacy and the effective functioning of legal, political, and governmental systems. The United Nations Educational, Scientific, and Cultural Organization (UNESCO) has played a critical role for decades in advocating for comprehensive media literacy education. UNESCO began fostering research on media literacy in the 1970s, and in 1982, it organized the International Symposium on Media Education. This symposium, which brought together representatives from 19 nations, resulted in the Grunwald Declaration on Media Education, which called for the development of comprehensive media education curricula, teacher training, support for media literacy education, and international cooperation (UNESCO, 1982). The declaration assigned responsibility for media literacy education to parents, teachers, media professionals, and policymakers. Its objective was "to develop the knowledge, skills and attitudes which will encourage the growth of critical awareness and, consequently, of greater competence among the users of electronic and print media" (UNESCO, 1982).

One author who traced the history of UNESCO's efforts in media literacy education described its progression from the 1950s onward (Altun, 2011). In the mid-20th century, news and information recipients were often viewed as blank slates needing protection from "bad media." By the 1970s, however, the media literacy agenda had shifted to a critical intelligence model, in which educators adopted a protectionist approach. Later, an empowerment model emerged, recognizing that consumers of news and other media engage with media sources and contribute to the production of meaning. A series of UNESCO conferences and initiatives following the 1982 Grunwald Declaration helped establish news and media literacy education as a "basic entitlement of every citizen, in every country in the world" (Altun, 2011). The international human right to news literacy is explored in detail in a subsequent section of this chapter.

The legal context of news literacy is rooted in a broader media literacy legal framework. The European Court of Human Rights has been particularly influential in shaping laws affecting media literacy education (Plotnikova et al., 2021). Its decisions, which balance fundamental rights such as freedom of expression, privacy, and reputation, provide a foundation for both news producers and consumers to understand the values and definitions of human rights, not only their own rights but also those of others (Plotnikova et al., 2021). While Article 10 of the European Convention for the Protection of Human Rights and Fundamental Freedoms guarantees free expression, it also requires that these rights be exercised responsibly, ensuring they do not infringe upon the rights of others. In this regard, media literacy education enables individuals to exercise their rights appropriately while critically evaluating how others do the same (Plotnikova et al., 2021).

The rise of misinformation and disinformation—or what some colloquially refer to as fake news—has led to legislative efforts in various countries aimed at curbing the spread of false information (Goldberg, 2018). Proposals for anti–fake news legislation have emerged in Germany, Ireland, Singapore, Cyprus, and California, among other places (Goldberg, 2018). The national security frame focuses primarily on the threat that foreign disinformation poses to domestic legal, political, and government systems (Levi, 2020). However, during the first administration of U.S. President Donald J. Trump, attention shifted to the internal threat to truth and good governance, particularly from attacks on journalists and their work, many of which originated from the federal executive branch itself (Levi, 2020). In response, renewed efforts were called for to strengthen journalism and enhance public understanding and support for it (Levi, 2020).

The potential for legal solutions to address the challenges posed by disinformation and misinformation continues to be proposed and debated. Proposals have included criminalizing the publication of "fake news for profit" as wire fraud (Size, 2020), accrediting journalists (Gonzalez & Shulz, 2017), and enacting disclosure and transparency laws for political messaging (Dawood, 2020), among others. Even while advocating legal approaches as partial solutions, legal scholars have acknowledged the bluntness of law as an instrument for social change. As a result, advocacy has increasingly shifted toward educational efforts (Goldberg, 2018). The international human rights law approach to news literacy takes a multi-pronged strategy, in which legal norms are adopted in treaty form but rely in part on education, voluntary compliance, and integration with economic and social development initiatives.

UNESCO has a critical mandate to lead international human rights law efforts in combating impunity for both digital and physical attacks on journalists. In 2018, UNESCO launched a database to track journalist killings and to document law enforcement efforts to achieve justice in cases of slain journalists. The UNESCO Observatory of Killed Journalists has recorded that, on average, a journalist is killed somewhere in the world every four days (UNESCO, 2018). Journalistic safety is a key issue for news literacy, as attacks on journalists create a chilling effect on news coverage, ultimately impacting the quality and content of news (Carter, 2023). While some journalist killings occur in conflict zones, the most common cases documented by UNESCO involve local journalists covering crime, corruption, government, and other local issues. The high-profile 2018 killing of journalist Jamal Khashoggi inside the Saudi Arabian consulate in Istanbul, carried out by agents of the Saudi government, raised public awareness, but lasting solutions remain elusive.

Generative AI presents thorny new problems for legal regulators, impacting news and a variety of other areas. For example, a group of authors, including John

Grisham, George R.R. Martin and Jodi Picoult, filed a class-action lawsuit against OpenAI in 2023 for copyright infringement, based on use of the authors' copyright-protected works to train ChatGPT. These issues are far from resolved, but questions have already arisen about whether copyright infringement liability could extend to users of AI programs. Intellectual property ownership of AI-generated content also remains unclear, although, thus far, judges and regulators in the United States have denied copyright ownership claims due to lack of originality (Student Press Law Center, 2024).

Regulation of AI for deception, including deepfakes, has preoccupied some U.S. state lawmakers in recent years. While the U.S. Congress has been mostly silent, and Presidents Biden and Trump adopted dueling executive orders that essentially canceled each other out, state legislatures have started to address the issue. The 2024 Utah Artificial Intelligence Policy Act, for example, requires regulated professionals—including lawyers and healthcare providers—to prominently disclose to consumers their uses of AI (White & Case, 2025). A California law requires online platforms to identify and block deepfakes relating to state elections during campaign seasons, and Tennessee's so-called ELVIS Act (Ensuring Likeness, Voice, and Image Security Act) prohibits unauthorized AI uses to mimic a person. Meanwhile, Colorado's comprehensive AI Act, scheduled to take effect in 2026, bans discrimination by AI against individuals in services relating to housing, education, health care, government, employment, insurance, and other areas (White & Case, 2025).

The prevalence of digital algorithms to determine the distribution of news and other content also has raised a variety of legal issues. Although much remains to be decided, the U.S. Supreme Court thus far has signaled its willingness to grant First Amendment protection to platform operations, including content algorithms (Carter et al., in press). In addition, Section 230 of the 1996 Communications Decency Act provides broad immunity to platforms for user-generated content misbehavior. But the unintended consequences of this immunity, which promise to greatly expand in the context of AI, have led to calls for revising Section 230 (Citron & Wittes, 2017).

INTERNATIONAL HUMAN RIGHTS LAW

Rights of Children to News Literacy

In the second half of the 20th century, the international community reached an agreement on nine foundational international human rights law treaties. One of these, the Convention on the Rights of the Child, has been signed and ratified by all United Nations member states except the United States, which has signed but not ratified the treaty (United Nations Children's Fund, n.d.). In total, 196 countries have committed to the treaty, including its provision in Article 28, establishing the right to compulsory and free education (United Nations General Assembly, 1989). The United Nations body responsible for interpreting and applying the Convention, the Committee on the Rights of the Child, issued an authoritative guideline in 2021 clarifying that Article 28's guarantee must include digital literacy education.

In General Comment No. 25, the Committee explicitly stated that news literacy is a key component of the digital literacy right. One rationale for this right came from a child's perspective shared with the Committee during its research leading up to General Comment No. 25, which established the need for governments, educators, and communication technology companies to "manage untrustworthy information online" (Committee on the Rights of the Child, 2021, para. 3). The right of children to access information includes an obligation for public authorities to ensure the availability of "age-appropriate and empowering digital content," including news about "civil and political affairs and children's rights" (Committee on the Rights of the Child, 2021, para. 51). Nations that are parties to the treaty have also committed to supporting the creation of news media content that is "diverse, accessible and beneficial" for children with disabilities and those from minority groups based on ethnicity, language, and other characteristics (Committee on the Rights of the Child, 2021, para. 52).

Misinformation and disinformation, among other types of harmful content, are identified as requiring official action to protect children (Committee on the Rights of the Child, 2021, para. 54). The quality of information is linked to its independence from commercial and political agendas. Digital algorithms that prioritize or recommend commercial and political content should be subject to government regulation to safeguard children's right to high-quality information (Committee on the Rights of the Child, 2021, para. 53). The treaty also places responsibility on the news industry to incorporate guidance into professional journalism codes of conduct regarding potential harms to children posed by digital communication technology. News reporting should take care not to reveal the identities of children who have been victimized and should also account for coverage of opportunities for children to benefit from digital content (Committee on the Rights of the Child, 2021, para. 57).

According to the Committee, digital literacy education should begin in preschool and continue throughout all years of schooling for those under age 18:

> *Curricula should include the knowledge and skills to safely handle a wide range of digital tools and resources, including those relating to content, creation, collaboration, participation, socialization and civic engagement. Curricula should also include critical understanding, guidance on how to find trusted sources of information and to identify misinformation and other forms of biased or false content, including on sexual and reproductive health issues, human rights, in-*

cluding the rights of the child in the digital environment, and available forms of support and remedy. (Committee on the Rights of the Child, 2021, para. 104)

Furthermore, digital literacy curricula should help children understand the risks and harms associated with cyberaggression and various forms of violence and abuse, including sexual exploitation and trafficking. The Committee's focus on the risks posed to children by digital technology is framed within a broader concern for child development. General Comment No. 25 emphasizes children's social, cognitive, and emotional development, recognizing that digital technology can both support and hinder this process. This emphasis on development is a recurring theme in international human rights law concerning news literacy.

Development, Education, and Freedom of Expression

The interaction between news media and development is a key concern in international human rights law. Development goals in sectors such as the economy, health care, and education are supported by independent and reliable news sources. At the same time, the development of news organizations and individual journalists capable of producing such news is itself a goal of sustainable development efforts within the international human rights law system. Media development requires citizens to be media literate (Scott, 2014). As citizens become critical media consumers, they can not only recognize hate speech and propaganda but also create media content, contributing to the development of their societies. As individuals and their communities strengthen media literacy, there is "an expectation and a demand among the public for a free and independent press" (Scott, 2014, p. 88).

In 2015, all UN member states adopted a set of objectives known as the 2030 Agenda for Sustainable Development, which includes 17 specific outcomes called the SDGs. SDG16 aims to "promote peaceful and inclusive societies for sustainable development, provide access to justice for all and build effective, accountable and inclusive institutions at all levels" (United Nations, n.d.). At its core, SDG16 seeks to establish the rule of law. One of its key targets, Target 16.10, is to "ensure public access to information and protect fundamental freedoms" (SDG16NOW, n.d.). Achieving this target requires international organizations and national human rights institutions to combat impunity for attacks on journalism. These attacks include both disinformation campaigns intended to discredit independent news reporting and physical violence against journalists (SDG16NOW, n.d.). The link to news literacy is evident in Target 16.10's mandate for national human rights institutions to educate the public about the "killings, fabricated legal charges, misuse of specific laws and other attacks" on journalists and human rights defenders (SDG16NOW, n.d.).

In the international human rights law system, education serves many purposes, but foremost among these is enabling "all persons to participate effectively in a free society" (UN General Assembly, 1976, art. 13). The right to education, like the right to freedom of expression, is not only inherently valuable but also instrumental in realizing other human rights (Committee on Economic, Social and Cultural Rights, 1999). Within this right to education, which is also reflected in SDG4, there is a specific emphasis on global citizenship education (UNESCO, n.d.). Education about journalism plays a crucial role in developing global citizens (Gerodimos, n.d.). As enshrined in Article 19 of the ICCPR, the right to freedom of expression depends on a well-informed and rational public that exercises its right to receive independent news content and act on it for the public good.

REGIONAL, NATIONAL, AND LOCAL NEWS LITERACY LEGAL STRUCTURES

The concept of information literacy as a human right was formalized in a non-binding 2005 declaration known as the Alexandria Proclamation, issued at a UNESCO conference called the High-Level Colloquium on Information Literacy. When applied to news literacy, this idea has since been incorporated into various regional, national, and local policies and legislation efforts.

The European Union, for example, introduced media literacy requirements in its 2018 Audiovisual Media Services Directive, mandating that member states engage in media literacy initiatives with their citizens and report progress regularly to the European Commission (Carter et al., in press). The directive set the goal of enabling "citizens to access information and to use, critically assess and create media content responsibly and safely" (European Union, 2018). Some EU countries, such as Finland, have developed well-organized national news literacy strategies that integrate efforts across education, governance, civil society, and voluntary collaboration with social media platforms. These initiatives aim to help citizens critically evaluate media content while advancing national objectives related to human rights and the rule of law (Carter et al., in press).

Meanwhile, the European Commission in 2021 proposed harmonized standards to be adopted by member states of the European Union specifically governing use of AI in commercial and other contexts (European Commission, 2021). The standards would prohibit use of AI in several ways, including use of subliminal techniques to distort an individual's behavior and cause harm; exploitation of vulnerabilities due to a person or group's age or disability; creation of social credit scores in certain contexts; and use of real-time remote biometric ID systems for law enforcement in public spaces unless aimed to search for certain crime victims or prevent imminent harm. In addition, the standards address data privacy and record-keeping, transparency, human oversight and other obligations of AI systems (European Commission,

2021). While the standards do not specifically address news, their application to prevent certain other practices could have broad implications for information and media literacy.

Meanwhile, some U.S. states have pursued media and news literacy legislation with mixed results (Chornoby et al., 2023). One study examined the motivations behind these state-level legislative efforts (Chornoby et al., 2023), though further research is needed to assess their impact.

WHAT LAW CONTRIBUTES TO THE DEFINITION OF NEWS

One of the uniquely valuable contributions of law and legal systems to news literacy is the definition of news. If citizens can distinguish high-value news from low-value information that sometimes masquerades as news, they may avoid confusion and related challenges. Although there is no single legal definition of news—and some lawyers, judges, and legal scholars refrain from defining it or believe doing so would undermine press independence—the reality is that certain areas of law do touch on its definition. For example, the legal protections afforded to journalists regarding confidential sources and other newsgathering information, known as reporter's privilege, require defining both journalism and journalists.

A key legal question in many jurisdictions is whether to define journalists functionally or formalistically for the purposes of reporter's privilege. In Alabama, for instance, the state shield law applies to anyone "engaged in, connected with or employed on any newspaper, radio broadcasting station or television station, while engaged in a newsgathering capacity" (Ala. Code § 12-21-142). This definition combines a functional element—"engaged in"—with a formalistic one—"newspaper, radio…or television." Because of this mixed approach, a magazine journalist was denied privilege protection since magazines were not explicitly included in the statute (*Price v. Time, Inc.*).

In many other jurisdictions, however, the functional definition prevails. For example, journalist privilege exists in international human rights law, where the protection extends to the function of journalism rather than formal employment by a news organization (Carter, 2017). Because this privilege protects the function of journalism, it applies not only to reporters but also to those who assist in gathering, producing, and distributing news (Carter, 2017). The international human rights law definition of journalism focuses on the independent pursuit and dissemination of relevant and truthful information in the public interest (Carter & Westenskow, 2020). This definition has several key components, including independence, relevance, a good faith effort to obtain and share truth, and service to the public interest. Within the international human rights law framework, this definition of journalism provides a relatively clear distinction from the broader right to freedom of expression, within which freedom of the press—or freedom of journalism—operates (Carter & Westenskow, 2020).

In the context of the First Amendment to the U.S. Constitution, "freedom of the press" is explicitly mentioned alongside the broader "freedom of speech." However, the U.S. Supreme Court has not interpreted the Press Clause as having independent meaning apart from the Speech Clause (Carter & Westenskow, 2020). In other words, journalists are entitled to the same rights—no more, no less—as everyone else. This approach has generally worked well for decades, as courts have still been able to account for the particular role of journalism in society through balancing tests, as discussed later in the section "Balancing of Interests and Values of Free Expression."

In the international human rights law system, the overarching balancing framework for freedom of expression is the proportionality test, established in Article 19 of the ICCPR. This test requires governments to ensure that any restrictions on free expression, including journalism, are proportional to the interest being served. In other words, government actions that limit journalism must be justified and proportionate to their intended purpose.

Some scholars argue that freedom of journalism in international human rights law is narrower but stronger than general freedom of expression. The UN Human Rights Committee, which oversees the implementation of Article 19 of the ICCPR, has stated that the proportionality test would never permit a government to engage in "a physical attack, arbitrary arrest, torture, threat to life, or murder of a journalist merely for doing journalism" (Carter & Westenskow, 2020, p. 131). Under international human rights law, protections for journalists reach near-absolute levels when they report on core topics "such as elections, politics and the performance of public officials" (Carter & Westenskow, 2020).

For news literacy, understanding the definition of journalism and the scope of its legal protections can help distinguish high-value news and information from low-value content. Much of what appears on cable television news channels and social media does not constitute core journalism, even when presented under the label of a news organization. Commentary, debate, discussion, and opinion are certainly valuable forms of freedom of expression. They may serve an informational role and even partially fulfill some of the key values of free expression—such as acting as a government watchdog, truth-seeker, or educating the public—discussed below. However, they do not represent the core function of independent reporting, that delivers truthful and relevant information in the public interest. News-literate readers should be able to distinguish between those forms of communication and core journalism itself.

THE LEGAL DISTINCTION BETWEEN DISINFORMATION AND MISINFORMATION

The concept of freedom of expression aims to facilitate the pursuit of truth, but paradoxically, achieving this goal requires news consumers to tolerate the possibility of falsehoods. However, this tolerance should be nuanced enough to distinguish between intentionally false statements (disinformation or lies) and unintentionally false statements (misinformation or errors). If society is rational enough to recognize and reject false statements, then official censorship is not justified.

This idea has ancient roots, appearing in the teachings of Gamaliel, a leading judicial and religious authority in Jerusalem. When Peter and the apostles of Jesus Christ were arrested, Gamaliel counseled the Sanhedrin to show restraint (Schechter & Bacher, 1909; *New Testament King James Version*, 2013, Acts 5). Rather than condemning the apostles for unorthodox preaching, he argued that if their message was true, it should not be opposed, and if it was false, it would "come to nought" on its own (*New Testament King James Version*, 2013, Acts 5:38).

A similar sentiment emerged in the 19th-century writings of John Stuart Mill (2002), who argued that opposing viewpoints are essential for correcting potential misperceptions held by the majority. However, Mill also acknowledged that society has a right to curtail individual speech when it reaches the point of causing harm. U.S. Supreme Court Justice Oliver Wendell Holmes, influenced by the economic free-market theories of Adam Smith, among others, advocated for a "free trade in ideas" in his dissenting opinion in the 1919 case *Abrams v. United States*. Holmes' concept, now known as the marketplace of ideas, assumes that rational citizens will reject falsehoods in favor of truth.

Modern scholars, however, have recognized that market failures can occur for various reasons and that falsehoods sometimes overpower truth in an unregulated marketplace shaped by commercial forces (Barron, 1967; Hopkins, 1996).

NEW YORK TIMES CO. V. SULLIVAN AND THE ACTUAL MALICE STANDARD

In this landmark Supreme Court case on freedom of the press, the ability of news consumers to recognize and discount relatively harmless errors while relying on prevailing truth played a central role. The Court's 1964 ruling in *New York Times Co. v. Sullivan* established a crucial distinction between intentional or reckless falsehoods and unintentional or merely negligent falsehoods. The decision effectively protected not only truthful speech under the First Amendment but also a margin of unintentional and non-reckless falsehoods surrounding the truth. Since "erroneous statement is inevitable in free debate," Justice William J. Brennan explained, this protection was necessary to provide freedom of expression with enough "breathing space…to survive" (*New York Times Co. v. Sullivan*, 1964, p. 272).

The facts of the *Sullivan* case, which arose during the civil rights movement, are essential to understanding the legal principle that has guided American news consumers toward truth for six decades, even in a media landscape where falsehoods exist. Montgomery Police Commissioner Lester B. Sullivan sued *The New York Times* and four Black clergy in Alabama for defamation, claiming that a newspaper advertisement carrying their names, along with those of 60 other civil rights leaders, had harmed his reputation.

The ad, titled "Heed Their Rising Voices," was published in the *Times* on March 29, 1960. It asserted that civil rights activists in the South were "engaged in wide-spread non-violent demonstrations in positive affirmation of the right to live in human dignity as guaranteed by the U.S. Constitution and the Bill of Rights" but that they were "being met by an unprecedented wave of terror by those who would deny and negate that document" (*New York Times Co. v. Sullivan*, 1964, p. 256). The advertisement also appealed for donations to support the civil rights cause and the legal defense fund for Martin Luther King, Jr.

The ad contained some inaccuracies, some serious and some benign. It stated that students sang "My Country 'Tis of Thee" on the Alabama State Capitol steps when, in fact, the song was the national anthem. Students had not been padlocked out of the Alabama State College dining hall, and police did not form a "ring" around the entire campus, as the ad claimed. King had been arrested four times rather than seven, and police had not been involved in placing a bomb at his home.

The ad did not specifically identify Sullivan, referring only to police and "Southern violators" as antagonists of civil rights advocates. However, Sullivan argued that the ad nonetheless harmed his reputation because, as police commissioner, he would be identified as the person responsible. A state court jury in Alabama found the newspaper and the ministers liable, imposing a $500,000 judgment without requiring any proof of intent or carelessness on the part of *The New York Times*. The verdict was upheld on appeal in the state courts, but the U.S. Supreme Court took a different view.

Justice Brennan's majority opinion first asserted that the advertisement was entitled to First Amendment protection because it expressed an advocacy message on an issue of great public concern. The country, Brennan said, had developed "a profound national commitment to the principle that debate on public issues should be uninhibited, robust, and wide-open, and that it may well include vehement, caustic, and sometimes unpleasantly sharp attacks on government and public officials" (*New York Times Co. v. Sullivan*, 1964, p. 270). The Court criticized Alabama's libel law for failing to protect critics of official conduct from self-censorship and for effectively requiring speakers to prove the truth of their statements. Instead, Brennan wrote, the First Amendment required a public official suing for defamation to prove not only that the statement was false but also that it was made with "actual malice," which he defined as "knowledge that it was false or...reckless disregard of whether it was false or not" (*New York Times Co. v. Sullivan*, 1964, p. 280). Since *The New York Times* neither knew the claims in the ad were false nor acted recklessly, the damage award was reversed.

The *Sullivan* precedent has implications for AI applications impacting news and information. News organizations using AI journalism content, for example, could be liable for defamation of public officials or public figures only if those plaintiffs could prove that false statements in the AI journalism content were made with knowledge of their falsity, or recklessness. Those plaintiffs would likely point to evidence of the known unreliability, or frequent errors, of AI-generated text. Journalists who treat AI content as more than merely suggestive could open themselves up to liability in this regard. But journalists who made good-faith attempts to verify the accuracy of AI-generated content before news publication would seemingly then benefit from the protection of the First Amendment under the *Sullivan* rule.

International Human Rights Law's "Error but Without Malice" Standard

National courts outside the United States have not widely adopted the rule established in *Sullivan*. However, the premier international human rights law body for freedom of expression has embraced a similar principle: "error but without malice." That language appears in General Comment No. 34, the UN Human Rights Committee's (2011) official explanation of the freedom of expression and freedom of press rights under Article 19 of the ICCPR. Similar to the U.S. Supreme Court's approach, the Committee limits the application of this rule to plaintiffs who hold political office or are well-known enough to justify prioritizing free expression on public affairs over individual reputation. As a result, a certain amount of false speech—if made without malice or intent—remains protected under Article 19, placing the responsibility on the public to act in good faith, both in expressing themselves and assessing the validity of others' speech.

Ramifications for News Literacy of the Actual Malice and Error but Without Malice Rules

The concept of good faith is the key takeaway for news literacy from both the actual malice and error but without malice standards. If a speaker is attempting to ascertain and communicate the truth in good faith, then the law protects their speech from a defamation claim by a public official or public figure, even if the statement turns out to be false and causes reputational harm. While the law is not without critics, including at least two current U.S. Supreme Court justices who have suggested they would like *New York Times Co. v. Sullivan* to be reconsidered, the point of the decision is not to encourage false or harmful statements about public officials. Rather, it promotes the idea of popular sovereignty—that a self-governing populace must be free to discuss the performance of those in positions of power and influence. This free discussion should aim at the truth but is safeguarded from punishment, even if it sometimes misses the mark, as long as the misstep is unintentional or not reckless.

The effect of this legal standard protecting unintentional false speech is to draw a clear distinction between disinformation and misinformation in terms of what the public in a democracy can and should tolerate. Not all lies can be criminalized or made subject to civil liability. However, the actual malice and error but without malice rules establish the principle that some lies—specifically those that harm reputation—can be subject to civil liability and possibly criminal sanction. The disinformation increasingly permeating social media platforms threatens to distort the marketplace of ideas, ultimately undermining its viability as a means of discovering truth. As algorithm-driven social media content reinforces echo chambers and often amplifies intentional falsehoods, the ability and willingness of users to distinguish and prioritize high-value, sometimes challenging, information over readily available, pleasing, low-value information seems to be declining. The profit-driven motives of social media platforms, combined with the rise of intentional falsehoods, have led to the emergence of a new framework: the anti-marketplace of ideas (Carter et al., in press).

The concept of the anti-marketplace of ideas is derived from the economic anti-marketplace articulated by 20th-century French historian Fernand Braudel. In his study of the economic history of multiple societies from the 15th to the 18th century, Braudel identified three zones of economic activity. The first is material life, where individuals primarily produce goods for their own use. Next is economic life, where individuals begin to trade and sell goods in local, transparent transactions. In this zone, minimal government regulation is needed or desirable because individuals can assess the quality of items and the fairness of transactions on their own. Free-market philosophies, such as Adam Smith's invisible hand, align with this middle zone of economic life. Finally, capitalism—the zone of the anti-market—comprises large-scale, non-transparent interactions such as those conducted by multinational corporations. In this capitalist context, government regulation is not only desirable but essential for the system's proper functioning.

When applying Braudel's three zones of economic life to freedom of expression and journalism, the idea is that government generally should not censor ideas exchanged in local, transparent settings. If speakers and listeners can reliably judge the quality of content because they are visible and audible to one another, then freedom from government regulation in the marketplace of ideas is justified. However, in the context of large-scale, non-transparent interactions like those conducted by social media platforms, some form of government regulation is not only desirable for the public interest but also necessary for the system to function (Carter et al., in press). While local marketplaces of ideas can exist within user interactions on social media platforms—provided those users are identifiable and act in good faith to share truth—the platforms themselves should not be seen as part of the marketplace of ideas. Instead, they represent a zone of speech capitalism, where the public interest calls for targeted and careful regulation by public authorities acting wisely (Carter et al., in press).

It is important to acknowledge, however, that the U.S. Supreme Court has, so far, treated platform operations—such as content moderation and algorithms that prioritize content—as free-speech activities deserving of First Amendment protection (Carter et al., in press). The continued protection of social media platforms from liability for user-generated content under Section 230 of the Communications Decency Act has contributed to the spread of disinformation and misinformation, further exacerbating the decline of high-quality news sources. Section 230, adopted by Congress in 1996 to foster the growth of the Internet, has resulted in a lack of incentives for social media platforms to ensure the quality of information. This absence of responsibility has been detrimental to journalism and truth, as platforms have been allowed to pursue purely commercial goals—maximizing user attention—without significant pressure to promote the kind of independent, relevant, and truthful information identified earlier in this chapter as essential to the public interest. The issues are likely to persist and grow in the AI context.

CONTRIBUTIONS OF FOUNDATIONAL LEGAL CONCEPTS TO NEWS LITERACY

Burden of Proof

Few concepts in law are as familiar yet as mysterious as the concept of proof. Legal dramas in television shows, movies, and streaming platforms have introduced the public to the oath administered to witnesses in courtrooms: "Do you solemnly swear that the testimony you are about to give in this cause shall be the truth, the whole truth, and nothing but the truth?" However, a leading law school textbook on legal evidence—after citing this very oath—includes an epigram from Carl Sandburg's 1936 poem "The People, Yes," which suggests that a witness cannot know the whole truth but can only “tell you what I saw and what I heard and I’ll swear to that…” (Younger et al., 2000).

Despite this qualification, the law has a well-developed process for ascertaining the closest possible approximation of truth through a complex series of evidentiary rules and burdens of proof. In a civil case, the plaintiff bears the burden of proving their assertions by a preponderance of evidence, meaning that their evidence outweighs the opposing side’s evidence. In a criminal case, the prosecution must meet the higher standard of proving guilt beyond a reasonable doubt. Judges and juries assess the evidence presented and determine whether the relevant burden has been met.

News consumers seeking literacy could apply the lesson of these concepts, if not the exact legal principles themselves, in weighing and judging the content of news presented to them. However, in line with the principle expressed in the Sandburg poem, the news consumer may be unable to ascertain the whole truth. Instead, the news consumer can consider the burden of proof carried by the news conveyer: Has the news producer sufficiently provided evidence to meet a certain burden—perhaps more than a preponderance and approaching beyond a reasonable doubt—to justify trust or belief in the validity of the assertions in the news content? That epistemological approach would prevent news consumers from believing many of the outlandish, unsupported assertions on social media platforms.

Some further thoughts from evidentiary admissibility may be useful in a news literacy context. For evidence to be admissible in court, it must be “relevant, material, and competent” (Younger et al., 2000, p. 30). Relevance and materiality refer to whether the evidence being presented makes a difference or matters to the determination of the issue at hand. Competence means the evidence was obtained properly, such that reliability is likely. To the extent that journalists can be more transparent about how they obtain the information in their news content, they provide consumers with a basis to form conclusions about competence and reliability. News consumers may need to consult sources outside the specific news content they are viewing to judge for themselves the relevance and materiality of the facts being asserted.

A final evidentiary concept to consider in the context of news literacy relates to the cross-examination of witnesses and the hearsay rule. Given the goal of obtaining truth—or the closest possible version of it—the common-law rules of evidence, developed over hundreds of years, place a high value on first-hand witness testimony presented in court, where the first-hand witness can be cross-examined by the party who stands to be harmed by the testimony (Younger et al., 2000). However, first-hand witnesses are sometimes unavailable, raising the question of whether another person who heard the first-hand witness discuss the matter can present what they heard, essentially acting as a second-hand witness to the ultimate truth of the matter. Generally, the rule against hearsay prevents second-hand testimony, but exceptions exist. These exceptions apply when the need is great and the reliability is high (Younger et al., 2000).

Like judges and juries, news consumers would be best served by first-hand witness testimony. However, journalists are almost always interposed between the first-hand witness and the news consumer. In many cases, it would be difficult or impossible for news sources—those with first-hand knowledge of events—to speak directly to news consumers. Thus, the journalist's role parallels the exceptions to the hearsay rule—journalists are traditionally deemed reliable, and the need for their second-hand testimony is often significant. However, modern communication technology gives the appearance of direct access to first-hand witnesses or news sources, suggesting authenticity and reliability. Figures like Trump have used social media platforms to reach the public directly, bypassing journalists. The problem is that the appearance of authenticity does not guarantee the reliability of information when the source is motivated by factors like power, greed, or political agenda rather than a commitment to truth.

As a result, news-literate citizens should consider the role of journalists as more than just an intermediary for convenience. Journalists not only fulfill the practical role of conveying information from first-hand witnesses to the public when direct contact is not possible, but they also ensure the reliability of the information before choosing to relay it. The epistemology of journalism is verification (Kovach & Rosenstiel, 2001). As long as news consumers can identify real journalism, as defined and discussed above, they should be able to trust its reliability without feeling compelled to trust every random person's perspective, particularly when those individuals lack first-hand knowledge of the matter. The introduction of AI journalism, however, presents additional complications because the AI systems are not first-hand witnesses or even, sometimes, second-hand witnesses. Instead, they could be considered third-hand witnesses because they essentially are scraping online sources for information, and some of those sources are not based on first-hand knowledge. So, the application of evidentiary legal principles to AI journalism would indicate a degree of caution is necessary, and this should be incorporated into news literacy curricula.

Standard of Review and Deference

An appellate court's role is to review the actions of a lower court, with the primary guideline being to ensure fairness (Luyster, 2007). To ensure fairness, the appeals court identifies errors committed by the lower court but only takes action if the error is deemed reversible. Some errors are considered harmless because they did not affect the outcome, while other actions by the lower court are considered to be within the court's discretion, prompting the appeals court to apply deference.

The lens through which the appeals court views the lower court's actions is called the standard of review. Applying a "thick lens" results in close or careful scrutiny of the lower court's actions, making reversal more likely. In contrast, using a "thin lens," or more deferential scrutiny, reduces the likelihood of reversal.

The areas where a trial judge is entitled to deference relate directly to the competence or expertise of the trial court (Luyster, 2007). For example, a trial judge can directly observe a witness's demeanor and credibility, so determinations on those issues are entitled to deference by an appeals court. However, a legal conclusion by the trial court may not be entitled to any particular deference on appeal, as appellate judges are just as capable of analyzing the legal issue. In such cases, the appeals court may review the issue *de novo*, essentially reconsidering it. Similarly, courts have long deferred to the expertise of administrative agencies, which are staffed by subject-matter experts. However, the doctrine of administrative deference has changed following the Supreme Court's decision in the 2024 case *Loper Bright Enterprises v. Raimondo*.

Nevertheless, even *Loper Bright* recognizes that administrative agencies are entitled to respect when acting within their statutory authority (Teichert, 2025). The principle of deference also applies to news literacy. Experts quoted in the news, or expert journalists themselves, could be entitled to deference by news consumers on certain issues. This does not mean that readers and viewers of news cannot make their own decisions about what or whom to believe. Despite the rise of anti-intellectualism and anti-expert sentiment in some circles, the prudent course remains to trust the expertise of individuals and institutions who are highly competent in their fields and have proven to be worthy of trust. However, the adoption of artificial intelligence by government agencies raises questions about the reliability of their exercise of discretion. Two scholars have argued that automation of the administrative state undermines their supposed expertise and necessitates skepticism relating to their processes and decisions (Calo & Citron, 2021).

Balancing of Interests and Values of Free Expression

The common law is full of balancing tests. Judges must weigh various interests in deciding cases, and lawyers conduct similar balancing analyses in constructing arguments for their clients. The interests of various parties are compared and weighed, then either accepted, rejected, or accommodated (Aldisert, 1996). According to Aldisert (1996), "an interest is a social fact, factor or phenomenon reflected by a claim or demand or desire which human beings, either individually or as groups or associations or relations, seek to satisfy and which has been recognized as socially valid by authoritative decision makers in society" (p. 489). Interests may be primarily individual, public, or social. For example, all members of a society have interests in collective security, stability of social institutions, and general progress. Individuals within those general interests may have specific interests in personal privacy or reputation (Aldisert, 1996, p. 490).

In the context of news literacy, some highly relevant interests to understand and weigh or consider are the values of freedom of expression. At times, these interests or values may be outweighed by other interests, which is normal because no particular interest will always prevail. The values of free expression can be described as the benefits to society and individuals of safeguarding the rights of journalists and others to communicate publicly. One interest highly relevant to news is the role that freedom of expression and freedom of the press play in checking the government's use of power (Blasi, 1977). This is sometimes referred to as the watchdog function of journalism. Through investigative and other forms of news reporting, journalists work on behalf of the public to hold government officials and institutions accountable. The public receives the information needed to advocate, lobby, vote, and otherwise act for change in policies and elected officials as necessary. The news-literate citizen does well to identify when journalism is filling this function and to support it.

Other values of news or freedom of the press include facilitating the search for truth in the marketplace of ideas, as discussed previously in connection with the *Abrams* case, and enabling democratic decision-making (Meiklejohn, 1961). Journalism is not perfect and may be tied to a commercial imperative to support its news reporting. However, in general, journalists are progressive reformers whose primary goal is to highlight flaws and needs in society so those problems can be resolved and conditions improved for everyone (Gans, 1979). Journalists are altruistic and believe that public servants should be, too (Gans, 1979). So, when journalists critique public officials, it can stem from a sense of righteous indignation and optimism that things can be made better. Freedom of the press and the work of journalists may also promote tolerance in society for minority perspectives (Bollinger, 1988). Meanwhile, individuals who engage in journalism may find a self-fulfillment or autonomy interest served (Richards, 1974).

News literacy should account for these and other values or interests of journalism. In a given case, the interests of journalism may be outweighed by national security, individual reputation, or another interest, but that determination requires careful weighing of the purposes and impacts on both sides. Judges and lawyers are not computers who merely perform calculations and produce "mechanical" jurisprudential answers (Aldisert, 1996, p. 493). The weighing of interests is a human enterprise that should be principled but also nuanced and responsive to human needs. Applying the law mechanically must sometimes be balanced against doing individual justice: "And the result should meet the test of the ends of law… that the decision should contribute to the establishment and preservation of a social environment in which the quality of human life can be spirited, improving and unimpaired" (Aldisert, 1996, p. 495).

In balancing interests surrounding communication in a technology-driven environment, news-literate consumers must account for the increasing secrecy of surveillance and other corporate and government practices. The legal scholar Frank Pasquale has called this the "knowledge problem," or the black box (Pasquale, 2015). Even though technology promised to democratize information, the reality is that transparency is not the goal of many corporations and governments who prioritize other agendas. News literacy curricula should account for these phenomena.

Logical Reasoning and Analogies

The common-law legal system, originating in England and passed on to the United States, relies heavily on the concept of precedent. Put simply, a precedent is a binding legal rule established in a previous case. Judges, lawyers, and litigants in a common-law system are bound by precedential rules established in prior cases they did not participate in but must respect and follow. The binding nature of a precedent, or legal rule, hinges on the similarity between the underlying facts of the precedent case and the current case at hand. A leading authority explained it this way: "If facts in the putative precedent are identical with or reasonably similar to those in the compared case, the precedent is recognized as legitimate, and it is applied" (Aldisert, 1996, p. 313).

This concept has several potential applications in the context of news literacy. A favorite pastime of social media users, including some journalists, is comparing the behavior of one political party or individual to another and then drawing conclusions about the ramifications of that behavior. For example, much debate has taken place over the similarities and differences between Hillary Clinton's use of an apparently unsecured and unapproved email account to conduct official business as Secretary of State and Trump's taking of boxes of classified documents from the White House to his Mar-a-Lago residence after losing the 2020 presidential election. Were those two actions comparable? Should federal prosecutors have charged Clinton with crimes, as they did Trump? The key to answering these questions is logical reasoning, specifically analogy. Drawing analogies is a staple of legal decision-making. If the facts of Clinton's case are very different from those of Trump's, then the rule applied to Clinton need not be the same as the rule applied to Trump. But if the facts are the same or very similar in the necessary ways, then the rule should be the same.

According to Aldisert (1997), analogy is the core of the Socratic method, frequently used in U.S. law school classrooms. Analogy is a form of, or at least similar to, inductive reasoning. In both inductive reasoning and reasoning by analogy, one begins with specific facts and then reasons toward a generally applicable rule. While the value of inductive generalization depends on the quantity of cases, the value of an analogy depends on the quality of the resemblance to another case (Aldisert, 1997, p. 51). Savvy news consumers must be able to determine when an attempted analogy is not valuable due to significant differences between the two sets of facts being compared.

Beyond reasoning by analogy, numerous concepts from logical reasoning could be relevant in the context of news literacy. Sources quoted or paraphrased by journalists may engage in a variety of logical fallacies, and the journalist may recognize them as such but still relay them to readers out of a duty to convey what the source said while withholding value judgments. The journalist's choice to leave those value judgments up to readers and viewers can be challenging for recipients, however, if they do not have full access to the information necessary to assess the circumstances. Still, the ability to recognize logical fallacies can aid news consumers in the age of AI and algorithms. Among these common fallacies that may appear in news content are *argumentum ad verecundiam*, or the appeal to prestige; *argumentum ad hominem*, or the appeal to personal ridicule; *argumentum ad populum*, or the appeal to the masses; *argumentum ad terrorem*, or the appeal to terror; and *argumentum ad ignoratiam*, or the appeal to ignorance (Aldisert, 1997, p. 144).

Reasonable Person Standard

The law often requires judgments to be made using both subjective and objective standards. For example, when a person is sued for harming someone else due to negligence, the law examines both the defendant's subjective conduct and an objective standard of conduct that would have been followed by a hypothetical "reasonable person." The reasonable person standard is used not only in negligence analysis but also in areas such as self-defense analysis in criminal law, determining whether sexual harassment has created a hostile work environment, and addressing questions of constitutional equality (Moran, 2010). Despite critiques that the reasonable person standard allows legal decision-makers to impose their own values and perspectives, the reasonable person has been called "the common law's most enduring legal fiction" (Moran, 2010, p. 1234).

The reasonable person has common, ordinary qualities (Moran, 2010). In the famous 1837 case *Vaughan v. Menlove*, the reasonable person standard played a key role. Vaughan and Menlove had cottages near each other in rural western England, and Menlove had a large haystack near the cottages. Vaughan warned Menlove that the haystack could catch fire and cause damage, which indeed occurred. In the ensuing tort litigation, Menlove claimed he was not intelligent and had exercised his best efforts to avoid causing harm. However, the court applied the reasonable person standard and concluded that Menlove should have heeded the warning about the haystack and taken action to avoid the risk of fire. As a result, Menlove was liable for damages.

In news literacy, applying the reasonable person standard could be beneficial in several ways. A news consumer might engage in a thought experiment about what a reasonable journalist would have done in a given circumstance and then reach judgments accordingly. Sometimes, journalists face digital and physical attacks, deadline pressure, or difficulty obtaining relevant information. In such cases, the actions of a reasonable journalist could be viewed with some level of understanding and even leniency compared to those of a large news organization with abundant resources, time, and access to information. The reasonable person standard could also be applied to the news consumer. This would require consumers to step outside their own subjective perspectives or biases and consider the perspective of a hypothetical objective person acting reasonably under the specific circumstances presented.

One common charge against journalists today is bias. While it is true that all human beings are influenced by their subjective experiences and personal values, the oft-forgotten corollary is that news consumers also bring their own biases to the interaction. A consumer's conclusion about a journalist's bias may be as much influenced by the consumer's own biases as by the journalist's. This is not necessarily problematic as long as it is recognized and accounted for. One way to address this is for both journalists and consumers to consider what a reasonable person in their shoes—or the other party's shoes—would do. In addition, the fact that AI regulation in Colorado and other places has banned discrimination in AI systems indicates that bias exists in those systems, and news literacy curricula should address that fact.

CONCLUSION

The legal context of news literacy is an important area for academic study and public understanding, particularly given the characteristics of AI, deepfakes and digital algorithms. The news-literate citizen does well to critically evaluate not only the content of news but also the interaction of journalism and news content with the constitutional, legal, and regulatory environment in which it exists. Journalists and the journalism they produce are both privileged and targeted within legal systems. Evaluating the legal context of news literacy requires an understanding of legal concepts such as balancing of interests, legal reasoning using analogies, and others. The legal context of news literacy also extends across international, regional, and national policy, treaty, and legislative efforts. News literacy is a global concern for the international human rights community, and several binding international human rights agreements address news literacy as a fundamental right for all citizens that governments are obligated to protect, respect, and fulfill. The legal context of news literacy deserves further study and attention, particularly as the legal protections and regulations for social media platforms are revised to meet the changing needs of society and evolving communications technology.

REFERENCES

Abrams v. United States, 250 U.S. 616, 630 (1919) (Holmes, J., dissenting).

Alabama Code § 12-21-142. (2023).

Aldisert, R. J. (1996). *The judicial process: Text, materials and cases*. West Publishing Co.

Aldisert, R. J. (1997). *Logic for lawyers: A guide to clear thinking*. National Institute for Trial Advocacy.

Altun, A. (2011). An overview of UNESCO activities in connection with media literacy (1977–2009). *Journal of National Education, 191*, 86–107. https://milunesco.unaoc.org/mil-articles/an-overview-of-unesco-activities-in-connection-with-media-literacy-1977-2009/

Barron, J. (1967). Access to the press—A new First Amendment right. *Harvard Law Review, 80*(8), 1641–1678. DOI: 10.2307/1339417

Blasi, V. (1977). The checking value in First Amendment theory. *American Bar Foundation Research Journal. American Bar Foundation, 1977*(3), 521–649. DOI: 10.1111/j.1747-4469.1977.tb01008.x

Bollinger, L. C. (1988). *The tolerant society*. Oxford University Press.

Calo, R., & Citron, D. K. (2021). The automated administrative state: A crisis of legitimacy. *Emory Law Journal, 70*, 797.

Carter, E. L. (2017). "Not to disclose information sources": Journalistic privilege under Article 19 of ICCPR. *Communication Law and Policy, 22*(4), 399–426. DOI: 10.1080/10811680.2017.1364912

Carter, E. L., Larsen, A. R., & Lambert, E. (2024, Oct). The anti-marketplace of ideas and the right to news literacy. *Communication Law and Policy, 29*(4), 205–236. DOI: 10.1080/10811680.2025.2511045

Carter, E. L., & Westenskow, R. (2020). Freedom of journalism in international human rights law. *Communication Law and Policy, 25*(2), 113–143. DOI: 10.1080/10811680.2020.1735188

Chornoby, J., Florence, T., Linkenhoker, A., Meier, M., Simeone, M., Wray, M., & Napoli, P. M. (2023). *Media literacy as media policy: An assessment of state-level legislative activity* [Paper presentation]. Law and Policy Division of the Association for Education in Journalism & Mass Communication Conference.

Citron, D. K., & Wittes, B. (2017). The Internet will not break: Denying bad Samaritans § 230 immunity. *Fordham Law Review, 86*, 401.

Committee on Economic. Social and Cultural Rights. (1999). *General comment no. 13: The right to education.* UN Office of the High Commissioner for Human Rights. https://www.refworld.org/legal/general/cescr/1999/en/37937

Committee on the Rights of the Child. (2021). *General comment no. 25 on children's rights in relation to the digital environment.* United Nations Office of the High Commissioner for Human Rights. https://www.ohchr.org/en/documents/general-comments-and-recommendations/general-comment-no-25-2021-childrens-rights-relation

Dawood, Y. (2020). Protecting elections from disinformation: A multifaceted public–private approach to social media and democratic speech. *Ohio State Technology Law Journal, 16*, 639–668.

European Commission. (2021). *Laying down harmonised rules on artificial intelligence (Artificial Intelligence Act) and amending certain Union legislative acts.* (Document 52021PC0206). EUR-Lex. https://eur-lex.europa.eu/legal-content/EN/TXT/?uri=celex:52021PC0206

European Union. (2018). *Directive (EU) 2018/1808 of the European Parliament and of the Council of 14 November 2018 amending Directive 2010/13/EU on the coordination of certain provisions laid down by law, regulation or administrative action in Member States concerning the provision of audiovisual media services (Audiovisual Media Services Directive) in view of changing market realities* (Publication No. 32018L1808). EUR-Lex. https://eur-lex.europa.eu/eli/dir/2018/1808/oj

Gans, H. J. (1979). *Deciding what's news: A study of CBS Evening News, NBC Nightly News, Newsweek and Time*. Random House.

Gerodimos, R. (n.d.). Journalism students as global citizens and mediators. *Journalism Education, 1*, 70–86. https://journalism-education.org/wp-content/uploads/2012/04/1-1-Global-Citizens.pdf

Goldberg, D. (2018). Responding to "fake news": Is there an alternative to law and regulation? *Southwestern Law Review, 47*, 417–447.

Gonzalez, A., & Shulz, D. (2017). Helping truth with its boots: Accreditation as an antidote to fake news. *Yale Law Forum, 127*, 315–336.

Hopkins, W. W. (1996). The Supreme Court defines the marketplace of ideas. *Journalism & Mass Communication Quarterly, 73*(1), 40–52. DOI: 10.1177/107769909607300105

Human Rights Committee. (2011). *General comment no. 34 on Article 19: Freedoms of opinion and expression.* United Nations Office of the High Commissioner for Human Rights. https://www.ohchr.org/en/documents/general-comments-and-recommendations/general-comment-no34-article-19-freedoms-opinion-and

Kovach, B., & Rosenstiel, T. (2001). *The elements of journalism: What newspeople should know and the public should expect.* Three Rivers Press.

Levi, L. (2020). Media literacy beyond the national security frame. *Utah Law Review, 2020*(4), 941–985.

Meiklejohn, A. (1961). The First Amendment is an absolute. *The Supreme Court Review, 1961*, 245–266. DOI: 10.1086/scr.1961.3108719

Mill, J. S. (2002). *The basic writings of John Stuart Mill.* Penguin Random House.

Moran, M. (2010). The reasonable person: A conceptual biography in comparative perspective. *Lewis & Clark Law Review, 14*, 1233–1283.

New York Times Co. v. Sullivan, 376 U.S. 254 (1964).

Pasquale, F. (2015). *The black box society: The secret algorithms that control money and information.* Harvard University Press. DOI: 10.4159/harvard.9780674736061

Plotnikova, M. V., Zavhorodnia, V. M., Degtyarez, S. I., & Polyakova, L. G. (2021). The role of decisions by the European Court of Human Rights in shaping the content of new media literacy education. *International Journal of Media and Information Literacy, 6*(2), 376–386.

Price v. *Time, Inc.*, 416 F.3d 1327, 1335–43 (11th Cir. 2005).

Richards, D. A. J. (1974). Free speech and obscenity law: Toward a moral theory of the First Amendment. *University of Pennsylvania Law Review, 123*(1), 45–91. DOI: 10.2307/3311577

Schechter, S., & Bacher, W. (1909). Gamaliel I. In *Jewish encyclopedia.* https://www.jewishencyclopedia.com/articles/6494-gamaliel-i

Scott, M. (2014). *Media and development.* Zed Books. DOI: 10.5040/9781350221314

SDG16NOW. (n.d.). *Target 16.10.* https://sdg16now.org/report/target16-10/

Size, R. (2020). Publishing fake news for profit should be prosecuted as wire fraud. *Santa Clara Law Review, 60*, 29–99.

Student Press Law Center. (2024). *Legal considerations of artificial intelligence for student journalists.* SPLC. https://splc.org/ai/

Teichert, J. (2025). Loper Bright and the ebbing tide of the administrative state. *Utah Bar Journal, 38*(2), 19–26.

The New Testament of Our Lord and Saviour Jesus Christ, King James Version. Acts 5. (2013). Intellectual Reserve, Inc. https://www.churchofjesuschrist.org/study/scriptures/nt/acts/5?lang=eng

Tully, M., Maksi, A., Ashley, S., Vraga, E. K., & Craft, S. (2022). Defining and conceptualizing news literacy. *Journalism, 23*(8), 1589–1606. DOI: 10.1177/14648849211005888

United Nations. (n.d.). *Goal 16.* Department of Economic and Social Affairs: Sustainable Development. https://sdgs.un.org/goals/goal16

United Nations Children's Fund. (n.d.) *Frequently asked questions on the Convention on the Rights of the Child.* UNICEF. https://www.unicef.org/child-rights-convention/frequently-asked-questions

United Nations Educational, Scientific, and Cultural Organization. (1982). *Grunwald declaration on media education.* https://milobs.pt/wp-content/uploads/2018/06/The-Grünwald-Declaration-on-Media-Education.pdf

United Nations Educational, Scientific, and Cultural Organization. (2018). UNESCO launches Observatory of Killed Journalists, tracking actions to punish crimes against media practitioners. https://www.unesco.org/en/articles/unesco-launches-observatory-killed-journalists-tracking-actions-taken-punish-crimes-against-media

United Nations Educational, Scientific, and Cultural Organization. (n.d.). *Unpacking sustainable development goal 4 education 2030.* https://www.gcedclearinghouse.org/sites/default/files/resources/190257eng.pdf

United Nations General Assembly. (1976). *International covenant on economic, social and cultural rights.* Office of the High Commissioner for Human Rights. https://www.ohchr.org/sites/default/files/cescr.pdf

United Nations General Assembly. (1989). *Convention on the Rights of the Child.* General Assembly Resolution 44/25. https://www.ohchr.org/en/instruments-mechanisms/instruments/convention-rights-child

Vaughan v. Menlove, 132 Eng. Rep. 490 (Court of Common Pleas 1837).

White & Case. (2025). *The global dash to regulate AI.* AI Watch: Global regulatory tracker—United States. https://www.whitecase.com/insight-our-thinking/ai-watch-global-regulatory-tracker

Younger, I., Goldsmith, M., & Sonenshein, D. A. (2000). *Principles of evidence*. Anderson Publishing Co.

KEY TERMS AND DEFINITIONS

Anti-Marketplace of Ideas: French historian Fernand Braudel popularized the concept of the anti-marketplace in economic history. He argued that societies have long developed material and economic zones where government regulation is largely unnecessary and undesirable, but that a layer of large-scale, non-transparent capitalism—or anti-market—does require government regulation. Applied to the speech context, this concept holds that the anti-marketplace of ideas consists of large social media platforms and necessitates targeted and prudent government regulation.

Balancing of Interests: In many jurisdictions, adjudications involve balancing competing interests. Judges, lawyers, and policymakers weigh the importance of individual and collective societal goals to determine which should prevail. In the context of news literacy, citizens need to understand the values and purposes of free expression and journalism.

Development: In international human rights law, development involves cultivating individual and societal capacity, participation, and agency. It is not confined to the economic realm but also encompasses education and capacity-building in other areas for individuals and institutions. In the context of news literacy, media development holds that governance systems and civil society should support news organizations and individual citizens in their efforts to produce and use news and information relevant to their broader goals.

Disinformation: False information that is known to be false by its producer or distributor.

International Human Rights Law: Under the auspices of the United Nations, countries have agreed to nine major international human rights law treaties delineating the fundamental rights of individuals and the obligations of states. Several of these treaties address news literacy and related topics.

Marketplace of Ideas: The metaphor of the marketplace of ideas has roots in history and philosophy dating back to ancient times. It was popularized in modern times by Justice Oliver Wendell Holmes's dissenting opinion in *Abrams v. United States* (1919). The marketplace metaphor asserts that truth is best determined through the absence of government regulation and reliance instead on the practical wisdom of information consumers.

Misinformation: False information that is not known to be false by its producer or distributor.

Transitional Justice: Societies emerging from periods of human rights abuses often turn to transitional justice principles to restore faith in governance and legal systems. The primary methods of transitional justice include reparations, institutional reforms to ensure non-recurrence, truth-telling initiatives such as truth commissions, and accountability through criminal investigations and prosecutions. Journalism can serve as a form of truth-telling within transitional justice, which, in turn, can help combat impunity for attacks on journalists.

Chapter 3

The Dual Impact of Social Media on Contemporary Society Opportunities, Challenges, and Societal Transformation

Iranna Ronad
https://orcid.org/0000-0002-8801-9501
Rani Channamma University, Belagavi, India

ABSTRACT

Social media today is incredibly influential and impactful. Having a pen to write with and paper to print on isn't sufficient if you're constantly weighing the advantages of social media. Meanwhile, studies carried out by various scholars demonstrate that social media can inflict significant and countless harm on large groups of people. Research indicates that 70 out of every 100 researchers are keen on exploring the negative impacts of these platforms. Although social media significantly contributes to organizing individuals in India, sharing vital information, educating, guiding, motivating, and influencing the community, its importance cannot be underestimated. Social media is essential in driving an educational, social, industrial, and political transformation. Platforms such as Facebook, Instagram, WhatsApp, Pinterest, TikTok, YouTube, Twitter, Snapchat, and others are well-known among community members today and are widely utilized every day.This research examined the impact of social media on individuals within the community. It investigate their influence on society

DOI: 10.4018/979-8-3373-0872-2.ch003

INTRODUCTION

The purpose of addressing social media in this chapter is due to its significant role in the ongoing process of globalization. Social media serves as a vital connection for individuals, acting as the primary instrument for rapidly and effectively sharing information and events from all areas of society, both locally and internationally. The global population of social media users continues to grow. Both those who are literate and illiterate are utilizing these platforms. In the 20th century, the domain of communication has gradually expanded its focus to other domains, including means of communication such as mass communication, interpersonal communication, and oral interpretation (Mohammad, 2020). Individuals ranging from young kids to women and the elderly, people of all ages, are increasingly becoming hooked on social media. There is a harsh debate that social media is consuming valuable time for individuals under the guise of entertainment. Social networking is rapidly becoming an integral aspect of contemporary life. Social media has become an undeniable force in shaping modern society (Shamim, 2024). Platforms like Facebook, Twitter, and Instagram revolutionized communication in the early 21st century (Omar & Ondimu, 2024). Social media serves as a space for both those who seek to gather information (receivers) and those who wish to disseminate it (senders), facilitating the sharing and acquisition of information within a community. They have established a communication network that fosters meaningful and effective interactions. Any individual can easily form friendships or romantic connections with others around the globe, transforming adversarial nations into allies or vice versa. People worldwide with similar interests, beliefs, aspirations, and goals can effortlessly connect and reap mutual advantages.

Social media has become an essential part of our contemporary existence, making it difficult to envision our lives without it. It has enhanced and streamlined the intensity, scope, and speed of communication, creating a platform for users around the world to exchange and access important information. Currently, social media has made a significant impact on individuals, communities, and society as a whole, altering their dynamics and perspectives. Its role in the social, educational, political, industrial, and cultural realms is undeniable. Social media is extensively utilized across various sectors, including public, social, political, and cultural areas. The negative consequences are just as significant as the positive effects. Although social media significantly contributes to organizing individuals in India, sharing vital information, educating, guiding, motivating, and influencing the community, its importance cannot be underestimated. Social media is essential in driving an educational, social, industrial, and political transformation. Platforms such as Facebook, Instagram, WhatsApp, Pinterest, TikTok, YouTube, Twitter, Telegram,

Snapchat, and others are well-known among community members today and are widely utilized daily.

OBJECTIVES OF THE STUDY

The present research seeks to explore the positive and negative impacts of social media on contemporary society. Its goal is to raise awareness among readers about both the beneficial and harmful effects. How can individuals reduce the risks associated with social media once they are informed of the dangers? By gaining knowledge, they can avoid negative influences and focus on the advantages, highlighting the importance of using these platforms in a careful and intentional manner at this time.

SIGNIFICANCE OF STUDY

Social media platforms have redefined how individuals connect, share information, and build communities. They enable instant global communication, fostering virtual communities that transcend geographical boundaries (Boyd & Ellison, 2007). Social media has positively impacted individuals in numerous ways. Research highlights both positive and negative effects of social media on mental health. Platforms can provide social support and reduce feelings of isolation (Primack et al., 2017). However, excessive use is linked to anxiety, depression, and reduced self-esteem, particularly among adolescents exposed to idealized self-presentations (Twenge & Campbell, 2019). It serves as a platform for online communication. Users have been able to discover necessary products, enjoy entertainment, connect with others, produce content, share information, and communicate. In essence, social media has enhanced people's lives, making it easier and better. However, it has also increased the risks associated with people's lives. This can be considered beneficial if social media usage is controlled, purposeful, and focused on personal growth. Nevertheless, the detrimental effects on individuals, groups, and families are undeniable, prompting this study to investigate the significance and negative consequences of social media.

LIMITATIONS OF STUDY

This section examines how social media influences contemporary society. It analyzes the effects, challenges, and possibilities presented by social media.

METHODOLOGY

The sought-after data and literature were gathered through platforms like ResearchGate, Google Scholar, SSRN, PubMed, and Google Search. Data, statistics, and pertinent literature were compiled using a range of keywords, including social media, influences of social media, impacts of contemporary social media, digital communication, applications of social media, adverse effects of social media, challenges posed by social media, and more. This information was subsequently reviewed and analyzed, with a methodological and updated summary and data being utilized for this scientific research.

REVIEW OF LITERATURE

Media has become an integral part of contemporary society, profoundly transforming communication, social behavior, political engagement, and cultural norms (Omar & Ondimu, 2024). Social networking sites are applications that enable users to connect by creating personal information profiles, inviting friends and colleagues to have access to those profiles, and sending e-mails and instant messages between each other (Kalpan & Haenlein, 2009). Social media refers to online social networking sites and is a broad example of Web 2.0, such as Twitter, YouTube, TikTok, Facebook, Snapchat, Reddit, Instagram, WhatsApp, and blogs (Kanchan & Gaidhane, 2023). Bhat (2024) found that social networking sites are web-based platforms that enable users to create personalized profiles with adjustable privacy settings based on individual preference. Fazil et al. (2024) reported that social media play a pivotal role in shaping global communication dynamics, offering unprecedented opportunities for intercultural dialogue and knowledge exchange. Understanding the influence of social media on cross-cultural communication is essential in today's interconnected world. Damota (2019) suggests that social media are the collective of online communication channels dedicated to community-based input, interaction, content sharing, and collaboration. Farooq et al. (2021) observe that social media is an advanced technology in which people share information and thoughts via digital networking. It safeguards a person's time. Yigit & Tarman (2013) believe that since the late 1990s, the impact of the internet on culture and commerce has been extensive. As more as blogs, video sharing sites, and social networks are being used more commonly among people.

IMPACTS OF SOCIAL MEDIA ON MODERN SOCIETY

The present review offers insights into the effects of social media on different populations. Social media engagement might either impact an individual or society as a whole. Some impacts may include depression, social media addiction, cyberbullying and cyber victimization, etc. (Soni et al., 2024). Typically, when individuals utilize social media for suitable intentions and specific objectives, the results tend to be beneficial, while the opposite holds true for adverse consequences (Damota, 2019). Social media has been shown to significantly enhance social capital by connecting users with supportive communities and fostering social engagement (Sabar et al., 2024). The influence of social media on communities is significant, as it brings numerous advantages and fosters collaboration among individuals in society. Conversely, many young people are becoming victims of the negative consequences of social media, jeopardizing their lives. For instance, issues such as crime, terrorism, sexual offenses, theft, smuggling, online addiction, and incitement to violence can be linked to social media use. Additionally, social media engages the public by offering entertainment content online, facilitating the buying and selling of products, materials and videos related to health, agriculture, industry, business, job opportunities, and fashion essentials. It allows individuals to share pictures and videos, maintain constant communication with friends, enhance political engagement, participate socially, conduct research, and pursue general learning, as well as engage in dance and music activities. There are many different types of social media, and they all share a common goal of facilitating communication and community building. While it has been associated with some negative impacts on mental health, it is important to acknowledge the many positive aspects of social media use (Kariya & Vidani, 2024).

Socialization and Individual Development

Social media has played a significant role in the socialization process for children and young adults. Platforms allow users to connect with friends, family, and like-minded individuals, reducing social isolation, particularly for those with limited physical access to social groups (Ellison et al., 2007). It has enabled them to reach their academic and career aspirations. In addition to offering valuable information, social media has assisted them in accomplishing their objectives. For instance, numerous YouTubers have transformed their lives by creating and sharing videos across various subjects on the prominent social media platform, YouTube. Platforms like YouTube and LinkedIn offer tutorials, professional networking, and knowledge-sharing opportunities, enhancing digital literacy and career development (Greenhow & Lewin, 2016). Social media represents a significant advancement in expanding their networks with influential individuals and well-known organizations within the same industry, contributing to the development of cinema by showcasing heroes and heroines, and introducing emerging talents, singers, and musicians, thereby achieving substantial success in the arts and film industries on a large scale.

Participation in Social and Political Activities

Sabar et al. (2024) describe that platforms provide a space for individuals to engage with political content, share their views, and mobilize around political causes. Social media represents a significant advancement for young people to immerse themselves in social service, gather support for charitable causes, participate in and inspire peers in philanthropy, social work, and community activities, as well as strengthen their connections with different people and organizations that have emerged in the same domain. Social media platforms, including Twitter and Facebook, have played a crucial role in movements like the Arab Spring and #BlackLivesMatter, enabling individuals to champion social and political transformation (Howard & Hussain, 2013; Mundt et al., 2018). In his article “The Impact of Social Media on Modern Society,” Turning (2024) proposes several social influences that social media has on today’s society.

Communication and Connectivity

Social networks have made communication more accessible to individuals previously excluded from traditional channels like newspapers, television, and radio in pre-information society (Vasylchyshyna et al., 2024). Social media serves as a vital means to communicate and engage with individuals globally. Social media platforms such as X, Facebook, and WhatsApp allow for instantaneous communication across geographical boundaries, linking individuals irrespective of their location. This promotes personal relationships, professional collaborations, and a heightened global awareness (Boyd & Ellison, 2007). They provide an easy way for effective communication and interaction among various countries and people. These platforms significantly aid in the sharing of essential information and ideas. The positive impact of social media on social interaction also includes increased social awareness. Social media has the power to influence public opinion in society (Nugraha et al., 2024). The ability to communicate globally has facilitated social, economic, political, and cultural exchanges between nations, cities, and regions and the establishment of a worldwide connectivity bridge. These social media sites possess the capability to broadcast and share information in real-time from event locations to audiences of all ages across the globe, complete with audio and visual elements.

Demographic Impact

Social media has created an avenue for people of all ages, from children to the elderly, to exchange experiences, ideas, and knowledge. This has resulted in social and cultural interactions and transformations. Democratization of information through social media encourages civic participation by enabling users to share and discuss public issues freely (Gil de Zúñiga et al., 2012). Social media platforms facilitate the democratization of information by enabling individuals to disseminate knowledge and coordinate movements without the interference of traditional gatekeepers (Shirky, 2011). Arranging content or information in a proper sequence can minimize miscommunication and bridge the generational divide. This serves as a vital resource for women and children who have faced exploitation, enabling them to seek justice and safeguard their rights while voicing their opposition to injustice. Social justice envisages an efficient social arrangement where the opportunity of leading a dignified life with good things and amenities of life is available for all (Nair, 2015). Turning (2024) explains that it has transformed into a space for underrepresented communities to elevate their voices and communicate their experiences. If marginalized communities understand and effectively harness the potential of social media, it can lead to their advancement. Social media can have both beneficial and detrimental effects on the population.

Business and Advertising

Numerous enterprises and businesses have turned to social media to enhance their profits and foster organizational growth, primarily for the effective promotion of their products and to build customer trust. Social media enables businesses to integrate traditional advertising with consumer-generated content, amplifying brand reach and engagement (Mangold & Faulds, 2009). Social media has transformed marketing, enabling targeted advertising and influencer-driven commerce, which significantly impacts consumer behavior (Kaplan & Haenlein, 2010). Businesses leverage platforms to engage customers, but this raises ethical questions about data privacy and manipulation (Zuboff, 2019).Various industries are focused on gaining visibility through social media, leveraging competitive advantages and pricing strategies for their offerings. Business utilizes web-based social networking to upgrade an association's execution in different ways, for example, to achieve business targets, expanding yearly offers of the association (Ename et al., 2022). This trend has resulted in a market transformation reminiscent of the Industrial Revolution. Consumers are left puzzled when it comes to selecting higher-quality and more affordable products. This situation affects both small businesses and large corporations alike. Targeted advertising on social media allows businesses to reach specific demographics, increasing marketing efficiency and sales (Tuten & Solomon, 2017). Products that resonate with consumers tend to maintain a strong presence in the market. Social media serves as a powerful tool for competitive marketing.

Democratization of Information

Social media democratizes information by lowering access barriers, allowing diverse groups to engage in civic discussions (Bimber et al., 2015). In earlier times, we depended on a range of tools for news and information. However, thanks to the social media revolution, everyone can now access the news they desire quickly through different platforms. By providing platforms for user-generated content, social media enhances democratic participation through widespread information sharing (Loader & Mercea, 2011). Individuals are not obligated to concur with others' opinions, thoughts, and perspectives on current events. Social media has created a platform for individuals to express their arguments through different channels. It has allowed for the free expression of personal opinions and ideas. Social media supports a networked public sphere, enabling collaborative knowledge creation and broadening access to information (Benkler, 2006).

Although it cannot be definitively stated that information shared on social media is accurate, it is frequently a topic of extensive discussion, and users are experiencing significant distress due to the proliferation of misinformation (Allcott & Gentzkow, 2017). As a result, they are beginning to lose trust in the media (Edelman, 2021).

Mental health and Well-Being

Organizations and influencers on platforms such as Instagram and YouTube disseminate content related to mindfulness, therapy, and stress management, thereby enhancing mental health literacy (Betton & Tomlinson, 2013). For those experiencing mental health difficulties, platforms such as Reddit or Facebook groups provide environments to exchange experiences and gain empathy, which can help reduce feelings of isolation (Naslund et al., 2016). This is especially advantageous for individuals who encounter stigma or physical obstacles to obtaining in-person support (Andalibi et al., 2016).This availability enables individuals to take proactive steps in managing their well-being (Lal et al., 2018). It has been noted previously that social media usage is increasing across all demographics. This surge is causing a decline in productivity and contributing to mental health issues for many individuals. With the rise of social media platforms such as TikTok,Instagram, and Snapchat, people are more connected than ever before. With this phenomenon being observed as the usage of social media has increased, there are concerns about its impact on mental health (Li, 2024). It is becoming an obsession for some. Various studies indicate that social media negatively impacts both physical and mental well-being. Alongside the benefits, social media presents dangers to adolescents. They are at risk if they engage with the internet at an age that requires parental approval (Tartari, 2015). Engaging excessively with social media can foster antisocial behaviors and may encourage undesirable habits. Utilizing social media out of necessity, in moderation, or with restriction enhances its benefits for users.

Privacy and Data Security

Social networking platforms offer innovative methods for self-construction and for establishing connections with individuals who visit these sites or possess similar interests (Ibrahim, n.d.). Malicious individuals exploit social media to acquire valuable personal information from others for fraudulent purposes and personal gain. When individuals believe that their personal data is secure, they are more inclined to share content and participate genuinely (Acquisti et al., 2015). For example, platforms that maintain clear privacy policies, such as those compliant with GDPR regulations, experience greater user retention as a result of enhanced trust (Goldfarb & Tucker, 2011). Social media poses significant challenges to privacy. Utilizing social media for the promotion of a brand, products, or services may also involve concerns regarding trust, privacy, and data security (Nadaraja & Yazdanifard, n.d.). Despite the implementation of various strategies, tools, and regulations to protect confidentiality, individuals remain highly susceptible to personal and financial fraud. This can resulte in substantial losses for social media users. It is essential for everyone to receive proper training to consistently follow privacy protocols.

Education and Development

Social media platforms enhance educational outcomes by enabling students to collaborate and access learning resources in informal settings (Greenhow & Lewin, 2016). Social media has offered significant advantages to students. They have aided in students' academic growth by simplifying the learning process. Everyone involved in education can easily access essential information and resources through social media. In their research, Timung et al. (2024) found that social media has a dual impact on learning behaviors. The use of social media is now part of life, and it is evident, most especially among the youth in the 21st century. Social media facilitates professional development by connecting educators and students with global networks for knowledge exchange (Manca & Ranieri, 2016). It is a complex part of education as it has positive and negative impacts on learning behaviors. This platform has widened the scope of knowledge, aiding in educational advancement. Social media play a crucial role in social and political movements. Engaging discussions and conversations, including those of diverse individuals, have helped facilitate dialogue. They have allowed leaders to maintain connections and inspire their followers and audiences via social media. These platforms have driven impactful social, economic, and political transformations.

Learning and Health Information

Social media offers numerous learning opportunities for students, researchers, and learners. It goes without saying that the majority of educators and students use social media in the classroom and own cellphones. Actually, there are websites and applications that provide social media in the context of education (Hattikar & Bagi, 2024). The various programs shared on social media provide substantial guidance to individuals in developing their future plans. Platforms provide users with the opportunity to develop skills ranging from coding to language acquisition in adaptable, self-directed formats (Greenhow & Lewin, 2016). For instance, YouTube channels focused on educational material have demonstrated an ability to improve digital literacy and critical thinking skills among a variety of learners (Ito et al., 2009). Social media serves as an excellent platform for boundless information, creativity, patience, collaboration, personal development, skill acquisition, and the learning of new languages and subjects. Creative writers assess current or pertinent information on blogs, Facebook, Twitter, and other platforms, disseminating insights and engaging in discussions with anonymous users in various ways, thereby making the information seem beneficial. Platforms like Reddit or specialized forums allow individuals to exchange knowledge on topics ranging from academic subjects to health management, fostering a culture of collective learning (Selwyn & Stirling, 2016). This peer-driven approach enhances understanding and engagement, particularly for complex health topics (Naslund et al., 2016). Resources related to mental health, sexuality, and general health are accessible to support countless individuals.

Social Movements and Activism

Social media empowers social movements by providing platforms for rapid information sharing and grassroots organizing, as seen in global protests (Tufekci, 2017). Social media is utilized to raise awareness and foster support among individuals, contributing to global change. It serves as a powerful tool for uniting people through social movements, rallying resources, addressing injustices, and advancing social justice. Social media has transformed social participation, offering both opportunities and challenges for young adults (Sabar et al., 2024). Social media supports activism by enabling activists to coordinate efforts and share information, even under restrictive regimes (Breuer & Farooq, 2012). Social media is vital for articulating the fundamental needs and aspirations of the populace, thereby capturing the government's attention. During critical times, it plays a crucial role in safeguarding the community by providing essential guidance

Influence on Policy

It is helpful to create appropriate policies and acts against or mitigate new and existing social problems and challenges through social media. Kanchan & Gaidhane (2023) asserted that sharing arguments in favor of or against health policies with the general public, decision-makers, and other important stakeholders is made possible by social media.

RISKS OF USING SOCIAL MEDIA

The intersections between risk and digital technologies function in multiple ways. Firstly, the phenomena and individuals categorized as 'risks' or 'risky' are progressively shaped and replicated through digital media, devices, and software (Lupton, 2016). The growth of digital technology has affected numerous areas of adolescent lives. Nowadays, teenagers' use of social media is one of their most apparent characteristics (Khalaf et al., 2023). Many elders, parents, and veterans living at home, outside of their homes, and within the community oppose the extensive use of social media due to its potential negative impacts on individuals, families, communities, and relationships, as well as the contradictions it can create, leading to various physical and psychological health issues (Twenge et al., 2018). A significant number of parents and guardians disapprove of their children engaging with social media in home and school settings due to the potential for substantial time loss, exposure to negative behaviors, identity suppression, dysfunction, and feelings of depression (Odgers & Jensen, 2020). The extensive use of social media is turning into a growing trend among both teenagers and adults for numerous reasons, or sometimes for no particular reason at all (Vogel et al., 2014). It is being used while walking, traveling, working, conversing, eating, and even while resting (Przybylski et al., 2013). Young people, particularly young women, as well as individuals from different age groups, excessively engage with various social media platforms such as Facebook, YouTube, Twitter, and Instagram, often losing track of time and experiencing an increase in unproductivity, stress, and depression (Primack et al., 2017). Today's youth are part of a modern society, but when they neglect their personal and family responsibilities and immerse themselves in social media, numerous conflicts and negative outcomes can arise, which is quite concerning (Shensa et al., 2018).

According to a study conducted by Naslund and Aschbrenner (2019), it was discovered that among 90 individuals identifying as having schizophrenia spectrum disorders (40%), bipolar disorder (37%), or major depressive disorder (23%), over one-third (36%) voiced concerns regarding privacy risks associated with social media usage (Naslund & Aschbrenner, 2019). Continuous engagement with social media can foster an addiction that is challenging to break (Andreassen & Pallesen, 2014). Social media contributes to heightened stress, depression, anxiety, and various physical and mental health issues in children, young adults, young women, adults, and mothers (Kross et al., 2013; Primack et al., 2017). The emergence of new social media platforms, in addition to those already available, facilitates the formation of new friendships, leading individuals to spend excessive time scrolling and monitoring these connections, which results in considerable time loss, with repeated engagement fostering a stronger dependence on them (Vogel et al., 2014). Being absorbed in social media, individuals often drift away from reality, leading to occasional incidents and mishaps (Billieux et al., 2015). Even when taking a break from it, the desire to use it tends to intensify, highlighting a fixation and reliance on it (Andreassen et al., 2016). Numerous research studies suggest that social media promotes detrimental aggressive behaviors among individuals (Greitemeyer & Sagioglou, 2016). In contemporary society, children are increasingly drawn to online games and platforms like TikTok, Facebook, and YouTube, leading to the emergence of apps and the provision of internet services, which various mobile companies are profiting from, but the greatest loss is being experienced by children and other individuals (Twenge & Campbell, 2019).

In an article published in Gulf News, installing the following 11 game apps on mobile and blindly following their instructions puts children at the highest risk (Gulf News report, 2023).

1) Blue Whale
2) Fire Fairy
3) Cinnamon Challenge
4) Choking Game
5) Mariam's Game
6) Tide Pod Challenge
7) Five Finger Fillet
8) Gallon Challenge
9) The Cutting-Edge challenge
10) The Salt and Ice Challenge
11) Charlie Charlie

Criminals engage in a range of activities on online social networks, which encompass communication, planning, and the execution of criminal acts (de Mendonça et al., 2020). Humiliation and intimidation are key elements of aggressive behaviors observed in social interactions (Smith & Jones, 2019). Threats and insults often manifest as aggressive actions directed at an individual or group, aimed at perpetrating harm (Anderson & Bushman, 2020). A concerning aspect of these behaviors is that innocent individuals can become victims, experiencing significant psychological distress (Brown et al., 2021). Another negative consequence of social media is slander, where individuals exploit social platforms to tarnish the reputation of their adversaries (Lee & Kim, 2022). This practice infringes on personal rights and can lead to severe reputational damage (Johnson, 2023). Both individual and group threats are frequently observed in daily life, exacerbating social conflicts (Taylor & Miller, 2018). Another perilous facet of social media is the swift embrace of this platform by terrorist organizations (Damota, M. D. (2019).

Terrorist organizations are increasingly leveraging social media platforms to advance their malicious objectives, effectively recruiting numerous young individuals into their ranks (Hamm & Spaaij, 2017). The threat posed by terrorism remains extremely grave, with social media serving as a powerful tool for radicalization and mobilization (Klausen, 2015). These groups exploit social media for personal and collective benefits, including propaganda dissemination and network expansion (Weimann, 2016). Various Islamic extremist groups persist in their activities across both developing and developed nations, adapting their strategies to local contexts (Awan, 2017).

In today's world, social media is extensively utilized by everyone from young children to women and the elderly. With the advent of technology, various companies have launched mobile phones and smartphones at competitive prices and discounts. This accessibility allows all segments of society, regardless of wealth, to engage with social media. Social media can easily tarnish an individual's reputation by fabricating a false narrative and disseminating it across various online platforms (Akram & Kumar, 2017). Political, entertainment, social, economic, and other important issues spread rapidly through these platforms. The capacity of social media as a tool for propaganda is enormous. Any piece of content can quickly gain traction, resulting in it being widely shared in a short time. Threatening messages, alarming information, and rumors can be disseminated to the public to create disturbance and chaos within society (Akram & Kumar, 2017).

CHALLENGES AND OPPORTUNITIES

In an increasingly interconnected world, the role of social media in facilitating global communication has become paramount (Fazil et.al., 2024). Social media has encountered numerous difficulties at various levels since its inception. For instance, the spread of false information, lack of public trust, mistakes in communication, breaches in privacy, and prevalence of eco chambers and noise pollution all pose serious threats to the safety of personal data. Nevertheless, these issues also create opportunities to leverage social media for fostering meaningful conversations and addressing societal issues (Fazil et al., 2024). Kalpan & Haenlein (2010) describe various types of social media uses, including collaborative projects like Wikipedia, blogs that enable individuals to discuss a wide range of topics content communities compassing sites such as YouTube, Flicker, and slide share social networking platforms like Facebook, Twitter (X) and Google+ as well as virtual game worlds and social environments. They emphasize that each of these platforms presents significant opportunities and challenges for social media.

Research conducted by Shroff et al. (2021) indicates that individuals on social media frequently engage in challenges to fulfill their desire for belonging and to highlight their personal abilities, which sheds light on the consistent popularity of this type of content. Fashion is a popular subject on social media, making it one of the greatest challenges in social media, as it constantly aligns with current trends and the interests of its audience (Kalemi, 2024).

Privacy Concerns and Misuse of Information

Even with the appropriate management of user data, social media platforms often tend to exploit and misuse that information. As a result, many users are at risk of having their data compromised and misappropriated. Inadequate privacy settings or ambiguous policies expose users to the risk of unauthorized data sharing, thereby undermining their autonomy (Acquisti et al., 2015). Notable events, like the 2017 Equifax breach associated with social media data, highlight the susceptibility of personal information kept on platforms that lack sufficient security protocols (Culnan & Williams, 2009). These breaches diminish user confidence and result in considerable personal damage (Dinev & Hart, 2006). Protecting their data requires enhanced security measures and reassurance. This situation has prompted necessary examination and oversight over time.The misuse of information on social media spreads misinformation, as bad actors exploit user data to create false news or targeted propaganda. This harms public discussion and can impact elections or health outcomes, as seen during the COVID-19 pandemic (Allcott & Gentzkow,

2017). The boosting of deceptive content by algorithms worsens these issues and decreases trust in society (Pariser, 2011).

Misinformation and Fake News

Rahaman et al. (2024) describe that the content of social media reflects millions of tweets, core genres, regional differences, and social and emotional consequences for users. The internet has changed the polarization of communication, allowing email sending to groups, bulletin boards, specialized forums, chat rooms, and blogging. Malicious actors utilize social media to disseminate inaccurate or misleading information regarding events, facts, and issues currently making headlines. Messages and rumors that instill fear can be disseminated to the public, causing disruption and chaos within society (Akram & Kumar, 2017). One significant drawback of social media is the prevalence of false information and misinformation. Individuals, either intentionally or unintentionally, post inaccurate or deceptive content. This misinformation can spread rapidly, leading to confusion and misconceptions among users (Sunkad, 2023). With social media reaching vast audiences and more individuals engaging by sharing information, the speed at which information spreads has accelerated significantly (Perrin & Anderson, 2019). This rapid dissemination of information has contributed to heightened anxiety and fear infiltrating the general population, adversely affecting mental well-being (Primack et al., 2021). The pervasive nature of social media exacerbates these effects, as constant exposure to negative content can intensify psychological distress (Karim et al., 2020).

Cyberbullying and Harassment

Cyberbullying has emerged as a significant problem among young people over the past few decades, as it enables victims to have their experiences shared publicly among their peers, leading to humiliation (Damota, 2019). Isolation exacerbates feelings of loneliness and can damage relationships, particularly among youth who rely on social media for social validation (Tokunaga, 2010). Social media have been perpetually inducing fear, anxiety, and harassment among its users. This has led to ongoing negative impacts on both the physical and mental well-being of individuals and society as a whole. Consequently, this has created a breeding ground for an increase in cybercrimes. In recent times, there has been a notable rise in cyber threats. Social media platforms have become hotspots for such threats and harassment. Individuals who are victimized frequently endure extended emotional turmoil as a result of the ongoing and visible characteristics of online harassment (Hinduja & Patchin, 2010). For example, research indicates that teenagers who are targeted on social media platforms such as Instagram or Snapchat exhibit increased levels of suicidal thoughts and emotional distress (Kowalski et al., 2014). Online safety training programs are crucial in mitigating these cyber risks. The anonymity provided by social media fosters escape behaviors among users. Consequently, this negative impact amplifies the dissemination of harmful messages. It is nearly impossible for social media companies to hold their users accountable for the adverse effects that arise. Ultimately, these companies contribute to the negative consequences stemming from individual mistakes.

Negative Impact on Addictive Behavior and Mental Health

The frequent engagement with social media negatively affects individuals' mental health. As adolescents navigate their sexuality and identity on social media platforms, they might share images, videos, or text that allude to hazardous behaviors such as substance abuse,sexual activity, and violence (Reid & Weigle, 2014). Its prolonged use can lead to compulsive behavior or addiction. Social media significantly influence the addictive behaviors of users. Regrettably, many individuals become aware of these effects only after a considerable delay. The design of social media platforms is intentionally crafted to stimulate dopamine release in users' brains, which induces pleasurable sensations. This mechanism can foster addictive tendencies as users engage with these platforms repeatedly. Social media promote prolonged scrolling, leading users to frequently check their various accounts, including social media and banking. Such habits contribute to the development of addictive behaviors, which in turn can result in anxiety and depression, adversely affecting self-esteem. The use of social media also offers an opportunity for emotional turmoil as a result of receiving threatening, harassing, or degrading messages from another young person (Tartari, 2015). The tendency to compare one's life with others on social media hinders the ability to appreciate one's own life (Vogel et al., 2014). Excessive use of social media can detrimentally affect both physical and mental health, manifesting in issues such as sleep disorders (Levenson et al., 2016). Therefore, it is crucial to thoroughly assess the serious implications of social media on health before engaging with these platforms (Woods & Scott, 2016).

DISCUSSION

Social media currently holds immense influence, comparable to that of an elephant. Media-society relations involve complex events, behaviors and processes. For this reason, it can be examined from different angles and dimensions (Okumus, 2024). Social media today is incredibly influential and impactful. Through modes like audio and visual, critical issues and facts have been effectively communicated to the public quickly. This has enabled communities to maintain strong connections with the wider world. They assist individuals in obtaining relevant information promptly, aiding those in need. These platforms have contributed to uniting people from various parts of the globe. They have made the world feel more interconnected. They offer an excellent avenue for individuals to engage with and succeed in real-time. Having a pen to write with and paper to print on isn't sufficient if you're constantly weighing the advantages of social media. Numerous studies demonstrate that social media can inflict significant harm on large groups, contributing to issues such as misinformation and psychological distress (Allcott & Gentzkow, 2017). Conversely, students and educators in academia now have easier access to a diverse array of resources through social media platforms, facilitating knowledge sharing (Greenhow & Lewin, 2016). In addition to fostering intellectual and educational growth, these platforms have played a pivotal role in the globalization of education (Selwyn, 2012). Innovative strategies, such as interactive learning communities and open-access resources, have enhanced the benefits of social media (Tess, 2013). This study examines the multifaceted influence of social media in the 21st century, investigating its impact on individuals within communities and the broader consequences for societal dynamics (Kaplan & Haenlein, 2010).

The increase in digital communication has made direct, in-person conversations less frequent, pointing to difficulties in building strong relationships. Personal interactions and deep discussions may become weakened, resulting in misunderstandings and a diminished emotional bond (Turning, 2024). Individuals are constantly using social media to introduce themselves, create profiles, and express their identities on popular platforms worldwide (Boyd & Ellison, 2007). However, these activities can harm personal interests through risks such as information leakage and misuse (Reyns & Henson, 2016). Cybercrime, including identity theft and data breaches, is a growing concern in this context (Holt & Bossler, 2014). While social media facilitates constant communication with friends and family, its adverse effects on society, such as increased vulnerability to cyber threats, cannot be overlooked (Saridakis et al., 2016). Social media has profoundly influenced the psychological dimensions of society, impacting every social, political, and cultural event and behavior in today's world. How does public opinion arise concerning each of these facets? What is the role of social media within them? To what degree does this influence exist? It is crucial to examine and comprehend this phenomenon. Social media has emerged as a portal for extensive global communication. A discourse that presents evidence of emerging social issues fosters a global perspective in the digital era, highlighting the potential for understanding the interconnectedness of social media influences.

Social media has significantly impacted the lives of individuals, groups, and communities. Media is a tool that can stimulate and influence the attitudes and behaviors of individuals or communities that embrace all aspects of human life. It also plays a role in establishing a nation's identity and culture for its overall development (Arisukwu et al.,2022). It has altered social interactions and developed its distinct processes. It has contributed to shaping communication methods. It has positively influenced how people socialize. Many individuals utilize social media to engage in entertainment and discover new ideas while connecting with the world around them. Today, social media is a vital component of our everyday lives. Adolescents increasingly find it difficult to picture their lives without social media (Khalaf et al., 2023). It has become central to the priorities of the younger generation. Social networks are an essential component of the lives of young people in the 21st century, influencing different aspects of their subjectivity, communication, and interaction (Timung et al., 2024). It has changed people's views, opinions, and behaviors across all areas of life. Social media is one of the favored choices for individuals who now follow innovative trends as part of globalization. Their gestures, personalities, speech styles, language, fashion, food choices, and all other aspects have been affected and adopted. The increase in the use of social media sites will allow researchers to observe the behaviors of the population engaging in social media (Das, 2018).

FINDINGS AND SOLUTIONS

1) Social media has become a widely used tool that plays a crucial role in our daily lives.
2) Currently, the number of social media users is on the rise across all age demographics.
3) Both individuals and society at large are affected by the impact of social media.
4) Social media has both beneficial and detrimental effects on individuals, families, communities, and society.
5) When used mindfully and within reasonable limits, social media can yield positive outcomes. Conversely, failing to manage its use may lead to increased negative repercussions.
6) It is essential for social media to enhance its positive impacts while addressing challenges and minimizing negative effects, as well as fostering trust and popularity.
7) The influence and significance of social media are substantial across various sectors, including social, economic, political, cultural, and familial realms.
8) Social media is vital in shaping public opinion, bringing people together, and finding solutions to the issues faced by the populace.

OPPORTUNITIES FOR FUTURE RESEARCH

"The influence of social media on contemporary society" is an intriguing research topic. This study delves into the effects of social media on today's society, as previously mentioned. The potential for future research in this domain is extensive, given that the variety of social media platforms continues to expand, along with their influence. The repercussions of social media on individual lives, family dynamics, social interactions, health, education, business sectors, community well-being, and other facets are on the rise. How can upcoming researchers address the adverse effects associated with these emerging social media platforms? Additionally, emphasis can be placed on enhancing their utility in the present. Social media centers can be considered to alleviate their negative effects. Their credibility and relevance to the public can be highlighted.

CONCLUSION

This paper explores the effects of social media on different facets of society, including education, social interactions, politics, health, employment, business, and human attitudes. Social networks wield significant influence across various facets of societal existence in the contemporary digital landscape (Vasylchyshna et al., 2024). Social media has impacted society primarily in two ways: positively and negatively. Social media is impacting both positively and negatively on Indian society (Sunkad, 2023). When individuals utilize social media for personal growth, it can lead to beneficial effects and advancements; conversely, if used for harmful intentions, it can result in negative consequences and undesirable changes. In general, neither individuals nor society can escape the influence of social media. It's fair to consider it one of the most significant components of everyday life. Nowadays, people, particularly adolescents, are undergoing so many changes that they find it hard to detach from their mobile devices, social media, and the Internet. Social media has become an integral component of daily life, shaping how individuals interact and perceive the world. It is accurate to acknowledge that while social media can engender challenges, it also offers potential solutions to these issues (Smith & Anderson, 2018). Social media platforms have profoundly influenced individuals, reshaping their perspectives and mindsets (Valkenburg & Peter, 2013). However, while these platforms often generate significant financial benefits for their creators, they have also been associated with persistent negative impacts on users' mental health and well-being (Twenge et al., 2019).

REFERENCES

Acquisti, A., Brandimarte, L., & Loewenstein, G. (2015). Privacy and human behavior in the age of information. *Science, 347*(6221), 509–514. DOI: 10.1126/science.aaa1465 PMID: 25635091

Akram, W., & Kumar, R. (2017). A study on positive and negative effects of social media on society. *International Journal on Computer Science and Engineering, 5*(10), 351–354. DOI: 10.26438/ijcse/v5i10.351354

Allcott, H., & Gentzkow, M. (2017). Social media and fake news in the 2016 election. *The Journal of Economic Perspectives, 31*(2), 211–236. DOI: 10.1257/jep.31.2.211

Andalibi, N., Haimson, O. L., De Choudhury, M., & Forte, A. (2016). Understanding social media disclosures of mental illness: Stigma, support, and identity. *Proceedings of the 2016 CHI Conference on Human Factors in Computing Systems*, 1352-1363.

Anderson, C. A., & Bushman, B. J. (2020). Human aggression. *Annual Review of Psychology, 53*(1), 27–51. DOI: 10.1146/annurev.psych.53.100901.135231 PMID: 11752478

Andreassen, C. S., Billieux, J., Kuss, D. J., Griffiths, M. D., Mazzoni, E., & Pallesen, S. (2016). The relationship between addictive use of social media and video games and symptoms of psychiatric disorders: A large-scale cross-sectional study. *Psychology of Addictive Behaviors, 30*(2), 252–262. DOI: 10.1037/adb0000160 PMID: 26999354

Andreassen, C. S., & Pallesen, S. (2014). Social network site addiction—An overview. *Current Pharmaceutical Design, 20*(25), 4053–4061. DOI: 10.2174/13816128113199990616 PMID: 24001298

Arisukwu, O., (2022). *Access Usage and Influence of Mass Media on Students Academic Performance: A Private University Experience*. Information & Communication Technology in Education., DOI: 10.1080/2331186X.2022.2102117

Awan, A. N. (2017). Jihadism transformed: Al-Qaeda and Islamic State's global battle of ideas. *Journal of Conflict and Security Law, 22*(3), 415–436. DOI: 10.1093/jcsl/krx005

Benkler, Y. (2006). *The wealth of networks: How social production transforms markets and freedom*. Yale University Press.

Betton, V., & Tomlinson, V. (2013). Social media and mental health: Opportunities and risks. *The Lancet. Psychiatry, 1*(2), 131–132.

Bhat, S. (2024). Impact of Social Media on Society, International Research Journal on Advanced Engineering Hub (IRJAEH) ISSN: 2584-2137Vol. 02 Issue: 03 March 2024, Page No: 473-480 https://irjaeh.com DOI: 10.47392/IRJAEH.2024.0068

Billieux, J., Philippot, P., Schmid, C., Maurage, P., De Mol, J., & Van der Linden, M. (2015). Is dysfunctional use of the mobile phone a behavioural addiction? Confronting symptom-based versus process-based approaches. *Clinical Psychology & Psychotherapy*, *22*(5), 460–468. DOI: 10.1002/cpp.1910 PMID: 24947201

Bimber, B., Flanagin, A. J., & Stohl, C. (2015). Reconceptualizing collective action in the contemporary media environment. *Communication Theory*, *25*(4), 365–388. DOI: 10.1111/j.1468-2885.2005.tb00340.x

Boyd, D. M., & Ellison, N. B. (2007). Social network sites: Definition, history, and scholarship. *Journal of Computer-Mediated Communication*, *13*(1), 210–230. DOI: 10.1111/j.1083-6101.2007.00393.x

Breuer, A., & Farooq, M. (2012). Online political participation: The impact of social media on political mobilization in the Middle East. *Journal of Communication*, *62*(5), 870–888. DOI: 10.1111/j.1460-2466.2012.01663.x

Brown, R., Smith, T., & Davis, L. (2021). The psychological impact of victimization through social aggression. *The Journal of Social Psychology*, *161*(3), 345–360. DOI: 10.1080/00224545.2020.1765234

Culnan, M. J., & Williams, C. C. (2009). How ethics can enhance organizational privacy: Lessons from the ChoicePoint and TJX data breaches. *Management Information Systems Quarterly*, *33*(4), 673–687. DOI: 10.2307/20650322

Damota, M. D. (2019). The effect of social media on society. *New Media and Mass Communication*, *78*, 12–17. DOI: 10.7176/NMMC

Damota, M. D. (2019). The Effect of Social Media on Society, New Media and Mass Communication, www.iiste.org, ISSN 2224-3267 (Paper), ISSN 2224-3275 (Online), DOI: , Vol. 78, 2019.DOI: 10.7176/NMMC

Das, A. (2018). Role of Mass Media in Fostering Values Among Students, JETIR August 2018, Volume 5, Issue 8 www.jetir.org (ISSN-2349-5162).

De Mendonça, R. R., de Brito, D. F., Rosa, F. de F., dos Reis, J. C., & Bonacin, R. (2020). A framework for detecting intentions of criminal acts in social media: A case study on Twitter. *Information (Basel)*, *11*(3), 154. DOI: 10.3390/info11030154

Dinev, T., & Hart, P. (2006). An extended privacy calculus model for e-commerce transactions. *Information Systems Research*, *17*(1), 61–80. DOI: 10.1287/isre.1060.0080

Edelman. (2021). Edelman Trust Barometer 2021. https://www.edelman.com/trust/2021-trust-barometer

Ellison, N. B., Steinfield, C., & Lampe, C. (2007). The benefits of Facebook "friends": Social capital and college students' use of online social network sites. *Journal of Computer-Mediated Communication, 12*(4), 1143–1168. DOI: 10.1111/j.1083-6101.2007.00367.x

Ename, A. A. et al. (2022). A Study on Positive and Negative Effects of Social Media on Society, IJARCCE, International Journal of Advanced Research in Computer and Communication Engineering, ISSN (O) 2278-1021, ISSN (P) 2319-5940, ISO 3297:2007, Vol. 11, Issue 5, May 2022, DOI: .DOI: 10.17148/IJARCCE.2022.115161

Farooq, K. et. al. (2021). The Study on the Role of Social Media in Social Change in Society, International Journal of Innovation, Creativity, and Change, Volume 15, Issue 2.

Fazil, A. W., (2024). Exploring the Role of social media in Bridging Gaps and Facilitating Global Communication, Studies in Media, Journalism, and Communications Journal, www.al-kindipublisher.com/index.php/smjc, SMJCDOI: DOI: 10.32996/smjc

Gil de Zúñiga, H., Jung, N., & Valenzuela, S. (2012). Social media use for news and individuals' social capital, civic engagement, and political participation. *Journal of Computer-Mediated Communication, 17*(3), 319–336. DOI: 10.1111/j.1083-6101.2012.01574.x

Goldfarb, A., & Tucker, C. (2011). Privacy regulation and online advertising. *Management Science, 57*(1), 57–71. DOI: 10.1287/mnsc.1100.1246

Greenhow, C., & Lewin, C. (2016). Social media and education: Reconceptualizing the boundaries of learning. *Learning, Media and Technology, 41*(1), 1–6. DOI: 10.1080/17439884.2015.1064954

Greenhow, C., & Lewin, C. (2016). Social media and education: Reconceptualizing the boundaries of formal and informal learning. *Learning, Media and Technology, 41*(1), 6–30. DOI: 10.1080/17439884.2015.1064954

Greitemeyer, T., & Sagioglou, C. (2016). Subjective well-being and social media use: Do personality traits moderate the relationship between social media use and subjective well-being? *Social Media + Society, 2*(3), 1–9. DOI: 10.1177/2056305116665859

Gulf News report,(2023, Jul 18) https://gulfnews.com,

Hamm, M. S., & Spaaij, R. (2017). *The age of lone wolf terrorism.* Columbia University Press., DOI: 10.7312/hamm18174

Hattikar, A. A., & Bagi, J. S. (2024). The Influence of social media on Education, International Journal of Innovative Science and Research Technology, Volume 9, Issue 8, August – 2024, ISSN No: -2456-2165, https://doi.org/, International Journal of Innovative Science and Research Technology, Volume 9, Issue 8, August – 2024, ISSN No: -2456-2165, https://doi.org/,DOI: 10.38124/ijisrt/IJISRT

Hinduja, S., & Patchin, J. W. (2010). Bullying, cyberbullying, and suicide. *Archives of Suicide Research, 14*(3), 206–221. DOI: 10.1080/13811118.2010.494133 PMID: 20658375

Holt, T. J., & Bossler, A. M. (2014). An assessment of the current state of cybercrime scholarship. *Deviant Behavior, 35*(1), 20–40. DOI: 10.1080/01639625.2013.822209

Howard, P. N., & Hussain, M. M. (2013). *Democracy's fourth wave? Digital media and the Arab Spring.* Oxford University Press. DOI: 10.1093/acprof:oso/9780199936953.001.0001

Ibrahim, Y. (n.d.). *The new risk communities: Social networking sites and risk.* University of Brighton.

Ito, M., Horst, H. A., Bittanti, M., Boyd, D., Herr-Stephenson, B., Lange, P. G., & Robinson, L. (2009). *Living and learning with new media: Summary of findings from the Digital Youth Project.* MIT Press. DOI: 10.7551/mitpress/8519.001.0001

Johnson, M. (2023). Defamation in the digital age: Legal and ethical implications. [https]. *Communication Law and Policy, 28*(2), 89–110.

Kalemi (2024). Publer, https: publer.io/blog/social-media-challenges

Kanchan, S., & Gaidhane, A. (2023). *Social media and Its Impact on Public Health: A Narrative.* Cureus, Open Access Review Article Review., DOI: 10.7759/cureus.33737

Kaplan, A. M., & Haenlein, M. (2010). Users of the world, unite! The challenges and opportunities of social media. *Business Horizons, 53*(1), 59–68. DOI: 10.1016/j.bushor.2009.09.003

Kaplan, A. M., & Haenlein, M. (2010). The challenges and opportunities of social media, Business Horizons (2010) 53, 59-68, Kelley School of Business, Indiana University, .DOI: 10.1016/j.bushor.2009.09.003

Karim, F., Oyewande, A. A., Abdalla, L. F., Ehsanullah, R. C., & Khan, S. (2020). Social media use and its connection to mental26 mental health outcomes: A systematic review. *Frontiers in Psychiatry, 11*, 573326. DOI: 10.3389/fpsyt.202sexuality2020.573326://

Kariya, R., & Vidani, J. (2024). The Positive Aspects of Social media Use: Examining Social Support and Mental health Benefits, Journal of Advanced Research in Economics and Business Management, Volume 7, Print Issue 1 - 2024, Pg. No. 37-43

Khalaf, A. M., Alubied, A. A., Khalaf, A. M., & Rifaey, A. A. (2023). An Impact of social media on the Mental health of Adolescents and Young adults. *Systematic Reviews*. DOI: 10.7759/cureus.42990 PMID: 37671234

Klausen, J. (2015). Tweeting the Jihad: Social media networks of Western foreign fighters in Syria and Iraq. *Studies in Conflict and Terrorism, 38*(1), 1–22. DOI: 10.1080/1057610X.2014.974948

Kowalski, R. M., Giumetti, G. W., Schroeder, A. N., & Lattanner, M. R. (2014). Bullying in the digital age: A critical review and meta-analysis of cyberbullying research among youth. *Psychological Bulletin, 140*(4), 1073–1137. DOI: 10.1037/a0035618 PMID: 24512111

Kross, E., Verduyn, P., Demiralp, E., Park, J., Lee, D. S., Lin, N., Shablack, H., Jonides, J., & Ybarra, O. (2013). Facebook use predicts declines in subjective well-being in young adults. *PLoS One, 8*(8), e69841. DOI: 10.1371/journal.pone.0069841 PMID: 23967061

Lee, H., & Kim, S. (2022). Social media and reputational harm: The role of online slander. *Cyberpsychology, Behavior, and Social Networking, 25*(4), 201–209. DOI: 10.1089/cyber.2021.0156

Levenson, J. C., Shensa, A., Sidani, J. E., Colditz, J. B., & Primack, B. A. (2016). The association between social media use and sleep disturbance among young adults. *Preventive Medicine, 85*, 36–41. DOI: 10.1016/j.ypmed.2016.01.001 PMID: 26791323

Li, A. (2024). The Effects of social media on Mental Health: A Study of Young Adults in the United States, *Proceedings of the 2nd International Conference on Interdisciplinary Humanities and Communication Studies*, DOI: DOI: 10.54254/2753-7064/27/20232070

Loader, B. D., & Mercea, D. (2011). Networking democracy? Social media innovations and participatory politics. *Information Communication and Society, 14*(6), 757–769. DOI: 10.1080/1369118X.2011.592648

Lupton, D. (2016). Digital risk society. In Burgess, A., Alemanno, A., & Zinn, J. (Eds.), *The Routledge handbook of risk studies* (pp. 301–309). Routledge.

Manca, S., & Ranieri, M. (2016). Facebook and the others. Potentials and obstacles of social media for teaching in higher education. *Computers & Education, 95*, 216–230. DOI: 10.1016/j.compedu.2016.01.012

Mangold, W. G., & Faulds, D. J. (2009). Social media: The new hybrid element of the promotion mix. *Business Horizons, 52*(4), 357–365. DOI: 10.1016/j.bushor.2009.03.002

Mohammad, W. (2020). Traditional media versus social media: challenges and opportunities, Technium Vol. 4, No. 10, pp. 145-160, ISSN: 2668-778X, Marwan Al-Quran International Media Cultural Work (M.A), Hochschule Darmstadt, University of Applied Sciences.

Mundt, M., Ross, K., & Burnett, C. M. (2018). Scaling social movements through social media: The case of Black Lives Matter. *Social Media + Society, 4*(4), 1–12. DOI: 10.1177/2056305118807911

Nadaraja, R., & Yazdanifard, R. (n.d.). *Social media marketing: Advantages and disadvantages. Center of Southern New Hampshire University (SNHU).* Help College of Arts and Technology.

Nair, P (2015). Study on Social Justice to Women Through Judicial Activism in India, Deeksha, Bi-annual Journal of Social Work, Volume 13, Number 01, February, 2015, ISSN-2250-3919, pp. 63-76.

Naslund, J. A., & Aschbrenner, K. A. (2019). Risks to privacy with use of social media: Understanding the views of social media users with serious mental illness. *Psychiatric Services (Washington, D.C.), 70*(7), 561–566. DOI: 10.1176/appi.ps.201800520 PMID: 30947635

Naslund, J. A., Aschbrenner, K. A., Marsch, L. A., & Bartels, S. J. (2016). The future of mental health care: Peer-to-peer support and social media. *Epidemiology and Psychiatric Sciences, 25*(2), 113–122. DOI: 10.1017/S2045796015001067 PMID: 26744309

Nugraha, A. P., (2024). The Impact of Social Media on Social Interaction and Self Identity in Indonesian Society, P-ISSN: 2827-9832, E-ISSN: 2828-335x, http://ijsr .internationaljournallabs.com/index.php/ijsr, DOI: . v3i9.2254, LicenseCC BY-SA 4.0DOI: 10.55324/josr

Odgers, C. L., & Jensen, M. R. (2020). Annual research review: Adolescent mental health in the digital age: Facts, fears, and future directions. *Journal of Child Psychology and Psychiatry, and Allied Disciplines*, *61*(3), 336–348. DOI: 10.1111/jcpp.13190 PMID: 31951670

Okumus, E. (2024). *Media Society Relationships in the Context of Politics*. University Journal of Social Sciences Institute., DOI: 10.30794/pausbed.1430267

Omar, A. S., & Ondimu, K. O. (2024). The Impact of Social Media on Society: A Systematic Literature Review, The International Journal of Engineering and Science (IJES), Volume 3, Issue 6, ISSN (e): 2319-1813

Pariser, E. (2011). *The filter bubble: What the internet is hiding from you*. Penguin Press.

Perrin, A., & Anderson, M. (2019). Social media usage: Trends and implications. Pew Research Center. https://www.pewresearch.org/wp-content/uploads/2019/02/Social-Media-Update-2019-FINAL.pdf

Primack, B. A., Feinberg, M. E., & Hollon, C. J. (2021). Social media use and mental health among young adults: A longitudinal study. *Computers in Human Behavior*, *114*, 106526. DOI: 10.1016/j.chb.2020.106526

Primack, B. A., Shensa, A., Sidani, J. E., Whaite, E. O., Lin, L. Y., Rosen, D., Colditz, J. B., Radovic, A., & Miller, E. (2017). Social media use and perceived social isolation among young adults in the U.S. *American Journal of Preventive Medicine*, *53*(1), 1–8. DOI: 10.1016/j.amepre.2017.01.010 PMID: 28279545

Przybylski, A. K., Murayama, K., DeHaan, C. R., & Gladwell, V. (2013). Motivational, emotional, and behavioral correlates of fear of missing out. *Computers in Human Behavior*, *29*(4), 1841–1848. DOI: 10.1016/j.chb.2013.02.014

Rahaman, V. et al. (2024). Perspective Chapter: Social media through Digital Humanities – Why Not Educate the Non-Engineering Students Intech Open, License CC BY 3.0, DOI: DOI: 10.5772/intechopen.1006346

Reyns, B. W., & Henson, B. (2016). The thief of time? An examination of the relationship between social media use and cybercrime victimization. Computers in Human Behavior, 65, 194–200. DOI: 10.1016/j.chb.2016.08.028

Reid, D., & Weigle, P. (2014). Social media use among adolescents: Benefits and risks. *Adolescent Psychiatry (Hilversum, Netherlands)*, *4*(2), 73–80. DOI: 10.2174/221067660402140709115810

Sabar (2024). The Impact of Social Media on Mental Health of Young Adults: A Literature Review, Information Management and Business Review (ISSN 2220-3796), Vol. 16, No. 3S(a), pp. 447-460

Saridakis, G., Benson, V., Ezingeard, J. N., & Tennakoon, H. (2016). Individual information security, user behaviour and cyber victimisation: An empirical study of social networking users. *Technological Forecasting and Social Change, 102*, 320–330. DOI: 10.1016/j.techfore.2015.08.012

Selwyn, N. (2012). Social media in higher education. *The Europa World of Learning*, *62*(1), 1–10. DOI: 10.4324/9781857436211

Selwyn, N., & Stirling, E. (2016). Social media and education: Now the dust has settled. *Learning, Media and Technology*, *41*(1), 1–5. DOI: 10.1080/17439884.2015.1115769

Shamim, M. I. (2024). How social media is Reshaping Society: A Look at Connection, Communication, and Change, Non-Human Journal, Vol. 1, No. 2; April; 2024.

Shensa, A., Sidani, J. E., Dew, M. A., Escobar-Viera, C. G., & Primack, B. A. (2018). Social media use and depression and anxiety symptoms: A cluster analysis. *American Journal of Health Behavior*, *42*(2), 116–128. DOI: 10.5993/AJHB.42.2.11 PMID: 29458520

Shirky, C. (2011). The political power of social media: Technology, the public sphere, and political change. *Foreign Affairs*, *90*(1), 28–41. https://www.foreignaffairs.com/articles/2010-12-20/political-power-social-media

Smith, A., & Anderson, M. (2018). Social media use in 2018. Pew Research Center. https://www.pewresearch.org/internet/2018/03/01/social-media-use-in-2018/

Smith, J., & Jones, K. (2019). Humiliation and intimidation in interpersonal conflicts. *Journal of Interpersonal Violence*, *34*(5), 987–1005. DOI: 10.1177/0886260516645573

Soni, P.. (2024). *Deciphering the Psychological Implications of social media, In book: Mindful Media: Mental Health Challenges in the Digital AgePublisher*. Blue Rose Publishers.

Sunkad, G. (2023). The Impact of Social media on Society, International Journal of Social health, https://ijsh.ph/index.php/rp Volume 2, Number 10, October 2023, E-ISSN: 2984-7079.

Tartari, E. (2015). Benefits and risks of children and adolescents using social media. *European Scientific Journal*, *11*(13), 321–332. https://eujournal.org/index.php/esj/article/view/5650

Taylor, P., & Miller, R. (2018). Social conflicts and group dynamics in the digital era. *The Sociological Review, 47*(2), 123–140. DOI: 10.1080/00380253.2018.1436942

Tess, P. A. (2013). The role of social media in higher education classes (real and virtual)—A literature review. *Computers in Human Behavior, 29*(5), A60–A68. DOI: 10.1016/j.chb.2012.12.032

Timung, B., (2024). *The influence of social media on learning behaviors: A social science perspective, Intercontinental Social Science Journal 6(1), 2024.* Pierre Online Publications Ltd., DOI: 10.62583/rjzw8r96

Tokunaga, R. S. (2010). Following you home from school: A critical review and synthesis of research on cyberbullying victimization. *Computers in Human Behavior, 26*(3), 277–287. DOI: 10.1016/j.chb.2009.11.014

Tufekci, Z. (2017). *Twitter and tear gas: The power and fragility of networked protest.* Yale University Press.

Turning (2024). The impact of social media on modern society, https://medium .comTwenge, J. M., Joiner, T. E., Rogers, M. L., & Martin, G. N. (2019). Increases in depressive symptoms, suicide-related outcomes, and suicide rates among U.S. adolescents after 2010 and links to increased new media screen time. Clinical Psychological Science, 6(1), 3–17. DOI: 10.1177/2167702617723376

Tuten, T. L., & Solomon, M. R. (2017). *Social media marketing* (3rd ed.). Sage Publications.

Twenge, J. M., & Campbell, W. K. (2019). Media use is linked to lower psychological well-being: Evidence from three datasets. *The Psychiatric Quarterly, 90*(2), 311–331. DOI: 10.1007/s11126-019-09630-7 PMID: 30859387

Valkenburg, P. M., & Peter, J. (2013). The differential susceptibility to media effects model. *Journal of Communication, 63*(2), 221–243. DOI: 10.1111/jcom.12024

Vasylchyshyna et al. (2024). Social media as a factor in the transformation of public administration, justice and legality, Multidiscip. Rev. (2024), Published Online: June 12, 2024, DOI: 10.31893/multirev.2024spe039

Vogel, E. A., Rose, J. P., Roberts, L. R., & Eckles, K. (2014). Social comparison, social media, and self-esteem. *Psychology of Popular Media Culture, 3*(4), 206–222. DOI: 10.1037/ppm0000047

Weimann, G. (2016). *Terrorism in cyberspace: The next generation.* Woodrow Wilson Center Press., DOI: 10.7312/weim17172

Woods, H. C., & Scott, H. (2016). #Sleepyteens: Social media use in adolescence is associated with poor sleep quality, anxiety, depression, and low self-esteem. *Journal of Adolescence*, *51*(1), 41–49. DOI: 10.1016/j.adolescence.2016.05.008 PMID: 27294324

Yigit, M. F., & Tarman, B. (2013). The Impact of Social Media on Globalization, Democratization, and Participative Citizenship, Journal of Social Science Education, JSSE 2013, Volume 12, ISSN-1618-5293.

Section 2

Navigating Contemporary Media Literacy Through Different Generations

Chapter 4
Young People and Social Cohesion:
Shaping Media Literacy in Postdigital Societies

Johannes Gemkow
https://orcid.org/0000-0002-0203-6467
University Leipzig, Germany

ABSTRACT

The impact of public communication media on social cohesion is multifaceted, primarily by facilitating the visibility, accessibility, and openness to dialogue of society itself. Social media, in particular, has been instrumental in enabling widespread par-ticipation of individuals and organisations in public discourse, thereby enriching the diversity of opinions expressed. However, concomitantly, these platforms have also given rise to socio-technical environments that foster the networking of anti-democratic actors and the propagation of disinformation and uncivil communication. The profound shifts in social participation engendered by social media have precipitated a dynamic shift in socialisation authority, particularly among younger people. This transformation is substantiated by the theory of post-digitality and articulated in the context of the concept of social cohesion. The article employs the German con-ception of media competence to advocate for a more expansive interpretation of me-dia literacy.

POST-DIGITALITY AS A THEORETICAL FRAMEWORK

Post-digitality refers to the cultural, artistic, and theoretical condition that emerges following the widespread integration of digital technologies into everyday life. This

DOI: 10.4018/979-8-3373-0872-2.ch004

concept challenges the traditional dichotomy between the digital and the analogue, emphasising their convergence. It signifies a shift from the novelty of digital innovations to a critical engagement with their pervasive presence and implications. From one perspective, the exploration of the digital's restructuring of quotidian life is central to the post-digital theoretical framework. Conversely, a critical stance towards prevailing media literacy models is implied, as the purported transformation of daily life gives rise to novel challenges pertaining to social cohesion. In this regard, media literacy is inextricably linked to social cohesion.

The term "post-digital" initially gained prominence in the early 21st century, particularly within the domain of art and design. Post-digital aesthetics encompass a fusion of digital and analogue techniques, frequently accentuating the imperfections and glitches that emerge from technological processes. This approach challenges the pursuit of digital perfection, instead emphasizing the unique qualities that emerge from the interplay of different media. The employment of glitches – defined as unanticipated errors in digital processes – as artistic components serves to critique the notion of flawless digital reproduction, emphasising the materiality and fallibility of digital media (Cascone, 2000; Kemper, 2023).

Subsequently, post-digitality was adopted by media science. The post-digitality concept does not signify a disconnection from digitality; rather, it underscores the inevitability of the prefiguration of the living world through digital technology and algorithms. Digital technology is not a recent phenomenon; it is an emergent element that has already had a profound impact on all facets of life (Berry, 2024).

The consequences of digitality can be observed in three key characteristics of post-digital societies.

THE UBIQUITY OF DIGITAL TECHNOLOGIES

In Germany, 96 per cent of young people aged between 12 and 19 have an internet-enabled smartphone (Medienpädagogischer Forschungsverbund Südwest, 2024), and the daily internet usage time is 434 minutes (Beisch & Koch, 2023), of which 120 minutes is spent using social media (Bitkom Research, 2024).

Digital tools and platforms have become so pervasive that they are taken for granted. This ubiquity reduces the sense of awe associated with digital advances, prompting a shift in focus from the technology itself to how it shapes culture, behaviour, and society.

Hybrid Media Practices

Not only do artists, designers, or creators increasingly combine analogue and digital techniques in their work, but the usage of social media is integral for follow-up communication among young people. The integration of social media in the lives of young people is a critical aspect of their socialisation process. Furthermore, social media platforms have the capacity to influence certain practices, such as challenges, livestreams, and trends, and to nurture attitudes, including the fear of missing out and even political orientation.

Changeability of Political Socialisation

Post-digitality has the potential to catalyse societal change, particularly in relation to the emergence of new political movements. Movements such as the Arab Spring, #MeToo, and Black Lives Matter demonstrate how post-digital activism combines online platforms (e.g., social media, petitions) with offline actions. Adolescents engage in the politicisation process within "communities of practice" (CoP) (Wenger-Trayner et al., 2010, p. 1), characterised by robust conduct yet an absence of member regulation or socially deterministic influence on the lifeworld of youth (e.g., local party offices, cultural or youth centres, municipalities, etc.).

Post-digitality encapsulates the evolving relationship between digital technologies and cultural practices. It reflects a shift from seeing digital media as novel and distinct to recognising their seamless integration into the fabric of everyday life. In the context of post-digitality, digital technologies influence not only modes of action or organizational forms but also cultural norms and political stability. Within this interplay between culture and politics, new forms of negotiation emerge. These are characterized by the fact that, situated between the poles of disinformation and populism on the one hand, and increasingly power-concentrated communication spaces on the other, they create new conditions for political socialization.

This chapter discusses political socialization as a symptom of societal crisis, one that affects social cohesion on multiple levels. It is argued here that social cohesion must also be understood through the transformations of the media landscape, with a particular focus on the logics and practices of social media. Building on this, the chapter examines key characteristics of political socialization in times of post-digitality, with the aim of demonstrating how media education can respond to these developments.

This contribution also aims to highlight a gap in media education research. This gap does not lie in a lack of engagement with aspects of post-digital transformation, but rather in the currently underdeveloped connection to the concept of social cohesion. To date, cohesion itself has only been addressed sporadically (Jandura et al.,

2017; Webster & Ksiazek, 2012; Weichert, 2008). While discussions surrounding the characteristics of digitalization and social media as 'neo-institutions' are both current and intense (Eisenegger, 2021; Jarren, 2017), they have not yet been situated within the framework of the concept of cohesion.

This chapter discusses the post-digital transformation through three key aspects: network transformations, social media politics, and social media intermediaries. It then examines German-language theories of media literacy to explore the extent to which media literacy as a theoretical construct must evolve in order to remain relevant. Finally, the chapter proposes a media literacy framework that draws on the three aspects – network transformations, social media politics, and social media intermediaries – and seeks to distinguish itself from the limitations of German-language literacy theories. This discussion remains at a theoretical level; the effectiveness of pedagogical interventions is not addressed.

SOCIAL COHESION AND SOCIAL MEDIA

Social cohesion is currently a multifaceted concept in Europe. However, its definition remains extremely vague.

There are a number of normative concepts that frame the idea of cohesion. These include concepts that interpret cohesion either *ex positivo* or *ex negativo*, the latter being much more common. *Ex negativo* refers to problematic crises that threaten cohesion. Research using this concept focuses, for example, on conflict, populism or group-based hostility. Conversely, *ex positivo* cohesion is associated with desirable features that aim to promote solidarity through forms of social bonding, such as youth milieus, neighbourhoods, or professional associations.

The normatively charged distinction between problematic and desirable forms of cohesion is also evident in the public use of the term. In their quantitative content analysis of the term's usage, Quent et al. (2020) demonstrated that discourse in selected newspaper articles divides into a desirable "political top-down framing" and a conflict-laden "bottom-up framing" (Quent et al., 2020, p. 87) by social movements.

The study of the role of the media in shaping social cohesion reveals a plethora of approaches. This stems from the simple, social constructivist assumption that social cohesion and the processes and practices that constitute it are communicatively constructed. This leads to both discursive and structural points of reference between the media and social cohesion. Examining structural changes in young people's lives highlights the transformation of their networks, the cultural impact of politics in social media, and the economic-technological model of social media intermediaries.

Network Transformations

The addition of social media to social capital has sometimes been viewed ambivalently (Mahrt, 2019, p. 35). In her study on the integrative potential of the internet, Mahrt (2019, p. 163) showed that the internet does not have a detrimental effect on bonding capital, with traditional mass media having a stronger integrative power compared to fragmented internet use (Mahrt, 2019, p. 165). Positive effects of the internet on bonding capital have already been identified for specific target groups in specific contexts. For older family members, an increase in bonding capital has been demonstrated through mobile use of social media (Zhao et al., 2021), with the positive effects on bridging capital being higher (Zhao et al., 2021, p. 397). Similarly, a mediating function of bridging capital between WhatsApp use and social integration was shown in U.S. and Pakistani students (Bano et al., 2019). However, there are also findings that differentiate the effect of the internet on bonding capital. For example, excessive internet use reduces the possibility of building up bonding capital (Guo et al., 2014, p. 81).

Building up bonding capital via the internet and social media is always problematic when it is accompanied by 'radicalisation [...] of extreme and fringe positions, including conspiracy theories and hate messages' (Task Force FGZ-Datenzentrum, 2022, p. 15). Extremist, especially right-wing extremist content (Reinemann et al., 2019, p. 30), recruitment attempts (Charlie Winter et al., 2020, p. 8), and communities have gained in importance in recent years due to their communication on social media (Schemer et al., 2018).

Furthermore, the relevance of social media for young people leads to "social pressure [...] to use certain services and be in communities" (Hoffmann, 2018, p. 690). At the same time, almost a third of young people describe the fear of missing out on something if they are not on social media (Feierabend, Sabine, Rathgeb, Thomas, Gerigk, Yvonne & Glöckler, 2024, p. 28). This suggests that socialisation via social media imposes various social constraints on young people. Based on qualitative interview data from young people, Winstone et al. (2021) describe the perceived obligation to be available to others and the need to find excuses for not fulfilling this obligation (Winstone et al., 2021, pp. 6–7).

Haythornthwaite (2002) has previously demonstrated the feasibility of establishing so-called 'weak-ties' through the Internet, a concept that extends to both the utilisation of social media (Donath & Boyd, 2004; N. B. Ellison et al., 2007) and to offline follow-up communication (Hampton & Wellman, 2003). Social media has been demonstrated to play a substantial role in the cohesion of social movements by facilitating the establishment and maintenance of networks characterised by a high degree of participation (Hwang & Kim, 2015, p. 486). The development of bridging capital has been demonstrated to be supported by certain personality traits, including agreeableness, a high degree of conscientiousness (Ma & Leung, 2019, p. 1073), and self-efficacy (Jin, 2015, p. 514). However, the findings of Valenzuela et al. (2009) suggest a lack of evidence to support the hypothesis that Facebook usage among U.S. students is associated with their social capital. Sajuria et al. (2015) come to similar conclusions, showing that bridging capital online is based on an intentional motivation: "The alleged horizontal and spontaneous nature of online interactions might not be enough to produce, without intention, bridging social capital." (Sajuria et al., 2015, p. 733). This assertion is further corroborated by the findings of Zhao et al. (2021), which demonstrate that older family members deliberately sought to establish networks, thereby augmenting bridging capital through social media.

Social Media Politics

The structural change of the public sphere is also associated with 'disinhibited [...] discourses shielded against dissonant opinions and criticism' (Habermas, 2022, p. 47). One crystallisation point of this development can be seen in the formation of a 'long tail' public sphere (Anderson, 2007). This concept refers to a scenario in which the public sphere maintains a significant presence in the front area, often termed the 'long tail', while concurrently experiencing a decline in the variety of content available in the rear area, which is characterised by a proliferation of low-reach information.

The proliferation of pseudo-journalistic content is facilitated by the rise of peer-to-peer politics on social media platforms. The conventional journalistic quality standards are no longer applicable in this environment, and the traditional gatekeepers of journalistic content are becoming obsolete, enabling the unfiltered circulation of narratives centred on scandal and outrage (Emmer, 2017, p. 85).

Populist movements benefit from this with their communication on social media. Negative, personalised, fast-moving and simplistic political reporting reinforces existing mistrust of politics. In this sense, the internet can contribute to a segregation of the public sphere, in which "certain user groups tend to see such network publics as a place for the creation of counter-publics" (Emmer, 2017, p. 94).

Populism is widely regarded as a significant challenge for liberal democracies, and its ramifications are intricate. A prevailing viewpoint is that populism possesses the capacity to polarize public sentiment, creating dichotomous camps of pro- and anti-populist factions. Furthermore, populism has been observed to capitalize on the latent conflict potential inherent in social crises, frequently engendering adverse attitudes towards politics and outgroups. (Sheets et al., 2016)

The strategic exploitation of emotionality, often characterised by exaggerations, attributions of blame, and simplifying metaphors, is a hallmark of populist communication strategies.

The functional logic of social media in particular has a positive effect for them, as success is measured by the categories of attention and reach: 'As numerous studies have now shown, this economy of attention promotes the communicative (often satirical) intensification and polarisation of political issues and social discourse' (Dittrich, 2017, p. 2). However, it should also be noted that the concepts of echo chamber and filter bubble themselves carry a simplifying impetus, which Bruns describes as 'ill-defined ideas' (2019, p. 117). This is based on the assumption that the two concepts themselves are not clearly defined and oversimplify human information appropriation. Stark et al. (2021) do not yet see any empirical evidence for the existence of confirming information environments. Rather, the use of social media seems to lead to an increasing number of confrontational opinions. However, this is not accompanied by a deliberative negotiation process, but rather a distortion of the climate of opinion into polarised fronts. This, in turn, leads to a perceived weakening of social cohesion as a whole while at the same time strengthening group-related 'internal cohesion'.

This phenomenon of group-related behaviour is comprehensively delineated within the theoretical framework of communitisation (Hepp et al., 2014, p. 185). Communitisation, predicated on the logic of shared values, is inherently a community of meaning, thus giving rise to an apparent ambivalence. On the one hand, the online realm offers a plethora of communal interpretations, while on the other hand, mediatisation engenders a marked increase in individual rationalisation. The aggregation of data gives rise to the creation of metric constructions of reality, as evidenced by the emergence of practices such as quantified self, lifelogging (Selke, 2014), and various rankings and scores (Mau, 2017). In other words, mediatisation creates an apparent contradiction between a surplus of meaning and a simultaneous push that, if not suggests, then at least enables individuals to rationalise their lives. This contradictory situation gives rise to an experience of powerlessness in the face of rationality, which is not only evident in the discussions about polarisation, populism and post-factuality, but is also part of the alternative facts (Kumkar, 2022), all of which oppose the compulsion of the rational. When the constraint of the rational falls away, the desire for the emotional increases. As a result, mediatised communities become extremely staged. To attribute the increase in staged representations to the egocentric networks would therefore be tantamount to a reduction. It is also a crisis of the rational that favours emotional representations. The communalisations do not follow shared interests; they create them. More precisely, joining in the action is all there is to share' (Bauman, 1995, p. 354). And 'sharing' on social media is always an act of staged attention.

Social Media Intermediaries

Mediatised communities not only change relationship practices, but also the structural conditions under which they are constituted. Intermediaries fulfil central functions of public and private communication: they "constitute two-sided markets, connect provider and user interests and receive resources (money, data, etc.) from both sides in return" (Jarren, 2021, p. 46).

The convergence of technologies by intermediaries, coupled with their provision of algorithmic selection, aggregation, and distribution services, results in the systematic mixing of different sub-areas and forms of use, such as interpersonal and public communication, politics, entertainment, and culture. Consequently, relationship practices occur within a space that is inherently politically, culturally, and consumeristically charged, rendering socialisation processes increasingly dependent on the surrounding topics of the respective social media platform, such as taking sides in wars or aligning with aesthetic trends.

Furthermore, intermediaries regulate opportunities for participation through their data-economic subject orientation, which links the extended ability to act with the economic ecosystems of the intermediaries. In mediatised communities, digital participation opportunities meet data-driven profiling, revealing a dissolution of the pure tool understanding of media as a means of communication. This reveals a dissolution of the pure tool understanding of media as a means of communication. Insofar as media are "digitalised and integrated into comprehensive communication infrastructures, they are also a means of algorithmised reality construction" (Hepp, 2016, p. 230), which is reflected, for example, in Google search results, the Facebook newsfeed or Amazon's shopping recommendations.

The hybridity of intermediary platforms is also evident in the normative question of the distinction between privacy and the public sphere. For communities, social media represent a space for gaining status and recognition. As a result of the fundamental scarcity of attention in social media, communities follow stronger staging logics. The advent of social media has led to the proliferation of diverse communities of meaning, including prominent examples such as 'Fridays for Future', 'Black Lives Matter' and 'MeToo'. These staged collective communities of meaning play a significant role in the formation of young people's identities during periods of heightened individualisation. The dynamic nature of these communities on social media is facilitated by their ability to organise themselves swiftly. However, participation in these communities is often limited in duration, as the interests and forms of organisation that are sometimes global have no socially deterministic influence on young people's lives (such as a local party office, cultural or youth centres, communities, etc.).

Political Socialisation through Social Media

The present study hypothesises that young people are particularly affected by the aforementioned structural changes, due to both the quantitative argument, which concerns their frequent use of social media – no other age group uses social media as intensively – and the qualitative argument, which points to the connection between young people's political opinion formation and their social media use. Young people rely heavily on social media for political information and opinion-building. The social-psychological argument emphasises the orientational role of social media in shaping young people's (political) identities, with the medium providing reference points for issues such as body image, success, and self-esteem through social comparison.

It is imperative to acknowledge that young people do not constitute a homogeneous group, exhibiting uniform behaviour and attitudes. Irrespective of the age group in question, whether 12 to 19 (Feierabend, Sabine, Rathgeb, Thomas, Gerigk, Yvonne & Glöckler, 2024) or 14 to 17 (Kruger et al., 2021), it is imperative to recognise the heterogeneity of the target group (Hugger, 2014).

Adolescent behaviour, whether in socialisation contexts or in communities, can only ever be derived to a certain extent from age. Other aspects, such as social background, number of and ties to siblings, gender, or place of residence, also play a role in the analysis. Nevertheless, the utilisation of age as a primary analytical framework is a recurring element in youth studies, either as an attempt to extract generalised statements from data (Scherr, 2009, p. 24) or to emphasise the multiple contexts that become visible in a psychological and sociological context of youth.

Researching youth in the context of social cohesion always necessitates disciplinary, or at least thematic, categorisation, as research on social cohesion itself is still very young and heterogeneous and also has an adult focus (Bauer & Ertugrul, 2023, p. 10). This remains a complex endeavour.

The concept of socialisation, as outlined by Hurrelmann and Bauer (2015, p. 97), acknowledges the processual nature of personal and social factors influencing adolescent development. This highlights that socialisation does not occur in isolation, but rather "takes place in various social contexts" (Paus-Hasebrink, 2017, p. 107). Potential socialisation contexts encompass familial, peer, and educational environments. The relevance of social contexts is emphasised in particular by Grundmann (2006), who sees socialisation as a "social practice [that] [...] is established through people living together, whereby experiences, skills and knowledge are exchanged and cultivated between people" (Grundmann, 2006, p. 30). Accordingly, socialisation describes the "'production' of social connectedness and realisation" (Grundmann, 2023, p. 30). Through behaviour that is attuned to one another within the framework of social relationships, young people are encouraged to recognise other people's interests, assert their own and find compromises (Gerris & Grundmann, 2002, p. 7). These competencies are initially cultivated within the family environment through intergenerational learning processes (Grundmann & Wernberger, 2015, p. 423), and subsequently applied in peer relationships and other secondary socialisation contexts, such as educational institutions (e.g., at school) (see Grundmann, 2002, p. 43).

In the context of socialisation as a social relationship practice, social media has become institutionalised in the lives of young people. They create a ubiquitous framework for observing oneself and others and are inextricable from everyday activities. In addition to maintaining social relationships, they fulfil functions such as consumer entertainment and the organisation of everyday life. They are also a central starting point for changes in the socialisation of young people, which will be discussed below.

The profound and constantly evolving nature of societal participation in the digital age has led to a dynamic and ever-changing process of socialisation for young people, combining emotionalisation, commodification and dramatisation with practices of inclusion and exclusion, resulting in a performative compulsion. In this sense, social media can be regarded as a volatile "significant other," functioning as a marketplace for fluid identities that intrude on the psychosocial moratorium of adolescence.

During the process of socialisation, young people acquire worldviews and self-conceptions, engage in conflicts and competition over these, and experiment with new concepts of coexistence. The focus here is on young people's current ways of understanding the world, their guiding orientations and attitudes, as well as the narratives, images, and ideologies they produce and stabilise in their everyday lives. The future of these individuals is inextricably linked to the present crises and ongoing processes of transformation, within which their agency is limited (Calmbach et al., 2024; M. Ellison et al., 2020). The examination of processes and practices of politicisation in their early stages offers a valuable insight into their orientations and attitudes towards societal hierarchies and power structures, along with the conflicts over symbolic and material resources embedded within them. Early observations facilitate the adoption of a societal perspective on generationally driven value shifts and the decoding of emerging patterns of societal transformation.

THE GERMAN CONCEPT OF MEDIA LITERACY

The strong integration of social media into the everyday lives of many young people remains a relatively recent phenomenon. Certain frameworks for constructive coexistence still need to be learned to some extent. The German-language concept of media literacy (or media competence) serves here as a theoretical point of departure from which the challenges and conditions of a post-digital understanding of media literacy can be developed.

The linguist Noam Chomsky originally linked the concept of competence with language acquisition, defining it as the ability to learn language. In Chomsky's theory, language is regarded as a system of signs organised hierarchically and according to rules, with the regularity of a language referred to as generative grammar. The competence of humans, according to this theory, is the ability to learn generative grammar solely through their generic affiliation. Chomsky refers to first language acquisition. Children have "an innate theory of potential structural descriptions" (Chomsky, 1970, p. 49). This is the only way to explain why children can speak sentences that they have never heard before. Chomsky's concept of competence is not geared towards actual use but represents a theoretical model for an unconscious anthropological ability. Consequently, competence becomes an ideal and subject-centred concept.

Building on this, Habermas refers to the concept of competence in his theory of communicative action. However, Habermas shifts the concept of competence from a biological to a sociological understanding. For Habermas, competences are no longer only given by nature but are also socially structured. Competence thus refers not only to the ability "to produce grammatically correct sentences, but also includes the ability to relate to the world around us in interaction" (Kurtz, 2010, p. 11). Habermas assumes an ideal speech situation for human interaction (Habermas & Luhmann, 1971, p. 136). Expressions of uncertainty regarding assertions of validity, such as truth and truthfulness, are concomitantly manifestations of doubt concerning their communicative competence. According to Habermas, such uncertainty should be subjected to closer scrutiny through a discursive examination. However, discourse itself constitutes a speech act, which can itself be doubted, necessitating the presence of a superordinate discourse that examines the validity claims of the original discourse. This process constitutes an infinite regress of verification. According to Habermas, this infinite process is not necessary, as an ideal speech situation is assumed in every communication between people (ibid., 136). Consequently, Habermas also retains the idealistic, subject-centred impetus of competence.

Building on Habermas, Dieter Baacke sees the need for communicative competence. According to Baacke (1975, p. 363), man is a 'homo educandus,' i.e., a living being capable of education, but also in need of education. The development of communicative competence remains 'a human leeway for the formation of an infinite number of sentences as well as for potentially unlimited communicative behaviour' (ibid., p. 101f.). In this sense, competence again appears as an idealistic, subject-centred concept, as it assumes that people are competent and thus makes this a fundamental anthropological characteristic.

According to Baacke, media literacy is now understood as part of communicative competence. Baacke defines media literacy as 'the ability to use all types of media for the communication and action repertoire of people in a way that actively appropriates the world' (Baacke, 1996b, p. 8).

The concept of media literacy has been linked to generative grammar and universal grammar, which were developed by Chomsky. These grammars are considered to be fundamentally universal and idealistically subject-centred. The attributes of generative grammar and universal grammar can be seen in Habermas' concept of communicative competence, Baacke's concept of media competence, and in the media pedagogical understanding of media competence.

A plethora of approaches have been developed that link media literacy with the challenges posed by social media, including data literacy, social media literacy and news literacy. However, there is still a paucity of a comprehensive concept that views societal challenges, such as polarization and right-wing populism, as part of the logic of social media and translates these challenges into the lived realities of young people. The present study proposes a novel approach to media literacy that is not merely an extension of the existing practices but rather a critical examination of the interplay between social media and the prevailing societal challenges, particularly those pertaining to polarization and right-wing populism. This approach aims to integrate the technological dimensions of social media with the political rhetorics and aesthetics that are shaped by the inherent logic of these platforms.

The crux of the issue concerning social cohesion does not lie in the implementation of overly stringent filters or one-sided informational behaviour. Instead, the critical problems pertain to the absence of distance from one's own opinions, a paucity of empathy and communicative accessibility for alternative viewpoints, and an insufficiency of understanding regarding the function of a shared public sphere. It is evident that social media frequently exacerbates these issues. It is therefore essential that a media literacy approach takes into account the post-digital entanglements of political media socialisation if it is to positively influence democratic opinion formation in a holistic manner.

The concept of media literacy has been the subject of considerable criticism.

The concept of media literacy has been the subject of repeated criticism in academic discourse, with three fundamental points of criticism emerging: (1) theoretical foundation, (2) empirical emptiness and (3) lack of media specificity. These criticisms will be discussed in detail below.

1) Theoretical Foundation

The linguistic root of media literacy remains focused on language and writing, which is why, for example, visual language is not taken into account (Moser, 2010,

p. 243). The original competence concept emphasised grammatical and pragmatic grammatical and pragmatic aspects of language, which are neither in a pedagogical nor in a medial context. Habermas, who explicitly refers to Chomsky, does not mention media. Rather, Habermas sees media as a hindrance to the structure of communicative competence (Vollbrecht, 1999, p. 14). Even in Baacke's fundamental work on communicative competence (1975), the term media competence does not appear.

The universal and normative orientation of media literacy can be seen as a further heir of communicative competence. The universal level of communicative competence can be found in the concept of media literacy in the inclusion of all media. Accordingly, media literacy addresses 'the electronic-technical handling of media of all kinds' (Baacke, 1998b).

The claim to universality makes it difficult to connect media literacy to educational discourse and practice (Gapski, 2001, p. 71).

Media literacy was defined by Baacke (1998a, p. 26) as a 'normative ideal'. The idealistic vein takes over media competence from communicative competence, while the pedagogical orientation represents a normative. The normative and universal orientation of the concept of media literacy harbours the danger of overlooking media-specific aspects.

To a certain extent, this creates an ambivalence "between the descriptive and normative levels of the concept" (Groeben, 2002a, p. 12). What is meant by this is finding a balance between dynamically orienting media literacy towards specific aspects (such as the concept of media, the individual, specific contexts or the situation) without violating a normative ideal. However, such a balance seems to be anything but self-evident. Gapski and Gräßer (2007, p. 26) make the following judgement: 'If the respective concept of media literacy focuses too strongly on specific technical application skills, it moves away from the normative ideal of the competent person'. In this sense, media literacy always harbours a normative-dynamic ambivalence.

This normative-dynamic ambivalence is reflected in the distinction between competence and performance. For Chomsky, competence refers to an unconscious ability to dispose of language. This interpretation seems downright disastrous for media competence. On the one hand, because an unconscious ability to deal with language would now have to be transferred to another (technical) medium. Secondly, because media literacy should refer to acting in communication contexts. Here, however, media competence would have to be orientated towards the specific constellation of the action (e.g. medium, subject, situation) in order to actually trace the dynamic, performative act (action) back to the normative ideal (competence).

The theoretical foundation of the concept of media literacy, therefore, does not appear to be stringent. The linguistic and nativist roots are difficult to summarise within a pedagogical framework. The focus on language seems to make it difficult to transfer the concept to other or 'all' media. Furthermore, it remains unclear whether media literacy is seen as a prerequisite or a goal. Finally, the universal, normative ideal of competence collides with the dynamic and descriptive level of media behaviour (performance). This normative-dynamic ambivalence is ultimately reflected in the difficulty of operationalising media literacy.

2) Empirical Emptiness

The universal and idealistic legacy of media literacy leads to the difficulty of operationalising and empirically assessing it. These difficulties are reflected in two different aspects: theorising conceptualisation and universality. Baacke (2007, p. 100) already warned against a theorising conceptualisation of media literacy by calling for media literacy not to be interpreted in a 'rationalistically narrow way'. With this rationalistic narrowing, Baacke addresses the convention of always conceptualising or operationalising skills from a theoretical position.

Media-specific, subjective, individual or even situational contexts are often ignored. This is clearly reflected in the existing models of media literacy (such as Baacke, 1996a; Groeben, 2002b; Pöttinger, 1997; Schorb, 1997; Theunert, 1999; Tulodziecki, 1998). All the models mentioned have been conceptualised from a theoretical position.

In Chomsky's sense, one could now argue that this theorisation is entirely consistent. For Chomsky, it is the competences that remain on an idealistic, i.e., theoretical level, while performance is empirically observable. However, this argument does not exclude the possibility that empirical competences could also be conceptualised via performance in conjunction with theoretical arguments.

The aspect of the universality of media literacy also leads to its empirical emptiness. The claim to provide a standardised concept for all media across all target groups makes empirical implementation difficult. Even in the theoretical operationalisation by Treumann et al. (2007, p. 35), the authors admit that 'an empirical investigation of all these facets [...] does not appear to be feasible within the framework of an empirical research project'. An often unclear definition of the term medium makes a clear demarcation difficult (Schiefner-Rohs, 2012, p. 67).

With the universal and theorising orientation of media literacy, the concept all too quickly becomes a 'meaningless universal goal' (Kübler, 2001, p. 21). This not only makes it difficult to scientifically substantiate and differentiate media literacy but also makes it impossible to transfer it into practice with practical recommendations for action.

3) Lack of media specificity

The lack of media specificity in the concept of media literacy results from its subject-centred and universal orientation. As already seen in the point of criticism (1), the theoretical foundation, media literacy, is in principle aimed at media of all kinds. In this context, the normative-dynamic ambivalence was mentioned. This ambivalence leads, on the one hand, to the problem of reconstructing competences and, on the other, to the theoretical definition of aspects of competence.

For the concept of media literacy, it is therefore necessary to determine the balance between pedagogical normativity and the changing subject matter. The subject matter of media literacy can be understood in very different ways. The contexts of the subject, the situation to be grasped or the specifics of the media each form different approaches here. The lack of media specificity is not only a consequence of the universal claim of media competence, but also of the original pedagogical impetus to place the subject at the centre.

When publishing his media literacy model, Baacke (1996a, p. 120) had already warned that media literacy should "not be reduced to a subjective-individualistic approach." Instead, he recommended "including all economic, technical, social, cultural and aesthetic problems" (Baacke 1996a, p. 120). The inclusion of all these fields, in turn, reflects the universal claim of media literacy. If only one of these fields is focused on, such as media specificity, the subject matter can be restricted. What remains mandatory is how the concept of media is to be specifically differentiated with regard to the respective field (cf. Schiefner-Rohs 2012, p. 72).

The reference to media specificity in the debate on media literacy is made more difficult by the rapid change in media communication technology.

Post-digitality has revealed the lack of media-specificity in the concept of media literacy. The favouring of a static, idealistic construct can therefore not be maintained in the context of post-digitality. The originally subject-centred, universal and idealistic concept of media literacy prevents the adequate inclusion of media-specific aspects.

MEDIA LITERACY FOR SOCIAL COHESION

These aspects, with which media literacy is associated in Germany are certainly justified. An autonomous subject, who is in principle competent with all media is an understandable focus from an educational perspective. The theory-based conceptualisations and dimensionalisations in the media competence models (e.g., Baacke 1996; Schorb 1997; Tulodziecki 1998; Aufenanger 1999; Groeben 2002b) are also comprehensible. The dimensions of the models reflect fundamental pedagogical norms and are therefore also justified.

In contrast to the German understanding of literacy in media education, the theoretical basis of literacy is based on the concept of U.S.-American pragmatism.

This focuses on actions as a central factor for problem-solving. The focus on actions is also not foreign to the German understanding of competence. In the pragmatism-based concept of media literacy, however, actions are still linked to media messages, in contrast to the German understanding of media literacies. The link with media messages can be traced back to the pioneering work on media literacy by Len Masterman. In one of his seminal works on media literacy entitled "Media Awareness Education: Eighteen Basic Principles" (1989), Masterman placed media at the centre of his considerations:

> *"The central unifying concept of Media Education is that of representation. The media mediate. They do not reflect but re-present the world. The media, that is, are symbolic sign systems that must be decoded. Without this principle, no media education is possible. From it, all else flows" (Masterman, 1989).*

This reveals the fundamental difference from the German concept of media literacy. The German-language discourse, shaped by the theoretical origins of the term "competence," favours a subjectivist-idealist understanding of competence (Gapski 2001), whereas media literacy emphasizes the media-conditioned nature of communication as central. This understanding of media literacy is also reflected in its various definitions and models. Many media literacy models (Aspen Media Literacy Institute, 2003; Potter, 2004), as well as models of information literacy (Eisenberg & Berkowitz, 1990; SCONUL, 2011), are structured around the step-by-step decoding of media-specific codes. These models formulate standardized sequences of action. One of the most frequently cited definitions of media literacy comes from the Aspen Media Literacy Institute. According to this definition, media literacy is "the ability to access, analyze, evaluate and create messages in a variety of forms" (Livingstone, 2004, p. 3).

Another influential definition of media literacy is provided by W. James Potter (2004, pp. 36–38), who outlines seven core skills within his conceptual model. These include standardized cognitive operations such as:

- "breaking down the message,
- judging its value,
- identifying commonalities among elements,
- generalizing patterns across all elements,
- applying general principles to specific instances,
- reorganizing elements into a new structure, and
- generating an accurate description that captures the essence of a message."

Potter's framework exemplifies an effort to formulate intersubjective, procedural strategies for the decoding of media messages. In contrast to the German understanding of competence, rooted in subject-centered and constructivist educational theory, this approach shifts analytical attention beyond the sender and content to the medium itself and its specific modes of encoding. Such a media-oriented perspective is foundational to the differentiated analysis of various media formats within the broader discourse on media literacy.

The expansion of individual agency through communicative media technologies gives rise to new spheres of action that simultaneously offer opportunities and impose demands. These spheres of action are pre-structured, with such pre-structuring being specific to each platform or media environment, thereby shaping both the conditions and possibilities for action. These possibilities are often strategically influenced by the data-economic intentions of various stakeholders. Moreover, such action spaces are fundamentally structured by capitalist market mechanisms. As a result, media literacy must engage with the specific characteristics of each medium. It is essential to critically examine the given media environments, as the structures of action spaces can only be meaningfully analysed within their concrete medial contexts.

AN APPROACH TOWARDS A POST-DIGITAL MEDIA LITERACY

The post-digital approach refers to cultural, political, and economic transformations. Yet it is precisely these transformations that engage subjective interpretive horizons, enabling both empowerment and resentment. These forms of transformation – and the ways individuals relate to them – are simultaneously central concerns of media education. The concept of post-digitality does not imply a separation of digital spaces and practices from the non-digital; rather, it underscores the inevitability of life-world prefiguration by digital technologies and algorithms. Post-digitality describes the evolving relationship between digital technologies and cultural practices, reflecting the shift from viewing digital media as novel and unusual to acknowledging their full integration into everyday life (Berry, 2024).

In response to the altered roles of subject and medium and the so-called "material turn" (Coole, 2014, p. 29), media education has developed corresponding theories and concepts. In recent years, approaches have emerged that are no longer strictly social-constructivist or institutionalist. Notably, this includes Actor-Network Theory (Gentzel, 2015) and materialist phenomenology (Hepp, 2018). For media literacy, this signifies a departure from "classical notions such as the autonomous, rational, reflexive subject" (Bettinger & Jörissen, 2022, p. 83).

In the context of social cohesion, this trajectory entails an inquiry into the social enactments of materially charged spaces. For example, one might explore how media aesthetics and algorithmic filtering emerge as epistemic forces. In doing so, media education accompanies the digital transformation in the spirit of an empirical Zeitgeist science.

In the final section, a model for media literacy is outlined that builds on post-digital transformations and integrates considerations of social cohesion. The goal is to design a model that incorporates democratic practices and frameworks and can be used by educators and multipliers. The model is built on three pillars: network transformations, social media politics, and media intermediaries. Its content is informed by theoretical and empirical research conducted at the Research Institute Social Cohesion and the experiences of young people with political media socialisation (Gemkow, 2023). These three pillars demonstrate that media literacy must not be reductively individualistic but rather situated within the activities that occur between medium and subject.

Media Literacy and Network Transformations

Digitalisation has fundamentally changed the way people communicate. Social media in particular influence political opinion-forming, identity construction and social interaction. Two key challenges in this context are the risk of radicalisation through extremist ideas and the psychological pressure to be constantly online. A comprehensive media literacy concept must develop strategies to protect users from both ideological manipulation and digital stress.

Radicalisation is defined as a process in which individuals increasingly adopt extremist positions and may resort to violence (Neumann, 2013). Digital media play a central role in this process, as they can act both as a recruitment platform (Reinemann 2019) and as an echo chamber.

Radical groups leverage online platforms to communicate, organise, and disseminate their ideologies. The absence of content moderators, the heightened visibility of actors, and the algorithmic construction of reality on social media platforms have led to an increase in the visibility and contact with radical ideologies. Furthermore, extremist groups employ gamification strategies, draw upon youth culture, and utilise emotional appeal to attract followers. The dangers associated with online radicalisation include creeping manipulation and social isolation of those affected.

In Germany, young people are particularly vulnerable to extremist content, as they use social media more frequently than other demographic groups to access information (Die Medienanstalten, 2023). This media use coincides with young people's constant online presence, which is characteristic of the post-digital era. In Germany, young people spend approximately five hours online per day (Beisch & Koch, 2023). This raises concerns not only about the risk of radicalisation, but also the social pressure to be constantly online. It is therefore important to emphasise that the political socialisation of young people is significantly influenced by online communities. These communities have a fundamental effect on young people's behaviour, often making polarised social conflicts visible.

Furthermore, social media engenders a perpetual need for social affirmation through likes, comments and notifications, which can result in increased stress, sleep disorders and reduced self-esteem (Twenge, 2017). The challenges of increasing radicalisation, as well as polarisation, via social media cannot be disentangled from the latent pressure on young people to be active online.

A synthesis of existing concepts is required to effectively address the challenges of the digital world, and a comprehensive approach is enabled by the combination of different programmes:

- **Prevention** of online radicalisation (such as Counter Extremism Project, RAN): Early identification of extremist content and training in counter-speech techniques.
- **Critical thinking** and digital reflection (such as Be Internet Citizens, MediaSmarts): Developing skills to recognise manipulative content and conscious media use. Reflecting on one's own usage behaviour in order to regularly analyse which platforms young people use, for how long and for what reasons.
- **Ambiguity tolerance** literally means tolerating ambiguity. The concept of ambiguity tolerance entails the capacity to manage contradictory or ambiguous information without resorting to negative or positive reactions. This skill is particularly pertinent in contemporary times, characterised by diverse and contradictory representations of reality, a phenomenon that is exacerbated by social media. The ability to navigate ambiguity competently appears to be of paramount importance.
- **Psychological** and **social support** (such as Common Sense Media, Screen Time Awareness Initiatives): Strategies for coping with FOMO and promoting a healthy approach to digital media.

The digital realm presents a duality of opportunities and challenges, and to counteract radicalisation tendencies and mitigate the psychological distress associated with social media, a comprehensive and holistic media literacy education is imperative. Educational institutions, political entities, and society at large must collaborate to ensure that individuals are equipped with the capacity to utilise the digital landscape in a critical and reflexive manner.

Media Literacy and Social Media Politics

In the context of digital media environments and political content, the question of whether competence is a solely subjective disposition is a contentious one. The question of the regulation of digital media environments arises anew, especially in light of individual experiences of information overload (Wissing & Häseler-Bestmann, 2022) and the communicative noise of alternative facts (Kumkar, 2022). This perspective emphasizes the dual aspect of media literacy, encompassing both the subjective dimension and the virtual domains of knowledge. This emergent form of media literacy, understood as the capacity to navigate and engage with these spaces, is inextricably linked to the broader concept of social media competence. The advent of social media platforms has rendered these virtual domains susceptible to the proliferation of alternative facts, largely unfiltered and unmoderated.

In the context of populism, resilience against persuasion and manipulation can be achieved by inoculating communicative strategies. This involves the use of educational videos that address emotionalised language, simplified dichotomies, and the populists' blame game (Roozenbeek et al., 2022). In the context of conspiracy theories, a method referred to as 'off-ramping,' initially developed in the field of radicalisation research, has shown efficacy in online settings (Mölders, 2023). This approach involves the targeted dissemination of content that denounces specific radicalisation themes in forums dedicated to radical ideologies. A notable example of this strategy can be seen in the case of Google Jigsaw's efforts to counter the recruitment of IS supporters in certain forums. The dissemination of videos featuring former extremists, statements by imams denouncing the corruption of Islam by ISIS, and clandestinely recorded footage showcasing various internal deficiencies within IS have been instrumental in mitigating recruitment (The Brookings Institution, 2016).

In the context of preventing fake news, 'accuracy prompts' have been shown to be a technical solution (Capraro & Celadin, 2023; Pennycook & Rand, 2021). These prompts, which are software-controlled, are designed to identify links to text that have been shared but not yet clicked on, thereby significantly reducing the spread of disinformation, which has a tendency to circulate more rapidly on social media platforms in comparison to authentic information. These prompts are designed to stimulate judgement rather than entrusting the decision to independent authorities.

The concept of 'accuracy prompts' is a notable example of this, as it involves the deliberate and strategic introduction of accuracy checks to digital systems. From a media education perspective, this approach necessitates a re-evaluation of media literacy, which was previously confined to specific subjects. However, the ongoing convergence of various domains, such as private and public spheres, entertainment and education, or subject matter and technology, underscores the need for a more comprehensive re-framing of media literacy. In this context, a hybrid subjectivity emerges during the acquisition of information, with technology playing a pivotal role through algorithmic personalisation. Addressing communicative spaces with the concept of media literacy can not only contain the crisis phenomena but also introduce media-pedagogical issues into the regulation of corporate platforms. This can serve as a crucial building block for fostering a public and epistemic reality consensus.

The issue of political content on social media, which is often characterised by its staged nature, polarisation, and populism, also necessitates social attention. The primary socialisation instance for young people is the parental home. In Germany, the family home is not only the main source of political content (Medienpädagogischer Forschungsverbund Südwest, 2024, p. 45), but also the central instance for political socialisation and media socialisation. A concept of media literacy that aims to achieve social cohesion through the media must therefore also take into account the collective aspect of socialisation. Parents, as the primary educators and guardians of their children, assume a pivotal role in shaping young individuals' media literacy, particularly in navigating and assessing media content that may pose potential risks or harms. The following criteria are identified as pivotal for the efficacy of media education:

1. Understanding and a willingness to talk

Young people who do not feel understood by their parents or caregivers are more receptive to negative content and themselves report experiencing little or no support when they have come into contact with this content.

2. Diversity of media education activities

A flexible repertoire of media education strategies is required, including protection against media content that is harmful to development by means of rules of use, as well as education about negative consequences, peer pressure and the interests of the platforms. 'Remedial media education' is also important in this context, with the aim of taking up the media experiences of young people and helping them process them. It should be noted that the understanding of risk can vary greatly between parents/guardians and young people. This discrepancy in understanding leads to variations in the perceived risks, with certain aspects being less problematised by young people than by parents, such as sexual content or contact with strangers, and vice versa, including cyberbullying and psychological violence.

3. Shared media use

The establishment of rules of use can be trialled and supported by shared experiences through shared media use, and if shared use is embedded in a positive emotional setting, trust arises. Based on a relationship of trust, children also dare to tell when they come across problematic content.

4. An authoritative parenting style

An authoritative parenting style has proven to be an essential protective factor against harmful media content. With this educational attitude, parents/educators recognise media education as their own area of competence. They create transparent rules, do not avoid conflicts and have a positive attitude towards the potentials of media and the medial interests of young people.

Another important player in the political media socialisation of young people is the school, because here, in addition to political content, a political culture can be cultivated. However, more than two-thirds of young people state that they are confronted with restrictions in school when it comes to media socialisation. Only a quarter state that the school provides information about certain content and interdependencies and encourages young people to take action online themselves. Teachers are only a point of contact for support for seven per cent (Hasebrink et al., 2019, p. 42). Furthermore, teachers are associated with a lack of knowledge about digital techniques and practices, which delegitimises them as contact persons.

In addition, there is the perception that young people have few opportunities for democracy in school. For example, the role of student government often remains unclear, and their perceived right to a say is marginal. (Calmbach et al., 2024) The diversity of the school's mission in the lives of young people and the range of support that already exists cannot be discussed in detail here. But in the case of political media socialisation, school still has the potential to develop from a place of restriction to a place of education.

Finally, individual aspects of media literacy are also important. These include understanding how to counter speech and digital civil courage. This refers to actively speaking out against hate speech, which can slow down radicalisation processes (Bartlett & Krasodomski-Jones, 2015). Furthermore, an awareness of algorithms is needed. Young people should understand how platforms filter content and what effects this has on their own perception.

Media Literacy and Media Intermediaries

Expanding the existing concept of media literacy from Germany to encompass the design of the communicative spaces of platforms (see above: media literacy) would allow for the application of platform literacy to areas such as algorithm design, data individualisation and globalisation.

This pertains to the utilisation of bridging algorithms as a solution to the escalating polarisation observed on social media (Bertelsmann Stiftung, 2025). The prevailing recommendation algorithms employed by social media platforms are optimised to maximise user engagement by suggesting content that aligns with the existing views and interests of users. These algorithms are designed to facilitate interaction between users, either directly or via content shared by friends or followers. However, this approach can potentially lead to the formation of echo chambers, where users are exposed exclusively to content that aligns with their existing views, thereby reinforcing polarisation and the dissemination of content that is sensational or scandalous in nature. In contrast, bridging algorithms propose content that aims to establish connections between diverse groups and opinions, thus fostering a more inclusive and balanced discourse.

One such algorithm might, for instance, be designed to suggest content from users or media outlets that adopt a moderate opinion or present diverse perspectives on a given issue. This approach aims to foster a more balanced discourse on political and social issues, thereby counteracting polarisation. Initial studies demonstrate that users exhibit a greater propensity to embrace alternative opinions when these are presented within a context that fosters understanding and factual discussion (Wojcik et al., 2022).

A further issue with current social media platforms pertains to the personalised delivery of content, which frequently employs non-transparent criteria. The implementation of data individualisation has the potential to assist in ensuring that users encounter content that aligns with their interests. However, it also carries the risk of users becoming isolated from alternative perspectives.

One potential enhancement would be to empower users with individualised control over data presentation, enabling them to influence the algorithms. Platforms could offer transparency tools that allow users to specify their preferences, whether they prefer to see diverse content or content tailored to their opinions. Similarly, platforms could introduce explicit labelling of algorithmically selected content to show the origin and possibilities for manipulation.

Another approach that could be adopted is the implementation of a so-called 'democratic feed,' which systematically shows users content from different political spectrums. This could be realised by labelling and classifying sources and by using mechanisms to integrate different perspectives in a targeted way.

The global reach of social media platforms is counterbalanced by the local or national nature of political and social discourse, which gives rise to challenges concerning the management of culturally divergent communication styles, political regulation, and freedom of expression.

One potential enhancement could be the promotion of intercultural exchange through content filtration according to linguistic and geographical criteria, as well as the deliberate incorporation of foreign perspectives into the discourse. For instance, platforms could develop mechanisms to facilitate interaction between users from diverse countries and cultural backgrounds. This could be supported by machine translations, dedicated discussion forums on specific topics, or international collaborations with fact-checking organisations.

The question of regulation is crucial, and national legislation differs greatly, particularly with regard to freedom of expression, data protection and disinformation. One possible improvement would be the development of global ethical standards for social media platforms that are aligned with fundamental democratic values. Close cooperation between platforms, governments and civil society organisations could help to ensure that social media becomes a place where fair and transparent discourse is possible.

The implementation of effective moderation strategies is paramount to nurturing constructive online discourse and shaping the conditions of young people's political socialisation. The following three strategies have demonstrated efficacy in this regard. However, it is imperative to recognise that these strategies should never be considered in isolation, but rather as a cohesive whole.

The first strategy is collaborative moderation, as exemplified by Community Notes on the X platform, which involves active user participation in the monitoring of discussion quality. Users can report (i.e., 'flag') problematic comments, which are then either automatically removed or forwarded to moderators for manual review. This system enables a faster response to rule violations and promotes a shared sense of responsibility for the discussion culture.

Empirical studies show that this form of moderation strengthens the sense of community among users and leads to more active participation in discussions (Ziegele & Heinbach, 2021). Since the community itself is involved in the regulation, users perceive the system as more transparent and fair. In addition, the need for direct intervention by platform operators is reduced because problematic content is detected early on.

The second strategy is content moderation, which is carried out by professional moderators who identify and remove inappropriate comments. This can be done either before publication (pre-moderation) or afterwards (post-moderation). Pre-moderation prevents harmful content from being visible in the first place, but it can restrict freedom of expression and lead to delays in the discussion. Conversely, post-moderation enables a more dynamic exchange of ideas by retrospectively removing or correcting problematic posts. Research indicates that both approaches result in higher-quality comments that are less hostile and more civilised.

In contrast to the passive intervention of post-moderation, interactive moderation, as a third strategy, relies on the active participation of moderators in the discussions. This form of moderation includes the provision of additional information, the mediation of conflict between parties, and targeted intervention in problematic discussions.

Research findings indicate that the active involvement of moderators, notably journalists and reporters in news forums, substantially mitigates incivility in comments (Ksiazek, 2018; Stroud et al., 2015). When moderators respond to uncivil comments in an impartial and courteous manner, moderated discussions are often perceived as more favourable than unmoderated ones. This fosters an environment where users are less inclined to contribute in a destructive manner, as they observe the efforts of competent actors to ensure a fair and respectful debate.

Social media platforms can make a decisive contribution to improving democratic discourse if they implement mechanisms that counteract polarisation, promote transparency and user control, and improve intercultural exchange. Bridging algorithms could help to link different opinions, while customisable data individualisation could increase the diversity of the content presented. At the same time, it is necessary to develop global standards to address the opportunities and challenges. Furthermore, the combination of collaborative, content-related and interactive moderation has been shown to contribute to a constructive and civilised online discourse. Collaborative moderation strengthens the sense of community, content moderation improves the quality of comments, and interactive moderation reduces incivility by actively involving moderators. Social media platforms should therefore make greater use of these measures to promote open and respectful digital discourse.

The intermediaries thus reproduce the pressing question of the control of privately owned media organizations. This question now arises in a significantly more comprehensive manner for the following reasons:

- Intermediaries already possess a dominant market share, which other actors in the public sphere both orient themselves toward and are compelled to do so. The fact that U.S. presidents communicate via X is as much an indicator of this as the necessity for traditional media outlets to use intermediary platforms to maintain reach.
- Through the logic of intermediaries, not only do technologies converge, but boundaries between different sectors and forms of use—such as politics, entertainment, and culture—systematically blur. This convergence is accompanied by the commodification of politicized domains such as gender, language, or humour. The process of commodification often occurs at the expense of politically relevant, deliberative processes. While intermediaries are not the sole drivers of this development, they contribute to it through their algorithmic practices of selection, aggregation, and distribution.
- Intermediaries indirectly regulate the possibilities for participation in a digital public sphere through their data-economic orientation toward the subject. This orientation intertwines individual agency with the economic ecosystems of the intermediaries (Couldry & Mejias, 2019). For instance, digital opportunities for participation are confronted with data-driven profiling, which includes political attitudes (Youyou et al., 2015).

In the age of digitization, the concept of digital sovereignty is increasingly gaining significance. It refers to the ability of states, companies, and individuals to maintain control over their digital resources, data, and technologies, and to shape their digital infrastructures autonomously. Digital sovereignty encompasses not only the assurance of data protection and security but also the promotion of independence in a digital world that is increasingly dominated by international conglomerates. Thus, digital sovereignty is a key term for media literacy, as it positions the perspective of competence between individual capabilities and the technical, social, and legal aspects of media intermediaries (Benenson et al., 2022).

CONCLUSION

The discussion in this paper centered on the challenges posed by social media to the political socialization of young people, under the assumption of the existence of post-digital life worlds for this demographic. The political socialization of young people is identified as a crucial factor in the development of a democratic and cohesive society. Social media is seen to pose specific challenges to social cohesion, and the discussion in this article is grounded in the concepts of network transformations, social media politics, and the role of media intermediaries. The discussion then turned to the German concept of media literacy, highlighting the challenges in its conceptualisation. The paper put forward an expanded understanding of media literacy that encompasses various actors and addresses specific actionable dimensions.

In contradistinction to the individualistic understanding of media literacy previously delineated, it is imperative to extend its scope to encompass additional actors, thereby ensuring a comprehensive grasp of media literacy in the context of social cohesion. These supplementary actors encompass not only the individual but also the media platform and other socialisation instances experienced by young people. The question of competence thus always pertains to the meaningful interaction between subject and medium, emphasizing the concept of "media-as-activities" (Fastrez et al., 2022, p. 74).

The present thesis contends that, in an era of post-digitality, the endeavour to facilitate democratic political socialisation among young individuals cannot be confined to an individualistic conception of media literacy. In the interest of fostering social cohesion, it is imperative that media literacy be evaluated in the future by the interaction of multiple actors and their contribution to the common good.

For the conceptualization of media literacy, it is essential to compile transdisciplinary empirical findings that, first, enable the differentiation of media education competence models based on the concrete interplay of medium, subject, and society (e.g., social media, adolescents, and social cohesion), in order to adequately address post-digital transformation. Second, there is a need for empirical evidence on the regulatory possibilities of social media, as well as best practice examples of their democratic use.

The chapter, therefore, advocates for an empirically grounded differentiation of media competencies that is oriented toward diverse contexts of action.

Acknowledging the ambiguities inherent in social media's role in fostering social cohesion is imperative. A notable development is the emergence of previously marginalised voices through social media platforms, leading to the creation of novel forms of mediatised social bonding (Dolata and Schrape, 2018; Hepp and Sinner, 2025). This phenomenon, while inclusive in nature, as it expands the public sphere and amplifies the voices of diverse individuals and groups, is not without its complexities. Conversely, there is an emergence of practices entailing exclusion and discrimination, along with other disruptions to societal self-understanding, such as the propagation of misinformation, conspiracy narratives, and authoritarian radicalisation.

These developments point to a fundamental transformation of the culture of participation and the order of communication in society, closely intertwined with media change. This transformation forms the framework for the emergence of shared worldviews and the democratic negotiation of collectively binding decisions. The traditional authority of political representatives, arbitral institutions, officeholders, scientific experts, and journalistic gatekeepers is being challenged. Concurrently, novel forms of identity-based engagement, the cultivation of shared knowledge, and societal debate are emerging.

REFERENCES

Anderson, C. (2007). *The Long Tail: Der lange Schwanz. Nischenprodukte statt Massenmarkt. Das Geschäft der Zukunft* [Nachdr.]. Hanser.

Aspen Media Literacy Institute. (2003). *Literacy for the 21st Century. An Overview.* https://www.medialit.org/sites/default/files/mlk/01_MLKorientation.pdf

Baacke, D. (1975). *Kommunikation und Kompetenz: Grundlegung e. Didaktik d. Kommunikation u. ihrer Medien* (2nd ed.). Juventa-Verlag.

Baacke, D. (1996a). Medienkompetenz – Begrifflichkeit und sozialer Wandel. In Rein, A. v. (Ed.), *Theorie und Praxis der Erwachsenenbildung. Medienkompetenz als Schlüsselbegriff* (pp. 112–124). Klinkhardt.

Baacke, D. (1996b). Medienkompetenz als Netzwerk. Reichweite und Fokussierung eines Begriffs, der Konjunktur hat. *Medien Praktisch, 20*(78), 4–10.

Baacke, D. (1998a). Medienkompetenz - Herkunft, Reichweite und strategische Bedeutung eines Begriffs. In H. Kubicek (Ed.), *Jahrbuch Telekommunikation und Gesellschaft: Vol. 6. Lernort Multimedia* (pp. 22–27). v. Decker.

Baacke, D. (1998b). *Zum Konzept der Operationalisierung von Medienkompetenz.* https://www.produktive-medienarbeit.de/ressourcen/bibliothek/fachartikel/baacke_operationalisierung.shtml

Baacke, D. (2007). *Medienpädagogik* [Nachdr.]. *Grundlagen der Medienkommunikation: Vol. 1.* Niemeyer.

Bano, S., Cisheng, W., Khan, A. N., & Khan, N. A. (2019). WhatsApp use and student's psychological well-being: Role of social capital and social integration. *Children and Youth Services Review, 103*, 200–208. DOI: 10.1016/j.childyouth.2019.06.002

Bartlett, J., & Krasodomski-Jones, A. (2015). *Counter-speech examining content that challenges extremism online.* https://www.demos.co.uk/wp-content/uploads/2015/10/Counter-speech.pdf

Bauer, U., & Ertugrul, B. (2023). Gesellschaftlicher Zusammenhalt, Sozialisation und generationaler Wandel – Konturen eines Forschungsproblems. In Ertugrul, B., & Bauer, U. (Eds.), *Sozialisation und gesellschaftlicher Zusammenhalt: Aufwachsen in Krisen und Konflikten* (pp. 9–28). Campus Verlag.

Bauman, Z. (1995). *Postmoderne Ethik.* Hamburger Ed.

Beisch, N., & Koch, W. (2023). ARD/ZDF-Onlinestudie: Weitergehende Normalisierung der Internetnutzung nach Wegfall aller Corona-Schutzmaßnahmen: Aktuelle Aspekte der Internetnutzung in Deutschland. *Media Perspektiven*, (23), 1–9.

Benenson, Z., Freiling, F. C., & Meyer-Wegener, K. (2022). Soziotechnische Einflussfaktoren auf die »digitale Souveränität« des Individuums. In G. Glasze, E. Odzuck, & R. Staples (Eds.), *Politik in der digitalen Gesellschaft. Was heißt digitale Souveränität?* (Vol. 3, pp. 61–88). transcript Verlag. DOI: 10.14361/9783839458273-003

Berry, D. M. (2024). *Post-Digital Humanities: Computation and Cultural Critique in the Arts and Humanities.* https://arxiv.org/pdf/2407.05922

Bettinger, P., & Jörissen, B. (2022). Medienbildung. In Sander, U., von Gross, F., & Hugger, K.-U. (Eds.), *Handbuch Medienpädagogik* (pp. 81–93). Springer VS., DOI: 10.1007/978-3-658-23578-9_10

Bitkom Research. (2024). *Kinder- & Jugendstudie 2024.* https://www.bitkom.org/sites/main/files/2024-08/240806bitkom-chartskinderundjugend2024.pdf

Bruns, A. (2019). *Are filter bubbles real?* Polity Press. https://ebookcentral.proquest.com/lib/kxp/detail.action?docID=5887595

Calmbach, M., Flaig, B. B., Gaber, R., Gensheimer, T., Möller-Slawinski, H., Schleer, C., & Wisniewski, N. (2024). *Wie ticken Jugendliche? 2024: Lebenswelten von Jugendlichen im Alter von 14 bis 17 Jahren in Deutschland. Schriftenreihe / Bundeszentrale für Politische Bildung: Band 11133.* Bundeszentrale für politische Bildung. https://www.bpb.de/system/files/dokument_pdf/u18_SINUS-Jugendstudie_Wie-ticken-Jugendliche_2024_Print_24-06-07_Sperrfrist_12.06.24_12.00.pdf

Capraro, V., & Celadin, T. (2023). "I Think This News Is Accurate": Endorsing Accuracy Decreases the Sharing of Fake News and Increases the Sharing of Real News. *Personality and Social Psychology Bulletin*, *49*(12), 1635–1645. DOI: 10.1177/01461672221117691 PMID: 35993352

Cascone, K. (2000). The Aesthetics of Failure: "Post-Digital" Tendencies in Contemporary Computer Music. *Computer Music Journal*, *24*(4), 12–18. DOI: 10.1162/014892600559489

Chomsky, N. (1970). *Aspekte der Syntax-Theorie* (1st ed.). *Sammlung Akademie-Verlag / Sprache Series: v.6.* Walter de Gruyter GmbH. https://ebookcentral.proquest.com/lib/kxp/detail.action?docID=31605869

Coole, D. (2014). Der neue Materialismus und Politik der Materialisierung. In Witzgall, S., & Stakemeier, K. (Eds.), *Schriftenreihe des cx centrum für Interdisziplinäre Studien der Akademie der Bildenden Künste München. Macht des Materials - Politik der Materialität* (1st ed., pp. 29–46). Diaphanes.

Couldry, N., & Mejias, U. A. (2019). Data Colonialism: Rethinking Big Data's Relation to the Contemporary Subject. *Television & New Media, 20*(4), 336–349. DOI: 10.1177/1527476418796632

Dittrich, P.-J. (2017). *Populismus im Netz: Im europäischen Vergleich liegt die AfD zurück.* Jacques Delors Institut – Berlin. https://www.hertie-school.org/fileadmin/user_upload/20170917_PopulismusWahleninDeutschland_Dittrich.pdf

Donath, J., & Boyd, D. (2004). Public Displays of Connection. *BT Technology Journal, 22*(4), 71–82. DOI: 10.1023/B:BTTJ.0000047585.06264.cc

Eisenberg, M., & Berkowitz, R. (1990). *Information problem-solving: The Big Six Skills approach to library & information skills instruction. Information management, policy, and services.* Ablex Pub. Corp. http://www.loc.gov/catdir/enhancements/fy1511/90022681-b.html

Eisenegger, M. (2021). Dritter, digitaler Strukturwandel der Öffentlichkeit als Folge der Plattformisierung. In Eisenegger, M., Prinzing, M., Ettinger, P., & Blum, R. (Eds.), *Digitaler Strukturwandel der Öffentlichkeit* (pp. 17–39). Springer Fachmedien Wiesbaden. DOI: 10.1007/978-3-658-32133-8_2

Ellison, M., Pollock, G., & Grimm, R. (2020). Young people's orientations towards contemporary politics: Trust, representation and participation. *Zeitschrift für Erziehungswissenschaft, 23*(6), 1201–1226. DOI: 10.1007/s11618-020-00984-4

Ellison, N. B., Steinfield, C., & Lampe, C. (2007). The Benefits of Facebook "Friends:" Social Capital and College Students' Use of Online Social Network Sites. *Journal of Computer-Mediated Communication, 12*(4), 1143–1168. DOI: 10.1111/j.1083-6101.2007.00367.x

Emmer, M. (2017). Soziale Medien in der politischen Kommunikation. In Schmidt, J.-H., & Taddicken, M. (Eds.), *Handbuch soziale Medien* (pp. 81–100). Springer VS. DOI: 10.1007/978-3-658-03765-9_5

Fastrez, P., Lacelle, N., Bihl, J., Gladu, E., Delamotte, E., Delarue-Breton, C., Ronveaux, C., & Sutter Widmer, D. (2022). The Media Literacy of Teenagers: An international study of Competence in Information Search and Multimodal Production. *Educare (San José)*, (1), 71–104. DOI: 10.24834/educare.2022.1.4

Feierabend, Sabine, Rathgeb, Thomas, Gerigk, Yvonne, & Glöckler, S. (2024). *JIM-Studie 2024: Jugend, Information, Medien. Basisuntersuchung zum Medienumgang 12- bis 19-Jähriger in Deutschland.* https://mpfs.de/app/uploads/2024/11/JIM_2024_PDF_barrierearm.pdf

Gapski, H. (2001). *Medienkompetenz: Eine Bestandsaufnahme und Vorüberlegungen zu einem systemtheoretischen Rahmenkonzept.* Diss. Westdt. Verl.

Gapski, H., & Gräßer, L. (2007). Medienkompetenz im Web 2.0 – Lebensqualität als Zielperspektive. In L. Gräßer & M. Pohlschmidt (Eds.), *Schriftenreihe Medienkompetenz des Landes Nordrhein-Westfalen: Vol. 7. Praxis Web 2.0: Potenziale für die Entwicklung von Medienkompetenz* (pp. 11–34). kopaed.

Gemkow, J. (2023). Polarisierung durch oder auf soziale(n) Medien? In Institut für Demokratie und Gesellschaft (Ed.), *Wissen schafft Demokratie. Schwerpunkt Netzkulturen und Plattformpolitiken* (pp. 44–57).

Gentzel, P. (2015). *Praxistheorie und Mediatisierung: Grundlagen, Perspektiven und eine Kulturgeschichte der Mobilkommunikation.* Springer VS. https://gbv.eblib.com/patron/FullRecord.aspx?p=1998476 DOI: 10.1007/978-3-658-08994-8

Gerris, J. R. M., & Grundmann, M. (2002). Reziprozität, Qualität von Familienbeziehungen und die intergenerationale Transmission von Beziehungskompetenz. *ZSE: Zeitschrift für Soziologie der Erziehung und Sozialisation, 22.* (ZSE: Zeitschrift für Soziologie der Erziehung und Sozialisation 22 (2002) 1, S. 3-24). DOI: 10.25656/01:8925

Groeben, N. (2002a). Anforderungen an die theoretische Konzeptualisierung von Medienkompetenz. In Groeben, N., & Hurrelmann, B. (Eds.), *Medienkompetenz: Voraussetzungen, Dimensionen, Funktionen* (pp. 11–22). Juventa-Verl.

Groeben, N. (2002b). Dimensionen der Medienkompetenz: Deskriptive und normative Aspekte. In Groeben, N., & Hurrelmann, B. (Eds.), *Medienkompetenz: Voraussetzungen, Dimensionen, Funktionen* (pp. 160–197). Juventa-Verl.

Grundmann, M. (2006). *Sozialisation: Skizze einer allgemeinen Theorie. UTB Soziologie* (Vol. 2783). UVK Verl.-Ges. DOI: 10.36198/9783838527833

Grundmann, M. (2023). Sozialisation als Beziehungspraxis. Sozialkonstruktive Dynamiken und Gestaltungsmöglichkeiten in Kindheit und Jugend. In Scheid, C., Silkenbeumer, M., Zizek, B., & Zizek, L. (Eds.), *Rekonstruktive Sozialisationsforschung. Sozialisationstheorie und -forschung revisited* (pp. 27–41). Springer Fachmedien Wiesbaden., DOI: 10.1007/978-3-658-36002-3_2

Grundmann, M., & Wernberger, A. (2015). Familie und Sozialisation. In *Handbuch Familiensoziologie* (pp. 413–435). Springer VS., DOI: 10.1007/978-3-658-02276-1_14

Guo, Y., Li, Y., & Ito, N. (2014). How do different internet use functions affect bridging and bonding social capital? an empirical study of the chinese international students in japan. *International Journal of Cyber Society and Education*, *7*(1), 71–88. DOI: 10.7903/ijcse.1074

Habermas, J. (2022). *Ein neuer Strukturwandel der Öffentlichkeit und die deliberative Politik* (1st ed.). Suhrkamp.

Habermas, J., & Luhmann, N. (1971). Theorie der Gesellschaft oder Sozialtechnologie: Was leistet die Systemforschung? (1. Aufl.). *Theorie Theorie-Diskussion*. Suhrkamp.

Hampton, K., & Wellman, B. (2003). Neighboring in Netville: How the Internet Supports Community and Social Capital in a Wired Suburb. *City & Community*, *2*(4), 277–311. DOI: 10.1046/j.1535-6841.2003.00057.x

Hasebrink, U., Lampert, C., & Thiel, K. (2019). *Online-Erfahrungen von 9- bis 17-Jährigen: Ergebnisse der EU Kids Online-Befragung in Deutschland 2019. eukidsonline.net.* Verlag Hans-Bredow-Institut. https://epub.sub.uni-hamburg.de/epub/volltexte/2022/132004/

Haythornthwaite, C. (2002). Strong, Weak, and Latent Ties and the Impact of New Media. *The Information Society*, *18*(5), 385–401. DOI: 10.1080/01972240290108195

Hepp, A. (2016). Kommunikations- und Medienwissenschaft in datengetriebenen Zeiten. *Publizistik*, *61*(3), 225–246. DOI: 10.1007/s11616-016-0263-y

Hepp, A. (2018). Von der Mediatisierung zur tiefgreifenden Mediatisierung. In Reichertz, J., & Bettmann, R. (Eds.), *Kommunikation – Medien – Konstruktion* (pp. 27–45). Springer Fachmedien Wiesbaden., DOI: 10.1007/978-3-658-21204-9_2

Hepp, A., Berg, M., & Roitsch, C. (2014). *Mediatisierte Welten der Vergemeinschaftung*. Springer Fachmedien Wiesbaden., DOI: 10.1007/978-3-658-02425-3

Hoffmann, D. (2018). Kinder, Jugend und Medien. In Lange, A., Reiter, H., Schutter, S., & Steiner, C. (Eds.), *Handbuch Kindheits- und Jugendsoziologie* (pp. 681–692). Springer Fachmedien Wiesbaden., DOI: 10.1007/978-3-658-04207-3_59

Hugger, K.-U. (2014). Digitale Jugendkulturen. In Hugger, K.-U. (Ed.), *Digitale Jugendkulturen* (pp. 11–28). Springer Fachmedien Wiesbaden., DOI: 10.1007/978-3-531-19070-9_1

Hurrelmann, K., & Bauer, U. (2015). *Einführung in die Sozialisationstheorie: Das Modell der produktiven Realitätsverarbeitung* (9th ed.). Beltz Verlag.

Hwang, H., & Kim, K.-O. (2015). Social media as a tool for social movements: The effect of social media use and social capital on intention to participate in social movements. *International Journal of Consumer Studies, 39*(5), 478–488. DOI: 10.1111/ijcs.12221

Jandura, O., Wendelin, M., Adolf, M., & Wimmer, J. (Eds.). (2017). *Medien - Kultur - Kommunikation. Zwischen Integration und Diversifikation: Medien und gesellschaftlicher Zusammenhalt im digitalen Zeitalter.* Springer VS. DOI: 10.1007/978-3-658-15031-0

Jarren, O. (2017). Strukturwandel der Öffentlichkeit unter digitalen Bedingungen. *Frankfurter Hefte*, (9), 46–50.

Jarren, O. (2021). Öffentlichkeitswandel durch Social Media – Auswirkungen der Plattformisierung auf die gesellschaftliche Vermittlungsstruktur. In Eisenegger, M., Prinzing, M., Ettinger, P., & Blum, R. (Eds.), *Digitaler Strukturwandel der Öffentlichkeit* (pp. 41–63). Springer Fachmedien Wiesbaden., DOI: 10.1007/978-3-658-32133-8_3

Jin, C.-H. (2015). The role of Facebook users' self-systems in generating social relationships and social capital effects. *New Media & Society, 17*(4), 501–519. DOI: 10.1177/1461444813506977

Kemper, J. (2023). Glitch, the Post-digital Aesthetic of Failure and Twenty-First-Century Media. *European Journal of Cultural Studies, 26*(1), 47–63. DOI: 10.1177/13675494211060537

Kruger, S., Walper, S., & Rauschenbach, T. (Eds.). (2021). *Aufwachsen in Deutschland 2019: Alltagswelten von Kindern, Jugendlichen und Familien: AID:A 2019.* wbv. https://elibrary.utb.de/doi/book/10.3278/9783763966325

Ksiazek, T. B. (2018). Commenting on the News. *Journalism Studies, 19*(5), 650–673. DOI: 10.1080/1461670X.2016.1209977

Kübler, H.-D. (2001). Neue Medien – neues Lernen? Perspektiven und Bedingungen des Lernens mit „Neuen Medien". In K.-D. Felsmann (Ed.), *Neue Medien - neues Lernen? Erweiterte Dokumentation 2000; Buckower Mediengespräche (4)* (pp. 17–36). kopaed.

Kumkar, N. C. (2022). *Alternative Fakten: Zur Praxis der kommunikativen Erkenntnisverweigerung* (Originalausgabe). Suhrkamp Verlag. https://www.content-select.com/index.php?id=bib_view&ean=9783518774731

Kurtz, T. (2010). Der Kompetenzbegriff in der Soziologie. In *Soziologie der Kompetenz* (pp. 7–25). VS Verlag für Sozialwissenschaften., DOI: 10.1007/978-3-531-91951-5_1

Livingstone, S. (2004). Media Literacy and the Challenge of New Information and Communication Technologies. *Communication Review*, *7*(1), 3–14. DOI: 10.1080/10714420490280152

Ma, S. Q., & Leung, L. (2019). The Impacts of Personality Traits, Use Intensity and Features Use of LinkedIn on Bridging Social Capital. *Applied Research in Quality of Life*, *14*(4), 1059–1078. DOI: 10.1007/s11482-018-9635-y

Mahrt, M. (2019). *Beyond Filter Bubbles and Echo Chambers: The Integrative Potential of the Internet.* Habilitationsschrift (Digital Communication Research 5). https://www.ssoar.info/ssoar/bitstream/handle/document/61606/ssoar-2019-mahrt-Beyond_Filter_Bubbles_and_Echo.pdf?sequence=1&isAllowed=y&lnkname=ssoar-2019-mahrt-Beyond_Filter_Bubbles_and_Echo.pdf DOI: 10.17174/dcr.v5.0

Masterman, L. (1989). *Media Awareness Education: Eighteen Basic Principles.* https://www.medialit.org/reading-room/media-awareness-education-eighteen-basic-principles

Mau, S. (2017). *Das metrische Wir: Über die Quantifizierung des Sozialen* (Erste Auflage, Originalausgabe). *Sonderdruck edition suhrkamp*. Suhrkamp.

Medienanstalten, D. (2023). *Mediengewichtungsstudie 2023-II.* https://www.die-medienanstalten.de/forschung/mediengewichtungsstudie/

Medienpädagogischer Forschungsverbund Südwest. (2024). *JIM 2024: Jugend, Information, Medien Basisuntersuchung zum Medienumgang 12- bis 19-Jähriger in Deutschland.* https://mpfs.de/app/uploads/2024/11/JIM_2024_PDF_barrierearm.pdf

Mölders, M. (2023). Das umgelenkte Publikum? In Muhle, F., Sutter, T., & Wehner, J. (Eds.), *Das sichtbare Publikum?* (pp. 145–166). Springer Fachmedien Wiesbaden., DOI: 10.1007/978-3-658-41172-5_6

Moser, H. (2010). *Einführung in die Medienpädagogik: Aufwachsen im Medienzeitalter* (5., durchgesehene und erweiterte Auflage). *Lehrbuch*. VS Verlag für Sozialwissenschaften.

Neumann, P. (2013). Radikalisierung, Deradikalisierung und Extremismus. *Bundeszentrale Für Politische Bildung*. https://www.bpb.de/shop/zeitschriften/apuz/164918/radikalisierung-deradikalisierung-und-extremismus/?utm_source=chatgpt.com

Paus-Hasebrink, I. (2017). Praxeologische (Medien-)Sozialisationsforschung. In D. Hoffmann, F. Krotz, & W. Reißmann (Eds.), *SpringerLink Bücher. Mediatisierung und Mediensozialisation: Prozesse - Räume - Praktiken.* Springer Fachmedien Wiesbaden.

Pennycook, G., & Rand, D. G. (2021). The Psychology of Fake News. *Trends in Cognitive Sciences, 25*(5), 388–402. DOI: 10.1016/j.tics.2021.02.007 PMID: 33736957

Potter, W. J. (2004). *Theory of Media Literacy: A Cognitive Approach.* SAGE Publications, Inc., DOI: 10.4135/9781483328881

Pöttinger, I. (1997). *Lernziel Medienkompetenz: Theoretische Grundlagen und praktische Evaluation anhand eines Hörspielprojekts.* Diss. kopaed.

Quent, M., Salheiser, A., & Weber, D. (2020). Gesellschaftlicher Zusammenhalt im Blätterwald: Auswertung und kritische Einordnung der Begriffsverwendung in Zeitungsartikeln (2014–2019). In Deitelhoff, N., Groh-Samberg, O., & Middell, M. (Eds.), *Gesellschaftlicher Zusammenhalt: Ein interdisziplinärer Dialog* (pp. 73–88). Campus.

Reinemann, C., Nienierza, A., Fawzi, N., Riesmeyer, C., & Neumann, K. (2019). *Jugend - Medien - Extremismus.* Springer Fachmedien Wiesbaden., DOI: 10.1007/978-3-658-23729-5

Roozenbeek, J., van der Linden, S., Goldberg, B., Rathje, S., & Lewandowsky, S. (2022). Psychological inoculation improves resilience against misinformation on social media. *Science Advances, 8*(34), eabo6254. Advance online publication. DOI: 10.1126/sciadv.abo6254 PMID: 36001675

Sajuria, J., van Heerde-Hudson, J., Hudson, D., Dasandi, N., & Theocharis, Y. (2015). Tweeting Alone? An Analysis of Bridging and Bonding Social Capital in Online Networks. *American Politics Research, 43*(4), 708–738. DOI: 10.1177/1532673X14557942

Schemer, C., Wirth, W., Wettstein, M., Müller, P., Schulz, A., & Wirz, D. (2018). Wirkung populistischer Kommunikation. Populismus in den Medien, Wirkungen und deren Randbedingungen. *Communicatio Socialis, 51*(2), 118–130. DOI: 10.5771/0010-3497-2018-2-118

Scherr, A. (2009). *Jugendsoziologie: Einführung in Grundlagen und Theorien* (9., erw. und umfassend überarb. Aufl.). *Lehrbuch.* VS, Verl. für Sozialwiss.

Schiefner-Rohs, M. (2012). *Kritische Informations- und Medienkompetenz: Theoretisch-konzeptionelle Herleitung und empirische Betrachtungen am Beispiel der Lehrerausbildung.* Diss. Waxmann.

Schorb, B. (1997). Medienkompetenz durch Medienpädagogik. In Wessler, H. (Ed.), *Perspektiven der Medienkritik: Die gesellschaftliche Auseinandersetzung mit öffentlicher Kommunikation in der Mediengesellschaft; Dieter Roß zum 60. Geburtstag* (pp. 275–285). Westdt. Verl. DOI: 10.1007/978-3-322-85097-3_27

SCONUL. (2011). *The SCONUL Seven Pillars of Information Literacy. Core Model for Higher Education.* https://www.sconul.ac.uk/sites/default/files/documents/coremodel.pdf

Selke, S. (2014). *Lifelogging: Wie die digitale Selbstvermessung unsere Gesellschaft verändert*. Econ.

Sheets, P., Bos, L., & Boomgaarden, H. G. (2016). Media Cues and Citizen Support for Right-Wing Populist Parties. *International Journal of Public Opinion Research, 28*(3), 307–330. DOI: 10.1093/ijpor/edv014

Stark, B., Magin, M., & Jürgens, P. (2021). Maßlos überschätzt. Ein Überblick über theoretische Annahmen und empirische Befunde zu Filterblasen und Echokammern. In Eisenegger, M., Prinzing, M., Ettinger, P., & Blum, R. (Eds.), *Digitaler Strukturwandel der Öffentlichkeit* (pp. 303–321). Springer Fachmedien Wiesbaden., DOI: 10.1007/978-3-658-32133-8_17

Stiftung, B. (2025). *Bridge-building instead of polarization: How algorithms can improve digital discourse.* https://bridging.reframetech.de/

Stroud, N. J., Scacco, J. M., Muddiman, A., & Curry, A. L. (2015). Changing Deliberative Norms on News Organizations' Facebook Sites. *Journal of Computer-Mediated Communication, 20*(2), 188–203. DOI: 10.1111/jcc4.12104

Task Force FGZ-Datenzentrum. (2022). *Gefährdeter Zusammenhalt? Polarisierungs- und Spaltungstendenzen in Deutschland: ausgewählte Ergebnisse der FGZ-Pilotstudie 2020.* SOCIUM; Forschungsinstitut Gesellschaftlicher Zusammenhalt. https://doi.org/DOI: 10.26092/elib/1739*

The Brookings Institution. (2016). *Disrupting ISIS Recruitment Online*, Washington D.C. https://www.brookings.edu/wp-content/uploads/2016/09/20160907_disrupting_isis_transcript.pdf

Theunert, H. (1999). Medienkompetenz: Eine pädagogische und altersspezifisch zu fassende Handlungsdimension. In F. Schell, E. Stolzenburg, & H. Theunert (Eds.), *Medienkompetenz: Grundlagen und pädagogisches Handeln* (pp. 50–59). kopaed.

Treumann, K. P., Meister, D. M., Sander, U., Burkatzki, E., Hagedorn, J., Kämmerer, M., Strotmann, M., & Wegener, C. (2007). *Medienhandeln Jugendlicher: Mediennutzung und Medienkompetenz. Bielefelder Medienkompetenzmodell.* VS Verlag., DOI: 10.1007/978-3-531-90509-9

Tulodziecki, G. (1998). Entwicklung von Medienkompetenz als Erziehungs- und Bildungsaufgabe. *Pädagogische Rundschau, 52*(6), 693–709.

Twenge, J. M. (2017). *Igen: Why today's super-connected kids are growing up less rebellious, more tolerant, less happy-and completely unprepared for adulthood*: *(and what this means for the rest of us)* (First Atria Paperback edition). Atria Paperback.

Valenzuela, S., Park, N., & Kee, K. F. (2009). Is There Social Capital in a Social Network Site? Facebook Use and College Students' Life Satisfaction, Trust, and Participation. *Journal of Computer-Mediated Communication, 14*(4), 875–901. DOI: 10.1111/j.1083-6101.2009.01474.x

Vollbrecht, R. (1999). Medienkompetenz als kommunikative Kompetenz. *Rückbesinnung und Neufassung des Konzepts.*, (43), 13–18.

Webster, J. G., & Ksiazek, T. B. (2012). The Dynamics of Audience Fragmentation: Public Attention in an Age of Digital Media. *Journal of Communication, 62*(1), 39–56. DOI: 10.1111/j.1460-2466.2011.01616.x

Weichert, S. A. (2008). Krisen als Medienereignisse: Zur Ritualisierung mediatisierter Kommunikation im Fernsehen. In Winter, C., Hepp, A., & Krotz, F. (Eds.), *Medien - Kultur - Kommunikation. Theorien der Kommunikations- und Medienwissenschaft: Grundlegende Diskussion, Forschungsfelder und Theorieentwicklungen* (pp. 311–328). VS Verl. für Sozialwissenschaften. DOI: 10.1007/978-3-531-90778-9_16

Wenger-Trayner, É., McDermott, R. A., & Snyder, W. (2010). *Cultivating communities of practice: A guide to managing knowledge* [Nachdr.]. Harvard Business School Press.

Winstone, L., Mars, B., Haworth, C. M. A., & Kidger, J. (2021). Social media use and social connectedness among adolescents in the United Kingdom: A qualitative exploration of displacement and stimulation. *BMC Public Health, 21*(1), 1736. DOI: 10.1186/s12889-021-11802-9 PMID: 34560872

Winter, C. [Charlie], Neumann, P., Meleagrou-Hitchens, A., Ranstorp, M., Vidino, L., & Fürst, J. (2020). Online Extremism: Research Trends in Internet Activism, Radicalization, and Counter-Strategies. *International Journal of Conflict and Violence (IJCV), 14*(2), 1–20. DOI: 10.4119/ijcv-3809

Wissing, C., & Häseler-Bestmann, S. (2022). Engagement im Digitalen Raum. Ein interdisziplinärer Blick auf Chancen und Risiken. In Bush, A., & Birke, J. (Eds.), *Nachhaltigkeit und Social Media* (pp. 17–35). Springer Fachmedien Wiesbaden., DOI: 10.1007/978-3-658-35660-6_2

Wojcik, S., Hilgard, S., Judd, N., Mocanu, D., Ragain, S., Hunzaker, M. B. F., Coleman, K., & Baxter, J. (2022, October 27). *Birdwatch: Crowd Wisdom and Bridging Algorithms can Inform Understanding and Reduce the Spread of Misinformation.* http://arxiv.org/pdf/2210.15723

Youyou, W., Kosinski, M., & Stillwell, D. (2015). Computer-based personality judgments are more accurate than those made by humans. *Proceedings of the National Academy of Sciences of the United States of America, 112*(4), 1036–1040. DOI: 10.1073/pnas.1418680112 PMID: 25583507

Zhao, L., Liang, C., & Gu, D. (2021). Mobile Social Media Use and Trailing Parents' Life Satisfaction: Social Capital and Social Integration Perspective. *International Journal of Aging & Human Development, 92*(3), 383–405. DOI: 10.1177/0091415020905549 PMID: 32098476

Ziegele, M., & Heinbach, D. (2021). *Hallo liebe Community! Konstruktive Online-Debatten fördern durch bestärkende Moderation.* www.medienanstalt-nrw.de/fileadmin/user_upload/NeueWebsite_0120/Zum_Nachlesen/WhitePaper_HalloLiebeCommunity_DIGITAL_210518.pdf

Chapter 5
Content Creators or Careless Curators?
The Rise of YouTubers and Its Impact on Gen Z

K. K. Nikhitha
https://orcid.org/0009-0005-6024-9996
Amrita Vishwa Vidyapeetham, Kochi, India

A. P. Prasanth
https://orcid.org/0009-0006-0288-6150
Amrita Vishwa Vidyapeetham, Kochi, India

ABSTRACT

This paper aims at analyzing the relationships between YouTubers and Generation Z in India and the effects of YouTubers including the positive and negative aspects. The case study reveals that Gen Z could not afford to lose YouTubers as they play a critical role in educating, entertaining, and connecting young people. In particular, the platform's contribution to making education more accessible and spreading community feel among young Indians cannot be overlooked. However, this study also shows are the negative characteristics, such as the distribution of fake news, bullying, and consumerism. This article analogizes these problems and presents examples from the Indian experience for comparison with the tendencies in the world.

INTRODUCTION

Understanding the profile of Gen Z in India is vital because the demographic comprises nearly 472 million people born between the mid-1990s and early 2000s,

DOI: 10.4018/979-8-3373-0872-2.ch005

who have been subjected to a myriad of internet and mobile technologies. (Hameed & Mathur, 2020). They have been brought up this way, and according to a survey, more than half of Gen Z in India have access to Over-the-Top (OTT) platforms, as they are their preferred choice for on-demand content. (Kumar & Mathew, 2023). Studies indicate that a typical Generation Z user spends more than six hours a day on their mobile phones, which makes the highly fluid and flexible nature of the YouTube platform suitable for the generation. (Chandhok & Nithya, 2019; Cismariu et al., 2019; Kang, 2022; Zhitomirsky-Geffet & Blau, 2016).

In recent years, there has been a significant rise in the number of YouTubers and viewers in India. (Avinaash & Jayam, 2019; Lowe et al., 2019). Bidav and Mehta, (2024) reveal that the Indian YouTube creators had made a direct impact of 6,800 crore on the Indian GDP in 2020, and there existed 6,83,900 full-time equivalent jobs. The report also stresses a significantly impressive rise in the number of YouTube channels that have over one million subscribers, with only 20 such channels in 2016, while in 2020, such channels were over 4,500 (Bidav & Mehta, 2024).

This paper identifies some forces that have led to the exponential growth of the YouTube community, namely, the increasing internet access in India (Avinaash & Jayam, 2019). According to Malhotra et al. (2021), the number of active internet users in India is expected to rise from 600 million in 2020 to 900 million by 2025. The availability of inexpensive data plans from telecommunication firms has also advanced this growth, as they have provided the majority of the population with a chance to access online content affordably (Colohan et al., 2016; Roy et al., 2022).

The huge viewer base of YouTube in India has led to the production of more content, which has encouraged new YouTubers to want to create content since the platform is fairly easy to use and can go viral (Ilangovan et al., 2021; Prachi et al., 2024). The realisation of content creation has led to the development of a new paradigm of the influencer's role; YouTubers are not only entertainers but also experts, opinion-makers, and examples for Generation Z (del Pilar Gutiérrez Arenas et al., 2022a; Martínez-Sanz, 2021; Weerasinghe & Wijethunga, 2022).

Since entertainment and advertisement have merged, there is a need to closely examine the role which YouTubers play in shaping the consumption patterns and contributing to the personal development of Generation Z (Park & Chun, 2020). As YouTubers occupy an important position in the lives of the Indian Gen Z audience, this paper analyses the various implications of YouTube content. We discuss the benefits, which are skill development and community formation, as well as the limitations, which are the inaccuracy of content and irresponsible behaviour. Analysing these aspects will help to explain the interconnection between YouTubers and Gen Z viewers in India.

POSITIVE IMPACTS OF YOUTUBERS ON GEN Z IN INDIA: LEARNING, ENTERTAINMENT, AND INSPIRATION

It has been seen that the burgeoning YouTube landscape has become a platform of many positive impacts on Gen Z in India. It is not just an entertainment portal, but the YouTubers are emerging as teachers, community leaders and even mentors, leading and influencing the lives of young audiences in a big way (García et al., 2023; Park & Chun, 2020; Pattier, 2024).

The evolution of YouTube from a simple video-sharing site to a complex environment has influenced the interaction of Gen Z in India more than any other platform, the way they learn new information, and their social networking (Agarwal & Kayal, 2024; Malhotra, 2022). This, the 'net generation' has grown up with YouTube and uses it as a regular means of sourcing information, being entertained, and so on. Nowadays, their availability and openness of materials have emerged as great equals, giving chances for skills enhancement to anyone eager to acquire knowledge, cutting across social statuses (Roodt et al., 2017).

These creators have earned the regular audience's trust when it comes to the complex and constantly developing world of the Internet, where they receive instructions in various areas of knowledge, practical careers, self-improvement, and social problems. Due to the social interactions such as comments section, live chats and community posts, it suggests that the service provides young users a sense of belongingness, which is often missing in their lives.

Learning and Skill Development:

A shift in learning styles identified among Generation Z in India is the use of YouTube for education, as well as other learning materials, which traditional classrooms cannot offer (LeAnne Basinger et al., 2021). Educational and learning channels like Khan Academy India, Mathigon, Learn Vern, etc., have interesting lessons and practice questions in K-12 education, which make Gen Z students independent learners and allow them to learn what has not been taught in school (Mellman et al., 2021).

The results of a survey conducted in 2019 by H., Buddayya and Gujjarappa, (2019) capture the importance of the YouTube platform in students' education, especially to Gen Z in India. The platform also allows people with unique skills to post and showcase their expertise to others, and provide how-to guides in different areas, including computer programming, visual arts and graphic design (Chintalapati & Daruri, 2017; Maynard, 2020). This helps Gen Z gain new, relevant knowledge and experience on what can be expected in such occupations (Kim & Kim, 2021; Lee et al., 2023).

Besides organised curriculum knowledge, the platform has become impactful for learning practical education among Gen Z in India. This way, the concept becomes much easier and more fun to understand than reading lengthy text about them on traditional learning interfaces. (Szymkowiak et al., 2021). Children and teenagers prefer tutorials that show them the process by demonstrating how to do something, while the child can replay the lessons in case they missed or did not understand a certain point. This concept has been more useful with more practical subjects, maybe computer programming, music, cooking, and personal finance (D'Angelo et al., 2022; Kellems et al., 2024).

It is their specificity that makes YouTube a valuable source of knowledge for millions of people who could never afford any courses or even go to a professional requesting their help. Through the e-learning facility, rural-based students who may not be able to afford or do not have access to quality education facilities in their areas can study the same as those in urban areas (Asselin et al., 2011; Chhachhar et al., 2022). This has helped in increasing the social mobility of Gen Z from humble backgrounds in ways that have never been seen before. For the same reason, the recommendations given by the platform introduce young learners to related concepts and areas of learning, which enhances their creativity and cross-disciplinary reasoning skills. The comment sections also serve the purpose of a posting section or a discussion forum, where one can ask questions, gain further clarification, and brainstorm with other members, including students from different parts of the world. The incorporation of collaboration in YouTube learning closely relates to the workplace environment that Gen Z will be practising in and discourages them from just mastering techniques, but instead prepares them for working in teams, which is a key factor to success.

Entertainment and Community:

YouTube is indeed the all-in-one entertainment channel for Gen Z with diverse interests, using a variety of hilarious sketches and gameplay (Adelhardt & Eberle, 2022). It fits well with their generation's penchant for rapid consumption of concise material, such as short clips. In India specifically, ByteDance, the parent company of TikTok, stated that the generational constants' concentration rate is as low as 8 seconds; hence, popular digital platforms such as YouTube suit their entertainment requirements (Jaffar et al., 2019).

Apart from the entertainment value, the platform is also very community-oriented for Generation Z users. There are possibilities for comments and live streaming to present the ideas of being in one community and sharing similar experiences of the Creators with the targeted audience. (Dutta & Manna, 2024a; Lange, 2021)

YouTube, as a social platform of the new generation youth, has not just been the source of entertainment but has become the foundation of virtual communities among the youth of India. Unlike their predecessors who were only bourgeoisie consumers of media productions that are primarily radio, television and newspapers, etc., Gen-Z consumes media actively by commenting, liking, sharing, and co-creating content on YouTube (Chau, 2010; Sambhanthan et al., 2020). There is a list of such corresponding cultures; people who continue a certain train of discussion and have a mutual list of values, jokes, answers and questions, and generally, feel like the chosen members of an elite. For the First Generation youth in India, particularly those from rural areas or who are not socially active physically due to various reasons, such as lack of transport, these social online sites offer vital social affiliation (Amudhan et al., 2024; Gataullina et al., 2024).

YouTubers have leveraged this community-building opportunity and have employed more engaging formats such as question-and-answer sessions, challenges involving the community's suggestions in DVDs, and premium services where the YouTubers stream privately and also post community material (C. W.-Y. Chen, 2020; McRoberts et al., 2016). These helped create intimacy or interaction between the creators and the audiences of the pieces they published. Parasocial interaction forms a support network among the youth within the teenage years and young adulthood. Some feel that creators speak about issues that they sometimes cannot in Indian households, like exercising one's right to seek help for mental health, sensual desires and job insecurity. Such have made entertainment not to be one-sided, but to embody a process of self-enrichment and coming together as people, a reality that previous generations could never fathom (Jarzyna, 2021).

Role Models and Career Inspiration:

Inspiring success stories of popular YouTubers in India have become one of the influential enablers of the entrepreneurial mindset in the Gen Z population, as well as vivid examples of how hobbies can be transformed into profitable businesses (Anggadwita et al., 2023; Desai-Stephens, 2022). Instances like Dhvani Bhanushali, a talented singer who started her career by posting song covers on her YouTube channel and is now a fast-rising music star, show us the extent of the influence of the platform in getting talent into the entertainment industry.

The real-life example of U.S.-based YouTuber Bethany Mota, who turned fashion and beauty content into a $1 million clothing line, is another real-life example that shows that the interests of Gen Z are a strong foundation for real occupations.

Similarly, a lot of Indian YouTubers have spoken and stood up for various social issues and encouraged the listeners to make a change. For instance, the channel that goes by the name "Be YouNick" has been speaking more about mental health, while

"Mumbiker Nikhil" has been advocating for what we should embrace when on the road, safe riding, to be precise.

As for life values, to which YouTubers represent an inspiration, they transcend professional dreams and actions for the benefit of society (del Pilar Gutiérrez Arenas et al., 2022b). They also play a significant role in the purchase choices and brand leanings of Gen Z consumers (Bezbaruah & Trivedi, 2020; Dutta & Manna, 2024b).

However, it is imperative to be aware of its adverse impacts and to consider the following as potential disadvantages or shortcomings. The experiences shared and the feeling that one perpetually needs to create more content to attract and retain fans can negatively affect mental health (Sangeorzan et al., 2019); one example is that of a 16-year-old Indian TikTok star, Siya Kakkar, who committed suicide. Specifically, a 2023 study by the National Institute of Mental Health and Neurosciences (NIMHANS) indicated that 35% of Indian YouTubers felt highly stressed and burned out (Albiez, 2020a). We note the immediate need for improved support for content creators in covering their mental health costs through their revenue share.

Understanding this positive influence is of immense importance to educators, parents, and policymakers. Schools and other learning institutions can also incorporate educational materials that abound on YouTube to supplement traditional learning and teaching processes. Regarding the output, parents can help their children become more wise and selective consumers by using YouTube channels; thus, parents can assist their children in developing media literacy skills.

Digital Literacy and Information Authentication

Fact-checkers and digital literacy instructors on YouTube have established a new culture for Generation Z for information consumption. Platforms such as *Soch* by Mohak Mangal have stood as the harbinger of digital journalism with over 2.5 million subscribers in the early period of 2024. A recent show featuring cryptocurrency scams aimed at young investors was a perfect example of what the platform was capable of in terms of safeguarding the members of the Gen Z population from online scammers. Likewise, Internet Said So, gaining more than 1 million subscribers in late 2023, was creating awareness among the young generation, distinguishing between real and fake news through its formats.

This generation of digital literacies is cropping up at a perfect time, given the scenario that Gen Z is currently grappling with fake news and misinformation. (Prelog & Bakic-Tomic, 2020). Given that fake news can be easily produced and shared through applications and social media, YouTubers assume the role of guardians, teaching their young audiences skills that formal school education does not prepare them for. Social media channels like *Dhruv Rathee* and *The Logical Indian* have replicated this style, where they explain political and social issues in a simple manner that is fashionable to Gen Z by using videos.

What makes these digital literacy YouTubers especially helpful is the fact that these individuals are familiar with the medium, the formats, as well as the genres that Gen Z thrives on (Alruthaya et al., 2021; Dezuanni, 2019). Instead of presenting information through a didactic and commanding manner, they use jokes, films, television shows, life stories and other easy-to-understand real-life scenarios to demystify the machinations of misinformation.

They also encourage active learning in which the viewers are invited to analyse the sources of the information presented, check other platforms for information, and engage in discussions in the comment section in a civilised manner. This kind of engagement assists in converting mere content consumers into critical thinkers who use it on other platforms apart from YouTube. It is noteworthy that modern schools and colleges are beginning to appreciate the effectiveness of such channels, to introduce their materials into the material on media literacy discussion.

Digital literacy, YouTubers are getting the Gen Z generation engaged with social responsibility while understanding that critical thinking for themselves and being able to distinguish between fake news is not just a self-service but a service to society (Gonzalez-Mohino et al., 2023; Van Der Merwe, 2014). They do this by showcasing how misinformation harms the public by causing the pandemic and escalating ethnic tensions, so young audiences feel compelled to fight misinformation with facts within their interpersonal relationships by debunking myths in the sources provided by relatives or friends. These effects further expand the influence of these creators beyond their direct audience and may redefine how an entire generation of internet users consumes information in the developing context of India.

Healthcare Awareness and Mental Wellness

More physicians and pharmacists have become YouTubers, and this change has raised the level of healthcare literacy of Gen Z. Dr. Cuterus (Tanaya) gained 1.5 million subscribers in 2024 and addressed taboos on sexual health. Her recent campaign on menstrual health with UNICEF India reached over 10 million youth in India. Also, the channel of the psychiatrist Dr. Alok Kanojia (Healthy Gamer GG), found popularity in India and focuses on such topics as the negative consequences of video games and the mental problems Gen Z faces, which became more significant after people turned to games during the pandemic.

The participation of healthcare professionals on YouTube has changed the landscape of Gen Z's health information-seeking behaviour in India (Jiao et al., 2023). Because many of these health conditions are kept concealed in society, mainly due to cultural barriers, prejudice, and shame, these medical YouTubers provide open, unidentified avenues through which youth can gain information on some topics they cannot discuss with their parents, family or even physicians. It is not just about sharing information with this population, as these individuals are altering the way that a future generation of Indians approaches healthcare and personal wellness (Colditz et al., 2018).

Mental health vloggers such as Shwetabh Gangwar and Ankur Warikoo have been more impactful, thereby becoming trendsetters, changemakers in addressing the mental health issues Gen Z is going through in India because of competition in academics, job insecurity and comparison given the availability of social media platforms. Through discussing symptoms and possible ways to cope with anxiety, depression, and burnout, these creators have contributed to demystifying the stigma clouding mental health issues in India. Much of it is based on a kind of experiential authority, providing young audiences with a mix of medical understanding and emotional insight they might not have the means to access from their healthcare providers (Daniel et al., 2021; Maulik et al., 2020).

Cultural Preservation and Modern Interpretation

Current Gen Z YouTubers are the link between the conventional culture and the new age perception. The channel "*Heritage Connect*" rose to fame in the year 2024 due to the series made on the lost Indian art forms, where the young artist explains the process of earning money by promoting the art via social media platforms. Recently, a documentary was produced on a '22-year-old Madhubani artist' who sells art online successfully through Instagram, which has garnered 5,00,000 views only; such a documentary encourages many young talents to go online for traditional art.

These YouTube creators connect the old and new generations by presenting Indian culture's arts, crafts, rituals and practices to viewers online (Raji et al., 2025; Wettstein, 2019). The use of different strategies in 'Indian Aesthetic' and 'Culture Capsule' motivates Gen Z viewers to explore India's traditions. Using immersive content, young Indians can observe folk arts, regional dances and weaving of Banaras saris without visiting cultural centres in person.

Financial Independence and Investment Education

The recent growth of retail investment among Gen Z has been driven to a significant extent by YouTubers who cover financial news. Platforms such as "Invest Buddy" emerged as popular after the 2023 small-cap market rally for making the market easy to understand for young investors. One of their founders is 25-year-old Ankita Mehta, recently rewarded by SEBI for inspiring young people to engage in responsible investment. The channel has provided a series of "First-Time Investor

Guides" for Gen-Z investors and has supported more than 200,000 young investors to begin investing safely.

NEGATIVE IMPACTS OF YOUTUBERS ON GEN Z IN INDIA: A LOOK BEYOND THE SHINE

Although the impact of YouTubers on Generation Z in India is vastly progressive and multifold, it cannot be neglected that there is another side of YouTubers that is less viewed and spoken of. The same tool that has opened up a new world of information, education and fun has posed an equal amount of threats and complications to children and adolescents. Given the fact that the platform had already seeped into almost all fields and facets of Gen Z's daily activities, commercial, educational, and otherwise, the prospects for adverse effects are equally possible. These concerns cannot be explained just as moral panic or technophobia, but are valid issues that need to receive proper critical attention and meaningful intervention.

Content Inauthenticity and Pressure:

YouTube has become one of the most popular platforms for sharing videos, and due to that, most of the people who create content are under pressure to constantly share materialistic and peculiar content (Chandiwala et al., 2022; Gajanayake & Sandanayake, 2020; Raju et al., 2018). Some of these YouTubers might end up producing fake or deceiving content just to gain views, likes, or even subscribers (Castaldo et al., 2024; L. Chen et al., 2015; Dutta et al., 2021; Kuchhal & Li, 2022). Studies by Dureja & Tanwar (2024) and Pandit (2020) Indian YouTube users sought fake news. This is worrying at a time when Indian Gen Z is using YouTube as their main source of news, as pointed out (Bute, 2014).

The pressure that is exerted to produce viral content can also result in the advancement of reckless and dangerous activity (Alfano et al., 2021; Alshanqiti et al., 2020; Seeley et al., 2019). The recent issue of Indian YouTuber Sanju Techy from Kerala, who drove a car containing a swimming pool inspired by a movie, indicates the outlook of YouTubers regarding content creation. Similar observations were also made in other countries, as in the USA, known as the "*Bird Box Challenge*," where a teenager crashed her car while attempting a stunt based on the popular Netflix movie.

This pressure for sensationalism has only grown more intense with the shift in the recent algorithm that favours engagement over quality. Certainly, Indian YouTubers experience certain issues unique to contestation on the social media platform, given that there are over 40 million active creators alongside fellow content producers on a global platform for content sharing (Mehta, 2020). It is a financial pressure that cannot be dismissed; the monetisation options brought the content creation from the sphere of personal interest to a way to get money for many people. When people's bread is buttered with viewership, it becomes virtually impossible not to make news a platform for sentiments over issues.

The recent incidents of a YouTuber from Kerala, India, named Sanju Techy, are not a one-off incident of the initiation of dangerous stunts in India's YouTube community. Some of the most popular include 'extreme' human behaviour, inclined towards performing stunts by swimming with crocodiles, walking on the rooftops of tall buildings, as well as consuming substances that may be poisonous just for the sake of getting views on the internet. These stunts have resulted in several cases of various injuries and at least half a dozen deaths among the Indian content creators since 2020. More disturbing is one that several accidents were recorded, whereby young people try to emulate those videos on YouTube with dangerous stunts; in 2023, three teenagers from Mumbai had to be admitted to the hospital after trying to emulate the "fire challenge.

Cyberbullying and Negativity:

The nature of YouTube comments, where individuals can leave comments unknown and, therefore, free from any control, can quickly turn into cyberbullying and negativity (Abdullah et al., 2018; Valpadasu et al., 2023). Such negativity becomes very dangerous to the mental health of both the content creators and the viewers (Jaiswal et al., 2023). In a rather unfortunate event, Indian YouTuber Siya Kakkar, who had over one million followers on the TikTok app, committed suicide at the age of 16, because of bullying.

As has been observed, the effects of cyberbullying are not restricted to the Indian territory. Studies report that many students have been involved in either cyberbullying or have been bullied through cyberspace in their lifetime (González Arévalo, 2013; Matos et al., 2018; Mura & Diamantini, 2013; Olumide et al., 2016; Shin & Ahn, 2015).

The possibility of an authenticity crisis does not simply lie in spectacular stunts such as jumping over helicopters, but in other, less obvious fakes. Several Indian YouTubers have been caught in fake 'social experiments,' or deceiving their viewers as millionaires or sharing fake success stories, or peddling fake cures for various ailments using certain products. These are especially misleading to the Gen Z audience since they rarely realise the difference between a real story and fake news or deep fakes.

Consumerism and Impulse Buying:

Phenomena such as 'haul' videos, which feature the YouTuber purchasing items and showcasing them to the viewers, are a clear indication that YouTubers are affecting consumerism (Che et al., 2015; Cheng et al., 2013). Haul videos were rated by consumers as having an important impact on purchasing behaviour, and respondents revealed their purchase decisions were influenced by these videos (Cheng et al., 2022; Shi et al., 2021).

The purchase choices of Gen Z in India have been significantly shaped by YouTubers in light of the increased use of the influencer marketing industry, which is now a multi-billion-rupee industry. Current successful Indian lifestyle YouTubers charge hefty fees for sponsored content, and numerous of them created their successful YouTube channel around consumer products. Such are the methods that this commercialisation has escalated itself to the point where, even if ASCI rules, which require sponsors to strictly state that the content in question is sponsored, are in force, the true intent of the video may be lost.

A notable effect is that Indian Gen Z respondents seem to be more financially insecure than others, owing to their age. A large number of youth from the middle class get entrapped in conspicuous consumption beyond their financial capability (Fadjar et al., 2022; Sundie et al., 2011; Suryandari & Jeon, 2016). Financial literacy studies have noted that young people seeking to imitate the lifestyles depicted in these works are subsequently accumulating credit card debts. It is not only limited to luxury items, but also applies to everyday consumer products, where fast fashion videos received significant attention, especially from Indian YouTubers. These videos often involve massive clothing hauls, which pose dangerous ideals for audiences, especially from ultra-fast fashion brands with adverse environmental and social impact. What makes this influence even more potent is the parasocial interaction called influence from content creators, and advice from friends on products, which feels like recommendations and incites impulse purchasing behaviour.

Dangerous Challenges and Life-Threatening Content

Due to the many fatal dangers posted on YouTube recently, it is clear that this recipe is threatening many lives. The same goes for the "*Train Reels Challenge*," which entailed filming near moving trains, due to which, there were several deaths in 2023; one of them was the unfortunate incident that occurred in Hyderabad, in which three teenagers died when attempting to recreate a scene from a certain vlogger.

The psychological factors that underlie the desire of members of Gen Z to participate in potentially hazardous stunts are rather diverse and interrelated. The developmental phase of adolescence involves a certain desire to take risks, searching for approval among peers, and identification – all those things are used by dangerous YouTube challenges (Cash & Schwab-Reese, 2020; Walsh et al., 2024). It also fulfils status needs for young viewers, where they get a sense of being in a group of people in a viral challenge and the possibility of being valued and acknowledged by likes and shares. This indeed holds particularly true for the Indian context, in which other forms of status acknowledgement are being rapidly replaced by technological advancement, and fame through digital media gives a new way for recognition.

What makes these challenges especially more dangerous is the fact that they are presented in some way as fun or as hazing activities. Some YouTubers are more risk-takers, will intentionally ignore the risks, and at other times, they will even 'mask the danger' through editing.

Mental Health Crisis and Burnout Culture

Social media influencers have been subjected to high pressure regarding posting on their online platforms, thereby exacerbating mental health issues among those individuals. Content producers experience a severe mental health problems since YouTube's creator business brings threats to their success, even when algorithm updates and audience preferences change rapidly (Albiez, 2020b; Kingsley et al., 2022). YouTube demands permanent content updates and inventions through its platform design because creators experience major audience and monetary losses when taking small breaks. The system forces creators to work endlessly, even when their mental and emotional state needs attention. In India, mental illness stigmas stop creators from sharing their problems until they need urgent help (da Silva & Gómez, 2024; Zhang, 2022).

The burnout culture hurts both content producers and viewers of Gen Z, especially because they start believing that creation success needs to be their future. Their limited exposure to select positive stories about content creators prevents them from seeing how this career harms mental health until they face it personally. Only after experiencing severe problems do successful content producers share their reality, which keeps viewers blind to the true work of being an online creator.

Academic Performance and Attention Span Issues

One disappointing development observed in the 2023 board examinations was students' surrender to YouTube tutorials, instead of books, ending up partially informed. The National Education Alliance also surveyed teachers who noticed that a large number of students who excessively use short-form content have shortened attention spans (Haliti-Sylaj & Sadiku, 2024; Lin et al., 2024).

The cognitive implications of YouTube consumption patterns among Gen Z students extend beyond mere academic performance metrics to fundamental shifts in information processing and learning approaches (Dani, 2015; Jang & Chiang, 2024). Educational psychologists at the Indian Institute of Psychology have documented what they term "fragmented learning syndrome," where students increasingly struggle with sustained engagement with complex concepts. This manifests as difficulty maintaining focus during lectures lasting more than 15-20 minutes, resistance to reading longer academic texts, and a preference for visual information delivery over text-based learning.

Financial Exploitation and Scams

There are worrying incidents of financial fraud due to some YouTubers who focus on finance. From an annual report of the SEBI, it was reported that cases of unauthorised financial advice through YouTube have increased by 150% in 2023, targeting mostly individuals between 18-25 years of age.

The susceptibility of Gen Z to financial scams on YouTube is due to several factors peculiar to this generation and the platform. India's youth are relatively more financially independent than the older generation, and handling of these funds from part-time earnings, scholarships or allowances before developing financial knowledge (Barrichello et al., 2024; Yuvaraja & Perumandla, 2023). They are also trying to manage their finances in an ever-changing market with such instruments as cryptocurrencies, NFTs, or algorithmic trading that had no existence in their parents' reality; thus, the notion of a generational gap emerged, with different generations seeking help online.

Internet fraudsters who target young users of the YouTube platform have adopted new techniques that are effective on Gen Z. Using mechanisms such as production quality and social proof, they seek to provide a credible and respectable image. Many of the scammers post images of luxurious lifestyles that were supposedly earned through their investment schemes (Na et al., 2023). Some financial YouTubers initially offer basic investment guidance, followed by relatively safer approaches, but change the angle gradually to a few charged investments in which the influencers have a vested interest. One example of such a scheme was the "*Wealth Creators Network*" that became a scandal in late 2023, in which several connected YouTubers first taught basic financial literacy and then invited the audience to invest at least 750 million, from which the scheme was built with the help of a majority of young people.

Digital Addiction and Social Isolation

The NIMHANS survey conducted in 2024 also showed that more youth were addicted to YouTube and spent an average of four and a half hours on the platform in 2024 as compared three hours in 2022. The same social workers stated that they identified 70% more cases of young people's social isolation arising from the excessive use of YouTube in 2023.

Clinicians at hospital group Fortis Healthcare explained that young people aged 18 and under exhibit symptoms such as restlessness, anxiety, and an inability to concentrate when they cannot access videos from the site. These symptoms resemble other dimensions of behavioural addictions and illustrate the brain rewiring to Dopamine responses evoked by content presentation on the platform. Marital and family therapists mention that this addiction escalates to isolation, whereby face-to-face interactions are shunned progressively to continue with YouTube viewing.

Misinformation and Radicalisation

Misinformation that circulates through YouTube has become more prominent issue now. As many as 1,218 YouTube channels were referred to the Election Commission during the 2024 state elections for telecom misinformation to voters. One example was an array of several YouTube channels which collectively accounted for 10 million subscribers to their programs, which promoted conspiracy theories regarding scientific truths, which in turn influenced young adults' reluctance to get vaccinated. According to the Internet and Mobile Association of India, young Generation Z users are 40% more likely to rely on YouTubers than traditional media.

The problem one can find in it is that the key feature of the platforms – algorithmic amplification as well as watching time instead of attention as a metric – makes YouTube potentially an ideal tool for misinformation. For instance, a study conducted by the Digital Democracy Initiative showed that 'news' videos which display misinformation as opposed to accurate information on matters that are emotionally taxing receive 65% more engagement from the public on similarly themed Indian YouTube channels; this means that creators of content shape the development of the former by creating more such videos rather than informative ones due to the incentives it offers. This is particularly a cause for concern in the Indian context, where other traditional journalistic intermediaries are being 'bypassed,' and where appropriate mechanisms of checks and balances have not been established to meet this vacuum.

The process described regarding radicalisation through the algorithm of 'suggestions' on YouTube is a rather dangerous perspective. Research conducted by CIS outlined above reveals how people first watched videos that may contain a relatively moderate level of politicisation can be gradually steered to far-right content through a series of links provided to similar videos. This process is known as confirmation bias, and is alarmingly common not only in 'extreme right' political stands but also in nationalist, religious or other 'extreme left'. The online survey of 5,000 young people in India demonstrated that students watching moderate political content were recommended extreme content within a month, with a probability of 28%.

Body Image Issues and Unrealistic Standards

In the current world, beauty and lifestyle YouTubers have affected the self-image of Gen Z worryingly. A literature review of ICMR in 2024 pointed out that eating disorders have grown in teenagers by 65%, influenced by beauty influencers. Further controversy regarding authentic content delivery came with the popularity of YouTuber '*GlamGirl*' and her 1.5 million subscribers confessed that she uses heavy filters and editing in all the videos she posts. It reveals that a dermatologist noticed an 80% rise in young patients in pursuit of unnecessary cosmetic procedures due to the influence of YouTubers.

Privacy and Data Security Concerns

Recent events have shown that young people who share videos on YouTube are also unfairly exposed to threats to their privacy. In February 2025, several teenage content creators from Mumbai found themselves victims of doxxing attacks, having their details posted online. In 2023, the Cyber Crime Cell also indicated a 90% rise in privacy concerns among young content providers. Further, the real incidence of a young YouTuber who had faced stalking issues in Delhi, and had shifted her house with her family due to these issues, also depicts the reality of being exposed on social media.

Cultural Degradation and Value Erosion

People have recently developed fears regarding the loss of various cultural values through materials posted on YouTube. The situation with the channel "*Prank Star India*" (3 million subscribers) in late autumn of 2023, when their immoral pranks in religious places caused people's anger, demonstrated this problem. According to the Ministry of Culture, more than 5,000 violations of traditional values were addressed in 2023, as disrespect for the content of YouTube with youth-oriented videos.

Economic Pressure and Career Misconceptions

This is mainly driven by the fact that the glamour of the YouTuber lifestyle has made many people perceive YouTubing as a glamorous career. One of the most important things that can hide behind the glamour of popular YouTubers is the economic state of content creation (Kim, 2025; Qian & Jain, 2024; Ren, 2024). Who can forget seeing creators with a hundred thousand or millions of subscribers, company deals, and a luxurious lifestyle, which are a representation of average statistics? According to the study conducted by the Indian Creator Economy Forum, out of about 4 million YouTubers in India, only a few can earn more than the median income of the country from the videos they post. This "creator economy inequality" is even more power-law distributed than conventional entertainment industries, but it isn't apparent to aspiring creators who only see what looks like successful perspectives about the platform.

Youths belonging to the lower-middle class feel especially threatened by economic challenges because they pin their hopes on YouTube to achieve upward social mobility. More students now switch away from following standard educational routes because they believe content creation will generate unrealistic income levels, according to career counselling reports. A Pune-based vocational guidance centre examined how five neighbourhood adolescents walked away from college to launch YouTube careers after one locally successful creator prompted them to do so, but they failed to establish sustainable earnings after two years, while three ran up large debts while making content.

CONCLUSION

India-based Gen Z's interaction with YouTubers can be described in a somewhat mixed fashion; it has its benefits and drawbacks. As the platform has offered exposure to education, entertainment, and social interaction, it has raised issues about the legitimacy of the content, the abuse of social networking as a tool for bullying, and the social construction of values concerning consumerism.

If it is desirable to harness the positive one and avoid the negative consequences of YouTube, it is necessary to mobilise the efforts of educators, parents, legislators, and creators of the site. Inclusion of media literacy into school learning aspirations, parents' and children's free discussion on appropriate uses of YouTube and putting down principles and regulations to govern YouTubers are very significant in defining a secure and empowering new age for Gen Z.

It is only by understanding how other countries have dealt with some of these difficulties and applying the lessons learnt that it will be possible to try to unlock

YouTube to its full capacity, to be a tool for education and development, as well as to limit its effects, which bring about negative changes in Gen Z.

In conclusion, it can be said that the presence of YouTubers plays a twofold role within India, as both a threat that can potentially influence the character of the country's development and as a blessing since the young generation is the driving force behind the constant progress. Knowledge exchange is thus important and through promoting responsible content creation and critical consumption, as well as embracing discussion about sensitive and complex matters, Gen Z will be better prepared for that reality and other forms of connectedness in the future world.

YouTube creates these impacts on Gen Z in India as society experiences swift technological progress alongside significant social conflicts. YouTube functions as a platform that both empowers people with diverse knowledge and distributes false information, while it permits community connections, yet creates social detachment and generates economic breakthroughs with unattainable expectations. A well-structured strategic framework needs to leverage YouTube's valuable advantages by developing protective safeguards against its dangerous aspects within this intricate environment.

REFERENCES

Abdullah, A. O., Ali, M. A., Karabatak, M., & Sengur, A. (2018). A comparative analysis of common YouTube comment spam filtering techniques. *6th International Symposium on Digital Forensic and Security, ISDFS 2018 - Proceeding, 2018-Janua*, 1–5. DOI: 10.1109/ISDFS.2018.8355315

Adelhardt, Z., & Eberle, T. (2022). YouTube as a Source of Educational Content in Teenagers' Learning Practices. *9th European Conference on Social Media, ECSM 2022*, 277–279. DOI: 10.34190/ecsm.9.1.267

Agarwal, S., & Kayal, S. (2024). Mapping of Learning Efficacy Through YouTube: An Empirical Study of Media Learners in Kolkata. *International Journal of Media and Information Literacy*, *9*(1), 4–16. DOI: 10.13187/ijmil.2024.1.4

Albiez, M. (2020a). Systemic, social and emotional challenges and magic moments in the professional life of full-time and part-time YouTubers: "Have fun and work at the same time" | Systemische, soziale und emotionale Herausforderungen und Glücksmomente im beruflichen Alltag. *Gruppe. Interaktion. Organisation. Zeitschrift Fur Angewandte Organisationspsychologie*, *51*(4), 457–468. DOI: 10.1007/s11612-020-00534-w

Albiez, M. (2020b). Systemic, social and emotional challenges and magic moments in the professional life of full-time and part-time YouTubers: "Have fun and work at the same time" | Systemische, soziale und emotionale Herausforderungen und Glücksmomente im beruflichen Alltag. *Gruppe. Interaktion. Organisation. Zeitschrift Fur Angewandte Organisationspsychologie*, *51*(4), 457–468. DOI: 10.1007/s11612-020-00534-w

Alfano, M., Fard, A. E., Carter, J. A., Clutton, P., & Klein, C. (2021). Technologically scaffolded atypical cognition: The case of YouTube's recommender system. *Synthese*, *199*(1–2), 835–858. DOI: 10.1007/s11229-020-02724-x

Alruthaya, A., Nguyen, T.-T., & Lokuge, S. (2021). The Application of Digital Technology and the Learning Characteristics of Generation Z in Higher Education. *ACIS 2021 - Australasian Conference on Information Systems, Proceedings*.

Alshanqiti, A., Bajnaid, A., Gilal, A. R., Aljasir, S., Alsughayyir, A., & Albouq, S. (2020). Intelligent parallel mixed method approach for characterising viral youtube videos in Saudi Arabia. *International Journal of Advanced Computer Science and Applications*, *11*(3), 661–671. DOI: 10.14569/IJACSA.2020.0110382

Amudhan, S., Chavadi, C. A., Poojara, R., Shakila, P., & Poornima, J. (2024). Beyond City Limits: Exploring the Untapped Potential of Social Media in Rural Karnataka: A Structural Equation Model Analysis. In *Studies in Systems, Decision and Control* (Vol. 537). DOI: 10.1007/978-3-031-62106-2_34

Anggadwita, G., Ramadani, V., & Navarrete, S. R. (2023). FROM MINUS TO HERO: IDENTIFYING SUCCESSFUL ENTREPRENEURIAL FACTORS USING SEMANTIC NETWORK ANALYSIS OF YOUTUBE CONTENT | IŠ DUGNO Į AUKŠTUMAS: SĖKMINGŲ ANTREPRENERYSTĖS VEIKSNIŲ NUSTATYMAS NAUDOJANT „YOUTUBE" TURINIO SEMANTINIO TINKLO ANALIZĘ. *Transformations in Business & Economics*, *22*(1), 165–183.

Asselin, M., Dobson, T., Meyers, E. M., Teixiera, C., & Ham, L. (2011). Learning from YouTube: An analysis of information literacy in user discourse. *ACM International Conference Proceeding Series*, 640–642. DOI: 10.1145/1940761.1940851

Avinaash, M., & Jayam, R. (2019). Analyzing the video consumption pattern of indian consumer using big data. *Journal of Advanced Research in Dynamical and Control Systems, 11*(3 Special), 1590–1598.

Barrichello, D. Elvin, Martin, K., Lasmy, & Bagaskara, J. (2024). Analysis of Determinants Influencing Victims' Interest in Illegal Investments. *2024 3rd International Conference on Creative Communication and Innovative Technology, ICCIT 2024*. DOI: 10.1109/ICCIT62134.2024.10701140

Bezbaruah, S., & Trivedi, J. (2020). Branded Content: A Bridge Building Gen Z's Consumer–Brand Relationship. *Vision (Basel)*, *24*(3), 300–309. DOI: 10.1177/0972262920930167

Bidav, T., & Mehta, S. (2024). Peripheral Creator Cultures in India, Ireland, and Turkey. *Social Media + Society*, *10*(1), 20563051241234693. DOI: 10.1177/20563051241234693

Bute, S. (2014). The role of social media in mobilizing people for riots and revolutions: Four case studies in India. In *Public Administration and Information Technology* (Vol. 13). DOI: 10.1007/978-3-319-04666-2_19

Cash, S. J., & Schwab-Reese, L. (2020). When adolescent offline risks behaviors go online. In *Technology and Adolescent Health: In Schools and Beyond*. DOI: 10.1016/B978-0-12-817319-0.00003-7

Castaldo, M., Frasca, P., Venturini, T., & Gargiulo, F. (2024). Fake views removal and popularity on YouTube. *Scientific Reports*, *14*(1), 15443. DOI: 10.1038/s41598-024-63649-w PMID: 38965242

Chandhok, G. A., & Nithya, V. (2019). Short-lived content, a social media platform it's purpose, perspective of generation z. *International Journal of Scientific and Technology Research*, *8*(12), 761–768.

Chandiwala, J., Agrawal, S., & Agarwal, S. (2022). Descriptive and Comparative Analysis of YouTube Trending Videos. In *Lecture Notes in Electrical Engineering* (Vol. 939). DOI: 10.1007/978-981-19-4364-5_61

Chau, C. (2010). YouTube as a participatory culture. *New Directions for Youth Development*, *2010*(128), 65–74. DOI: 10.1002/yd.376 PMID: 21240954

Che, X., Ip, B., & Lin, L. (2015). A Survey of Current YouTube Video Characteristics. *IEEE MultiMedia*, *22*(2), 56–63. DOI: 10.1109/MMUL.2015.34

Chen, C. W.-Y. (2020). Learning through participation: A case study on the affordances of making YouTube tutorial videos. *The JALT CALL Journal*, *16*(1), 51–67. DOI: 10.29140/jaltcall.v16n1.259

Chen, L., Zhou, Y., & Chiu, D. M. (2015). Analysis and detection of fake views in online video services. *ACM Transactions on Multimedia Computing Communications and Applications*, *11*(2), 1–20. DOI: 10.1145/2700290

Cheng, X., Liu, J., & Dale, C. (2013). Understanding the characteristics of internet short video sharing: A youtube-based measurement study. *IEEE Transactions on Multimedia*, *15*(5), 1184–1194. DOI: 10.1109/TMM.2013.2265531

Cheng, Z., Shao, B., & Zhang, Y. (2022). Effect of Product Presentation Videos on Consumers' Purchase Intention: The Role of Perceived Diagnosticity, Mental Imagery, and Product Rating. *Frontiers in Psychology*, *13*, 812579. Advance online publication. DOI: 10.3389/fpsyg.2022.812579 PMID: 35250742

Chhachhar, A. R., Chachar, A. A., & Arbab, N. F. (2022). Usage of YouTube for Academic Purpose Among University Students in Time of COVID-19. *International Journal of Media and Information Literacy*, *7*(1), 38–47. DOI: 10.13187/ijmil.2022.1.38

Chintalapati, N., & Daruri, V. S. K. (2017). Examining the use of YouTube as a Learning Resource in higher education: Scale development and validation of TAM model. *Telematics and Informatics*, *34*(6), 853–860. DOI: 10.1016/j.tele.2016.08.008

Cismariu, L., Ciurel, D. L., & Hosu, I. (2019). Generation Z and Social Media. *Proceedings of the International Conference on Virtual Learning*, 367–373.

Colditz, J. B., Woods, M. S., & Primack, B. A. (2018). Adolescents seeking online health information: Topics, approaches, and challenges. In *Technology and Adolescent Mental Health*. DOI: 10.1007/978-3-319-69638-6_2

Colohan, A., Freir, T., & Finlay, D. (2016). Optical wavelength ratiometric monitoring system for data centre CWDM applications. *Proceedings - 2016 51st International Universities Power Engineering Conference, UPEC 2016, 2017-Janua*, 1–7. DOI: 10.1109/UPEC.2016.8113984

D'Angelo, S., Marcus, R., & Ngabonzima, E. (2022). Teaching and learning for life skills development: Insights from Rwanda's 12+ programme for adolescent girls: Special Issue Youth & Adolescent Skills Development: Preparing young people for diverse global challenges. *Development Policy Review*, *40*(S2), e12622. DOI: 10.1111/dpr.12622

da Silva, A. H. B., & Gómez, Á. H. (2024). What's Behind the 'Likes'? – Development of Self-Image in Young YouTubers | O que está por trás dos "likes"? – Desenvolvimento da autoimagem em jovens youtubers. *Rotura: Journal of Communication, Culture and Arts, 4*(1), 64–79. DOI: 10.34623/qa6g-hn70

Dani, E. (2015). The HY-DE model: An interdisciplinary attempt to deal with the phenomenon of hyperattention. *6th International Multi-Conference on Complexity, Informatics and Cybernetics, IMCIC 2015 and 6th International Conference on Society and Information Technologies, ICSIT 2015 - Proceedings, 2*, 211–216.

Daniel, M., Maulik, P. K., Kallakuri, S., Kaur, A., Devarapalli, S., Mukherjee, A., Bhattacharya, A., Billot, L., Thornicroft, G., Praveen, D., Patel, A., & Peiris, D. (2021). An integrated community and primary healthcare worker intervention to reduce stigma and improve management of common mental disorders in rural India: Protocol for the SMART Mental Health programme. *Trials*, *22*(1), 179. DOI: 10.1186/s13063-021-05136-5 PMID: 33653406

del Pilar Gutiérrez Arenas, M., García, A. R., & Reifs Ruíz, R. M. (2022a). Generation Z wants to be a youtuber and/or influencer. Factors that determine this trend | A Geração Z quer ser um youtuber e/ou influenciador. Factores que determinam esta tendência | La generación Z desea ser youtuber y/o influencer. Factores que determ. *Icono14, 20*(2). DOI: 10.7195/ri14.v20i2.1882

del Pilar Gutiérrez Arenas, M., García, A. R., & Reifs Ruíz, R. M. (2022b). Generation Z wants to be a youtuber and/or influencer. Factors that determine this trend | A Geração Z quer ser um youtuber e/ou influenciador. Factores que determinam esta tendência | La generación Z desea ser youtuber y/o influencer. Factores que determ. *Icono14, 20*(2). DOI: 10.7195/ri14.v20i2.1882

Desai-Stephens, A. (2022). The Infrastructure of Engagement: Musical Aesthetics and the Rise of YouTube in India. *Twentieth-Century Music*, *19*(3), 444–471. DOI: 10.1017/S1478572222000299

Dezuanni, M. (2019). Children's minecraft multiliteracy practices and learning through peer pedagogies. In *Multiliteracies and Early Years Innovation*. Perspectives from Finland and Beyond., DOI: 10.4324/9780429432668-11

Dureja, V., & Tanwar, S. (2024). Detection of False Information on Social Media. *2024 11th International Conference on Reliability, Infocom Technologies and Optimization (Trends and Future Directions), ICRITO 2024*. DOI: 10.1109/ICRITO61523.2024.10522238

Dutta, H. S., Jobanputra, M., Negi, H., & Chakraborty, T. (2021). Detecting and Analyzing Collusive Entities on YouTube. *ACM Transactions on Intelligent Systems and Technology*, *12*(5), 1–28. DOI: 10.1145/3477300

Dutta, S. K., & Manna, S. (2024a). Role of youtube and instagram advertising in attracting gen-z consumers in delhi-ncr. In *Consumer Experience and Decision-Making in the Metaverse*. DOI: 10.4018/979-8-3693-4167-4.ch012

Dutta, S. K., & Manna, S. (2024b). Role of youtube and instagram advertising in attracting gen-z consumers in delhi-ncr. In *Consumer Experience and Decision-Making in the Metaverse*. DOI: 10.4018/979-8-3693-4167-4.ch012

Fadjar, A., Hartini, S., & Astuti, S. W. (2022). Instagram Usage Behavior: Does It Aim to Look More Attractive? *Quality - Access to Success*, *23*(189), 67–73. DOI: 10.47750/QAS/23.189.09

Gajanayake, G. M. H. C., & Sandanayake, T. C. (2020). Trending pattern identification of youtube gaming channels using sentiment analysis. *20th International Conference on Advances in ICT for Emerging Regions, ICTer 2020 - Proceedings*, 149–154. DOI: 10.1109/ICTer51097.2020.9325476

García, A. R., Arenas, M. P. G., & Moreno, M. G. (2023). Children want to be celebrities. Is it compatible with school engagement? | Los menores desean ser celebrities. ¿Es compatible con el compromiso escolar? *Revista Complutense de Educacion*, *34*(4), 755–767. DOI: 10.5209/rced.80039

Gataullina, L. N., Tuktarova, G. M., Nezhmetdinova, F. T., & Fassakhova, G. R. (2024). Socialization of rural youth issues in the development of agricultural industry and society. *BIO Web of Conferences, 103*. DOI: 10.1051/bioconf/202410300068

González Arévalo, B. (2013). [Cyberbullying at school]. | Cyberbullying en el colegio. *Revista de Enfermeria (Barcelona, Spain)*, *36*(10), 16–21. PMID: 24354128

Gonzalez-Mohino, M., Rodriguez-Domenech, M. Á., Callejas-Albiñana, A. I., & Castillo-Canalejo, A. (2023). Empowering Critical Thinking: The Role of Digital Tools in Citizen Participation. *Journal of New Approaches in Educational Research, 12*(2), 258–275. DOI: 10.7821/naer.2023.7.1385

H., R. B., Buddayya, R., & Gujjarappa, N. L. (2019). Benefits of videos in youtube for the undergraduate students in engineering and technology in India. *Webology, 16*(2), 57–71.

Haliti-Sylaj, T., & Sadiku, A. (2024). Impact of Short Reels on Attention Span and Academic Performance of Undergraduate Students. *Eurasian Journal of Applied Linguistics, 10*(3), 60–68. DOI: 10.32601/ejal.10306

Hameed, S., & Mathur, M. (2020). Generation Z in India: Digital Natives and Makers of Change. In *The New Generation Z in Asia: Dynamics, Differences, Digitalization*. DOI: 10.1108/978-1-80043-220-820201010

Ilangovan, A., Beswick, P. R., & Sarojini, B. (2021). The Impact of YouTube Personalization Algorithm on User-Generated Content Creation in India. *Proceedings of the 2021 2nd International Conference on Communication, Computing and Industry 4.0, C2I4 2021*. DOI: 10.1109/C2I454156.2021.9689393

Jaffar, B. A., Riaz, S., & Mushtaq, A. (2019). Living in a moment: Impact of TicTok on influencing younger generation into micro-fame. *Journal of Content. Community and Communication, 10*(5), 187–194. DOI: 10.31620/JCCC.12.19/19

Jaiswal, A., Porwal, P., Singh, A., Kumari, P., Bhalla, P., & Sachdeva, N. (2023). Empirical Analysis of Depression Detection Using Deep Learning on Twitter. In *Lecture Notes in Networks and Systems* (Vol. 787). LNNS., DOI: 10.1007/978-981-99-6550-2_23

Jang, Y.-T., & Chiang, I.-T. (2024). Incorporating desire and persistence into understanding Gen Z learners' continuance intention toward using Youtube for learning in digital learning context. *Education and Information Technologies, 29*(8), 10043–10068. DOI: 10.1007/s10639-023-12202-9

Jarzyna, C. L. (2021). Parasocial Interaction, the COVID-19 Quarantine, and Digital Age Media. *Human Arenas, 4*(3), 413–429. DOI: 10.1007/s42087-020-00156-0

Jiao, W., Chang, A., Ho, M., Lu, Q., Liu, M. T., & Schulz, P. J. (2023). Predicting and Empowering Health for Generation Z by Comparing Health Information Seeking and Digital Health Literacy: Cross-Sectional Questionnaire Study. *Journal of Medical Internet Research, 25*, e47595. Advance online publication. DOI: 10.2196/47595 PMID: 37902832

Kang, M., & Kang, M. (2022). Daily Behavior of Generation Z Using a Smart Phone App for Content Recommendation based on Context Awareness. *Archives of Design Research, 35*(1), 277–295. DOI: 10.15187/adr.2022.02.35.1.277

Kellems, R. O., Steinburg, M., Bahr, D., & Hansen, B. D. (2024). Using Video Modeling Via iPads to Teach Multiplication to Struggling Learners. *Journal of Special Education Technology, 39*(1), 67–78. DOI: 10.1177/01626434231180584

Kim, D. (2025). Selling Otherness on YouTube: Digital inter-Asian Orientalism and YouTube monetization system. *International Journal of Cultural Studies, 28*(1), 39–55. DOI: 10.1177/13678779241240780

Kim, S., & Kim, H.-C. (2021). The benefits of youtube in learning english as a second language: A qualitative investigation of korean freshman students' experiences and perspectives in the U.S. *Sustainability (Basel), 13*(13), 7365. Advance online publication. DOI: 10.3390/su13137365

Kingsley, S., Sinha, P., Wang, C., Eslami, M., & Hong, J. I. (2022). 'give Everybody [.] a Little Bit More Equity': Content Creator Perspectives and Responses to the Algorithmic Demonetization of Content Associated with Disadvantaged Groups. *Proceedings of the ACM on Human-Computer Interaction, 6*(CSCW2). DOI: 10.1145/3555149

Kuchhal, D., & Li, F. (2022). A View into YouTube View Fraud. *WWW 2022 - Proceedings of the ACM Web Conference 2022*, 555–563. DOI: 10.1145/3485447.3512216

Kumar, P., & Mathew, A. O. (2023). EXAMINING CUSTOMER SATISFACTION AND BRAND LOYALTY OF GENERATION Z CUSTOMERS IN OTT MEDIA SERVICES. *Proceedings of the International Conferences on E-Society 2023, ES 2023 and Mobile Learning 2023, ML 2023*, 235–242.

Lange, P. G. (2021). Conceptualizing communities of truth on YouTube. *Explorations in Media Ecology, 20*(1), 33–54. DOI: 10.1386/eme_00071_1

LeAnne Basinger, K., Alvarado, D., Ortega, A. V., Hartless, D. G., Lahijanian, B., & Alvarado, M. M. (2021). Creating ACTIVE Learning in an Online Environment. *ASEE Annual Conference and Exposition, Conference Proceedings*. DOI: 10.18260/1-2--36870

Lee, C. S., Yeo, R. Q. Y., Zhang, S., Goh, D. H.-L., Ang, R. P., & Ng, B. (2023). Gen Z Transitions to University: A Preliminary Study on Everyday Information-Seeking Practices. In *Lecture Notes in Computer Science (including subseries Lecture Notes in Artificial Intelligence and Lecture Notes in Bioinformatics): Vol. 14457 LNCS*. DOI: 10.1007/978-981-99-8085-7_23

Lin, B.-H., Chung, Y.-J., Cheng, H.-Y., Yen, Y.-T., Li, C.-C., & Cherng, F.-Y. (2024). Understanding the Effects of Short-Form Videos on Sustained Attention. *Conference on Human Factors in Computing Systems - Proceedings*. DOI: 10.1145/3613905.3651018

Lowe, D., Galhotra, B., & Ahuja, Y. (2019). Unfurling the latest patterns of entertainment consumption by indian audience: A twitter sentiment analysis. *International Journal of Recent Technology and Engineering*, *7*(6), 135–139.

Malhotra, S. (2022). The Youtube Companion to Film Education. *Studies in Media and Communication*, *10*(2), 320–334. DOI: 10.11114/smc.v10i2.5748

Malhotra, S., Sharma, K., & Dogra, S. (2021). Introduction: Inhabiting Cyberspace in India: Theory, Perspectives, and Challenges. In *Inhabiting Cyberspace in India: Theory, Perspectives, and Challenges*. DOI: 10.1007/978-981-15-9934-7_1

Martínez-Sanz, R. (2021). Communication of minor influencers: Measuring their impact in the medium term | La comunicación de los influencers menores de edad: Medición de su impacto en el medio plazo. *Observatorio (OBS*)*, *15*(3), 22–36. DOI: 10.15847/obsOBS15320211739

Matos, A. P. M., Vieira, C. C., Amado, J., Pessoa, T., & Martins, M. J. D. (2018). Cyberbullying in Portuguese Schools: Prevalence and Characteristics. *Journal of School Violence*, *17*(1), 123–137. DOI: 10.1080/15388220.2016.1263796

Maulik, P. K., Devarapalli, S., Kallakuri, S., Bhattacharya, A., Peiris, D., & Patel, A. (2020). The systematic medical appraisal referral and treatment mental health project: Quasi-experimental study to evaluate a technology-enabled mental health services delivery model implemented in Rural India. *Journal of Medical Internet Research*, *22*(2), e15553. DOI: 10.2196/15553 PMID: 32130125

Maynard, A. D. (2020). How to Succeed as an Academic on YouTube. *Frontiers in Communication*, *5*, 572181. Advance online publication. DOI: 10.3389/fcomm.2020.572181

McRoberts, S., Bonsignore, E., Peyton, T., & Yarosh, S. (2016). 'Do it for the viewers!' Audience engagement behaviors of young YouTubers. *Proceedings of IDC 2016 - The 15th International Conference on Interaction Design and Children*, 334–343. DOI: 10.1145/2930674.2930676

Mehta, S. (2020). Localization, diversification and heterogeneity: Understanding the linguistic and cultural logics of Indian new media. *International Journal of Cultural Studies*, *23*(1), 102–120. DOI: 10.1177/1367877919880304

Mellman, L., Williams, M. K., & Slykhuis, D. A. (2021). Using generation Z's learning approaches to create meaningful online learning. In *Handbook of Research on Transforming Teachers' Online Pedagogical Reasoning for Engaging K-12 Students in Virtual Learning*. DOI: 10.4018/978-1-7998-7222-1.ch008

Mura, G., & Diamantini, D. (2013). Cyberbullying among colombian students: An exploratory investigation | El ciberacoso entre los estudiantes de colombia: Una investigación exploratoria. *European Journal of Investigation in Health, Psychology and Education, 3*(3), 249–256. DOI: 10.3390/ejihpe3030022

Na, S. H., Cho, S., & Shin, S. (2023). Evolving Bots: The New Generation of Comment Bots and their Underlying Scam Campaigns in YouTube. *Proceedings of the ACM SIGCOMM Internet Measurement Conference, IMC*, 297–312. DOI: 10.1145/3618257.3624822

Olumide, A. O., Adams, P., & Amodu, O. K. (2016). Prevalence and correlates of the perpetration of cyberbullying among in-school adolescents in Oyo State, Nigeria. *International Journal of Adolescent Medicine and Health, 28*(2), 183–191. DOI: 10.1515/ijamh-2015-0009 PMID: 26251981

Pandit, S. (2020). Mapping the mechanics of truth: Fake news and suburban young adult news consumers in India. In *Information Nightmare*. Fake News, Manipulation and Post-Truth Politics in the Digital Age.

Park, J., & Chun, J. (2020). How does watching YouTube fashion content impact perception of appearance: A phenomenological study of Korean women in Generation Z. *Humanities & Social Sciences Communications, 7*(1), 161. DOI: 10.1057/s41599-020-00652-2

Pattier, D. (2024). Communication and Emerging Teaching Models: A Study on Youtubers Teachers | Comunicación y Modelos Docentes Emergentes: un Estudio sobre los Profesores Youtubers. *Multidisciplinary Journal of Educational Research, 14*(1), 1–16. DOI: 10.17583/remie.9887

Prachi, S. Deepa, & Manju. (2024). Exploring Regression Models for Youtube Views Prediction with Interpretable Insights. *2024 IEEE 9th International Conference for Convergence in Technology, I2CT 2024*. DOI: 10.1109/I2CT61223.2024.10544146

Prelog, L., & Bakic-Tomic, L. (2020). The perception of the fake news phenomenon on the internet by members of generation Z. *2020 43rd International Convention on Information, Communication and Electronic Technology, MIPRO 2020 - Proceedings*, 452–455. DOI: 10.23919/MIPRO48935.2020.9245169

Qian, K., & Jain, S. (2024). Digital Content Creation: An Analysis of the Impact of Recommendation Systems. *Management Science, 70*(12), 8668–8684. DOI: 10.1287/mnsc.2022.03655

Raji, T. A., Udorah, D. C., & Akinpelu, A. M. (2025). *Digitalisation of Yorùbá Culture in YouTube Children's Performances.* English Academy Review., DOI: 10.1080/10131752.2025.2466885

Raju, R., Qbrien, B., & Kalaiselvi, R. (2018). Detection and Prevention of Copywriting Multimedia Contents in Youtube Using Multi-Keyword Ranking Algorithm. *7th IEEE International Conference on Computation of Power, Energy, Information and Communication, ICCPEIC 2018*, 197–202. DOI: 10.1109/ICCPEIC.2018.8525154

Ren, Q. (2024). Advertising and Content Creation on Digital Content Platforms. *Marketing Science, 43*(4), 734–750. DOI: 10.1287/mksc.2022.0387

Roodt, S., Harry, N., & Mwapwele, S. (2017). The effect of using youtube in the classroom for student engagement of the net generation on an information systems course. In *Communications in Computer and Information Science* (Vol. 730). DOI: 10.1007/978-3-319-69670-6_4

Roy, D. R., Sinha, S. K., & Veenadhari, S. (2022). Big Data Analytics Based Recommender System for Tele-Communication Industry. *PDGC 2022 - 2022 7th International Conference on Parallel, Distributed and Grid Computing*, 525–530. DOI: 10.1109/PDGC56933.2022.10053201

Sambhanthan, A., Thelijjagoda, S., Good, A., & Scupola, A. (2020). Virtual community based destination marketing with youtube: Investigation of a typology. In *Destination Management and Marketing* (Vol. 2–2). Breakthroughs in Research and Practice., DOI: 10.4018/978-1-7998-2469-5.ch065

Sangeorzan, I., Andriopoulou, P., & Livanou, M. (2019). Exploring the experiences of people vlogging about severe mental illness on YouTube: An interpretative phenomenological analysis. *Journal of Affective Disorders, 246*, 422–428. DOI: 10.1016/j.jad.2018.12.119 PMID: 30599364

Seeley, J. S., Wickens, C. M., Vingilis-Jaremko, L., Fleiter, J., Yildirim-Yenier, Z., Grushka, D. H., & Vingilis, E. (2019). Street racing, stunt driving and ghost riding YouTube videos: A descriptive content analysis. *Transportation Research Part F: Traffic Psychology and Behaviour, 63*, 283–294. DOI: 10.1016/j.trf.2019.04.012

Shi, W.-Q., Cheng, F., Zhan, H.-Y., Liu, J., Zhou, Y.-P., & Gu, Z.-H. (2021). Influence of Short Video on Apparel Consumers' Purchase Intention | . [Natural Science Edition]. *Journal of Beijing Institute of Clothing Technology, 41*(1), 67–72.

Shin, N., & Ahn, H. (2015). Factors Affecting Adolescents' Involvement in Cyberbullying: What Divides the 20% from the 80%? *Cyberpsychology, Behavior, and Social Networking*, *18*(7), 393–399. DOI: 10.1089/cyber.2014.0362 PMID: 26167838

Sundie, J. M., Kenrick, D. T., Griskevicius, V., Tybur, J. M., Vohs, K. D., & Beal, D. J. (2011). Peacocks, Porsches, and Thorstein Veblen: Conspicuous Consumption as a Sexual Signaling System. *Journal of Personality and Social Psychology*, *100*(4), 664–680. DOI: 10.1037/a0021669 PMID: 21038972

Suryandari, R. T., & Jeon, S. (2016). Consumers' Conspicuousness and its Underlying Traits. In *Developments in Marketing Science: Proceedings of the Academy of Marketing Science*. DOI: 10.1007/978-3-319-24148-7_52

Szymkowiak, A., Melović, B., Dabić, M., Jeganathan, K., & Kundi, G. S. (2021). Information technology and Gen Z: The role of teachers, the internet, and technology in the education of young people. *Technology in Society*, *65*, 101565. DOI: 10.1016/j.techsoc.2021.101565

Valpadasu, H., Chakri, P., Harshitha, P., & Tarun, P. (2023). Machine Learning based Spam Comments Detection on YouTube. *Proceedings of the 7th International Conference on Intelligent Computing and Control Systems, ICICCS 2023*, 1234–1239. DOI: 10.1109/ICICCS56967.2023.10142608

Van Der Merwe, P. (2014). How could life orientation teachers in secondary schools make use of the proposed digital media literacy program for teaching and learning? *International Journal of Pedagogy and Curriculum*, *20*(2), 89–109. DOI: 10.18848/2327-7963/CGP/v20i02/48961

Walsh, L. C., Regan, A., Okabe-Miyamoto, K., & Lyubomirsky, S. (2024). Does putting down your smartphone make you happier? the effects of restricting digital media on well-being. *PLoS ONE, 19*. DOI: 10.1371/journal.pone.0306910

Weerasinghe, K., & Wijethunga, C. (2022). Child Influencers in the Creator Economy – The Good, the Bad and the Ugly. *ACIS 2022 - Australasian Conference on Information Systems, Proceedings*.

Wettstein, M. (2019). YouTube and the rising trend of indigenous folk dance: The case of the sakela dance of the Rai in Nepal and their diaspora. In *Media*. Indigeneity and Nation in South Asia., DOI: 10.4324/9780429424649-12

Yuvaraja, N., & Perumandla, S. (2023). Financial knowledge and online payment decisions of Generation Z consumers: An empirical study using SEM approach. *International Journal of Process Management and Benchmarking*, *15*(2), 198–217. DOI: 10.1504/IJPMB.2023.133153

Zhang, H. (2022). Contextual Factors behind Audience Engagement Behaviours of YouTube Vloggers: A Case Study. *9th European Conference on Social Media, ECSM 2022*, 284–287. DOI: 10.34190/ecsm.9.1.105

Zhitomirsky-Geffet, M., & Blau, M. (2016). Cross-generational analysis of predictive factors of addictive behavior in smartphone usage. *Computers in Human Behavior, 64*, 682–693. DOI: 10.1016/j.chb.2016.07.061

Chapter 6
Boomers Need New Skills: Teaching Modern Media Literacies for the New Media Landscape

Barbara Ruth Burke
https://orcid.org/0000-0002-9906-448X
University of Minnesota, Morris, USA

ABSTRACT

Educational opportunities for older adults seeking to understand today's media are necessary. It may be assumed Boomers already know media literacy, but the skills of their youth do not match contemporary citizenry needs. Contrasting the American media landscapes of the 1950s-60s, the 1970s-1990s, and the 2010s-today, this chapter highlights media literacy challenges US Boomers (aged 60 and older) now face. Explanations of varied contemporary pedagogical approaches for teaching about media and algorithmic literacies are introduced, with the Critical Media Literacy perspective being promoted as the broadest and best option to apply to educate this vital population today.

INTRODUCTION

In the U.S., Boomers and their elders (born before 1963) represent about 30% of the population (Neilsberg, 2025). They have enjoyed the benefits of being a demographic "bulge" in the lived experiences of everyone in the United States, have had a significant cultural impact in society, affecting housing, work/occupations, educational institutions, the arts and music scene, fashion, interpersonal relations, and politics, and exert economic and political importance even beyond their numbers. While other media literacy scholars may recognize the attention given to educating school children, teens, and young adults, this chapter recognizes that, unfortunately,

DOI: 10.4018/979-8-3373-0872-2.ch006

less attention is given today to instruction and educational opportunities for this age cohort. Elders may be addressed in the news when "scam-prevention" is discussed as a media literacy topic, but otherwise, the broader, more general kinds of literacies which all citizens need are not explicitly taught in ways that target this influential population. It may be assumed that Boomers already know what is necessary, but in fact, the skills learned in their youth do not match the citizenry needs of the contemporary, "AI-enhanced" media landscape.

Therefore, in this chapter, with a discussion of the history of media technologies, media users, and media literacy scholarship, Boomers remain the people of primary interest for the core argument, which relies on the assertion that people educated in the 1960s-early 1970s, and then removed from formal instructional opportunities, will need to learn new things fifty years later. To make the point, explaining why this cohort deserves age-appropriate training, the following chapter identifies the characteristics of the mid/late 20th century American mediated experience, contrasting the media literacy educational goals of that period with the goals of the intervening years, and with a discussion of some media elements that are now "new" and thus need additional, explicit educational attention tailored to this population.

Understanding Generative AI's current uses and potentials are important for all citizens, and this chapter does not seek to diminish the urgency with which concerned scholars, educators, policymakers, and the general public of all ages should develop better understandings of the ways this new communication technology will have impacts. However, by highlighting the particular demographic of elders, many of whom are eager to learn more about AI, this chapter asserts that this group of Americans could use some targeted help in making sense of what is happening. Admittedly, my interest in elder education is self-serving in two ways: I have been a media professional and then a media scholar and educator for students from middle-school-aged to retirees, and have spent over 40 years working predominantly in higher education. Seeing the many changes in media education goals and perspectives over time has broadened my views about what is taught and what we should be teaching. Furthermore, as is probably obvious for anyone doing math after reading the last sentence, I myself am an American Baby Boomer. My peers in life have maintained keen interests, and many have not stopped engaging with media– they want to know how to access, review, critique, interpret, evaluate, and create media. We elders recognize the ubiquity of mass media and do not, generally, want to be left behind or fooled by the media.

The media technology history and the related media and educational theories of the relevant eras–of Boomer childhoods, the intervening years, and Boomer retirements–are described in detail in the next sections of this chapter and are presented to highlight contrasts between older and more modern media experiences and contemporary life. It is through an understanding of the opportunities, habits, instructional practices and theories of an earlier era that the distinctiveness of now requiring new media and information literacy skills related to Generative AI become particularly problematized. The chapter ends by suggesting some ways to approach the challenges of instructing elders and ways to broaden and enhance the instruction of media and information literacies in the United States.

SELECTIVE HISTORY–US, 1950s-1960s

Media Landscape

In the late 20th century, the American mass media were dominated by an increasingly consolidated marketplace of a few, multi-platformed media corporations. (Campbell, Martin & Fabos, 2016; Journalist's Resource, 2013). Researchers of agenda-setting (e.g., McCombs, 2005; McCombs & Shaw, 1993) in this era examined content from print outlets with large national audiences, such as newspapers *The Washington Post, The New York Times, The LA Times*, and national magazines *Time* and *Newsweek*. These media were selected for many studies about media influence on public ideas about what constituted true, reliable, and necessary information about reality. Because these publications were read by the most influential members of society and were cited and reprinted at regional and local levels, they were among the "supercultural seven" media in the US, which set the agendas for newspapers and magazines nationwide (Breed, 1955, Burke, 1995; Howenstein, 1987). During this period, trust in the news media was correlated with their political independence, professional reporters were expected to objectively gather and summarize information, and news photos were seen as verification of details and experiences. As Hallin (1985) claimed, it was during this era that "the news tells us not only what happened in the world today but who we are in relation to that world" and conveys the nature of politics and the citizens' responsibilities (p. 123).

The American television news offerings during the same mid-20th century era were dominated by the three New York-based broadcast networks–CBS, NBC, and ABC. "On Sept. 2, 1963, what had been, since 1948, a 15-minute broadcast, anchored first by Douglas Edwards and then Walter Cronkite, doubled to 30 minutes overnight" (Pelly, 2013). Cronkite was often referred to as 'the most trusted man in America' "and for two of the most tumultuous decades in American history, he was the authoritative voice of news in America, the man who told viewers that President John F. Kennedy had been assassinated, that men had walked on the moon and that the Vietnam War couldn't be won" (Galant, 2012). Boomers who recall important national events of their youth usually remember the ways the news told them about what happened, and how they should feel–seeing a news anchor cry on camera left an indelible impression for many. Boomers may also recall when their families first got televisions, and if they were among the first or the later members of their social circle to have the increasingly popular technology. The accelerated rate of the adoption of television sets during this period, noted in the transition from being a household status symbol to being a necessary device for members of American society, is well-documented. It is not an exaggeration to say that people enthusiastically embraced television in the U.S.; 55% of households had a TV set in 1956 and 87% had one in 1960 (DeFleur & Ball-Rokeach,1989). "The media flood was just getting started, however. As television's reach continued to grow – 97 percent of U.S. homes had a TV set by 1974, and in 2001 the U.S. Census Bureau estimated that U.S. households averaged 2.4 TV sets apiece" (Roberts & Foehr, 2010).

Media Uses and Users

Given the small number of TV channels in the earliest days, and the limited quantity, quality, and diversity of voices available for us to culturally decode in the first decades of the medium, one might infer that older forms of broadcast TV content would have a smaller social influence. However, the opposite seemed to occur for Boomers during our youth, as the dominant culture's responses to TV programming and commercials included the everyday, personal, and interactive uses of TV slang, catch phrases, and story/ character types widely known nationally across the US. The assorted mass media were perceived at that time, by the people who grew up then, to be abundant, and were viewed as so much more diverse and immersive than what our parents and the previous generation experienced with only print, radio, and film as entertainment and information options. We felt like we lived in a time in which it was possible to spend a lot of hours watching and reading, and thus, when personal computers became available during the early-adult period of Boomers' lives, many of us became enthusiastic, news and entertainment-seeking purchasers of this newest of technologies, which we may or may not have understood in the pre-World Wide web era. As evidence of the rapid adoption of this technology, in 1984, 8.2% of households in the US had a personal computer; by 2003, 61.8% did so (Alsop, 2020). Boomers consequently came to believe that in a future with continued progress in inventions and with the rapid increase in technology adoption, the American media landscape would continue adding content and/or access choices but would essentially remain comprehensible.

For Boomers, use of media was one of the most popular diversions in their youth. Through formal and informal instruction, and from our own experimentation (usually trial and error), we knew how to access "our media" and knew what we liked, and we thought we knew who and what to believe–oftentimes we felt well prepared to interpret and act on mass mediated messages.

Media and Educational Themes and Theories

The media scholars of the mid- to late-20th century included university faculty (from a diverse range of academic appointments), independent and industry-supported researchers, and media professionals. Although the phrase "media literacy" was not explicit in most of their published research studies in the 1940s and 1950s, the gallery of "grandparents of media literacy" (Hobbs, 2021) suggests that prominent thinkers were seeking ways to explore and investigate the expansive uses and influences of the mass media.

The mass media research of this period, conducted by political scientists, cultural critics, and psychologists explored the particular ways selected media might impact people, generally or in different instances, and/or in response to particular historical situations. Reports of this work, shared widely in popular media, made claims about media strength or potencies, direct or indirect effects, large, moderate, or small effects, and universal or differentiated effects (Severin & Tankard, 2001). Media effects research of this era was often built upon social science assumptions, which had been honed post-World War II. The methods of the era were used to address several interests related to propaganda efficacies, the evils of comic books, the influence of crime stories on the radio, and the dawn of television; the scholars applied experiments and/or surveys to describe media impacts on individuals and identifiable groups (Sparks, 2015). Additionally, in the 20th century, qualitative studies of the influence of media could be found in cross-disciplinary works by notable "scholars like Walter Ong, Louis Mumford, Jacques Elul, Roland Barthes, Harold Innis and Marshall Mcluhan" (Hobbs & Jensen, 2009, pp. 2-3).

When summarizing a diverse collection of research on media impacts, from before 1960, Wartella & Reeves (1985) suggest that several of the conclusions of adult studies were used to design social and instructional settings, although the research community may have cautioned against such applications. Persuasively, Liebert, Sprafkin & Davidson (1982) would also assert that several popularly-discussed media research studies from a similar period offered provocative findings, but that some of their recommendations for societal, instructional, and parental practice were derived from studies with adults. They therefore promoted that scholars interested in teaching children the skills needed to use and understand media would necessarily require different strategies and evaluations.

Hobbs & Jensen (2009) explain this shift in focus which occurred during the late-1960s, "It is hardly unusual for society to engage in vigorous debate about the implications of new media forms, and sooner or later educators become part of that conversation" (p. 3). In response, in the United States during the Boomer school years, increasingly children were addressed as a specific research focus area, and a particular media audience with identifiable and unique needs and interpretation skills.

Research involving children, media, and instruction targeted each adopted technology, and devoted significant focus toward the influence a given media might hold on their moral, ethical, and/or intellectual development. The research related to children and movies, or radio, or comic books, thus considered cognitive, social, intellectual and mental and physical health impacts. When, in the mid-1960s, TV was added to the list of media to be studied, because television was considered the dominant entertainment of the time, scholars revisited several of the same variables related to potential influences and impacts that had been investigated with earlier communication technologies.

In the 1960s, many media studies still did not use the vocabulary which is found in the Media Literacy academic field, but nonetheless, the earlier works offer several of the research questions which will be continually explored in that period and in the following decades. Furthermore, "Another likely influence of the whole body of research on media and youth is the social reform movement" (Wartella & Reeves,1985, p.129).

To illustrate this point, the *National Society for the Study of Education (NSSE) Yearbook*, "Mass Media and Education" section (Henry, 1954), "acknowledged the growing impact of movies and newspapers on American society and thus on schooling" and suggested "media had expanded to the point that "contents and effects of messages disseminated through the mass media" needed to be "viewed in the light of their social values" (p. vii, cited by Schwartz, 2005, pp. 7-8). Regarding specific in-school activities, Forsdale (1955) said, "we may hasten the inevitable maturation of the newer media and help our students gain necessary multimedia literacy. Is there an educational job to be done which has a higher priority?" Classroom instructional materials, created by education experts during the 1950s and 1960s, were disseminated by various channels during the Boomer school years. For instance, in 1950 Spence wrote for the *Wisconsin Association for Better Radio Listening*, and published with the National Council of Teachers of English; as Chair of Education for the Wisconsin Association for Better Radio and Television in 1952, she expanded her ideas to include television, in a booklet titled *Let's Learn to Look and Listen*, featuring a slogan on the front cover which said "Radio-TV: Everyone's Responsibility" (as cited in Jolls & Wilson, 2014). Classrooms throughout the US had teachers of Language Arts, Health, Home Economics, "Social Studies" and other subjects adopt the suggested strategies after reading these materials and/or attending workshops advocating media instruction as curricular supplements to their programs.

Media literacy competencies were, during the 1960s and 1970s, sometimes an inferred outcome rising from a logical mode of defense we Boomers might have been taught to use to counter sensationalism, propaganda, and, to some extent, advertising. The practice of media instruction in mid-century America was sometimes also associated with skills related to: guiding younger children to distinguish between "pretend" and "real" media content (Buckingham, et al., 2005); recognizing advertising versus program content and distinguishing between paid spokespersons and authentic endorsements (Aufderheide, 1993); acknowledging the compositional and selective aspects of news story creation; identifying photo editing practices that were "acceptable/ not-acceptable" (Scott, 1994); and the recognition that some types of stories were less-often told/shared because they were deemed less-worthy by those holding social/cultural power. When media critics noted that some sources were always asked, and others were never asked (e.g., Brown, et al., 1987; Gitlin, 1980), the analysis was based on the belief that the functions of the news (surveillance, correlation, and integration (Lippmann, 2020)) were legitimate, and that the role of media included providing the necessary information the public needed. When normative criticism of the 20th century said the media were failing, it was seen to be due to errors related to investigative skills or corporate-influenced silencing, rather than to the argument that the basic news activities were inappropriate for society. The critical thinking skills championed by Nussbaum (2010) and others reflect what guided the ways we were taught to understand linking news messages, decoding, and ethics to democratic activities.

THE "INTERVENING YEARS" – 1970s-1990s

Media Landscape

In the 1970s, television maintained dominance as the most-used mass media in the United States, with nearly every household having at least one TV, and by the early 1980s, "the overwhelming majority of households have a color receiver" (Liebert, Sprafkin, & Davidson, 1982, p. 2). Their TVs were turned on about six hours per day, in the average household (Steinberg, 1980; Broadcasting Yearbook, 1980).

Further responding to technological changes of this era, with the diffusion of systems that expanded access, Americans began to have more opportunities to view more news and entertainment offerings. The 1984 Cable Act allowed for new TV networks to emerge and hence, through the decade, over 70 new networks launched that focused on niche, "boutique", and specially-targeted markets (Gerhardt, 2024). This availability of "narrowcasting for a price" and the expanded access to remote TV stations got more people spending more time watching television, much to the concern of educators, parents, and, therefore, policymakers. Legislatures during that time had challenges regulating the creation and distribution of content that was not broadcast (the FCC and its predecessor FRC regulated broadcasting with the reasoning that signals traveled by air, and that the air was considered a public resource under government purview, but cable came to homes by wires; see FCC, 2022).

The urban and small-town television network affiliates of CBS, NBC, and ABC continued to have their news programming repeat/rebroadcast segments from the national evening news and public affairs programs, adding only minimal local news content, such as mayoral and city-council politics, school information, sports, and weather, to the mix of news messages most people in the late 20th century consumed. This added content, which stylistically matched the "parent company", attempted to mimic the values that earned national reporters the public's trust, and from my experiences, even journalism students of the era who were interned to smaller stations were taught the importance of adopting the professional value of objective storytelling. CNN launched in 1980 as a 24-hour news option, and "in April 1981, CNN successfully sued the Big Three television networks and the Reagan administration for equal representation in the White House press corps" (Troy, 2005). CNN disrupted the American patterns of news timing and news interview program lengths but adhered to the same news values of the major networks and thus earned public trust. Collectively, the most-viewed American news media during this era remained firmly grounded in a sensibility that their presentations of news and public affairs would stress "objectivity," reflecting the liberal sensibilities of the accepted role of the press in society. The presented messages often supported the strength of existing systems of government, valued the input of experts, industry leaders, scholars, and authorities, and/or maintained the status quo.

Regarding their consumption of entertainment-media content, the older portion of the Boomer cohort was raised in an era of radio dramas aimed to a general audience but popular among children, family television viewing of assorted broadcast programs including sports, Westerns, crime dramas, and variety shows, and some limited TV programming "for children" such as puppet shows or host-introduced cartoon reels. As stated by Palmer & Fisch (2001), "children's television programs of the 1950s and 1960s duplicated 'prior media forms'" (p. 6). Skills related to accessing, understanding, and applying knowledge about how and when to use these legacy-media content systems were taught through the instruction and experiences described in the earlier section of this paper.

The 1970s marked a distinct change in the media programming landscape in the United States. Children's television became a newly imagined, specialized content form, with a unique grammar and style, due to the introduction of *Sesame Street*, an instructional program for preschoolers shown on Public Broadcasting System stations. This milestone is important for understanding the growth in the number of academic studies and the intensified interests of educators examining the influences of TV.

Media Uses and Users

By 1970 (when the average age of motherhood in the US was 21, see Chernikoff, 2024), the early Boomers were parents; some may have even watched *Sesame Street* with *their* children. Even many younger members of this post-war generation were "too old" for *Sesame Street* by the time it became widely distributed to regional PBS stations. Thus, people born between 1945 and 1964 may have been no longer getting explicit media education from schools, at this pivotal moment when the Media Literacy movement, as a specialized focus, began to be considered seriously in the US (Schwartz, 2005).

In response to this change in programming and other child-centered instructional innovations in media content, the National Society for the Study of Education (NSSE) Yearbook (1974) addressed the growing influence of "new" media on education, with ideas from media experts. This yearbook called for study specifically into "the structure of the symbols that make up such an important part of our environment, the media that propagate those symbols, and the cognitive consequences of exposing children to them" (Olson, 1974, p. 9 as cited in Schwartz, 2008, p. 8).

As the next part of this chapter describes, in between the mid-1970s and the 1990s, scholars and practitioners within the growing field of media literacy, and writers of related policy initiatives, gained worldwide recognition. In the United States, they worked to clarify definitions, establish theoretical positions, refine research perspectives, and develop instructional goals. The provided, selective summary of academic and public activities is useful for understanding the relevant and resilient modes of thought and the social concerns related to media literacy from this era, but the described issues and controversies likely happened beyond the awareness of many of the Baby Boomer cohort. This period's review is offered to establish a foreground for some of the ideas we find present in discussions about today's media literacy challenges.

Media Literacy Themes and Theories

The UNESCO declaration of 1978 stated that the mass media have an essential part to play in the education of young people, and must be used to strengthen and promote peace, justice, freedom, human rights, and international understanding. In response, during the 1970s and thereafter, several "nations have reacted to the explosion of new media by including media literacy (through media education or media studies) in the school curriculum" and, according to Ferrington and Anderson-Inman (1996), "Australia, Great Britain, Norway, and Canada have had extensive K-12 media education programs for years" (p. 668, cited in Schwartz, 2008, p. 7).

Finland, France, and Germany began creating their own national educational programs in this period as well (Leedom, 2024).

The American media literacy movement also grew significantly, and by the 1990s, integrated the ideas of many media effects research scholars, social critics, educational theorists, concerned teachers and parents, and others. Conceptualizing media literacy education as a mixed-disciplinary interest, implementation of initiatives occurred within the newly-understood "hybrid field with roots in many areas, including but not limited to: semiotics, film studies, cultural studies, educational technology, instructional technology, information literacy, and many more" (Thoman & Jolls, 2004, p. 25). Considine (2002) notes that, during that time, media literacy also received broad public attention–it was endorsed by the U.S. Secretary of Education and the U.S. Secretary of Health and Human Services; it was featured on public TV in *Media Literacy: The New Basic?* (PBS,1996) and reported on in *Great Transitions: Preparing Youth for the 21st Century* (Carnegie Council on Adolescent Development,1995).

Although the public interest and international and national pronouncements gave media literacy much-needed attention in these intervening years, what actually counted as "media literacy" was contested and refined during this time, through discussions (and disputes) at various conferences and meetings and in editorial articles in public and academic channels. Deliberations involved identifying relevant educational goals, the types of media content and/or technologies to be examined, the tools that should be introduced in instructional settings, and the appropriate processes for obtaining and assessing relevant skills and knowledge. Some people suggested the goals of media literacy education in the United States could be simply understood by the alliterative mnemonic, "protection, preparation and pleasure" (Considine, 2002, pp.11-12, as cited in Stein & Prewett, 2009, p. 113). After the 1992 National Conference on Media Literacy, the Aspen Institute attendees' consensus definition of media literacy was that it was "the ability to access, analyze, and produce information for specific outcomes" (p. v), and they later elaborated that Media Literacy education involves instruction in the ability "to decode, analyze, evaluate and produce communication in a variety of forms" (Aufderheide, 1993). This, however, was not the final version of a definition.

To integrate social/cultural views, some media literacy educators embraced McLuhan's contention that every medium reproduces and reflects assumptions that influence the unwary (McLuhan, 1964/2002, p.15). If we are looking at larger systems of society, Livingstone (2004) says the "access, analysis, evaluation, and content creation" definition is incomplete, because "(n)ot only does a skills-based definition of literacy focus on users to the neglect of text and technology, it also prioritizes the abilities of the individual over the knowledge arrangements of society" (p. 11). Rubin (1998) further asserts that media literacy "is about understanding the sources and technologies of communication, the codes that are used, the messages that are produced, and the selection, interpretation, and impact of those messages" (p. 3). As Schwartz (2004) attempts to smooth out disagreements, she suggests that "these disagreements can be problematic… Nevertheless, it is doubtful if anyone would disagree…: At the heart of all the various elements of media literacy is critical analysis" (pp.12-13).

To clarify and possibly resolve this discussion, Potter (2010) provides an outstanding summary of the ideas of the era, by noting and contrasting several definitions of media literacy from seven articles (Adams & Hamm, 2001; Anderson, 1981; Aufderheide, 1993; Barton & Hamilton, 1998; Hobbs, 2001; Sholle & Denski, 1995; and Silverblatt & Eliceiri, 1997) and sixteen citizen action groups including, for example: the Action Coalition for Media Education; the Center for Media Literacy; Citizens for Media Literacy; the Media Awareness Network; Media Watch; the National Leadership Conference on Media; and others (pp.677-678). After this extensive review, Potter offered the recommendation that media literacy should be approached by asking the key questions: "what are the media?"; "what do we mean by literacy?"; and "what is the purpose of media literacy?", and concluded that the answers will emerge from common, although perhaps situational, themes and goals which could be addressed by reviewing case studies, employing direct education, and/or user interventions. Using Potter's position would mean media literacy instruction, tools, and skills could be applied to any or all of the following: defending against evils; empowering students to be critical thinkers; and/or engaging with social justice and equity activities.

Television remained, at the end of the intervening era, the primary medium of entertainment, and thus of media literacy attention. Furthermore, "(t)he most common targets of media literacy intervention studies are children" (Potter, 2010, p. 285). Because children were seen as the core audience of concern, schools were given primary responsibility for educational programs. Media would be used in schools in a variety of classrooms, as a subject of study, as an information-delivery system, as a tool for creativity, and as diversion/reward. Regarding children, Buckingham (1993) was somewhat positive about the social and developmental potentials of television, while Postman (1986) saw TV as providing a curriculum which educators would need to review and counter.

Meanwhile, regarding media literacy, parents and grandparents would be offered supporting roles by the end of this era, being told to discuss content and arrange co-viewing if or when needed. It is important at this point, however, to (re)emphasize that this chapter is about Baby Boomers and their needs. That population, who grabbed so much social, cultural, economic, and political attention and focus in the earlier decades (and earlier sections of this chapter) had been, in the 1970s-1990s, relatively ignored by many in the Media Literacy movement, by educational and social institutions, and by policymakers and social service providers. As discussed here, this "middle period" when Media Literacy theories and strategies developed and gained significant attention was when Boomers were active in the workforce or recently retired. Some of these possible learners may have disengaged; others may have been given meager technical media or communication instruction or provided with a few directions and given an unclear role regarding supporting media uses by themselves or family members. The years of media literacy scholarship and the pedagogical theory debates went largely unnoticed by our cohort, even though during these decades, media availability expanded. Instead, this was when our skills for acquiring, organizing, and evaluating message sources became dated. Furthermore, during this time, as content became varied, greater in number, and increasingly made by a much wider variety of people, companies, and organizations, our interpretive knowledge structures were not prepared to do the relevant analysis, decoding, and critique of the messages that the new media provided. In many ways, therefore, Boomers were poorly equipped to teach others or to implement media literacies in our own lives. Furthermore, as time passed, we moved into roles as "elders" without anticipating the significant changes that would come in the upcoming years, including broadened use of the Internet, mobile communications, "smart" technologies, and the rising technical ways to create and spread disinformation/misinformation.

SELECTIVE HISTORY–US, EARLY-21st CENTURY

Media Landscape

The early-21st-century media environment is much more complex than the American media landscape of 30-50 years ago (the educational and working decades of current Boomers). The apparent number of available message sources has grown beyond count, while the legacy media's explicit influence becomes dwarfed by many other choices, easily available to people with increasingly affordable technologies and internet access. These new options for programming and "news" (necessarily in scare-quotes as the very definition of what constitutes news has shifted) have provided a potential audience with customizable access to topics and voices. Because the powers and wealth associated with the obscure clusters of ownership of media distribution outlets and technologies have become increasingly hidden, many older consumers are unaware of the nature of the reach of American media industries and are thus challenged to keep track of the small number of very influential corporations sending messages related to social values across the plethora of sponsored or supported modalities. The level of print subscriptions for magazines and newspapers is so low that many outlets have embraced online-only services (for the number of newspapers closing, see Fu, 2023). In regard to TV viewership, Boomers remain cable or dish customers at levels higher than other age groups–only 3% of people aged 50-55 and 21% of people over age 55 receive streaming-only video media (Stoll, 2024). The phenomenon of being cable TV "cord-cutters" seen as normal by many, has been less enthusiastically embraced by elders, with broadcasting and cable providing many of the choices in news and entertainment involving legacy media channels, distant stations, and the "interest stations" (shopping, gardening, religious, etc.) which Boomers have grown to love.

Media Uses and Users

Today's elders are avid media consumers–like all age groups, they are getting entertainment and information from online sources, which are variously transparent when telling about their biases, loyalties, sponsors, and world views. Despite the media literacy education of their past, which taught Boomers about signals they could use to identify advertising, they sometimes lack the second-level skills to do similar discernments when online (suggested by Nunan & Di Domeco, 2019). The sheer quantity of today's offered mass media content choices also leads casual consumers of programming to rarely scrutinize the real abundance of sameness which arises from content franchises and spinoffs, and which promote ideological values supporting the status quo, consumerism, specified gender roles and beauty ideals, and/or racial depictions (Laughey, 2010). While more-attentive, younger, media literate consumers may articulate a conclusion that many mass media messages align with the views of socially-dominant message makers, identifying preferred/socially acceptable readings (e.g., Hall, 1980), that critical thinking exercise known to younger consumers is unknown to many elder media users.

Furthering complications for media literacy come from the additions to the recognizable news media of the previous era. The cry of "fake news" has been applied to all kinds of messages from a huge number of skeptical and discerning public and corporate sources, and instead of objectivity as a standard expectation, bias has become the assumed norm. Thus, individual fact checking, verification, and reasoned analysis have become more difficult for many, especially in an environment where rumor and hearsay are easily shared and conspiracies infiltrate legacy media sites; nonetheless, there is still a public interest in understanding news. Boomers in their youth and young adulthood may have felt competent to evaluate message sources, but now, because there is also the online assortment of blogs, sites, substacks, streams, and social media created and disseminated by a wider range of people, with various goals beyond performing the functions of the traditional news and information providers, Boomers may be easily misled or deceived by misinformation and/or disinformation. The Boomers who have been educated in earlier decades and have not been given updated instruction or opportunities for engagement with diverse media are oftentimes not prepared to keep up with the new systems of information access and lack the new media literacy skills of discerning fact from "alternative fact" or manipulation, misinformation, or disinformation. When identifying and countering misinformation, recent reports show a pattern in which older media users are worse at recognizing misinformation but have a greater hand in spreading it (Gottfried & Grieco, 2018).

Furthermore, contemporary emerging media and information literacy challenges related to AI can be linked to the need for integrated "multiple literacies" (Livingstone, 2005, p. 9), blending the skills and knowledge required for media and information literacies with cyber-literacy/Internet literacy/network literacy, digital literacy, and visual literacy to make sense of AI-generated messages, which provide new complexity. Furthermore, all consumers, but especially elders, need some understanding of political literacy, environmental literacy, financial literacy, and health and emotional literacy. Thus, as the next section of this chapter explains, following Mallik et al.'s (2022) assertion, "it is necessary to facilitate the digital literacy of citizens and raise awareness about AI as a collective issue and cross-sectional matter" (p. 202).

The conversation about dangers and potential gains posed by algorithmic transformation is filled with what linguists would call 'false friends'– words in a foreign language that despite bearing resemblance to words in one's native language have an entirely different meaning...each framing carries a set of values, explicit and implicit expectations and assumptions about the technology itself as well as – more fundamentally – the world around us (Malik, et al., 2022, p.193).

We elders may be said to be the digital immigrants, learning the new language while struggling in a world of "digital natives" (Barlow, 1996; Prensky, 2001), and although many exceptions and outliers can be found to the reductionist assumptions of such classifications, we do form a sizeable cohort of people who need guidance and direction in regard to understanding the influences of Generative AI on, and in, the media. Boomer-focused AI-acknowledging media literacy instruction is therefore particularly important in the contemporary landscape. While programs for adults need to highlight the changes in the availability and quantity of content which comprises the new experiences of contemporary life, educators face a multi-pronged challenge– systems of adult education need to focus on persuading people that they, really, need to be (re)instructed and they need to develop new competencies; that they need to understand and care about *why* this matters; and that they would benefit by knowing the details of who or what controls the media they consume, and creates the messages they interpret. This means older adults may have to be persuasively approached regarding learning about 21st-century media and information literacies, including Generative AI uses in society.

Media and Educational Themes and Theories

Instead of looking at TV as the new media, by 2000, Wartella and Jennings and other media literacy experts were testing assumptions related to media influences by exploring the ways computers, mobile technologies, and other new technologies were affecting 21st-century children. The argument that children were different than adults was the impetus for much of the theory-building related to targeted media literacy education in the 1950s through 1990s, and many of the prominent scholars from the past continue their focus on children. Therefore, these experts are no longer looking at us, the "former children" who have disengaged from media literacy instruction and other educational opportunities during our working years. Nonetheless, the Baby Boomer cohort has continued our earlier enthusiastic technology adoptions and are exploring computers and AI without structured instructional attentions geared to our specific interests and needs. Expanding the logic of the media literacy field, with necessities created by the contemporary media landscape, suggests the premise that older adults (who are not the same as contemporary adults nor children) should not receive the same kinds of instruction that "youngers" require, but instead get targeted instruction.

The Boomers/ elders can be understood as a particular population, with many exhibiting specific learning differences which impact the ways we should consider offering media and information literacy instruction. Main (2022) asserts that elders can not be effectively instructed by lessons which have been designed for school-aged learners, or for young(er) adults. Cognitive Load Theory (CLT), described by Bannert (2002) and Sweller (1994), explains that this is because older adults have working memory limitations or "cognitive loads" which are generally greater for elders than for other learners, and affect the capacity to process and store information. The types of cognitive loads which create "processing bottlenecks" and memory challenges may be intrinsic (related to the complexity of the learning material), extraneous (related to the poor design of instructional materials and lessons), and/ or germane (related to the mental effort involved with making connections and developing schemas). CLT further suggests that compared to other learners, elders often have increased sensitivity to extraneous load and diminished attention control.

Furthermore, unlike younger people who may prefer to learn through experimentation, elders are found to prefer learning from structured, sequential, written instructions, with multiple repetitions of information, more time to process and encode learning, and opportunities for practice (Chen, Paas & Sweller, 2023). Also, older learners prefer to have explanations of the reasons they are being taught, and to be told about the ways the new information builds on prior knowledge (Flauzino, et al., 2020)

CLT scholars suggest that addressing the specific needs of elder learners can be achieved by implementing deliberate lesson strategies. Chandler & Sweller (1991) cautiously recommend encouraging duo processing optimization, with instructors offering information in multiple modalities, such as visual and verbal, to suggest two possible paths to have knowledge move into long-term memory. Goad & Homes (2022) offer several recommendations for elder-focused pedagogy, including: needs-based learning, focusing on the learner not the technology; essential skills instruction, focusing on skills that will enhance the learners' participation in society; and familiar device instruction, teaching people to use what they have, rather than giving group instruction in tools provided for lessons. Instruction in explicit "chunking" (the meaningful grouping of information, see Thalmann, Souza, & Oberauer, 2019) is also a strategy to reduce intrinsic load and to enhance memory storage, as is "scaffolding" (involving visual cueing and learner-centered directing, see van Nooijen, et al., 2024).

Additionally, when designing instruction for elders it is necessary to acknowledge their possible psychological barriers to media, information, and digital literacies. The digital divide, often recognized as the gap between those with and those without access to and skills for the newest technologies, can be influenced by age (e.g., Mubarak & Suomi, 2022). Some Boomers may have technology comfort and confidence issues; while some experience specific-device fears, others have generalized technophobia. For instance, only about 18% of elders feel comfortable learning about ways to use features of their phones and other devices (Goad & Homes, 2022),

In addition to the above-described pedagogical design specifics, media and information literacy initiatives for seniors should "meet the people where they are" while also addressing what may be considered the most pressing of societal needs. In response, some adult media literacy instruction of late has focused on news message bias identification, tied to "responsible citizenship". Sorted classifications of right-leaning or left-leaning publications/ media channels serve as markers; standing for the interests of owners, publishers and producers which are understood in relation to how they align and affiliate with political parties, and which have created different understandings and definitions of what can be seen to constitute reality, useful information, and reliable facts. Those bias charts may be read to suggest that a well-informed person is to consume options across the continuum, or to find "central" sources that combine information sources and present "both sides" of an issue and have fact-checked their messages for consumers. The Los Angeles Times owner Soon-Shiong has said that he "wants to integrate an AI-powered 'bias meter' into the paper's coverage, in an apparent effort to make its reporting more politically neutral" (Ropek, 2024). This insertion of a technical fix for a social problem replaces employees, and their human opinions, while promoting a problematic belief that machines are better at understanding messages than trained professionals and an educated public. Ignored in this application of an AI tool are the embedded biases that come from using training data which comes from a collection of previously published and tagged articles. Much as legal and financial decisions coming from algorithmic logics (e.g., Burrell, 2016; O'Neil, 2017) neither provide opaque reasoning nor relevant guidance regarding future decisions; this use of AI may instead create narrowing, recycled, or recursive thinking. Consequently, this means the solution to the dissolution of trust in news media is now a social and cultural problem, whose solution will not be found in, just, investigating the "black box" containing the decision-making heuristics behind the implemented AI.

Tufekci (2015) has identified several possible harms caused by algorithmic manipulation of mediated messages; these harms are frequently present in the data-driven personalization and recommendation algorithms offered on social media sites and through search engine responses to prompts derived from browser tracking. Looking at the centrality of these message-sifting and -presenting technologies in regards to the social and political processes, and the influences of these applied technologies on knowledge, discourse, and social decision-making, it thus may be argued that the use of algorithmic technologies creates new relationships of power, drives uneven participation in social life, and thus poses a threat to social justice (Cinnamon, 2017).

EXPANDING RESPONSES TO TODAY'S MEDIA & INFORMATION LITERACY NEEDS

As Thoman & Jollis (2004) state: "Adults, too, need the opportunity to gain the skills they now find missing in their educational background" (p. 22). Many Boomers are retired, so now they are active and engaged community members who now have the time to learn new things, develop skills and take on hobbies or volunteer work. With advanced media and information literacies, they have the potential to be, still, vital members of society. But, as this chapter has asserted, the current media landscape is so different from the one which was prevalent in the Boomers' formative years, without new instruction, they may not be able to effectively face this opportunity. It has been reasoned: What one learns in compulsory secondary school sets one up for early-adult life. What happens educationally during adulthood is shaped, oftentimes, by the necessities of work, community, and family obligations. The specific literacy skills and tools which are needed for success in adulthood are explored and mastered, as needed, while other technologies may be ignored or dismissed. Adult education that is not explicitly for skills related to new occupations, is oftentimes provided as merely an opt-in experience. Hence, due to the variety of life experiences and needs, this means, for instance, some Boomers are more engaged with their mobile phone's various capabilities, while others are challenged by their TV remotes.

Gabaree (2022) offers an instructional guide advocating for metacognitive approaches to educating for 21st-century media and information literacy. For instance, his pedagogy offers a remedy to reduce the spreading of misinformation, and while designed for teens, his curricular strategies can be adapted readily to reflect CLT-logic and used with Boomers. His plans highlight the identification of the interests and social goals of media users (interests held by oneself and/or others), and through attention, clarify online accessing habits and practices; information seeking and verification intentions, and/or reasoning that verification may not be necessary; an emotional analysis of how linking, sharing or replying feels; and an articulation of the social needs which may be met with media engagement, which are perceived when others evaluate the clicks and replies. In this environment, forward-facing instruction for Boomers should also provide elders with opportunities to discuss the many ways technologies capture, focus, and monetize media uses and users, with particular attention on how these new modes of activities occur within the contemporary media landscape.

Furthermore, a well-designed program in elder media literacy instruction will also need to: highlight algorithmic "suggestion" filters that direct people in non-neutral ways to sponsored content over criteria-driven sites and streams; include instruction about finding the best sources and links in online searches; and provide directions in the ways online users can seek better offerings of additional, truly similar and/or related content on streaming sites. As noted in the section of this chapter about the early media landscape, among Boomers, there persists technological enthusiasm and amazement; unfortunately, this thinking results in naive assumptions that computers are rational and neutral, and can make good if not better comparisons than people may (Bowles, 1996). The not-generally-transparent, often obscure or hidden programming and machine learning training data behind the suggestion systems are based on sometimes problematic assumptions, which consequently may create and perpetuate AI-supported information filter bubbles. These bubbles can then offer limited options for public entertainment and information/ knowledge formation. The ramifications of living within smaller and smaller information clusters, which provide merely ideology, political mindset, or culture-reinforcing content from less diverse sources, do not benefit a society that depends on varied opinions and voices from and in the media. While the ability to curate and amplify or eliminate news topics is variously championed as empowerment (e.g., Beer, 2009, arguing for a post-hegemonic media) and vilified as "mind-closing" (Harris, 2017; Pariser, 2011), information/content access filter bubbles, created by algorithms, function as invisible and unaccountable entertainment, news, and information gatekeepers. There are clear demographic differences in the understanding of algorithms and their applications on social media (Gran, Booth, & Bucher, 2021). In particular, elders have a deficit of understanding why, when, and how they are receiving incomplete and/or biased information. There are abundant, sometimes sensational anecdotes suggesting Boomers in particular fall into traps of misinformation and disinformation that make them susceptible to conspiracy theories, which can be found repeated circularly from cable news to social media to the "dark web" and podcasts (see McCammon, 2021 for an example). In some of those instances when people are misled or confused, when elders say they are "doing my own research", they need to be helped to understand that what they are finding does not yield strong reasoning, but merely confirmation of already held incorrect and/or incomplete suppositions.

It is thus imperative that Boomers are persuaded that they need to revise their skills associated with abilities to identify and respond to potentially harmful GAI-created and algorithmically suggested misinformation and disinformation which they encounter online, and it is the scholar/educators' duty to design media literacy interventions that can explicitly assist Boomers. As an example, Fryer (2024) addresses some ways media literacy education about conspiracies and culture wars should be discussed, specifically to improve the quality of public discourse and the decisions of citizens. Similarly, deeply-detailed discussions of the ways media-delivered data are understood are provided through channels such as the Media Education Lab's online series (e.g., Hoechsmann, Kumaran, & McKee, 2024, demonstration of an example of small-scale "big data" analysis, which also offers socio-cultural commentary on the complications of public discourse in the "mirror world", a concept defined by Klein, 2023). Additionally, in an effort to address weak research and information filtering and interpreting skills, excellent webinars and supporting materials for public and community/ adult education instructors teaching Boomers 21st-century media and AI-based literacies may be found on a variety of websites, such as those hosted by the American Library Association, 2024; and by UNESCO, 2024/25. The (U.S.) National Association of Media Literacy Education (NAMLE), although focused mostly on youth, has several resources which can be adapted for multi-generational learning.

American Boomers also need renewed instruction related to their visual literacy/ image-interpretative skills, which are tightly associated with media and information literacies. Because we were raised in a particular historic moment, during the Cold War, we might have been taught about instances found in the international news media, and imported books, wherein awkward and easily detectable manipulations were used to create propagandistic images (see Soviet examples, e.g., Blakemore, 2022) which we were told to mock and deride. This generation might have also been taught about classical fine arts paintings in which artists did creative representations of seemingly "almost realistic" natural and human forms, in ways that were thereafter replicated in modern instances of "simple photo adjusting" (e.g Berlatsy,

2013); these manipulations we were taught to see as acceptable artistic visions or versions of "reality". As examples, for understanding and critiquing images used in entertainment and for commercial purposes, in my own experiences in an American, midwestern public, secondary school we had units in "girls' health", in which we received detailed and explicit instructions telling us that we should exercise skepticism regarding images of thinness and to be cautious regarding inexpert recommendations for unhealthy dieting (Burke,1974). At the same school during that era, in "home economics" classes we were instructed to interrogate pictures of women's bodies in fashion magazines and to study the "enhanced"/artificial versions of food in advertisements and commercials with skepticism. These lessons contained arguments later widely recognized by feminists, such as Pollay (1986), as marketing distortions.

During the late-20th century, photo "touch-ups" thus became topics of some conversations and cursory studies, although in most instances, simple cropping, color enhancement, and red-eye removal in news photos were considered generally acceptable as news practices (Sullivan, 2009). In our personal making and sharing of images, by the turn of the century, many family photographers (even Boomers) had the ability to easily adjust and add filters to images of ourselves and our surroundings. Because we had come to accept that image cropping and brightening by the news media was increasingly "normal", we began considering that these practices were also OK for making personal pictures better, despite the fact that the manipulated photos and video created a resultant disconnect from actual lived experiences, and despite the fact that the photos and videos thereafter became the "saved records" that shaped our memories of what happened. A significant shift in the ways we now can possibly create and interact with images and messages from news and from other sources has occurred with the introduction of AI. Although we had some training in propaganda detecting, which we learned in our youth, and some experiences with the photo manipulation techniques we may have practiced in the past, we now encounter more sophisticated, more prevalent, and also more difficult to identify 21st century version of image and video manipulation resulting from the use of GAI.

The quantity and quality of misleading images, spread from the larger-than-ever assortment of sources, for news/ "news", entertainment, advertising, and creating social connection, potentially fosters wide-spread confusion among Boomers. It is important, therefore, to educate older people to recognize today's manipulated images, disseminated from a variety of official and informal sources which look trustworthy and perhaps appear news-like or from "friends," or real people, but are instead from various political, corporate, or other sources. Perhaps one's "newsfeed" messages come with biased or nefarious agendas, misinformation and misleading images, which are designed to spread quickly, for as Oremus (2024) reports, studies show that (message content-based) outrage fuels significant misinformation sharing, especially among less mindful media users. In today's media landscape, this means older media users must be instructed and encouraged to begin decoding all mediated messages with skepticism. The necessity to be investigative or suspicious of news and entertainment is not a perspective often associated with Boomers, who may be proud of their self-perceived savvy as media consumers.

To understand AI images in particular, formal pedagogy and informal messaging about modern media literacy, therefore, need to emphasize that the skills for evaluating today's mediated experiences are far different than what was used in the past. Boomers may be comfortable in relation to their reasoning associated with applying the older practices they have been taught for reviewing the meanings of images. They have been taught the importance of attending to the text associated with news photos, and of addressing the diminished thinking associated with when the juxtaposition of words and images gives greater validity to the image. The "eye wins every time" the White House Press secretary of the Reagan administration, Deaver, is said to have stated in reference to the interplay of "bad news" and uplifting posed photos of a happy-looking or confident president (as referenced in Bunton, et al., 1999). It also means however that some people who may still believe the idiom that 'a picture is worth one-thousand words' (e.g., see Lester, 1996) or that 'pictures do not lie' particularly need to be systematically educated to ask new questions and apply new reasoning and tools to understanding the new media landscape of today with AI images in news, entertainment, advertising and social media. Boomers in particular may be reluctant to see that they need visual media literacy instruction, so as a cohort they may need convincing that the contemporary, image-rich media environment, of real, realistic, and imagined images, needs new forms of scrutiny, and those who are the first of their social circle or community to gain understanding can become opinion-leaders and socially-elevated.

Highly technical reports have attempted to be comprehensive in providing guidance in AI detection (e.g., Lin et al., 2024). This kind of work will not serve media and information literacy scholars/educators addressing the majority of Boomers. Online, one can find web pages inviting self-education for motivated learners (e.g., Bartels, 2023; Benson, 2024). However, Benson (2004) reports, apparently from such lessons, "AI-savvy adults correctly identified AI-generated images only about half the time", and thus more work is needed to address elders' message decoding skills. What seems to be more effective is offering supportive workshops and creative opportunities for elders. Classes specifically designed to address seniors and their media literacies are offered across the U.S., and "Experts from the National Council on Aging, an organization established in 1950 to advocate for seniors, said classes on AI at senior centers have increased in recent years and are at the forefront of digital literacy efforts" (Merica, 2004). In the U.S., the AARP has offered a variety of in-person and online courses which have been well-publicized (AARP, nd). At the state and national levels, however, there is no consistent or standardized instructor training nor widely-adopted curriculum for scholar/educators to use; instead, it seems the piece-meal efforts and observed outcomes for this important work and the assessment of these initiatives rely on assorted organizations and public entities serving the elderly, and from "continuing education" options from schools, universities, and public libraries.

Regarding identifying and giving recognition for instances of the accomplished work related to designing, implementing and assessing programs of media literacy education for senior citizens, there are few academic reports. Rasi, Vuojärvi, & Rivinen, (2021) in their international, comparative meta-analysis of the ways people over age 60 have been explicitly educated in seventeen different countries suggest, and in follow-up reports (Rasi-Heikkinen, et al., 2025) offer that "interventions aimed at fostering ML in older people need further development and creative enrichment in terms of aims, content, providers, recipients, and pedagogical approaches". Notley, Chambers, Park & Dezuanni (2021), and Notley, Hourigan & Thomson (2025), as researchers from the Institute for Culture & Society, assert that, because misinformation can harm democratic processes, social cohesion and public health outcomes, workshops in partnership with cultural organizations and public entities are best evaluated using an evidence-informed approach with a connected learning approach to ensure that learning initiatives are aligned with people's interests, and are embedded in their everyday media activities, which include a diversity of goals, practices, technologies and interpretative reasonings. As these scholars have found, there have been many good attempts at addressing AI and media and information literacy for elders, but more work needs to be done to promote relevant skills related to AI and media.

As the following section of this chapter explains, our responsibility is therefore to broaden our pedagogical assumptions and instructional approaches, in order to address the needs of adult and elder learners, and to provide guidance for ways Boomers may continue to effectively and ethically engage in the new media landscape. Furthermore, as Moss (2022) notes, "We live in a time where digital algorithms are woven throughout our society, often making vital decisions in areas including, but not limited to, education, commerce, politics, justice, and employment". Therefore in addition to expanding traditional media literacy perspectives, we should embed algorithmic literacy into our instructional programs.

RECOMMENDATION FOR AN EXPANSION OF APPROACHES

Among the best strategies to holistically address the many new challenges presented by AI's influence on media is to begin thinking more openly about ways to apply several arguments from Critical Media Literacy. This broad-ranging, progressive approach situates generalized literacy education within ideological investigations, aiming to apply a multi-perspectival approach to reconceptualize Dewey's ideals related to public engagement for democracy, and to articulate "relationships between media and audiences, information and power" (Kellner & Share, 2007, p. 59). Whereas, in the US and many Western countries, 20th century media education goals, strategies, and practices were varied, and were responding to competing interests (Hobbs, 1998), a few core themes of the past perspectives have been identified and added to local and regional curricula in a piece-meal fashion, some of which were described earlier in this chapter, recounting the author's personal experiences. The perspectives in this chapter are: the protectionist approach; media aesthetics and "media studies"; media production skills training; and media and algorithmic literacy. Each is described by past or current concerns, and then the extension of Critical Media Literacy arguments is attached. Realistically, in many instances, scholars/educators may work within several of these perspectives, or have blurred the categorical distinctions, but the listing nonetheless functions here to systematically address possible expansions for consideration.

The "protectionist approach" responded to public and educational fears related to the mass media, especially as television gained prominence (Postman, 1985). Boomers (today's elders), who were said to be the first generation who grew up with TV, were the subjects of the socially-conveyed worries saying that media would undermine family and institutional influence (Genner & Süss, 2017; Kammerl & Kramer, 2016; Kelly & Donohew, 1999), that children would lose text-literacy skills (Furedi, 2016; Van Peer, 1988), that youth would not play outdoors or socialize (Newell, 2007; Nossek & Adoni, 2001), and that attention spans (Bodensteiner, 1995; Subramanian, 2018) would greatly diminish as media consumption increased. Although these concerns are familiar to scholars of media history, who may retort that the same fears were popular when radio gained its audience (e.g., Dennis, 1998), and when mass marketed "dime novels" and comic books were growing in popularity (Tilley, 2012; Wertham, 1954), television's rapid adoption did press the questions to the forefront of educational interest, and hence political interest. The present environment, with the additions of new media, social media, and AI, should be pushing some of the same concerns even farther, with a mixture of curiosity and caution. This theme of protectionism which has begun to be reinvigorated in the AI era we now face, should not be seen to advocate reducing the multi-faceted media experience, and should be approached from a position of considering comparative historical insights in order to suggest future actions. Critical Media Literacy scholars thinking more broadly about the communicative landscape we face today, who suggest that the mass media teach and reinforce increasing consumerism and promote values supporting the status quo, should be actively engaged in joining this broad cultural conversation, in light of the nature of and abundance of available messages. Experiences with artificial videos, AI-produced memes and simple games, and manipulated images are easily available for the curious and the unwary, including many Boomers, and can be focal topics for instruction and discussion.

A second approach, employed in the past and making a resurgence in respect to AI-created media, may be deemed "media aesthetics". It is focused on the appreciation of media as an artistic form of expression. Expanding on the reasoning often found in "Languages and literature" classes, this instructional strategy is taught to children and adults as "film studies" and "popular culture criticism". The possibility to see and classify works in relation to previous forms of (high) art, and the relevant vocabulary to talk about methods of image and message production, may be stressed. Expanding this approach by adding the Critical Media Literacy perspective to aesthetics would enable us to interrogate privileges associated with a selection of works deemed "worthy" of study, the underlying economic and political ramifications of inclusion/exclusion of types of images, and the presence/absence of underrepresented people and groups in the canon. In regard to serving the new needs of Boomers facing an AI-filled environment, this perspective, with the addition of a critical lens, can consider ways image analysis can be used to scrutinize examples in light of their truth and/or beauty, and could include teaching about using particular AI-detection tools. Applications of this enlarged perspective can then address factors regarding AI in the media, and can also be considered in light of in other social/cultural/scientific domains into which AI has been inserted, such as racial profiling of suspects, geographic assumptions of credit-worthiness based on identifiable "ethnic neighborhoods", and medical errors derived from race-biased, or race blind, tools used for detections of serious ailments (Benjamin, 2019; Tacheva & Ramasubramanian, 2023).

A third popular approach to media education prioritizes the teaching of the technical aspects of media production and applies a logic which sees mechanical competency as a precondition for vocational (re)training with the applied set of skills. This mode of instruction often serves a population of retirees who want to do additional work and who see media production fluency as a marketable skill set they can use for part-time work and (virtual) consulting. Alternatively, production technology uses can be instructionally integrated with training in seeing self-made, or group-made, mediated communication as a creative outlet, to bring participants a form of joy. In this situation, such instruction for Boomers may, for instance, take the form of workshops for gathering attributes, photographing and scanning documents, recording and editing audio files, and designing graphics to make a "personal history story recording", a digital scrapbook for family members, or a blog with insights and wisdom from one's long life. Such classes are especially popular with elders and do give them an opportunity for the creation of a legacy, with their personal ideas being organized into shareable, attractive form(s) for descendants, friends, and their communities. The challenge faced by education related to this perspective is that broader social and cultural questions are not usually directly addressed in practical training. Adding Critical Media Literacy concerns to this approach would necessarily include embedding discussions which advocate that production is not isolated and neutral but instead needs to be contextualized within historical practices in contemporary society. Additionally, learners would be guided to seek communicative models from socially aware, cultural and economic investigations of alternative media and their audiences. In the presence of AI's simplifying and reductionistic influences in this area, the "preferred tools" for elders to understand media production logics thus need to also go beyond the mechanics and software of story production and become prominent in the relevant questions learners ask about surrounding the reproduction of hegemonic conclusions and dominant ideologies which are found in common media-crafting instructions and serve to become formulaic and diminish audience expectations.

Additionally, when considering the teaching of media literacy using any, or a blend of, the above perspectives, forward-thinking adult instructional practices which address GAI and media should include extending the widely used evaluative frameworks for reviewing information literacy instruction and competencies to include Algorithmic Literacy components into all levels of education. Applying the Association of College & Research Libraries (ACRL, 2015) framework to include new, AI-specific "threshold concepts", key ideas, and associated knowledge practices to the frames "Authority is constructed and contextual", "Information has value", and "Searching as strategic exploration (as advocated by Archambault, 2023) can reasonably be said to formulate learning objectives and/or learner goals that apply beyond the university context to include motivated, independent learners across the lifespan, including elders. This type of instruction would not only make systems of information organization explicit and transparent but would also be useful for articulating ways machine learning informs present and future interactions people may have with the mediated environments which affect them privately, interpersonally, and socially. For instance, as Frau-Meigs (2024) contends, there is a need to study "how to design learner-centred interventions that foster increased user understanding of algorithms and better respond to disinformation spread by such processes" (p.512).

Basic algorithmic literacy which would be central to understanding the uses of GAI, although becoming increasingly important, is not often well-defined in traditional media literacy instructional programs. Oeldorf-Hirsch & Neubaum (2025), while acknowledging that the media literacy skills better-known to elders of finding, consuming, evaluating, and producing media which we have been previously taught are useful beginnings, suggest that additional research is needed for scholar/educators to better understand what may be successful tactics for instructing older people, and people of all ages, with the necessary new literacy skills for the new era. Using various testing and self-reporting scales which operationalize specified tasks and modes of thinking/reasoning, several assessments of levels of algorithmic literacy show there are age-based gaps in knowledge and proficiencies, with younger computer users out-performing the elders (Cotter & Reisdorf, 2020). The model of thinking about pedagogy offered by Oeldorf-Hirsch & Neubaum (2025, p. 685), involving cognitive, affective, and behavioral dimensions, illuminates an excellent possibility for moving forward, with specific suggestions regarding ways to narrow this identified knowledge divide, and to remedy several of the specific media-created challenges that the elderly face. To address common algorithmic literacy gaps which affect media and information literacies and knowledge-element deficits of Boomers, we should apply expansive pedagogical perspectives to create deliberate multi-faceted instructional frameworks which explicitly focus on AI, while also aligning our teaching, and research, strategies with Critical Media Literacy and its emphasis on justice, reasoning, and critical thinking. Some practical work in this vein can be found in smaller-scale lesson examples, which have been described by instructors with backgrounds in computer sciences and/or communication studies. These projects also suggest ways to teach learners about "decision trees" and sorting (e.g., Burke, & Machkasova, 2020; Valtonen, Tedre, Mäkitalo, & Vartiainen, 2019) and give students practice in designing and interpreting the processes of machine learning programs, which are essential exercises for teaching about the ways AI operate. Additionally, the work of librarians includes outstanding leadership in this area, hosting webinars (e.g., Spikes & Calvert, 2024) and in-personal workshops on ChatGPT and conversational AI, to teach elders about how text and visual messages are made and how they are spread. These are first-step suggestions–there are other examples, as noted by the examples reviewed by colleagues from Finland (Rasi-Heikkinen & Luksua, 2023), and Australia (Notely, Hourigan & Thomson, 2025) which can be adapted for U.S.-based instructions for adult learners.

If we truly plan to create a strong educational program for elders which integrates algorithmic literacy with Critical Media Literacy, this means we should also be thinking about ways scholar/educators should be highlighting the many media-created and AI-exacerbated gaps and biases which have been discussed in this chapter. We cannot fully anticipate future technologies and applications; nonetheless, we can be creating pathways for giving people relevant skills and knowledge to interrogate the sources and perpetuating factors related to the inequalities and injustice arising from the implementation of GAI in the contemporary, increasingly complex media landscape. Through highlighting systematic AI bias, which excludes entire groups from receiving information, or being represented in considered content, algorithmic symbolic annihilation (involving detrimental assumptions about information-seekers), and interpretation bias embedded in the design and display of information (which is trained by humans with biased examples), we can aid Boomers, and all learners, in interrogating the ethics of GAI (Danks & London, 2017; Tsamados, et al., 2021) through the application and extension of the concerns articulated by the Critical Media Literacy perspective.

Furthermore, with the Critical Media Literacy perspective, the competencies associated with (general) media literacy, such as the abilities to access, analyze, evaluate, and communicate, become deepened by critical thinking that leads to understandings of, and critiques of, mainstream message making, and introduces the possibilities for alternative and oppositional readings (e.g., Hall, 1980), which can result in social and cultural change. In the investigation of the influences of AI on the media landscape, a Critical Media Literacy focus can thus see positive, rather than solely negative, opportunities; and can offer systemic, rather than merely personal, interrogations to cultural and historical trends regarding seeing, reading, thinking, and being that are emerging in the 21st century. According to several assessments, some excellent instruction which has adopted the interests of Critical Media Literacy for teaching elders has been facilitated by cultural institutions in Australia. With government support for adult education, targeted programs teaching about the media which adults regularly use, yielding promising results regarding successes in fostering deeper involvement with and improved levels of scrutiny of media content. Hobbs (2025) has encouraging results from teaching diverse ages of adults applied skills in media and information literacy "Courageous Conversation" sessions, focused on fostering intellectual humility, reducing defensiveness and increasing active listening in the U.S. Park, et al., (2023) specifically tie together relevant variables in their data, including demographic sorts for people aged 40+ and 60+, to discern links between online interactions and civic engagement, suggesting "social media literacy" works well among older people, for it helps to create skills and positive attitudes regarding their competencies in creating and evaluating online messages.

CONCLUSION

This chapter started with a discussion of adult learners and why a special focus has to be given to the population group we think of as Boomers/ elders. This particular generational cohort in the US grew in educational, social, cultural, political, and economic influence from their birth through their school years and working years during the mid-1960s through the early/mid 2000s, and due to their relative size in the population, are accustomed to having their particular needs being addressed. About one out of every five Americans today is a Boomer (Bump, 2025), or counted as a Boomer and an elder (World Bank, 2025).

A comparative, historical discussion of media landscapes was described in this chapter. The reason the points of contrast were highlighted was to emphasize that Boomers grew up in a very different world than that which we live in today. The past dominance of print newspapers and magazines, merely, three TV stations, and the trust of the public in the idealized goal of "objective" news was specific to the era. The educational opportunities for many Boomers to learn about media during their school years were small and specific, but nevertheless, this generation entered the workforce, established homes and communities, in many instances, raised children, and contributed to society while thinking their skills were sufficient to function as information seekers and message evaluators. But the world kept changing–technological innovations introduced new mediated forms of communication, and increased possibilities for a wider number of people to create and disseminate media for personal, interpersonal, group, and mass communication. Meanwhile with the wide-scale use of AI, now there are also abundant real and imaginary images and texts that have been made which create additional perplexing and potentially troubling media content. Elders are more likely to misunderstand messages, share or spread misinformation, fall prey to conspiracy theories, and lack nuanced understandings of the ways algorithms filter messages. Technologically enthusiastic, Boomers have attempted to use the new media, but many lack the educational background to do so effectively. There is a need and an opportunity to educate this population of eager, life-long learners.

As discussed in the recommendation section of this chapter, meeting this pedagogical imperative is possible, with modifications to the instructional perspectives which have been embedded parts of traditional media literacy instruction for the last several decades. Each perspective has a wealth of documentation and available supportive materials that can be found online, so to add to the conversation this chapter stressed the addition of Critical Media Literacy to encourage broader thinking about the purposes and goals of what we may implement. The argument has been made that American culture has been influenced by intersections between slices of ingenuity and more-widely-distributed, marginalized voices previously drowned out by the repeated, multiply-offered dominant ideological images, messages, sounds, and resultant conclusions (e.g., Lull, 2002) but Critical Media Literacy highlights and provides counterpoint skills to address this situation.

The chapter's discussion of algorithmic literacy and its connection to media literacies for elders is brief yet important. There is a growing need to educate the public in the emerging, rapidly changing world of AI. Some noteworthy works and manifestos for response were published in the last year (e.g., Bozkurt et al., 2024), but more statements of "best practices" of AI in educational, social communication, and news situations are still being written. The suggestions offered in this chapter, therefore, merely reflect some attempts at showing the current state of what is available, but realistically, vast adoption and new uses of AI are likely to be at the edge of the next new media landscape, which is yet to be developed and explored. Perhaps the next edition of this book will have more to say on this communicative innovation.

In closing, the Critical Media Literacy perspective described in this chapter as a response to Boomers' educational needs should be embedded in our thinking about media literacies for the 21st century. It must be acknowledged that Critical Media Literacy as an applied, instructional practice has obstacles to overcome. The political climate in the US limits what is and can be taught to children in schools, but may have fewer complaints about what can be taught to or discussed with adults, which opens possibilities for thinking about elder education courses and webinars in ways this chapter describes. To implement this perspective, instructors need to be confident in questioning social and cultural structures, and in investigating ways things may be rather than just creating descriptions of the way media currently shapes and reinforces culture. Honestly, to do this work a scholar/educator also likely needs to rely on a supportive educational system or a community which understands the value of education as a whole-life experience which creates liberatory opportunities for learners to create and negotiate meanings, and to empower members of a variety of publics to "speak out"/ "speak up" in a variety of ways.

When we respond to our duties, by teaching about media understanding as a form of civic, democratic duty or responsibility, we are servicing a greater good for our scholarship, our students, and our society. Ignoring any age cohort or population eager to learn about media literacy is a poor strategy for scholar/educators, and deleterious for a society that needs to address ways we can strengthen public media literacies regarding information, disinformation, and misinformation. Dependency on media may weaken our active participation, but wise media uses may expand participation. The society promoted by Critical Media Literacy encourages people to create honest messages, to be able to evaluate messages for truth, and beauty, to create messages of care and connection, and to facilitate involvement with social and community issues.

REFERENCES

AARP. (n.d.) *Learn About AI, Technology, Digital Safety & More!* AARP. https://states.aarp.org/new-york/educational-workshops-on-all-things-technology

Alsop, T. (2020, May 1). *Percentage of households in the United States with a computer at home from 1984 to 2016.* Statistica. https://www.statista.com/statistics/214641/household-adoption-rate-of-computer-in-the-us-since-1997/

American Library Association. (2024, Oct). *Media Literacy Education for Adult Audiences: Demystifying AI.* [Video]. Programming Librarian. https://programminglibrarian.org/learn/media-literacy-education-adult-audiences-demystifying-ai

Archambault, S. G. (2023). Expanding on the frames: Making a case for algorithmic literacy. *Communications in Information Literacy*, *17*(2), 530–553. DOI: 10.15760/comminfolit.2023.17.2.11

Aufderheide, P. (1993). National leadership conference on media literacy. In *Conference report. Washington, DC: Aspen Institute.*

Bannert, M. (2002). Managing cognitive load—Recent trends in cognitive load theory. *Learning and Instruction*, *12*(1), 139–146. DOI: 10.1016/S0959-4752(01)00021-4

Barlow, J. P. (2016, Jan 20). *A Declaration of the Independence of Cyberspace.* Electronic Frontier Foundation. https://www.eff.org/cyberspace-independence

Bartels, M. (2023, Mar 31). *How to Tell If a Photo Is an AI-Generated Fake.* Scientific American. https://www.scientificamerican.com/article/how-to-tell-if-a-photo-is-an-ai-generated-fake/

Beer, D. (2009). Power through the algorithm? Participatory web cultures and the technological unconscious. *New Media & Society*, *11*(6), 985–1002. DOI: 10.1177/1461444809336551

Benjamin, R. (2019). Assessing risk, automating racism. *Science*, *366*(6464), 421–422. DOI: 10.1126/science.aaz3873 PMID: 31649182

Benson, M. (2024, Feb 13). *"Real or AI" Quiz: Can You Tell the Difference?* Britannia Education. https://britannicaeducation.com/blog/quiz-real-or-ai/

Berlatsy, N. (2013, May 3). *The Ethics of Fashion Photo Manipulation.* Center for Digital Ethics & Policy. https://digitalethics.org/essays/ethics-fashion-photo-manipulation

Blakemore, E. (2022, Apr 11). *How photos became a weapon in Stalin's great purge*. History.com. https://www.history.com/news/josef-stalin-great-purge-photo-retouching

Bodensteiner, C. A. (1995). Predicting Public and Media Attention Span for Social Issues. *Public Relations Quarterly*, *40*(2).

Bowles, M. D. (1996). US technological enthusiasm and British technological skepticism in the age of the analog brain. *IEEE Annals of the History of Computing*, *18*(4), 5–15. DOI: 10.1109/85.539911

Bozkurt, A., Xiao, J., Farrow, R., Bai, J. Y., Nerantzi, C., Moore, S., & Asino, T. I. (Eds.). (2024). The manifesto for teaching and learning in a time of generative AI: A critical collective stance to better navigate the future. *Open Praxis, 16*(4), 487-513.

Breed, W. (1955). Newspaper 'opinion leaders' and processes of standardization. *The Journalism Quarterly*, *32*(3), 277–328. DOI: 10.1177/107769905503200302

Broadcasting Yearbook. (1980). Broadcasting Publications, Inc.

Brown, J. D., Bybee, C. R., Wearden, S. T., & Straughan, D. M. (1987). Invisible power: Newspaper news sources and the limits of diversity. *The Journalism Quarterly*, *64*(1), 45–54. DOI: 10.1177/107769908706400106

Buckingham, D. (1993). *The development of television literacy: talk, text and context* (Doctoral dissertation, Institute of Education, University of London).

Buckingham, D., Banaji, S., Carr, D., Cranmer, S., & Willett, R. (2005). The media literacy of children and young people: A review of the research literature.

Bump, P. (2025, Jan 18). *Baby boomers*. Encyclopedia Britannica. https://www.britannica.com/topic/baby-boomers

Bunton, K., Connery, T., Kanihan, S., Neuzil, D. M., & Nimmer, D. (1999). *Writing across the media*. Bedford/St. Martin's.

Burke, B.R. (1974). Assorted Class Notebooks [Personal collection].

Burke, B. R. (1995). *A shifting nature of understanding: Media coverage of environmentalism during the early 1990s*. [Unpublished dissertation]. Purdue University, West Lafayette, Indiana, United States.

Burke, B. R., & Machkasova, E. (2020). Critical media, information, and digital literacy: Increasing understanding of machine learning through an interdisciplinary undergraduate course. *Irish Communication Review*, *17*(1), 1.

Burrell, J. (2016). How the machine 'thinks': Understanding opacity in machine learning algorithms. *Big Data & Society*, *3*(1), 2053951715622512. DOI: 10.1177/2053951715622512

Campbell, R., Martin, C. R., & Fabos, B. (2016). *Media essentials: A brief introduction* (3rd ed.). Bedford/ St. Martins.

Chandler, P., & Sweller, J. (1991). Cognitive load theory and the format of instruction. *Cognition and Instruction*, *8*(4), 293–332. DOI: 10.1207/s1532690xci0804_2

Chen, O., Paas, F., & Sweller, J. (2023). A Cognitive Load Theory Approach to Defining and Measuring Task Complexity Through Element Interactivity. *Educational Psychology Review*, *35*(2), 1–18. DOI: 10.1007/s10648-023-09782-w

Chernikoff, S. (2024, May 18). The average age of first-time mothers continues to rise. *USA Today*, https://www.usatoday.com/story/news/health/2024/05/18/graphics-show-changing-trend-average-age-parents/73707908007/

Cinnamon, J. (2017). Social injustice in surveillance capitalism. *Surveillance & Society*, *15*(5), 609–625. DOI: 10.24908/ss.v15i5.6433

Considine, D. (2002). Media literacy: National developments and international origins. *The Journal of Popular Film and Television*, *30*(1), 7–15. DOI: 10.1080/01956050209605554

Cotter, K., & Reisdorf, B. C. (2020). Algorithmic knowledge gaps: A new horizon of (digital) inequality. *International Journal of Communication*, *14*, 21.

Danks, D., & London, A. J. (2017, Aug). Algorithmic bias in autonomous systems. *IJCAI (United States)*, *17*, 4691–4697.

DeFleur, M. L., & Ball-Rokeach, S. (1989). *Theories of mass communication* (5th ed.). Longman.

Dennis, P. M. (1998). Chills and thrills: Does radio harm our children? The controversy over program violence during the age of radio. *Journal of the History of the Behavioral Sciences*, *34*(1), 33–50. DOI: 10.1002/(SICI)1520-6696(199824)34:1<33::AID-JHBS3>3.0.CO;2-K PMID: 9487691

FCC. US government (2022 Sep). *The Public and Broadcasting*. Federal Communications Commission. https://www.fcc.gov/media/radio/public-and-broadcasting#ACT

Flauzino, K. D. L., Pimentel, M. D. G. C., Batistoni, S. S. T., Zaine, I., Vieira, L. O. B., Rodrigues, K. R. D. H., & Cachioni, M. (2020). Digital Literacy for Older Adults: Perceptions about teaching-learning. *Educação e Realidade*, *45*, e104913. DOI: 10.1590/2175-6236104913

Forsdale, L. (1955). *Multi-media Literacy. Better Broadcasts Newsletter, 8(4).* American Council for Better Broadcasts.

Frau-Meigs, D. (2024). Algorithm Literacy as a Subset of Media and Information Literacy: Competences and Design Considerations. *Digital, 4*(2), 512–528. DOI: 10.3390/digital4020026

Fryer, W. (2024). Conspiracy & culture wars. https://medialiteracy.wesfryer.com/concw

Fu, A. (2023, Nov 16). *US lost more than two local newspapers a week this year, new Medill report finds.* Poynter Institute. https://www.poynter.org/business-work/2023/2023-news-deserts-report-penny-abernathy-medill/

Furedi, F. (2016). Moral panic and reading: Early elite anxieties about the media effect. *Cultural Sociology, 10*(4), 523–537. DOI: 10.1177/1749975515626953

Gabaree, S. (2022). A metacognitive approach to reduce the spread of online misinformation. *The Journal of Media Literacy.* https://ic4ml.org/journal-article/a-metacognitive-approach-to-reduce-the-spread-of-online-misinformation/

Galant, R. (2012, Jun 5). *The most trusted man in America.* https://www.cnn.com/2012/06/05/opinion/brinkley-walter-cronkite/index.html

Genner, S., & Süss, D. (2017). Socialization as media effect. *The International Encyclopedia of Media Effects, 1*(15), 1-16.

Gerhardt, M. (2024). *1980s television.* History of American Pop Culture https://www.explorepopculture.com/unit-6-1980s/1980s-television

Gitlin, T. (1980). Making democracy safe for America. *Columbia Journalism Review, 18*(6), 53.

Goad, A., & Homes, O. (2022). Bridging the digital divide: an evaluation of existing elderly digital literacy education.

Gottfried, J., & Grieco, E. (2018) *Younger Americans Are Better than Older Americans at Telling Factual News Statements from Opinions.* Pew Research Center. https://www.pewresearch.org/fact-tank/2018/10/23/younger-americans-are-better-than-older-americans-at-telling-factual-news-statements-from-opinions/

Gran, A.-B., Booth, P., & Bucher, T. (2021). To be or not to be algorithm aware: A question of a new digital divide? *Information Communication and Society, 24*(12), 1779–1796. DOI: 10.1080/1369118X.2020.1736124

Hall, S. (1980). Encoding/decoding. In *Culture, Media, Language. S.* Hall, D. Hobson, A. Lowe, A. and P. Willis (Eds.), *Culture, Media, Language* (pp.128-138). Hutchinson Press.

Hallin, D. C. (1985). The American news media: A critical theory perspective. *Critical Theory and Public Life, 121*, 146.

Harris, T. (2017, Apr). *How a handful of tech companies control billions of minds every day*. [Video]. TED Conferences. https://www.ted.com/talks/tristan_harris_how_a_handful_of_tech_companies_control_billions_of_minds_every_day

Henry, N. B. (1954). *Mass Media and Education. Fifty-Third Yearbook of NSSE (National Society For The Study Of Education), Part II*. University of Chicago Press.

Hobbs, R. (1998). The seven great debates in the media literacy movement. *Journal of Communication, 48*(1), 16–32. DOI: 10.1111/j.1460-2466.1998.tb02734.x

Hobbs, R. (2021). *Gallery of grandparents of media literacy*. Grandparents of Media Literacy. https://grandparentsofmedialiteracy.com/

Hobbs, R. (2025, Apr 27). How Media Literacy Education for Adults Advances Active Listening & Intellectual Humility. American Educational Research Association Annual Conference. Denver. https://aera25-aera.ipostersessions.com/default.aspx?s=85-AA-15-20-82-7B-5D-E2-EA-64-C6-4D-F3-53-7C-6C

Hobbs, R., & Jensen, A. (2009). The Past, Present, and Future of Media Literacy Education. *The Journal of Media Literacy Education, 1*(1), 1–11. DOI: 10.23860/jmle-1-1-1

Hoechsmann, M., Kumaran, B., & McKee, M. (2024, Jan). *What conspiracy? Media education in/and the mirror world* [Video]. Media Education Lab webinar. https://youtu.be/xyKSST3CRP0?si=jKbkU2GBnVOhjnZP

Howenstine, E. (1987). Environmental reporting: Shift from 1970 to 1982. *The Journalism Quarterly, 64*(4), 842–846. DOI: 10.1177/107769908706400425

Jolls, T., & Wilson, C. (2014). The core concepts: Fundamental to media literacy yesterday, today and tomorrow. *The Journal of Media Literacy Education, 6*(2), 68–78. DOI: 10.23860/jmle-6-2-6

Journalist's Resource. (2013, Aug 28). *The decline of big media, 1980s-2000s: Key lessons and trends*. Journalist's resource. https://journalistsresource.org/media/covering-america-journalism-professor-christopher-daly/

Kammerl, R., & Kramer, M. (2016). The changing media environment and its impact on socialization processes in families. *Studies in Communication Sciences, 16*(1), 21–27. DOI: 10.1016/j.scoms.2016.04.004

Kellner, D., & Share, J. (2007). Critical media literacy: Crucial policy choices for a twenty-first-century democracy. *Policy Futures in Education*, *5*(1), 59–69. DOI: 10.2304/pfie.2007.5.1.59

Kelly, K., & Donohew, L. (1999). Media and primary socialization theory. *Substance Use & Misuse*, *34*(7), 1033–1045. DOI: 10.3109/10826089909039395 PMID: 10359221

Klein, N. (2024). *Doppelganger: A trip into the mirror world*. Random House.

Laughey, D. (2010). *Key themes in media theory*. Open University Press.

Leedom, F. (2024, Feb 29). "Building media literacy into school curriculums worldwide". News Decoder. https://news-decoder.com/building-media-literacy-into-school-curriculums-worldwide/

Lester, P.M. (1996). "Digital hegemony: The clash between words and pictures". Speech given during the "Spring Forum" at Middle Tennessee State University, Murfreesboro, Tennessee, reprinted in the Instructor's Manual for Harris and Lester's *Visual Journalism* (2001).

Liebert, R., Sprafkin, J., & Davidson, E. (1982). *The early window: Effects of television on children and youth* (2nd ed.). Pergamon.

Lin, L., Gupta, N., Zhang, Y., Ren, H., Liu, C. H., Ding, F., . . . Hu, S. (2024). Detecting multimedia generated by large AI models: A survey. *arXiv preprint arXiv:2402.00045*. DOI: 10.36227/techrxiv.170723324.44685515/v1

Lippmann, W. (2020). *Liberty and the news* (p. 47). mediastudies. Press.

Livingstone, S. (2005). Media literacy – challenges ahead. London: LSE Research Online. http://eprints.lse.ac.uk/archive/00000551

Lull, J. (2002). Superculture for the communication age. In *Culture in the Communication Age* (pp. 142–174). Routledge. DOI: 10.4324/9780203136188-11

Main, P. (2022, Jan 17). *Cognitive Load Theory: A teacher's guide*. Retrieved from https://www.structural-learning.com/post/cognitive-load-theory-a-teachers-guide

Malik, H. M., Lepinkäinen, N., Alvesalo-Kuusi, A., & Viljanen, M. (2022). Social harms in an algorithmic context, *Justice. Power and Resistance*, *5*(3), 193–207. DOI: 10.1332/OYUA8095

McCammon, S. (2021, Jan 30). *Combating Misinformation When A Loved One Is Caught In A Web Of Conspiracies*. National Public Radio. https://www.wabe.org/combating-misinformation-when-a-loved-one-is-caught-in-a-web-of-conspiracies/

McCombs, M. (2005). A look at agenda-setting: Past, present and future. *Journalism Studies*, *6*(4), 543–557. DOI: 10.1080/14616700500250438

McCombs, M. E., & Shaw, D. L. (1993). The evolution of agenda-setting research: Twenty-five years in the marketplace of ideas. *Journal of Communication*, *43*(2), 58–67. DOI: 10.1111/j.1460-2466.1993.tb01262.x

McLuhan, M. (1964/2002). *Understanding media: The extensions of man*. MIT Press.

Merica, D. (2024, Aug 13). *Classes across the country help seniors interact with a world altered by AI.* AP News. https://apnews.com/article/seniors-artificial-intelligence-deepfake-education-classes-bc30958c273af7c79bfe77d321617738

Moss, S. (2022). The Prevalence of Artificial Intelligence, Surveillance Capitalism, Disinformation, and Biased Algorithms Amplify the Need for Critical Skills Applied to Media. *International Council For Media Literacy: Bridging Academia to Action* (online journal). https://ic4ml.org/journal-article/the-prevalence-of-artificial-intelligence-surveillance-capitalism-disinformation-and-biased-algorithms-amplify-the-need-for-critical-skills-applied-to-media/

Mubarak, F., & Suomi, R. (2022). Elderly forgotten? Digital exclusion in the information age and the rising grey digital divide. *Inquiry : a Journal of Medical Care Organization, Provision and Financing*, *59*, 00469580221096272. DOI: 10.1177/00469580221096272 PMID: 35471138

Neilsberg Research. (2025, Feb 22). *United States population by age - 2025 update*. Neilsberg. https://www.neilsberg.com/insights/united-states-population-by-age/

Newell, J. (2007). Revisiting Schramm's Radiotown: Media displacement and saturation. *Journal of Radio Studies*, *14*(1), 3–19. DOI: 10.1080/10955040701301722

Nossek, H., & Adoni, H. (2001). The New Media Consumers: Media Convergence and the Displacement Effect. *Communications*, *26*(1).

Notley, T., Chambers, S., Park, S., & Dezuanni, M. (2021). *Adult media literacy in Australia: Attitudes, experiences and needs. Research Report.* Western Sydney University.

Notley, T., Hourigan, A., & Thomson, T. J. (2025). *Addressing everyday experiences with misinformation* [Conference presentation]. Media Education Forum (online conference).

Nunan, D., & Di Domenico, M. (2019). Older Consumers, Digital Marketing, and Public Policy: A Review and Research Agenda. *Journal of Public Policy & Marketing*, *38*(4), 469–483. DOI: 10.1177/0743915619858939

Nussbaum, M. C. (2010). The liberal arts are not elitist. *The Chronicle of Higher Education*, 28.

O'Neil, C. (2017). *Weapons of math destruction*. Penguin Books.

Oeldorf-Hirsch, A., & Neubaum, G. (2025). What do we know about algorithmic literacy? The status quo and a research agenda for a growing field. *New Media & Society*, *27*(2), 681–701. DOI: 10.1177/14614448231182662

Olson, D. R. (1974). Media and symbols: The forms of expression, communication, and education. In Olson, D. R. (Ed.), *The 73rd Yearbook of the NSSE*. part 1 (pp. 1–24). National Society for the Study of Education.

Oremus, W. (2024, Dec 4). *Outraged? You're more likely to share misinformation, study finds.* Washington Post. https://www.washingtonpost.com/politics/2024/12/04/foreign-disinfo-2024-election-outrage-science-study/?itid=hp_latest-from-the-post_p003_f007

Palmer, E., & Fisch, S. M. (2001). The Beginnings of Sesame Street Research. In Fisch, S. M., & Truglio, R. T. (Eds.), *G" is for growing:Thirty years of research on children and Sesame Street* (pp. 3–24). Lawrence Erlbaum Publishers.

Pariser, E. (2011). *The filter bubble: What the Internet is hiding from you.* Viking/Penguin Press.

Park, S., Lee, J. Y., Notley, T., & Dezuanni, M. (2023). Exploring the relationship between media literacy, online interaction, and civic engagement. *The Information Society*, *39*(4), 250–261. DOI: 10.1080/01972243.2023.2211055

Pelly, S. (2013, Sep 2). *"Evening News" marks golden anniversary of 30-minute broadcast.* CBS News https://www.cbsnews.com/news/evening-news-marks-golden-anniversary-of-30-minute-broadcast/

Pollay, R. W. (1986). The distorted mirror: Reflections on the unintended consequences of advertising. *Journal of Marketing*, *50*(2), 18–36. DOI: 10.1177/002224298605000202

Postman, N. (1985). *Amusing ourselves to death: Public discourse in the age of show business*. Penguin.

Potter, W. J. (2010). The state of Media Literacy. *Journal of Broadcasting & Electronic Media*, *54*(4), 675–696. DOI: 10.1080/08838151.2011.521462

Prensky, M. (2001, Sep). Digital Natives, Digital Immigrants Part 1. *On the Horizon*, *9*(5), 1–6. https://revistas.ucm.es/index.php/ESMP/article/view/58020. DOI: 10.1108/10748120110424816

Rasi, P., Vuojärvi, H., & Rivinen, S. (2021). Promoting media literacy among older people: A systematic review. *Adult Education Quarterly*, *71*(1), 37–54. DOI: 10.1177/0741713620923755

Rasi-Heikkinen, P. (2025), *Promoting Older People's ML* [Conference session]. Media Education Forum, Online conference.

Rasi-Heikkinen, P., & Luksua, T. (2023). Increasing seniors' resilience against mis- and disinformation. Benchmarking report of training and materials provided for seniors in Europe. https://www.wearesum.eu/wp-content/uploads/SUM_D2.1_Updated-Benchmarking-report.pdf

Roberts, D. F., & Foehr, U. G. (2010, Apr). *Youth: Trends in Media Use*. CYC Net. https://cyc-net.org/cyc-online/cyconline-apr2010-roberts.html

Ropek, L. (2024, Dec 6). *Billionaire owner of LA Times plans to use AI-powered 'bias meter' on news*. Gizmodo. https://gizmodo.com/the-la-times-billionaire-owner-plans-to-use-an-ai-powered-bias-meter-on-editorials-2000535126

Rubin, A. M. (1998). Media literacy. *Journal of Communication*, *48*(1), 3–4. DOI: 10.1111/j.1460-2466.1998.tb02732.x

Schwarz, G. (2005). Overview: What is Media Literacy, who Cares, and Why? *Teachers College Record*, *107*(13), 5–17. DOI: 10.1177/016146810810701301

Scott, L. M. (1994). Images in Advertising: The Need for a Theory of Visual Rhetoric. *The Journal of Consumer Research*, *21*(2), 252–273. DOI: 10.1086/209396

Severin, W. J., & Tankard, J. W. (2001). *Communication theories: Origins, methods, and uses in the mass media*. Longman.

Sparks, G. G. (2015). *Media effects research: A basic overview* (5th ed.). Thomson/Wadsworth Press.

Spikes, M. A., & Calvert, K. (2024, Dec 11). *Media Literacy Education for Adult Audiences: Exploring ChatGPT and Conversational AI*. Programming Librarian - ALA. [Webinar] https://events.callacademy.org/event/media-literacy-education-adult-audiences-exploring-chatgpt-and-conversational-8698

Stein, L., & Prewett, A. (2009). Media literacy education in the social studies: Teacher perceptions and curricular challenges. *Teacher Education Quarterly*, *36*(1), 131–148.

Steinberg, C. S. (1980). *TV facts*. Facts on File, Inc.

Stoll, J. (2024, Nov 9). *Breakdown of cord cutters in the U.S. 2022, by age*. Statistica. https://www.statista.com/statistics/782564/usa-cord-cutter-distribution-by-age/

Subramanian, K. R. (2018). Myth and mystery of shrinking attention span. *International Journal of Trend in Research and Development*, *5*(3), 1–6.

Sullivan, A. (2009, Sep 26). *The daily dish: The ethics of photo cropping*. The Atlantic. https://www.theatlantic.com/daily-dish/archive/2009/09/the-ethics-of-photo-cropping/196090/

Sweller, J. (1994). Cognitive load theory, learning difficulty, and instructional design. *Learning and Instruction*, *4*(4), 295–312. DOI: 10.1016/0959-4752(94)90003-5

Tacheva, J., & Ramasubramanian, S. (2023). AI Empire: Unraveling the interlocking systems of oppression in generative AI's global order. *Big Data & Society*, *10*(2), 20539517231219241. Advance online publication. DOI: 10.1177/20539517231219241

Thalmann, M., Souza, A. S., & Oberauer, K. (2019). How does chunking help working memory? *Journal of Experimental Psychology. Learning, Memory, and Cognition*, *45*(1), 37–55. DOI: 10.1037/xlm0000578 PMID: 29698045

Thoman, E., & Jolls, T. (2004). Media literacy—A national priority for a changing world. *The American Behavioral Scientist*, *48*(1), 18–29. DOI: 10.1177/0002764204267246

Tilley, C. L. (2012). Seducing the innocent: Fredric Wertham and the falsifications that helped condemn comics. *Information & Culture*, *47*(4), 383–413. DOI: 10.1353/lac.2012.0024

Troy, G. (2005). *Morning in America: how Ronald Reagan invented the 1980s*. Princeton University Press.

Tsamados, A., Aggarwal, N., Cowls, J., Morley, J., Roberts, H., Taddeo, M., & Floridi, L. (2021). The ethics of algorithms: key problems and solutions. *Ethics, governance, and policies in artificial intelligence*, 97-123.

Tufekci, Z. (2015) Algorithmic harms beyond Facebook and Google: emergent challenges of computational agency. *Colorado Technology Law Journal*, (13) 203. https:// ctlj.colorado.edu/wp-content/uploads/2015/08/Tufekci-final.pdf

UNESCO. (1978/79). Mass Media Declaration. *Journal of Communication*, *29*(2), 190–191.

UNESCO. (2024/25). *Media and Information Literacy Course for Adult Educators launched* https://www.uil.unesco.org/en/articles/media-and-information-literacy-course-adult-educators-launched

Valtonen, T., Tedre, M., Mäkitalo, K., & Vartiainen, H. (2019). Media Literacy Education in the Age of Machine Learning. *The Journal of Media Literacy Education, 11*(2), 20–36. DOI: 10.23860/JMLE-2019-11-2-2

van Nooijen, C. C., de Koning, B. B., Bramer, W. M., Isahakyan, A., Asoodar, M., Kok, E., van Merrienboer, J. J., & Paas, F. (2024). A Cognitive Load Theory Approach to Understanding Expert Scaffolding of Visual Problem-Solving Tasks: A Scoping Review. *Educational Psychology Review, 36*(1), 12. DOI: 10.1007/s10648-024-09848-3

Van Peer, W. (1988). Reading, culture and modern mass media. *Journal of Information Science, 14*(5), 305–309. DOI: 10.1177/016555158801400508

Wartella, E., & Reeves, B. (1985). Historical Trends in Research on Children and the Media: 1900–1960. *Journal of Communication, 35*(2), 118–133. DOI: 10.1111/j.1460-2466.1985.tb02238.x

Wartella, E. A., & Jennings, N. (2000). Children and computers: New technology. Old concerns. *The Future of Children, 10*(2), 31–43. DOI: 10.2307/1602688 PMID: 11255707

Wertham, F. (1954). V The Curse or the Comic Books: The value patterns and effects of comic books. *Religious Education (Chicago, Ill.), 49*(6), 394–406. DOI: 10.1080/0034408540490605

KEY TERMS AND DEFINITIONS

:

Boomers: A slang expression for "Baby Boomers", referring to people born in the US before 1963.

Critical Media Literacy: Understood in relation to the writings of Kellner & Share (2007), this approach to literacy studies merges with critical cultural studies, and interrogates ways power relationships are created and perpetuated.

Media Aesthetics: A perspective in pedagogy which is interested in understanding media content and products as forms of creative expression

Media Landscape: The combination of available media options at a given time. This may include experiences with communication tools used by or for mass media, for group and/or interpersonal communication, or for creative expression.

Media Production Technology Training: A perspective in pedagogy which is interested in training learners to obtain practical and/or vocational skills related to making media.

Protectionist Approach to Media Literacy: A perspective in pedagogy which is interested in protecting media users from harms associated with media exposures and uses.

Section 3
Education on the Edge: Teaching Transformative Media Literacy

Chapter 7
Critical Thinking, Media, and Smart Technologies:
Edu-Communication the New Frontier of Digital Literacy

Daniele Battista
https://orcid.org/0009-0005-8418-8374
University of Salerno, Italy

Francesca Cubeddu
IRPPS-CNR of Rome, Italy

Lucia Picarella
University of Foggia, Mercato San Severino, Italy

ABSTRACT

Contemporary societies are increasingly shaped by participative and interconnected logics, with digital platforms playing a key role in reshaping social, cultural, and economic interactions. These platforms are spaces for exchange and the redefinition of data flows, where two-way interaction between consumption and production is central. Digital platforms have gained importance in education, especially through media literacy programs. This article explores the diffusion of edu-communication in Latin America, based on liberative education, popular communication, and cultural studies. It analyzes edu-communication as a tool to enhance intersubjectivity, focusing on the individual and media interactions, and reframing socio-cultural practices with political implications. The article is divided into three parts: challenges of digital media in education, the need for new media education, and the Latin American perspective on edu-communication.

DOI: 10.4018/979-8-3373-0872-2.ch007

INTRODUCTION

Digital platforms and technologies have acquired strategic value in reshaping the ways in which social, cultural and economic interaction takes place in modern societies, where participation and interconnectedness are increasingly prevalent. Information and communication technologies (ICT) have revolutionised many universal perspectives (Castells, 1996). The online ecosystem has established itself as a global interconnected network in which the elements and content of many types are generated, disseminated and reproduced seamlessly (Salzano et al. 2023). The digital revolution and the resulting transformations undoubtedly raise numerous questions and issues relating to the crossroads between communication processes and new frontiers such as intelligent systems, the significant socio-cultural impact, and the reconstruction of traditional paradigms of authority and power. With specific reference to the subject of this study, there is the ability to outline the centre of future trajectories in education.

In this context, the internet has established itself as the new organisational model of our society. The democratisation of access to technology has fostered the promotion of individual and collective empowerment, creating the possibility for everyone to be an active part of the information society. Digital ecosystems and the virtual sphere have replaced offline social spaces for public relations. They have allowed individuals to interact on an equal footing that transcends any space-time barriers. Furthermore, cutting-edge devices and technologies not only facilitate the use of content but also allow users to participate actively, enabling them to play the dual role of both producers and consumers of information. The two-way interaction between consumption and production is one of the most significant features supporting the development of a real collective digital culture. Digital platforms and ecosystems have become both places where social reality can be discussed, redefined and re-signified, as well as catalysts in the field of education and training.

Boccia Artieri's (2012) observation regarding the redefinition of the dynamics of the production, distribution and consumption of symbolic forms of society through blogs, social networks, and wiki-style cooperative production provides an important basis when analysing the educational potential of digital applications. Numerous studies, particularly those which use the social learning and connectivism approach, such as Siemens (2005), have highlighted the advantages that such platforms can bring to learning and teaching. They emphasise how beneficial it is to work together in learning environments designed with specific educational objectives and environments created for recreational and social purposes. Digital media and smart technologies diversify and amplify the ways in which learning objectives are achieved. They offer a wide range of spaces and support that facilitate the creation of personalised pathways that are extremely well suited to specific needs. Furthermore, they are enhanced by educational innovations introduced by artificial intelligence, which increase the effectiveness of the search for more accessible and practical training pathways by tailoring each stage to the specific requirements of each element, along with intelligent tutoring systems based on machine learning algorithms.

However, the growing importance of studies on this topic also highlights the presence of more sceptical positions within the broader context of the research. The current debate is characterised by a careful assessment of the strengths and weaknesses, as well as the prospects and risks arising from the implementation of these tools in educational design.

In this sense, to develop more informed and balanced educational strategies, we highlight the complex dynamics of addiction (Kuss & Griffiths, 2017) that can emerge when attempting to incorporate social networks into education. Similarly, the introduction of artificial intelligence into the educational world is seen as a frontier between benefits and risks (Yue et al. 2022). This is due to the absence of any significant comprehensive information on measuring the impact of these resources, along with the difficulty of resolving issues of ethics, privacy, authenticity and autonomy of learning. There are also problems concerning the excessive standardisation of the educational experience caused by the automation of the training process to the detriment of the development of creativity and originality. This misalignment shows the complexity of the problem as well as the need for a joint effort between the educational, socio-political and technological spheres to create shared standards that balance innovation and responsibility. It should allow for the impact of digital technology on learning to be assessed in an objective and cross-cutting way.

Digital technology has played an important role in the transformation of educational processes in recent years, offering new opportunities to rethink the various methodologies currently in use. Consequently, the integration of new technologies in educational contexts is essential to not only achieve new learning objectives but also to replace or complement traditional educational practices. This intersection should critically and consciously consider the role of education and communication in the age of technological innovation. It should leave aside any excessive enthusiasm or, conversely, radical opposition, since the open questions related to digital technology in the socio-educational field are growing rapidly as its impact is becoming increasingly evident.

While on the one hand, the growing dependence on technology has led to distortions in learning, in the dissemination of information, in the perception of the individual, as well as in social relations. On the other hand, there is a need expressed by young people to conceive a more interactive approach, typical of their everyday lives, to the dynamics of study and learning. If used properly, the adoption of educational technologies can be an opportunity to reinvent the concept of education and bring it closer to the needs of today's societies. In this sense, digital ecosystems and platforms can be used not only to facilitate access to information, but above all to promote the development of critical, creative and communication skills. To stop any problems and negative effects, it is therefore essential to implement digital literacy aimed at investing in education, along with a critical understanding of the potential of digital environments and technologies.

Digital literacy involves the spread of digital systems, language and communication processes. There is widespread use of media, but above all, their potential for communication as a bridge and link between different realities (Boccia Artieri, Colombo & Gili, 2022; McLuhan, 1964). Improving both individual and collective knowledge as well as awareness transforms digital literacy into an incisive and transformative variable with a significant impact in terms of reducing social inequalities and marginalisation, i.e., creating a more equitable and resilient education system to face future developments. Only through digital equity is digital education and digital systems possible (Tirocchi, 2013; Belluati, Tirocchi, 2023).

Reducing digital inequality and increasing the awareness of digital systems, communication, and interaction is a point of contact with the Latin American vision of edu-communication. A field of study and experience based on the theoretical currents of liberating education, popular communication and cultural studies. The mission of Latin American edu-communication has traditionally been to foster active and participatory citizenship through dynamic and interactive educational methods, along with learning practices aimed at creating collective and group knowledge. The two-way, participatory communication component linked to the use of audiovisual and digital technologies accompanies teaching and learning processes, intertwining them with a high degree of critical reflection in a cultural, social and political sense.

In the complex scenario of Latin America, edu-communication has therefore integrated digital literacy with a set of dialogical and conceptualising strategies. Its aim is to transform the vision of education into a vehicle for social justice as well as the extension and protection of human rights into praxis, thus representing a tool of opposition and resistance to neoliberal models and logics (Antonucci, Sorice, Volterrani, 2024). Considering the challenges posed by the platformisation of today's societies, edu-communication, understood as a dialogic process inseparable from critical educational and communicative practice, can represent a new frontier in the debates on digital and AI literacy, pointing towards alternative perspectives, approaches and proposals that are more responsive to the evolutionary complexity of the contemporary world.

EDUCATION, DIGITAL MEDIA AND SOCIAL MEDIA: CHALLENGES AND OPPORTUNITIES FOR DIGITAL LEARNING

Some platforms and social media are relatively new, but their evolution has been a significant technological phenomenon of the last century. Despite this, there is still no agreement on how to comprehensively assess the effects of these technologies. The words used to describe the problem of addiction to digital media, and social media in particular, vary widely (Varona *et al.* 2022). Most of the studies have focused on the consequences that this addiction can have on people's mental health and well-being (Elmer *et al.* 2020). However, an analysis of the data on the use and spread of not only mobile devices but also digital and social platforms is essential to fully understand the extent of this phenomenon.

The latest edition of the Digital 2024 report reveals that the number of social media users has reached a new record of 5.04 billion, equivalent to 62% of the world's population. The average time people spend online each day has reached 6 hours and 40 minutes, and of this time, a full 2 hours and 23 minutes are spent on social media, thus confirming the steady growth of these platforms as the main source of information, entertainment and communication at the expense of traditional mass media such as television, which continues its downward trend. Among the platforms that keep us glued to our screens, TikTok stands out with 34 hours per month and YouTube with 28 hours per month.

Williams (2018) had already presented worrying information about growing addiction, highlighting the degree of user participation. On average, people check their mobile phones 150 times a day and touch them 2,600 times a day. Furthermore, estimates indicate that mobile devices are the last thing people look at before going to sleep. The importance of a comprehensive understanding of the effects of digital ecosystems on everyday life is made clear by these data and the growing research being conducted on this topic. The ever-increasing prevalence of these technologies and digital media requires a critical analysis and awareness of the risks associated with their excessive use. This implies the urgency of additional studies and research to address this phenomenon effectively and comprehensively. In addition to this fundamental consideration, it is necessary to highlight the essential assumption that digital media and social platforms have become an essential and inescapable part of contemporary human existence, significantly influencing social, cultural, psychological and ethical systems in modern society. The proliferation of these platforms has led to a variety of complex dynamics that affect the way people communicate, relate to each other and share information, creating not only new opportunities but also significant challenges. Regarding the latter, the main issues include privacy management, the spread of disinformation, the creation of information bubbles and how we perceive ourselves in relation to others through dynamics of exhibitionism and social comparison. While it is undeniable that these platforms have had a significant impact on contemporary human life, it is equally important to consider the wide range of problems arising from this phenomenon, which go far beyond personal use.

To fully understand the role and impact of this technology in modern society and to develop appropriate strategies and policies to address the challenges and maximise the benefits of this increasingly widespread technology, a multidimensional approach is needed. The ongoing digital transition poses new challenges, making innovation a cross-cutting issue, while reshaping all the models and forms of social organisation. Consequently, the models of analysis, research and dissemination in the humanities are all influenced to a greater or lesser extent by digitalisation and the essential components of the new knowledge society. Current scientific debates are taking place in an increasingly complex and rapidly evolving context. It is characterised by the growth of sophisticated technologies and the explosion of digital media and social networks, which have profoundly reconfigured the ways of interacting and communication processes both online and offline.

The Internet era of the 2010s, the age of social media, differs significantly from the Internet era of the 1990s and 2000s, the age of cyberspace (Smith *et al.* 2021). The Internet of 2012 can no longer be traced back to a linear, unidirectional system of operation, in which a single user passively receives data, information and resources from a relatively limited and selected number of content providers. Today's Internet can be driven (and to some extent defined) by the activities of ordinary users, a concept known as 'many-to-many' rather than 'one-to-many' (Gillespie, 2010). Moreover, users in the context of digital ecosystems have undergone a significant transformation. They are no longer considered mere passive consumers of content, but rather actively involved in the mutual creation of content and digital interaction. Users connect to the network with the intention of sharing, evaluating, incorporating, remixing, making friends and participating in emerging trends.

In many ways, all these activities can be conceived as genealogical archiving processes, i.e. acts that include sharing content, establishing interpersonal connections, evaluating cultural elements and actively producing digital content (Poell *et al.* 2021). In this new digital dynamic, users have become active agents and participants in the construction and circulation of knowledge. Their involvement is no longer limited to a passive role of reception but rather encompasses a wide range of creative and relational activities. This phenomenon reflects a trend towards a user-centric culture, in which the creation and distribution of content are democratised, allowing individuals to have a central impact on the production and circulation of information.

It is clear that new technologies and digital means of communication are becoming increasingly integrated into everyday practices. They affect profound and complex experiences such as education and learning, knowledge exchange, human relationships and hybrid human-machine relationships (Castells, 2000; Boccia Artieri 2006,

2018; Van Dijck *et al.* 2018). The impressive evolution of educational paradigms has been observed in contemporary societies around the world. There is a growing commitment to open educational policies as well as to promote access to education through a greater use of digital media and technologies. The intrinsic goal of these initiatives is to eliminate inequalities in education by removing traditional barriers to access to formal schools.

Digital and social media platforms, which serve as digital ecosystems where people can interact, collaborate and share content, have shown tremendous potential as a driving force for open access to education in this context. It is therefore essential to analyse the specific resources and functionalities of these platforms to facilitate the distribution and sharing of educational resources. It is also important to highlight the advantages of an open and collaborative approach to learning, since access to high-quality educational resources can act as a catalyst for bridging gaps in formal education while offering opportunities for personalised and flexible learning.

Given that these platforms are widely used and easily accessible, some studies seem to find limited benefit in terms of learning from their interaction (Amsalem & Zoizner, 2023). This assertion plays a crucial role in creating a solid conceptual framework as well as in gaining an in-depth understanding of the underlying phenomena under investigation. The starting point is the awareness that one of the main challenges in contemporary education is the need to redefine and reconfigure the educational space to adapt it to a constantly evolving society. In this context, digital media and social media, which are one of the distinctive features of the Web 2.0 paradigm, must be subject to an in-depth analysis that goes beyond the apparent perception of mass distraction devices, especially considering their undeniable appeal among the younger generations (Battista, 2024). On the contrary, they should be understood as an educational resource since they are characterised by their fundamental focus on interaction and their ability to facilitate immediate and persuasive communication (Salzano & Battista, 2022). Greenhow (2011), for example, expresses appreciation for the pedagogical adaptation of open social network environments. She considers these platforms capable of initiating a learning process in various ways because they have the potential to generate social and civic benefits, both online and offline, with significant positive implications for the field of education.

Some also highlight how digital ecosystems can encourage people to share their personal and professional interests and aspirations, which are often neglected in traditional study contexts. At the same time, these tools allow online resources created by external participants to be catalogued, organised and annotated, thus extending sharing beyond the limits imposed by conventional educational and training courses. In line with these observations, it is emphasised that their conscious use can provide a socio-relational substrate, ranging from informal relationships to links with professional communities, and a cognitive substrate, through the exchange of knowledge and skills, which can be effectively integrated with formal e-learning courses (Salzano & Battista, 2023).

These approaches confirm the important role that these structures can play in learning, providing a dynamic and socially interactive learning environment that goes beyond traditional educational approaches, while promoting the development of personal and professional skills. For this reason, the reality of constant change requires a critical and thoughtful perspective on the use of digital ecosystems in the educational context. They can represent a vast territory of opportunities for learning. Their intrinsic ability to facilitate interaction and promote rapid and effective communication provides fertile ground for the implementation of innovative teaching strategies.

For some time now, there has been a growing urgency to effectively address the inherent challenges posed by these tools, with an emphasis on integrated approaches aimed at creating more sophisticated educational contexts that are conducive to interaction and learning activities, while always taking into account the digital divide that prevents widespread penetration (Ragnedda, 2017). It is also worth recalling that access to information is no longer a simple passive reception of content, but rather a dynamic process in which the production, consumption and circulation of news take place on interactive digital platforms. The transformations in the way news is created and shared — often by non-professional users — require new skills to navigate a complex and sometimes opaque information ecosystem.

The challenges associated with disinformation, the algorithmic manipulation of content and the emergence of generative artificial intelligence systems urgently raise the issue of news literacy, i.e. the critical ability to evaluate, interpret and contextualise information (Koltay, 2011). In this scenario, media literacy is integrated with AI literacy, offering an educational model that not only enables the decoding of media messages but also the understanding of the technological processes that regulate their dissemination (Su et al., 2023). This imperative considers the growing awareness that the adoption of technological and online resources in the educational context requires a comprehensive strategy that goes beyond a fragmented approach. Such a strategy must be conceived as a coherent and synergistic system capable of harmonising the various dimensions of technology-mediated education. It is a call to consider these tools not only as mere means of communication or sharing, but also as an integral part of a broader and well-structured educational environment.

From this perspective, it is possible to identify the fundamental characteristics of any practice related to digital media and social platforms, such as large-scale socialisation and mass participation. These characteristics refer to the ability to exploit the power of collective actions undertaken by groups of online users, in which actions are closely intertwined with the dynamics of social participation and relationality (Dolata & Schrape, 2016). From this perspective, it is a question of understanding communication and educational ecosystems in virtual environments, creating actions, and promoting innovative strategies through a renewed vision of media education and digital literacy that also takes into account the new challenges posed by developments in artificial intelligence applications. Latin America, in this sense, offers a fertile ground for analysing edu-communicative practices which, rooted in a critical and participatory perspective, promote media literacy geared towards social transformation and awareness (Mateus, et al. 2019). Including the topic of news and information in this framework means not only strengthening the critical dimension of education but also reaffirming the role of the media as spaces for the democratic and dialogic construction of reality.

FROM DIGITAL LITERACY TO AI LITERACY FOR EDUCATION IN NEW MEDIA

The first section analysed the evolution of digital systems and how they have brought about social and cultural change. Their evolution follows that of the social system and *vice versa*. The media are a means of "cultural expression and communication" that enable active participation in social life. They are also «the most significant agent of socialisation in contemporary society and have now taken the place of the family, the church and the school» (Buckingham, 2003, p. 23). They are increasingly pervasive in people's daily lives and activities (Rampazzo Gambarato, Heuman, 2024), to the extent that they are considered possible tools (Pelaez et al., 2021) applicable both at work and in the organisation of daily life, in the management of relationships and social dynamics. Digital platforms have replaced real environments, becoming true "social spaces beyond the virtual" (Castells, 2001).

Digital media and social media can not only be a potential resource for communication and an open space for socialisation (Boyd, 2014), but also a place of risk (Livingstone, Haddon, 2009; Smahel et al., 2020), where the vulnerabilities of certain social groups are more evident and targeted. In light of the importance but also the significant effects that digital platforms and technologies have acquired over the years in the social and cultural sphere, the educational sector has also begun to question the negative and positive effects of the use and application of new technologies and digital platforms, highlighting the urgent need to define models of knowledge and education of digital ecosystems, their use and their activities. It is precisely in the management of the effects and future impacts mentioned in the first paragraph that the urgent need has been identified to develop educational programmes that focus on digital literacy geared towards the implementation of a praxis of digital media and platforms. In this perspective, the importance of an educational approach that insists on promoting critical thinking with regard to the use of and actions carried out in the media and digital platforms is emphasised in order to counteract, through education, the various negative effects (Frizzo, 2024; Cubeddu, Scocco, 2024) encapsulated, for example, in the macro-phenomenon of cyberviolence.

This phenomenon is a multidimensional construct that represents numerous phenomena with specific characteristics such as cyberbullying, cyberstalking, and hate speech dynamics (Backe Backe, Lilleston, McCleary-Sills, 2018; Peterson, Densley, 2017; Hellsten et al., 2021). These are trends that have specific characteristics. They are distinguished by being rooted in power/domination dynamics and social inequality, in which power disparities between different social groups emerge strongly (Waldron, 2012). When a dominant group perceives a threat to its status or privileges, it can use hate speech as a means of belittling and marginalising groups perceived as 'other' (Delgado, Stefancic, 2017).

Online hate speech (Cubeddu, Scocco, 2024), due to its digital nature, has specific characteristics. The vastness and anonymity of the web can amplify the reach and intensity of hate speech, making victims more vulnerable and perpetrators often unpunished (Petrilli 2019; Ferrini, Paris, 2019). Considering it as a subset of cyberviolence, it can be understood as a form of digital attack which, although based on words, can have tangible and harmful consequences (Barendt, 2019), including social exclusion, psychological damage and, in some cases, violent actions in the real world.

In light of the above, digital education has established itself over time as one of the main variables in combating these dynamics, encouraging interaction with young people to understand the practice and relationship between digital technologies and the social and cultural system. As early as 1985, British scholar Len Masterman considered "media as symbolic or representational systems", focusing on the representational dimension of digital media, viewing them as languages, images that narrate a referent outside themselves. This is another representation of the self that requires a specific language, interpretation and decoding. These skills must be acquired by individuals not only through the use of digital media and platforms, but also through an understanding of language, its meaning and its construction. This is a communication process that belongs to a digital culture and distinguishes only those who have a conscious knowledge of its application.

Digital media are a central element in the social system and in the lives of individuals, as they condition their socialisation. It is for this reason that they are an element on which to educate (Tirocchi, 2013; Belluati, Tirocchi, 2023). Young people grow up in contact with the media and quickly learn how to use them without being aware of their effects and impact. With the *Grünwald Declaration on Media Education and the subsequent International Congress on Media Education*, held in Germany in 1982, media education began to be proposed as an educational tool for young people. It was recognised that exposure to the media and digital platforms entails numerous risks, especially for the youngest (Livingstone, Blum-Ross, 2020). In June 2007, UNESCO promoted a meeting in Paris to celebrate the anniversary of the Grünwald Declaration (Germany), emphasising that political and educational systems must promote a critical understanding of the phenomenon of modern communication determined by the media and social media.

Twelve recommendations have been drawn up with the aim of identifying the relationship between education and the media[1](UNESCO, 2007). The innovation brought about by these twelve points laid the foundations for *digital literacy*, focusing on media literacy and studies, the relationship between digital skills and education systems, media studies and evaluation through widespread media education and, finally, raising awareness and mobilising political actors. These points sought to highlight how it is necessary not only to strengthen educational awareness of the media but also to seek to understand how important it is to raise awareness and mobilise the various social actors to educate and generate a culture of change. This includes the dual nature of the media, which is to disseminate information, create communication networks and bring cultures closer together. While at the same time having various negative impacts caused by the loss of one's own reality and the definition of the boundary between the real world and the digital world.

Media education aims to create media literacy and empowerment (Doni, 2015) through education *about* the media, education *with* the media, and education *for* the media. These three different approaches aim to help young people, including through school education, to acquire the appropriate tools to recognise and counteract the negative effects of the media. According to UNESCO (2024), through Media and Information Literacy (MIL), it is possible to create societies in which people, through competence in information, communication and technology, participate consciously in social activities because they understand their importance and opportunities. This type of education aims to enable citizens of all levels and ages (UNESCO, 2021a) to think critically and interact consciously and ethically with applications and their content.

Educational support enables people to learn about and be aware of both the potential and the risks. This allows for a change in access to and use of information. As the media are now an integral part of our lives, it is important at an educational and social level to consider media education as a form of civic education for the new millennium, understanding the distinctive differences between reality and virtual reality (Rivoltella, Rossi, 2019). It is through media education that it is possible to understand the language used in and by the media and digital platforms to then be able to communicate correctly and use these systems correctly (Friesem, Raman, Kanižaj & Choi, 2023; Landry & Fastrez, 2023). According to Gálik (2017), digital ecosystems, platforms and cyberspace in general influence educational processes in terms of the organisation, planning, learning and understanding of information, since they have immediate effects and future impacts not only on learning ability, but also on communication, expression and interpretation. Digital platforms and different media have evolved over the years, to the point where we now talk about new digital media that aim for immediacy and immediate results, as is the case with artificial intelligence, where the solution is immediate and at our fingertips.

With the spread of artificial intelligence, questions are being asked about its effects and impact. Attention is beginning to shift from digital media to AI. The advent of artificial intelligence raises other issues – relating to ethics, privacy and the authenticity of learning – which are leading to the development of specific regulatory frameworks, methodologies and educational processes. A process of digital media literacy is beginning to spread, focusing specifically on artificial intelligence as a new digital tool. Artificial intelligence opens new horizons, revealing different aspects, the first of which is a tendency to replace the human mind with an artificial one in various everyday activities. Although humans have always used technology to help them carry out their work, with AI they have reached the pinnacle of being able to interact on equal terms with a mind that uses their own language and with which they can discuss different topics.

A second application of Artificial Intelligence is the ability to manage large amounts of data and to bring together different elements to build a database of information, which, however, is not always correct. While it is used to create, formulate and solve (texts, images, problems, calculations), these materials are not always correct. Only if this application is used correctly is it possible to obtain products that are unique but also real and truthful.

Artificial intelligence is a tool with great potential that can be used to study different applications, but at the same time, it needs to be understood. While other digital media as a whole are now more understandable and definable, artificial intelligence still requires precise study aimed at understanding how it works, evaluating its algorithms and developing an awareness of its uses and applications. This makes it possible to use the machine's full potential by knowing how to guide it towards the correct application. Knowledge of the mechanisms involved leads to the successful development of products, avoiding negative effects such as ethical issues and the spread of false and untruthful information (Joyce, Cruz, 2024).

Investments in Artificial Intelligence have led to the creation of software applications ranging from clinical algorithms and autonomous vehicles to generative AI tools (GAI) such as ChatGPT. In 2021, the first studies on data policy, algorithms and code, and the social formation of Artificial Intelligence in practice emerged (Joyce et al., 2021). Political institutions themselves have shown considerable interest in artificial intelligence, which has also led to growing cultural and educational interest. Today's artificial intelligence is an evolution of the same, and its central element is its self-learning, which conditions its use (UNESCO, 2021b) and also determines its applicability in the educational context (Miao, Holmes, 2023; DNE-TN2, 2024).

There is a growing amount of research on the positive applications of AI, which can be used as a learning tool to assist teachers and stimulate learners (Nabeel Gillani *et al.* 2023; Miao, Holmes, 2023; DNE-TN2, 2024) or as cognitive assistance in knowledge development (Scott, 2022). In its definition of *Media and Information Literacy* (MIL), UNESCO (2024) observes it as a combined set of skills, knowledge and attitudes aimed at the process of learning and applying critical thinking for the creation and dissemination of digital information and content. Furthermore, the use of artificial intelligence by all individuals is an element of evaluation and analysis of the educational process, since it takes into account the ethical aspects of its use, both in terms of its application and usefulness as well as in terms of the relationship between human capabilities and artificial intelligence. With the advent of artificial intelligence, the definition of AI literacy (Long & Magerko, 2020, p. 2) has also been established, which aims to teach the skills necessary to critically evaluate different artificial intelligence technologies, while at the same time consciously understanding the possible positive and negative applications of AI in everyday life.

The use of media and artificial intelligence puts the role of education at the centre, which must be critical and based on different educational plans. Firstly, starting from a consideration of the knowledge and methods of use of technologies, different media, social media, and digital technologies. Secondly, an analysis of the acquisition of skills and knowledge, including how these technologies can be exploited. Finally, ensuring that everyone can use them in order to disseminate these educational processes. These three perspectives generate awareness of the use of technology and digital media, while also promoting the development of new skills and a new method of learning.

Education plays a central role not only in providing individuals with the skills they need to navigate this intricate digital sea (Lee, 2014; Guèvremont, Brin, 2024) but also in educating them on how to use it. Technological and digital literacy is both a resource for improving learning and a determining factor for individual success and the reduction of social inequalities, to the extent that it stands out as an incisive and transformative factor for reaching as yet unknown frontiers (Reddy, 2020). Digital media education aims to promote forms of critical literacy, raise awareness, educate on use and, finally, evaluate the benefits and possible negative effects.

Digital literacy is, therefore, a fundamental element in understanding both the benefits produced by digital media and technology as well as the negative effects and impacts not only from applications and prolonged use but also from communication, from the products created (taking artificial intelligence into account) and, finally, from digital inequality, determined by the possibility of access to certain technologies. The ability to understand communication ecosystems in virtual environments, creating actions and promoting strategies, including through the ability to analyse the media, i.e. through media education, involves analysing learning dynamics and utilising and implementing its benefits, which can be expressed through the practice of *edu-communication* (Antonucci, Sorice, Volterrani, 2024), which is highly active and critical in Latin America. The aim is therefore to promote digital media and artificial intelligence education to generate social inclusion and spread a culture of equity in the use of such systems.

CRITICAL DIGITAL EDUCATION AND COMMUNICATION IN LATIN AMERICA

Education goes far beyond the mere transmission of knowledge, ensuring the development of socio-emotional skills, critical thinking, creativity and civic awareness. The «artifactual and infrastructural dimension of culture» (Dussel and Trujillo Reyes, 2018, p. 171) highlights the configuration of our present and shows the different trajectories of how cultural practices in general, and digital media in particular, enter the educational sphere. The combination of human interaction and new digital technologies during the learning process enhances opportunities for access. However, in the Latin American context, its full expression in education often comes up against structural limitations related to overcoming the digital divide, the lack of infrastructure and specialised human capital, the lack of accessibility and interoperability, along with the updating of legislation on gender equality, interculturalism and human rights.

The debate in Latin America seems to be polarised between proponents of AI and new technologies as tools for universalising education, and critics who, on the contrary, see them as risks that could exacerbate existing inequalities. With the aim of harnessing the potential offered by the application of AI and new technologies and reducing their negative impacts, joint action is needed between the state as an agent of development, dissemination and guarantee of the right to education, and in particular, the educational sphere linked to training, learning, and the promotion of critical thinking.

The complexity of Latin American societies makes it imperative to make strategic choices to ensure equity and social justice, transformed into practice through education, which must be understood first and foremost as a human right. If we consider education as the only tool capable of fostering an effective relationship between the social system and the individual (Durkheim, 1922), and therefore as a transformative factor for socio-cultural progress, it becomes necessary to reflect on what perspectives and methods can promote its transformation from a privilege for the few to a human right as well as a social right.

Historically, this reflection has been even more pressing for Latin America, which has identified critical edu-communication as the tool and sphere of transformative practice for achieving social justice, inclusion, respect for human rights and fundamental freedoms, and democratisation. In the Latin American view, the democratisation of education implies a reinterpretation of the entire field of education and communication processes in a humanistic and not merely professionalising sense, to build different social alternatives through the enhancement of individuals' critical abilities and their conscious participation in society.

Critical edu-communication originated in the popular and community movements of Latin America, from the practical experience of educator-communicators who see the relationship between communication and education as a critical and transformative field of action (Toth et al., 2012). In this perspective, the basic theoretical and methodological framework of Latin American critical edu-communication represents the crossroads between progressive visions of education as a social process of democratisation, inclusion and resistance (Dewey, 1997; de Sousa Santos, 2009), the critical approach of the Frankfurt School and Cultural Studies, and the dialogical-participatory criteria of Liberation Theology, Liberation Pedagogy and Freirean Pedagogy of the Oppressed (Freire, 1998; 2005).

The correlation between these perspectives shifts the focus of Latin American edu-communication towards forms of education and pedagogy of communication and learning processes, marking an epistemological and methodological departure from European (Picarella, 2024a) and Anglo-Saxon (Fraser, Wardle, 2013) perspectives. Latin American critical edu-communication considers an important but often overlooked detail, namely that "communication has an educational intention" (Gué-Martini, 2020, p. 680), which therefore implies the search for a dialogue between communication and education and continues to be an area undergoing constant reformulation.

In light of the logic of today's digitalised and platformised societies, understanding the complex risks of digital ecosystems is becoming a central issue in the Latin American context. The focus is on strengthening the ability to discern the quality of information sources, hegemonic forms of production and dissemination of digital messages and content, as well as the relationship between power, the market and digitalised communication processes and their marginalising effects.

The Latin American critical edu-communication project assumes that the simple production/publication of a message or digital content is not synonymous with active and democratic participation. From this perspective, its development is framed within the socio-cultural and socio-political sphere. It has the aim of building a communicative citizenship. Critical edu-communication, therefore, allows us to re-examine conceptual interactions and interpretations within digital ecosystems, transforming itself into a powerful means of socio-political intervention. This is because it is based on not only an emphasis on the concepts of counter-hegemony and power/subordination, but also of social intervention. It corresponds to a precise conception of educational and communicative practices and, above all, of collective socio-community actions oriented towards co-creation and co-construction through a constant critical and dialogical flow of symbolic and communicative re-signification (Aparici, 2010; Kaplún, 1998).

Latin American critical digital edu-communication transcends the boundaries of literacy understood as simple knowledge of digital media and new technologies, or the acquisition of specific results-oriented skills. Clearly, the constellation of projects and experiences that characterise the region demonstrates that the overlap between the edu-communicative vision and the potential offered by digital media has become an interesting combination in terms of liberation, equity and human rights (Picarella, 2024b). The Latin American perspective is therefore oriented towards a critical reading of communication and media processes, proposing to move away from a vision of education based solely on the unidirectional and vertical transmission of information and content. It is moving towards an interdisciplinary and transdisciplinary vision based on the union between the dialogic mediation of educational processes and the critical use of digital communication tools and technologies in order to strengthen teaching-learning processes. According to Kendall and McDougall (2012), this is a form of pedagogy strongly oriented towards the practical process.

The numerous Latin American practices of critical edu-communication (Picarella, 2025) are united by the use of educational and communicative strategies based on the link between traditional participatory-dialogic methodology and the conscious use of audiovisual tools, digital media, platforms, and social media. Their aim is to democratise the educational sphere by creating opportunities for formal and informal access as well as promoting alternative modes of learning and relating to the socio-cultural environment that are capable of producing, through a different and non-passive use of digital ecosystems, transformative cultural narratives and experiences. The debate on the use of generative AI technologies in education also falls within this perspective. The region's ministries of education are working on guidelines and investments to promote the integration of AI at all levels of education, not only to incorporate new technologies into the classroom, but also to foster development capabilities aligned with local needs, along with an ethical and sustainable approach.

They also want to close the digital knowledge gap. Latin America is launching learning and training experiments aimed at educating a critical digital citizenry to identify and respond to algorithmic challenges through the design of educational models that strengthen deep critical thinking, computational skills, and problematisation. An interesting example is the private comprehensive school Educare in

Guadalupe (Mexico), where artificial intelligence is integrated to personalise and optimise the learning process, adapting to the needs of each student and improving their academic development. The physical school has been complemented by the creation of its online version, Educare Online School, to improve education through technology. It is focused on creating innovative educational solutions to enable new generations to contribute to the transformation of their reality[2].

The Educare project focuses on several key aspects: a) personalisation of learning through the EDUCARE.ai platform with the aim of adapting educational content to the individual needs of each student through the use of methodologies such as flipped learning and project-based learning; b) inclusion and equity to reduce disparities in academic performance through the personalisation of e-learning; c) the transformative role of teachers, who are no longer limited to transferring content but act as learning facilitators, guiding students in the use of digital tools and specialised virtual profiles. This approach combines cutting-edge technology with the personalised human support that is essential in education; d) emotional and psychological development under the supervision of psychologists who carry out diagnostic assessments through specialised platforms; e) creation of an app that integrates and simplifies the management of the institution's educational model.

This AI-powered application enables personalised learning and the real-time monitoring of students' academic and socio-emotional progress. Thanks to its ability to connect with all the members of the educational community – students, teachers and parents – the application fosters closer collaboration and more efficient learning. Parents can follow their children's progress, teachers can adapt their teaching strategies thanks to accurate data, and students receive personalised support based on their emotional and academic needs, ensuring a comprehensive and inclusive educational experience.

Among the programmes offered are IT and Technology, "The fun way to learn technology", which develops critical thinking skills and the correct use of technology in primary school students, and Robotopia Maker, "You make it Real", an educational robotics programme that aims to promote a passion for STEM subjects through the construction of mechatronic models. Both are based on the methodology and key aspects of the *Educare.ai* educational project.

The example considered summarises the trends that are characterising the Latin American context, highlighting once again the region's strategic choice in terms of critical digital edu-communication. In the age of hyperconnectivity, the Latin American vision once again takes on a liberating role in shaping a critical citizenry capable of transforming its own reality by achieving greater levels of social justice and guarantees of respect for human rights – such as education – because, especially for the Global South, hyperconnectivity does not necessarily mean the resolution of systemic problems and empowerment.

The digital transition in education systems and programmes can broaden access to educational opportunities and promote inclusion, as well as improve the quality of learning. However, for this transition to be feasible, it is essential to have full and equitable access to digital infrastructure. In the Latin American context, there is still considerable inequality in access to digital infrastructure by socioeconomic level. In general, countries with lower access to the Internet and digital technologies and devices have a greater gap in terms of socioeconomic status. Although most countries in Latin America and the Caribbean have achieved full primary education coverage, some still have shortcomings (Arias Ortiz, Dueñas, Giambruno, López, 2024).

This framework also includes the most recent and multifaceted reflections on the integration of artificial intelligence into educational and communication processes (Torres-Toukoumidis, Santín-Picoita, Henríquez Mendoza, 2024). Its confluence is based on three central axes, namely AI support for learning processes, the urgent need to educate ourselves about artificial intelligence, and the need to adapt to coexisting with more intelligent autonomous entities in the near future. Nevertheless, Latin American digital edu-communication prioritises the promotion of skills and abilities inherent to human beings. Therefore, the intertwining of digital edu-communication and artificial intelligence is set to outline a path that focuses on training human beings capable of facing the many facets of the current century and interacting with the challenges of the platform society through reflective thinking and the capacity for originality and authentic innovation.

The social and humanising approach proposed by the Latin American vision becomes the reference framework for the proposal of media education and media literacy for equality, social justice, the reduction of gaps and the promotion of greater access. It aims to critically analyse content, narratives and representations, focusing on practical methods that value creativity and free expression so that individuals can become conscious and responsible actors in society, as well as creators and producers of content as part of the educational-media-digital empowerment process. Criticism and citizen empowerment are therefore the pillars of Latin American digital edu-communication. The aim is to reconstruct the social, ethical and political dimension of communication and digitalisation education based on a philosophical-practical concept that complements static educational processes with dynamic-participatory ones, thus guiding towards the construction of digital media skills and narrative and critical (re)signifying thinking.

CONCLUSION

Over the last few decades, debates on media education have focused on the importance of developing a greater awareness of the role of the media and its effects and impact on society. In the current scenario of technological and digital saturation, the goal of promoting an awareness of the opportunities offered by new technologies and digital media has guided visions of digital literacy and AI literacy, which have highlighted the need for skills, knowledge, and attitudes aimed at the process of learning and applying critical thinking for the creation and dissemination of digital information and content. Furthermore, through a critical form of media education, it is also possible to increase the empowerment (Doni, 2015) of individuals by aiming for media education that takes a different approach to the study of media, i.e. education with and for the media.

Digital ecosystems, platforms, social networks and the latest innovations in AI, as participatory environments that users choose spontaneously, can form the basis for the creation of new inclusive educational projects aimed at democratising education through an effective combination of formal and informal educational and learning strategies. However, it is essential that the integration of educational and communication processes and digitalisation be rooted in an environment capable of stimulating critical reflection and oriented towards meaningful learning. The link between critical thinking, media, and intelligent technologies should be able to combine digital skills with the methodological reflexivity, awareness and critical sense typical of mature knowledge.

The integration of media literacy, AI literacy and edu-communication is emerging as a strategic educational response to the challenges of the contemporary information system. In Latin America, the critical pedagogical tradition offers valuable tools for reflecting on how news is produced, interpreted and contested in social contexts characterised by information inequalities, monopolised media and distrust of institutions. Training citizens to critically read information, recognise manipulative practices, and actively participate in the construction of public discourse is now a global educational priority (Hobbs, 2008). Within this trajectory, news is not just content to be decoded but becomes a pedagogical object with which to exercise awareness, agency, and critical thinking. Educational pathways that integrate the edu-communication approach with tools for analysing the information ecosystem — including the algorithmic dimensions and implications of artificial intelligence in the selection and dissemination of news — create spaces for active, emancipated citizenship that is attentive to the socio-cultural processes in which information is embedded.

This balance between digital ecosystems and educational processes is essential to ensure that new learning strategies have a lasting and profound impact in terms of training citizens who are able to respond critically and consciously to the challenges of the future, but also to promote the ongoing democratisation of education, reduce digital divides and break down systemic barriers that limit opportunities for access to education. In other words, to build a more equitable and high-quality education system for all. In this perspective, as also stated by Pope Francis (2024), media education must show the means of communication and new technologies for what they are, namely, useful means for creating communication based on proximity, sharing and encounter.

It is therefore essential to create an educational praxis of communication to understand the innovative and different uses of media, digital platforms, and artificial intelligence and maximise their benefits while limiting their negative effects on the social and cultural system. Education and critical knowledge of digital media allow for the development of discernment skills and promote pluralism rather than monism, as well as representing and signifying the complexity of reality.

This approach, linked to critical digital edu-communication in its Latin American form, guides the co-construction of communities and the breaking down of socio-cultural, educational and socio-economic domains. In the Latin American context, the pervasiveness of digitalisation and platformisation has been permeated by critical digital edu-communication practices that involve the formation of meaningful learning networks, collaboration, and communities of practice, to strengthen access and construction – often as an alternative to formal institutions – of the knowledge needed in the digital age, filtered through the lens of dialogic, reflective and participatory communication and training methodologies. From a Latin American perspective, critical education in digital media involves the acquisition of skills and knowledge that can promote social justice through the critical and conscious use of new technologies and digital media.

This peculiarity of the Latin American vision can be explained by reference to the systemic and structural problems of the region, which have fuelled exclusion, marginalisation, violence, and limitations on the guarantee of human rights. If education is conceived not only as a social right but also, and above all, as a human right, it is understandable how the experiences and practices guided in particular by communities and social opposition movements, linked to Freirean theoretical currents of liberating education, popular communication, and cultural studies, have worked towards democratisation by focusing on critical education and communication as tools and vectors of democratisation and liberation. This perspective also includes the most recent experiences of critical digital edu-communication, whose strategies contribute to the development of digital skills and knowledge through the use of teaching methodologies focused on the development of a critical understanding of the media and the management of technological tools themselves, collective dialogic reflection on information, the ability to analyse digital messages and content, socialisation and meaning-making, the development of empathy for normal coexistence in online and offline environments, combined with the use of the attractive means and tools of digital ecosystems and platform societies.

The concluding reflection of this analysis is justified, which considers Latin American critical digital edu-communication as an interesting frontier of digital literacy, because in the Latin American context, the emancipation and liberation of subjectivity through alternative educational and communicative experiences and methodologies intertwined with the conscious use of new technologies and digital communication media have become a powerful weapon for social pacification, the extension of human rights, and the construction of a more equitable, inclusive and high-quality educational future.

REFERENCES

Amsalem, E., & Zoizner, A. (2023). Do people learn about politics on social media? A meta-analysis of 76 studies. *Journal of Communication, 73*(1), 3–13. DOI: 10.1093/joc/jqac034

Antonucci, M. C., Sorice, M., & Volterrani, A. (2024). *Confini invisibili. Comunità liminali e pratiche di resistenza nella città neoliberista*. Meltemi.

Aparici, R. (Ed.). (2010). *Educomunicación: más allá del 2.0*. Gedisa.

Arias Ortiz, E., Dueñas, X., Giambruno, C., & López, Á. (2024). *El estado de la educación en América Latina y el Caribe 2024: la medición de los aprendizajes*. Banco Interamericano de Desarrollo, División de Educación.

Backe, E. L., Lilleston, P., & McCleary-Sills, J. (2018). Networked individuals, gendered violence: A literature review of cyberviolence. *Violence and Gender, 5*(3), 135–146. DOI: 10.1089/vio.2017.0056

Barendt, E. (2019). What is the Harm of Hate Speech? *Ethical Theory and Moral Practice, 22*(3), 539–553. DOI: 10.1007/s10677-019-10002-0

Battista, D. (2024). TikTok Politics: Influenze e interazioni sociali. *Mimesis*.

Belluati, M., & Tirocchi, S. (2023). *Sociologia della comunicazione e degli ambienti mediali*. Pearson.

Bloomfield, B. P. (2020). *The Question of Artificial Intelligence. Philosophical and Sociological Perspectives*. Routledge.

Boccia Artieri, G. (2006). Farsi media. Consumo e media-mondo: tra identità, esperienza e forme espressive. In E. Di Nallo, R. Paltrinieri, *Con sumo, Prospettive di analisi del consumo nella società globale*. FrancoAngeli.

Boccia Artieri, G. (2012). *Stati di connessione. Pubblici, cittadini e consumatori nella (Social) Network Society*. Franco Angeli.

Boccia Artieri, G., Colombo, F., & Gili, G. (2022). *Comunicare. Persone, relazioni, media*. Laterza.

Boyd, D. (2014). *It's Complicated. The social life of networked teens*. Yale University Press.

Buckingham, D. (2003). Media Education: Literacy, Learning and Contemporary Culture. *Polity*.

Castells, M. (1996). *The Rise of the Network Society: The Information Age: Economy, Society, and Culture*. Wiley.

Castells, M. (2000). Materials for an exploratory theory of the network society1. *The British Journal of Sociology*, *51*(1), 5–24. DOI: 10.1111/j.1468-4446.2000.00005.x

Castells, M. (2001). *The Internet Galaxy: Reflections on the Internet*. Oxford University Press. DOI: 10.1007/978-3-322-89613-1

Castells, M. (2010). Globalisation, networking, urbanisation: Reflections on the spatial dynamics of the information age. *Urban Studies (Edinburgh, Scotland)*, *47*(13), 2737–2745. DOI: 10.1177/0042098010377365

Cubeddu, F., & Scocco, M. (2024). Online Hate Speech as a Form of Cyberviolence: Communication Practices, Social Perception and Vulnerabilities in the Experience of Young People. In Gualda, E. (Ed.), *Teorias de la conspiraòn y discursos de odio en linea en la Sociedad de las plataformas. Comparación de pautas en las narrativas y redes sociales sobre COVID-19, inmigrantes, refugiados, estudios de género y personas LGTBIQ+* (pp. 221–235). Dykinson. DOI: 10.14679/2761

de Sousa Santos, B. (2009). *Una Epistemología del Sur. La reinvención del conocimiento y la emancipación social*. Clacso/Siglo XXI Editores.

Delgado, R., & Stefancic, J. (2017). *Critical race theory: An introduction*. NYU Press.

Dewey, J. (1997). *Democracy and Education*. Free Press.

DNE-TN2 (2024). Intelligence artificielle et éducation: apports de la recherche et enjeux pour les politiques publiques: édition trilingue 2024. *Éducation, numérique et recherche*. DOI: 10.58079/vq06

Dolata, U., & Schrape, J. F. (2016). Masses, crowds, communities, movements: Collective action in the internet age. *Social Movement Studies*, *15*(1), 1–18. DOI: 10.1080/14742837.2015.1055722

Doni, T. (2015). *Dalla Media Education alla New Media Education. Cinema e dintorni*. Rassegna CNOS.

Durkheim, E. (1922). *Éducation et sociologie*. PUF.

Dussel, I., & Trujillo Reyes, B. F. (2018). ¿Nuevas formas de enseñar y aprender? Las posibilidades en conflicto de las tecnologías digitales en la escuela. [– IISUE – UNAM.]. *Perfiles Educativos*, *XL*(159), 201. DOI: 10.22201/iisue.24486167e.2018.Especial.59182

Elmer, T., Mepham, K., & Stadtfeld, C. (2020). Students under lockdown: Comparisons of students' social networks and mental health before and during the COVID-19 crisis in Switzerland. *PLoS One*, *15*(7), e0236337. DOI: 10.1371/journal.pone.0236337 PMID: 32702065

Fraser, P., & Wardle, J. (Eds.). (2013). *Current Perspectives in Media Education: beyond the Manifesto*. Palgrave McMillan. DOI: 10.1057/9781137300218

Freire, P. (1998). *Pedagogy of Freedom: Ethics, Democracy, and Civic Courage*. Rowman & Littlefield Publishers.

Freire, P. (2005). *Pedagogy of the Oppressed*. The Continuum Publishing Company.

Friesem, Y., Raman, U., Kanižaj, I., & Choi, G. Y. (2023). *The Routledge Handbook of Media Education Futures Post-Pandemic*. Routledge.

Frizzo, G. B. (2024). *Digital Media and Early Child Development. Theoretical and Empirical Issues*. Springer. DOI: 10.1007/978-3-031-69224-6

Gálik, S. (2017). Influence of cyberspace on changes in contemporary education. *Communication Today*, *8*(1), 30–38.

Gillani, N., Eynon, R., Chiabaut, C., & Finkel, K. (2023). Unpacking the 'Black Box' of AI in Education. *Journal of Educational Technology & Society*, *26*(1), 99–111.

Greenhow, C. (2011). Online social networks and learning. *On the Horizon*, *19*(1), 4–12. DOI: 10.1108/10748121111107663

Gué - Martini. R. (2020). Educomunicación: ¿Contracampo o intersección? In I. Aguded; A. Vizcaìno Verdù (Eds.). *Redes sociales y ciudadanía: hacia un mundo ciberconectado y empoderado*. Grupo Comunicar Ediciones (pp. 677-685).

Guèvremont, V., & Brin, C. (2024). *Intelligence artificielle, culture et médias*. Éthique, IA et société – OBVIA.

Guilherme Goulart Righetto, G. G. (2021). Imbecilization in the disinformation society: What can information literacy do about it? *Investigación Bibliotecológica*, *35*(87), 33–55. DOI: 10.22201/iibi.24488321xe.2021.87.58310

Hellsten, L. M., Crespi, I., Hendry, B., & Fermani, A. (2021). Extending the Current teorization on Cyberbullying: Importance of Including Socio-Psychological Perspectives. *Italian Journal of Sociology of Education*, *13*(3), 85–110.

Hobbs, R. (2008). Debates and challenges facing new literacies in the 21st century. *International Handbook of Children, Media and Culture. Sage (Atlanta, Ga.)*, 431–447.

Joyce, K., & Cruz, T. M. (2024). A Sociology of Artificial Intelligence: Inequalities, Power, and Data Justice. *Socius: Sociological Research for a Dynamic World, 10*, 23780231241275393. DOI: 10.1177/23780231241275393

Joyce, K., Smith-Doerr, L., Alegria, S., Bell, S., Cruz, T. M., Hoffman, S. G., Noble, S., & Shestakofsky, B. (2021). Toward a Sociology of Artificial Intelligence: A Call for Research on Inequalities and Structural Change. *Socius: Sociological Research for a Dynamic World, 7*, 2378023121999581. DOI: 10.1177/2378023121999581

Kaplún, M. (1998). *Una pedagogía de la comunicación*. Ediciones de la Torre.

Kendall, A., & McDougall, J. (2012). Critical media literacy after the media. [Alfabetización mediática crítica en la postmodernidad]. Comunicar. *Revista Científica de Comunicación y Educación*, *19*(38), 21–29. DOI: 10.3916/C38-2012-02-02

Koltay, T. (2011). The media and the literacies: Media literacy, information literacy, digital literacy. *Media Culture & Society*, *33*(2), 211–221. DOI: 10.1177/0163443710393382

Kuss, D. J., & Griffiths, M. D. (2017). Social networking sites and addiction: Ten lessons learned. *International Journal of Environmental Research and Public Health*, *14*(3), 3–11. DOI: 10.3390/ijerph14030311 PMID: 28304359

Landry, N., & Fastrez, P. (2023). *Media Literacy and Media Education Research Methods: A Handbook*. Routledge.

Lee, S. H. (2014). Digital literacy education for the development of digital literacy. [IJDLDC]. *International Journal of Digital Literacy and Digital Competence*, *5*(3), 29–43. DOI: 10.4018/ijdldc.2014070103

Livingstone, S., & Blum-Ross, A. (2020). *Parenting for a Digital Future: How Hopes and Fears about Technology Shape Children's Lives*. Academic., DOI: 10.1093/oso/9780190874698.001.0001

Livingstone, S., & Haddon, L. (Eds.). (2009). *Kids online: Opportunities and risks for children*. Policy Press.

Masterman, L. (1985). *Teaching the Media*. Routledge., DOI: 10.4324/9780203359051

Mateus, J. C., Andrada, P., & Quiroz, M. T. (Eds.). (2019). *Media Education in Latin America*. Routledge. DOI: 10.4324/9780429244469

McLuhan, M. (1964). *Understanding Media: The Extensions of Man*. Gingko Press.

Miao, F., & Holmes, W. (2023). *Guidance for generative AI in education and research*. UNESCO. https://unesdoc.unesco.org/ark:/48223/pf0000386693

Pelaez, A. L., Diaz, H. L., Servos, C. M., & Castillo de Mesa, J. (Eds.). (2021). Digital Social Work: Challenges, Trends and Best Practices. *Journal of Sociology and Social Welfare*, *XLVIII*(3).

Peterson, J., & Densley, J. (2017). Cyber violence: What do we know and where do we go from here? *Aggression and Violent Behavior*, *34*, 193–200. DOI: 10.1016/j.avb.2017.01.012

Picarella, L. (2024a). Critical education between social justice and dialogic cultural action. *The Lab's Quarterly*, XXVI(2), 65-89. DOI: https://doi.org/DOI: 10.13131/unipi/z182-yb80

Picarella, L. (2024b). Critical Education and Digital Media: A Binomial for the Exercising of Human Rights. *REVIEW OF HUMAN RIGHTS*, *10*(1), 86–114. DOI: 10.35994/rhr.v10i1.272

Picarella, L. (2025). Processi educativi e comunicativi orientati alla giustizia sociale in America Latina. In E. Mangone, E. Martini & A. Volterrani (a cura di), *Società frammentata e traiettorie educative. Disuguaglianze, giustizia sociale e intelligenza artificiale* (pp. 21-44). Mimesis.

Poell, T., Nieborg, D. B., & Duffy, B. E. (2021). *Platforms and cultural production*. Wiley.

Pope Francis. (2024). *Artificial Intelligence and the Wisdom of the Heart: Towards a Fully Human Communication. Message for the 58th World Day of Social Communications*. https://www.vatican.va/content/francesco/en/messages/communications/documents/20240124-messaggio-comunicazioni-sociali.html

Ragnedda, M. (2017). *The third digital divide: A Weberian approach to digital inequalities*. Routledge. DOI: 10.4324/9781315606002

Rampazzo Gambarato, R., & Heuman, J. (2024). *Streaming Media and Cultural Memory in a Postdigital Society*. Taylor & Francis. DOI: 10.4324/9781032690872

Reddy, P., Sharma, B., & Chaudhary, K. (2020). Digital literacy: A review of literature. [IJT]. *International Journal of Technoethics*, *11*(2), 65–94. DOI: 10.4018/IJT.20200701.oa1

Rivoltella, P. C., & Rossi, P. G. (2019). *Il corpo e la macchina. Tecnologia, cultura, educazione*. Morcelliana.

Salzano, D., & Battista, D. (2023). Social network e generazione Z: Tra empowerment e rischi educativi. *Q-TIMES WEBMAGAZINE*, *1*, 47–59.

Salzano, D., Scognamiglio, I., & Battista, D. (2023). La rispazializzazione digitale nelle aree interne del Sud Italia= Digital respazialization in the inland areas of Southern Italy. *H-ermes. Journal of Communication*, *24*, 51–72.

Scott, K. (2022). I Do Not Think It Means What You Think It Means: Artificial Intelligence, Cognitive Work & Scale. *Daedalus*, *151*(2), 75–84. DOI: 10.1162/daed_a_01901

Siemens, G. (2005). Connectivism: A learning theory for the digital age. *International Journal of Instructional Technology and Distance Learning*, *2*(1).

Smahel, D., Machackova, H., Mascheroni, G., Dedkova, L., Staksrud, E., Ólafsson, K., Livingstone, S., & Hasebrink, U. (2020). *EU Kids Online 2020: Survey results from 19 countries*. London School of Economics and Political Science.

Smith, D., Leonis, T., & Anandavalli, S. (2021). Belonging and loneliness in cyberspace: Impacts of social media on adolescents' well-being. *Australian Journal of Psychology*, *73*(1), 12–23. DOI: 10.1080/00049530.2021.1898914

Su, J., Ng, D. T. K., & Chu, S. K. W. (2023). Artificial intelligence (AI) literacy in early childhood education: The challenges and opportunities. *Computers and Education: Artificial Intelligence*, *4*, 100124. DOI: 10.1016/j.caeai.2023.100124

Tirocchi, S. (2013). *Sociologie della Media education. Giovani e media al tempo dei nativi digitali*. FrancoAngeli.

Torres-Toukoumidis, Á., Santín-Picoita, F. G., & Henríquez Mendoza, E. (2024). Inteligencia Artificial y Educomunicación. In A. Torres-Toukoumidis, T. León-Alberca, (coords.), *ComunicAI. La revolución de la Inteligencia Artificial en la Comunicación*. Comunicación Social Ediciones y Publicaciones.

Toth, M., Mertens, F., & Rodrigues Makiuchi, M. F. (2012). Novos espaços de participação social no contexto do desenvolvimento sustentável: As contribuições da Educomunicação. *Ambiente & Sociedade*, *15*(2), 113–132. DOI: 10.1590/S1414-753X2012000200007

UNESCO. (2007). *Paris agenda or 12 recommendations for media education. Paris Conference*. UNESCO. http://www.ifap.ru/pr/2007/070625ba.pdf

UNESCO. (2021a). *Media and information literate citizens: think critically, click wisely!* UNESCO. https://www.unesco.org/mil4teachers/en/curriculum

UNESCO. (2021b). *IA et éducation: Guide pour les décideurs politiques*. UNESCO. https://unesdoc.unesco.org/ark:/48223/pf0000380006

UNESCO. (2024). *Operational Guidelines Constructing UNESCO Media and Information Literacy Cities.* UNESCO. https://unesdoc.unesco.org/ark:/48223/pf0000391748

Van Dijck, J., Poell, T., & De Waal, M. (2018). *The platform society: Public values in a connective world.* Oxford University Press. DOI: 10.1093/oso/9780190889760.001.0001

Varona, M. N., Muela, A., & Machimbarrena, J. M. (2022). Problematic use or addiction? A scoping review on conceptual and operational definitions of negative social networking sites use in adolescents. *Addictive Behaviors, 134*, 107400. DOI: 10.1016/j.addbeh.2022.107400 PMID: 35820296

Waldron, J. (2012). *The harm in hate speech.* Harvard University Press. DOI: 10.4159/harvard.9780674065086

Weeks, B. E., Ardèvol-Abreu, A., & Gil de Zúñiga, H. (2017). Online influence? Social media use, opinion leadership, and political persuasion. *International Journal of Public Opinion Research, 29*(2), 214–239.

Williams, J. (2018). *Stand out of our light: Freedom and resistance in the attention economy.* Cambridge University Press. DOI: 10.1017/9781108453004

Yue, M., Jong, M. S. Y., & Dai, Y. (2022). Pedagogical design of K-12 artificial intelligence education: A systematic review. *Sustainability (Basel), 14*(23), 15620. DOI: 10.3390/su142315620

ENDNOTES

1 The twelve recommendations proposed in the 2007 UNESCO Report are: «*1. Adopt an inclusive definition of media education; 2. Strengthen the links between media education, cultural diversity and human rights; 3. Define the skills to be acquired and formulate assessment systems; 4. Integrate media education into basic teacher training; 5. Develop appropriate and evolving teaching methods; 6. Mobilise key actors in the education system; 7. Mobilise other key actors in society; 8. Introduce media education into lifelong learning; 9. Develop media education and research in higher education; 10. Create exchange networks; 11. Organise and give visibility to international exchanges; 12. Raise awareness and mobilise political actors*» (UNESCO, 2007).

2 For further information, please refer to the page: *Instituto Educare, Homepage. Educare Online School* - https://sites.google.com/institutoeducare.edu

.mx/educarehomeschool/p%C3%A1gina-principal/educare-online-school (last accessed on 10 May 2025).

Chapter 8
Rhetoric, Technology, and the Digital Online Media Literacy Assessment Framework in Grant Writing

Ronald B. Cole
https://orcid.org/0009-0007-2646-817X
University of Cincinnati, USA

Lauren N Maher
https://orcid.org/0009-0002-7525-8025
Texas Tech University, Lubbock, USA

Rich Rice
https://orcid.org/0009-0005-3801-199X
Texas Tech University, Lubbock, USA

ABSTRACT

The rapid pace of technological change, marked recently by advances in artificial intelligence (AI), is transforming society, including writing (Abbass, 2021; Fowler, 2003). AI tools offer opportunities to enhance grant writing, but they also present new challenges regarding ethical and effective communication. Grant writers must develop algorithmic and media literacy skills to engage with AI-generated content and ensure content produced is persuasive and strategic. The shift necessitates an approach that considers digital, online, media, and critical literacies. DOMLA, the Digital Online Media Literacy Assessment framework, when applied to grant writing,

DOI: 10.4018/979-8-3373-0872-2.ch008

helps us understand ways in which writers may understand and refine their work. Strategies include optimizing media components, using digital tools, navigating online grant platforms, and critically assessing AI-generated content. By incorporating these approaches, grant writers may craft more compelling and strategic proposals that align with the goals and objectives of the funder, the applicant, and beneficiary communities.

INTRODUCTION

We are living in a time of great change. The First Industrial Revolution started with the invention of the steam engine in 1760 and lasted over a hundred years, transforming industry and society as it unfolded. The second and third industrial revolutions, which propelled advancements in production, energy, and information technologies, each took only a few decades (Xu, David, & Kim, 2018, pp. 90–91) but dramatically shifted knowledge making and global economies as they progressed. Currently in the fourth revolution and on the brink of the fifth, new advances continue to push society forward at an accelerated pace, marked by breakthroughs in artificial intelligence (AI), robotics, biotechnology, and the Internet of Things. And as converging technologies sprint toward quantum computing and advanced AI, they impact media literacy in increasingly significant ways.

Three relevant technologies and practices are AI, machine learning (ML), and algorithms (Chaka, 2020, p. 370; González-Pérez & Ramírez-Montoya, 2022, p. 2). These technologies have necessitated Industry 5.0's refocusing, where human-centricity (the concept of human needs being at the center of a multidimensional framework that includes the design, development, and implementation of technological solutions) has been put forth alongside resilience and sustainability as three important pillars of the coming age (DG RTD, 2024; European Commission, 2021; Ivanov, 2023, p. 1683). Further, as "educational revolutions" are directly correlated to developments in industrial revolutions (Becker, Hornung, & Woessmann, 2011; Hussin, 2018), these technologies in turn necessitate significant shifts in learning structures wherever they are implemented.

Core Grant Concepts

Maintaining human-centricity is critical to core concepts that form the grant ecosystem to ensure valid, reliable, and rhetorically effective communication. The funder (often referred to as grantmaker) establishes the priorities and criteria for securing a grant. The opportunity (often referred to as Request for Proposal or RFP) represents the formal announcement of the grant and an invitation to submit a proposal. The opportunity outlines eligibility requirements, evaluation criteria, and proposal submission instructions. The grant proposal is the persuasive bridge between applicant and funder. These core concepts remain throughout the evolution of technological assistance in planning, drafting, and revising grant proposals.

Grant writing is the practice of developing structured, persuasive documents that advocate for funding projects. It relies on both technical precision and rhetorical strategy. It is an inherently situated genre. The use of AI affords valuable opportunities to strengthen proposals and to deepen quality and impact on readers, but AI adds ethical, writing style, and other technological challenges that require writers to practice and refine their media literacy skills.

A NEW DIGITAL MEDIA LITERACY

One framework that can be used to understand these adapting literacy skills is Digital Online Media Literacy Assessment (DOMLA) (Hallaq, 2016). In the context of grant writing, "digital" literacy involves using tools to streamline the writing process. AI and other natural language processing models help writers draft proposals, generate content, and tailor applications based on funder preferences and needs. "Online" literacy in grant writing might pertain to the ability to navigate the digital ecosystem of grant portals, RFP opportunities, search tools, keywords, grant parameters, and funding patterns. Further, different forms of "media"—such as the written, the visual, the multimodal, and interacting with stakeholders—are routinely used in the grant writing process, and AI can help create, optimize, and analyze media used in these writing processes. Sound decisions involving rhetorical moves can be created and augmented through algorithmic "literacy," which, with the DOMLA, relates specifically to understanding how to use AI tools that maintain ethical and effective communication. Understanding media literacy principles of validity, reliability, triangulation, and misinformation is directly related.

By leveraging the DOMLA media literacy principles, grant writers can use AI to enhance their work in specific ways. Increasing digital literacy ensures grant writers understand the technologies and the tools that may be available, which might include AI-driven searches, grammar checkers, proposal structure analyzers, and content generators. Online literacy helps grant writers understand how to use AI to navigate online grant platforms and databases with greater efficiency and increased likelihood of funder-organization mission matching. Media literacy helps grant writers refine and improve media elements in proposals, better aligning expectations of funders and stakeholders. And critical literacy aids grant writers in evaluating AI-generated content. Seckel et al. (2024) highlight an important tension in grant writing—balancing personal voice and originality with the potential risks of using AI. Proposals should reflect unique ideas, style, and personality, and AI is a tool that, when used strategically, can enhance a personal imprint rather than dilute it. Research required in effective grant writing is contextual and situational; the DOMLA framework equips grant writers to engage with AI in strategic ways.

The current chapter treats AI as a team member who can be prompted to help the grant writer work better, faster, and smarter. AI has the potential to democratize grant writing in this way, by helping nonprofits and researchers with limited resources develop proposals that can compete with those from applicants who may have a dedicated grant writing team or extensive administrative support. Many smaller (or leaner) organizations and early-career researchers struggle to secure funding. Their projects do not lack merit; applicants struggle to navigate the highly technical, competitive, and time-intensive grant writing processes. Godwin et al. (2024) reference the Matthew Effect, which is the tendency for people with advantages to accumulate more advantages over time, and cite a parallel phenomenon in research grant writing in which researchers who find early success experience an increased chance of future success:

> *The gap between those who do and those who do not find early success often widens, as researchers whose scores fall just outside of funding thresholds are less likely to apply in the future [...] while the grant writing process and what is required to write an effective grant has been detailed, there has been little development of infrastructure to facilitate writing the application. (p. 1)*

AI can provide an equalizing infrastructure, potentially mitigating disparities between well-funded applicants and those who may be under-resourced. However, realizing potential requires writers to develop specific competencies.

The AI Literacy in Grant Writing Rubric, adapted from Hallaq's (2016) DOMLA framework (see Table 1), provides a structured approach to using and evaluating AI-assisted grant writing for practitioners, students, and instructors. The rubric promotes engaging with AI utilities with intention and efficacy to underscore the importance of the grant writer's responsibility for that engagement. It supports the writer's accountability for ethical implications of employing AI tools. Rather than presenting these constructs as binary competencies that are either absent or present, the rubric encourages a developmental continuum in which grant writers progress toward greater literacy practices. Mastery may be iterative as it develops through practice, reflection, peer feedback, and adaptation to changing technologies.

Table 1. AI Literacy in Grant Writing Rubric, Adapted from Hallaq's (2016) DOMLA Framework

Constructs	1	2	3	4
Media Awareness (MAw)	Shows no understanding of the grant writer's responsibility for ensuring AI prompt quality and mitigating generic content.	Shows a developing understanding of the grant writer's responsibility for ensuring AI prompt quality and mitigating generic content.	Shows proficient understanding of the grant writer's responsibility for ensuring AI prompt quality and mitigating generic content.	Shows exceptional understanding of the grant writer's responsibility for ensuring AI prompt quality and mitigating generic content.
Media Access (MAc)	Shows no understanding of available platforms' strengths and limitations resulting in the ability to select and use the most appropriate AI tool.	Shows a developing understanding of available platforms' strengths and limitations resulting in the ability to select and use the most appropriate AI tool.	Shows proficient understanding of available platforms' strengths and limitations resulting in the ability to select and use the most appropriate AI tool.	Shows exceptional understanding of available platforms' strengths and limitations resulting in the ability to select and use the most appropriate AI tool.
Ethical Awareness (EA)	Shows no understanding of the potential for bias in AI-generated or AI-revised content, the need to review credibility of source material, and the need to disclose AI use.	Shows a developing understanding of the potential for bias in AI-generated or AI-revised content, the need to review credibility of source material, and the need to disclose AI use.	Shows proficient understanding of the potential for bias in AI-generated or AI-revised content, the need to review credibility of source material, and the need to disclose AI use.	Shows exceptional understanding of the potential for bias in AI-generated or AI-revised content, the need to review credibility of source material, and the need to disclose AI use.
Media Evaluation (ME)	Shows no understanding of persuasive devices, adjustments for grant funder priorities and application instructions, and/or reflecting the applicant organization's authenticity.	Shows developing an understanding of persuasive devices, adjustments for grant funder priorities and application instructions, and/or reflecting the applicant organization's authenticity.	Shows proficient understanding of persuasive devices, adjustments for grant funder priorities and application instructions, and/or reflecting the applicant organization's authenticity.	Shows exceptional understanding of persuasive devices, adjustments for grant funder priorities and application instructions, and/or reflecting the applicant organization's authenticity.
Media Production (MP)	Shows no understanding of opportunities to automate or delegate to AI assistance.	Shows developing an understanding of opportunities to automate or delegate to AI assistance.	Shows proficient understanding of opportunities to automate or delegate to AI assistance.	Shows exceptional understanding of opportunities to automate or delegate to AI assistance.

The rubric encourages grant writers to explore strategic multiple prompting beyond surface-level engagement with AI to produce more targeted results. The following AI literacy definitions have been adapted from original Hallaq's (2016) DOMLA constructs as examples. Specifically:

- *Media Awareness (MAw):* The knowledge of how AI tools analyze and process information, including the ability to recognize AI's potential impact on grant writing practices. Such awareness includes how AI interprets grant project requirements provided through various media. Awareness also includes how AI generates content based on the quality and content of user prompting, such as specificity and detail that helps the AI tool avoid generic content and incorporate important organizational culture nuances.

- *Media Access (MAc):* The ability to select and effectively use appropriate AI tools or platforms for specific grant writing tasks. Doing so requires the application of knowledge regarding the strengths and limitations of available platforms (e.g., purpose, functionality, accuracy, and language processing/ generation). It also encompasses ways in which grant writers access tools that augment expertise rather than replace critical thinking, creativity, and authenticity.
- *Ethical Awareness (EA):* Knowledge of ethical implications using AI in grant writing (e.g., transparency about its use, hallucinations, bias, and confidentiality). Demonstrated disclosure communicating the extent of AI use and compliance with usage policies if applicable.
- *Media Evaluation (ME):* The construct requires grant writers to make informed decisions about what AI content or assistance to incorporate, modify, or reject. These decisions are based on an ability to critically assess AI-generated content for accuracy, relevance, and alignment with organizational voice and funder expectations, whether through the solicitation or research intelligence.
- *Media Production (MP):* The ability to use AI to automate and expedite proposal management tasks. The ability may also entail the ability to use AI to produce templates formatted to the funder's submission requirements, including proper headings, font point size, and style guide if specified.

RHETORIC IN GRANT WRITING

Writing grant proposals requires careful consideration of digital tools, navigating various online platforms, examining the potential impact of different media forms, and critically engaging with media content to effectively use rhetoric and technology for problem-solving. Because words hold both literal (denotative) and implied (connotative) meanings, making successful grant writing highly contextual. It is essential to know what to write, where to understand significance, and how to address the knowledge and needs of the audience to succeed (Moravec et al., 2025).

In the end, grant writing is a form of rhetorical writing (Koutsantoni, 2009; Kessler, 2020; Nabhan et al., 2025; van den Besselaar & Mom, 2022).

Rhetoric is the art of persuasion, which requires knowing what to say, how much to say, and when to say it—a concept known as *kairos*. For grantmakers, the "right thing" often means demonstrating a high return on investment by showcasing significant impact and well-founded, reliable plans for sustainability. Funders want to ensure their resources are used as efficiently as possible. Mastering *kairos* is essential for crafting successful grant proposals. Should writers rely on logic, emotion, or an appeal to authority or urgency? A successful proposal presents a practical solution to a specific problem or need, while also convincing potential funders that the idea is worthy of investment.

To persuade grantmakers, the proposal writer must understand both the reasons their organization is seeking funding and the motivations of the grantmaker. Such understanding allows the creation of a proposal that aligns the missions of both parties. It's important to acknowledge that the grantor may not interpret the proposed solution in the same way the writer intends. For instance, grant management software used by funders might strip formatting or alter fonts, causing the proposal to appear different from the original. Similarly, jargon and specialized terminology might demonstrate the applicant's expertise but could confuse reviewers who lack that specific knowledge, potentially leading to rejection. To avoid this, proposal writing often employs plain language, visuals, and timely references to reduce confusion. These elements—how information is perceived, experienced, and understood—should be thoroughly researched and carefully considered during both the development and presentation of the proposal.

The DOMLA can guide writers in integrating rhetorical strategies, motivations, and modalities into their proposals. Key components of the proposed solution, such as the applicant, the problem, the location, and the beneficiaries, require careful consideration. Beneficiaries are those who will receive something because of the grant, whether directly (such as receiving funds or services) or indirectly (like gaining knowledge or seeing improvements in their communities). The group may also include the grantmakers themselves, as they are working to fulfill their own missions. It is important to recognize how beneficiaries could contribute to the solution in both generative and sustained ways, as doing so helps highlight the localized or situated assets of the project. The problem/solution framework in the proposal encompasses goals, objectives, tasks, activities, measurement plans, and outcomes, detailing what will be done and why. Location refers to where project activities will take place, where they may be sustained long-term, and how the background experiences of participants may influence effectiveness. The use of Generative AI can also help better assess the viability of variables within each problem/solution framework that can lead to project success.

A key aspect of demonstrating a strong return on investment and a credible sustainability plan is understanding the instrumental dynamics between the applicant and the community. AI can be particularly useful in developing this understanding. A proposal that emphasizes community should go beyond simply stating, "this is what we do," and instead illustrate how the applicant (whether an individual or organization) is embedded within and actively engages with the community. Consider prompting AI to generate ideas about strengths, weaknesses, opportunities, and threats (SWOT). The approach can lead to showing that the applicant is not only part of the community but also serves it. Using technology in a rhetorically effective way is crucial for crafting this narrative. It provides a foundation for highlighting the unique, personal interactions that take place when addressing both location and beneficiaries.

Consider the classic 5Ws+ of writing (who, what, when, where, why, and how). Specifically, what are the connections between the applicant and the community? Reflect on who is implementing the project, the broader what the organization does as opposed to just what the project will do. AI can be particularly helpful in generating related questions to further explore these connections:

- How does the applicant exist in the community? Where does it exist in relation to the community? Why?
- What does the applicant do for the community? For example, an Area Agency on Aging might run a community center that provides older adults with activities and nutritional support.
- How long has the applicant been in the community? How has it responded to events in the community in the past?
- Are those applying for the grant full members of the community? Where do they live? Are members of the applicant's leadership team present in the community?

These questions can be difficult to answer, requiring thorough research and often uncovering complexities that are more intricate and context-dependent than initially thought. In the end, it is critical to assess whether there are elements of the application that offer a unique or valuable perspective on community engagement. Such engagement could include factors such as the applicant's experience, diversity, credibility, or other characteristics that enhance the likelihood of the project's success.

A proposal emphasizing community as an asset contributing to a return on investment should highlight both unique features of the location and general characteristics of the community. What sets this place apart from many others? Why is it essential for the project to be funded here? While demographic data may be part of the answer, the proposal should also include stories and the history of the area to convey its distinctiveness. The location's characteristics are crucial because they can have a significant impact on the needs of the community and the interactions within it, making a detailed description necessary. The project's impact extends beyond individuals to support families and neighbors, contributing to a broader impact. By addressing the problem effectively, the project generates widespread, lasting effects. Identifying beneficiaries helps answer the question of who benefits from the project, and why the project is important. Consider the following questions in engineering prompts:

- Who directly benefits from what is produced by the funded proposal/project?
- Why would this help them? For how long?
- Who is connected to those who benefit, and how will their lives improve as a consequence of the funding of the proposal?
- How might the larger community benefit?

Such insight may be applied, adapted, or replicated in other project components or communities to extend impact. Grant writing mechanisms that facilitate replicability include a well-documented methodology, a sound implementation plan, clear quality assurance and surveillance plans, a logical outline moving from goals through projected outcomes, and identification of scalable project elements, particularly as they relate to economies of scale. Rhetoric, as art of persuasion, includes strategic organization, optimizing return on investment for funder, smart prompt engineering, and even purposeful writing style.

GRANT WRITING STYLES

Choice of writing style impacts how a grant proposal communicates need, capacity, and impact. In addition to rhetorical devices, compelling and successful proposals may also adopt a writing style that aligns and presents the organization's culture, funder expectations, and the nature of the project as well as proposal reviewer evaluation criteria. Below, four key grant writing styles are outlined: 1) asset-based framing, 2) plain language, 3) scientific writing, and 4) storytelling. For each style, an overview of relevant contexts for which the style may be appropriate, examples of the style in use, and identification of the style's strengths and challenges in an application are provided. Consider ways in which AI could help make best practice decisions easier.

Asset-Based Framing

Asset-based framing showcases a community or organization's strengths and resources (Salib, de la Garza, & Kapadia, 2024, p. 1190). It positions funding to enhance these assets for positive outcomes in a defined service area, encouraging funders to invest in what is already working to further support community improvement. Asset-based framing is particularly effective with grantmakers who value resilience and prioritize sustainability as well as long-term capacity building. Grant writers using this style of writing position their agency as a capable partner committed to excellence rather than an entity in crisis. The strategy treats applicant communities as agents of change rather than with significant deficits. The shift in perspective can be obvious; for instance, instead of "*we provide ultrasounds in prenatal care to prevent infant mortality*," writing "*our program expands access to prenatal care in rural communities by equipping mobile units with ultrasound technology*." Or a subtle reorienting from "*the communities we serve*" to "*the communities with which we partner*." In areas like health and human services where the dominant narrative revolves around need, prevention, intervention, and service, asset-based writing can really stand out (Martin-Kerry et al., 2023). In research grant applications, the applicant may emphasize institutional expertise, reinforcing credibility and likelihood in successfully executing the proposed project. While some funding opportunities may still require a clear articulation of the unmet need (through a problem or needs statement, for example), grant writers using asset-based strategic thinking can reframe the problem or need within the context of existing successes.

If a writer applies for a grant to support maternal health by mitigating infant morbidity and mortality, instead of emphasizing that clients in a rural health program are struggling with transportation barriers to access specialized prenatal care, an asset-based proposal might highlight the program's existing mobile medical unit that is staffed by skilled healthcare professionals and is already reaching underserved populations. The proposal would then position the request as an opportunity to enhance and expand its successful services, such as acquiring a new ultrasound machine to provide on-site imaging. Rather than identifying the deficits and shortcomings, this stylistic approach identifies ways in which additional financial support expands the project's proven impact by overcoming current constraints on growth. And it demonstrates a model of success already in place. This writing style can build confidence in the applicant's ability to deliver meaningful, lasting impact, appealing to funders who prefer investments in sustainable growth over short-term interventions.

Plain Language

Plain language is a writing style that helps ensure writing is free from unnecessary complexity (plainlanguage.gov, 2011; Willerton, 2015; Mateeva et al., 2017). The style is useful when proposals are reviewed by non-experts in the subject area, by multidisciplinary panels, when space or knowledge of contextualize language may be limited, when clarity over content is especially critical, or by funders who support a wide array of initiatives (such as private foundations or corporate philanthropies). A goal is to make complex ideas understandable without oversimplifying key elements such as project design or delivery. Strong plain language proposals avoid jargon, use active voice, avoid potentially ambiguous gerunds or referents, and incorporate simple sentence structure. A plain language proposal might facilitate multiple uses, such as informing the public and Congress about a project's significance (NIH, 2024).

Consider a grant proposal to a private foundation focused on disaster recovery. Rather than using technical language to describe federal assistance eligibility or the role of repopulation in economic recovery, a simpler approach might state: "*After Hurricane Harvey, survivors face delays and complexity in accessing federal aid, which often doesn't meet their needs. This initiative provides direct financial support to Aransas County residents, helping them replace essentials, secure temporary housing, and begin rebuilding. With creative solutions and flexible funding, we help survivors return, regain stability, and support the local economy.*" This approach ensures clarity for foundation board members who may not be familiar with federal disaster aid complexities and highlights the foundation's critical role in supporting the region. While some funders may prefer more technical language, plain language enhances readability and engagement for diverse grant reviewers.

Scientific Writing

Scientific writing is highly structured and methodologically rigorous. Unlike many other writing styles, it typically assumes that both the author and the audience have a background in science or technical information, though levels of expertise may vary. The style often requires empirical evidence and peer-reviewed studies. Additional nuances, such as the use of either active or passive voice, also exist, and perceptions of rhetorical effectiveness can differ between funders. Research-focused funders may also require proposals to adhere to specific formats that include Introduction, Methods, Results, and Discussion (IMRaD) (Wu, 2011) and comply with additional guidelines contained in discipline-specific style guides.

Consider a proposal seeking funding for high-consequence infectious disease research. It could potentially rely on historical epidemiological data, statistical models, and controlled experiments to demonstrate significance and justify funding. The proposal would also need to follow the funder's style guide to comply with formal requirements and increase chances of being awarded. The strength of this writing style is perceived objectivity. Despite the National Science Foundation's push for clarity and simplicity in scientific communication, NSF continues to reward conformance to the discipline's established writing paradigm that favors text length, complexity, and specialized terminology (Markowitz, 2019). Markowitz's study revealed that more lengthy grant abstracts with predominantly technical language that are written with an assertive voice received more money (over $370 *per one-word increase*). These financially successful linguistic patterns (e.g., passive voice) and technical language for which the discipline is known reinforce ways in which the hallmarks of scientific writing continue to signify expertise and credibility rhetorically, even when these elements may limit a broader understanding of the research by non-specialist reviewers. The style requires writers to balance the expected technical lexicon with readability, particularly with a multi- or interdisciplinary review panel.

Storytelling

Storytelling is another stylistic choice in grant writing that can amplify immediate and long-term impact on individuals and communities. Stories do more than just relay facts; they provide context, meaning, and emotional engagement, which are crucial to reviewer engagement, particularly as the audience's response relates to decision making about an award (Mosier, 2002; Clarke, 2009; Seeger & Sellnow, 2016; Altshuler, 2022). Drawing from research in crisis communication, stories that use familiar arcs elicit varying levels of audience engagement. For instance, victim-to-hero transformations result in heightened positive emotional responses. By contrast, narratives centered solely on victims tend to generate a more negative emotional response (Shanahan et al., 2019). For this reason, storytelling is particularly effective in service-based grants, social impact initiatives, and community-driven or collaborative projects, where funders want to see how their investment will directly impact lives. A compelling grant story may take the form of a real-life client testimonial, a composite narrative, or an anecdotal need or success story that demonstrates the transformational impact of the proposed project.

A strength of storytelling is its ability to forge an emotional connection with reviewers, making the proposal more memorable throughout the review process. In a proposal for training on emergency medical sheltering operations, for instance, an applicant leveraged their own real-world experience managing a 500-bed shelter in an austere disaster area by sharing several real-world (sometimes painful) lessons learned, best practices, and glimpses of some of the challenges they encountered. The stories resonated deeply with the funder, who cited them as a key factor in awarding the bid. Rather than emphasizing the typical "heartstring pull" seen in most examples of storytelling in proposals, this was a story that resulted in credibility and established the applicant as a relatable, trusted partner who could deliver practical, actionable training rather than just theory. Funders may prioritize objectivity and quantifiable, replicable impact over narrative, making it the grant writer's responsibility to balance storytelling with data and logical argumentation. Storytelling does not replace the need for supporting data; rather, it makes the data more relatable and emotionally compelling by humanizing the project that then contextualizes inputs, outputs, and outcomes. When used strategically, the writing style puts a face to the numbers, helping funders visualize benefactors of their investments.

Writing styles are powerful rhetorical tools that can significantly influence how reviewers engage with and evaluate proposals. Grant writers should approach style decisions with intentionality, carefully considering rhetorical contexts. The most effective and successful proposals demonstrate a sophisticated understanding of when to deploy stylistic elements based on the field, the project, the funder, and the responding organizational culture. Technical precision in scientific writing that lacks a human connection may risk producing sterile proposals that fail to resonate with reviewers. Yet, emotional appeals without evidence to support the claims may lack credibility. Skilled grant writers may look to blend styles, gaining insight from AI in addition to training and practice to satisfy reviewers.

ARTIFICIAL INTELLIGENCE AND GRANTS

The growing availability, use, and capabilities of AI have increased the public's need to become more media literate. Several definitions of media literacy inform rhetorical and ethical best practices of AI use with grant writing (Aufderheide, 1993; Buckingham, 2007, p. 44; Potter, 2010, pp. 676–678; Potter, 2022; Wuyckens, Landry, & Fastrez, 2022, pp. 173–174). Aufderheide's (1993) definition, which is the ability to access, analyze, and produce information for specific outcomes, is one of the most widely used (p. 6). It aligns well with Hallaq's (2016) DOMLA framework, which includes media awareness (MAw), media access (MAc), ethical awareness (EA), media evaluation (ME), and media production (MP) (p. 65).

For digital literacy in AI and its utility in grant writing, we focus on 1) understanding the capabilities of AI, 2) AI's role in the grant proposal writing process, and 3) limitations of the technology in this context. Within each of the three focus areas, we integrate relevant constructs of the DOMLA framework, demonstrating how media awareness, ethical awareness, media evaluation, and media production intersect with AI's role in grant development. The approach allows us to critically assess both the advantages and challenges AI presents in the field and within the grant writing practice.

The Capabilities of AI

A simple definition of AI is that it is "the automation of cognition" (Abbas, 2021, p. 1). While there are many types and classes of AI, two relevant to grant writing are Generative and Discriminative. Discriminative AI establishes boundaries between classes of data to predict the conditional probability of a given data point falling into a certain class (Jebara, 2004, p. 21; IBM, n.d.; Rybiński, 2025). These models excel at sorting data. Generative AI models, on the other hand, predict the joint probability of a given data point appearing in a particular area (Jebara, 2004, p. xiii; IBM, n.d.). The high-probability predictions of Generative AI models lend themselves to the creation of new material.

Significant advances have been made possible through the concept of the *transformer*, which is a neural network architecture based on attention mechanisms, as presented in Vaswani et al.'s (2017) "Attention is All You Need." The transformer is often combined with what are known as large language models (LLMs), which are AI models trained on large text datasets to facilitate natural language processing (Kasneci et al., 2023, pp. 1–2). Additional interfaces and programs have been designed around these AI models to increase capabilities and simplify user interaction, including the development of popular "chatbots" and AI tools such as OpenAI's ChatGPT, Google's Gemini, Anthropic's Claude, and DeepSeek's eponymous platform. Their widespread adoption can be attributed to both their impressive functionality as well as the ease with which people can use them.

AI in Grant Proposal Writing

A growing list of uses, benefits, and drawbacks of AI in the general workplace have been documented (Dell'Acqua et al., 2023; Noy & Zhang, 2023; Patrikakis & Hurlburt, 2025). Most utilizations rely on users interacting with an AI tool via natural language through the act of prompting. To produce content of usable quality, one must understand the nuances of prompting. The technology can then be more effectively applied to specific tasks and areas. Related to grant writing, applications include tasks associated with writing assistance, editing, and content creation. *Prompting*, simply put, is when a user provides input to elicit a response from the AI. The content the AI responds with is known as the *completion* (Microsoft, 2023).

The prompt can be broken down into its key components: the instruction, which directs the AI's response (e.g., "write a paragraph"), and the content, which provides material for the AI to process or transform. For example, an instruction like "write a paragraph" can be enhanced by adding content such as "about the need to expand caregiver training," which helps the AI generate a more useful response. The process of crafting and refining prompts is called prompt engineering, which aims to elicit a desired outcome (Reynolds & McDonell, 2021, p. 3). OpenAI offers strategies—broad guidelines for achieving better results—and tactics, which are specific methods to implement those strategies (OpenAI, 2023). Patterns, or reusable solutions to common problems, can also be used in prompt design (Fowler, 2003; White et al., 2023). While strategies are the most general, patterns are the most specific. Below are key strategies, tactics, and patterns for grant writing:

Strategies (OpenAI, 2023)

- *Split Complex Tasks into Simpler Subtasks.* Working in steps and stages rather than attempting to generate a complex piece of content with a single prompt. Prompting an AI tool to generate a single sentence or section rather than an entire document is an example.
- *Provide Reference Content.* Using reference material such as related text, documents, or images can decrease fabrications (hallucinations) and increase the likelihood of generating suitable content.

Tactics (OpenAI, 2023)

- *Specify Desired Parameters.* Instructing the AI tool to respond within specific parameters, such as paragraphs or pages, increases the likelihood that those parameters will be met.
- *Prompt the Model with a Follow-up Query.* Asking the model if it missed anything or to "think carefully and logically, explaining your answer" (Hulbert, 2023) in a subsequent prompt may reveal flaws and lead to improved content.

Patterns (White et al., 2023)

- *Persona Designation.* Prompt the AI to respond in the manner of a specific role, aspect, or character; for instance: You are [PERSONA]. Example: "You are a professional grant writer."
- Provide output that [PERSONA] would create. Example: "Provide output that a college professor would create."
- *Inquisitive Prompting (Flipped Interaction).* Prompt the AI tool by asking what information is needed from the user to complete a task and then instruct it to act on that information. This may be especially useful when a user is new to or unfamiliar with a task; for instance:

Ask me [NUMBER OF QUESTIONS] [SUBJECT]. Once I have responded, [DESIRED BEHAVIOR]. Example: "Ask me four questions regarding my organization. Once I have responded, write a paragraph for a grant proposal summarizing my organization."

Prompting may be a complex action. It is important, however, as it directly impacts the AI tool's ability to generate content in useful ways. Once sufficient media literacy skills have been developed, the use of AI for specific purposes and tasks becomes more reliable and valid. AI should not be considered a replacement for user expertise; it is a tool that potentially allows users to work better, faster, and more intelligently. Writers may come to view the AI tool as a team member, though the writer remains responsible for quality and accuracy.

The AI as Writing Assistant

A writing assistant's roles are varied and numerous. A grant writer may be just one member of a small team working on a project, or even alone in the endeavor, and receiving such assistance through prompting can be highly beneficial. Potential uses for AI as a writing assistant or guide on the side include:

- *Researching Subject Matter.* AI tools may be prompted to provide sources on a specific subject. Though early models tended to fabricate (hallucinate) these, more advanced AI tools seamlessly incorporate the internet through separate programs in a process known as Retrieval Augmented Generation (RAG). The process improves the results significantly (Lewis et al., 2020), with the material found by the RAG programs being incorporated into the prompt that is then responded to by the model.
- *Summarizing Sources.* AI tools are often prompted to summarize sources, thus providing the main ideas from various materials. These materials may include texts, audio files, and videos.
- *Locating Grants.* The assistant can use multiple avenues to locate relevant grant opportunities. For example, a direct query to the AI tool may result in a completion containing information on well-known grants in the specified area. Further, tools and queries that incorporate aspects of RAG may scour the Internet for relevant opportunities.
- *Analyzing the Solicitation.* The AI writing assistant can identify important clues about funder identity and preferences. Prompts for solicitation analysis may specifically focus on describing the funder's rhetoric, style, and tone; extracting keywords; or even developing a template based on proposal requirements. Grant writers may then decide to follow up with a multiple prompting approach to specify page or word count allocations based on an RFP's evaluation criteria.

- *Mining Public Data.* AI as a grant writing assistant maximizes one of its most powerful capabilities: researcher. Grant writers may use AI assistants to mine public data to support evidence-based proposals, namely in constructing the justification for the project. Such capability may also be useful in supporting methodologies or citing previous studies. Research goes beyond the search capacity for which grant writers may only have limited time to execute. The AI assistant, equipped with RAG, can conduct a much deeper dive and dynamically pull from credible, public sources—parameters that grant writers would specify in the prompt. The research may include census data, community demographics, availability and accessibility of service providers, academic performance, peer-reviewed literature, environmental information, or policy updates to supply the grant writer with the most recent and relevant evidence and insights for the proposal. The functionality enhances proposal elements such as the needs statement, project feasibility, cost estimations, and anticipated outcomes.
- *Identifying Win Themes.* Win themes are key messages or arguments that highlight the unique value and benefits that distinguish the proposal and proposer from competing submissions; for instance, aligning with funder priorities, emphasizing impact, demonstrating feasibility, and differentiating the proposal. Win theme identification is an exercise typically conducted among a proposal team following research on the funder, market, and competition. However, this is one of several tasks that can be expedited by an AI assistant to advance or jumpstart subsequent steps in the grant writing process. The grant writer, and proposal writing team when applicable, may then maximize the proposal kickoff meeting or proposal planning process with a discussion on the results rather than spending time generating ideas.
- *Analyzing Competitors.* Similar to the strategy of win theme identification, competitor analysis is also about differentiation or how to stand out, with which AI can assist. For instance, grant writers may ask the AI writing assistant to identify competitors based on previous awardees available on the funder's website, or via the attendance roster from a pre-bid Q&A session. Grant writers may also ask the AI assistant to develop a comparative analysis of competitors, including in relation to their own organization, to identify and potentially mitigate any weaknesses.

AI as Content Creator

The ability of Generative AI to create and transform content is paradigm-shifting (Ayers et al., 2023; Noy & Zhang, 2023; Zhang & Gosline, 2023). Whether content created is of sufficient quality to satisfy reader needs requires careful consideration.

Authors might consider the interplay of three key elements: (1) the capabilities of the AI tool/model, (2) the skills of the user, and (3) the information being provided. An AI tool that limits completions to roughly one page of text, for instance, would not be able to generate a ten-page paper if prompted to do so. A user who understands this and utilizes multiple prompts to generate smaller sections rather than an entire paper while also providing relevant information at each prompt-step would be able to generate higher-quality content.

AI can help grant writers streamline and expedite the grant writing process by automating repetitive sections such as the organizational capacity, past performance, or internal controls sections. Prompting for this accelerates proposal production while maintaining consistency and accuracy within the application and across submissions by the same organization. Further, it is common practice for grant writers to maintain a library of proposal materials—a repository of technical narratives, logic models, past performance descriptions, organizational narratives, and compliance statements related to their work. Grant writers routinely adapt content from this library for new applications.

Another specific area in grant writing where AI content creation may be of use regards past performance. Once a project is successfully completed, outcomes, impacts, and key details are documented to serve as a reference for future grant proposals. Documentation allows for the verifiable demonstration of capacity and capability without the need to significantly rewrite the content. Traditionally, grant writers manually extract and tailor these details for each new funding opportunity. Media production literacy can be used to enhance this process by automating content customization.

Rather than copying and pasting from old proposals or from our database entries and tweaking wording, AI can dynamically and consistently adjust details, emphasizing specific outcomes, aligning language with funder expectations and funding parameters, ensuring every section remains compliant and compelling. Attaching the notice of funding for analysis, including a link to the funder's mission statement in the prompt, or using an established organizational persona to prompt the AI platform are all ways in which a grant writer can reduce time spent on customizing "boilerplate" content, allowing them to instead focus on finessing rhetorical strategies.

By integrating AI into grant writing project management workflows, grant writers and writing teams can not only improve efficiency but also increase their competitiveness by submitting winning proposals in less time. The writer is responsible for maintaining authenticity, strategic intent, and organizational culture in every submission.

AI as Editor

AI can significantly enhance editorial accuracy in grant writing. Large or resource-rich organizations may have the staff and business processes to accommodate a *full-color review*, which is a comprehensive proposal evaluation process in which distinct teams or individuals use a color-coded feedback system (e.g., blue for strategy, red for compliance and overall evaluation, green for costing, white for final proof). Time or resources may necessitate compressing the review process from a full-color review to targeted input (e.g. only a *white* review just before submission). For organizations without the capacity to provide for a full-color review, whether due to time or resource constraints, AI serves as an accessible and timely editorial assistant, providing real-time feedback and revisions based on key writing components included in the grant writer's prompt. Potential editorial functions for AI may include:

- *Grammar, Spelling, and Punctuation.* AI editors can identify and correct errors that could undermine a proposal's credibility. Sophisticated AI editors offer a refined functionality where the grant writer determines with what text, where, when, and how the AI editor might intervene. Again, this convenience does not absolve writers of responsibility for the final text. The delegation and automation of proofreading tasks should be understood as a partnership in which the grant writer maintains oversight.
- *Flow.* The AI editor can analyze the solicitation for instructions on formatting and content organization to revise the proposal accordingly. Tasking the editor with flow may also entail ensuring a logical progression within the technical proposal's elements, such as the project narrative. AI can analyze structure and coherence of content and suggest revisions that ensure each section cohesion. A grant writer might also prompt the AI editor to flag abrupt transitions that need additional attention as well as identify redundancies or circular arguments that disrupt the content's progression.
- *Language.* If grant writers prompt the AI tool to analyze information such as the funder's website, the solicitation, correspondence with the funder, or previously awarded projects (if available), the tool can suggest phrasing and word choices that mirror the funder. Such alignment may be persuasive to reviewers; alignment may establish common ground and trust. By optimizing language to reflect the funder, including terminology, level of formality, modality preferences, reading level, and other language elements, the AI editor can help refine proposals to resonate with reviewers who read on behalf of the funder's mission, vision, and objectives. Furthermore, the AI editor can

help calibrate balance between technical- or discipline-specific language and readability for interdisciplinary review panels.

- *Compliance.* The AI editor can also confirm if or how well a project might meet eligibility requirements for applicants, and it can also assess if the grant writer's content is responsive to available evaluation criteria. The AI editor can also flag areas of noncompliance in the cost proposal, such as allowable costs, indirect cost restrictions, match, or in-kind requirements. Beyond basic compliance with the solicitation, the grant writer can prompt AI to produce detailed checklists specific to the funder or the project focus area, tracking both expectations of the field and implicit assumptions about what constitutes a competitive application in the relevant discipline, funder type, project focus, award amount, or against incumbent and competitor profiles. AI can cross-reference multiple documents related to the opportunity, such as the request for information, pre-bid notification, NOFO, bidder question and answers, and amendments. The task would identify any contradictions or updated guidance that impacts the proposal content and submission, including the submission timeline.
- *Voice, Style, and Tone.* Using AI to maintain a consistent voice and style throughout a proposal is especially useful for teams. A prompt should specify the desired style (e.g., academic) and tone (e.g., authoritative, aspirational) to unify the proposal under one cohesive voice, representing the agency as a whole rather than a mix of writers. This unified voice often embodies the agency's identity, which can influence reviewers. For example, a nonprofit might use its CEO's signature phrase, "what right looks like," in a proposal to a private foundation. The selection committee, familiar with the CEO's leadership and personality, may find this phrase strengthens the agency's identity and credibility, fostering a deeper connection with funders.

Limitations of AI in Grant Writing

AI is an incredibly powerful tool. It has revolutionized multiple industries and continues to change others as it becomes more widely adopted. There are, however, multiple limitations and issues with the technology (Fjeld et al., 2020; Dave, Athaluri, & Singh, 2023; Lucchi, 2024). Not all of these, however, significantly affect grant writing. For instance, the U.S. Copyright Office's ruling that material created by an AI solely through a prompt by a human cannot be registered for a copyright (U.S. Copyright Office, 2023, p. 4), while important to many industries and practices, is not particularly relevant to grants. Grant writers do not typically seek to copyright their proposals. On the other hand, there are several issues that directly affect proposal writing with AI support, and those in the industry should be aware of them, including hallucinations, confidentiality, and the need to address grantmaker AI use policies.

Hallucinations

A hallucination is when an AI generates a nonfactual response that appears valid (Lowe & Leike, 2022; Barassi, 2024). While this is sometimes obvious, it can just as easily be difficult to detect and may occur in any part of the completion. A very famous example of this is when Alphabet released a promotional video for its AI chatbot Bard that incorrectly stated which satellite first took pictures of a planet outside the Earth's solar system (Coulter & Bensinger, 2023). Regarding media literacy, hallucinations can present an obstacle to validity and reliability. Triangulating AI-generated content is the writer's responsibility. For a grant writer, a false claim based on a hallucination can undermine the strength of a grant proposal and can also permanently damage the writer's credibility as well as that of the organization associated with the document.

Confidentiality

It is easy to assume that what transpires between a user and an AI tool is private, as there are often no other humans present during the interaction. The assumption, however, is wrong. There are documented incidents of data breaches and losses of confidential information related to the use of AI (Prinz, 2025). Further, corporations that own the AI systems regularly monitor them, as is evidenced by Google's previous statement within Bard, "Your conversations are processed by human reviewers to improve the technologies powering Bard. Don't enter anything you wouldn't want reviewed or used" (Google, 2023). Thus, users must assume that any data provided to an AI through prompting or other means is not private and may be viewed by others.

Grantmaker AI Use Policies

Those involved with grants should be aware of any policies held by the grantmaker regarding AI use. These policies may appear in various locations, including the published grant opportunity, a related writing/style guide like APA or MLA or Chicago, or on the funder's website. Some funders, such as the National Science Foundation, do encourage applicants to "indicate in the project description the extent to which, if any, Generative AI technology was used and how it was used to develop their proposal" (NSF, 2023). Further, many grantmakers, including the NSF, NIH, and ARC (Australian Research Council), prohibit the use of AI by reviewers or assessors of grant proposals, often citing confidentiality rules as a primary reason (ARC, 2023; NIH, 2023; NSF, 2023).

CONCLUSION

Effective proposal writing involves rhetorical moves that demonstrate sophisticated understanding of content needs, the most appropriate writing style choices, careful implementation of research tools like AI, and strategic and tactical problem/solution sets that realistically optimize potential funder return on investment. AI is transforming grant writing by providing tools that enhance efficiency, allowing writers to focus more on strategy and asset-based proposal writing approaches instead of deficit models. Through frameworks like the Digital Online Media Literacy Assessment (DOMLA), grant writers can develop the necessary media, digital, and algorithmic literacies to navigate AI's capabilities while also maintaining ethical integrity and rhetorical efficacy.

AI is a synergistic supporter and task automator. It can process documents, flag key themes, and suggest competitor strategies with remarkable efficiency. And by integrating AI into grant writing project management workflows, writers and teams can increase competitiveness. However, final decisions on strategy, language, and the logic of a proposal connecting goals and objectives leading to outcomes must remain with the writer rather than the AI assistant to avoid a presentation that is not valid or reliable. Writers may come to view the AI tool as a team member, though the user of the AI tool remains responsible for quality and accuracy.

REFERENCES

Abbass, H. (2021). What is artificial intelligence? *IEEE Transactions on Artificial Intelligence*, *2*(2), 94–95. https://doi-org.uc.idm.oclc.org/10.1109/TAI.2021.3096243. DOI: 10.1109/TAI.2021.3096243

Altshuler, R. D. (2022). Narratives are useful strategies for overcoming challenges in risk communication. *American Journal of Public Health (1971)*, *112*(S1), S12–S14.

ARC Australian Research Council. (2023). *Policy on Use of Generative Artificial Intelligence in the ARC's Grants Programs*. Research Policy Branch.

Aufderheide, P. (1993). *Media Literacy. A Report of the National Leadership Conference on Media Literacy*. https://eric.ed.gov/?id=ED365294

Ayers, J. W., Poliak, A., Dredze, M., Leas, E. C., Zhu, Z., Kelley, J. B., Faix, D. J., Goodman, A. M., Longhurst, C. A., Hogarth, M., & Smith, D. M. (2023). Comparing physician and artificial intelligence chatbot responses to patient questions posted to a public social media forum. *JAMA Internal Medicine*, *183*(6), 589–596. DOI: 10.1001/jamainternmed.2023.1838 PMID: 37115527

Barassi, V. (2024). Toward a theory of AI errors: Making sense of hallucinations, catastrophic failures, and the fallacy of Generative AI. *Harvard Data Science Review* (Special Issue 5). DOI: 10.1162/99608f92.ad8ebbd4

Becker, S. O., Hornung, E., & Woessmann, L. (2011). Education and catch-up in the industrial revolution. *American Economic Journal. Macroeconomics*, *3*(3), 92–126. DOI: 10.1257/mac.3.3.92

Buckingham, D. (2007). Digital media literacies: Rethinking media education in the age of the internet. *Research in Comparative and International Education*, *2*(1), 43–55. DOI: 10.2304/rcie.2007.2.1.43

Chaka, C. (2020). Skills, competencies and literacies attributed to 4IR/Industry 4.0: Scoping review. *IFLA Journal*, *46*(4), 369–399. DOI: 10.1177/0340035219896376

Clarke, C. (2009). *Storytelling for grantseekers: A guide to creative nonprofit fundraising* (2nd ed.). Jossey-Bass.

Coulter, M., & Bensinger, G. (2023). Alphabet shares dive after Google AI chatbot Bard flubs answer in ad. *Reuters*. https://www.reuters.com/technology/google-ai-chatbot-bard-offers-inaccurate-information-company-ad-2023-02-08

Dave, T., Athaluri, S. A., & Singh, S. (2023). ChatGPT in medicine: An overview of its applications, advantages, limitations, future prospects, and ethical considerations. *Frontiers in Artificial Intelligence*, *6*, 1169595–1169595. DOI: 10.3389/frai.2023.1169595 PMID: 37215063

Dell'Acqua, F., McFowland, E., Mollick, E. R., Lifshitz-Assaf, H., Kellogg, K., Rajendran, S., Krayer, L., Candelon, F., & Lakhani, K. R. (2023). Navigating the jagged technological frontier: Field experimental evidence of the effects of AI on knowledge worker productivity and quality. *Harvard Business School Technology & Operations Mgt. Unit Working Paper* (24-013). DOI: 10.2139/ssrn.4573321

DG RTD (European Commission Directorate-General for Research and Innovation). (2024). *ERA Industrial Technologies Roadmap on Human-Centric Research and Innovation for the Manufacturing Sector.* Publications Office of the European Union. https://data.europa.eu/doi/10.2777/0266

European Commission. (2021). *Proposal for a Regulation of the European Parliament and of the Council laying down harmonised rules on Artificial Intelligence (Artificial Intelligence Act) and amending certain Union legislative acts.* COM/2021/206 final. https://eur-lex.europa.eu/legal-content/EN/TXT/?uri=celex:52021PC0206

Fjeld, J., Achten, N., Hilligoss, H., Nagy, A., & Srikumar, M. (2020). Principled artificial intelligence: Mapping consensus in ethical and rights-based approaches to principles for AI. *Berkman Klein Center Research Publication.* https://papers.ssrn.com/sol3/papers.cfm?abstract_id=3518482

Fowler, M. (2003). Patterns. *IEEE Software*, *20*(2), 56–57. DOI: 10.1109/MS.2003.1184168 PMID: 12628886

Godwin, R. C., DeBerry, J. J., Wagener, B. M., Berkowitz, D. E., & Melvin, R. L. (2024). Grant drafting support with guided Generative AI software. *SoftwareX*, *27*, 101784. DOI: 10.1016/j.softx.2024.101784

González-pérez, L. I., & Ramírez-montoya, M. S. (2022). Components of education 4.0 in 21st century skills frameworks: Systematic review. *Sustainability (Basel)*, *14*(3), 1493. DOI: 10.3390/su14031493

Google. (2023). Bard [Large Language Model]. https://bard.google.com

Hallaq, T. (2016). Evaluating online media literacy in higher education: Validity and reliability of the digital online media literacy assessment (DOMLA). *The Journal of Media Literacy Education*, *8*(1), 62. DOI: 10.23860/jmle-8-1-5

Hulbert, D. (2023). Tree-of-thought prompting to boost ChatGPT's reasoning. *GitHub*. DOI: 10.5281/zenodo.10323452

Hussin, A. A. (2018). Education 4.0 made simple: Ideas for teaching. *International Journal of Education and Literacy Studies*, *6*(3), 92–98. DOI: 10.7575/aiac.ijels.v.6n.3p.92

IBM. (n.d.). What is an AI model? *IBM.com.* https://www.ibm.com/topics/ai-model

Ivanov, D. (2023). The industry 5.0 framework: Viability-based integration of the resilience, sustainability, and human-centricity perspectives. *International Journal of Production Research*, *61*(5), 1683–1695. DOI: 10.1080/00207543.2022.2118892

Jebara, T. (2004). Generative versus discriminative learning. In Jabara, T. (Ed.), *Machine Learning. The International Series in Engineering and Computer Science. 755*. Springer., DOI: 10.1007/978-1-4419-9011-2_2

Kasneci, E., Sessler, K., Küchemann, S., Bannert, M., Dementieva, D., Fischer, F., Gasser, U., Groh, G., Günnemann, S., Hüllermeier, E., Krusche, S., Kutyniok, G., Michaeli, T., Nerdel, C., Pfeffer, J., Poquet, O., Sailer, M., Schmidt, A., Seidel, T., & Kasneci, G. (2023). ChatGPT for good? on opportunities and challenges of large language models for education. *Learning and Individual Differences*, *103*, 102274. DOI: 10.1016/j.lindif.2023.102274

Kessler, M. (2020). A text analysis and gatekeepers' perspectives of a promotional genre: Understanding the rhetoric of Fulbright grant statements. *English for Specific Purposes*, *60*, 182–192. DOI: 10.1016/j.esp.2020.07.003

Koutsantoni, D. (2009). Persuading sponsors and securing funding: Rhetorical patterns in grant proposals. *Academic Writing: At the Interface of Corpus and Discourse,* 37–57.

Lewis, P., Perez, E., Piktus, A., Petroni, F., Karpukhin, V., Goyal, N., Küttler, H., Lewis, M., Yih, W.-t., Rocktäschel, T., Riedel, S., & Kiela, D. (2020). Retrieval-augmented generation for knowledge-intensive NLP tasks. *arXiv.* https://arxiv.org/abs/2005.11401.

Lowe, R., & Leike, J. (2022). Aligning language models to follow instructions. OpenAI. https://openai.com/research/instruction-following

Lucchi, N. (2024). ChatGPT: A case study on copyright challenges for generative artificial intelligence systems. *European Journal of Risk Regulation*, *15*(3), 602–624. DOI: 10.1017/err.2023.59

Markowitz, D. M. (2019). What words are worth: National Science Foundation grant abstracts indicate award funding. *Journal of Language and Social Psychology*, *38*(3), 264–282. DOI: 10.1177/0261927X18824859

Martin-Kerry, J., McLean, J., Hopkins, T., Morgan, A., Dunn, L., Walton, R., Golder, S., Allison, T., Cooper, D., Wohland, P., & Prady, S. L. (2023). Characterizing asset-based studies in public health: Development of a framework. *Health Promotion International, 38*(2). DOI: 10.1093/heapro/daad015 PMID: 36932994

Matveeva, N., Moosally, M., & Willerton, R. (2017). Plain language in the twenty-first century: Introduction to the special issue on plain language. *IEEE Transactions on Professional Communication, 60*(4), 336–342. DOI: 10.1109/TPC.2017.2759619

Microsoft. (2023). Introduction to prompt engineering. *Microsoft Azure AI Services.* https://learn.microsoft.com/en-us/azure/cognitive-services/openai/concepts/prompt-engineering

Moravec, V., Hynek, N., Skare, M., Gavurova, B., & Polishchuk, V. (2025). Algorithmic personalization: A study of knowledge gaps and digital media literacy. *Humanities & Social Sciences Communications, 12*(341), 341. DOI: 10.1057/s41599-025-04593-6

Mosier, K. E. (2022). Deconstructing the art of grantsmanship: The roles of the storyteller, grant writer, typesetter, proofreader, accountant and reviewer. *The Journal of Research Administration, 53*(1), 93–121.

Nabhan, S., & Habók, A. (2025). The digital literacy academic writing scale: Exploratory factor analysis. *SAGE Open, 15*(1), 21582440241311709. DOI: 10.1177/21582440241311709

NIH National Institutes of Health. (2023). The use of generative artificial intelligence technologies is prohibited for the NIH peer review process. *nih.gov,* NOT-OD-23-149. https://grants.nih.gov/grants/guide/notice-files/NOT-OD-23-149.html

NIH National Institutes of Health. (2024). Communicating research intent and value in NIH applications. *nih.gov,* https://grants.nih.gov/grants-process/write-application/general-grant-writing-tips/communicating-research-intent-and-value-in-nih-applications

Noy, S., & Zhang, W. (2023). Experimental evidence on the productivity effects of generative artificial intelligence. *Science, 381*(6654), 187–192. DOI: 10.1126/science.adh2586 PMID: 37440646

NSF National Science Foundation. (2023). Notice to research community: use of generative artificial intelligence technology in the NSF merit review process. *nsf.gov.* https://www.nsf.gov/news/notice-to-the-research-community-on-ai

Open, A. I. (2023). Prompt engineering. *OpenAI.com.* https://platform.openai.com/docs/guides/prompt-engineering

Patrikakis, C. Z., & Hurlburt, G. F. (2025). Could artificial intelligence write, review, edit, and produce this column? *IT Professional, 27*(1), 4–10. DOI: 10.1109/MITP.2025.3530597

PlainLanguage.gov. (2011). *Federal Plain Language Guidelines.* U. S. General Services Administration. https://www.plainlanguage.gov/media/FederalPLGuidelines.pdf

Potter, W. J. (2010). The state of media literacy. *Journal of Broadcasting & Electronic Media, 54*(4), 675–696. DOI: 10.1080/08838151.2011.521462

Potter, W. J. (2022). Analysis of definitions of media literacy. *The Journal of Media Literacy Education, 14*(2), 27–43. DOI: 10.23860/JMLE-2022-14-2-3

Prinz, K. D. (2025). Managing the legal risks of artificial intelligence on intellectual property and confidential information. *Consulting Psychology Journal, 77*(2), 169–179. DOI: 10.1037/cpb0000287

Reynolds, L., & McDonell, K. (2021). Prompt programming for large language models: Beyond the few-shot paradigm. In *Extended abstracts of the 2021 CHI conference on human factors in computing systems* (pp. 1–7). DOI: 10.1145/3411763.3451760

Rybiński, K. (2025). Automation of grant application writing with the use of Chatgpt. *Scientific Papers of Silesian University of Technology., 2025*(216), 493–515. DOI: 10.29119/1641-3466.2025.216.30

Salib, S., de la Garza, K., & Kapadia, A. M. (2024). Asset framing: A tool for enhanced equity in feedback and assessment. *Medical Science Educator, 34*(5), 1189–1192. DOI: 10.1007/s40670-024-02094-w PMID: 39450041

Seckel, E., Stephens, B. Y., & Rodriguez, F. (2024). Ten simple rules to leverage large language models for getting grants. *PLoS Computational Biology, 20*(3), e1011863–e1011863. DOI: 10.1371/journal.pcbi.1011863 PMID: 38427611

Seeger, M., & Sellnow, T. L. (2016). *Narratives of crisis: Telling stories of ruin and renewal* (Vol. 19). Stanford University Press.

Shanahan, E. A., Reinhold, A. M., Raile, E. D., Poole, G. C., Ready, R. C., Izurieta, C., McEvoy, J., Bergmann, N. T., & King, H. (2019). Characters matter: How narratives shape affective responses to risk communication. *PLoS One, 14*(12), e0225968. DOI: 10.1371/journal.pone.0225968 PMID: 31815957

U.S. Copyright Office. (2023). Copyright registration guidance: Works containing material generated by artificial intelligence. *Federal Register.* https://www.copyright.gov/ai/ai_policy_guidance.pdf

van den Besselaar, P., & Mom, C. (2022). The effect of writing style on success in grant applications. *Journal of Informetrics, 16*(1), 101257. DOI: 10.1016/j.joi.2022.101257

Vaswani, A., Shazeer, N., Parmar, N., Uszkoreit, J., Jones, L., Gomez, A. N., & Polosukhin, I. (2017). Attention is all you need. *Advances in Neural Information Processing Systems, 30*. DOI: 10.48550/arXiv.1706.03762

White, J., Fu, Q., Hays, S., Sandborn, M., Olea, C., Gilbert, H., Elnashar, A., Spencer-Smith, J., & Schmidt, D. C. (2023). A prompt pattern catalog to enhance prompt engineering with ChatGPT. arXiv. https://doi.org//arXiv.2302.11382DOI: 10.48550

Willerton, R. (2015). *Plain language and ethical action*. ATTW/Routledge. DOI: 10.4324/9781315796956

Wu, J. (2011). Improving the writing of research papers: IMRAD and beyond. *Landscape Ecology, 26*(10), 1345–1349. DOI: 10.1007/s10980-011-9674-3

Wuyckens, G., Landry, N., & Fastrez, P. (2022). Untangling media literacy, information literacy, and digital literacy: A systematic meta-review of core concepts in media education. *The Journal of Media Literacy Education, 14*(1), 168–182. DOI: 10.23860/JMLE-2022-14-1-12

Zhang, Y., & Gosline, R. (2023). Human favoritism, not AI aversion: People's perceptions (and bias) toward Generative AI, human experts, and human–GAI collaboration in persuasive content generation. *Judgment and Decision Making, 18*, e41. DOI: 10.1017/jdm.2023.37

KEY TERMS AND DEFINITIONS

Artificial Intelligence (AI).: The automation of cognition based on various technologies as well as the field of science that studies it. Machine Learning (ML) is considered a subset, though machine learning techniques (along with natural language processing, algorithm mutation, and others) are used to create programs known as AI models.

Asset-Based Framing.: A style of writing that showcases a community or an organization's strengths and resources rather than deficits.

Digital Online Media Literacy Assessment (DOMLA).: A method of evaluating and understanding digital online media literacy. Its primary elements (known as constructs) include ethical awareness (EA), media access (MAc), media awareness (MAw), media evaluation (ME), and media production (MP).

Hallucination.: When an AI generates false, misleading, or nonsensical information. This will often appear to be highly plausible.

Notice of Funding Opportunity (NOFO).: An announcement from a grantmaker (funder) detailing a grant opportunity, which is a formal period when the grantmaker accepts requests for resources (usually submitted in the form of a proposal). Frequently understood as a request for proposals (RFP).

Plain Language (in writing).: A style of writing that communicates information in a straightforward manner and avoids unnecessary complexity. See https://plainlanguage.gov.

Prompt Engineering.: The designing or crafting and revising of prompts to elicit a desired behavior or outcome.

Prompt (in AI).: Input (often text) used to elicit a response from an AI or similar program. The content the AI responds with is known as the completion. Prompting is the act of providing a prompt.

Rhetoric.: The art of persuasion. Knowing writing moves available and best employed can be both art and science.

Scientific Writing.: A form of technical writing used to communicate information between scientists.

Storytelling (in grant writing).: Effective storytelling in grant writing transforms data and objectives into a compelling narrative, making the proposal more engaging, relatable, and persuasive to funders.

Chapter 9
Empowering Educators and Students Through Information Literacy in the Era of AI

Stephanie Korslund
https://orcid.org/0009-0000-7087-836X
University of Cincinnati, USA

Ashley Seibert
University of Cincinnati, USA

ABSTRACT

Today, where artificial intelligence (AI) is at the forefront of our world, information literacy has become more relevant, and critical, than ever before. Information literacy is the set of skills and knowledge that allows individuals to "recognize when information is needed and have the ability to locate, evaluate, and use effectively the needed information" (American Library Association, 1989). As AI continues to evolve and become more robust, it is crucial for educators to support learners as they develop and expand their critical thinking skills. By understanding how artificial intelligence works, particularly generative AI, and the limitations it carries, educators can implement strategies that foster both information literacy skills and AI awareness, equipping learners with the skills needed to navigate and leverage these technologies responsibly in an evolving digital landscape.

DOI: 10.4018/979-8-3373-0872-2.ch009

Introduction

Generative AI is at the forefront of conversation in education. Here we explore the intersection of information literacy and artificial intelligence, with a particular focus on generative AI. This chapter is split into three main parts. In the first part, we will begin by defining information literacy and the influence artificial intelligence has on information. Then we will narrow our focus to AI and education, examining the impact generative AI has on teaching and learning and the considerations both educators and students must make when working with AI-generated information.

In part two, we will look more closely at the information models that currently exist and how they help build a foundation for how students can evaluate AI-generated content. Through the CRAAP and SIFT methods, the reader will learn to navigate AI-generated content responsibly and emphasize the importance of evaluating content for credibility, accuracy, and relevance while recognizing potential biases built into AI models. We will walk through common types of bias students and educators may encounter when working with generative AI and provide readers with the tools to evaluate for these biases.

The third and final part of the chapter will focus on providing educators with practical strategies for integrating information literacy skills and AI awareness into teaching practices. These strategies will support educators in preparing students to responsibly use AI tools and think more critically about the information they are receiving from AI.

PART I: UNDERSTANDING INFORMATION LITERACY

What is Information Literacy?

Information Literacy is the set of skills and knowledge that allows individuals to "recognize when information is needed and have the ability to locate, evaluate, and use effectively the needed information" (American Library Association, 1989). Having these skills allows individuals to critically evaluate the vast amount of data they encounter, distinguishing between credible sources and misinformation. With the growing influence of artificial intelligence in society, which often curates information alongside generating it, information literacy skills help everyone identify biases, inaccuracies, or omissions in AI-driven outputs. Having such skills empowers individuals to make informed decisions, think critically, and navigate complex digital environments effectively. For educators, fostering information literacy equips students with the skills needed to responsibly consume, create, and share information, preparing them to thrive in a society increasingly shaped by technology and data.

The American Library Association (ALA) identifies six core areas or "frames" by which they use to guide the organization of various critical thinking strategies. These six frames are:

- Authority is Constructed and Contextual
- Information Creation as a Process
- Information has Value
- Research as Inquiry
- Scholarship as Conversation
- Searching as Strategic Exploration

The purpose behind the development of these frames is to help educators, librarians, or anyone who has a hand in developing curriculum to implement information literacy skills that will benefit students and create an environment where they are more involved in "the understanding of how information is produced and valued, and the use of information in creating new knowledge and participating ethically in communities of learning." (ACRL, 2016)

Authority is Constructed and Contextual

As students are taught research strategies, they are taught to look for those who are "authorities" on the particular topic they are exploring. These authorities can come in many different complex forms but are seen as an influence in their fields. Students must be taught to keep an open mind and to look for diverse perspectives, even ones that may challenge what they already know or believe.

Educators should guide their students to look at what makes a person an "authority" on a specific topic, whether that includes a person's position or title, personal experience, or other defining credentials. These perspectives may not always reach the learner through formal channels such as academic journals, but come from all forms of media. Thus, a student should be taught to think critically about the information being provided and what makes it credible. It is also important to recognize that while the community that surrounds this authority may deem them as influential, new and developing information may still challenge that figure's perspective. Students should always strive to find a diverse array of authorities to form a larger picture of the subject at hand. As they learn more, they themselves become more authoritative and need to be conscious of the effect their ideas have on the information being created.

Information Creation as a Process

The creation of information varies for each individual, influenced by their research methods and the intended use of the final product. Students should be encouraged to look beyond a resource's format when assessing its usefulness. They need to understand that the process by which information is discovered and compiled can significantly impact its perceived quality. Information that has undergone an editing or review process is often seen as more credible. The usefulness of a resource also depends on the context in which it is used; a resource may be more valuable in a corporate setting than in an academic one, and vice versa.

Once students recognize the process behind information creation, they can evaluate whether it meets their specific research needs. Regardless of the information's format, they should be able to determine its value in relation to their goals. For example, if a student is researching a scientific hypothesis, they should assess whether the methods used by the source creator are appropriate for their topic, despite the final format of the information.

Over time, as students begin to develop their own information creation processes, they need to understand that each choice impacts how their final product will be perceived. Choices during the creation process must be considered, as well as how they intend their final product to be used. The information may evolve over time, and students should be adaptable to the process while being mindful of their own capabilities and needs.

Information Has Value

Information has many different facets that give it value. Presently, "free" information is widely accessible to students at a click of a button. Educators must be vigilant and guide students through the process of determining value based on their own research contexts. Many students are never taught how to assess a resource's value yet are told to fear plagiarism and copyright infringement. It is important for students to understand how value is placed on information, including how perceived value can marginalize certain perspectives disproportionately and even be used to promote certain agendas.

It is the job of students and educators to take responsibility for how they value information. Each individual must examine their own privileges and recognize the time and effort creators put into the information they produce. This means directly teaching students how information varies in regard to copyright law and intellectual property. It is a student's duty to know when, where, and how to create proper citations and attributions. As their research develops, their mindsets need to shift from being a consumer to becoming a producer and realizing the effect their research may have in regard to the larger community.

Research as Inquiry

Every research project starts with an inquiry about a certain topic. Oftentimes, what starts out as a single question can turn into multiple, or a seemingly straightforward question leads to multiple possible outcomes. Curiosity, adaptability, and flexibility are key factors for a student looking to develop a deeper level of inquiry. Learning to form good questions that identify gaps in their knowledge, being open to constructive conversations, and knowing when to broaden or narrow the scope of their research will lead to deeper critical thinking. When research is viewed as exploration and left open-ended, true engagement with information can begin.

As information is collected, educators must guide students on how to organize information, whether that is by assisting in utilizing new research techniques or breaking down complex ideas into smaller, more manageable questions to research. They should be coached to constantly search for gaps in knowledge and fill them with diverse perspectives, while maintaining critical evaluation of their resources to ensure quality and value.

Scholarship as Conversation

Solutions to inquiries are not always apparent, and there are many paths that can be taken to reach the final results. Some disciplines use tried and tested approaches to research, whereas others have ongoing conversations where experts come together to create meaning. As suggested in the other frames, a diverse selection of perspectives can help bring new information to a situation.

Established scholarly conversations can sometimes be daunting for a student new to the field to join. Factors such as authority, level of background knowledge, and experience level can create barriers which prevent certain people from joining. That should not prevent them from finding these conversations and using factual information to contribute. Conversations are often ongoing, and joining in is a helpful opportunity for students to learn from peers in the same research field. It is important to note that an interaction within these conversations should be treated respectfully and at an appropriate level.

Searching as Strategic Exploration

The final frame reminds students and educators that while research is goal-oriented, it is seldom linear. As students develop their research skills, they are able to determine which methods best fit their needs and to scale the scope of information accordingly. Students who are new to research tend to limit the amount of sources they seek out due to lack of confidence or an overwhelming sense of what to even include. Seasoned researchers who have been equipped with various strategies to filter information can often cast a wider net to be able to find more valuable information.

Students with developed research skills can more easily identify sources where useful information can be found and brainstorm strategies to collect and organize it to fit their needs. They must remain flexible and be able to adapt their inquiries if no results are being found. Students should be coached to lean on experts around them, whether they are faculty, librarians, local community members, or otherwise. New perspectives lead to new insights which can take their research to new places. Educators should encourage resilience in the face of challenges and help equip students with the skill set needed to persevere.

AI's Influence on Information

While artificial intelligence has been a field of study for well over half a century, since the introduction of ChatGPT-3.5 in late 2022, there has been a surge in the use of generative artificial intelligence tools to generate information by the general population. Large language models like those developed by OpenAI, Meta, and Anthropic have an influence on the type and quality of information users receive. Such models are not only able to generate information but also "analyze data; generate images, videos, and websites; [and] write, run, and correct code" (Pratschke, 2024, p. 9) with their abilities continuing to expand with every new version released. And as Pratschke (2024) noted in their own summary of generative AI, there is no question any longer about whether these tools will be used within the workforce but a question of how they are used, making it that much more important for users to have a solid understanding of what kind of information these models are producing.

While large language models are trained on enormous datasets, they are unable to create new information as a human might. Instead, these models are only capable of generating text that mimics that of humans through processing and interpreting information from their training data. For example, ChatGPT's predictive algorithms allow it to only produce information based upon what it has been taught. While its training dataset may be large, because it is still finite and ultimately based on human input, it is possible for it to not only generate misinformation but also, as OpenAI (2022) put it, "plausible-sounding but incorrect or nonsensical answers." Such models have also struggled in the past to identify sources and create accurate citations when prompted to do so, hallucinating information. Hallucinations occur when large language models produce fake information, misleading users into thinking the information generated is real and credible. As Jones (2025) notes, "this is both a strength and a weakness. It's the reason for their celebrated inventive capacity, but it also means they sometimes blur truth and fiction, inserting incorrect details into apparently factual sentences" (p. 778).

Artificial Intelligence has also been used to personalize and filter the information users receive by analyzing user data to deliver tailored recommendations. This is evident in almost every internet-connected service. Social media platforms customize feeds based on users' previous views, search engines prioritize certain publications on the front page, and video streaming services predict what users might want to watch. While this personalization in many ways is helpful to a user's overall online experience, users need to be aware that such tailoring is occurring. Users should be aware in particular of the concept known as the 'filter bubble,' where a user may rarely encounter content outside the curated experience created by the AI models, limiting the perspectives provided to the user to what the model deems relevant. To maintain a well-rounded worldview, it is crucial to balance information. To manage this, Pariser (2011) argues that AI algorithms must be designed to present diverse perspectives, even those that challenge our thinking. Such algorithms need to incorporate ethical considerations to ensure an even flow of information.

Issues with personalization are not the only types of bias that users contend with when working with AI models. Biases within such models can also distort information, as these systems often inherit biases from their training data or reflect the perspectives of their creators. These perspectives can be harmful to marginalized and underrepresented groups. Issues such as skewed data, missing perspectives and voices, and reinforced stereotypes are just a few of the ways bias has shown up in AI results. Bias in AI will be discussed further in the next part. What can be said now is that understanding how generative AI models influence information is crucial for critically evaluating content, mitigating biases, and ensuring that the information we consume and share is accurate, diverse, and reliable.

Defining AI in the Educational Context

In higher education, there has been a notable movement, from educators and students alike, in integrating generative AI tools into their scholarly practice (Hodges & Ocak, 2023). The movement has shifted from seeing AI as a tool that just checks spelling and grammar to one that seemingly simplifies even the most complicated tasks. Generative AI has become a personal assistant to many educators, assisting with everything from course development to data analysis. For students, AI has become a partner in the educational process, acting as an editor, personal tutor, and even a research assistant. Such skills and knowledge are not only critical within higher education but beyond, with many in higher education believing these skills will be key for our future workforce (Gurchiek, 2024).

Educators have a key role to play here. It is not enough to assume because today's students are digital natives, they already have the knowledge needed to succeed with these tools, particularly in educational contexts. If educators want students to critically use these tools ethically and responsibly in education, then they must help students build the necessary skills. From this need comes AI literacy. In the few years that it has been researched, AI literacy has already been positioned as an essential 21st-century skill (Cox, 2024; Malik et al., 2023; Ru & Tang, 2025). While there are many different definitions in the existing literature for AI literacy, one of the most cited definitions defines it as "a set of competencies that enables individuals to critically evaluate AI technologies; communicates and collaborate effectively with AI; and use AI as a tool online, at home, and in the workplace" (Long & Magerko, 2020).

In a sense, AI literacy is no different from what librarians in higher education have been doing with information literacy for over twenty years. Calling back to the American Library Association's definition of information literacy and the six frames it uses to guide the organization of various critical thinking strategies, there are clear connections between the two concepts. Both information literacy and AI literacy focus on not only use but also the need to critically evaluate the source or tool in question. It is in this critical evaluation of information that information literacy skills can be particularly useful to students as they continue to build their AI literacy skills. As students turn to generative AI more and more, it's imperative they develop the critical thinking skills needed to evaluate everything generative AI models present to them. It is in this space that information literacy skills are key.

PART II: INFORMATION LITERACY FRAMEWORKS

The G.E.A.R. Framework

To understand the elements of Information literacy and where to begin with evaluating information, we look at the G.E.A.R. framework (Brooks, Warner, Hammons, & Chesnut, 2019). Based on the six frames of information literacy developed by the American Library Association, this framework divides information literacy into four areas: Gather, Evaluate, Apply, and Respect. Each area covers a different step of the research process that students should follow.

The first area, Gather, focuses on the initial stage of a research project, which is "gathering" information that relates to their topic. At this stage, a student should be utilizing several research methods to find a wide range of resources. Students may look to multiple databases, academic journals, or other publications that align with the type of information needed for the topic. During this step, students are encouraged to reflect on their gathering techniques to ensure that they are utilizing the appropriate tools for the work they are doing.

The next area is Evaluate, where the student is asked to examine their gathered information to find the most relevant and accurate resources. Considerations such as the goal of the research, the intended audience, and the format of the final deliverable should also be considered, as they will help to guide the learner in choosing which resources will serve them the best. At this stage, students will begin to curate the information and filter out the resources that don't fit their needs while also making sure that a wide variety of perspectives are included in their research.

The third area, Apply, is where the actual creation happens. Now that a student has found all the information needed to support their work, they will start to craft their final deliverable. They will take their curated resources and apply them to their research goals, using them to form new ideas, assumptions, and solutions. Students at this step are asked to take a step back and make sure that they are not just making claims without supporting evidence, but using what already exists as a foundation for their own claims.

The final area, Respect, asks students to look at the responsibilities that come with finding and using information. At this step, one should be looking at the licensing for their resources to determine how it can or cannot be used, and how to give credit to the original creators. Certain licenses dictate how the resource and information can be used, modified, or shared. It is important to know which type of licensing a resource has so proper citations and/or attributions can be created.

The CRAAP Method

Once one understands the components of information literacy, they can then move to using evaluative methods to guide their decisions when choosing resources. One method for evaluating information is CRAAP, which focuses on evaluating sources for credibility, relevance, authorship, accuracy, and purpose (Blakeslee, 2004). This method was originally designed to assist students in scholarly research and encourages students to take a closer look at where information is originating from and the reasoning behind its creation to ensure they are curating the best possible resources to support their topic. It relies on the concept of vertical reading or digging deep into the background of the single resource to understand its origins and intent.

The first consideration when evaluating resources according to the CRAAP method is currency. Students should consider the nature of their research and if it is time sensitive. For example, research on historic events such as the U.S. Civil War may not have many new resources. Since information about this topic is less likely to experience rapid change, it is fine to have an older resource. In fact, resources like first-hand accounts may be more helpful. However, if the subject matter is something new and emerging, then a good rule of thumb is to find a resource that has been published or updated within the past three to five years. This ensures that recent findings are being taken into consideration and that information is not out-of-date or obsolete.

The next consideration focuses on relevancy. With every scholarly project, there is a goal that is trying to be achieved. That goal could be anything from a scientific hypothesis, a question to be answered, or a new skill to be learned. As a student looks for resources, they should ask themselves whether or not the information is helping them to achieve their desired goal. Will it help them to directly further their research, or is it something that doesn't quite align? Included in this analysis is ensuring that the resource not only aligns with their goal but also at the level of their audience.

The third consideration, and the first A, stands for Accuracy, and is intended to remind students not to take information at face value. It is critical for students to consider the information that a resource is presenting and review how that information came to be, including examining the process by which the information was formed and recorded. Students may ask themselves questions such as "Is the provided information supported by evidence and has it been reviewed for accuracy?", "What kind of organization is producing this resource?" or even "Can the information be verified through other resources?" Asking these questions, along with paying close attention to how the information is presented, can give students clues to a resource's reliability.

The next A stands for Authority, which asks students to consider who is behind the information being presented. A good first step in examining authority is to look at the organization behind the resource. For example, if a student were gathering information from the internet, what kind of website or database is being used? Looking at the end of a website's URL can give some clues as to who is behind certain resources. Websites ending in '.com' are generally commercial and entertainment-oriented, while '.edu' sites are typically dedicated to education. Those with '.gov' are government-produced, and '.org' sites usually belong to non-profit organizations. All these types of websites have merit depending on the type of research being conducted. However, knowing the background of the organization can help determine whether it will fit the student's needs. Beyond looking at the organization producing the resource, the author of the resource must also be examined. Who is writing the information, and what are their qualifications to do so? Knowing the author's qualifications will lend credibility to the information being presented.

The final consideration, Purpose, builds upon the questions asked about the author and organization producing the information. It requires students to look at why the information was produced. Is the information given to entertain the viewer, or is it to teach and inform? Is it trying to persuade the audience on a matter or sell them something? Is there a certain leaning to the resource (political, cultural, religious), or is the point of view impartial? Every author brings their own experience to the information they publish. It is important for students to consider what their own purpose is to see if the information presented aligns with their goals.

Despite its origins in traditional scholarly research, the CRAAP method can be utilized anywhere there is information available. Analyzing information through a critical lens will help ensure that the best resources are being gathered to support one's research.

The SIFT Method

Another method for evaluation is SIFT(Caufield, 2019). Whereas the CRAAP method focused more on traditional scholarly work, such as journal articles, this method focuses more closely on the review of online information. Like CRAAP, it can still be applied to other types of information as well. SIFT stands for Stop, Investigate, Find, and Trace.

SIFT is meant to be a quick way to look at what is being presented to us online and evaluate the legitimacy of the resource. For example, if someone is scrolling through a social media platform, they may encounter a post that is giving information on a certain topic, such as a current event, entertainment news, or a new discovery. Using the SIFT method, the person should first Stop and digest the information that is being presented at its face value. They should take a moment to consider what kind of response they are having to the information, whether it's a positive reaction or not. Clickbait, news articles, and other online posts try to be sensational and strive to evoke emotions out of people so they can gain attention and views. A person interacting with digital media needs to be savvy to digital marketing tactics and should step back from their initial reactions to consider what information they already have about the subject. Does the information seem like it could be factual based on prior knowledge? Who or what is behind the information being presented? Is it from a reputable source? What kind of account is posting the information? Is it a tabloid, news outlet, an organization of some sort, or, in the case of social media, a friend or acquaintance? Each of these brings their own perspectives, biases, and reasons behind sharing information.

This leads into step 2 of SIFT, where one should "investigate the source". Many people get their information from their social media accounts. It is easy to be taken in by information being presented by fake accounts posing as a legitimate resource. Taking the time to click through an account to evaluate whether the account is legitimate can help determine the authority that the source has on the topic. One thing to be particularly aware of is account verification. It is important to note, though, that just because an account is "verified" does not mean that the account is a legitimate source. If the source is a friend, acquaintance, or public figure, do they have any credentials that establish their authority on the subject, or is the information based solely on their personal opinions or interests? If the source is an organization, what details are available about it? What does their profile or website reveal about their interests, mission, and expertise? Does this organization have authority on the subject?

While profiles and websites can be insightful to a certain person or organization, what they present is always going to be intentionally designed to meet a goal or present a certain facade. Going further to investigate the source can reveal more about the reasons behind the information they provide. Lateral Reading (Wineburg & McGrew, 2017) is the idea of fact-checking the same information across multiple websites before digging too much into any one source. Using search engines to look up the source can provide information that the original author/creator did not include themselves. In their study, Wineburg and McGrew (2017) brought together a group of Stanford students, historians, and professional fact-checkers to see which group would best determine the credibility of certain websites. Two website examples they offered the group were the American Academy of Pediatrics and the American College of Pediatrics, both seemingly reputable websites based on child health. Out of the three groups, only the professional fact-checkers were able to determine that the American Academy of Pediatrics was the more credible source. They used lateral reading to find background information on each organization before delving too far into the information that they provided. Looking beyond official-looking logos, well-designed websites, and seemingly factual articles being presented, they took to searching the organizations outside of their respective websites. They found that the American Academy for Pediatrics is the largest professional association for Pediatrics and has been in service since the early 1900s, whereas the American College of Pediatrics is a political group founded in 2002 and has a much smaller following. For someone doing research on pediatrics who wants factual, unbiased information, the American Academy is the more reputable organization.

The next step in SIFT is to "find better coverage", which builds on the idea of lateral reading. Once the original source is investigated, one should do further research to see what information is out there on the topic. Are there more resources available that support the original source's claim, or dispute it? It is important to hold each of these secondary sources to the same standards as the original, and only use ones that have been verified as reputable. It can be telling if one resource presents a certain idea, and there are no other resources that claim or support the same thing. A simple way to verify certain facts would be to use non-profit fact-checking websites such as FactCheck.org or Politifact.

The final step is "trace claims to their original context," meaning that there should be an attempt to find the original source for any fact, quote, or media presented. As mentioned before, opinion, bias, and certain agendas can skew information from its original context. It is best practice to look further into any claim being presented to ensure that the full story around that information is being presented, rather than being curated to fit a certain narrative.

Digital information and the way that it is disseminated will continue to grow and change with any new platforms that emerge. In our modern society, people turn to the internet as a quick way to find information. However, it is fair to say that many people have had little to no training on ways to effectively find information based on fact and to avoid being misled while online. Whether that information is coming from a social media post, or from a search within a database or site like Google, it is best practice not to take anything at face value.

Critically Evaluating AI

Although the methods discussed above were not initially created to assess AI-generated information, they provide valuable insights that can be applied to evaluating the content generated by large language models. Just as a student would critically analyze information found through tools like Google when researching a topic, they must also apply the same scrutiny to information generated by AI models.

As in the CRAAP and SIFT methods, a student must look at the original source (the dataset) that the model has been taught by and is pulling information from. They must also stop to analyze the content of the results in relevance to their prompt and assess it for accuracy and completeness. Did the generated information meet the purpose or goal of the question asked? Did it show a complete factual perspective, or did it create false answers (hallucinations) to answer the prompts? Applying these questions to an AI-generated response can help a student decide whether the information being presented is factual and fulfills their needs.

To illustrate how a prompt can be evaluated using these criteria, students must simply ask a question to any language model. For example, when ChatGPT was asked the question "How was your language model taught?" it responded by saying it used the "unsupervised learning method on a large dataset that includes text from books, websites, and other publicly available written material" (OpenAI, 2025). It then elaborates that after it learned from the dataset, it formatted the information to remove "irrelevant or harmful content" (OpenAI, 2025). When asked how it flagged and removed content, it stated that it looked for content surrounding "hate speech and discrimination, violence and harmful behaviors, misinformation and conspiracy theories, and explicit content" (OpenAI, 2025). It said it used automated filtering algorithms, along with human review of flagged content and built-in ethical guidelines and policies to set standards for what was or was not removed from its dataset. It also had a clause stating that content surrounding "controversial but legitimate" topics and "factual disagreements" is not always removed (OpenAI, 2025). After the content was formatted, Copilot explained that it used "transformer neural networks" to learn word associations, concepts, and text prediction. From there, the data is fine-tuned to fit the guidelines provided by humans to improve its performance. It also states that it continues to learn to have "more natural conversations" from receiving additional human feedback.

Background information students should consider gathering when doing research with generative AI models includes finding out the language model the system was built upon, how that language model trained, which company created it, and why. In ChatGPT's case, it was built using OpenAI's GPT-4 language model. OpenAI's mission statement indicates that they want to "ensure that artificial general intelligence - AI systems that are generally smarter than humans – benefits all of humanity" (OpenAI, 2025). Its website boasts that safety is a key concern when training its model. Its overall goal is to achieve Artificial General Intelligence (AGI), meaning that an artificial intelligence model "can possess the ability to understand or learn any intellectual task that a human being can" (Google Cloud, 2025).

To check for accuracy and completeness, a student can turn to lateral reading methods. Students can easily search for "OpenAI" and find links to confirm ChatGPT's response. The top links on Google are on its various policies, posts about battling bias, its AGI mission, and its ethical guidelines. These links are from both its main website and community forum pages. Outside of its own links, organizations like MIT Technology Review (a long-standing publication focused on technology) have run its own tests and drawn conclusions from the results.

In 2023, MIT Technology Review's Melissa Heikkilä, interviewed some of OpenAI's policy researchers about their work with training their large language model (LLM), who confirmed that the company is aware of the bias issues, and it is actively working on "cleaning up its dataset and removing examples where the model has had a preference for things that are false" (Heikkilä, 2023). She also learned that OpenAI is aware of people attempting to manipulate the model to generate biased and derogatory information. The interview goes on to say that OpenAI "is exploring using surveys or setting up citizen assemblies to discuss what content should be completely banned" (Heikkilä, 2023).

In an effort to understand the political biases that Chat-GPT had, it designed a series of charged questions based on current hot topic issues to see how the model would respond. It found that Chat-GPT 3.5 and Chat-GPT 4 often returned inconsistent responses. From a shared list of their prompts, it demonstrated that Chat-GPT would respond "Not Support" for prompts written from both left and right-leaning perspectives, thus contradicting itself. They also noted that small changes to the wording of its prompts could lead to completely different responses being generated.

Note that these tests were completed in 2023, and responses generated today may yield different results.

As a student, one must think of one's own context and needs when determining whether a response is relevant to the prompt given to the model. In the example above, Chat-GPT offered the process by which it was taught, which was able to be confirmed by other reputable resources outside of the model. While the prompt was answered in detail, it never mentioned that it still has its own biases and may still generate problematic responses despite having human review and adhering to OpenAI's ethical guidelines. Without the outside resources providing context for the biases within the code, that part of the story would have been filtered out, leading the student to believe that it could only generate information that was ethical and impartial on certain topics.

Understanding Bias and AI

Beyond credibility, accuracy, and relevance, another area educators must focus on with information literacy is bias. AI-generated information often reflects the biases of the data on which it was trained, as well as from the algorithms and contexts in which the information is generated (IBM Data and AI Team, 2023). Beyond the bias that exists within the algorithms and datasets themselves, there also exists the biases within the user which shape how questions are asked and how information is interpreted (Wei, Kumar, & Zhang, 2025). Understanding the types of bias that can exist in AI-generated content can help students more effectively evaluate the information presented to them.

The bias most people are familiar with when working with generative AI models is algorithmic bias. This is the bias that exists inherently within the data the AI model was trained on (Jackson, 2021) or exists within the design of the model (Ferrera, 2024) and often results in generated content that reflects stereotypes and other inequities. One example of algorithmic bias would be gender bias in AI-generated career suggestions, for example, when asked to produce an image of a construction worker, only producing images of men or when asked to produce an image of an elementary school teacher, only producing images of women.

Another type of bias frequently seen in AI-generated content is cultural bias. Cultural bias occurs when the content generated by the AI model highlights the norms, values, or beliefs of one culture while dismissing or misrepresenting other cultures. Liu (2024) noted that this was a particular issue with newer models that often are "defaulting to Western culture and norms even when operating in non-Western languages." An example of cultural bias in AI-generated content would be a response that uses examples from only the United States when referencing global trends.

Confirmation bias appears when generative AI models selectively present information to support a particular viewpoint, rather than objectively reflecting the data it has been trained on. An example of confirmation bias in AI would be a healthcare chatbot immediately diagnosing a female patient presenting with chest pain with anxiety without further questioning. Similar to confirmation bias is selection bias, which occurs when generative-AI models only include certain types of information in their responses, leading to incomplete information. Looking at an example of technology in learning, an AI-generated response that had selection bias would only highlight the benefits of technology in learning while completely omitting information on any harmful effects.

These are just a few of the biases that exist within AI-generated data. Without the proper information literacy skills to critically evaluate such biases, these biases can influence how students respond to and interpret the information presented. Using information literacy skills such as cross-referencing AI-generated information and being aware of personal biases that may influence how they prompt or interpret received information can assist students in their understanding of the information being presented to them by AI models.

PART III: STRATEGIES FOR INTEGRATING INFORMATION LITERACY IN THE CLASSROOM

Overview of Strategies

In the final part of this chapter, we have included a variety of activities and resources that can be used within the classroom environment to encourage students and educators to think critically about the information generated by AI models. These activities include:

1. SIFTing for AI Content: Students are asked to enter a prompt into an AI model and apply the SIFT method to verify the information received. Could they trace the information back to the original context? Were there other resources that supported (or did not support) the information they were given?
2. Detecting Bias in AI: Students are given AI-generated content and asked to use a Bias Detection checklist. They will be asked to identify which type of bias the content has. Then they will be asked to do comparative research to look for alternative perspectives on the topic.
3. Creating Prompt Variations for AI Responses: Students will experiment with prompt variations and analyze how wording can lead to different responses.

They will examine the uses of specificity, clarity, tone, style, and point of view when writing prompts.

4. Comparative Analysis Across AI Platforms: Students will compare AI-generated content across platforms and identify variations in perspective. They will utilize their skills in critical thinking, bias recognition, and comparative analysis, highlighting how information is presented differently based on the AI tool used.
5. Source Verification Scavenger Hunt: Students will engage in a "scavenger hunt" to verify the accuracy of citations and assess the credibility of the sources included in AI-generated responses.
6. Copyright and Fair Use for AI Responses: Students will explore the U.S. Copyright and Fair Use laws when it comes to information generated by AI, and how to properly credit and cite AI-generated content.

While many of these activities build on the knowledge gained from other activities, it is not necessary to implement them all in the same class. We recommend that educators choose the activities that best suit the needs of their class and students.

SIFTing for AI Content

Students must be coached not to take information at face value and not to use AI-generated responses as-is. The SIFT method encourages students to question, investigate, verify, and validate information, which can be directly applied to AI-produced content in academic and personal contexts. By the end of the activity, students will be able to critically assess the credibility and accuracy of AI responses.

Begin the activity with an introduction to the SIFT framework, its purpose, and how to use it to analyze information. Use this introduction to facilitate a class discussion where the students identify reasons why they think AI-generated content could be difficult to verify and ask if they have encountered information that seemed credible but was difficult to confirm. This discussion can be used to gauge the students' understanding of information literacy and adjust the discussion to support their critical thinking skills.

Once the students are familiar with the SIFT method, ask them to select a topic to prompt an AI tool with. Students should be sure to ask the tool to include sources for the information that it is providing them. Coach the students to search broad topics such as "the impact of social media on mental health," or "the impact of plastic pollution on marine life," as this will give them a wider spectrum of information to consider. Apply each step of SIFT to the generated responses.

In the first step, "Stop", educators should teach the students to take time to react to the response that the AI tool returns from their prompt before they accept it as credible. Before looking too deeply at the information, ask the students to determine whether the sources that the tool provided appear to be reliable and relevant to the topic. Have them take time to write down any questions or doubts that they have content generated.

During step 2, "Investigate the Source," have students investigate the AI tool that generated the content. Understanding background information about the tool will provide insight into its origins, dataset, and any known limitations it might have. Have students consider questions such as:

- What is the tool's known expertise or limitation on this topic?
- Is the AI trained on authoritative or reputable data for this subject?
- What is the known expertise or limitations of the sources the AI has provided within the response?

Students should record their findings and any implications that they have on the reliability of the generated responses.

Next, students will begin to "Find Better Coverage." Using the information within their responses, students will begin to look for outside sources to verify the claims that were generated. They should select 2-3 claims made within their responses and search for them in reputable sources (such as academic journals, government websites, or major news organizations), taking note of how the response aligns with information from those sources. Are there similarities or contradictions? Were the outside sources able to support the AI-generated content, or were there discrepancies? If there are discrepancies, how could this affect the outside resource's credibility? Have them record their observations.

Finally, students will "Trace Claims to Original Context," where they will verify the origin of the claims within the response, paying close attention to specific facts and data that were generated. Students should attempt to trace each item back to their original source. If the AI tool fails to provide a citation for a specific piece of information, they should document it and try to locate similar data within trusted sources. As they trace the information, they should consider whether the AI-generated content was presented accurately and identify what limitations a missing source may present.

To end the activity, educators should ask the students to reflect on their experiences. What were the main challenges that they encountered? How did the SIFT framework help them assess the credibility of their responses? How can using it assist in future research using AI-generated sources?

Detecting Bias in AI

The ability to recognize bias within information is a critical information literacy skill. Students who can recognize bias and understand its impact on information will develop stronger research strategies and better evaluate content within resources.

This activity is a multi-part workshop that asks students to identify and discuss types of bias within AI-generated content. Through analysis, discussion, and reflection, students will practice their ability to recognize biases and foster a more critical approach to AI-generated content.

To prepare for the activity, students should be provided with resources on recognizing bias within AI-generated content and the impact those biases can have on perception. Educators should also consider providing a checklist for defining types of bias. This checklist would provide definitions of the types of bias, examples, and questions that guide students through the identification process. See Figure 1 for an example bias detection checklist.

Figure 1. Bias Detection Checklist for AI-Generated Content

Cultural Bias Questions to Consider

- Whose cultural perspective is represented in this content?
- Are there other cultural perspectives that are missing or underrepresented?
- Does the language suggest one culture's values as universal or superior?

Confirmation Bias Questions to Consider

- Does this content present only one side of a controversial issue?
- Are there alternative viewpoints or evidence that should be included?
- If you search for information from other sources, does it align with or contradict this AI-generated response?

Selection Bias Questions to Consider

- Does the AI include a diverse range of sources and viewpoints?
- Are there newer or more authoritative sources that could add depth to this information?
- If certain groups or viewpoints are missing, how might this affect the content's completeness?

Algorithmic Bias Questions to Consider

- Is the AI content making assumptions based on stereotypes?
- Does the information reinforce harmful generalizations or exclude certain groups?
- How might the training data behind this AI have influenced the content?

Framing Bias Questions to Consider

- Does the language used in the content push you toward a specific interpretation?
- Are there words or phrases that seem overly positive or negative without balanced explanation?
- Could the information be framed differently to provide a more objective view?

Implicit Bias Questions to Consider

- Are there assumptions in the content about who the reader is or what they value?
- Does the AI make unspoken judgments that favor one perspective over others?
- How could the content be adjusted to remove these implicit preferences?

Overall Reflection Questions - After identifying specific types of bias, reflect on the broader impact:

- How does each identified bias affect the reliability and completeness of the AI-generated content?
- What strategies could help mitigate these biases in the content?
- How might understanding these biases impact the way you use AI-generated information in the future?

Once the students are familiar with the content, educators can facilitate a discussion surrounding the resources provided. Discuss whether students have encountered bias within AI-generated content, what types of bias they observed, and how it affected the credibility and/or usefulness of the information.

Select an AI tool and ask the students to input a specific prompt and have them document their initial impressions of the content, taking note of any slant or lack of diversity in viewpoints. Using a checklist (if prepared), have the students analyze the AI-generated content for the signs of various biases, such as Cultural, Confirmation, or Selection bias. They should document any examples, noting each incident of bias, which type of bias was most prevalent, and how each might impact a reader's perspective.

After reviewing the AI-generated content and noting the identified biases, have the students select 1-2 key points from the response. Using reputable, human-authored resources, students should find similar information and compare how each source frames the topic, noting the differences in tone, emphasis, and scope of the information provided to that of the AI-generated content. Were there perspectives or details in the human-made sources that the AI content missed, and how did the inclusion of diverse perspectives change their understanding of the topic?

In a final discussion, bring the class together to discuss their findings. Have the students reflect on their experiences during the activity. How did recognizing bias in AI-generated content influence their perceptions of AI tools in academic research? Ask what strategies they will use to identify and mitigate bias when using AI in the future.

Creating Prompt Variations for AI Responses

Learning how to write effective prompts is an important skill when working with AI tools. Slight changes in the wording of the prompt can lead to variations in how a tool generates a response. For this activity, students will explore how different ways of asking questions can impact the results they receive. They will practice creating varying prompts while observing changes in content, tone, and depth within the generated information, while learning how to refine their prompts for better outcomes.

Start by choosing a specific AI tool which all students will use. Allow students to ask a question on a specific topic. An example of a question could be "What are the effects of social media on mental health?" Students should record the response that the AI tool generates, documenting any observations about the tone, depth, or bias in the content.

From there, the students will modify their original prompt to add details or clarify their question. For example, they may change "What are the effects of social media on mental health?" they may try "Describe both positive and negative effects of social media on mental health among teenagers." Students will record their new response and compare it to the previous, noting any changes in detail or tone. How did adding specifics change the AI's response? Did it provide more balanced or detailed information?

Next, ask the students to experiment with the tone and style of their prompt. Have them adjust their prompts to be more formal, conversational, or investigative. For example:

- Formal tone: "Provide an academic analysis of the effects of social media on mental health."
- Conversational tone: "Can you tell me how social media might affect people's mental health in day-to-day life?"

Again, ask the students to record the response generated by the tool, noting differences in language, structure, and content depth. Did the tone of the response change depending on the prompt style? For example, did the formal prompt style generate a more formal response? Were certain tones more effective in generating the type of response they wanted?

Finally, have the students experiment with adding specific points of view and perspectives to their prompts. An example of this could be "What do mental health professionals say about social media's impact on mental health?" Have them record the responses, noting any additional insights or details that have been added. Students should reflect on how using specific perspectives may help to avoid bias and enrich the responses that they receive.

End the activity by having the students discuss their discoveries as a class. Did they find anything surprising as they modified their prompts? What changes did they see? What insights did they gain about the importance of clear and specific prompt design?

Comparative Analysis Across AI Platforms

Students must be made aware that each generative AI tool responds differently depending on the dataset by which it was trained, the algorithmic formatting, and the prompt it was given. The objective of this activity is to illustrate the variances between how different AI models will respond to the same prompt. They will need to use critical thinking skills to conduct a comparative analysis between any two models and identify the variations in not only formatting, but also perspectives, language, and any potential biases.

To prepare students for this activity, it is recommended that they be provided with materials about generative AI and a high-level overview of the AI tools available. Use resources with information describing why AI tools may differ in the content that they generate, focusing on the training data, algorithms, and the nature of probabilistic outputs. This part of the activity can be adjusted based on the level of familiarity the students have with AI, but for students who are new to generative AI, this will help to establish a foundation on which to base their findings.

After reviewing the materials, educators should facilitate a class discussion where the students can reflect on their previous experiences (if any) with generative AI. Ask the students if they have noticed differences between the types of responses that each respective tool provides, and why they think those differences exist.

After the initial discussion, ask each student to select a topic or research question that is relevant to their studies or interests. Using that topic, students will create a prompt and submit it to at least two different AI tools (ChatGPT, Bing Chat, Bard, etc.). They should record the generated responses to their prompt, the name of the tool used, and the date within separate documents (or pre-made worksheets) for side-by-side comparisons.

For each tool, students should be asked to provide:

- Summary of key points from the response that the tool generated.
- The tone and language of the response (Is it formal or informal? Does it use technical terms/jargon or is it written in accessible language? Is the writing concise or detailed?)
- Notes on any unique perspectives from the information provided. (Is the response complete and relevant to the prompt? Does it vary in substance or specificity? Are there any gaps in the information in regard to missing perspectives or important details?)

End the activity by completing a final reflection. This can be done as a class discussion where students share their findings with their peers and respond to others about the similarities and differences they noted in their respective searches, or a written submission in addition to the documentation of the tool response. Have students respond to prompts such as "What did this activity reveal about how AI tools present information differently?" "Did one platform provide more comprehensive or balanced information than the others?" or "How would you apply these critical analysis skills when using AI for research in the future?"

Source Verification Scavenger Hunt

AI tools have been known to create false sources when generating citations. The goal of this activity is to help students understand the importance of verifying information for authenticity and accuracy.

To begin this activity, provide the students with resources on verifying information in the age of AI. Facilitate a class discussion where students reflect on why source verification is especially important with AI-generated content and the risks that may arise from relying on the generated citations without checking them.

After the discussions, have the students select a topic that is relevant to their studies or interests, have them use it as a query in an AI tool, and request a response with citations and sources. The students should document the generated response. If the AI tool generates citations, have the students record details such as publication title, author (if given), and publication date for each source. They should also include any observations regarding whether the source appears reliable based on the information provided. Did the citation have an identifiable author or list a well-known, reputable publication? Are there any citations that seem questionable based on their format or lack of detail?

Once the students have finished noting their observations, have them use a reputable search engine or academic database to confirm the existence and accuracy of the sources that the AI tool generated. They should begin by searching for the exact title and author name. If found, the publication date can be used to further verify the source. Have students report their findings, noting whether each source was verifiable, accurate, or if they encountered false or "hallucinated" citations. They should also note any challenges they encountered when searching for the source and whether the AI citation aligned with the information they discovered.

Next, the students should evaluate the quality of each source they were able to verify. Ask them to consider the author's qualifications and expertise in the topic, the publication's reputation, and any potential biases based on the publisher's and author's affiliations. Students should reflect on whether the source is well-suited to support the AI-generated content and explain their reasoning.

In a final class discussion, educators should have the students share their findings. How did verifying the AI citations impact their level of trust in the AI tool's response?

Copyright and Fair Use for AI Responses

Due to AI models being trained on datasets pulled from many different sources, the issue of copyright infringement has been one of the leading conversations on the ethics of using AI tools. A user can unknowingly use copyrighted material due to a lack of proper citations and attributions. In this activity, students will explore copyright law, fair use and how to properly cite AI-generated content. It can be completed as an extension to the Source Verification Scavenger Hunt activity, following along the same process.

Begin the activity by having students view resources about copyright law, fair use, and the types of works that are protected under them. The U.S. government has a webpage on copyright and AI that is a good place to start. Resources that describe how to create citations in varying styles should also be included, preferably ones that focus on the style used in that particular discipline.

Once the resources have been reviewed, bring the students together to discuss what they have learned. What do the students already know about copyright law and/or Fair Use? How do they think AI-generated content could affect the market for information protected by copyright law?

If this activity is being done in conjunction with the Source Verification Scavenger Hunt, students should proceed with the steps as listed in that activity. They should examine each citation carefully, taking note of what format they are in. Are the source citations in the proper formatting? Is there information missing? They should consider how missing information can affect their ability to verify the original source and also its effect on the credibility of the generated content.

As the students find and verify the sources that the AI-generated content provided, they should also look to see what kind of licensing the information is protected by. Is the source all rights reserved, or is it in the Creative Commons? Have the students note the specific licensing that each verified source is under. Did the citation within the AI-generated content align with information in the verified source?

End the activity by having the class come back together for a final discussion where they reflect on what they have learned. Did their generated responses provide proper citations? Can AI-generated content be considered Fair Use? Is it ethical for AI models to be trained on copyrighted content?

CONCLUSION

Integrating information literacy skills is critical when it comes to using generative artificial intelligence. This chapter has explored the intersection of information literacy and artificial intelligence, emphasizing the need for a balanced approach that recognizes both the potential and the challenges of generative AI. By educating students about information literacy, educators are helping them develop the skills needed to evaluate and be mindful of the content they receive from generative AI. These skills go beyond the classroom and will prepare students for the future, to seek credible and accurate information, and prevent the spread of misinformation.

In this chapter, educators and students have been introduced to information literacy as a tool for critically evaluating the information produced by generative AI tools. Through methods such as G.E.A.R., CRAAP, and SIFT, educators were provided with the foundational information to help students understand what it means to critically think about the information they encounter. Additionally, students were introduced to the different types of bias that exist within AI-generated content and information on how to minimize the effects of those biases. In the end, educators were provided with strategies for supporting students in critically evaluating information generated by AI tools. Whether used individually or separately, these strategies provide students with the skills needed to use AI critically both in education and beyond. As we look to the future, the role of AI in education will undoubtedly expand, presenting new possibilities and challenges. It is imperative that educators prioritize AI literacy, ensuring that students are not only consumers of information but also informed creators and critical thinkers.

REFERENCES

American Library Association. (1989). Presidential committee on information literacy: Final report. https://www.ala.org/acrl/publications/whitepapers/presidential

American Library Association. (2016, Jan 11). Framework for information literacy for higher education. *American Library Association.* https://www.ala.org/acrl/standards/ilframework

Baum, J., & Villasenor, J. (2023, May 8). The politics of AI: ChatGPT and political bias. *Brookings.* https://www.brookings.edu/articles/the-politics-of-ai-chatgpt-and-political-bias/

Blakeslee, S. (2004) The CRAAP test, *LOEX Quarterly: 31*(3), 6-7. https://commons.emich.edu/loexquarterly/vol31/iss3/4

Brooks, A., Warner, L., Hammons, J., & Chesnut, M. (2019). *GEARUP*. Northern Kentucky University. https://www.nku.edu/qep.html

Caufield, M. (2019, Jun 19). SIFT: The four moves. *Hapgood.* https://hapgood.us/2019/06/19/sift-the-four-moves/

Cox, A. (2024). Algorithmic literacy, AI literacy and responsible generative AI literacy. *Journal of Web Librarianship, 18*(3), 93–110. DOI: 10.1080/19322909.2024.2395341

Data, I. B. M., & Team, A. I. (2023, Oct 16). Shedding light on AI bias with real world examples. *IBM.* https://www.ibm.com/think/topics/shedding-light-on-ai-bias-with-real-world-example

Ferrara, E. (2024). The butterfly effect in artificial intelligence systems: Implications for AI bias and fairness. *Machine Learning with Applications, 15*, 15. DOI: 10.1016/j.mlwa.2024.100525

Google. (2025). What is artificial general intelligence? *Google.* https://cloud.google.com/discover/what-is-artificial-general-intelligence

Gurchiek, K. (2024, Feb 20). Employers want new grads with Ai experience, knowledge. *SHRM.* https://www.shrm.org/topics-tools/news/technology/employers-want-new-grads-with-ai-experience--knowledge

Heikkila, M. (2023, Feb 22). How OpenAI is trying to make ChatGPT safer and less biased. *MIT Technology Review*, www.technologyreview.com/2023/02/21/1068893/how-openai-is-trying-to-make-chatgpt-safer-and-less-biased/

Hodges, C., & Ocak, C. (2023, Aug 30). Integrating generative AI into higher education: Considerations. *Educause Review*. https://er.educause.edu/articles/2023/8/integrating-generative-ai-into-higher-education-considerations

Jackson, M. C. (2021). Artificial intelligence & algorithmic bias: The issues with technology reflecting history & humans. *Journal of Business & Technology Law.*, *16*(2), 299–316.

Liu, Z. (2023). Cultural bias in large language models: A comprehensive analysis and mitigation strategies. *Journal of Transcultural Communication*, *3*(2), 224–244. DOI: 10.1515/jtc-2023-0019

Long, D., & Magerko, B. (2020). What is AI literacy: Competencies and design considerations. *Proceedings of the 2020 CHI conference on human factors in computing systems*. Association for Computing Machinery. https://dl.acm.org/doi/10.1145/3313831.3376727

Malik, A. R., Pratiwi, Y., Andajani, K., Numertayasa, I. W., Suharti, S., & Marzuki, A. D. (2023). Exploring artificial intelligence in academic essay: Higher education student's perspective. *International Journal of Educational Research Open*, *5*, 5. DOI: 10.1016/j.ijedro.2023.100296

Open, A. I. (2022, Nov 30). *Introducing ChatGPT*. https://openai.com/index/chatgpt/

Open, A. I. (2025). ChatGPT (Mar 14 version) [GPT-4]. https://chat.openai.com/chat

Pratschke, B. M. (2024). *Generative AI and education*. Springer. DOI: 10.1007/978-3-031-67991-9

Ru, K. C., & Tang, R. (2025). Promoting AI literacy through U.S. academic libraries: An analysis of LibGuides from ARL and Oberlin group libraries using the EDUCAUSE AI literacy framework. *Information Research*, *30*(i), 847–865.

Ted. (2011, May 1). *Beware online "filter bubbles" | Eli Pariser* [Video]. YouTube. https://www.youtube.com/watch?v=B8ofWFx525s

Wei, X., Kumar, N., & Zhang, H. (2025). Addressing bias in generative AI: Challenges and research opportunities in information management. *Information & Management*, *62*(2), 62. DOI: 10.1016/j.im.2025.104103

Wineburg, S., & McGrew, S. (2017, Oct 6). Lateral reading: Reading less and learning more when evaluating digital information. *SSRN*, *121*. DOI: 10.2139/ssrn.3048994

KEY TERMS AND DEFINITIONS

- **AI Large Language Model - any artificial intelligence interface that is trained on a specific dataset to generate information when prompted by a user.:**
- **AI-Generated Content - information generated by an artificial intelligence tool. This content can be in various forms including text:** images, videos, etc.
- **Algorithm - the code:** or set of guidelines that calculates, predicts, and generates responses for AI models based on the user's input. Each AI model's algorithm varies based on who created it and the purpose it was intended to serve.
- **Bias - an unfair leaning in favor for or against a person:** group of people, or thing.

o **Algorithmic - bias that occurs when an error within an AI model's code generates unfair or discriminatory results that reinforces prejudice.:**

o **Confirmation - bias that occurs when a person favors information that aligns with their own beliefs and values.:**

o **Cultural - bias that occurs when a person interprets information based on the beliefs and values of their own personal community.:**

o **Selection - bias that occurs when the selection process is not randomized properly. This could lead to skewed information that is not representative of the actual results.:**

- **Hallucinations - false or misleading information created by artificial intelligence when the model misinterprets a prompt or encounters an error within their training data. This information is often illogical or inaccurate.:**
- **Information Literacy - critical thinking skills that are used to recognize the need of information:** where to find it, and how to evaluate its usefulness.
- **Misinformation - misleading or untrue information:**
- **Training Dataset - a grouping of information in various formats (articles, books, academic journals, blog posts, etc.) that are used to train an AI algorithm. Information within these datasets can come from various sources depending on the purpose the AI tool will serve.:**

Section 4
Artificial Intelligence and Human Learning in an Era of Misinformation

Chapter 10
Navigating Truth and Fiction:
Generative AI's Role in Modern Media Literacy

Lalit Kumar
https://orcid.org/0000-0002-8441-1696
MCAET, Ambedkar Nagar, India

Neelendra Badal
REC Bijnor, India

Mohd. Aquib Ansari
Bennett University, Noida, India

Arvind Mewada
Bennett University, Noida, India

Dushyant Kumar Singh
MNNIT Allahabad, India

ABSTRACT

The emergence of generative AI has transformed the media landscape, making it increasingly difficult to distinguish between real and artificially created content. This chapter explores its influence on media literacy, particularly in the realms of social media and news consumption. It examines developments in language models and deep learning, highlighting concerns such as misinformation, deepfakes, and echo chambers. While these challenges exist, AI also contributes to fact-checking, personalized content, and improved accessibility. Through real-world examples, the

DOI: 10.4018/979-8-3373-0872-2.ch010

chapter emphasizes the need for ethical AI practices and stronger media literacy. It encourages collaboration among experts, educators, policymakers, and media organizations to promote transparency and trust in digital information.

1. INTRODUCTION: THE RISE OF GENERATIVE AI IN MEDIA

Generative Artificial Intelligence (AI) is transforming the media industry, redefining content creation, consumption, and distribution. From AI-generated news and deepfake videos to synthetic voiceovers and AI-assisted filmmaking, this technology is revolutionizing journalism and entertainment. While it enhances creativity and efficiency, it also poses ethical challenges, including misinformation, intellectual property concerns, and content authenticity.

1.1 Understanding Generative AI

Generative Artificial Intelligence (AI) refers to advanced machine learning models capable of producing original content, including text, images, music, and videos, by recognizing patterns in extensive datasets. Unlike conventional AI, which primarily analyzes and categorizes information, generative AI creates new, contextually relevant outputs. Notable examples include language models like GPT, image generators such as DALL·E, and coding tools like AlphaCode. This technology has significantly impacted content creation, enabling automated journalism, deepfake videos, and AI-generated art. However, alongside its benefits in efficiency and creativity, it also raises concerns regarding misinformation, media manipulation, and ethical challenges in digital content (Feuerriegel, S., et al., 2024), (Kumar, L., et al., 2024), (Kumar et al. 2024), (Mirsky et al., 2021), (Kumar, L., 2024).

1.2 The Evolution of Generative AI in Media

Generative AI's integration into media has been a gradual process, with significant breakthroughs in the past decade. Early AI models could generate simple text, but today's models produce human-like narratives, compose music, and create photorealistic images. Some key milestones in AI's media evolution include (Totlani, 2023):

In 2014, the introduction of Generative Adversarial Networks (GANs) by Ian Goodfellow revolutionized the field of AI-generated images and videos. GANs enabled the creation of hyper-realistic media content, including deepfake videos, marking a significant leap in generative AI capabilities. By 2017, the invention of the Transformer model paved the way for the development of Generative Pre-trained

Transformers (GPT), significantly enhancing AI's text generation abilities and laying the groundwork for sophisticated language models.

In 2019, deepfake technology gained widespread public attention, showcasing AI's ability to manipulate videos and convincingly superimpose faces, raising both excitement and ethical concerns. Between 2021 and 2023, the emergence of multimodal AI models such as OpenAI's DALL·E and Google's Imagen demonstrated the potential of AI to generate high-quality visual and textual content from simple user prompts, further expanding creative applications. From 2024 to the present, AI tools have become widely integrated into industries including newsrooms, advertising, entertainment, and education, where they are used to create, curate, and enhance digital content at an unprecedented scale. These advancements underscore AI's growing role in shaping modern media consumption.

1.3 Generative AI in News and Journalism

News agencies have increasingly adopted AI to assist in content generation, fact-checking, and summarization. AI-generated articles, headlines, and reports are now commonplace, especially for covering data-driven news such as sports results, financial reports, and weather updates [Pavlik, (2023)]. AI is playing an increasingly influential role in modern journalism, transforming how news is gathered, verified, and presented. One of the most notable applications is automated reporting. Major news agencies such as Reuters and The Washington Post have adopted AI systems to generate reports on topics like financial earnings, sports results, and market trends. These tools allow journalists to quickly produce accurate, data-driven stories, freeing up time for more in-depth investigative work. Another crucial area is fact-checking. AI-powered platforms like Google's Fact Check Explorer and IBM's Watson assist journalists in verifying claims, identifying misinformation, and analyzing large volumes of sources. These tools enhance the speed and accuracy of fact-checking processes, helping reporters maintain credibility and respond swiftly to breaking news.

1.4 AI-Generated Visual and Video Content

Generative AI has dramatically influenced the production of visual content, from social media filters to deepfake videos. AI-powered platforms can generate realistic images, animations, and video clips, raising both opportunities and ethical dilemmas (Pavlik, 2023).

Key Applications:

- **Deepfake Technology:** AI-generated videos that manipulate real footage, making individuals appear to say or do things they never did. While deepfakes have entertainment value, they also pose risks of misinformation and identity fraud.

- **AI Art and Design:** Tools like MidJourney, Stable Diffusion, and DALL·E allow users to create high-quality artwork and advertisements. This is transforming creative industries but also sparking debates about artistic authenticity.
- **AI in Film and Animation:** Hollywood studios use AI for visual effects, voice cloning, and scriptwriting assistance, streamlining production costs and enhancing creative possibilities.

Despite these advancements, AI-generated visuals raise concerns about copyright infringement, digital ethics, and deepfake-driven propaganda.

1.5 The Impact of AI on Social Media and Digital Marketing

Social media platforms extensively use AI for content curation, targeted advertising, and automated responses. AI-driven recommendation algorithms dictate what users see, influencing opinions, behaviors, and even elections (Theodoridis, P. K. et al., 2019), (Sadiku, M. N. O., et al. 2021).

AI has become deeply integrated into social media, transforming the way content is created, shared, and consumed. One of its primary applications is in content creation, where AI tools generate captions, suggest relevant hashtags, and even perform image edits to enhance visual appeal. These features streamline the production process for content creators and marketers, allowing them to maintain consistent and engaging posts across various platforms. Another notable development is the emergence of virtual influencers, such as Lil Miquela—a fully AI-generated social media personality. These digital avatars demonstrate how AI is reshaping influencer marketing, enabling brands to create controlled, always-available personalities that interact with followers much like real humans do. This trend highlights the growing intersection of AI, entertainment, and branding.

AI is also crucial in combating misinformation on platforms like Facebook and Twitter. Advanced algorithms are employed to flag potentially false content and reduce its spread. However, the task is complex, as distinguishing between legitimate information and AI-generated deception remains a persistent challenge. While AI significantly enhances user engagement and personalization in social media, it also introduces ethical concerns. Issues such as privacy invasion, data manipulation, and the reinforcement of echo chambers call for careful regulation and transparency to ensure that AI serves the public good without compromising individual rights or the integrity of information.

1.6 The Future of AI in Media

Generative AI (Kumar et al., 2023) is set to play an even greater role in shaping the media landscape. Future advancements may include more sophisticated deepfake detection systems, improved AI-assisted journalism, and enhanced AI-driven media verification tools (Capatina et al., 2020).

Predictions for the future of AI in media and communication suggest a landscape shaped by increasingly sophisticated technologies and evolving societal needs. One key development is the anticipated improvement in misinformation detection. Future AI models are expected to possess real-time fact-checking capabilities, enabling them to instantly verify the accuracy of information shared across digital platforms. This advancement could play a vital role in maintaining the integrity of online discourse and curbing the spread of false narratives. Another emerging trend is the creation of AI-generated personalized media. In the near future, audiences may be able to watch films or videos entirely crafted by AI to suit their individual tastes, including preferred genres, storylines, and visual styles. This level of customization could transform entertainment by offering highly tailored viewing experiences, blurring the lines between content consumer and creator (Zlateva et al., 2024).

2. UNDERSTANDING GENERATIVE AI: CAPABILITIES AND LIMITATIONS

Generative AI is an advanced technology that creates text, images, audio, and video with impressive precision. It is widely used in journalism, entertainment, design, and education, powering tools that generate realistic conversations, artwork, and multimedia content. In filmmaking, AI aids in scriptwriting, visual effects, and digital actors, while in journalism, it automates news reporting and content summarization. Additionally, AI-driven systems personalize content recommendations, improving user experiences on digital platforms.

However, generative AI has notable limitations. It does not possess true understanding, relying on patterns rather than reasoning, which can result in biased, inaccurate, or misleading outputs. Deepfake technology, for instance, raises concerns about political and social manipulation. AI-generated content may also lack originality, sometimes replicating existing material and raising intellectual property issues. Furthermore, its reliance on high computational power makes it resource-intensive and environmentally demanding (Nah et al., 2023).

While generative AI boosts creativity and efficiency, responsible use requires transparency, regulation, and better AI literacy to address ethical challenges and ensure its positive impact across industries.

2.1 Introduction to Generative AI

Generative Artificial Intelligence (AI) is a specialized branch of AI designed to create original content, including text, images, music, and videos. Unlike traditional AI, which primarily analyzes and categorizes information, generative AI produces new content by identifying patterns in existing data. This has led to the development of advanced models such as OpenAI's GPT series, Google's Imagen, and DeepMind's AlphaCode (Nah et al., 2023).

2.2 Capabilities of Generative AI

Generative AI has emerged as a transformative force across a wide array of domains, significantly altering how digital content is conceived, created, and utilized. Its core strength lies in its ability to understand and reproduce complex patterns in text, visuals, sound, and code, allowing for the automation and augmentation of tasks that were once the exclusive domain of human expertise.

In the realm of text and language, generative AI has made major strides through models capable of producing coherent, contextually relevant written content. These models not only generate new text based on prompts but also perform nuanced tasks like summarizing dense documents, translating languages with high accuracy, and powering intelligent virtual assistants. Such advancements have found practical applications in journalism, customer service, education, and marketing. Despite these benefits, there is still a risk that these systems may generate plausible but factually incorrect content, a phenomenon known as AI hallucination, which underscores the need for vigilant human review.

The visual arts have also been deeply impacted by generative AI. Tools that interpret textual prompts to generate detailed images or videos are now being employed in graphic design, digital storytelling, and advertising. Additionally, AI is contributing to the entertainment industry by streamlining visual effects production and even creating lifelike animations and short films. However, as the technology becomes more sophisticated, concerns about authenticity and ethical use—particularly in the context of deepfakes—have grown more pronounced, highlighting the fine line between creative innovation and potential misuse.

In the field of audio, generative models are pushing creative boundaries by composing original pieces of music and synthesizing voices that closely mimic human speech. These capabilities are being integrated into multimedia production, voiceover generation, and personalized soundscapes for various forms of digital media. Yet, as AI systems learn from pre-existing musical works, issues around intellectual property rights and artistic authorship present ongoing challenges that the creative industry must address. The influence of generative AI extends into the realm of software development, where it is reshaping how programmers write and test code.

In scientific research, generative AI is accelerating progress by analyzing complex datasets and making novel predictions. In biology and medicine, for instance, models can predict protein folding structures or suggest new molecular compounds for drug development [Gangwal et al. (2024)]. These tools are also being applied in disciplines such as climate science and genomics to uncover patterns that would be difficult for humans to discern manually. While the potential for discovery is vast, the scientific community must continue to validate AI-generated results rigorously to ensure they meet established standards of reliability and reproducibility.

Overall, generative AI's diverse capabilities are enabling new modes of creation and discovery across disciplines. However, with these innovations come critical responsibilities—ensuring ethical usage, maintaining transparency, and embedding human oversight to manage the limitations and risks associated with automated generation.

2.3 Limitations of Generative AI

Despite its remarkable capabilities, generative AI is not without limitations. Some of the key challenges include (Feuerriegel et al., 2024), (Kumar et al. 2024), (Kumar & Singh, 2024), (Mirsky & Lee, 2021), (Kumar & Singh, 2024), (Totlani, 2023):

Generative AI has opened up new avenues for content creation and automation, but it also brings with it a set of significant challenges that need careful attention. One of the most critical issues is the generation of misinformation and factual inaccuracies. AI systems operate by predicting patterns based on data rather than understanding context or truth. As a result, they may fabricate facts, present unverified health advice, or even produce convincingly realistic but false video content through deepfakes. These outputs, while technically impressive, can mislead audiences, distort public discourse, and contribute to the spread of disinformation.

Beyond factual errors, the ethical implications of generative AI are profound, particularly concerning embedded biases. Since these models learn from human-generated datasets, they inevitably absorb and replicate existing societal prejudices. This can manifest in content that reinforces stereotypes or unfairly influences automated decision-making processes in sensitive areas like recruitment or legal assessments. Moreover, when AI imitates human artistic styles, it raises difficult questions about authorship and originality, challenging the boundaries of intellectual property rights and ethical use.

The infrastructure required to support generative AI also presents a sustainability concern. Developing and running these models demands substantial computational power, which not only incurs high financial costs but also contributes to significant energy usage and environmental impact. As these models become more advanced, the barrier to entry for small-scale researchers and organizations grows, threatening to widen the digital divide. Consequently, the pursuit of more efficient and environmentally sustainable AI technologies is essential to balance innovation with accessibility and ecological responsibility.

Legal frameworks are still catching up to the realities of AI-generated content. Issues around copyright and ownership remain unresolved, especially when AI systems learn from vast repositories of existing, and often copyrighted, material. The lack of clarity regarding who holds rights to machine-generated work—whether it's the user, the developer, or neither—has led to growing concerns among artists, publishers, and policymakers. Addressing these ambiguities is vital for ensuring fair use and protecting creative industries.

Finally, while generative AI excels at mimicking patterns, it lacks the intrinsic creativity and emotional intelligence that characterize human expression. Its outputs, though coherent and aesthetically appealing, often fall short in terms of originality, subtlety, and contextual awareness. AI struggles to grasp cultural nuances, irony, or the emotional weight of certain expressions, leading to content that may seem superficial or repetitive. This underscores the ongoing need for human guidance and curation in leveraging AI tools effectively, ensuring that technological progress enhances rather than replaces authentic creative expression.

2.4 The Future of Generative AI: Overcoming Limitations

As AI research progresses, efforts are being made to overcome these limitations. Some key advancements include:

- **Improving fact-checking mechanisms** to reduce misinformation.
- **Enhancing AI explainability** to make AI decisions more transparent.
- **Developing energy-efficient AI models** to reduce computational costs.
- **Refining ethical AI frameworks** to ensure fairness and accountability.

Generative AI has revolutionized various domains, from media and entertainment to science and software development. However, despite its remarkable capabilities, it also comes with significant limitations, including misinformation, bias, high computational costs, and ethical concerns. Addressing these challenges will be crucial in ensuring AI remains a beneficial tool for society. As AI technology evolves, a balanced approach—leveraging AI's strengths while mitigating its risks—will be essential for a responsible and ethical digital future.

3. DETECTING AI-GENERATED CONTENT

As generative AI advances, distinguishing between human-created and AI-generated content is becoming increasingly difficult. AI can produce highly realistic text, images, videos, and audio, raising concerns about misinformation, digital manipulation, and ethical challenges in journalism, social media, and entertainment.

Efforts to detect synthetic media include deepfake detection algorithms, watermarking techniques, and AI-powered verification tools, but these methods struggle to keep pace with AI's rapid improvements. Deep learning models continuously refine their ability to mimic human-like outputs, making detection an ongoing challenge.

Emerging solutions involve blockchain-based content verification, AI-generated content disclosures, and collaboration among governments, tech companies, and researchers to strengthen detection frameworks. Additionally, media literacy programs and awareness initiatives help individuals critically evaluate digital content. While AI-driven misinformation presents risks, continuous research and policy efforts are crucial for promoting transparency and accountability. A multi-faceted strategy combining technology, regulation, and education will be essential to addressing the challenges posed by AI-generated media (Chaka, 2023).

3.1 Challenges in Detecting AI-Generated Content

Detecting AI-generated content is a growing challenge due to the sophistication of deep learning models. The main difficulties include:

3.1.1 Increasingly Realistic AI Models

Artificial intelligence models such as OpenAI's GPT-4, Meta's LLaMA, and Google's Gemini have reached a level of sophistication that allows them to generate text closely mimicking human writing. These models can interpret context, tone, and even humor, producing outputs that are nearly indistinguishable from those written by humans. In parallel, deepfake technologies powered by models like StyleGAN and DeepFaceLab are capable of generating highly realistic images and videos. The realism achieved through these tools makes it increasingly difficult to detect fabricated media, raising concerns about authenticity and trust in digital content.

3.1.2 Lack of Clear Digital Signatures

Traditional media manipulation techniques, such as those performed in Photoshop, often leave detectable traces, like lighting inconsistencies or pixel distortions. In contrast, images generated by Generative Adversarial Networks (GANs) are created at the pixel level, leaving little to no detectable artifacts, thereby complicating identification efforts. Similarly, AI-generated text has evolved to the point where grammar, coherence, and narrative flow are so refined that traditional markers of artificial content are no longer reliable. This lack of digital signatures makes distinguishing AI-generated content from authentic human output a significant challenge.

3.1.3 Rapid Advancements in AI Models

The rapid pace at which AI technology evolves creates a continuous struggle between the development of detection tools and the improvement of generative models. As soon as new methods are developed to identify AI-generated content, AI models are updated to circumvent these detection mechanisms. This ongoing cycle of "detection versus evasion" severely limits the long-term effectiveness of any single detection technique. For example, deepfake detection tools that proved effective in 2022 became considerably less accurate by 2023 due to advances in synthetic image generation technologies.

3.1.4 Contextual and Psychological Biases

Beyond technical limitations, psychological and contextual biases significantly hinder the identification of AI-generated misinformation. People are more likely to accept and believe content that aligns with their preexisting beliefs, a phenomenon known as confirmation bias. This cognitive bias makes it particularly difficult for individuals to critically evaluate AI-generated content that supports their viewpoints. For instance, politically charged deepfake videos generated by AI can manipulate public opinion by exploiting these biases, making them highly effective tools for propaganda and disinformation.

3.2 Current Techniques for Detecting AI-Generated Content

Despite the challenges, researchers have developed various detection methods. These can be categorized into text detection, image/video forensics, and audio analysis.

3.2.1 AI-Generated Text Detection

Detecting AI-generated text involves a combination of linguistic pattern analysis, coherence evaluation, and the application of statistical metrics. Several methods and tools have been developed to distinguish AI-authored content from human-written text.

A) Linguistic Analysis and Stylometry

One of the key approaches is linguistic analysis and stylometry. AI-generated text often exhibits repetitive sentence structures and an overuse of particular phrases. These texts may also lack emotional depth or demonstrate inconsistencies in narrative flow. For example, while an AI might begin a story with logical progression, it may falter in maintaining coherence over longer passages, leading to illogical or disjointed conclusions. Such limitations serve as potential indicators of machine-generated content.

B) Perplexity and Burstiness Metrics

Statistical properties like perplexity and burstiness provide another layer of detection. Perplexity measures how predictable a sequence of words is within a language model. AI-generated text typically has lower perplexity scores, indicating higher predictability compared to human writing. Burstiness, on the other hand, examines variations in sentence structure and length. Human writing tends to exhibit more variation, whereas AI output often maintains uniformity, which can be a red flag.

C) AI Detection Tools

Several tools have emerged to automate the identification of AI-written content. GPTZero, for instance, is specifically designed to detect text produced by ChatGPT by analyzing sentence complexity and linguistic patterns. OpenAI's own AI Text Classifier attempts to distinguish between AI- and human-generated texts, though it struggles with shorter excerpts. Additionally, Hugging Face offers transformer-based detectors that use deep learning models to identify synthetic text with varying levels of accuracy (Chaka, 2023).

3.2.2 AI-Generated Image and Video Detection

As generative AI tools advance in producing hyper-realistic images and videos, the need for robust detection methods has become more critical. Techniques range from forensic image analysis to deep learning-based models (Bai et al., 2024), (Baraheem et al. 2023).

A) Visual Artifacts and Inconsistencies

AI-generated images, particularly those created using GANs, often contain visual anomalies. These may include unnatural blurring around facial features, inconsistent lighting, or unrealistic reflections in the eyes. Another telltale sign is asymmetry—GANs sometimes produce mismatched earrings or differently sized eyes. Additionally, AI models frequently struggle with human hands, resulting in unnatural finger shapes or even extra digits. These artifacts can help forensic analysts determine the authenticity of visual content.

B) Deepfake Detection Algorithms

To combat deepfakes, several algorithmic solutions have been developed. DeepForensics uses convolutional neural networks (CNNs) to identify generated facial features. FaceForensics++ goes further by analyzing facial expressions and frame-by-frame inconsistencies in video footage. Intel's FakeCatcher takes an innovative approach by measuring subtle changes in blood flow across facial skin pixels, which AI models typically fail to replicate accurately.

C) Reverse Image Search and Metadata Analysis

Basic yet effective methods like Google Reverse Image Search can help verify whether a suspicious image has a prior digital footprint. Furthermore, examining metadata, particularly EXIF data embedded in image files, can expose anomalies or missing information that may suggest AI generation or manipulation.

3.2.3 AI-Generated Audio Detection

With AI-generated speech achieving near-human realism through models such as WaveNet, Tacotron, and VALL-E, detecting synthetic audio has become increasingly sophisticated and essential (Frattolillo, 2020), (Shao et al. (2022).

A) Acoustic Fingerprints and Spectrogram Analysis

Forensic audio techniques like spectrogram analysis—visual representations of sound frequency over time—can reveal subtle abnormalities in synthetic speech. AI-generated voices may exhibit robotic inflections or lack natural breathing patterns, which are typically present in human speech. These irregularities often show up in the spectrogram as unnatural frequency distributions.

B) Deep Learning Models for Audio Detection

Several deep learning tools have been developed for identifying AI-generated voices. One such tool, Resemblyzer, analyzes vocal characteristics and compares them to known samples to detect synthesis. Other AI speech classifiers assess pitch, tone, and rhythm to flag anomalies indicative of machine-generated audio.

3.3 Emerging AI Detection Models

Given the continuous advancements in generative AI, new strategies and technologies are emerging to improve detection accuracy and resilience.

3.3.1 Blockchain and Cryptographic Watermarking

One promising solution is to embed cryptographic watermarks in AI-generated content at the time of creation. These watermarks can be used later to verify authenticity. For example, OpenAI is developing methods to include hidden watermarks in its text outputs, enabling clearer differentiation from human writing. This could become a standard practice for ensuring accountability in AI-generated media.

3.3.2 AI Detecting AI

A particularly innovative frontier is using AI to detect other AI-generated content. Self-supervised learning models are trained on both synthetic and real data to learn the subtle distinctions between the two. These systems become increasingly adept at recognizing generative model patterns. For instance, deepfake detection AIs are specifically trained to identify unique characteristics embedded in manipulated videos.

3.3.3 Federated and Community-Based Detection

Crowdsourcing detection efforts can also play a vital role. By encouraging users to report suspected deepfakes or misinformation, platforms can improve the accuracy and responsiveness of detection systems. Furthermore, federated learning enables models to be trained on diverse datasets from multiple sources without centralizing sensitive data. This enhances the generalization capability of detection models while preserving user privacy.

3.4 The Future of AI-Generated Content Detection

The future of AI-generated content detection will rely on a combination of advanced machine learning models, blockchain verification, and regulatory frameworks to combat misinformation and synthetic media. As AI continues to improve in generating realistic text, images, and videos, detection systems must evolve to keep pace. Researchers are developing more sophisticated deepfake detection algorithms, AI-driven watermarking techniques, and digital provenance tracking to verify content authenticity. Blockchain technology offers potential solutions by creating immutable records of original content, helping distinguish real from AI-generated media. Additionally, major tech companies and governments are working on global AI transparency standards, such as mandatory labelling of AI-generated content.

4. AI AND MEDIA LITERACY EDUCATION

As AI-generated content becomes more prevalent, integrating AI literacy into media education is essential to help individuals critically engage with digital media. Traditional media literacy focused on evaluating sources, fact-checking, and identifying biases, but the rise of generative AI introduces new challenges, such as deepfakes, AI-generated misinformation, and algorithm-driven content manipulation. Educators must equip students with the skills to recognize AI-generated content, understand how AI algorithms shape information consumption, and critically assess digital narratives. Schools and universities are beginning to introduce AI literacy programs that cover topics such as deepfake detection, ethical AI use, and algorithmic bias. Additionally, governments and tech companies are collaborating to develop educational initiatives that promote AI transparency and responsible media consumption. Tools such as AI-powered fact-checking systems and watermarking technologies are also being integrated into media literacy curricula to help individuals verify content authenticity. Beyond formal education, public awareness campaigns and online resources play a crucial role in educating the general population about AI's impact on media. As AI continues to evolve, media literacy education must adapt to ensure that individuals have the knowledge and critical thinking skills to navigate the increasingly AI-driven information landscape responsibly (Shalevska, 2024).

4.1 Why Media Literacy Needs an AI Focus

Media literacy has always been crucial for navigating information in the digital age, but with the rapid rise of AI-generated content, it now requires a stronger focus on AI (Shalevska, 2024).

4.1.1 The Evolution of Media Literacy

Traditionally, media literacy focused on analyzing newspapers, television, and online news sources for bias, credibility, and misinformation. However, the rise of generative AI has fundamentally changed how content is created, distributed, and consumed.

Media literacy now requires a technical understanding of AI—how it generates content, the ethical implications, and methods for detecting synthetic media.

Without this, individuals are vulnerable to misinformation, deepfakes, and AI-generated propaganda.

4.1.2 The Rise of AI-Generated Misinformation

AI-generated misinformation is becoming a major concern in the digital information ecosystem. Deepfake technology has been exploited to impersonate politicians, celebrities, and public figures, often with the intent to alter public perception or influence political outcomes. These fabricated visuals and audio recordings can create convincing yet entirely false representations, undermining public trust. In addition, AI-written news articles have been used to spread misinformation while mimicking the tone and structure of legitimate journalism, making them difficult to detect. Compounding the issue, AI-powered bots on social media platforms engage in conversations, promote specific viewpoints, and disseminate false information to manipulate public opinion. Without adequate education on media literacy, individuals may find it increasingly difficult to differentiate between authentic and AI-generated content, leading to significant trust issues in journalism, politics, and social media.

4.1.3 Ethical Implications of AI in Media

The use of AI in media also raises important ethical questions. One major concern is consent and privacy—AI can now generate hyper-realistic images and videos of individuals without their permission, infringing on personal rights. Additionally, bias is a prevalent issue, as AI models trained on biased datasets can unintentionally reinforce harmful stereotypes related to race, gender, or political beliefs. Another ethical dilemma involves job displacement. As AI tools become more proficient in creative tasks like writing, graphic design, and video production, professionals in journalism, art, and filmmaking face increasing job insecurity. These developments highlight the urgent need for media literacy education that addresses the ethical use of AI, its limitations, and its broader societal consequences.

4.2 Teaching Critical Thinking and Evaluation Skills

To effectively navigate a media environment shaped by AI-generated content, individuals must cultivate strong critical thinking and content evaluation skills. These skills are essential for analyzing digital content, verifying sources, and making informed decisions in an era where synthetic media is widespread.

4.2.1 Source Verification: How to Identify Trustworthy Sources

One of the most effective ways to combat AI-generated misinformation is through robust source verification. AI-generated content can convincingly fabricate entire narratives, making it essential for media literacy programs to teach specific verification strategies. These include checking the authenticity of URLs and domains—fake news sites often use URLs that closely resemble legitimate ones, such as "cnn-news.com" instead of "cnn.com." Analyzing the credibility of the author is also important; this involves researching their professional background and cross-referencing their work. Cross-referencing information with multiple reputable sources ensures that a story is corroborated before being accepted as true. Furthermore, using established fact-checking platforms like Snopes, FactCheck.org, or Reuters Fact Check helps verify the accuracy of news content.

4.2.2 Understanding AI Content Generation

Another critical aspect of media literacy is understanding how AI creates content. Educators should explain the underlying mechanisms of AI-generated text, images, and videos so that students can better recognize artificial media. For instance, AI-written articles often mimic human language patterns and writing styles, making them difficult to distinguish without close inspection. Deepfake videos, meanwhile, manipulate visual and auditory elements to deceive viewers by altering facial expressions, voices, and movements. AI-generated images may appear realistic at first glance, but often include subtle flaws, such as distorted hands or mismatched facial features. Gaining an understanding of how AI operates helps individuals' question and analyze the authenticity of media more effectively.

4.2.3 Identifying AI Bias and Manipulation

AI-generated content is not immune to bias. Because AI models are trained on large datasets collected from the internet, they inherit the prejudices and inaccuracies present in that data. As a result, AI-generated content may unintentionally amplify stereotypes or present skewed narratives. Media literacy education should therefore include lessons on detecting bias, such as evaluating whether a piece of content presents a balanced perspective or leans toward a particular ideology. Understanding dataset bias is also critical—learners should recognize that AI outputs are only as unbiased as the data used to train the model. Moreover, awareness of how social media algorithms influence content visibility is essential. These recommendation systems, driven by AI, shape users' perceptions by selectively curating what they see, often reinforcing preexisting beliefs and echo chambers.

4.3 Digital Literacy and Ethical Awareness

Digital literacy is the ability to effectively use digital tools, evaluate online information, and navigate the digital world responsibly. It involves understanding how technology works, critically assessing digital content, and ensuring cybersecurity. Ethical awareness in the digital space means recognizing the impact of one's online actions, respecting privacy, avoiding misinformation, and adhering to ethical guidelines in communication and data usage. Together, digital literacy and ethical awareness empower individuals to engage safely and responsibly in the digital era, fostering informed decision-making, respectful interactions, and a secure online environment.

4.3.1 The Role of Digital Literacy in Identifying AI Content

Digital literacy today goes beyond basic computer skills; it encompasses the ability to interact with, evaluate, and create digital media responsibly and critically. In a world increasingly influenced by AI, being digitally literate also means being capable of recognizing and responding to AI-generated content. One crucial skill is the ability to detect manipulated images and videos. AI-generated media, such as deepfakes, often contain subtle but telltale errors—unnatural movements, mismatched reflections, or inconsistencies in facial features—that digitally literate individuals should learn to identify.

4.3.2 Ethical Considerations in AI Usage

As AI becomes more integrated into content creation and communication, it raises complex ethical questions. One major concern is the role of AI in journalism. AI-generated news articles, while efficient, challenge traditional notions of transparency and editorial accountability. If readers are unaware that an article was written by an AI, trust in journalism may erode. Therefore, ethical frameworks must be developed to determine when and how AI should be used in news reporting.

Another ethical debate centers around the use of AI in the arts. Some AI models generate images or music by drawing from existing works, prompting concerns over plagiarism and copyright infringement. This raises the question: can AI-generated art be considered original, or is it merely a derivative of human creativity? Finally, the issue of labelling AI-generated content is becoming increasingly important. Some governments and organizations advocate for mandatory disclosure whenever media is produced by AI, arguing that transparency is essential for maintaining public trust and informed decision-making. These debates highlight the need for ongoing dialogue about the responsible use of AI across industries.

Media literacy education should encourage discussions on these ethical dilemmas and help students form informed opinions.

4.4 Case Studies and Examples of AI in Media Literacy

AI plays a crucial role in media literacy by helping users identify misinformation, analyze media bias, and improve digital content understanding. For example, Google's Fact Check Explorer uses AI to verify news sources, while tools like OpenAI's GPT-based models assist in summarizing and analyzing articles for credibility. Deepfake detection systems, such as Microsoft's Video Authenticator, help combat manipulated media by identifying AI-generated content. Additionally, AI-driven platforms like NewsGuard provide credibility ratings for news websites, helping users distinguish between reliable and misleading information. These AI applications enhance media literacy by enabling critical evaluation of digital content and fostering informed consumption.

4.4.1 The 2016 U.S. Elections and AI-Generated Fake News

During the 2016 U.S. elections, AI-powered bots spread political misinformation on social media. This highlighted the dangers of AI-driven propaganda and the need for stronger fact-checking measures (Kreps et al., 2022).

4.4.2 Deepfake Scandals in Politics

- In 2019, a deepfake video of Nancy Pelosi made her appear intoxicated. The video was widely shared on social media, influencing public perception (Hodge Jr et al., 2021).
- In 2023, a deepfake video of Ukraine's President Zelenskyy surfaced, falsely stating that Ukraine had surrendered to Russia (Apăteanu, 2022).

These incidents illustrate the real-world dangers of AI-generated deception and why media literacy programs must address deepfake detection.

4.4.3 AI in Journalism and Education

- The BBC and Reuters have started training journalists on AI detection techniques to prevent the spread of misinformation.
- Universities like MIT and Stanford now offer courses on AI in media ethics, helping students understand the evolving media landscape.

4.5 Government and Institutional Roles in AI Literacy

As AI reshapes media, education, and communication, governments and institutions play a critical role in promoting AI literacy. Their responsibilities include policy-making, education initiatives, regulation, and public awareness campaigns to ensure ethical and responsible AI usage (Dakhel et al., 2024), (Gangwal & Lavecchia, 2024), (Chaka, 2023), (Bai et al. 2024), (Baraheem & Nguyen, 2023), (Frattolillo, 2020), (Shao et al. 2022), (Shalevska, 2024), (Hodge Jr et al. 2021), (Apăteanu, 2022), (Neuwirth et al. 2024).

4.5.1 The Role of Schools and Universities

Education systems should integrate AI media literacy into school curricula by:

- Offering critical thinking courses focused on AI-generated content.
- Teaching hands-on AI detection skills (e.g., using AI-detection software in classrooms).
- Encouraging discussions on the ethical implications of AI in media.

4.5.2 Tech Companies and AI Transparency

- Companies like Google, OpenAI, and Meta are working on AI detection tools to combat misinformation.
- Platforms like YouTube and TikTok are experimenting with AI-generated content labels to inform users when content is AI-created.

4.5.3 Government Policies and AI Regulation

- The European Union's AI Act proposes transparency requirements for AI-generated content.
- China now mandates that deepfake videos include a visible disclaimer to prevent misinformation.
- The U.S. Federal Trade Commission (FTC) is exploring regulations on AI-powered misinformation.

Regulating AI-generated media is complex but necessary to prevent widespread manipulation and deception.

4.6 The Future of Media Literacy in the AI Age

As AI continues to reshape media, the future of media literacy must evolve to address the challenges posed by AI-generated content. Traditional media literacy focused on identifying credible sources, recognizing bias, and fact-checking information. However, in the AI age, these skills must be expanded to include AI literacy—understanding how generative AI creates content, detecting deepfakes, and recognizing algorithmic influence on information consumption. Educational institutions will need to incorporate AI-focused media literacy programs, equipping individuals with the ability to critically evaluate AI-generated texts, images, videos, and audio. Additionally, emerging detection technologies, such as digital watermarking and blockchain-based verification, will play a crucial role in ensuring content authenticity. Governments, tech companies, and educators must collaborate to develop policies and tools that promote AI transparency and ethical use in media. Public awareness campaigns will also be essential in helping individuals navigate an increasingly AI-driven media environment. As AI continues to advance, media literacy must become a lifelong learning process, ensuring that people of all ages are equipped with the critical thinking skills needed to discern reliable information and engage responsibly in the digital world (Ali et al., 2021).

4.6.1 Adapting Education to Emerging AI Technologies

- AI tools like ChatGPT, MidJourney, and Synthesia will continue to evolve. Media literacy must keep up with these changes (Ali et al., 2021).
- Schools and universities need ongoing curriculum updates to address new AI threats.

4.6.2 Developing AI-Literate Societies

- Governments and educators must ensure citizens understand AI's impact on media and democracy.
- AI literacy programs should be made widely accessible, including online training courses and community workshops.

Media literacy in the AI era is no longer optional—it is essential. AI-generated content poses both opportunities and risks, and individuals must develop critical thinking skills to navigate an increasingly synthetic media landscape. By integrating AI-focused media literacy into education, enforcing ethical guidelines, and promoting public awareness, societies can become more resilient against AI-driven misinformation.

5. THE FUTURE OF MEDIA LITERACY IN AN AI-DRIVEN WORLD

The future of media literacy in an AI-driven world will be shaped by both opportunities and challenges as AI continues to influence how information is created, distributed, and consumed. AI-powered tools will enhance media literacy by providing real-time fact-checking, bias detection, and deepfake identification, helping users navigate the digital landscape more critically. However, the rise of AI-generated content also increases the risk of misinformation, making it essential for individuals to develop stronger analytical skills and ethical awareness. Educational institutions and policymakers will play a crucial role in integrating AI literacy into curricula, ensuring that people can discern credible sources and engage responsibly with digital media. Ultimately, media literacy in an AI-driven era will require a combination of technological solutions and human critical thinking to foster an informed and resilient society.

5.1 The Evolving Role of AI in Media Consumption and Production

Artificial Intelligence (AI) is reshaping the way media is consumed and produced, influencing journalism, entertainment, and digital communication. As AI technology advances, its role in both creating and curating content has expanded, raising opportunities and challenges for media literacy (Ali et al., 2021).

5.1.1 AI as a Content Creator

AI is rapidly becoming a dominant force in content creation. From automated journalism to AI-generated films and music, the boundaries between human and machine-produced media are increasingly blurred. As a result, future media literacy programs must adapt to this evolving landscape. Audiences need to understand how AI-generated news articles differ from those written by humans and recognize the inherent limitations and biases within AI content generation models. It is also essential to foster discussions about the ethical implications of AI-driven creativity (Briot et al., 2020).

Some of the most transformative AI applications in media include GPT-4 and its successors, which are capable of generating realistic articles, blog posts, and scripts; MidJourney and Stable Diffusion, which produce hyper-realistic AI-generated art and images; and deepfake technology, which allows AI to replicate voices and animate facial expressions convincingly. As these technologies advance, the ability to identify synthetic content will become a critical component of media literacy.

5.1.2 AI-Powered Personalization and Its Impacts

AI-driven algorithms are now central to how users experience digital content. These systems customize news feeds, recommend videos, and curate social media posts based on individual behavior and preferences. While this personalization enhances user experience, it also introduces risks such as filter bubbles—where users are only exposed to content that aligns with their views—and echo chambers, which reinforce existing beliefs and limit critical engagement. Additionally, AI can generate targeted misinformation, making it even more difficult to detect false narratives.

To address these issues, media literacy programs must educate users on how AI algorithms influence content consumption. Learners should understand the importance of diversifying their information sources and be equipped with tools to break free from algorithmic constraints, such as unbiased search engines and independent fact-checking platforms.

5.2 Emerging Threats: AI-Generated Misinformation and Manipulation

The rapid development of generative AI has introduced serious threats related to misinformation and media manipulation. AI-powered tools can produce hyper-realistic deepfakes, fabricate news stories, and generate misleading imagery or videos. This makes it increasingly challenging to discern authentic content from synthetic creations. Malicious actors may exploit these technologies to disseminate propaganda, sway public opinion, or manipulate financial markets. Such misinformation can deepen social divides, amplify conspiracy theories, and erode trust in journalism and democratic institutions (Mylrea, 2025).

5.2.1 Deepfake Technology and Its Societal Implications

Deepfake technology, which enables the creation of convincing synthetic videos and images, poses serious risks, including fraud, political propaganda, and reputational harm. Future threats may involve AI-generated political speeches spreading misinformation, synthetic identity fraud used in scams or disinformation campaigns, and even falsified evidence in legal proceedings. To prepare for these challenges, media literacy education should include training on AI-detection tools such as Deepware and Sensity AI. Legal and ethical discussions about AI-generated content must also be integrated into curricula, along with policy-based interventions like mandatory AI content labeling.

5.2.2 AI-Generated Propaganda and Political Influence

Governments and organizations are increasingly leveraging AI to manipulate public opinion. This includes using AI-powered fake social media profiles to engage in political discourse, orchestrating automated disinformation campaigns to influence elections, and distributing hyper-personalized political advertisements tailored to specific voter demographics. In response, media literacy initiatives must teach individuals how to recognize AI-generated propaganda, verify information sources before sharing content, and understand how AI is utilized in political messaging.

5.2.3 AI-Enhanced Cyber Threats and Scams

AI has dramatically improved the sophistication of cyber threats, making scams and identity theft more convincing. Common examples include AI-generated phone scams mimicking the voices of real individuals, fake emails impersonating CEOs or government officials, and AI-created influencers promoting fraudulent products. Media literacy programs should focus on helping users recognize these AI-generated threats. Training should emphasize the use of AI-detection tools and promote robust cybersecurity awareness to defend against these emerging risks.

5.3 AI and the Future of Journalism

Artificial intelligence is transforming journalism by automating repetitive tasks such as drafting financial reports, summarizing articles, and verifying facts. Leading news agencies like The Associated Press and Reuters already use AI systems for real-time updates on stock markets, sports, and weather. Moreover, AI enhances investigative journalism by analyzing large datasets and uncovering hidden trends. However, this transformation comes with challenges. AI-generated content raises concerns about accuracy, bias, and misinformation. Without adequate oversight, AI could propagate misleading narratives. The increasing use of deepfakes also threatens journalistic integrity. Additionally, automation may lead to job displacement in the media industry (Pavlik, 2023).

5.4 The Need for AI Media Literacy Policies and Regulations

5.4.1 Global AI Content Regulation

Governments around the world are drafting laws to promote AI transparency and accountability. Key proposals include mandatory labeling of AI-generated content (as seen in the EU AI Act), bans on AI-enabled disinformation campaigns, and tougher penalties for AI-related cybercrimes. However, creating balanced regulations that respect freedom of speech while addressing the harms of misinformation remains a complex challenge.

5.4.2 Ethical AI Development for Media

Technology companies play a vital role in shaping ethical AI practices. They must implement advanced AI content detection systems, follow ethical guidelines in media applications, and provide users with transparent reports on AI-generated content. Media literacy programs should help the public understand how ethical AI development and corporate responsibility impact the information they consume.

5.5 The Future of AI-Driven Media Literacy Education

AI-driven media literacy education is poised for a transformative future, marked by personalization, real-time analysis, and adaptive learning tools. AI-based platforms will offer tailored lessons through intelligent tutoring systems, helping students evaluate digital content more effectively. Technologies like AI-powered fact-checkers, deepfake detectors, and sentiment analysis software will support critical evaluation skills, while VR and AR can simulate media-rich scenarios for immersive learning.

6. ETHICAL CONSIDERATIONS AND CHALLENGES IN AI-GENERATED MEDIA

The rise of AI-generated media brings significant ethical concerns and challenges, particularly regarding misinformation, authenticity, intellectual property, and bias. One of the most pressing issues is the potential for AI-generated content to spread misinformation and manipulate public opinion. Deepfake technology, for example, can create realistic but entirely fabricated videos or audio recordings, posing risks to political discourse, journalism, and personal reputations. Without proper regulation, AI-generated misinformation could undermine trust in digital content and democratic institutions. Another major challenge is authenticity and authorship. As AI systems generate text, images, and videos that are indistinguishable from human-created content, questions arise about intellectual property rights and creative ownership. Should AI-generated works be attributed to their human developers, the AI system itself, or remain unprotected? Copyright laws must evolve to address these ambiguities and protect human creators from AI-driven plagiarism (Bekkar et al. (2025).

Bias in AI-generated media is another ethical concern. AI models are trained on vast datasets that may reflect existing societal biases, leading to content that reinforces stereotypes or excludes diverse perspectives. Ensuring fairness and inclusivity in AI-generated media requires continuous monitoring, diverse training datasets, and algorithmic transparency.

6.1 Ethical Dilemmas in AI-Generated Content

The rapid advancement of generative AI in media production has introduced several ethical dilemmas. While AI has the potential to enhance creativity, personalize content, and increase accessibility, it also raises critical ethical concerns about misinformation, consent, authorship, and accountability (Bekkar, 2025).

AI-generated content increasingly blurs the line between reality and fabrication. Synthetic media—such as deepfakes, AI-generated news, and virtual influencers—makes it difficult for audiences to distinguish between real and fake content. AI-generated journalism may lack essential elements like proper fact-checking and contextual understanding, potentially spreading misinformation. Additionally, AI tools can be used to manipulate historical records, either by altering old footage or generating entirely false narratives, thereby rewriting history in misleading ways.

To uphold ethical standards in media, several measures are necessary. Transparency mechanisms, such as watermarking AI-generated content, should be implemented to help users identify synthetic material. AI verification systems can assist in flagging and identifying AI-generated media. Furthermore, comprehensive educational programs are crucial for teaching the public how to critically analyze and verify content created using artificial intelligence.

6.2 The Role of Bias in AI-Generated Media

Bias in AI-generated media significantly impacts public perception, influencing narratives and potentially reinforcing harmful misinformation. AI models are trained on extensive datasets that often include historical and societal biases. As a result, outputs from these models—whether in news generation, content recommendation, or moderation—can be skewed. For example, AI may favor certain political ideologies, underrepresent marginalized communities, or perpetuate racial, gender, or cultural stereotypes. Technologies like deepfakes and AI-generated journalism further complicate the ethical landscape of content authenticity and fairness.

To address these issues, developers must ensure that training data is diverse and representative. AI systems should be developed with transparency and continuously audited by human overseers to maintain ethical standards. As AI technology becomes more influential in media creation, mitigating bias is essential for producing fair, accurate, and responsible content.

6.2.1 Bias in AI Training Data

AI systems trained on biased datasets can inadvertently perpetuate harmful stereotypes. These models may reflect and amplify existing social inequalities by reinforcing racial, gender, or cultural biases. They often Favor dominant languages and viewpoints while marginalizing others, influencing news coverage, hiring practices, and broader social narratives.

For example, AI image generators like MidJourney and DALL·E have been criticized for producing stereotypical depictions, such as portraying CEOs primarily as white men or generating hyper-sexualized images of women. They also underrepresent certain ethnic groups in visual outputs. To combat this, developers must ensure that datasets are inclusive and representative. Regular auditing of models, implementation of fairness constraints, and prioritization of ethical training practices are all necessary steps in reducing bias in AI-generated media.

6.2.2 AI Bias in Journalism and Political Content

AI-generated news and political content often reflect the biases present in their training data. This can lead to selective representation of facts, algorithmic favoritism towards particular political ideologies, and sensationalized content designed for engagement rather than accuracy. These issues undermine journalistic integrity and distort democratic discourse.

To mitigate these problems, collaboration between AI developers and fact-checking organizations is essential. AI-generated journalism should be clearly labelled and reviewed by human editors to ensure credibility. Additionally, promoting open-source AI models and transparent development practices will foster greater accountability and trust in AI-driven media.

6.3 Accountability and Legal Challenges

Determining accountability for harmful or misleading AI-generated content remains a major legal and ethical challenge. If an AI system produces false news, damaging deepfakes, or biased media, who should be held responsible? Possible accountable parties include the developers who train and deploy unsafe models, users who exploit AI tools to spread misinformation, and platform owners who fail to regulate the content effectively. Governments and tech companies must work together to establish clear legal frameworks that define liability in AI media. Policies should include guidelines for content moderation, ethical standards for AI-generated journalism, and mechanisms to trace and address misuse. Regulations concerning AI-generated media vary worldwide, but several significant legislative efforts have emerged. The European Union's AI Act aims to regulate high-risk AI applications, including those used for deepfake detection. In the United States, the Deepfake Law criminalizes malicious uses of deepfake technology. China has implemented strict regulations requiring government approval for AI-generated news.

6.4 Ethical AI Design and Policy Recommendations

Creating ethical AI systems requires a focus on transparency, fairness, and accountability. Developers must use diverse and representative datasets to reduce bias, ensure explainability in AI decision-making, and protect user privacy. Regular audits and fairness-aware algorithms can help identify and correct problems in AI models. Additionally, strong security measures are essential to prevent the misuse of AI technologies for spreading misinformation or enabling discriminatory practices.

Policy recommendations include implementing regulatory frameworks that enforce ethical standards, promoting AI ethics education among developers, and mandating that AI-generated content clearly disclose its automated origin. Governments and organizations should collaborate to establish accountability measures such as AI impact assessments and public bias audits. Public participation in AI policy discussions is vital to align technological advancements with societal values and human rights.

6.4.1 Developing Ethical AI for Media

To prevent misuse of AI in media, developers must prioritize core ethical design principles. Transparency should be maintained by disclosing when AI is used to create content. Fairness must be addressed by identifying and correcting biases in training datasets. Accountability should be enforced by making AI-generated misinformation traceable. Moreover, users must be given control over how their personal data is used in AI systems, including options to opt out.

6.4.2 Policy Recommendations for Ethical AI in Media

Policymakers should implement regulations to promote ethical practices in AI media development. These include mandatory content labelling for all AI-generated media, ethical standards for datasets used in training AI models, and public education programs aimed at improving AI literacy. Such initiatives will equip individuals with the tools needed to detect and critically evaluate synthetic content.

6.4.3 Corporate Responsibility in AI Media Development

Technology companies play a crucial role in shaping the ethical landscape of AI media. They should establish self-regulatory frameworks to prevent misuse, ensure diversity within AI research teams to reduce bias, and publish transparency reports detailing the extent and nature of AI-generated content. By taking responsibility, corporations can contribute to a more ethical and trustworthy media ecosystem.

6.5 The Path Forward: Balancing AI Innovation and Ethics

As AI continues to revolutionize media production, it is essential to balance innovation with ethical considerations. The future of AI-generated media must prioritize truth and authenticity, ensure fair and unbiased content, and establish clear mechanisms for accountability. To navigate this future responsibly, several key actions are necessary: always disclose and label AI-generated content, develop robust legal frameworks to address AI misinformation, correct biases in AI training data, educate users on AI media verification, and encourage collaboration between governments and tech companies on ethical policy development.

7. CONCLUSION AND FUTURE DIRECTIONS

The rapid advancement of generative AI has ushered in a profound transformation in the media landscape. From news reporting to entertainment, social media, and digital storytelling, AI technologies are reshaping the way content is created, shared, and consumed. These developments offer immense creative potential and operational efficiency, but they also raise complex challenges surrounding misinformation, authenticity, and ethical responsibility. As AI continues to blur the line between truth and fiction, cultivating media literacy and ethical awareness becomes increasingly vital.

One of the most significant disruptions caused by AI lies in its capacity to generate content that closely mimics human creation. Automated journalism, AI-generated videos, and synthetic voices are redefining traditional media workflows. While these tools can streamline reporting and boost creativity, they also complicate efforts to verify information and uphold journalistic integrity. Personalization algorithms, although designed to enhance user experience, often limit exposure to diverse viewpoints, contributing to ideological silos and reducing critical engagement with opposing perspectives. The rise of deepfakes and AI-generated propaganda has elevated concerns about the manipulation of public opinion. Highly realistic yet fabricated media can be weaponized for disinformation, especially in political and social contexts. This necessitates not only advanced detection tools and fact-checking systems but also a foundational shift in how audiences engage with digital content. Media consumers must develop the skills to critically assess sources and differentiate between authentic and AI-generated material. As these challenges grow more pronounced, addressing bias and accountability in AI becomes imperative. Algorithms trained on flawed or unrepresentative data can perpetuate harmful stereotypes and marginalize certain groups. Transparent AI development, ethical design principles, and oversight mechanisms are crucial for mitigating these risks. Moreover, current legal and regulatory structures are often inadequate to govern the nuances of AI-generated content, underscoring the urgency of policy innovation.

Looking to the future, the role of AI in content creation and journalism will expand even further. In journalism, AI is already streamlining routine tasks and offering new modes of storytelling. In creative industries, it provides novel tools for visualizing and producing content. However, regardless of the application, human oversight remains essential to preserve accuracy, fairness, and ethical standards. Editorial responsibility cannot be outsourced to algorithms. To protect the integrity of public discourse, stronger AI detection and verification mechanisms are needed. Watermarking AI-generated content and developing robust tools for deepfake identification are practical solutions that should be widely adopted. Simultaneously, governments and institutions must invest in research and infrastructure to support content authentication and media ethics. These efforts must be globally coordinated, as misinformation transcends national borders. International collaboration is crucial for crafting cohesive policies that govern AI in media. While national governments must enforce regulatory standards, tech companies also bear responsibility for ethical self-regulation. Public-private partnerships can drive the creation of industry-wide ethics guidelines, ensuring accountability without stifling innovation.

REFERENCES

Ali, S., DiPaola, D., Lee, I., Sindato, V., Kim, G., Blumofe, R., & Breazeal, C. (2021). Children as creators, thinkers and citizens in an AI-driven future. *Computers and Education: Artificial Intelligence*, *2*, 100040. DOI: 10.1016/j.caeai.2021.100040

Apăteanu, D. (n.d.). The disinformation in the case of the Ukraine war. In *The War in Ukraine* (p. 241).

Bai, J. (2024). AI-generated video detection via spatial-temporal anomaly learning. In *Chinese Conference on Pattern Recognition and Computer Vision (PRCV)*. Singapore: Springer Nature Singapore.

Baraheem, S. S., & Nguyen, T. V. (2023). AI vs. AI: Can AI detect AI-generated images? *Journal of Imaging*, *9*(10), 199. DOI: 10.3390/jimaging9100199 PMID: 37888306

Bayer, M., Kaufhold, M.-A., Buchhold, B., Keller, M., Dallmeyer, J., & Reuter, C. (2023). Data augmentation in natural language processing: A novel text generation approach for long and short text classifiers. *International Journal of Machine Learning and Cybernetics*, *14*(1), 135–150. DOI: 10.1007/s13042-022-01553-3 PMID: 35432623

Bekkar, A., & Aarab, F. (2025). Ethical challenges in artificial intelligence generated media content. *Revue de Recherches et Etudes Scientifiques*, *19*(1), 107–125.

Briot, J.-P., & Pachet, F. (2020). Deep learning for music generation: Challenges and directions. *Neural Computing & Applications*, *32*(4), 981–993. DOI: 10.1007/s00521-018-3813-6

Capatina, A., Kachour, M., Lichy, J., Micu, A., Micu, A.-E., & Codignola, F. (2020). Matching the future capabilities of an artificial intelligence-based software for social media marketing with potential users' expectations. *Technological Forecasting and Social Change*, *151*, 119794. DOI: 10.1016/j.techfore.2019.119794

Chaka, C. (2023). Detecting AI content in responses generated by ChatGPT, YouChat, and Chatsonic: The case of five AI content detection tools. *Journal of Applied Learning and Teaching*, *6*(2), 94–104.

Dakhel, A. M. (2024). Generative AI for software development: A family of studies on code generation. In *Generative AI for Effective Software Development* (pp. 151–172). Springer Nature Switzerland. DOI: 10.1007/978-3-031-55642-5_7

Feuerriegel, S., Hartmann, J., Janiesch, C., & Zschech, P. (2024). Generative AI. *Business & Information Systems Engineering*, *66*(1), 111–126. DOI: 10.1007/s12599-023-00834-7

Frattolillo, F. (2020). A watermarking protocol based on blockchain. *Applied Sciences (Basel, Switzerland)*, *10*(21), 7746. DOI: 10.3390/app10217746

Fui-Hoon Nah, F., Zheng, R., Cai, J., Siau, K., & Chen, L. (2023). Generative AI and ChatGPT: Applications, challenges, and AI-human collaboration. *Journal of Information Technology Case and Application Research*, *25*(3), 277–304. DOI: 10.1080/15228053.2023.2233814

Gangwal, A., & Lavecchia, A. (2024). Unlocking the potential of generative AI in drug discovery. *Drug Discovery Today*, *29*(6), 103992. DOI: 10.1016/j.drudis.2024.103992 PMID: 38663579

Hodge, S. D.Jr. (2021). Don't always believe what you see: Shallowfake and deepfake media has altered the perception of reality. *Hofstra Law Review*, *50*, 51.

Kreps, S., McCain, R. M., & Brundage, M. (2022). All the news that's fit to fabricate: AI-generated text as a tool of media misinformation. *Journal of Experimental Political Science*, *9*(1), 104–117. DOI: 10.1017/XPS.2020.37

Kumar, L., & Singh, D. K. (2023). A comprehensive survey on generative adversarial networks used for synthesizing multimedia content. *Multimedia Tools and Applications*, *82*(26), 40585–40624. DOI: 10.1007/s11042-023-15138-x

Kumar, L., & Singh, D. K. (2024). Diversified realistic face image generation GAN for human subjects in multimedia content creation. *Computer Animation and Virtual Worlds*, *35*(2), e2232. DOI: 10.1002/cav.2232

Kumar, L., & Singh, D. K. (2024). A novel aspect of automatic vlog content creation using generative modeling approaches. *Digital Signal Processing*, *148*, 104462. DOI: 10.1016/j.dsp.2024.104462

Kumar, L., Singh, D. K., & Ansari, M. A. (2024). Role of video content generation in education systems using generative AI. In *Integrating Generative AI in Education to Achieve Sustainable Development Goals* (pp. 354–368). IGI Global. DOI: 10.4018/979-8-3693-2440-0.ch019

Mirsky, Y., & Lee, W. (2021). The creation and detection of deepfakes: A survey. *ACM Computing Surveys*, *54*(1), 1–41. DOI: 10.1145/3425780

Mylrea, M. (2025). The generative AI weapon of mass destruction: Evolving disinformation threats, vulnerabilities, and mitigation frameworks. In *Interdependent Human-Machine Teams* (pp. 315–347). Academic Press. DOI: 10.1016/B978-0-443-29246-0.00007-9

Neuwirth, R. J. (2024). The global institutional governance of AI: A four-dimensional perspective. *International Journal of Digital Law and Governance*, *1*(1), 113–153. DOI: 10.1515/ijdlg-2024-0004

Pavlik, J. V. (2023). Collaborating with ChatGPT: Considering the implications of generative artificial intelligence for journalism and media education. *Journalism & Mass Communication Educator*, *78*(1), 84–93. DOI: 10.1177/10776958221149577

Sadiku, M. N. O. (2021). Artificial intelligence in social media. *International Journal of Scientific Advances*, *2*(1), 15–20.

Shalevska, E. (2024). The future of political discourse: AI and media literacy education. *Journal of Legal and Political Education*, *1*(1), 50–61. DOI: 10.47305/JLPE2411050sh

Shao, Z., Zhao, R., Yuan, S., Ding, M., & Wang, Y. (2022). Tracing the evolution of AI in the past decade and forecasting the emerging trends. *Expert Systems with Applications*, *209*, 118221. DOI: 10.1016/j.eswa.2022.118221

Theodoridis, P. K., & Gkikas, D. C. (2019). How artificial intelligence affects digital marketing. In *Strategic Innovative Marketing and Tourism: 7th ICSIMAT, Athenian Riviera, Greece, 2018* (pp. [pages if known]). Springer International Publishing. DOI: 10.1007/978-3-030-12453-3_151

Totlani, K. (2023). The evolution of generative AI: Implications for the media and film industry. *International Journal for Research in Applied Science and Engineering Technology*, *11*(10), 973–980. DOI: 10.22214/ijraset.2023.56140

Xu, T. (2024). From recorded to AI-generated instructional videos: A comparison of learning performance and experience. *British Journal of Educational Technology*.

Zlateva, P. (2024). A conceptual framework for solving ethical issues in generative artificial intelligence. In *Electronics, Communications and Networks* (pp. 110–119). IOS Press. DOI: 10.3233/FAIA231182

Chapter 11
Teaching Climate Change and Building Critical Dialoguing Skills in a Fake News and Misinformation Era

Adam J. Kuban
https://orcid.org/0009-0003-3084-9179
Ball State University, Muncie, USA

ABSTRACT

Climate change intersects many disciplines, and this chapter explores the nexus of the science of climate change with political and mediated interpretations of that science through a literacy course taught at the undergraduate level. It begets discussions of fake news and misinformation in the form of climate skepticism and denialism, which have permeated online and social-media spaces, and those discussions eventually help students develop their critical-dialoguing skills as a logical application of their refined critical-thinking capabilities. Major assessments include student presentations about climate change in connection to countries of their choice and a final synthesis paper, which is a cogent literature review that students compose from content that they have read, watched and/or discussed, looking for relationships around a predetermined theme. This best-practices chapter includes sections that identify lessons learned, and it contains appendices that offer rubrics and assignment exemplars that fulfill the book's objective for "applied learning and curriculum design."

DOI: 10.4018/979-8-3373-0872-2.ch011

INTRODUCTION

Preamble

Former President Obama once called climate change the "greatest threat to future generations" (United Nations Climate Change, 2015, para. 1). Late Oklahoma Senator James Inhofe, who served on the Senate Committee on Environment and Public Works, referred to it as the greatest hoax ever perpetrated on the American public (Eilperin & Dennis, 2017). President Trump said he did not think it is a hoax but that "it'll change back again" (Tutton, 2018, para. 1).

Whom do we believe?

In March 2017, more than 25,000 U.S. science teachers received a free book—Why Scientists Disagree About Global Warming—in the hope that they might use it with their students (Worth, 2018). It came with a cover letter from The Heartland Institute, a national nonprofit research and education organization and self-described think tank that rejects the scientific consensus on climate change, asking teachers to consider the possibility that the science is not settled (Idso et al., 2016). Meanwhile, as a counter effort, the Paleontological Research Institution, a Cornell University–affiliated publisher, produced The Teacher-Friendly Guide to Climate Change and distributed it to teachers nationwide (Worth, 2018). Another book, Understanding Climate Change, was released in early 2019 from the National Science Teachers Association (Tucker & Sherwood, 2019).

Whose information is most accurate?

The media often report sources from both the Intergovernmental Panel on Climate Change (IPCC) and the Nongovernmental International Panel on Climate Change (NIPCC) in an effort to appear fair and unbiased.

What is fact? What is fiction?

According to an October 2018 study conducted by the Association of College and Research Libraries, approximately 50% of the 6,000 American college students surveyed said they lacked confidence in discerning fake news (Head et al., 2018). Roughly 36% said the threat of disinformation made them trust all forms of media less. Current students with media-centric majors are not immune and are ultimately faced with an increasingly arduous task: evaluating sources that, at the surface, seem legitimate and equally credible, making it challenging to know which source(s) to cite in stories (Head et al., 2018). Years later, this challenge remains: The National Association for Media Literacy Education (2024) identified "discerning high-quality information" (p. 23) as the top concern. This phenomenon has also been explored more broadly and globally in Goldstein's (2020) book Informed Societies: Why Information Literacy Matters for Citizenship, Participation and Democracy, in which the chapters, authored by professionals in a range of disciplines, explain how information literacy can contribute to the fostering of attitudes, habits, and practices that underpin an informed citizenry.

We, as educators, must help students develop their critical thinking and critical dialoging skills. This chapter describes a climate change course taught at the undergraduate level to offer best practices that can address this pedagogical challenge.

Teaching climate change—an international, complex problem that requires interdisciplinary solutions to address it—exposes students to the political rhetoric and nuanced media framing that surrounds this contemporary issue. It affords them the chance to learn more not only about climate change itself but also about statistical manipulation, false equivalence, and varying degrees of truth in the content they consume—all 21st-century challenges amplified in our media-saturated, postmodern world.

As part of a 2-year fellowship with my university's Honors College, I devised a course to do this that included several media-focused students as well as students from political science, sociology, biology, math, early childhood education, and natural resource/environmental management departments. According to primary syllabi for courses within this honors curriculum, students should use multiple sources of information and knowledge to evaluate competing hypotheses and form judgments; evaluate the strengths and weaknesses of arguments and actions related to current societal topics; and articulate their thoughts through well-crafted discussions, writings, presentations, and projects.

The course is 16 weeks (i.e., a full academic semester), and it is directed at younger college-age undergraduates, although it is possible for a student at any stage in their respective program of study to enroll. Most of the time, I taught students in their first or second semester of college. For general reference, students enrolled in this 100-level honors course typically had exposure to or awareness of climate change as a topic, but they had little to no knowledge of either the science of climate change or its sociopolitical influences. In other words, their collective background was limited or superficial; they may have heard the term "climate change," and they may have been able to list a potential cause or consequence of it, but overall, they lacked any depth of knowledge of the subject. In my experience, most had rather indifferent opinions of climate change, or at least their subdued demeanor in class suggested that. It is possible that some had strong feelings about the topic but felt compelled to self-censor out of fear that their beliefs or stances might cause conflict among their peers or with me.

THE PRAGMATIC GOAL OF THIS CHAPTER

This chapter is not empirically driven; instead, it contributes to best practices that could help fellow educators and specifically focuses on the course's rationale, objectives, and design; forms of assessment, including emphasis on the final capstone; and lessons learned from teaching it.

Course Rationale

Manipulation of information about climate change is not new. For my master's thesis, I conducted a content analysis of the three legacy broadcast networks' primetime newscasts (ABC's "World News Tonight," CBS's "Evening News," and NBC's "Nightly News") in relation to sources cited in stories about climate change from January 2000–December 2005. In sum, these network newscasts consulted 250 sources throughout that analysis duration; politicians were cited the most. However, scientists were most often the sources of conflicting information about climate change, which demonstrates journalists' desire to pit credible albeit contradicting sources against each other with the rationale that the viewing audience will sort it out on their own. Conflict is, in fact, an enduring value within the industry to determine newsworthiness (Bender et al., 2019).

The qualification and quantification of what constitutes expertise has been increasingly blurred in recent years, and topics, such as climate change, that have sociopolitical repercussions are often pawns in the ensuing dialogue among conflicting sources that claim that they offer the real truth about said topic (Dessler, 2016). In other words, the relevant question is this: What makes somebody an expert about a certain topic? How does a layperson differentiate fact from fiction—or perhaps degrees of fact versus degrees of fiction? Rarely is any source, even a scientist, 100% accurate 100% of the time (Elkins, 2019). However, if a layperson does not understand how science works as a process to create new knowledge—that is, does not understand new facts or understandings about a given topic—then it becomes easier to manipulate that person into believing that a less credible source who projects their information more confidently is more correct (Iyengar & Massey, 2018; Kruger & Dunning, 1999).

Course Design

This is how my course begins. My students and I initially dissect the definitions of misinformation, disinformation, and fake news. Misinformation is "false information that is spread regardless of whether there is intent to mislead" (Campus Library, University of Washington Bothell and Cascadia College, 2020). In other words, the dissemination of incorrect information can be based on ignorance or negligence; it is not necessarily deliberate (BBC, 2025). Disinformation is "deliberately misleading or biased information; manipulated narrative or facts; or propaganda," and fake news is "purposefully crafted, sensational, emotionally charged, misleading or totally fabricated information that mimics the form of mainstream news" (Campus Libraries, University of Washington Bothell and Cascadia College, 2020).

Similarly, people often differentiate terminology associated with climate change, such as weather and global warming, interchangeably but incorrectly. My students and I review the Earth Science Literacy Principles outlined by the National Science Education Standards and the American Association for the Advancement of Science's Benchmarks for Science Literacy (University Corporation for Atmospheric Research, 2009). Weather pertains to current (i.e., hourly or daily) atmospheric conditions; global warming is "the increase in Earth's average surface temperature due to rising levels of greenhouse gases," and climate change is the "long-term change in the Earth's climate or of a region on Earth" (National Aeronautics and Space Administration). We also distinguish *summarize* from *analysis* from *synthesis*, which are degrees of critical thinking used throughout the course (University of Utah Electrical and Computer Engineering, n.d.). Finally, I explain how academe generally works, in particular what one must typically do to earn a terminal degree in their discipline, such as a PhD, an EdD, or an MFA, as one way to establish source expertise. This reinforces the basics of scientific research, which is a process that typically includes a review of the relevant literature, an articulation of the research questions or hypotheses, an outline of the methods used to collect and analyze data, and the identification and discussion of the findings. We discuss how "this process of testing, contesting, and reviewing is what gives scientists confidence in the state of knowledge at a particular time" and that "as new knowledge emerges, newer publications supersede older ones, and they become the new reference point" (Australian Academy of Science, n.d., para. 2). This introduces the concept of peer review, often unfamiliar or unknown to undergraduate students, whose purpose "is to evaluate the paper's quality and suitability for publication" and to act "as a form of quality control for academic journals" (Taylor & Francis Author Services, n.d., para. 4-5). I explain that published, peer-reviewed scientific research has undergone scrutiny and independent assessment by experts in the applicable field. Most important, I emphasize that scientists focus on aggregate evidence and not opinions and that scientific evidence continues to show that human activities (primarily the human burning of fossil fuels) have warmed Earth's surface and its ocean basins, which in turn have continued to impact Earth's climate (National Aeronautics and Space Administration).

Although this course exposes students from myriad majors to current scientific data and findings, it is not exclusively about the science of climate change; instead, the primary emphasis is on media-provided and political interpretations and impacts of this scientific inquiry. In the end, I want students to be better able to do three things: (a) comprehend the process of empirical scientific inquiry—that is, how scientists generate findings about climate change; (b) recognize degrees of truth or accuracy in media and political interpretations of these findings, explaining how or why certain interpretations are accurate or inaccurate; and (c) more competently articulate the nuances and complexities of climate change on the basis of their evaluation of source expertise.

Course Learning Objectives and Applications

The overarching student learning outcomes are as follows from my course syllabus:

- Identify key terms and vocabulary associated with climate change,
- Examine current representations and interpretations of information presented in media and political discourse about climate change and water resources,
- Articulate the connection of your major/field of interest to climate change and water resources, and
- Identify your own predispositions with respect to climate change, noting any/all change in perceptions as a result of course content and class discussion.

After introductory definitions, students read and analyze current scientific data and discussions regarding climate change, including the latest data available from the IPCC, a leading international organization of 195 countries as members whose scientists study this subject (IPCC, 2020). As a specific example, we begin with an analysis of a global study about climate change awareness and risk perception conducted by Lee et al. (2015). In general, to guide their respective analyses, I ask students to answer the following questions:

- What is the reason for this research? Why does it matter?
- What are the authors trying to do or trying to know? In other words, what are the goals of this research? (Note any/all specific research questions if emphasized in the study, which usually appear at the end of the literature review.)
- How did they collect data for their research? In other words, how did they go about finding out what they want to know or do? (This would be the method.)
- What key takeaways resulted from their research? In other words, what did they find out?
- What are the limitations of this study that the authors identified?
- What are the limitations of this study that you identify? Can you spot different or additional limitations?

- What did you learn from this research?
- What did you not understand as you read the article?

Other examples of studies that have focused on climate change awareness include Howe et al. (2015), Doll et al. (2017), Agee et al. (2016), and Feldman and Hart (2018). Howe et al. examined a combination of 12 nationally representative surveys (N = 12,061) from Yale University's Project on Climate Change Communication and the George Mason University's Center for Climate Change Communication to estimate public climate change beliefs, risk perceptions, and policy preferences. Doll et al. (2017) also examined beliefs about climate change but used different methods and a targeted sample size. In Agee et al.'s (2016) study, scientists used modeling data to map tornado frequency over 60 years and, as key takeaways, new data revealed a new geographical distribution of tornado activity for 1984–2013: The autumn season displayed "substantial increases" in both tornado counts (EF1–EF5) and significant tornado counts (EF2–EF5) in a region stretching from Mississippi to Indiana. Finally, Feldman and Hart (2018) conducted two online news-browsing experiments that assessed selective exposure to climate change news stories.

Analysis-focused assignments and subsequent class discussions gave me clues as to where students were lacking in their overall comprehension of the process of scientific inquiry. For example, while some studies overtly list limitations, others do not, and in those instances, many students struggle to independently and confidently identify limitations in that study's findings. In other words, students can be quick to accept a study's accuracy simply because it has been peer-reviewed. Analysis-focused assignments like this open the door to opportunities to explain the peer-review process and why it matters as part of scientific inquiry. However, as I explain to my students, there is no such thing as a perfect study—each inevitably has challenges and limitations as a result of established parameters. This also presents a chance to determine the extent to which the findings of any study are grounded by data versus those that may be extrapolated or even speculated.

I have found that students—even honors students—are generally overwhelmed by scientific and social scientific studies. This may not come as a surprise; however, it is an important observation because it speaks to the broader phenomenon whereby some in society hold a noticeable distrust in science and scientists perhaps because they do not understand how science works. As students in my course form a better understanding of the rigor and methodological processes to which scientists must adhere to formulate their findings, it fortifies their trust in the findings even in the presence of transparent limitations. That said, students also come to learn that some peer-reviewed, scientific studies about climate change are, in fact, more accurate and rigorous than others, which leads us into a discussion of additional tactics to establish source credibility and expertise, such as journal impact factors and individual author credentials.

As a journalism educator, I want my students to acknowledge that scientific findings rarely exist in a vacuum; instead, once published, they are interpreted by secondary sources, such as journalists and politicians. These interpretations are sometimes incorrect—innocuously so as a form of misinformation and intentionally as a form of fake news. This leads us into an introduction to agenda setting theory and framing theory, both of which are long-standing media-effects theories of content manipulation.

Underpinnings of Agenda Setting Theory and Framing Theory

Agenda-setting theory posits that increased media exposure to an event or a phenomenon will cause the media-consuming audience to perceive it as more important. It suggests that journalists exert their influence by telling us what to think about (McCombs & Shaw, 1972). Framing theory takes this to the next level, positing that specific tactics, depending on the medium—for example: placement, word count, word choice, use of images, use of particular sources—tells us what we should actually think or believe about the given phenomenon (Entman, 1991). Busch's (2016) and Feldman and Hart's (2018) articles are two examples of scholarly studies that explored the nexus of framing theory and climate change.

In most cases, even if students have not heard of these two theories by name, they are aware of their presence within media content that the public consumes. This is when the course transitions more into the social science realm, where we take our newfound understandings of the science of climate change and view it through the lens of the journalists and politicians who frame the findings. We read Iyengar and Massey's (2018) reflexive, scholarly essay, which contends the following:

> *Whenever scientific findings clash with a person or a group's political agenda, be it conservative (as with climate change and immigration) or liberal (as with genetically modified foods and vaccination risks), scientists can expect to encounter a targeted campaign of fake news, misinformation, and disinformation in response, no matter how clearly the information is presented. (p. 7661).*

As we look for and examine media stories related to the findings of the aforementioned scientific studies, we find that these secondary sources—journalists and politicians—either do not understand science in general or they attenuate the complexities of climate change. For example, rarely is an explanation offered in media stories about the relationship of sample size, population, and margin of error. Moreover, politicians, perhaps in an effort to fit a short statement into a broadcast clip or sound on tape, offer superlatives and generalizations about climate change that most scientists explicitly shun in their own discussions of the implications of their findings.

This also presents my class an opportunity to explore climate change denialism, especially content from the NIPCC. According to the European Center for Populism Studies (n.d.), climate change denial is

> *dismissal or unwarranted doubt that contradicts the scientific consensus on climate change, including the extent to which it is caused by humans, its effects on nature and human society, or the potential of adaptation to global warming by human actions. (para. 1)*

As mentioned, the IPCC consists of many scientists from around the globe whose research pertains directly or indirectly (e.g., marine biology) to climate change. Earlier in the semester, when we are still analyzing the science of climate change, students also explore the results and limitations of the three working groups affiliated with the IPCC:

- Working Group 1: The Physical Science Basis
- Working Group 2: Impacts, Adaptation, and Vulnerability
- Working Group 3: Mitigation of Climate Change

The NIPCC, on the other hand, exists to challenge or contradict the IPCC and its findings. Its distribution, in conjunction with The Heartland Institute, of free books to U.S. science teachers was viewed by some as an attempt to interject itself into the curriculum. This gives us yet another opportunity to examine source credibility, including a leaked confidential budget for The Heartland Institute that revealed the fiscal resources available to support its political agenda. It also speaks to the existence of false equivalence, whereby, in this specific instance, the NIPCC situates itself as a credible source compared with the IPCC, implying one should weigh their information equally when making decisions or forming beliefs about climate change.

My students and I also dissect *Climate Hustle* (Rogers 2016), a documentary about climate change denialism, identifying instances of misinformation or even disinformation based on scientifically produced data findings. Finally, we read the Union of Concerned Scientists' (2007) ExxonMobil analysis, which reveals a historic precedent for misinformation campaigns, specifically how Big Oil corporations, such as ExxonMobil, currently use Big Tobacco's tactics to manufacture uncertainty and distrust in scientists in the current climate change scenario.

Critical Dialoguing

Conversations about climate skepticism and denial are important in this course, so students see what this side says about the topic and can strategically correct erroneous statements. This also introduces them to the concept of critical dialoguing, as explained by Morris (2017):

> *Colleges now have a moral responsibility to move education beyond critical thinking to experience in critical dialogue, [which is] more than basic communication skills; it is an active group process and opportunity for students and faculty members to learn how to engage in civil, respectful, difficult conversations. (p. 377)*

Morris offered the mnemonic TOOLS (Talk, be Open and authentic, be Optimistic, Laugh, be Sensitive and strategic) as a way to further qualify critical dialoguing but noted that this is a process that may not build a consensus or bring disparate voices together. Still, critical dialoguing is a 21st-century skill that students need in order to live and work "in this maze of difference" (p. 377).

One assignment connected to this concept has students prepare to critically dialogue in a hypothetical discussion with a climate skeptic or denier. By this point in the semester, we have already identified several assertions commonly made by climate skeptics or deniers, and I have them pick three that they address with data-driven responses from numerous credible sources/experts. I also have them explain (after their response) how they know their cited sources are credible on the basis of tactics we have previously discussed. The following are common samples of skeptic/denier assertions from which students can select their three:

- "It's late March in Indiana. It's technically spring, but it just snowed 3 inches last night. I guess global warming isn't real after all."
- "I mean, plants need carbon dioxide to grow, right? So more carbon dioxide in the atmosphere just means plants have more food."
- "So another part of a glacier in Antarctica just broke off. So what? Glaciers are just ice—they always fluctuate between growing and receding. It doesn't mean climate change has anything to do with it."
- "Scientists don't know what they're talking about. Back in the '70s, maybe about 50 years ago, they were warning us about a global *cooling* trend. And now they've switched it up and said it's warming. Sounds bunk to me."
- "Isn't science complicated? Aren't there always new questions to study and research? Then how can anybody say 'the science is settled' or that scientists have a consensus about anything related to something as complex as climate change? I think the scientists aren't even sure."

- "The models are biased. We can't even accurately predict the weather for next week—how can somebody or something reliably predict climate patterns for 2050 or even later in the century?"
- "Climate change has always happened! Greenland used to be green. And what about that drought in the '30s that led to the Dust Bowl? Seems like it's always fluctuated; mankind can't make that big of a difference."
- "Water vapor is a greenhouse gas too. How come that doesn't get mentioned right alongside carbon dioxide? Seems like scientists are ignoring all greenhouse gases besides carbon dioxide."
- "Climate change is just an alarmist, liberal talking point. I mean, how many times have they said that the world was going to end if we didn't act now or by some arbitrary date in the future? And nothing's happened! I see no reason to take it seriously."
- "It's the developing nations like China and India that cause the most pollution that leads to climate change. They should be responsible—maybe even more—than we are for any changes to climate."

It helps to have students type their responses first so they can organize their thoughts. If time permits, I have them engage in a mock discussion, or debate, as an in-class exercise, and in this environment, we can provide feedback to each other, offering findings from other credible sources they might have forgotten in their original responses.

Climate change injustice also enters the course curriculum, in particular in the context of water, which serves as a specific exemplar of the damaging repercussions of climate change inaction. The existing climate change scenario indicates that by 2030, water scarcity in some arid and semi-arid places across the globe will displace between 24 million and 700 million people (United Nations, n.d.). According to another statistic, the global urban population facing water scarcity "is projected to double from 930 million in 2016 to 1.7–2.4 billion people in 2050. The growing incidence of extreme and prolonged droughts is also stressing ecosystems with dire consequences for both plant and animal species" (United Nations Educational, Scientific and Cultural Organization, 2023, para. 3). Another documentary that we watch is *Water & Power: A California Heist* (Zenovich, 2017), which basically claims how financial elites, recognizing the gradual scarcity of water, have commandeered it for personal profit. Climate change, exacerbating this evolving have/have-not scenario, creates injustice for those less affluent, not only in California but also in other areas where water is lacking in abundance.

Thus, this honors course does more than introduce just the current scientific findings about climate change: It also situates those findings in the context of media frames and political agendas, which in turn affect how society understands and perceives risk about this complex issue, which then influences how we (do not) critically dialogue about it in a meaningful way so as to create policy and substantive change to attenuate its adverse consequences, especially those faced by the most vulnerable communities worldwide.

Capstone Assignment

Students' final exam, or capstone, for this course is actually a synthesis of literature and content that we have covered, plus integration of any new credible sources that further support their results. In other words, for this final synthesis paper, students first revisit content that we have read, watched, and discussed, looking for relationships around a predetermined theme. I also want them to find and incorporate new sources that are based on their own research.

I give them a choice between two themes:

1. Perceptions of climate change (this is meant to be more sociocultural)
    - What do people think or believe? How has this evolved over time?
    - What about causes? Consequences? Potential solutions? How does this change when referring to themselves versus the globe?
    - Is there evidence of media frames? Of media agenda-setting? How much or little are people influenced by media about this topic?
2. Impacts of climate change (this is meant to be more social scientific)
    - What evidence is there for the impacts of climate change? How has the science pertinent to climate change impacts changed over time?
    - How have those impacts been communicated via media? Is there evidence of media frames? Of media agenda-setting? How has this evolved?
    - What are common limitations when discussing real or potential impacts of climate change?

Either of these options should be broad enough that students have ample source material to synthesize and cite in their resultant papers. It is possible that themes may overlap, and I tell them that, but I encourage them to try to focus on one theme as much as possible. I also provide them with a comprehensive list of references for course content, which helps them see some of the idiosyncrasies indicative of American Psychological Association (APA) style, which is how they format their papers.

I remind students that their goal is not to simply provide an organized essay of scholarly texts, chapters, and documentaries; instead, their overarching objective is to provide a cogent synthesis of the sources pertinent to their chosen theme. Out of this synthesis should emerge supported stances relative to either perceptions or impacts of climate change.

In terms of logistics, I require a minimum of three pages, not including their references, and a minimum of 10 sources. They need a 50- to 100-word abstract for their paper, and I want their references formatted in APA style, which, as previously mentioned, is modeled in the comprehensive list of sources that I provide to them. I ask them to structure their papers with subheads for greater organization as follows (and including my prompts, or hints, to them):

- Abstract: Think key words + key sources + key takeaways.
- Introduction: This is where you identify your chosen theme.
- Literature review: This should be the bulk of your written text, including copious in-text citations per APA style.
- Final statement: This should be one to two sentences that offer conclusive remarks based on your synthesized literature review about your chosen theme.
- References: Begin this list on a separate page, and be mindful of APA style, including idiosyncrasies such as capitalization (or not), italics, punctuation, and spacing. Consistency is important!

I have included my rubric for this capstone assignment in Appendix A.

Other Assessments

As one might surmise, we read a lot in this course, and we watch several documentaries. To help students organize their thoughts—and to remind them later of those thoughts, especially for the final synthesis capstone—I have created an assigned-reading outline as well as a documentary-analysis outline that students complete for most (but not all) readings and documentaries. I have included both templates in Appendix B (for assigned readings) and Appendix C (for documentaries).

Figure 1 contains a screenshot of a more reflexive assignment that I assign once at the beginning of the course and again at its conclusion. In essence, near the beginning of the course, I want them to think about their preconceived notions about climate change: what they believe about this subject and why. Then, as we are finishing the semester, I ask them the same questions so we can discern how and where their beliefs have evolved.

Figure 1. A Short Reflexive Exercise to Gauge Students' Knowledge and Potential Biases Regarding Climate Change at the Beginning of the Semester and to Assess (at the End of the Term) How Those Stances May Have Evolved

No question about it – climate change is a contentious, complicated sociocultural issue. Also potentially an economic one. On the one hand, you have former President Barack Obama say that climate change is the greatest threat to future generations ... but then, on the other hand, you have Oklahoma Sen. James Inhofe, who has served on the Senate Environment & Public Works Committee, refer to climate change as the greatest hoax ever perpetrated on the American public.

The same superlative – greatest – but at opposite ends. ***So where are YOU on this spectrum? Where do you lean? And how much or how little do you believe climate change impacts our water resources?***

I want you to think about this, documenting your thoughts for this reflexive assignment. In all fairness, I've already dropped some statistics and information that reveal where I stand on this topic, so I acknowledge that my asking you to do this assignment might seem like an academic "trap." It's not. In fact, as you'll see below, I actually want you to think about where your knowledge and understanding might be limited ... or where you think the science might be shady or less than trustworthy.

DUE on Sunday, Jan. 12, by 11:59 PM EST.

Use these questions to guide your resultant Word Doc that you'll submit via Canvas:

- Do you believe in the concept of climate change – in general?
  - Do you believe in anthropogenic (i.e., human-caused) climate change?
  - WHY do you believe whatever you believe?
- Based on your own skepticism and/or the skeptics (like Inhofe) that you've read or seen, where do you believe climate change & the science around it seems ... Confusing? Or contradictory? Or too much conjecture (& not enough fact)?
- To what extent do you believe climate change can impact our water resources?
  - Presuming you think there is a connection, then how worrisome is this in your opinion? For instance, some have posited that, as a way to combat the effect that climate change could have on our water, that we can invest in more desalinization plants to generate more freshwater from our abundant ocean waters.

Also, near the end of the semester, I have students assemble a presentation about climate change in connection to another country of their choice; specifically, I have them select a country for an exploration and analysis of climate change and water resources. The United States is not an option for this presentation, and ideally, I would prefer that they select a developing country because it is generally understood that these nations will be less able to adapt to the changes resulting from climate change (Dessler, 2016). Students then conduct independent research, locating credible source material to help them answer these questions:

- How has (or will) climate change affect this country?
- What is the status of water in this country: accessibility, quality, usage?
- How does this country's media describe climate change and its impact on water resources?
- How does this country's political landscape affect climate change and water policy?
- How does this country's citizenry generally react to concepts related to climate change?
- How is this country's water status, plus its media and politics regarding climate change and its impact on water resources, similar to or different from those of the United States?
- How does your academic discipline connect to this country's ongoing adaptation to climate change and/or water resources?

I have included my rubric for this capstone assignment in Appendix D.

In sum, as mentioned, the course typically contains about 13 weeks of instruction followed by 2 weeks of students' in-class presentations about their selected countries. I compute students' overall course grades on the basis of weighted percentages assigned to the following categories:

- 20%: Participation (attendance) points from aggregate class sessions
- 20%: Exam—final synthesis paper
- 40%: In-and out-of-class assignments, which may include but are not limited to
    - assigned reading checks/end-of-chapter problems (in the Dessler textbook),
    - documentary analyses,
    - scholarly text analyses, and
    - reflexive exercises.
- 20%: Final presentation on the country of your choice (besides the United States)

CONCLUSION

For this course, I initially used Dessler's (2016) *Introduction to Modern Climate Change* (2nd edition) as an anchor textbook. (A third edition became available in 2021.) I also have students purchase the *Publication Manual of the American Psychological Association* (7th ed., APA, 2020). I have found it is more beneficial to teach this 3-credit–hour course in two 75-minute class sessions per week, if possible, as opposed to three 50-minute class periods. The extra time per class session allows us to dig deeper into our discussions for a more cohesive classroom environment. Finally, I try to encourage my students to submit their final synthesis papers to a nearby university's undergraduate research symposium, which typically accepts empirical research but also considers well-constructed, thorough literature reviews. This allows these papers to "go somewhere" after the course concludes, providing students with more professional development experience.

Suggestions for Educators

Should one want to adopt this course or distill it into a series of pedagogical units within an existing course, it might be useful to first assess students' comprehension of climate change. This assessment tool could be informal, that is, not graded but administered toward the beginning of the semester or unit to further understand, for example, students' preconceived notions about climate change; their ability to detect misleading information and/or fake news; and their knowledge about media effects theories, such as agenda setting and framing.

Lessons Learned

I have noticed that most honors students, when asked to read and analyze a scholarly study, tend to dutifully begin with the abstract and then proceed to Paragraph 1 and Line 1 on Page 1, and so forth. This makes complete sense and is entirely logical; however, peer-reviewed studies can be 20 or more pages and rather dense, especially when they originate from the physical or natural sciences. Thus, they can overwhelm students who are not accustomed to this type of discourse, so I decided to offer them a strategy of my own in the hope that it would make these reading assignments less arduous. North Carolina State University Libraries (2009) offer a resource that effectively explains the typical parts of a scholarly study, and after we break down the sections that typically comprise scholarly manuscripts and discuss their importance, I advise them to start with the abstract and introduction so they understand the summary of the study as well as the reasons that led to it in the first place. After that, I suggest that they skip toward the end of the article, reading its final section, which is typically labeled either "Implications," "Conclusions," or "Discussion." This is usually where the authors articulate the importance of the findings. I tell students to then scan the middle sections: "Literature Review"/ "Theoretical Framework," "Method," and "Results." Other educators may have their own strategy for digesting scholarly research manuscripts, but I believe it is important to help students strategize how to read and comprehend these texts. It is reasonable to assume that many honors students will eventually apply to graduate programs, where they will likely have additional opportunity to apply this strategy again. Moreover, for students with media-centric majors whose careers will depend on deadlines, this strategy should help them more quickly discern what they are reading.

I also have noticed that after students have analyzed a scholarly study on their own, our in-class discussions are more productive when I use the think–pair–share tactic that is commonly practiced in group settings; specifically, after students have attempted their own analyses, I have them pair with a peer or assemble a small group to compare notes and check for comprehension before we engage in a full discussion. This seems to attenuate some apprehension and encourage more voices to contribute in the resultant conversations.

Small teams also work well when we have explored the three IPCC working groups. I have had students work in groups to prepare short presentations of their discoveries and key takeaways from each working group, and this has served as early practice for their individual presentations of selected countries toward the conclusion of the course. It also provides me with an opportunity to provide some professional-development feedback, such as in relation to their organization of content, audience engagement, and use of communications aids—all areas that I later included in my rubric (see Appendix D).

For students' synthesis papers, some simple exercises or assignments with APA style protocols (or another preferred style of the educator's choice) throughout the semester will reinforce key concepts, such as in-text citation format and parameters for the reference list. I did include these style protocols in my rubric (see Appendix A) because, as previously mentioned, I wanted students to submit these papers to an undergraduate research symposium, where reviewers would likely notice style errors.

To further elaborate on the participation points included as a weighted percentage in students' overall evaluation, they earn 10 points per class session: 5 points for their general presence in class and 5 points for their punctuality. They could not replenish missed points for an absence—excused or unexcused—unless it resulted from a documented university-related function. I did this to reward them for their constructive, consistent participation in our in-class discussions. If the course must be taught online asynchronously, then students' completion of the reading checks (see Appendix B) or completion of the documentary analyses (see Appendix C) could substitute for these participation points, and weighted percentages can be adjusted as desired.

In the end, the subject or topic is incidental. My course focuses on climate change; however, an educator could apply the activities, strategies, and rubrics outlined in this chapter to any topically driven course. Having taught this course for several semesters, I believe students, in particular aspiring journalists and media practitioners, need more in-depth knowledge in many subjects (outside of journalism and the media). That increased depth, or comprehension, should help them become better able to evaluate sources and the information they dispense and to recognize degrees of truth or accuracy in media and political interpretation of that information. Furthermore, in this era of fake news and misinformation, these budding media professionals need to be able to articulate and explain how or why certain interpretations are accurate or inaccurate so they can ultimately move away from the tired practice of simply pitting two opposing sources against each other, one of which may be more credible and legitimate than the other.

We must be more discerning than that, and we educators have a responsibility to help build students' confidence in this regard.

REFERENCES

Agee, E., Larson, J., Childs, S., & Marmo, A. (2016). Spatial redistribution of U.S. tornado activity between 1954 and 2013. *Journal of Applied Meteorology and Climatology*, *55*(8), 1681–1697. DOI: 10.1175/JAMC-D-15-0342.1

American Psychological Association. (2020). *Publication manual of the American Psychological Association* (7th ed.). https://apastyle.apa.org/products/publication-manual-7th-edition

Australian Academy of Science. (n.d.) *How does science work?* https://www.science.org.au/curious/policy-features/how-does-science-work

BBC. (2025, Jan). *Misinformation vs disinformation: What's the difference?* BBC Bitesize. https://www.bbc.co.uk/bitesize/articles/z3hhvj6

Bender, J., Davenport, L., Drager, M., & Fedler, F. (2019). *Writing & reporting for the media* (12th ed.). Oxford University Press.

Busch, K. (2016). Polar bears or people? Exploring ways in which teachers frame climate change in the classroom. *International Journal of Science Education. Part B. Communication and Public Engagement*, *6*(2), 137–165. DOI: 10.1080/21548455.2015.1027320

Campus Library, University of Washington Bothell and Cascadia College. (2020, Oct 26). *News: Fake news, Misinformation, & disinformation*. https://guides.lib.uw.edu/c.php?g=345925&p=7772376

Dessler, A. (2016). *Introduction to modern climate change* (2nd ed.). Cambridge University Press.

Doll, J., Petersen, B., & Bode, C. (2017). Skeptical but adapting: What Midwestern farmers say about climate change. *Weather, Climate, and Society*, *9*(4), 739–751. DOI: 10.1175/WCAS-D-16-0110.1

Eilperin, J., & Dennis, B. (2017, Mar 14). How James Inhofe is upending the nation's energy and environmental policies. *Washington Post*. https://www.washingtonpost.com/national/health-science/how-james-inhofe-is-upending-the-nations-energy-and-environmental-policies/2017/03/14/2bebdbfa-081c-11e7-a15f-a58d4a988474_story.html

Elkins, Z. (2019, Feb 26). Ask a scientist: Are we ever 100 percent sure? *Columbia Daily Tribune*. https://www.columbiatribune.com/story/lifestyle/family/2019/02/26/ask-scientist-are-we-ever/5830985007/

Entman, R. (1991). Framing U.S. coverage of international news: Contrasts in narratives of the KAL and Iran Air incidents. *Journal of Communication, 41*(4), 6–27. DOI: 10.1111/j.1460-2466.1991.tb02328.x

European Center for Populism Studies. (n.d.). *Climate change denial.* https://www.populismstudies.org/Vocabulary/climate-change-denial/

Feldman, L., & Hart, P. (2018). Broadening exposure to climate change news? How framing and political orientation interact to influence selective exposure. *Journal of Communication, 68*(3), 503–524. DOI: 10.1093/joc/jqy011

Gibney, A., & Kirby, L. (Executive Producers). (2017). *Water & power: A California heist* [Documentary]. Jigsaw Productions.

Goldstein, S. (2020). *Informed societies: Why information literacy matters for citizenship, participation and democracy.* Facet Publishing.

Head, A., Wihbey, J., Metaxas, P., MacMillan, M., & Cohen, D. (2018). *How students engage with news: Five takeaways for educators, journalists, and librarians.* Project Information Literacy. https://eric.ed.gov/?id=ED591129

Howe, P., Mildenberger, M., Marlon, J., & Leiserowitz, A. (2015). Geographic variation in opinions on climate change at state and local scales in the USA. *Nature Climate Change, 5*(6), 596–603. DOI: 10.1038/nclimate2583

Idso, C., Carter, R., & Singer, F. (2016). *Why scientists disagree about global warming: The NIPCC report on scientific consensus* (2nd ed.). The Heartland Institute.

Intergovernmental Panel on Climate Change. (2020). *About the IPCC.* https://www.ipcc.ch/about/

Iyengar, S., & Massey, D. (2018). Scientific communication in a post-truth society. *Proceedings of the National Academy of Sciences of the United States of America, 116*(16), 7656–7661. DOI: 10.1073/pnas.1805868115 PMID: 30478050

Kruger, J., & Dunning, D. (1999). Unskilled and unaware of it: How difficulties in recognizing one's own incompetence lead to inflated self-assessments. *Journal of Personality and Social Psychology, 77*(6), 1121–1134. DOI: 10.1037/0022-3514.77.6.1121 PMID: 10626367

Lee, T., Markowitz, E., Howe, P., Ko, C., & Leiserowitz, A. (2015). Predictors of public climate change awareness and risk perception around the world. *Nature Climate Change, 5*(11), 1014–1020. DOI: 10.1038/nclimate2728

McCombs, M., & Shaw, D. (1972). The agenda-setting function of mass media. *Public Opinion Quarterly*, *36*(2), 176–187. https://www.jstor.org/stable/2747787. DOI: 10.1086/267990

Morris, L. (2017). Moving beyond critical thinking to critical dialogue. *Innovative Higher Education*, *42*(5-6), 377–378. DOI: 10.1007/s10755-017-9413-z

National Aeronautics and Space Administration. (n.d.-a). *Scientific consensus*. https://science.nasa.gov/climate-change/scientific-consensus/

National Aeronautics and Space Administration. (n.d.-b). *What's in a name? Global warming vs. climate change*. https://gpm.nasa.gov/education/articles/whats-name-global-warming-vs-climate-change

National Association for Media Literacy Education. (2024). *State of media literacy education report 2024*. https://namle.org/state-of-media-literacy-report-2024/

North Carolina State University Libraries. (2009, Jul 13). *Anatomy of a scholarly article*. https://www.lib.ncsu.edu/tutorials/scholarly-articles/

Rogers, C. (Producer). (2016). *Climate hustle* [Documentary]. Fathom Events.

Taylor & Francis Author Services. (n.d.). *Understanding the peer review process*. https://authorservices.taylorandfrancis.com/publishing-your-research/peer-review/

Tucker, L., & Sherwood, L. (2019). *Understanding climate change*. National Science Teachers Association. https://static.nsta.org/pdfs/202002BookBeatFactOrPhony.pdf

Tutton, M. (2018, Oct 15). Donald Trump: Climate "will change back again." *CNN Politics*. https://www.cnn.com/2018/10/15/politics/trump-climate-change-60-minutes/index.html

Union of Concerned Scientists. (2007, Jul 16). *Smoke, mirrors, & hot air: How ExxonMobil uses Big Tobacco's tactics to "manufacture uncertainty" on climate science*. https://www.ucs.org/resources/smoke-mirrors-hot-air

United Nations. Climate Change. (2015, Jan 21). *President Obama: Climate change greatest threat to future generations*. https://unfccc.int/news/president-obama-climate-change-greatest-threat-to-future-generations

United Nations. (n.d.) *Water scarcity*. https://www.unwater.org/water-facts/scarcity/

United Nations Educational, Scientific and Cultural Organization. (2023, Mar 22). *Imminent risk of a global water crisis, warns the UN World Water Development Report 2023*. https://www.unesco.org/en/articles/imminent-risk-global-water-crisis-warns-un-world-water-development-report-2023

University Corporation for Atmospheric Research. (2009). *Earth science literacy principles: The big ideas and supporting concepts of earth science*. https://scied.ucar.edu/sites/default/files/2021-10/earth_science_literacy_brochure.pdf

University of Utah Electrical and Computer Engineering. (n.d.). *Summarizing, analyzing, synthesizing*. https://www.ece.utah.edu/wp-content/uploads/2012/10/Summary-Analysis-Synthesis-Definitions.pdf

Worth, K. (2018, Mar 23). Mailings to teachers highlight a political fight over climate change in the classroom. *PBS Frontline*. https://www.pbs.org/wgbh/frontline/article/mailings-to-teachers-highlight-a-political-fight-over-climate-change-in-the-classroom/

Zabel, I. (2017). *The teacher-friendly guide to climate change*. Paleontological Research Institution.

KEY TERMS AND DEFINITIONS

Climate Change: — An international, complex problem that requires interdisciplinary solutions to address it. The concept that increased concentrations of greenhouse gases impact climatological patterns, which can have adverse ecological and economic repercussions.

Climate Change Denialism: — Rejection or uncertainty of the scientific consensus on climate change, which has been generated and updated over time as more data become available by the Intergovernmental Panel on Climate Change.

Fake News: — Content that has been intentionally created to evoke sensationalism and emotionally charged reactions. It often masquerades as the "real" truth, imitating mainstream media outlets and containing fabricated information.

Misinformation: — False information that has been disseminated through social channels. There may or may not be intent to mislead the consumer.

Science Literacy: — Knowing how science works and how new knowledge is generated, which should lead to better, more-informed decision-making and improved critical thinking.

Media Framing: — A media-effects theory. Whereas agenda-setting theory posits that media organizations and practitioners tell consumers what to think *about*, framing theory pertains to media's ability to dictate what to actually *think* about a topic or concept.

Critical Thinking: — Developing cognitive aptitude to distinguish fact from opinion and degrees of expertise through analysis plus the ability to synthesize credible sources into a coherent stance.

Critical Dialoguing: — Actively listening and engaging in conversation, particularly regarding complex and perhaps controversial topics, articulating stances with facts and data from credible experts while acknowledging that the goal isn't persuasion or consensus.

APPENDIX A. FINAL SYNTHESIS PAPER RUBRIC

- **Did they submit a single Word Doc via Canvas BEFORE the established deadline?**
  → late-work penalty (-30% of total) applies if past deadline
      YES
      NO

- **Is their TITLE centered & italicized at the TOP of page 1? (no course #, prof name, etc.)**
  YES—4 points
  NO
- **Are page #s in the TOP RIGHT corner? Including default margins + 12-point font?**
  YES—4 points
  NO
- **Is their ABSTRACT immediately below the title? (~ 50–100 words)**
  YES—3 points
  NO
- **Do they have SINGLE-SPACED text? With ONE LINE of space between paragraphs?**
  YES—4 points
  NO
- **Do they include SUBHEADS: Introduction, Literature Review, Final Statement?**
  YES—4 points
  NO
- **Are IN-TEXT CITATIONS evident?**
  YES—3 points
  NO
- **Did they have a MINIMUM of 3 pages? (not including their Reference List)**
  YES—3 points
  NO
- **Does their Reference List begin on a SEPARATE page?**
  YES—3 points
  NO
- **Do they include AT LEAST 10 sources?**
  YES—4 points
  NO

- **Are at least TWO sources from peer presentations BOLDFACED in the Reference List?**
  YES—4 points
  NO

(=) ________ / 36 possible

More Subjective Criteria

Table 1. **[12 points]** *Abstract/Introduction—key terms, theme identification, overarching thesis*

Exemplary (4)	Sufficient (3)	Marginal (2)	Unacceptable (0)
Abstract is compelling. Key terms defined. Key findings and/or conclusion identified. Introduction also includes key terms with ample source citations. Theme is evident. Thesis is completely clear.	Abstract is compelling but might be vague or unclear in spots. Some key terms not defined. Conclusion identified. Introduction includes key terms but may lack source support. Theme & thesis evident but may not be clear.	Abstract exists. Not very compelling. Missing important elements. Conclusion unclear. Introduction is shaky at best: little explanation of key terms, too few sources cited, etc. Theme & thesis might be there but difficult to discern.	Abstract exists but offers little to no insight into rest of paper. Introduction needs much attention. Does not establish key terms and/or identify the theme chosen or thesis of the paper.

Table 2. **[28 points]** *Literature Review—depth of content*

Exemplary (4)	Sufficient (3)	Marginal (2)	Unacceptable (0)
Provides complete explanation of key findings, trends, concepts, etc. Connects to numerous, credible citations. Offers ample synthesis. Readers gain insights.	For the most part, paper sufficiently explains findings, trends, concepts, etc. Some connections to source material may not be clear. Could synthesize more.	Explanations lacking re: findings, trends, concepts, etc. Many sources / citations missing. Little or no synthesis made. Readers gain little.	General statements made re: findings, trends, concepts, etc. No citations evident. Sources generally unknown. Nothing gained.

Table 3. **[4 points]** *Final Statement—conclusion*

Exemplary (4)	Sufficient (3)	Marginal (2)	Unacceptable (0)
Clear conclusion. Logically summarizes the paper based on aggregate lit review. Stimulates thinking, e.g., suggesting areas for further exploration.	Clear conclusion. But might extrapolate or offer remarks NOT supported by lit review. Just ends without much stimulation.	Conclusion not clear. Illogical assertions made based on literature review.	Conclusion not clear. Assertions made that actually contradict lit review.

Table 4. **[12 points]** *Mechanics—spelling, grammar, usage, punctuation*

Exemplary (4)	Sufficient (3)	Marginal (2)	Unacceptable (0)
Perfect. Maybe 1 minor error. This could be published as submitted.	A few minor errors evident—but these do not tarnish overall quality of paper.	Errors mar the quality of the paper. Needs proofreading.	Errors present to the point where reader begins to focus on them rather than the message.

Table 5. **[8 points]** *APA style—in-text citations + references*

Exemplary (4)	Sufficient (3)	Marginal (2)	Unacceptable (0)
ALL In-text citations formatted correctly. Reference list consistent. A few style errors but effort evident.	In-text citations generally correct. Reference list consistent. Effort is there … but could have spent more time here.	In-text citations generally incorrect. Reference list inconsistent. Needs attention.	In-text citations evident but no evidence of APA. Reference list inconsistent. No evidence of APA.

(=) ________ / 64 possible

APPENDIX B. TEMPLATE FOR READING 'CHECKS'

Text Details: (2 points)

- Title/Chapter (from Dessler textbook) = ______________________________ ________________________

If this text is NOT from the Dessler (2016) textbook, then complete the following:

- Publication Title = ________________________________
- Publication Year = ________________________________
- Author(s) = ______________________________________
- Any sponsors/interests? Look for any "acknowledgments" at the bottom of page 1 or at the end of article.

Text "check": (8 points)

- What's the main thesis, or overarching point, of this/these text(s)?
  (For multiple texts, you can either outline the main thesis for each or synthesize into one overarching statement.)
- What did you learn?
  (For multiple texts, you can either outline what you learned for each or synthesize into one overarching statement.)
- How is this/these text(s) similar to or different from what you've previously read or known?
- After (re)reading it/them, what do you still not understand?
  (This question is more for you than it is for me. It's meant for you to identify where you might need to explore or investigate in greater detail. If I have an answer, then I'll note it in the "Comments" in Canvas when I grade.)

APPENDIX C. TEMPLATE FOR DOCUMENTARY ANALYSES

Documentary Details: (3 points)

- Title = ______________________________
- Director(s) = ______________________________
- Writer(s) = ______________________________
- Producer(s) = ______________________________
- Year released = ______________________________
- Any sponsors/interests? Look for any "special thanks'' in the credits.

Documentary Analysis: (27 points)

- From the opening sequence (which could be anywhere from ~ 1–10 minutes): What's the thesis, or overarching point, of this documentary?
- What technique(s) does the filmmaker use throughout the doc to communicate essential ideas or takeaways? How effective are this/these technique(s)? Consider production elements (e.g., order of content, graphics, music) but also emotion (anger, sadness, guilt, joy, etc.).
- Of the sources/experts/people included in the documentary, whose testimony did you find MOST COMPELLING? And why?
- Notes re: things you liked as presented in the doc—notable production elements or storytelling strategies that you found effective.
  - (open response)
  - (open response)
- Notes re: things you would challenge as presented in the doc—moments/aspects where you disagree with their production tactic(s) . . . and include HOW you might do it differently.
  - (open response)
  - (open response)
- What is YOUR reaction to this documentary? (specifically note highs & lows, i.e., WHERE/WHEN you started to lose interest in the narrative and/or WHERE/WHEN you were truly captivated . . . & why did this occur?)
- How do you think OTHERS might react to this documentary in a way that differs from the way you've reacted to it?
- Notes re: things you want to research further based on content presented in the documentary.
- THIS IS YOUR OWN RESEARCH: What's something that somebody said that you want to investigate? Or a statistic/graphic that you want to verify? Maybe you want to discover more about an interviewee?

- Whatever "things" you want to research further, replace the blank lines with your details. ALSO re: where you found it: This should be more descriptive than just Google or Wikipedia. We want credible sources.

Thing #1 = What did you find? Where did you find it?
Thing #2 = What did you find? Where did you find it?

APPENDIX D. FINAL PRESENTATION RUBRIC

- Did they submit a single Word doc with key takeaways & corresponding citations BEFORE the date/time of their presentation? → late-work penalty (-30% of total) applies if past deadline
  YES—4
  NO
- Did they have a MINIMUM of 3 takeaways?
  YES—3 points
  NO
- Did they finish their presentation before the 10-minute mark? Was it long enough?
  YES—7 points
  NO

More Subjective Criteria

Table 6. Organization—4 points

Exemplary (4)	Sufficient (3)	Marginal (2)	Unacceptable (0)
Presentation is clear. Listener can follow line of reasoning.	Presentation is generally clear. A few minor points may be confusing.	Listener can follow presentation with effort. Some points/areas not clear. Presentation seems haphazard overall.	Not clear. Listener typically confused.

Table 7. Engagement—8 points

Exemplary (4)	Sufficient (3)	Marginal (2)	Unacceptable (0)
Level of presentation is appropriate. Presentation is a planned conversation, paced for audience understanding. It is NOT a reading of slides or bullet points.	Level of presentation is generally appropriate. Pacing is sometimes too fast or slow. Instances where presenter relies too much on notes, etc.	Aspects of presentation are too elementary or too sophisticated. Pacing is sometimes too fast or slow. Much of the info is read.	Presentation consistently too elementary or too sophisticated. Pacing leads to boredom or confusion.

Table 8. Use of Communication Aid(s)—12 points

Exemplary (4)	Sufficient (3)	Marginal (2)	Unacceptable (0)
Aid(s)/Format enhance the presentation. Prepared & used in a professional manner: • Large-enough font • Main points emphasized • Relevance made obvious	Aid(s)/Format contribute to the quality of the presentation: • Minor font issues • Main points somewhat obscured • Relevance not always evident	Aid(s)/Format generally detract from the quality of the presentation: • Major font issues • Main points not clear • Relevance questionable in several instances	Aid(s)/Format are poorly prepared or utilized.

Table 9. Depth of Content—12 points

Exemplary (4)	Sufficient (3)	Marginal (2)	Unacceptable (0)
Presenter provides complete explanation of key findings, trends, concepts, etc. Connects to credible citations. Offers synthesis. Listeners gain insights.	For the most part, presenter sufficiently explains findings, trends, concepts, etc. Some connections to source material may not be clear. Could synthesize more.	Explanations lacking re: findings, trends, concepts, etc. Many sources/citations missing. Little or no synthesis made. Listeners gain little.	General statements made re: findings, trends, concepts, etc. No citations evident. Sources unknown. Nothing gained.

Table 10. Responsiveness to Audience—4 points

Exemplary (4)	Sufficient (3)	Marginal (2)	Unacceptable (0)
Summarizes. Breaks things down as necessary. Consistently clarifies and fully answers questions if applicable.	Some attempt to help listener make sense of content. Presenter might be unsure about some material. Answers to questions adequate if applicable.	Little attempt to help listener make sense of content. Presenter seems to lack confidence. Difficulty in communicating and/or answering questions.	No attempt to summarize or make sense of content. Discourages or deflects questions.

Score = ___________ / 50 points possible

ANY NOTES FROM ME

Chapter 12
Building a GenAI Socratic Chatbot for Critical Thinking:
Insights From Cross-Cultural Cocreation, Living Labs and Pilots

Edward De Vooght
https://orcid.org/0000-0001-8274-2478
Artevelde University of Applied Sciences, Gent, Belgium

Aline Duelen
https://orcid.org/0009-0003-5560-1954
imec-SMIT, Vrije Universiteit Brussel, Belgium

Georgios Petasis
National Center for Scientific Research Demokritos, Athens, Greece

Wendy Van den Broeck
imec-SMIT, Vrije Universiteit Brussel, Belgium

Laurien Desimpelaere
Artevelde University of Applied Sciences, Ghent, Belgium

Ike Picone
https://orcid.org/0000-0002-0423-3456
Vrije Universiteit Brussel, Belgium

Gian Andrea Giacobone
International Telematic University Uninettuno, Italy

Alessandro Pollini
International Telematic University Uninettuno, Italy

Dora Katsamori
National Center for Scientific Research Demokritos, Athens, Greece

Nicklas Bang Bådum
https://orcid.org/0000-0002-1611-8869
Foundation Democracy X, Copenhagen, Denmark

DOI: 10.4018/979-8-3373-0872-2.ch012

Giannis Stamatellos
https://orcid.org/0000-0003-2839-0218
Institute of Philosophy and Technology, Athens, Greece

Ioannis Elissaios Paparrigopoulos
https://orcid.org/0009-0000-5040-7376
National Center for Scientific Research Demokritos, Athens, Greece

Panayiotis (Panos) Kapetanakis
https://orcid.org/0000-0003-3122-9855
National Center for Scientific Research Demokritos, Athens, Greece

Eirini Papachristou
https://orcid.org/0009-0004-2763-9653
National Center for Scientific Research Demokritos, Athens, Greece

ABSTRACT

This chapter explores the challenges and opportunities of deploying generative AI to enhance critical thinking to fight disinformation, focusing on the TITAN project under Horizon Europe. The chapter conceptualizes a Socratic chatbot powered by generative AI, aiming to foster media literacy and resilience against disinformation among diverse user groups. This Socratic chatbot aims to enhance critical thinking skills by asking users questions about media content. Building upon user insights from cocreation, living labs and pilot testing conducted in higher education in Flanders, NGOs in Bulgaria, and migrant communities in Italy, the chapter critically examines the efficacy and potential of a Socratic chatbot. While the results of the pilots indicate a strong potential, the current state of chatbots like ChatGPT have altered the playing field. Users tend to search more for answers than they are willing to answer questions themselves. This chapter provides actionable insights into the design, implementation, and pedagogical value of generative AI tools in combating disinformation.

INTRODUCTION

Disinformation poses a significant threat to democratic values, social cohesion, and informed decision-making (McKay & Tenove, 2020). Efforts to halt the dissemination of fake news and disinformation may vary from system-level (i.e., platform-level fact-checking and debunking, legislation, policy regulation, etc.) to individual-level interventions (Kozyreva et al., 2024; Ziemer & Rothmund, 2024). System-level approaches to combating misinformation have shown mixed success and often lack long-term effectiveness compared to individual-level interventions (Ecker et al., 2022; Hoes et al., 2024; Koppel et al., 2023). Even effective debunking strategies, such as warning labels (Martel & Rand, 2024), require continuous efforts and do not eliminate the effects of falsehoods on group perceptions (Ecker et al., 2022).

Critical thinking, therefore, appears crucial as the challenge of disinformation is also a challenge of source credibility and public trust, which are fueled by the complexity of information disorders and multiple cognitive as well as socio-affective drivers. Source credibility is central, as individuals are more receptive to corrections from familiar and trusted sources, such as Twitter accounts they follow, over unfamiliar ones (Margolin et al., 2017). Additionally, trust in fact-checkers like Snopes and FactCheck.org is often limited, especially among conservatives who perceive them as politically biased (Brandtzaeg & Følstad, 2017; Walker & Gottfried, 2019). Maintaining objectivity in fact-checking is challenging due to the subjective nature of political issues, the risk of politicizing the fact-checking process, and the influence of large donors, like Meta (Roozenbeek et al., 2023). Moreover, disinformation spreads faster than corrections, making it difficult for fact-checkers to keep up (Vosoughi et al., 2018). This is worsened by skepticism toward mainstream media (Brandtzaeg & Følstad, 2017) and trust in figures who challenge facts, such as influential politicians during COVID-19 (Bauer & Clemm von Hohenberg, 2020). Algorithm-driven echo chambers (Zollo et al., 2017) and confirmation bias further limit exposure to effective corrections, as people prefer fact-checks that align with their existing beliefs (Hameleers & van der Meer, 2020).

Psychosocial factors also hinder fact-checking. The continued influence effect allows disinformation to persist despite corrections (Swire et al., 2017; Lewandowsky et al., 2012), while the backfire effect can reinforce false beliefs (Nyhan & Reifler, 2010). Repetition of disinformation leads to the illusory truth effect, where repeated exposure to false information makes it seem more credible (Fazio et al., 2015; Udry & Barber, 2024; Ecker et al., 2022). Emotionally charged content—especially fear, anger, and sadness—activates heuristic reasoning, diminishing critical evaluation and increasing belief in and sharing of false information (Martel et al., 2020; Chuai & Zhao, 2022; Han et al., 2020; Kwek et al., 2023). Motivated reasoning and identity protection further impede corrections, as individuals reject information that threatens group identity, favoring beliefs that maintain social belonging (Nickerson, 1998; Kahan, 2013; Pennycook & Rand, 2021).

Fact-checking is further complicated because disinformation often extends beyond fake news, encompassing content that defies simple true/false classification (Wardle & Derakhshan, 2017). Disinformation campaigns leverage sensationalized headlines, partial truths, and misleading narratives, using tactics such as discrediting, trolling, conspiracism, polarization, and science denialism (Harjani et al., 2022; Donovan et al., 2023; Kozyreva et al., 2020; European External Action Service, 2024). Their goals include manipulating public opinion, confusing audiences, attacking opponents and critics, mobilizing ideologies, undermining institutions, and deepening societal divides (Hameleers & van der Meer, 2020). These campaigns are amplified through technologies like bots, deepfakes, and fake websites (Wardle & Derakhshan, 2017; Murero, 2023; USAID, 2021).

Misinformation further complicates fact-checking, as media outlets face pressures that prioritize sensationalism and clickbait over accuracy to drive engagement (Staender et al., 2021; Jung et al., 2022). Fast-paced news cycles often result in rushed, less reliable reporting (Lewis & Cushion, 2009). Additionally, social media influencers, infotainment, and citizen journalism contribute to the erosion of factual accuracy (Hobbs, 2021). Despite the importance of critical thinking and media literacy, debates persist regarding their transferability and long-term impact (Roozenbeek et al., 2023). They also face scalability challenges, often requiring personalized instruction or being poorly adaptable across different media contexts (Roozenbeek et al., 2023). Also, well-designed, online media literacy initiatives (e.g., SIFT, Checkology, Civic Online Reasoning) teach practical skills but do not adequately address how to recognize common misinformation tactics, such as conspiracy theories, polarization, and trolling (DEPICT tactics), even though these are crucial to detecting misinformation (Wardle & Derakhshan, 2017). This is particularly evident when misinformation agents employ manipulative tactics such as emotional appeals, logical fallacies, rhetorical ploys, and misleading frames, rather than straightforward factual inaccuracies (Wardle & Derakhshan, 2017; Harjani et al., 2022).

This rapid proliferation of false information via digital platforms exacerbates the need for innovative tools to foster media literacy and critical thinking on a scalable level. Such tools encompass advanced technologies and methodologies specifically designed to combat disinformation, moving beyond conventional fact-checking methods to include cutting-edge approaches. AI-driven algorithms, such as those implemented in disinformation detection models (e.g., Grover; Zellers et al., 2019), can identify patterns, inconsistencies, and potential falsehoods in vast amounts of online content. Natural Language Processing (NLP) systems (e.g., OpenAI's GPT; Brown et al., 2020) can analyze text for indicators of disinformation, sentiment, bias, and credibility. Furthermore, crowdsourced fact-checking platforms (e.g., Factmata; Bhulai et al., 2019) can leverage collective intelligence to validate information. Social network analysis tools (e.g., Hoaxy; Shao et al., 2016) can explore how disinformation spreads across digital platforms and identify influential users involved in its dissemination. Blockchain-based verification systems (e.g., Po.et; Koster, 2018) can trace the origin of information and monitor how it propagates within digital ecosystems. Additionally, interactive educational platforms (e.g., Bad News; Roozenbeek & van der Linden, 2019) can simulate real-world scenarios to enhance critical thinking and media literacy skills. Gamified learning experiences (e.g., Cranky Uncle; Cook, 2020) make media literacy education engaging and accessible. Moreover, cross-platform tracking systems (e.g., NewsGuard; Brill, 2018) enable the monitoring and analysis of disinformation campaigns across multiple social media platforms and websites.

The TITAN project builds on this technological trend and combines it with multiple didactic frameworks to enhance critical thinking. In TITAN's theoretical framework, a critical media consumer must possess both media literacy and critical thinking skills, as these two elements are deeply intertwined. TITAN's proposed solution is **AI-powered Media Critical Thinking** because media literacy and critical thinking skills are deeply intertwined, and AI offers a scalable and personalized solution. The TITAN project harnesses the transformative potential of generative AI (GenAI) to provide scalable, personalized strategies that empower users to identify misinformation independently. By emphasizing the identification of manipulative tactics such as discrediting, emotional manipulation, polarization, impersonation, conspiracy theories, and trolling (DEPICT Model; Harjani et al., 2022; Roozenbeek et al., 2023; Donovan et al., 2023; Kozyreva et al., 2020; European External Action Service, 2024), TITAN's AI-powered chatbot helps users 'internalize' critical questioning techniques, enhancing their ability to detect misinformation. This process strengthens users' critical reflexes and reduces their susceptibility to manipulative content.

This chapter describes the user-centered design and evaluation of the TITAN project, discussing its mission to leverage AI for disinformation resilience through user-centric digital solutions. Central to the project is its generative AI chatbot, designed as a Socratic interlocutor to guide users in critically assessing online content. The chapter examines the potential of this approach, alongside its limitations, informed by Cocreation Sessions (CC), Living Lab (LL) and pilot testing (PT) in varied sociocultural settings. While AI-powered Socratic chatbots can support critical thinking, their effectiveness is limited by user preferences for direct answers over dialogue. The TITAN chatbot showed potential in structured settings but struggled with engagement and adaptability. Without significant refinements, AI chatbots may fall short as reliable tools for teaching critical thinking at scale.

1. THEORETICAL FRAMEWORK

The theoretical framework underpinning this chapter leverages insights from the TITAN socio-technical framework and relevant literature on critical thinking, media literacy. Critical thinking and media literacy serve as foundational pillars for combating disinformation (Kertysova, 2018). To effectively detect disinformation cues, citizens must adopt a critical thinking approach, allowing them to set aside their own perspectives and preconceived notions (Faragó et al., 2023). Drawing on established literature, critical thinking is defined as the capacity to evaluate information systematically, discern biases, and construct reasoned arguments (Facione, 2015). Media literacy extends this concept by emphasizing users' ability to navigate digital ecosystems and identify trustworthy information (Hobbs, 2017). Generative AI offers a unique opportunity to operationalize these principles by enabling interactive, adaptive learning experiences. However, AI's limitations in addressing ethical concerns, responsiveness, and engagement highlight the need for deliberate design and contextual adaptation (Floridi & Cowls, 2019).

1.1 Cognitive Foundations of Critical Thinking

Critical thinking and media/information literacy are widely recognized as essential skills for empowering individuals to navigate the infodemic (Marcos-Vílchez et al., 2024; Roozenbeek et al., 2023). These skills enable individuals to critically assess information and sources, i.e. detect signs of disinformation, recognize unreliable sources, scrutinize the validity of messages, recognize bias, understand the underlying motives behind various forms of media and resist manipulative narratives that threaten public health and democratic values (Traberg et al., 2023). Media literacy and critical thinking are mutually reinforcing: media literacy provides the domain-specific knowledge necessary for informed critical analysis of media information, while critical thinking ensures that media evaluations are conducted rigorously, with an emphasis on logic, objectivity, and evidence (Facione, 1990; Paul & Elder, 2020).

Most definitions of **Critical Thinking** (e.g. Duron, 2006; Ennis, 1996; Facione, 1990; Halpern, 1998, 2014; Paul & Elder, 2001; Sartori et al., 2022; Sternberg, 1986) agree that it is "self-regulatory judgment" (Facione, 1990) and "purposeful, reasoned, and goal-directed thinking" (Halpern, 1998, p. 4) "focused on deciding what to believe or do" (Ennis, 1991, p. 11). In other words, critical thinking helps us "achieve a desired outcome by thinking rationally in a goal-oriented fashion" (Halpern, 2014, p. 8). 'Thinking rationally' means that critical thinking allows individuals to arrive at sound judgments about what to *do* and what to *believe* (Ennis, 1987, p. 10; Bailin, 1999). In this respect, critical thinking is "an optimal decision-making competence" which allows individuals "to avoid cognitive errors and the use of heuristics" in daily decision-making and problem-solving (Sartori et al., 2022, p. 3). Critical thinking is also a metacognitive ability that enables individuals to be aware of their own thought processes, evaluate their strategies, and adjust them as necessary (Facione, 1990; Sartori et al., 2022).

Bailin et al. (1999) argue that effective critical thinking requires integrating domain-specific knowledge rather than relying solely on generic skills. Also, as Hitchcock (2024) underscores, "critical thinking abilities are not a magic elixir that can be applied to any issue whatsoever by somebody who has no knowledge of the facts relevant to exploring that issue." For instance, a doctor must not only apply general analytical skills but also have in-depth knowledge of medical conditions, treatments, and procedures to make sound clinical decisions.

Critical thinking consists of various **skills or abilities**. The critical thinking models, including Halpern's Model (Halpern Critical Thinking Assessment, 2007), Facione's Model (California Critical Thinking Skills Test, 1990, 1994), Paul-Elder Framework (2001), Watson-Glaser Critical Thinking Appraisal (1941; 1980 and 1994), and Cornell Critical Thinking Test (Ennis & Millman, 1971; 1985), share the following common abilities Argument Analysis, Inference, Decision Making, Identifying Assumptions, Evaluation of Evidence, Metacognition.

There is a general agreement among psychologists and educators that critical thinking encompasses not only a range of abilities and skills but also a specific mindset or intellectual dispositions that influence thinking performance (Butler & Halpern, 2020; Ennis, 1987; Facione et al., 1990, 2015; Paul & Elder, 2001). Effective critical thinking requires dispositions such as the following: truth-seeking, a commitment to pursuing objective knowledge; confidence in reasoning, trusting logical analysis; open-mindedness, a willingness to consider different perspectives; analyticity, the ability to evaluate complex information; systematicity, approaching problems in an organized manner; autonomy, thinking independently; and intellectual courage, the willingness to challenge assumptions and confront difficult ideas. In particular, critical thinking skills determine how well a person can manage a thinking task, while a critical mindset determines whether one is willing to engage thoroughly in the thinking process. Studies show that simply possessing critical thinking skills without actively seeking the truth or investing cognitive effort offers no benefit compared to those who lack these skills (Butler & Halpern, 2020; Facione, 2015; Rand & Pennycook, 2021; Kwek, 2023).

1.2 Understanding Media as a Crucial Aspect in Enhancing Media Literacy

Media literacy refers to the combination of knowledge, skills, and attitudes necessary for individuals to navigate, critically evaluate, and actively participate in a media-rich and dynamic world (Hobbs, 2024). This concept emphasizes awareness of media's societal impact, the ability to use media creatively and responsibly, and the importance of fostering social engagement. Media literacy encompasses two main competencies, understanding how media function and using media for personal and collective growth, as described in the Media Literacy Competence Model (Mediawijs,

2023, Seymoens, et. al. (2020). It plays a crucial role in fostering critical engagement with media's influence on society and individuals (Van Audenhove, et al., 2024).

Media Literacy is the ability to access, analyze, evaluate, and create media content across various formats, including digital, print, and broadcast media (Hobbs, 2010, 2021). It equips individuals with the skills to navigate today's complex media landscape, distinguishing credible information from misinformation and understanding how media messages are constructed and their potential influence (Potter, 2018). Key components of media literacy include **access**, which involves finding and using media effectively; **analysis**, the ability to critically examine content, identify biases, and recognize manipulative strategies; **evaluation**, which assesses the credibility, accuracy, and intent of media messages; **creation**, the skill to produce responsible and ethical media content while understanding its impact; and **reflection**, which considers the broader influence of media on individuals and society, including its role in shaping opinions, cultural norms, and public discourse (Buckingham, 2003; Hobbs, 2010; Kellner & Share, 2007; Potter, 2018).

Various media literacy interventions (e.g., educational curricula such as Stanford University's Civic Online Reasoning initiative https://cor.stanford.edu/) have been studied and were found effective at increasing lateral reading, click restraint, evidence evaluation and other strategies for navigating digital environments (Roozenbeek et al., 2023; Wineburg et al., 2022). In addition, media literacy interventions that include explicit instruction in critical thinking for the media were found to enhance individuals' ability to identify misinformation on platforms, like Facebook, and reconsider beliefs in pseudoscience or climate change (e.g. Al Zou'bi, 2022; Lantian et al., 2021; Lutzke et al., 2019; Dyer & Hall, 2018; Horn & Veermans, 2019; Lu et al., 2024; Jones-Jang et al., 2021). In addition, providing users with media-literacy tips for identifying false and misleading information in their newsfeeds improved discernment between mainstream and false news headlines (Guess et al., 2020).

Despite some reservations (Većkalov et al., 2024), research also suggests that priming individuals to use analytical thinking–i.e., the "propensity and competency in 'thinking carefully' about information" (Kwek et al., 2023), reduces belief in/or sharing of fake news (e.g., O'Mahony et al., 2023; Swami et al, 2014). This is crucial because simply having critical thinking skills without actively engaging in truth-seeking or applying cognitive effort is as ineffective as lacking these skills altogether (e.g., Pennycook & Rand, 2019; Kwek et al., 2023). In addition, media literacy has been found to improve meta-cognition (e.g., monitoring one's bias) and critical thinking dispositions, such as open-mindedness and skepticism, required for thinking performance (Jeong et al., 2012; Ku & Ho, 2010).

The TITAN chatbot specifically focuses on enhancing the 'understanding media' competency to encourage critical reflection on media content. Frameworks on media literacy highlight its essential role in preparing citizens for informed media consumption and production, promoting inclusion, and supporting democratic participation in an increasingly mediatized society (Hobbs, 2024). Van Audenhove et.al. (2024) further developed the media-literacy model into a data-literacy model, with a specific focus on skills required in a *datafied* society as well as including specific literacy requirements to engage with AI tools. Identified skills related to using data include more active and creative use of data, such as interpreting a table with environmental data, navigating a specific data source and finding the required information, collecting raw data or visualizing data in a graph. Understanding data, on the other hand, focuses more on 'the knowledge, skills and attitude required to critically and consciously assess the role of data' in society. This includes more critical thinking skills such as observing, analyzing, evaluating and reflecting on the role of data. This includes, for example, critical questions on the potential societal consequences of how data is being used and communicated. It is these skills in particular that are cultivated within TITAN project.

1.3. TITAN's Conception of Critical Thinking

TITAN adopts the DELPHI REPORT (Facione, 1990): critical thinking is "purposeful, self-regulatory judgment which results in interpretation, analysis, evaluation, and inference, as well as explanation of the evidential, conceptual, methodological, criteriological, or contextual considerations upon which that judgment is based [...] The ideal critical thinker is habitually inquisitive, well-informed, trustful of reason, open-minded, flexible, fair minded in evaluation, honest in facing personal biases, prudent in making judgments, willing to reconsider, clear about issues, orderly in complex matters, diligent in seeking relevant information, reasonable in the selection of criteria, focused in inquiry, and persistent in seeking results which are as precise as the subject and the circumstances of inquiry permit".

In particular, TITAN focuses on developing the following **six abilities** of critical thinking (Facione, 1990):

1. **Interpretation** (categorization, decoding significance, clarifying meaning)
2. **Analysis/ Deduction** (examining ideas, detecting arguments, analyzing arguments)
3. **Evaluation of arguments** (assessing claims, assessing arguments)
4. **Inference** (querying evidence, conjecturing alternatives, drawing conclusions)
5. **Explanation/Recognition of assumptions** (stating results, justifying procedures, presenting arguments)
6. **Self-regulation** (self-examination, self-correction)

TITAN brings together the above generic abilities with media literacy to perform domain-specific critical thinking, that is, **media critical thinking**. We define '*media critical thinking*' as the ability to evaluate the credibility of a media item and, in particular, the ability to identify disinformation tactics/techniques and narratives (Machete & Turpin, 2020). It encompasses several essential domain-specific skills that help the ability to detect, break down, and assess what we read in media and everyday arguments; to distinguish facts from opinions; to pinpoint common logical errors and ineffective persuasive tactics; to recognize and account for perceptual, cognitive, and social biases when evaluating evidence; to differentiate between the proper and improper use of statistical and causal reasoning; to distinguish deductive reasoning from inferential logic while understanding the limitations of the conclusions each supports; to evaluate the credibility of experts, authorities, and media sources; to discern scientifically sound claims from those rooted in pseudoscience; to recognizing signs of digital manipulation tactics, such as identity fraud and impersonation, etc. (Arke & Primack, 2009; Dyer & Hall, 2018; Hobbs & Frost, 2003; Koç & Barut, 2016; Machete & Turpin, 2020).

2. CONCEPTUALIZING THE SOCRATIC CHATBOT

The Socratic method, rooted in dialogic and systematic questioning, provides an ideal framework for fostering critical thinking (Le, 2019; Overholser, 1993). It originates in the "maieutic" inquiry and practices of the ancient Greek philosopher Socrates (c. 470–399 BCE), who challenged his fellow citizens through continuous questioning to instill doubt in their common beliefs and "bring to birth" their latent truths (Benson, 2010). The Socratic method is vividly depicted in Plato's dialogues (Cooper, 1997) and the works of Xenophon (Wright, 2009) and has had a notable revival in modern education and teaching methodologies (Brickhouse and Smith, 2009).

The Socratic method, by prompting individuals to critically examine assumptions and contradictions in their reasoning (Morrison, 2011), encourages self-discovery and reflection through questioning. Modern applications of the Socratic method include critical thinking education (Paul & Elder, 2006), coaching (Neenan, 2008) and Cognitive Behavioral Therapy (CBT; Padesky, 1993; Overholser & Beale, 2023) with the goal of promoting independent learning and increased awareness. A Socratic coach -such as TITAN -, can use this method to help individuals gain an understanding of their core values, goals, and obstacles by helping them enhance their abilities, learn new skills, and achieve personal growth (Neenan, 2008; Downey, 2003).

The ultimate goal of Socratic coaching and Socratic critical thinking education is to help people become independent thinkers by internalizing the questioning method. Socratic practitioners suggest that individuals are more likely to retain both the answers and the reasoning behind them when they arrive at conclusions independently, rather than being provided with the answers (Overholser & Beale, 2023). AI coaching, on the other hand, is believed to have a significant impact in developing and enhancing metacognitive and self-regulatory skills such as improvements in study habits, acquisition of real-world skills, critical engagement with theories and their underlying assumptions, personal and collective reflection, etc. (Navarro et al, 2024). Likewise, in Socratic coaching, "asking questions is the main but not the only role of a coach: instruction, feedback, clarification, pointing out inconsistencies, offering advice, and making suggestions" are also important (Neenan, 2008, p. 262). Socratic chatbots aim to facilitate the Socratic method in a "Socratic AI" modus operandi, serving as an emerging innovation in prompt engineering in education to foster critical thinking by encouraging students to question ideas, examine assumptions, and evaluate arguments from diverse perspectives (Misnevs, 2023; Le, 2019; Kim and Mejia, 2019).

Generative AI, specifically large language models, can simulate such interactions by dynamically generating questions, summarizing user input, and prompting reflection. The TITAN chatbot builds upon this premise, aiming to:

1. Guide users in evaluating the credibility of online content.
2. Encourage reflection through iterative questioning.
3. Enhance user agency in identifying and countering disinformation.

3. METHODOLOGY

This section outlines the methodological framework used in the TITAN project to design, develop, and evaluate a Socratic AI chatbot for critical thinking. It begins with the chatbot design, detailing how Socratic questioning, dialogue structuring, and support mechanisms were integrated to enhance critical thinking and media literacy. The methodology then follows a three-phased implementation approach, starting with co-creation workshops (Phase A) to gather user insights and define chatbot requirements, followed by Living Labs (Phase B) to refine the prototype based on real-world user feedback, and concluding with pilot studies (Phase C) to assess its effectiveness in diverse settings. By combining participatory research, iterative testing, and stakeholder engagement, this approach ensured that the chatbot was both technologically effective and aligned with user needs and societal values.

3.1 General Research Methodology for Building a Socratic Chatbot

To develop an AI-driven Socratic chatbot capable of fostering critical thinking, the TITAN project implemented a multi-faceted research approach. This involved systematically refining the chatbot's design and functionality through several key methodological components, including profiling disinformation tactics, applying the Socratic questioning method, structuring dialogues for optimal engagement, and integrating support mechanisms to enhance user interaction. Each of these methodological steps was designed to ensure that the chatbot effectively challenges users to critically evaluate media content while maintaining an intuitive and accessible user experience. The following sections outline these methodological components in detail, explaining how they contribute to the chatbot's capacity to support media literacy and disinformation resilience.

1. **Profiling:** We developed an innovative questioning methodology by leveraging a concept we refer to as "Tactics Profiling". This methodology involves extensive research from various credible sources to identify and categorize the warning signs of distinct misinformation tactics. For each tactic, we created detailed profiles comprising lists of warning signs. In particular, we arranged the most common warning signs in six blocks: definition, narrative structures, rhetorical ploys and logical fallacies, cognitive biases or other psychological mechanisms, agendas and targets. In line with inoculation logic and literature (e.g., Harjani et al., 2022), the sixth block contains material to pre-emptively refute the fallacy or rhetorical trick found in the sign. Also, it contains material to forewarn users. The profiling logic is to enable easy detection of deceptive content and critical thinking over media content. By structuring questions around these tactic-specific signs, the methodology enables a systematic and targeted approach to uncovering misinformation.
2. **Socratic Method:** Our questioning method is further grounded on the principles of Socratic critical thinking (Paul & Elder, 2012) and coaching (Neenan, 2008) and is designed to foster independent media critical thinking skills along Facione's six dimensions of critical thinking (Facione, 1990, 2015). Our method prompts users to interpret meanings, reflect on the importance of the questions, understand the implications of media messages, recognize assumptions, spot fallacies in the reasoning and evidence, and recognize purpose and hidden agendas. Last but not least, the Socratic method is infused as a support mechanism by providing pre-emptive refutations and explanations, encouraging users to generate their own counterarguments in response to persuasive tactics (Walsh & Sattes, 2011).

3. **Dialogue Design, the 2-Block Structure:** The dialogue design consists of a two-block structure which serves prebunking and critical media thinking. Block 1 employs passive prebunking through an infographic, while Block 2 uses an adaptation of the Socratic questioning method. The infographic describes unique warning signs for each tactic, supported by real-life, memorable examples (e.g., conspiracism signs: secret manipulation, evil motives, "us vs. them" narratives). The signs were sourced from the tactic profiles. The expected outcomes are to contribute to broader media literacy efforts and to prime users to use this information in Block 2 dialogues. Block 2 uses the structured questioning method to help users analyze both the source ("WHO" is behind a media item) and the content ("WHAT" is said/the message) of media items.
4. **The questioning Method:** The questioning method uses two kinds of questions. First, for the WHO part, we use questions that prompt users to evaluate the trustworthiness of the author/source. We have created eight "WHO" questions for websites/articles and six "WHO" questions for social media posts/accounts. The questions guide users to assess the author's identity and credentials, website or account credibility/authenticity, funding transparency, purpose/agenda, editorial policies, and activity patterns. The "WHO" questions are inspired by state-of-the-art, established media literacy protocols like SIFT, CRAAP Test, and SMART Check. However, the logic of selection was based on our Profiling Method. In particular, we researched the deceptive tactics related to the source and identity of media items and then profiled these signs of these deceptive tactics. Then, we tailored the protocol questions after these signs in order to create the fourteen "WHO" questions. These questions are designed to detect common source credibility issues found in trolling, conspiracism, propaganda, smear campaigns, etc.

We have created sets of WHAT Questions for each misinformation tactic found in the content (the "WHAT") of media items. Each question corresponds to a sign of the following tactics: Discrediting, Polarization, Conspiracism, Trolling, Pseudoscience, and Science Denialism.

The "WHAT" questions were sourced from our Profiling Method. Each sign addresses a misleading narrative structure, a rhetorical ploy or logical fallacy, or a psychological tactic. Then, the signs were converted into "WHAT" questions. The profiling logic is to enable easy detection of deceptive content. At the same time, each question fosters skills in interpreting arguments, identifying biases and hidden agendas, and spotting fallacies and rhetorical ploys.

5. **Support Mechanisms:** We also created three Support Mechanisms for the WHO and WHAT questions based on three state-of-the-art strategies:

- Explanations and Forewarnings. We provide the rationale for each question, thus forewarning users and encouraging their critical thinking (Harjani et al., 2022).
- Media literacy material. We offer definitions, examples and interactive tips to help low and medium-level literacy navigate media items and detect deceptive tactics (Guess et al., 2020).
- Preemptive refutations. We provide explanations of the narrative, logical, or psychological structure of each sign addressing common fallacies (Harjani et al., 2022). This encourages reflection and develops cognitive resistance to biased users.

These mechanisms align with the Socratic method: they help clarify meaning, they question the question, they probe implications, they analyze assumptions and evaluate reasoning and evidence, considering alternative viewpoints. Segmenting interactions into two parts (WHO and WHAT), with flexible entry/exit points and optional shorter versions, aims to sustain user interest.

To optimize the chatbot intervention, certain limitations must be addressed. Closed questions ensure quick and easy detection but may make interactions feel overly structured. Open-ended prompts, explanatory feedback, and advanced natural language processing are planned to enhance conversational flow. Cultural and linguistic diversity also may affect the chatbot's effectiveness, highlighting the need for localized content and examples. Over-reliance on the chatbot is another concern; thus, the chatbot emphasizes developing transferable critical thinking skills rather than replacing critical thinking. Confirmation bias among users resistant to questioning their beliefs may also reduce engagement. To address this, the chatbot uses non-confrontational language and examples of biases to encourage openness. Regular updates to misinformation materials and algorithms will ensure adaptability, while dynamic feedback mechanisms and simplified language enhance effectiveness and user experience.

3.2 Participatory Design for Citizens' Empowerment

A principal foundation of the TITAN project was the policy framework of the EU Commission regarding AI, namely that the technology should be developed to be trustworthy, human-centric and based on European values (European Commission, 2019; EU AI HLEG, 2019; EU AI Act, 2024). The TITAN project operationalized these high-level concepts in a co-creation methodology, taking the point of departure that if one is to base an AI system on European values, one way of going about that is to investigate how those abstract values are embodied in everyday practices of regular Europeans. Along those same lines, creating a system that is worthy of trust requires a multi-disciplinary understanding of trust, which takes both technical and legal properties into account, but trustworthiness is equally a social concept, and for this reason it is necessary to understand what characteristics the intended target groups of the TITAN-system, but also European citizens more broadly, perceive as being of pivotal importance for them to trust the system. Lastly, ensuring human centricity in developing AI systems in the TITAN context means engaging these users at the outset of the project, and giving them a central role in defining user requirements.

New technologies are increasingly being developed, implementing an open innovation approach and participatory research methods involving all stakeholders in the early stages of the technological design and development process (Westerlund et al., 2018). This, to ensure social acceptance, trustworthiness and usability by valorizing and considering the needs and opinions of a wide range of citizens (Ballon et al., 2018). Participatory research "encompasses research designs, methods, and frameworks that use systematic inquiry in direct collaboration with those affected by an issue being studied for the purpose of action or change" (Vaughn & Jacquez, 2020, p. 1). In the TITAN project, this approach has been operationalized in a co-creation methodology divided into three phases (i.e., phase A, phase B, and phase C). In phase A, citizens from 8 European countries were engaged in co-creation workshops with the purpose of understanding their values, concerns and requirements regarding the socio-political and socio-cognitive drivers of the problem of disinformation and how to utilize AI to fight disinformation in a trustworthy, ethically and societally acceptable way, which according to the EU Work Programme 2023-2025, 'Widening participation and strengthening the European Research Area (ERA)' is a major objective and demonstrates the necessity of broad and diverse citizen engagement (European Commission, 2024). Within TITAN, Citizens were therefore recruited to be demographically stratified lay people, and thus were intended to each represent a different societal point of view. The intention was thus not to achieve representativeness of the entire population, but rather, to gain an understanding of the different positions vis-à-vis an AI tool to combat disinformation. The output of these workshops was then synthesized and qualified in a stakeholder and expert workshop, which served to transform the normative outputs of the citizen workshops to user requirements that could be taken into account in the prototyping of the TITAN system.

The results of the co-creation phase A were used as first inputs for the technological development of a prototype of the Socratic AI-chatbot. In phase B, Living Labs with citizens were conducted to test this prototype and gather feedback on the usability, user friendliness, and effectiveness of the system in stimulating critical thinking and aiding the evaluation of online news credibility. The results of this second methodological stage (i.e., consisting of new user requirements and a validation of requirements from phase A) served as input for the technological development of the first release of the TITAN system. This first release was consequently tested with possible end-users during phase C (i.e., pilots). Phase C further consisted of phases of iterative testing and technological improvements.

Through the adoption of this participatory and iterative approach, citizens and stakeholders were engaged at every stage of the technological design process, from the initial exploration phase to the final evaluation phase (Schuurman et al., 2016). The overall project approach is characterized by a three-phased implementation methodology that focuses on the co-creation of the TITAN system to ensure the development of a citizen-centered system (see Figure 1). An open innovation approach was adopted to refine, test, co-create, and validate the system with users, starting from the early stages and continuing throughout the entire technological development process. (Schuurman et al., 2016)

Figure 1. TITAN's three phased implementation methodology

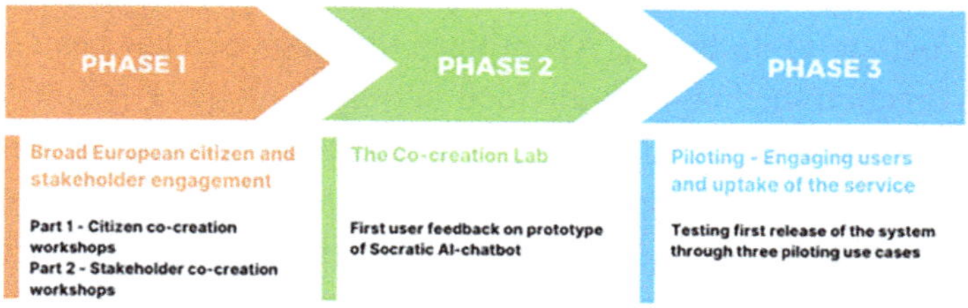

3.3. Setting the Scene Through Cocreation (Phase A)

The methodology of the co-creation session in the TITAN project followed a structured, multi-session workshop approach designed to engage citizens in shaping the AI-based TITAN system for combating disinformation. The methodology was developed through desk research and internal workshops with TITAN consortium partners, ensuring alignment with research objectives. It was implemented across eight European countries, with all workshops adhering to a standardized format.

3.3.1 Methodology

The co-creation session methodology of the TITAN project was designed to ensure a human-centered and participatory approach to developing an AI tool for combating disinformation. The methodology was standardized across eight European countries—Belgium, Bulgaria, Denmark, Ireland, Italy, Lithuania, Slovakia, and Spain—and involved 215 citizens in total, with an average of 27 participants per workshop. These participants were recruited through various channels such as social media, flyers, newsletters, and direct invitations to ensure diversity in age, gender, education, occupation, and geographical distribution. While the participants varied, there was an overrepresentation of women and students, with fewer participants from primary or vocational education backgrounds. The workshops were structured into four distinct sessions, each focusing on different aspects of news consumption, disinformation detection, AI system functionality, and potential risks. By structuring the process into interactive and reflective exercises, the methodology ensured a comprehensive understanding of citizen perspectives on AI-driven disinformation detection.

The first two sessions focused on citizens' existing digital habits and their ability to identify disinformation. In Session 1, participants created timelines of their daily routines, marking the points when they consumed news and information. This was followed by group discussions on how they shared news, both online and offline. Session 2 tested participants' ability to detect disinformation. A moderator presented ten news items, and participants had 30 seconds per item to judge whether it was real or false, simulating the rapid decision-making required when scrolling through online content. Afterward, participants discussed their reasoning in groups, reflecting on the signals they used to identify misinformation. The session concluded with the correct answers being revealed, highlighting the complexity and ambiguity of disinformation detection.

The third session introduced a scenario-based interactive game where participants engaged in a physical movement exercise to indicate their stance on various TITAN system functionalities. They were presented with different hypothetical scenarios related to AI interventions in news verification and were asked to position themselves according to their preferred approach. This method encouraged deeper engagement and reflection on AI's role in media literacy and disinformation combat strategies. After positioning themselves, participants had to justify their choices and discuss potential concerns. The interactive nature of this session helped uncover citizens' underlying attitudes toward AI interventions, privacy concerns, and trust in automated systems.

The final session encouraged brainstorming on potential risks and failures of the TITAN system. Participants were asked to identify reasons why the system might not succeed, clustering their answers into thematic categories. This exercise provided valuable insights into public skepticism, concerns about AI biases, and trust issues related to data privacy and misinformation mitigation strategies. The collected feedback from all four sessions was used to develop the design principles for the TITAN system, ensuring that it aligns with citizen needs and expectations. The results also informed subsequent stakeholder workshops, where experts and policymakers contributed further refinements. This structured co-creation methodology not only enhanced user engagement but also ensured that the TITAN system reflects the perspectives of diverse European citizens.

3.3.2 Results

The co-creation sessions of the TITAN project revealed critical insights into user perceptions of AI-driven disinformation mitigation and critical thinking support. Across the eight European countries involved, a key finding was the varying levels of trust in AI systems and their role in media literacy. Participants highlighted concerns about algorithmic bias, transparency, and data privacy—issues echoed in broader discussions about AI ethics and trustworthiness (AI HLEG, 2019). Furthermore, the sessions underscored the importance of integrating a human-centered design approach, ensuring that the chatbot aligns with users' cognitive processes and information consumption habits. These findings emphasize the necessity of designing AI interventions that account for diverse user experiences and expectations, particularly in politically and culturally heterogeneous environments (McKay & Tenove, 2020).

Another major finding from the co-creation sessions was the importance of fostering critical thinking through interactive and personalized engagement. Participants across different demographic groups expressed a preference for AI tools that not only challenge their reasoning but also provide context and explanation, aligning with existing research on media literacy interventions (Hobbs, 2017). The Socratic chatbot's questioning method was received positively in principle, but many participants struggled with its abstract nature, highlighting the need for adaptive and context-sensitive questioning strategies (Guess et al., 2020). Some users preferred structured, guided questioning paths, while others wanted more open-ended discussions, indicating that chatbot design must accommodate different cognitive and learning styles to be effective (Halpern, 2014).

A significant cultural and demographic difference emerged in how participants perceived AI's role in news verification and misinformation detection. In regions where media trust was lower, there was skepticism about the chatbot's neutrality, reinforcing existing research on trust and misinformation (Hameleers & van der Meer, 2020). Conversely, in contexts where users had higher confidence in institutional fact-checking, the chatbot was seen as a complementary tool rather than a replacement. These findings suggest that AI-driven interventions must be designed with flexibility, allowing users to choose their level of engagement and the degree of AI involvement in their verification process. Furthermore, co-creation results demonstrated that while users value AI assistance, they prefer tools that empower them rather than dictate conclusions, aligning with the principles of prebunking and media literacy education (Harjani et al., 2022).

Finally, the co-creation results reinforced the need for an iterative development process that incorporates continuous user feedback to refine chatbot functionality. Many participants highlighted the need for multilingual support, improved UI accessibility, and more engaging onboarding experiences, which align with broader findings from digital literacy research (Halpern, 2014). The chatbot's effectiveness was found to be contingent on clear communication of its purpose and limitations, as users who misunderstood its role were less likely to engage critically with its questions. This underscores the importance of transparency in AI system design and the need for continuous adaptation to user needs and evolving digital misinformation landscapes (Floridi & Cowls, 2019). Implementing these recommendations in the TITAN chatbot's development will be crucial to ensuring its impact on fostering critical thinking and resilience against disinformation.

3.4 Living Lab and Pilot Implementation (Phase B and C)

This section describes the implementation of TITAN's LLs, with 65 participants in 4 co-creation workshops, and pilot testing with 52 participants in 20 focus groups, focusing on three case studies:

The first Use Case is focused on higher education in Flanders and targets students who must enhance their critical thinking to become independent and critical citizens regardless of their academic discipline. The second Use Case targets members of NGOs in Southeast Europe who are often highly engaged and seek to expose malpractices from both governments and organizations, especially in the recent times of global spread of hostile disinformation and propaganda from authoritarian states. The third Use Case is concerned with disinformation about migration and refugees in Italy. UNINETTUNO launched the University for Refugees91 initiative in 2016, providing migrants and refugees access to degree program scholarships at UNINETTUNO. TITAN tool will support migrants, refugees and students' counter-narrative ideation and definition, providing support in verifying information, access to reliable sources, and describing how fake news spreads in social media.

Data collection included co-creation workshops, user observations, group discussions, and chatbot interaction analysis. These methods illuminated both the enablers and barriers to successful implementation, emphasizing the importance of contextual sensitivity in AI tool deployment.

3.4.1 Living Lab Methodology

The aim of the Living Labs was to gather insights on the usability, user experience and effectiveness of the Socratic AI-chatbot. A first prototype of the chatbot was tested in four European countries, i.e., Belgium, Bulgaria, Denmark, and Italy.

The Living Labs respectively engaged four target groups: students, citizenship at large, NGO members and active citizens, and migrants. During the workshops, four exercises were executed, each with its own focus and goal: First, participants tested the Socratic chatbot by completing a Critical Thinking Assessment (CTA), evaluating news articles, filling out an online questionnaire, and engaging in small group discussions to share feedback on usability and critical thinking stimulation. Second, using the Rose, Thorn, Bud method, participants identified strengths, weaknesses, and opportunities for improvement in the system's design and user experience. The third exercise involved prioritizing user requirements through the Island Approach, where participants ranked and categorized scenarios based on perceived importance. Finally, participants discussed key themes—engagement, effectiveness, context of use, and concerns around AI trustworthiness, privacy, and personalization—recording their insights on a structured template to inform future system development. Additionally, a mixed-method approach was applied, both qualitative (i.e., co-creation activities) and quantitative (i.e., survey research) research was conducted. The co-creation activities formed the foundation of the workshop, facilitating the collection of rich, qualitative data and in-depth insights. Complementing this, the survey research provided a means to quantify and validate these findings (Hossain et al., 2018). The full methodology is included in Appendix A.

3.4.2 Pilot Methodology

The pilots aimed to gather insights on the usability, functionality, user experience, and user attitudes toward the TITAN tools and its functions, as well as the ecosystem implementation of each use case. It targeted two main audiences: the target users and the ecosystem facilitators, both of whom must be considered to ensure a smooth implementation of TITAN solutions. To achieve this, a multimethod approach was used, consisting of three phases: In the first phase, participants engaged in structured tasks while being observed to identify user experience enablers and barriers, focusing on interactions with the chatbot and integration within the broader ecosystem. This was complemented by a post-activity survey assessing perceived impacts on critical thinking and fact-checking behavior. In the second phase, focus groups were held immediately afterward, allowing participants to reflect on their experiences, discuss the tool's usability, functionality, and contextual relevance, and provide targeted feedback on specific features and their implementation. The third phase involved chat analysis, where coders systematically examined transcripts of participant-chatbot interactions to identify communication patterns, misunderstandings, and positive user reactions, yielding detailed insights into areas for improvement in chatbot design and conversation flow. The full methodology is included in Appendix A.

4. RESULTS AND DISCUSSION

4.1 Opportunities and Impact

The following section highlights the opportunities and impact of the TITAN tools, focusing on its effectiveness in promoting critical thinking, supporting educational applications, and enhancing disinformation resilience. Initial user feedback across various Use Cases revealed that the TITAN tools, particularly the chatbot, successfully encouraged users to reflect critically on articles and arguments. By utilizing methods such as the Socratic approach, the chatbot fostered deeper analytical engagement and helped users evaluate reasoning more rigorously. Additionally, the chatbot's potential as an educational tool in controlled environments was emphasized, with particular value noted in its role in training critical thinking and combating disinformation.

First of all, the TITAN chatbot was promising in terms of fostering reflection: First of all, the TITAN chatbot showed promise in fostering reflection. Users across different Use Cases indicated that TITAN tools, such as the chatbot and the collaboration tool, motivated them to critically evaluate articles and arguments. Citizens highlighted that, where they would normally do a superficial reading of an online news article, TITAN encouraged them to do an in-depth and reflective reading of the content. In the Italian use case with students and migrants, the chatbot encouraged them to adopt a more reflective approach to news consumption. Rather than passively accepting information, they critically evaluated sources and arguments, reinforcing their fact-checking skills. They saw the chatbot as a structured tool for fostering critical thinking, particularly through its use of the Socratic method to scrutinize reasoning and deepen analytical engagement. As Joan, a lecturer in teacher education, noted, "*The concept of TITAN is good and valuable, and some of the questions are really good and precise to reach critical thinking.*" By encouraging users to question assumptions and seek corroborative evidence, the chatbot stimulated deeper analytical engagement. Simon, a psychology student, mentioned, "*The chatbot pushed me to read the article in depth, rather than doing a superficial or quick reading which I would normally do*". This aligns with empirical findings on AI's potential to support critical thinking (Sunstein, 2021).

Second, there appeared to be a clear value for educational applications. Feedback from higher education suggests that the chatbot is most effective within structured educational settings, where it complements existing curricula and benefits from facilitator oversight. Both lecturers and students alike identified its potential as a tool for training critical thinking, particularly in scrutinizing articles and identifying disinformation signals. Being able to learn more about specific disinformation signals, what they entail, and how to recognize them was highly valued by students. The chatbot's step-by-step guidance was especially appreciated in this context, as it helps users navigate complex articles while prompting them to ask the right analytical questions. Activists in Bulgaria who participated in training workshops found the chatbot useful in identifying disinformation tactics used in politically motivated narratives. They reported that the chatbot's questioning method helped them challenge misleading claims and verify the credibility of online sources. Additionally, its role as a goal-oriented, closed system was seen as a distinguishing factor that could enhance structured learning environments, such as training courses, EDUboxes, or facilitated classroom discussions. That was also acknowledged by media professionals who saw the value of the TITAN chatbot in controlled environments, "*for example, within a training course or an EDUbox*", where a facilitator could provide necessary context and guidance. It is clear that there is a potential contribution to media literacy education.

Third, the chatbot built disinformation resilience. It demonstrated promise in improving users' awareness of disinformation strategies, as reflected in pre- and post-intervention measures of critical thinking efficacy, such as Regulatory Self-Efficacy in Sharing Misinformation (RSESM) scores. Users themselves recognized TITAN's impact on their critical thinking skills. A quantitative survey assessing its preliminary effectiveness found that among 34 participants across three Use Cases, over 90% rated TITAN as at least somewhat effective in enhancing their critical thinking. Specifically, 37% deemed it moderately effective, 48% very effective, and 7% extremely effective. The Bulgarian use case provided evidence of the chatbot's application in professional fact-checking and advocacy. NGO members emphasized its potential in tackling coordinated disinformation campaigns, particularly in politically charged environments. Their feedback suggests that integrating the chatbot into structured fact-checking workflows could strengthen its impact on misinformation resilience. Findings from a separate survey conducted during the Living Labs indicated that participants anticipated adopting a more critical approach toward the news and information they consume online. Among the 65 respondents, 69% expressed agreement with this statement, 29% remained neutral, and 2% disagreed. Furthermore, 53% of participants agreed with the statement, "*The chatbot provided helpful guidance in evaluating the article.*" TITAN also fostered more critical and responsible engagement with disinformation. A preliminary quantitative analysis measured active and passive RSESM among 27 participants before and after interacting with TITAN. Results from exploratory paired-samples t-tests revealed significant improvements: active RSESM scores increased from 7.53 to 8.30 ($t(26)=-3.28$, $p=0.003$), while passive RSESM scores rose from 7.44 to 7.93 ($t(26)=-2.35$, $p=0.027$). These findings suggest that TITAN not only helps users recognize misinformation but also strengthens their commitment to refraining from sharing it and actively countering disinformation.

4.2. Challenges in Chatbot Design and Use

Despite the promising results highlighted in the previous section, where the TITAN chatbot demonstrated its potential to foster critical reflection, support educational applications, and strengthen disinformation resilience, this section outlines the challenges encountered in its design and use. User feedback revealed several shortcomings, including the chatbot's limited responsiveness, lack of unique value and immersion, and too complex language and tasks.

First, results demonstrated the issue of limited responsiveness, which led to frustration among users. Many users found the chatbot's repetitive questioning frustrating, feeling that it did not effectively respond to their inputs. Most participants felt that the chatbot resembled a checklist rather than a conversational coach. One participant, Dylan, a Graphical Design student, expressed, "*I don't feel heard. There is just a list of questions. It doesn't pick up on what I just said in the following question.*" This lack of adaptability resulted in miscommunication and missed learning opportunities. This shortcoming did not stimulate users to give well thought-out answers, as "*It doesn't take them into account anyway*" (Louise, Communication Sciences student). Users suggested that the chatbot should offer more guidance and support in finding the right answers. Many expressed a desire for the chatbot to coach them by providing feedback and building upon their responses. "*At one point I had the feeling 'When will this stop?'. There was just no goal-directedness to the exercise,*" noted Matt, a Marketing student, reflecting the sentiment of many users who felt the interaction lacked purpose and direction. Students described their experience as more of a questionnaire than an interactive conversation, lacking human-like language. The communication was largely one-sided, with the chatbot neither addressing specific user inputs nor building upon their responses. Some of the users ended up in a loop of repetitive questions, with the chatbot often repeating questions, offering praise without clear reason, and sometimes abruptly ending conversations. This underscores the need for enhanced interactivity and dynamic adaptability.

Second, the tool lacked immersion. To boost user engagement and enhance system interactivity, participants highlighted the importance of an innovative, clear, and engaging User Interface (UI). Providing improvements in elements such as fonts, colors, profile pictures, and features like notetaking was found necessary. Participants recommended the inclusion of more visuals (e.g., including pictures with news articles) and examples to enhance the user experience. Participants also emphasized the need to enhance the structure of the dialogue, suggesting the addition of subtitles in news articles and dialogues. They recommended providing more background information on disinformation signals and including a summary of key lessons at the end of the dialogue to improve interactivity and user engagement.

Participants proposed increasing the size of the article reading window and user input text boxes to enhance readability and ease of interaction. To improve accessibility, they suggested adding support for vocal messages, using a more readable and refined font, and offering user assistance by highlighting keywords and providing contextualized information within news articles. They also recommended incorporating greater language diversity and formulating clearer questions to address different user preferences and needs. Finally, participants advocated for a visual overview of disinformation signals at the end of dialogues and for adapting dialogues based on users' education levels, expertise, and the content of the articles.

Furthermore, there was a conceptual ambiguity among participants. A few of them compared the TITAN Chatbot to ChatGPT. "*In principle TITAN is a nice idea, but we are spoiled by ChatGPT, which makes TITAN fall short*", (John, lecturer in journalism and researcher on disinformation). Participants expect from any chatbot to behave like ChatGPT, directly answering questions and guiding them. This led on several occasions to parallel conversations and miscommunication as the chatbot was not responding to the input of the student. Therefore, participants deviated from the structural questioning of the chatbot not reaching any conclusion. One participant, who often experiments with ChatGPT to create prompts that make the chatbot engage in a critical dialogue, stated that he created a very functional prompt in ChatGPT that functions better and with less effort (one sentence prompt only). In this prompt, he asks ChatGPT to engage in a critical dialogue about an article in such a way that the user reaches certain critical reflections about the reasoning and trustworthiness of the article. Moreover, some participants indicated that existing tools such as riffbot.ai are doing something similar and provide a more pleasant user experience than TITAN. It is clear that the mismatch in user expectations became apparent, with some participants expressing frustration over the lack of clear responses. This indicates that participants struggled to discern the TITAN chatbot's unique value and intended purpose and suggests the need for a clearer value proposition and integration within specific pedagogical contexts (e.g., workshops).

Finally, there was an issue concerning complex language and tasks. The chatbot's academic language and task design often alienated less proficient users, particularly in non-academic settings. "*The chatbot uses very specific words that are difficult for me to understand, and this pushed me to read the same sentences several times*" (Samira, migrant). Simplifying language and tailoring tasks to diverse user competencies emerged as critical recommendations. In that respect, one of the participants underlined the need to follow the "Google-style" wording, using simple language (i.e., avoid jargon or overly complex words, and write in a way that anyone can understand) and short sentences to improve readability. The current complexity of the language and phrasing that the system employs was identified as a barrier to user engagement, limiting its reach to a broad and diverse audience. To improve the accessibility of TITAN, participants recommended providing multilingual support or integrating translation services.

4.3. Cross-Cultural Differences

The TITAN project sought to evaluate the effectiveness of a Socratic chatbot in fostering critical media literacy across diverse cultural and societal contexts. A comparative analysis of the pilot results, in combination with findings from the co-creation and living labs sessions, provides a deeper understanding of the extent to which cross-cultural differences influenced user engagement, effectiveness, and perception of the chatbot. While some context-specific variations emerged in the way participants interacted with and assessed the chatbot, there were no fundamental cultural barriers that hindered its broader applicability. Instead, differences in media literacy levels, trust in AI, and digital engagement habits shaped how participants from different regions responded to the chatbot.

4.3.1 Media Literacy and Digital Engagement

A key factor shaping user interactions with the chatbot was pre-existing media literacy levels. The co-creation and living labs sessions revealed that Belgian participants (mostly students) were already familiar with disinformation as a societal issue, which aligns with their exposure to critical media literacy education. As a result, they approached the chatbot as an extension of existing knowledge rather than a novel intervention. In contrast, Italian participants, particularly migrants and refugees, faced more significant challenges in navigating misinformation due to language barriers, limited access to reliable news sources, and unfamiliarity with AI-driven critical thinking tools. Living labs data showed that migrant participants struggled with the chatbot's language and complexity, indicating a need for linguistic adaptation and simplification in chatbot dialogues.

Similarly, Bulgarian participants, comprising NGO workers and activists, exhibited high skepticism toward AI-driven fact-checking tools. Co-creation sessions revealed concerns that AI could be manipulated to push specific political or ideological narratives, reflecting a broader mistrust in institutions and media organizations in the region. While Flemish students engaged with the chatbot with curiosity, Bulgarian users expressed a need for transparency regarding data use and the chatbot's information sources, suggesting that trust-building mechanisms should be embedded within the chatbot to foster credibility.

4.3.2 Interactions

Another key difference across the use cases was how users expected to interact with the chatbot. Belgian and Danish participants appreciated the Socratic questioning format and found it engaging, whereas Italian and Bulgarian users preferred more direct and instructional approaches. The living labs data confirmed that users often disengaged when the chatbot's questioning became too abstract or prolonged, indicating that while Socratic questioning is a valuable pedagogical method, it should be adapted to user preferences by offering options for shorter, more guided conversations.

Moreover, in Italy, users emphasized the need for visual cues and real-life examples to complement textual Socratic dialogues, suggesting that a multimodal learning approach—integrating images, videos, or infographics—could enhance effectiveness. In Bulgaria, participants found the chatbot's responses too rigid, noting that a more conversational and dynamic AI system would improve engagement. These findings suggest that while the Socratic method is a valuable strategy for critical thinking, its implementation must be flexible, allowing users to select between structured and open-ended questioning styles based on their preferences.

4.3.3 Usability and Accessibility

The co-creation and living labs findings highlight key usability concerns that could influence the chatbot's effectiveness across different cultural contexts. Technical barriers, such as slow response times, lack of personalization, and language difficulties, were consistently reported across all regions, though their impact varied. In Denmark and Belgium, users found the chatbot's interface intuitive but repetitive, while Italian and Bulgarian participants faced difficulties in navigating complex dialogue structures and understanding disinformation concepts.

A particularly striking finding from the living labs was the importance of adaptive onboarding. While Flemish students quickly grasped the chatbot's function, Italian and Bulgarian participants needed more structured guidance, reinforcing the need for localized onboarding experiences that gradually introduce users to the Socratic method and chatbot functionalities. This was particularly evident among migrant participants in Italy, who highlighted the need for multilingual support and simpler language structures to ensure accessibility.

4.3.4 Conclusions on the Cross-Cultural Dimension of TITAN

Overall, the results suggest that while cross-cultural differences exist, they do not fundamentally hinder the chatbot's effectiveness. The main variations stem from differences in digital literacy, AI trust levels, and user expectations rather than inherent cultural barriers. The chatbot's Socratic approach is broadly applicable, but tailored adaptations—such as customizable dialogue styles, visual aids, multilingual options, and transparent trust-building mechanisms—are essential to maximize engagement across diverse audiences.

The living labs and co-creation sessions provide clear recommendations for refinement, particularly in ensuring adaptability in user interaction, simplifying onboarding, and integrating context-sensitive disinformation detection mechanisms. Future iterations of the TITAN chatbot should prioritize a balance between Socratic questioning and structured guidance, ensuring that users from different backgrounds can effectively engage with the tool and strengthen their critical media literacy skills.

5. IMPLICATIONS FOR DESIGN AND IMPLEMENTATION

Based on living labs and pilot findings, the chapter proposes 4 key aspects of building AI-driven Socratic chatbots to enhance critical thinking.

Simplified Onboarding: A streamlined onboarding process is essential to ensure that users understand the purpose, functionality, and expectations of the chatbot from the start. During TITAN's pilot phase, participants expressed confusion about the chatbot's purpose and how to effectively engage with its Socratic questioning method. As noted in the results section, users who lacked prior experience with AI-driven tools struggled to grasp the chatbot's intended role as a critical thinking stimulator rather than a direct information provider. Implementing an interactive tutorial that introduces the chatbot's Socratic questioning approach, provides sample interactions, and sets clear expectations could mitigate this issue. Additionally, offering adaptive onboarding that tailors instructions based on users' familiarity with AI tools can make the process more engaging and intuitive. Simplified onboarding is crucial for AI-driven media literacy tools because it reduces cognitive overload, ensures user engagement from the outset, and enhances learning retention. Without a clear introduction, users may become frustrated or disengaged, limiting the chatbot's effectiveness in fostering critical thinking skills.

Dynamic Interactivity: To enhance engagement, the chatbot should incorporate adaptive questioning that adjusts to user responses, preventing conversations from feeling rigid or repetitive. The TITAN's results highlighted that some users found the chatbot's questioning style to be mechanical and repetitive, which reduced engagement and discouraged sustained interaction. By improving Natural Language Processing (NLP) capabilities, the chatbot could better recognize user input nuances and tailor its questioning strategy accordingly. Incorporating multi-turn dialogue structures, where previous answers inform follow-up questions, can create a more fluid and personalized learning experience. This was particularly noted in the results from Living Labs, where participants emphasized the need for conversations to feel natural and engaging rather than overly structured. Dynamic interactivity is vital for AI approaches in critical media thinking because it encourages active engagement, reduces frustration, and mimics real-world inquiry, making critical reflection a more immersive and meaningful process.

Integrated Learning Modules: Embedding the chatbot within structured learning modules—such as educational courses, workshops, or online curricula—can significantly enhance its impact. Results from TITANS's pilot testing showed that participants in higher education settings reported the greatest value when chatbot interactions were integrated into structured activities, such as classroom debates, case studies, or fact-checking exercises. This integration enabled users to apply their chatbot-guided reflections in real-life critical thinking contexts, reinforcing key skills. Integrating interactive media literacy lessons, providing contextual case studies, or allowing users to complete progressive challenges that reinforce critical thinking skills would further enhance this approach. By embedding the chatbot in a broader educational framework, its use becomes more than a standalone experience and instead evolves into a structured, goal-oriented learning process, strengthening users' ability to identify manipulative tactics in real-world media consumption.

Continuous Feedback and Iteration: For the chatbot to remain effective, it must incorporate ongoing user feedback and iterative improvements. Results from TITAN's Living Labs and pilot tests underscored that participants highly valued opportunities to share feedback about confusing or ineffective interactions with the chatbot. This feedback highlighted the need for improvements in response accuracy, question clarity, and adaptability to diverse conversation paths. Introducing a feedback mechanism that allows users to rate responses, provide qualitative feedback, and suggest improvements can directly address these concerns. Furthermore, AI-driven analytics tools could track engagement patterns, identifying points where users disengage or struggle, allowing developers to refine the chatbot's questioning techniques. Regular updates informed by user data and expert insights will help improve the chatbot's logic, enhance response precision, and ensure the tool remains relevant in an evolving disinformation landscape. Continuous feedback and iteration are crucial in AI-based media literacy training because they ensure the tool remains engaging, effective, and responsive to emerging challenges in digital information environments.

6. CONCLUSION

This chapter has explored the potential and challenges of using AI-driven Socratic chatbots to foster critical thinking and media literacy, particularly in combating disinformation. Findings from the TITAN project indicate that while the chatbot encouraged users to engage in reflective inquiry, many expected direct answers rather than critical dialogue. This tension between Socratic questioning and user expectations shaped by mainstream AI tools highlights both the promise and limitations of AI-driven interventions for media literacy. The co-creation, Living Labs, and pilot studies provided valuable insights into how users interact with the chatbot, demonstrating the importance of adaptability, engagement, and contextual integration in designing AI tools for critical thinking.

Despite these promising findings, this study has several limitations. First, the chatbot's effectiveness was tested in structured environments, which may not fully represent real-world, everyday media consumption habits. Additionally, while the chatbot's Socratic approach aimed to challenge users' cognitive biases, its current design struggles with interactivity and adaptability, making it less effective for users who expect more fluid AI interactions. Moreover, cultural and linguistic variations in how users interpret media content require further customization to ensure the chatbot remains relevant and engaging across different populations. Future research should explore how AI-driven adaptive questioning techniques, personalized learning paths, and multimodal content integration can enhance the chatbot's impact.

The importance of AI in training critical media thinking skills lies in its ability to scale, personalize, and adapt learning experiences in ways that traditional educational methods cannot. However, AI alone cannot replace human-led critical thinking training; rather, it should serve as an augmentative tool that enhances users' ability to analyze, question, and evaluate media content. As AI systems become more embedded in daily life, ensuring that they are designed to challenge misinformation rather than passively distribute content is crucial for an informed and resilient society. The TITAN chatbot represents an important step in this direction, but its long-term success depends on continuous iteration, user-driven improvements, and ethical AI deployment that prioritizes media literacy over mere information retrieval.

ACKNOWLEDGEMENT

TITAN project has received funding from the EU Horizon Europe research and innovation programme under grant agreement No.101070658, and by UK Research and innovation under the UK governments Horizon funding guarantee grant numbers 10040483 and 10055990 (https://www.titanthinking.eu/). Views and opinions expressed are however those of the authors only.

REFERENCES

AI HLEG. (2019). *Ethics guidelines for trustworthy AI.* European Commission. https://ec.europa.eu/digital-single-market/en/news/ethics-guidelines-trustworthy-ai

Al Zou'bi, R. M. (2022). The impact of media and information literacy on students' acquisition of the skills needed to detect fake news. *The Journal of Media Literacy Education, 14*(2), 58–71. DOI: 10.23860/JMLE-2022-14-2-5

Arke, E. T., & Primack, B. A. (2009). Quantifying media literacy: Development, reliability, and validity of a new measure. *Educational Media International, 46*(1), 53–65. DOI: 10.1080/09523980902780958 PMID: 21572920

Bailin, S., Case, R., Coombs, J. R., & Daniels, L. B. (1999). Conceptualizing critical thinking. *Journal of Curriculum Studies, 31*(3), 285–302. DOI: 10.1080/002202799183133

Ballon, P., Van Hoed, M., & Schuurman, D. (2018). The effectiveness of involving users in digital innovation: Measuring the impact of living labs. *Telematics and Informatics, 35*(5), 1201–1214. DOI: 10.1016/j.tele.2018.02.003

Bauer, P. C., & Clemm von Hohenberg, B. (2020). Believing and sharing information by fake sources: An experiment. *Political Communication, 38*(6), 647–671. DOI: 10.1080/10584609.2020.1840462

Benson, H. (2010). "Socratic Method." In D. Morrison (Author), *The Cambridge Companion to Socrates (Cambridge Companions to Philosophy*, pp. 179-200). Cambridge: Cambridge University Press. DOI: 10.1017/CCOL9780521833424.008

Binns, R. (2018). Fairness in machine learning: Lessons from political philosophy. *Proceedings of the 2018 Conference on Fairness, Accountability, and Transparency*, 149–159.

Brandtzaeg, P. B., & Følstad, A. (2017). Trust and distrust in online fact-checking services. *Communications of the ACM, 60*(9), 65–71. DOI: 10.1145/3122803

Brickhouse, Th. C., & Nicholas, D. Smith.(2010, 2 Jan.) "Socratic Teaching and Socratic Method." In Harvey Siegel (ed.), *The Oxford Handbook of Philosophy of Education*, Oxford Handbooks (2009; online edn, Oxford Academic.

Buckingham, D. (2003). *Media education: Literacy, learning, and contemporary culture*. Polity Press.

Butler, H. A., & Halpern, D. F. (2020). Critical thinking impacts our everyday lives. In Sternberg, R. J., & Halpern, D. F. (Eds.), *Critical thinking in psychology* (pp. 152–172). Cambridge University Press. DOI: 10.1017/9781108684354.008

Chuai, Y., & Zhao, J. (2022). Anger can make fake news viral online. *Frontiers in Physics (Lausanne)*, *10*, 970174. DOI: 10.3389/fphy.2022.970174

Cooper, J. (Ed.). (1997). *Plato: Complete Works*. Hackett.

Cybersecurity and Infrastructure Security Agency (CISA). (2021). *Tactics of disinformation*. https://www.cisa.gov/sites/default/files/publications/tactics-of-disinformation_508.pdf

Delic, H., & Bećirović, S. (2016). Socratic Method as an Approach to Teaching. *Evropejskij Issledovatel*, *111*(10), 511–517. DOI: 10.13187/er.2016.111.511

Donovan, J., Friedberg, B., & McCormick, K. (2023). *The Media Manipulation Casebook*. https://mediamanipulation.org/

Downey, M. (2003). *Effective coaching: Lessons from the coaches' coach* (2nd ed.). Texere.

Dyer, K. D., & Hall, R. E. (2018). Effect of critical thinking education on epistemically unwarranted beliefs in college students. *Research in Higher Education*, *60*(3), 293–314. DOI: 10.1007/s11162-018-9513-3

Ecker, U. K. H., Lewandowsky, S., Cook, J., Schmid, P., Fazio, L. K., Brashier, N., Kendeou, P., Vraga, E. K., & Amazeen, M. A. (2022). The psychological drivers of misinformation belief and its resistance to correction. *Nature Reviews Psychology*, *1*(1), 13–29. DOI: 10.1038/s44159-021-00006-y

Ennis, R. H. (1987). A taxonomy of critical thinking dispositions and abilities. In Baron, J., & Sternberg, R. J. (Eds.), *Teaching thinking skills: Theory and practice* (pp. 9–26). W.H. Freeman and Company.

Ennis, R. H. (1991). Critical thinking: A streamlined conception. *Teaching Philosophy*, *14*(1), 5–24. DOI: 10.5840/teachphil19911412

Ennis, R. H., & Millman, J. (1971). Manual for Cornell Critical Thinking Test, Level X, and Cornell Critical Thinking Test, Level Z. Critical Thinking Project, University of Illinois.

Ennis, R. H., Millman, J., & Tomko, T. N. (1985). *Cornell Critical Thinking Tests Level X & Level Z: Manual* (3rd ed.). Midwest Publications.

European Commission. (*2019). Communication From The Commission To The European Parliament, The Council, The European Economic And Social Committee And The Committee Of The Regions – Building Trust in Human-Centric Artificial Intelligence.* COM(2019) 168 final. https://eur-lex.europa.eu/legal-content/EN/TXT/PDF/?uri=CELEX:52019DC0168

European Commission. (2024). Horizon Europe Work Programme 2023-2025: Widening participation and strengthening the European Research Area. In *Research And Innovation: European Commission*. https://ec.europa.eu/info/funding-tenders/opportunities/docs/2021-2027/horizon/wp-call/2023-2024/wp-11-widening-participation-and-strengthening-the-european-research-area_horizon-2023-2024_en.pdf

European Commission High-Level Expert Group on AI. (2019). *Ethics Guidelines for Trustworthy AI.* https://ec.europa.eu/newsroom/dae/document.cfm?doc_id=60419

European Union. (2024). *Regulation (EU) 2024/1689 of the European Parliament and of the Council of 13 June 2024, laying down harmonised rules on artificial intelligence and amending various regulations and directives (Artificial Intelligence Act).* Official Journal of the European Union. https://eur-lex.europa.eu/legal-content/EN/TXT/PDF/?uri=OJ:L_202401689 European External Action Service. (n.d.). *Learn.* EU vs Disinfo. https://euvsdisinfo.eu/learn/

Facione, P. (1990). Critical thinking: A statement of expert consensus for purposes of educational assessment and instruction. *Research findings and recommendations* (p. 315).

Facione, P. A. (1990b). *California Critical Thinking Skills Test, CCTST – Form A.* The California Academic Press.

Facione, P. A. (1990c). *The California Critical Thinking Skills Test--College Level. Technical Report #3. Gender, ethnicity, major, CT self-esteem, and the CCTST.* ERIC Document ED326584.

Facione, P. A. (2015). *Critical thinking: What it is and why it counts.* Insight Assessment.

Faragó, L., Krekó, P., & Orosz, G. (2023). Hungarian, lazy, and biased: The role of analytic thinking and partisanship in fake news discernment on a Hungarian representative sample. *Scientific Reports, 13*(1), 178. Advance online publication. DOI: 10.1038/s41598-022-26724-8 PMID: 36604448

Fazio, L. K., Brashier, N. M., Payne, B. K., & Marsh, E. J. (2015). Knowledge does not protect against illusory truth. *Journal of Experimental Psychology. General, 144*(5), 993–1002. DOI: 10.1037/xge0000098 PMID: 26301795

Floridi, L., & Cowls, J. (2019). *A unified framework of five principles for AI in society. Harvard Data Science Review.Hanington, B., & Martin, B. (2022). The Pocket Universal Methods of Design, Revised and Expanded: 125 ways to Research Complex Problems, Develop Innovative Ideas, and Design Effective Solutions.* Rockport Publishers.

Glaser, R. (1984). Education and thinking: The role of knowledge. *The American Psychologist, 39*(2), 93–104. DOI: 10.1037/0003-066X.39.2.93

Guess, A. M., Lerner, M., Lyons, B., Montgomery, J. M., Nyhan, B., Reifler, J., & Sircar, N. (2020). A digital media literacy intervention increases discernment between mainstream and false news in the United States and India. *Proceedings of the National Academy of Sciences of the United States of America, 117*(27), 15536–15545. , D. F. (1998). Teaching critical thinking for transfer across domains: Dispositions, skills, structure training, and metacognitive monitoring. *American Psychologist, 53*(4), 449–455. DOI: 10.1073/pnas.1920498117

Halpern, D. F. (2014). *Thought and knowledge: An introduction to critical thinking* (5th ed.). Psychology Press.

Hameleers, M., Brosius, A., & de Vreese, C. H. (2022). Whom to trust? Media exposure patterns of citizens with perceptions of misinformation and disinformation related to the news media. *European Journal of Communication, 37*(3), 3. DOI: 10.1177/02673231211072667

Hameleers, M., & van der Meer, T. G. L. A. (2020). Misinformation and polarization in a high-choice media environment: How effective are political fact-checkers? *Communication Research, 47*(2), 227–250. DOI: 10.1177/0093650218819671

Han, J., Cha, M., & Lee, W. (2020). Anger contributes to the spread of COVID-19 misinformation. *Harvard Kennedy School Misinformation Review.* DOI: 10.37016/mr-2020-39

Harjani, T., Roozenbeek, J., Biddlestone, M., van der Linden, S., Stuart, A., Iwahara, M., Piri, B., Xu, R., Goldberg, B., Graham, M. (2022). A practical guide to prebunking misinformation.

Higdon, J. (2020). *The anatomy of fake news: A critical news literacy education*. Routledge.

Hitchcock, D. (2024). Critical thinking. In Zalta, E. N., & Nodelman, U. (Eds.), *The Stanford encyclopedia of philosophy* (Summer 2024 Edition)., https://plato.stanford.edu/archives/sum2024/entries/critical-thinking/

Hobbs, R. (2010). *Digital and media literacy: A plan of action*. Aspen Institute.

Hobbs, R. (2011). *Digital and Media Literacy: Connecting Culture and Classroom*. Corwin.

Hobbs, R. (2017). *Media literacy in the digital age*. Wiley-Blackwell.

Hobbs, R. (2021). *Media literacy in action: Questioning the media*. Rowman & Littlefield.

Hobbs, R. (2024). *Media Literacy in Action: Questioning the Media*. Rowman & Littlefield.

Hobbs, R., & Frost, R. (2021). *Mind over media: Propaganda education for a digital age*. W.W. Norton & Hobbs, R., & Frost, R. (2003). Measuring the acquisition of media-literacy skills. [Company.]. *Reading Research Quarterly*, *38*(3), 330–355. DOI: 10.1598/RRQ.38.3.2

Hoes, E., Aitken, B., Zhang, J., Gackowski, T., & Wojcieszak, M. (2024). Prominent misinformation interventions reduce misperceptions but increase skepticism. *Nature Human Behaviour*, *8*(11), 1545–1553. DOI: 10.1038/s41562-024-01884-x PMID: 38858544

Horn, S., & Veermans, K. (2019). Critical thinking efficacy and transfer skills defend against 'fake news' at an international school in Finland. *Journal of Research in International Education*, *18*(1), 23–41. DOI: 10.1177/1475240919830003

Hossain, M., Leminen, S., & Westerlund, M. (2018). A systematic review of living lab literature. *Journal of Cleaner Production*, *213*, 976–988. DOI: 10.1016/j.jclepro.2018.12.257

Jeong, M., Bae, R. E., & Kim, H. K. (2023). Psychological mechanisms of misinformation endorsement. *Journal of Health Psychology*, *28*(2), 179–196.

Jones-Jang, S.M., Mortensen & T., Liu, J. (2021). Does Media Literacy Help Identification of Fake News? Information Literacy Helps, but Other Literacies Don't. *American Behavioral Scientist. 65(*2), 371-388. DOI: 10.1177/0002764219869406

Jung, A. K., Stieglitz, S., Kissmer, T., Mirbabaie, M., & Kroll, T. (2022). Click me…! The influence of clickbait on user engagement in social media and the role of digital nudging. *PLoS One*, *17*(6), e0266743. DOI: 10.1371/journal.pone.0266743 PMID: 35767538

Kahan, D. M. (2013). Ideology, motivated reasoning, and cognitive reflection. *Judgment and Decision Making*, *8*(4), 407–424. DOI: 10.1017/S1930297500005271

Kapantai, E., Christopoulou, A., Berberidis, C., & Peristeras, V. (2021). A systematic literature review on disinformation: Toward a unified taxonomical framework. *New Media & Society*, *23*(5), 1301–1326. DOI: 10.1177/1461444820959296

Kellner, D., & Share, J. (2007). Critical Media Literacy, Democracy, and the Reconstruction of Education. In Macedo, D., & Steinberg, S. R. (Eds.), *Media Literacy: A Reader* (pp. 3–23). Peter Lang Publishing.

Kertysova, K. (2018). Artificial Intelligence and Disinformation. *Security And Human Rights*, *29*(1–4), 55–81. DOI: 10.1163/18750230-02901005

Kim, T. W., & Mejia, S. (2019). From Artificial Intelligence to Artificial Wisdom: What Socrates Teaches Us. *Computer*, *52*(10), 70–74. DOI: 10.1109/MC.2019.2929723

Koc, M., & Barut, E. (2016). Development and validation of New Media Literacy Scale (NMLS) for university students. *Computers in Human Behavior*, *63*, 834–843. DOI: 10.1016/j.chb.2016.06.035

Koppel, L., Robertson, C. E., Doell, K. C., Javeed, A. M., Rasmussen, J., Rathje, S., Vlasceanu, M., & Van Bavel, J. J. (2023). Individual-level solutions may support system-level change if they are internalized as part of one's social identity. *Behavioral and Brain Sciences*, *46*, e165. Advance online publication. DOI: 10.1017/S0140525X2300105X PMID: 37646255

Kozyreva, A., Lewandowsky, S., & Hertwig, R. (2020). Citizens versus the internet: Confronting digital challenges with cognitive tools. *Psychological Science in the Public Interest*, *21*(3), 103–156. DOI: 10.1177/1529100620946707 PMID: 33325331

Kozyreva, A., Lorenz-Spreen, P., Herzog, S. M., Ecker, U. K. H., Lewandowsky, S., Hertwig, R., Ali, A., Bak-Coleman, J., Barzilai, S., Basol, M., Berinsky, A. J., Betsch, C., Cook, J., Fazio, L. K., Geers, M., Guess, A. M., Huang, H., Larreguy, H., Maertens, R., & Wineburg, S. (2024). Toolbox of individual-level interventions against online misinformation. *Nature Human Behaviour*, *8*(6), 1044–1052. DOI: 10.1038/s41562-024-01881-0 PMID: 38740990

Ku, K. Y. L., & Ho, I. T. (2010). Dispositional factors predicting Chinese students' critical thinking performance. *Personality and Individual Differences*, *48*(1), 54–58. DOI: 10.1016/j.paid.2009.08.015

Kwek, A., Peh, L., Tan, J., & Lee, J. X. (2023). Distractions, analytical thinking and falling for fake news: A survey of psychological factors. *Humanities & Social Sciences Communications*, *10*(1), 319. DOI: 10.1057/s41599-023-01813-9 PMID: 37333884

Lantian, A., Bagneux, V., Delouvée, S., & Gauvrit, N. (2021). Maybe a free thinker but not a critical one: High conspiracy belief is associated with low critical thinking ability. *Applied Cognitive Psychology*, *35*(3), 674–684. DOI: 10.1002/acp.3790

Le, N. (2019). How do Technology-Enhanced learning tools support critical thinking? *Frontiers in Education*, *4*(126), 126. DOI: 10.3389/feduc.2019.00126

Lewandowsky, S., Ecker, U. K. H., Seifert, C. M., Schwarz, N., & Cook, J. (2012). Misinformation and its correction: Continued influence and successful debiasing. *Psychological Science in the Public Interest*, *13*(3), 106–131. DOI: 10.1177/1529100612451018 PMID: 26173286

Lewis, J., & Cushion, S. (2009). The thirst to be first: An analysis of breaking news stories and their impact on the quality of 24-hour news coverage in the UK. *Journalism Practice*, *3*(3), 304–318. DOI: 10.1080/17512780902798737

Livingstone, S. (2004). What is media literacy? *Intermedia*, *32*(3), 18–20.

Lu, C., Hu, B., Bao, M. M., Wang, C., Bi, C., & Ju, X. D. (2024). Can Media Literacy Intervention Improve Fake News Credibility Assessment? A Meta-Analysis. *Cyberpsychology, Behavior, and Social Networking*, *27*(4), 240–252. DOI: 10.1089/cyber.2023.0324 PMID: 38484319

Lutzke, L., Drummond, C., Slovic, P., & Árvai, J. (2019). Priming critical thinking: Simple interventions limit the influence of fake news about climate change on Facebook. *Global Environmental Change*, *58*, 101964. DOI: 10.1016/j.gloenvcha.2019.101964

Machete, P., & Turpin, M. (2020). The use of critical thinking to identify fake news: A systematic literature review. In Hattingh, M., Matthee, M., Smuts, H., Pappas, I., Dwivedi, Y. K., & Mäntymäki, M. (Eds.), Lecture Notes in Computer Science: Vol. 12067. *Responsible design, implementation and use of information and communication technology* (pp. 268–286). Springer., DOI: 10.1007/978-3-030-45002-1_20

Marcos-Vílchez, J. M., Sánchez-Martín, M., & Muñiz-Velázquez, J. A. (2024). Effectiveness of training actions aimed at improving critical thinking in the face of disinformation: A systematic review protocol. *Thinking Skills and Creativity, 51*, 101474. DOI: 10.1016/j.tsc.2024.101474

Margolin, D. B., Hannak, A., & Weber, I. (2017). Political fact-checking on Twitter: When do corrections have an effect? *Political Communication, 35*(2), 196–219. DOI: 10.1080/10584609.2017.1334018

Martel, C., Pennycook, G., & Rand, D. G. (2020). Reliance on emotion promotes belief in fake news. *Cognitive Research: Principles and Implications, 5*(1), 47. DOI: 10.1186/s41235-020-00252-3 PMID: 33026546

Martel, C., & Rand, D. G. (2024). Fact-checker warning labels are effective even for those who distrust fact-checkers. *Nature Human Behaviour, 8*(11), 1957–1967. DOI: 10.1038/s41562-024-01973-x PMID: 39223352

McKay, S., & Tenove, C. (2020). Disinformation as a Threat to Deliberative Democracy. *Political Research Quarterly, 74*(3), 703–717. DOI: 10.1177/1065912920938143

Mediawijs. (2023, 16 May). What is the Media Literacy Competency Model? https://www.mediawijs.be/en/competentiemodel

Misnevs, B. (2023). Socratic Method for Prompt Engineering – New Teching Desing. *STEP into the FUTURE, 18*(2), 10–11.

Morrison, D. R. (Ed.). (2011). *The Cambridge companion to Socrates*. Cambridge University Press.

Murero, M. (2023). Coordinated inauthentic behavior: An innovative manipulation tactic to amplify COVID-19 anti-vaccine communication outreach via social media. *Frontiers in Sociology, 8*, 1141416. DOI: 10.3389/fsoc.2023.1141416 PMID: 37006634

Neenan, M. (2008). Using Socratic questioning in coaching. *Journal of Rational-Emotive & Cognitive-Behavior Therapy, 27*(4), 249–264. DOI: 10.1007/s10942-007-0076-z

Nickerson, R. S. (1998). Confirmation bias: A ubiquitous phenomenon in many guises. *Review of General Psychology*, *2*(2), 175–220. DOI: 10.1037/1089-2680.2.2.175

Nyhan, B., & Reifler, J. (2010). When corrections fail: The persistence of political misperceptions. *Political Behavior*, *32*(2), 303–330. https://www.jstor.org/stable/40587320. DOI: 10.1007/s11109-010-9112-2

O'Mahony, C., Brassil, M., Murphy, G., & Linehan, C. (2023). The efficacy of interventions in reducing belief in conspiracy theories: A systematic review. *PLoS One*, *18*(4), e0280902. DOI: 10.1371/journal.pone.0280902 PMID: 37018172

Overholser, J. C. (1993a). Elements of the Socratic method: I. Systematic questioning. *Psychotherapy (Chicago, Ill.)*, *30*(1), 67–74. DOI: 10.1037/0033-3204.30.1.67

Overholser, J. C., & Beale, E. (2023). The art and science behind Socratic questioning and guided discovery: A research review. *Psychotherapy Research*, *33*(7), 946–956. DOI: 10.1080/10503307.2023.2183154 PMID: 36878221

Padesky, C. A. (1993, Sep). Socratic questioning: Changing minds or guiding discovery? Invited keynote address presented at the 1993 European Congress of Behaviour and Cognitive Therapies, London.

Paul, R., & Elder, L. (2020). *Fact over fake: A critical thinker's guide to media bias and political propaganda*. Rowman & Littlefield.

Paul, R. W., & Elder, L. (2006). *The Thinker's Guide to The Art of Socratic Questioning*. Foundation for Critical Thinking.

Pennycook, G., & Rand, D. G. (2019). Lazy, not biased: Susceptibility to partisan fake news is better explained by lack of reasoning than by motivated reasoning. *Cognition*, *188*, 39–50. DOI: 10.1016/j.cognition.2018.06.011 PMID: 29935897

Pennycook, G., & Rand, D. G. (2021). The psychology of fake news. *Trends in Cognitive Sciences*, *25*(5), 388–402. DOI: 10.1016/j.tics.2021.02.007 PMID: 33736957

Potter, W. J. (2018). *Media literacy*. SAGE Publications.

Roozenbeek, J., Culloty, E., & Suiter, J. (2023). Countering misinformation: Evidence, knowledge gaps, and implications of current interventions. *European Psychologist*, *28*(3), 189–205. DOI: 10.1027/1016-9040/a000492

Salinas Navarro, D. E., Vilalta-Perdomo, E., Michel-Villarreal, R., & Montesinos, L. (2024). Designing experiential learning activities with generative artificial intelligence tools for authentic assessment. *Interactive Technology and Smart Education*, *21*(4), 708–734. DOI: 10.1108/ITSE-12-2023-0236

Sartori, R., Tommasi, F., Ceschi, A., Falser, M., Genero, S., & Belotto, S. (2022). Enhancing critical thinking skills and media literacy in initial vocational education and training via self-nudging: The contribution of the NERDVET project. *Frontiers in Psychology*, *13*, 935673. DOI: 10.3389/fpsyg.2022.935673 PMID: 35992484

Schuurman, D., De Marez, L., & Ballon, P. (2016). The impact of living lab methodology on open innovation contributions and outcomes. *Technology Innovation Management Review*, *6*(1), 7–16. DOI: 10.22215/timreview/956

Seymoens, T., Van Audenhove, L., Van Den Broeck, W., & Mariën, I. (2020). Data literacy on the road: Setting up a large-scale data literacy initiative in the DataBuzz project. *The Journal of Media Literacy Education*, *12*(3), 102–119. DOI: 10.23860/JMLE-2020-12-3-9

Skovsgaard, M., & Andersen, K. (2020). Conceptualizing news avoidance: Towards a shared understanding of different forms of news avoidance. *Journalism Studies*, *21*(6), 768–782.

Staender, A., Humprecht, E., Esser, F., Morosoli, S., & Van Aelst, P. (2021). Is sensationalist disinformation more effective? Three facilitating factors at the national, individual, and situational level. *Digital Journalism (Abingdon, England)*, *10*(6), 976–996. DOI: 10.1080/21670811.2021.1966315

Stanford History Education Group. (2019). *Evaluating information: The need for critical thinking*. Stanford University.

Sunstein, C. R. (2021). *Liars: Falsehoods and free speech in an age of deception*. Oxford University Press.van Raemdonck, N., & Meyer, T. (2022). Why disinformation is here to stay: A socio-technical analysis of disinformation as a hybrid threat. In Lonardo, L. (Ed.), *Addressing hybrid threats: European law and policies*. Edward Elgar Publishing.

Swami, V., Voracek, M., Stieger, S., Tran, U., & Furnham, A. (2014). Analytic thinking reduces belief in conspiracy theories. *Cognition*, *133*(3), 572–585. DOI: 10.1016/j.cognition.2014.08.006 PMID: 25217762

Swire, B., Ecker, U. K. H., & Lewandowsky, S. (2017). The role of familiarity in correcting inaccurate information. *Journal of Experimental Psychology. Learning, Memory, and Cognition*, *43*(12), 1948–1961. DOI: 10.1037/xlm0000422 PMID: 28504531

Traberg, C. S., Harjani, T., Basol, M., Biddlestone, M., Maertens, R., Roozenbeek, J., & van der Linden, S. (2023). Prebunking Against Misinformation in the Modern Digital Age. In Purnat, T. D. (Ed.), *et al., Managing Infodemics in the 21st Century: Addressing New Public Health Challenges in the Information Ecosystem* (pp. 99–111). Springer. DOI: 10.1007/978-3-031-27789-4_8

Udry, J., & Barber, S. J. (2024). The illusory truth effect: A review of how repetition increases belief in misinformation. *Current Opinion in Psychology, 56*, 101736. DOI: 10.1016/j.copsyc.2023.101736 PMID: 38113667

United States Agency for International Development. (2021). *Disinformation primer*. https://www.usaid.gov/sites/default/files/2023-01/Disinformation-Primer.pdf

Van Audenhove, L., Vermeire, L., Van den Broeck, W., & Demeulenaere, A. (2024). Data literacy in the new EU DigComp 2.2 framework: How DigComp defines competences on artificial intelligence, internet of things and data. *Information and Learning Science, 125*(5/6), 406–436. DOI: 10.1108/ILS-06-2023-0072

Van Buggenhout, N., Van den Broeck, W., & Jennes, I. (2018). The Island Approach (TIA): a suited projective technique for evaluating a bevy of attributes. In *Research and Innovation Conference Proceedings 2018* (Vol. 2018, pp. 496-521). ENoLL - European Network of Living Labs. DOI: 10.5281/zenodo.1434994

Većkalov, B., Gligorić, V., & Petrović, M. B. (2024). No evidence that priming analytic thinking reduces belief in conspiracy theories: A registered report of high-powered direct replications of Study 2 and Study 4 from Swami, Voracek, Stieger, Tran, and Furnham (2014). *Journal of Experimental Social Psychology, 110*, 104549. DOI: 10.1016/j.jesp.2023.104549

Villi, M. (2019). News fatigue and emotional drivers in the age of information overload. *Journalism Studies, 20*(8), 1123–1139.

Vosoughi, S., Roy, D., & Aral, S. (2018). The spread of true and false news online. *Science, 359*(6380), 1146–1151. DOI: 10.1126/science.aap9559 PMID: 29590045

Walker, M., & Gottfried, J. (2019). Republicans far more likely than Democrats to say fact-checkers tend to favor one side. *Pew Research Center*. https://www.pewresearch.org/short-reads/2019/06/27/republicans-far-more-likely-than-democrats-to-say-fact-checkers-tend-to-favor-one-side/

Walsh, J. A., & Sattes, E. D. (2011). *Thinking through quality questioning: Deepening student engagement* (1st ed.). Corwin.

Wardle, C., & Derakhshan, H. (2017). *Information disorder: Toward an interdisciplinary framework for research and policy making*. Council of Europe Report. https://rm.coe.int/information-disorder-toward-an-interdisciplinary-framework-for-research/1680765e2b

Westerlund, M., Leminen, S., & Habib, C. (2018). Key Constructs and a Definition of Living Labs as Innovation Platforms. *Technology Innovation Management Review*, *8*(12), 51–62. DOI: 10.22215/timreview/1205

Wineburg, S., Breakstone, J., McGrew, S., Smith, M. D., & Ortega, T. (2022). Lateral reading on the open internet: A district-wide field study in high school government classes. *Journal of Educational Psychology*, *114*(5), 893–909. DOI: 10.1037/edu0000740

Wright, M. R. (2009). *Introducing Greek Philosophy*. Routledge. DOI: 10.1017/UPO9781844654390

Ziemer, C. T., & Rothmund, T. (2024). Psychological underpinnings of misinformation countermeasures: A systematic scoping review. *Journal of Media Psychology*, *36*(6), 397–409. DOI: 10.1027/1864-1105/a000407

Zollo, F., Bessi, A., Del Vicario, M., Scala, A., Caldarelli, G., Shekhtman, L., Havlin, S., & Quattrociocchi, W. (2017). Debunking in a world of tribes. *PLoS One*, *12*(7), e0181821. DOI: 10.1371/journal.pone.0181821 PMID: 28742163

APPENDIX A – METHODOLOGICAL DETAILS OF THE CO-CREATION, LIVING LABS, AND PILOT PHASES

Living Lab and Pilot Implementation (Phase B and C)

This section describes the implementation of TITAN's LLs, with 65 participants in 4 co-creation workshops, and pilot testing with 52 participants in 20 focus groups, focusing on three case studies:

The first Use Case is focused on higher education in Flanders and targets students who must enhance their critical thinking to become independent and critical citizens regardless of their academic discipline. The second Use Case targets members of NGOs in Southeast Europe who are often highly engaged and seek to expose malpractices from both governments and organizations and especially in the recent times of global spread of hostile disinformation and propaganda from authoritarian states. The third Use Case is concerned with disinformation about migration and refugees in Italy. UNINETTUNO launched the University for Refugees91 initiative in 2016, providing migrants and refugees access to degree program scholarships at UNINETTUNO. TITAN tool will support migrants, refugees and students' counter-narrative ideation and definition, providing support in verifying information, access to reliable sources, and describing how a fake news spread in social media.

Data collection included co-creation workshops, user observations, group discussions, and chatbot interaction analysis. These methods illuminated both the enablers and barriers to successful implementation, emphasizing the importance of contextual sensitivity in AI tool deployment.

Living Lab Methodology

The aim of the Living Labs was to gather insights on the usability, user experience and effectiveness of the Socratic AI-chatbot. A first prototype of the chatbot was tested in four European countries, i.e., Belgium, Bulgaria, Denmark, and Italy. The Living Labs respectively engaged four target groups: students, citizenship at large, NGO members and active citizens, and migrants. During the workshops, four exercises were executed, each with its own focus and goal. Additionally, a mixed-method approach was applied, both qualitative (i.e., co-creation activities) and quantitative (i.e., survey research) research was conducted. The co-creation activities formed the foundation of the workshop, facilitating the collection of rich, qualitative data and in-depth insights. Complementing this, the survey research provided a means to quantify and validate these findings (Hossain et al., 2018).

As an initial step in the Living Labs workshops, participants were invited to test the prototype of the Socratic chatbot. This process began with the Critical Thinking Assessment (CTA), followed by the evaluation of the chatbot using a set of predefined news articles. To ensure comprehensive coverage, a selection of ten articles was distributed among participants, with each article being tested at least once in each of the four workshops. Afterwards, each participant completed an online questionnaire designed to gather quantitative insights into their perceptions of the CTA and the effectiveness of the Socratic dialogue in promoting critical thinking, as well as the usability and user-friendliness of the TITAN system. Following the questionnaire, participants engaged in small group discussions to share their initial impressions of and feedback on the system.

During the second exercise, we evaluated the design of the TITAN prototype. The aim was to get insights into the positive and negative aspects of the design as well as opportunities to improve the User Interface (UI) and User Experience (UX). For this, we applied the Rose, Thorn, Bud Method (Hanington & Martin, 2022). We presented the participants with a visual of a rose and gave them red, yellow, and green post-it notes. Participants individually reflected on the design of the system and wrote positive aspects on the red post-it notes (i.e., representing the flower), negative aspects on the yellow post-it notes (i.e., thorns of the flower), and opportunities to improve on the green post-its (i.e., stem of the flower). Afterwards, participants engaged in a group discussion, presented their post-it notes to each other and placed them on the visual of the rose while clustering them in themes.

The aim of the third exercise was to gather feedback on earlier collected user requirements (i.e., collected during a literature review and the co-creation workshops in the earlier stages of the project), validate and prioritize them. For this exercise, we implemented The Island Approach (TIA) (Van Buggenhout et al., 2018). The participants received 10 user scenarios, based on a range of user requirements, and a visual template of the island (see Figure 2) in their group. Each spot of the island had a dedicated meaning: the beach chair was intended for the most important scenario, the palm tree for the second most important, and the 'exposed spot' at the bottom of the island was intended for the third most valued user scenario. The other seven scenarios were then divided between the lifebuoy (i.e., interesting but not necessary scenarios) and the crocodiles (i.e., scenarios that were not important). During the analysis of the Living Labs' results, we were then able to make a priority list of the user requirements that were linked to each scenario.

Figure 2. The Island Template used during exercise 3 of the Living Labs

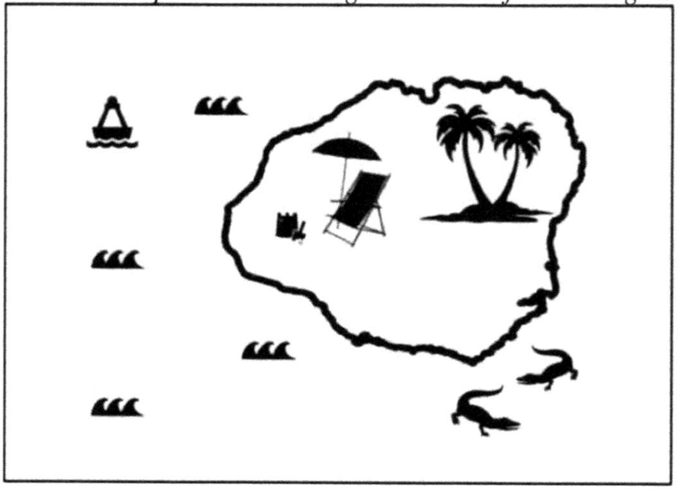

During the last exercise, the aim was to discuss remaining feedback and concerns around four topics: the engagement of the tool, the effectiveness of the tool in stimulating critical thinking, the context in which participants saw the tool being used, and concerns related to trustworthy AI, privacy, data, and personalization. The participants were asked to discuss these four topics in group and wrote keywords of the discussion on a provided template (see Figure 3).

Figure 3. Template used during exercise 4 of the Living Labs

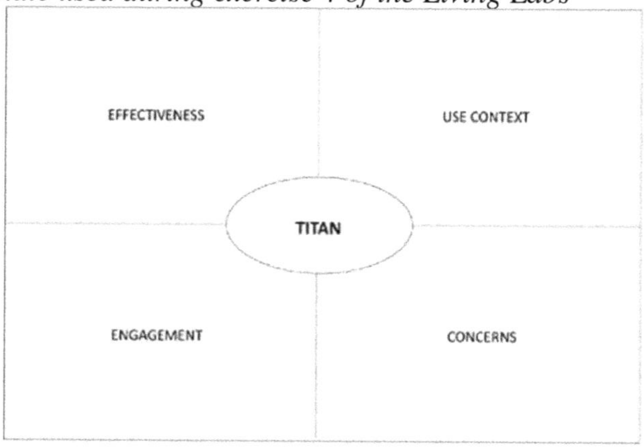

The questionnaire used in the Living Lab study consisted of six main sections. The first section, **Demographics**, included one item asking for the participant's full name to link data across phases, with the guarantee that all data would be anonymized afterward.

Item: What is your full name?

The second section, **Evaluation of the Critical Thinking Assessment**, contained nine items. Six used a five-point Likert scale to assess perceptions of the test's relevance, difficulty, willingness to retake it, interest in progress tracking, and emotional reactions such as insecurity or ethical concerns. Three open-ended questions invited participants to comment on the clarity of the test's statements, the questionnaire's length, and their overall experience.

Items:

- I feel like the questionnaire tested my critical thinking skills
- I found it hard to fill in the questions
- I would happily fill it in again to test my critical thinking skills
- I would like to be able to see the results and progress over time
- Filling out the questionnaire made me insecure
- Filling out the questionnaire raised some concerns or ethical questions
- What did you think about the statements and conclusions in the questionnaire?
- Explain more in detail what you thought about the statements and conclusions
- What is your opinion on the duration of this questionnaire?

The third section, **Evaluation of the Chatbot**, included both closed and open-format questions. Multiple-choice questions assessed usability, perceived user-friendliness, and dialogue length. Participants were then asked to reflect on their engagement with the chatbot, including whether they answered thoughtfully. Seven statements followed, each rated on a five-point scale, evaluating the chatbot's effectiveness in guiding critical thinking, identifying disinformation, supporting credibility assessments, raising awareness, and encouraging future vigilance and reflection.

Items:

- What do you think about the usability of the chatbot?
- Do you think the interface of the chatbot was user friendly?
- Could you explain why you perceived the interface as [user friendly / not / unsure]?
- What did you think about the length and duration of the dialogue?
- How would you describe the time you took and devoted to answering the chatbot's questions?
- The chatbot guided me in thinking critically about the information in the article
- The chatbot gave me a better idea of signals for disinformation
- The chatbot gave me good guidance in the evaluation of the article

- The chatbot helped me improve my skills for evaluating online news
- I am now more aware of the existence and dangers of online disinformation
- In the future, I will pay more attention to the possibility of encountering disinformation
- In the future, I will reflect more critically when reading online information and news

The fourth section, **Analytical and Critical Thinking Skills**, consisted of four logic-based, open-ended riddles. These included classic problems related to race position, sheep count, naming patterns, and spatial reasoning.

Items:

- If you're running a race and you pass the person in second place, what place are you in?
- A farmer had 15 sheep and all but 8 died. How many are left?
- Emily's father has three daughters. The first two are named April and May. What is the third daughter's name?
- How many cubic feet of dirt are there in a hole that is 3' deep x 3' wide x 3' long?

In the fifth section, **Value Placed on Truthfulness and Openness**, participants responded to four items using a ten-point scale. These measured the importance assigned to learning, truthfulness, self-questioning, and commitment to new knowledge, especially on topics of personal relevance.

Items:

- How important is it for you to learn new things about that topic, even when it requires a very big effort?
- To you, how important is truthfulness concerning that topic, even when it might lead to uncomfortable situations?
- How important is it for you to question your knowledge concerning that topic, even when it may involve a major change in your current perspective?
- To you, how important is acquiring new knowledge concerning that topic, even when it may involve a major commitment?

The final section, **Resistance to Disinformation Sharing**, included eight self-assessment items rated on a ten-point scale. These examined the participant's likelihood to avoid spreading dubious information under social pressure, popularity incentives, or personal bias, and to engage in source verification, critical sharing, and seeking out alternative perspectives.

Items:

- Avoid spreading it even if not doing so might lead to disagreements within your relevant group
- Choose not to share it even if spreading could enhance your popularity or influence
- Refrain from sharing it even when it seems to be a prevailing trend among your important peers
- Express your skepticism about the information even if your important peers seem to accept it
- Find and share credible and verified sources even if they may challenge the prevailing narrative in your group
- Refrain from sharing it even if it aligns with your pre-existing beliefs
- Search for different perspectives and sources on the same news story, even if doing so could question your beliefs
- Take the time to verify the information's sources even when it feels boring or time-consuming

Compilation of References

AARP. (n.d.) *Learn About AI, Technology, Digital Safety & More!* AARP. https://states.aarp.org/new-york/educational-workshops-on-all-things-technology

Abbass, H. (2021). What is artificial intelligence? *IEEE Transactions on Artificial Intelligence, 2*(2), 94–95. https://doi-org.uc.idm.oclc.org/10.1109/TAI.2021.3096243. DOI: 10.1109/TAI.2021.3096243

Abdullah, A. O., Ali, M. A., Karabatak, M., & Sengur, A. (2018). A comparative analysis of common YouTube comment spam filtering techniques. *6th International Symposium on Digital Forensic and Security, ISDFS 2018 - Proceeding, 2018-Janua*, 1–5. DOI: 10.1109/ISDFS.2018.8355315

Abrams v. United States, 250 U.S. 616, 630 (1919) (Holmes, J., dissenting).

Acquisti, A., Brandimarte, L., & Loewenstein, G. (2015). Privacy and human behavior in the age of information. *Science, 347*(6221), 509–514. DOI: 10.1126/science.aaa1465 PMID: 25635091

Adelhardt, Z., & Eberle, T. (2022). YouTube as a Source of Educational Content in Teenagers' Learning Practices. *9th European Conference on Social Media, ECSM 2022*, 277–279. DOI: 10.34190/ecsm.9.1.267

Agarwal, S., & Kayal, S. (2024). Mapping of Learning Efficacy Through YouTube: An Empirical Study of Media Learners in Kolkata. *International Journal of Media and Information Literacy, 9*(1), 4–16. DOI: 10.13187/ijmil.2024.1.4

Agee, E., Larson, J., Childs, S., & Marmo, A. (2016). Spatial redistribution of U.S. tornado activity between 1954 and 2013. *Journal of Applied Meteorology and Climatology, 55*(8), 1681–1697. DOI: 10.1175/JAMC-D-15-0342.1

AI HLEG. (2019). *Ethics guidelines for trustworthy AI.* European Commission. https://ec.europa.eu/digital-single-market/en/news/ethics-guidelines-trustworthy-ai

Akram, W., & Kumar, R. (2017). A study on positive and negative effects of social media on society. *International Journal on Computer Science and Engineering*, *5*(10), 351–354. DOI: 10.26438/ijcse/v5i10.351354

Al Zou'bi, R. M. (2022). The impact of media and information literacy on students' acquisition of the skills needed to detect fake news. *The Journal of Media Literacy Education*, *14*(2), 58–71. DOI: 10.23860/JMLE-2022-14-2-5

Alabama Code § 12-21-142. (2023).

Albiez, M. (2020a). Systemic, social and emotional challenges and magic moments in the professional life of full-time and part-time YouTubers: "Have fun and work at the same time" | Systemische, soziale und emotionale Herausforderungen und Glücksmomente im beruflichen Alltag. *Gruppe. Interaktion. Organisation. Zeitschrift Fur Angewandte Organisationspsychologie*, *51*(4), 457–468. DOI: 10.1007/s11612-020-00534-w

Aldisert, R. J. (1996). *The judicial process: Text, materials and cases*. West Publishing Co.

Aldisert, R. J. (1997). *Logic for lawyers: A guide to clear thinking*. National Institute for Trial Advocacy.

Alfano, M., Fard, A. E., Carter, J. A., Clutton, P., & Klein, C. (2021). Technologically scaffolded atypical cognition: The case of YouTube's recommender system. *Synthese*, *199*(1–2), 835–858. DOI: 10.1007/s11229-020-02724-x

Ali, S., DiPaola, D., Lee, I., Sindato, V., Kim, G., Blumofe, R., & Breazeal, C. (2021). Children as creators, thinkers and citizens in an AI-driven future. *Computers and Education: Artificial Intelligence*, *2*, 100040. DOI: 10.1016/j.caeai.2021.100040

Allcott, H., & Gentzkow, M. (2017). Social media and fake news in the 2016 election. *The Journal of Economic Perspectives*, *31*(2), 211–236. DOI: 10.1257/jep.31.2.211

Alruthaya, A., Nguyen, T.-T., & Lokuge, S. (2021). The Application of Digital Technology and the Learning Characteristics of Generation Z in Higher Education. *ACIS 2021 - Australasian Conference on Information Systems, Proceedings*.

Alshanqiti, A., Bajnaid, A., Gilal, A. R., Aljasir, S., Alsughayyir, A., & Albouq, S. (2020). Intelligent parallel mixed method approach for characterising viral youtube videos in Saudi Arabia. *International Journal of Advanced Computer Science and Applications*, *11*(3), 661–671. DOI: 10.14569/IJACSA.2020.0110382

Alsop, T. (2020, May 1). *Percentage of households in the United States with a computer at home from 1984 to 2016*. Statistica. https://www.statista.com/statistics/214641/household-adoption-rate-of-computer-in-the-us-since-1997/

Altshuler, R. D. (2022). Narratives are useful strategies for overcoming challenges in risk communication. *American Journal of Public Health (1971), 112*(S1), S12–S14.

Altun, A. (2011). An overview of UNESCO activities in connection with media literacy (1977–2009). *Journal of National Education, 191*, 86–107. https://milunesco.unaoc.org/mil-articles/an-overview-of-unesco-activities-in-connection-with-media-literacy-1977-2009/

American Library Association. (1989). Presidential committee on information literacy: Final report. https://www.ala.org/acrl/publications/whitepapers/presidential

American Library Association. (2016, Jan 11). Framework for information literacy for higher education. *American Library Association.* https://www.ala.org/acrl/standards/ilframework

American Library Association. (2024, Oct). *Media Literacy Education for Adult Audiences: Demystifying AI.* [Video]. Programming Librarian. https://programminglibrarian.org/learn/media-literacy-education-adult-audiences-demystifying-ai

American Psychological Association. (2020). *Publication manual of the American Psychological Association* (7th ed.). https://apastyle.apa.org/products/publication-manual-7th-edition

Amsalem, E., & Zoizner, A. (2023). Do people learn about politics on social media? A meta-analysis of 76 studies. *Journal of Communication, 73*(1), 3–13. DOI: 10.1093/joc/jqac034

Amudhan, S., Chavadi, C. A., Poojara, R., Shakila, P., & Poornima, J. (2024). Beyond City Limits: Exploring the Untapped Potential of Social Media in Rural Karnataka: A Structural Equation Model Analysis. In *Studies in Systems, Decision and Control* (Vol. 537). DOI: 10.1007/978-3-031-62106-2_34

Andalibi, N., Haimson, O. L., De Choudhury, M., & Forte, A. (2016). Understanding social media disclosures of mental illness: Stigma, support, and identity. *Proceedings of the 2016 CHI Conference on Human Factors in Computing Systems*, 1352-1363.

Anderson, C. (2007). *The Long Tail: Der lange Schwanz. Nischenprodukte statt Massenmarkt. Das Geschäft der Zukunft* [Nachdr.]. Hanser.

Anderson, C. A., & Bushman, B. J. (2020). Human aggression. *Annual Review of Psychology*, *53*(1), 27–51. DOI: 10.1146/annurev.psych.53.100901.135231 PMID: 11752478

Andreassen, C. S., Billieux, J., Kuss, D. J., Griffiths, M. D., Mazzoni, E., & Pallesen, S. (2016). The relationship between addictive use of social media and video games and symptoms of psychiatric disorders: A large-scale cross-sectional study. *Psychology of Addictive Behaviors*, *30*(2), 252–262. DOI: 10.1037/adb0000160 PMID: 26999354

Andreassen, C. S., & Pallesen, S. (2014). Social network site addiction—An overview. *Current Pharmaceutical Design*, *20*(25), 4053–4061. DOI: 10.2174/13816128113199990616 PMID: 24001298

Anggadwita, G., Ramadani, V., & Navarrete, S. R. (2023). FROM MINUS TO HERO: IDENTIFYING SUCCESSFUL ENTREPRENEURIAL FACTORS USING SEMANTIC NETWORK ANALYSIS OF YOUTUBE CONTENT | IŠ DUGNO Į AUKŠTUMAS: SĖKMINGŲ ANTREPRENERYSTĖS VEIKSNIŲ NUSTATYMAS NAUDOJANT „YOUTUBE" TURINIO SEMANTINIO TINKLO ANALIZĘ. *Transformations in Business & Economics*, *22*(1), 165–183.

Antonucci, M. C., Sorice, M., & Volterrani, A. (2024). *Confini invisibili. Comunità liminali e pratiche di resistenza nella città neoliberista*. Meltemi.

Aparici, R. (Ed.). (2010). *Educomunicación: más allá del 2.0*. Gedisa.

Apăteanu, D. (n.d.). The disinformation in the case of the Ukraine war. In *The War in Ukraine* (p. 241).

ARC Australian Research Council. (2023). *Policy on Use of Generative Artificial Intelligence in the ARC's Grants Programs*. Research Policy Branch.

Archambault, S. G. (2023). Expanding on the frames: Making a case for algorithmic literacy. *Communications in Information Literacy*, *17*(2), 530–553. DOI: 10.15760/comminfolit.2023.17.2.11

Arias Ortiz, E., Dueñas, X., Giambruno, C., & López, Á. (2024). *El estado de la educación en América Latina y el Caribe 2024: la medición de los aprendizajes*. Banco Interamericano de Desarrollo, División de Educación.

Arisukwu, O., (2022). *Access Usage and Influence of Mass Media on Students Academic Performance: A Private University Experience*. Information & Communication Technology in Education., DOI: 10.1080/2331186X.2022.2102117

Arke, E. T., & Primack, B. A. (2009). Quantifying media literacy: Development, reliability, and validity of a new measure. *Educational Media International*, *46*(1), 53–65. DOI: 10.1080/09523980902780958 PMID: 21572920

Aspen Media Literacy Institute. (2003). *Literacy for the 21st Century. An Overview.* https://www.medialit.org/sites/default/files/mlk/01_MLKorientation.pdf

Asselin, M., Dobson, T., Meyers, E. M., Teixiera, C., & Ham, L. (2011). Learning from YouTube: An analysis of information literacy in user discourse. *ACM International Conference Proceeding Series*, 640–642. DOI: 10.1145/1940761.1940851

Aufderheide, P. (1993). *Media Literacy. A Report of the National Leadership Conference on Media Literacy.* https://eric.ed.gov/?id=ED365294

Aufderheide, P. (1993). National leadership conference on media literacy. In *Conference report. Washington, DC: Aspen Institute.*

Australian Academy of Science. (n.d.) *How does science work?* https://www.science.org.au/curious/policy-features/how-does-science-work

Avinaash, M., & Jayam, R. (2019). Analyzing the video consumption pattern of indian consumer using big data. *Journal of Advanced Research in Dynamical and Control Systems, 11*(3 Special), 1590–1598.

Awan, A. N. (2017). Jihadism transformed: Al-Qaeda and Islamic State's global battle of ideas. *Journal of Conflict and Security Law*, *22*(3), 415–436. DOI: 10.1093/jcsl/krx005

Ayers, J. W., Poliak, A., Dredze, M., Leas, E. C., Zhu, Z., Kelley, J. B., Faix, D. J., Goodman, A. M., Longhurst, C. A., Hogarth, M., & Smith, D. M. (2023). Comparing physician and artificial intelligence chatbot responses to patient questions posted to a public social media forum. *JAMA Internal Medicine*, *183*(6), 589–596. DOI: 10.1001/jamainternmed.2023.1838 PMID: 37115527

Baacke, D. (1998a). Medienkompetenz - Herkunft, Reichweite und strategische Bedeutung eines Begriffs. In H. Kubicek (Ed.), *Jahrbuch Telekommunikation und Gesellschaft: Vol. 6. Lernort Multimedia* (pp. 22–27). v. Decker.

Baacke, D. (1998b). *Zum Konzept der Operationalisierung von Medienkompetenz.* https://www.produktive-medienarbeit.de/ressourcen/bibliothek/fachartikel/baacke_operationalisierung.shtml

Baacke, D. (2007). *Medienpädagogik* [Nachdr.]. *Grundlagen der Medienkommunikation: Vol. 1.* Niemeyer.

Baacke, D. (1975). *Kommunikation und Kompetenz: Grundlegung e. Didaktik d. Kommunikation u. ihrer Medien* (2nd ed.). Juventa-Verlag.

Baacke, D. (1996a). Medienkompetenz – Begrifflichkeit und sozialer Wandel. In Rein, A. v. (Ed.), *Theorie und Praxis der Erwachsenenbildung. Medienkompetenz als Schlüsselbegriff* (pp. 112–124). Klinkhardt.

Baacke, D. (1996b). Medienkompetenz als Netzwerk. Reichweite und Fokussierung eines Begriffs, der Konjunktur hat. *Medien Praktisch, 20*(78), 4–10.

Backe, E. L., Lilleston, P., & McCleary-Sills, J. (2018). Networked individuals, gendered violence: A literature review of cyberviolence. *Violence and Gender, 5*(3), 135–146. DOI: 10.1089/vio.2017.0056

Bai, J. (2024). AI-generated video detection via spatial-temporal anomaly learning. In *Chinese Conference on Pattern Recognition and Computer Vision (PRCV)*. Singapore: Springer Nature Singapore.

Bailin, S., Case, R., Coombs, J. R., & Daniels, L. B. (1999). Conceptualizing critical thinking. *Journal of Curriculum Studies, 31*(3), 285–302. DOI: 10.1080/002202799183133

Ballon, P., Van Hoed, M., & Schuurman, D. (2018). The effectiveness of involving users in digital innovation: Measuring the impact of living labs. *Telematics and Informatics, 35*(5), 1201–1214. DOI: 10.1016/j.tele.2018.02.003

Bannert, M. (2002). Managing cognitive load—Recent trends in cognitive load theory. *Learning and Instruction, 12*(1), 139–146. DOI: 10.1016/S0959-4752(01)00021-4

Bano, S., Cisheng, W., Khan, A. N., & Khan, N. A. (2019). WhatsApp use and student's psychological well-being: Role of social capital and social integration. *Children and Youth Services Review, 103*, 200–208. DOI: 10.1016/j.childyouth.2019.06.002

Baraheem, S. S., & Nguyen, T. V. (2023). AI vs. AI: Can AI detect AI-generated images? *Journal of Imaging, 9*(10), 199. DOI: 10.3390/jimaging9100199 PMID: 37888306

Barassi, V. (2024). Toward a theory of AI errors: Making sense of hallucinations, catastrophic failures, and the fallacy of Generative AI. *Harvard Data Science Review* (Special Issue 5). DOI: 10.1162/99608f92.ad8ebbd4

Barendt, E. (2019). What is the Harm of Hate Speech? *Ethical Theory and Moral Practice, 22*(3), 539–553. DOI: 10.1007/s10677-019-10002-0

Barlow, J. P. (2016, Jan 20). *A Declaration of the Independence of Cyberspace*. Electronic Frontier Foundation. https://www.eff.org/cyberspace-independence

Barrichello, D. Elvin, Martin, K., Lasmy, & Bagaskara, J. (2024). Analysis of Determinants Influencing Victims' Interest in Illegal Investments. *2024 3rd International Conference on Creative Communication and Innovative Technology, ICCIT 2024*. DOI: 10.1109/ICCIT62134.2024.10701140

Barron, J. (1967). Access to the press—A new First Amendment right. *Harvard Law Review*, *80*(8), 1641–1678. DOI: 10.2307/1339417

Bartels, M. (2023, Mar 31). *How to Tell If a Photo Is an AI-Generated Fake*. Scientific American. https://www.scientificamerican.com/article/how-to-tell-if-a-photo-is-an-ai-generated-fake/

Bartlett, J., & Krasodomski-Jones, A. (2015). *Counter-speech examining content that challenges extremism online*. https://www.demos.co.uk/wp-content/uploads/2015/10/Counter-speech.pdf

Battista, D. (2024). TikTok Politics: Influenze e interazioni sociali. *Mimesis*.

Bauer, P. C., & Clemm von Hohenberg, B. (2020). Believing and sharing information by fake sources: An experiment. *Political Communication*, *38*(6), 647–671. DOI: 10.1080/10584609.2020.1840462

Bauer, U., & Ertugrul, B. (2023). Gesellschaftlicher Zusammenhalt, Sozialisation und generationaler Wandel – Konturen eines Forschungsproblems. In Ertugrul, B., & Bauer, U. (Eds.), *Sozialisation und gesellschaftlicher Zusammenhalt: Aufwachsen in Krisen und Konflikten* (pp. 9–28). Campus Verlag.

Baum, J., & Villasenor, J. (2023, May 8). The politics of AI: ChatGPT and political bias. *Brookings*. https://www.brookings.edu/articles/the-politics-of-ai-chatgpt-and-political-bias/

Bauman, Z. (1995). *Postmoderne Ethik*. Hamburger Ed.

Bayer, M., Kaufhold, M.-A., Buchhold, B., Keller, M., Dallmeyer, J., & Reuter, C. (2023). Data augmentation in natural language processing: A novel text generation approach for long and short text classifiers. *International Journal of Machine Learning and Cybernetics*, *14*(1), 135–150. DOI: 10.1007/s13042-022-01553-3 PMID: 35432623

BBC. (2025, Jan). *Misinformation vs disinformation: What's the difference?* BBC Bitesize. https://www.bbc.co.uk/bitesize/articles/z3hhvj6

Beach, R., & Baker, F. W. (2011). *Why core standards must embrace media literacy*. Truth, and Verification.

Becker, S. O., Hornung, E., & Woessmann, L. (2011). Education and catch-up in the industrial revolution. *American Economic Journal. Macroeconomics, 3*(3), 92–126. DOI: 10.1257/mac.3.3.92

Beer, D. (2009). Power through the algorithm? Participatory web cultures and the technological unconscious. *New Media & Society, 11*(6), 985–1002. DOI: 10.1177/1461444809336551

Beisch, N., & Koch, W. (2023). ARD/ZDF-Onlinestudie: Weitergehende Normalisierung der Internetnutzung nach Wegfall aller Corona-Schutzmaßnahmen: Aktuelle Aspekte der Internetnutzung in Deutschland. *Media Perspektiven*, (23), 1–9.

Bekkar, A., & Aarab, F. (2025). Ethical challenges in artificial intelligence generated media content. *Revue de Recherches et Etudes Scientifiques, 19*(1), 107–125.

Belluati, M., & Tirocchi, S. (2023). *Sociologia della comunicazione e degli ambienti mediali*. Pearson.

Bender, J., Davenport, L., Drager, M., & Fedler, F. (2019). *Writing & reporting for the media* (12th ed.). Oxford University Press.

Benenson, Z., Freiling, F. C., & Meyer-Wegener, K. (2022). Soziotechnische Einflussfaktoren auf die »digitale Souveränität« des Individuums. In G. Glasze, E. Odzuck, & R. Staples (Eds.), *Politik in der digitalen Gesellschaft. Was heißt digitale Souveränität?* (Vol. 3, pp. 61–88). transcript Verlag. DOI: 10.14361/9783839458273-003

Benjamin, R. (2019). Assessing risk, automating racism. *Science, 366*(6464), 421–422. DOI: 10.1126/science.aaz3873 PMID: 31649182

Benkler, Y. (2006). *The wealth of networks: How social production transforms markets and freedom*. Yale University Press.

Benson, H. (2010). "Socratic Method." In D. Morrison (Author), *The Cambridge Companion to Socrates (Cambridge Companions to Philosophy*, pp. 179-200). Cambridge: Cambridge University Press. DOI: 10.1017/CCOL9780521833424.008

Benson, M. (2024, Feb 13). *"Real or AI" Quiz: Can You Tell the Difference?* Britannia Education. https://britannicaeducation.com/blog/quiz-real-or-ai/

Berlatsy, N. (2013, May 3). *The Ethics of Fashion Photo Manipulation*. Center for Digital Ethics & Policy. https://digitalethics.org/essays/ethics-fashion-photo-manipulation

Berry, D. M. (2024). *Post-Digital Humanities: Computation and Cultural Critique in the Arts and Humanities*. https://arxiv.org/pdf/2407.05922

Bettinger, P., & Jörissen, B. (2022). Medienbildung. In Sander, U., von Gross, F., & Hugger, K.-U. (Eds.), *Handbuch Medienpädagogik* (pp. 81–93). Springer VS., DOI: 10.1007/978-3-658-23578-9_10

Betton, V., & Tomlinson, V. (2013). Social media and mental health: Opportunities and risks. *The Lancet. Psychiatry*, *1*(2), 131–132.

Bezbaruah, S., & Trivedi, J. (2020). Branded Content: A Bridge Building Gen Z's Consumer–Brand Relationship. *Vision (Basel)*, *24*(3), 300–309. DOI: 10.1177/0972262920930167

Bhat, S. (2024). Impact of Social Media on Society, International Research Journal on Advanced Engineering Hub (IRJAEH) ISSN: 2584-2137Vol. 02 Issue: 03 March 2024, Page No: 473-480 https://irjaeh.com DOI: 10.47392/IRJAEH.2024.0068

Bidav, T., & Mehta, S. (2024). Peripheral Creator Cultures in India, Ireland, and Turkey. *Social Media + Society*, *10*(1), 20563051241234693. DOI: 10.1177/20563051241234693

Billieux, J., Philippot, P., Schmid, C., Maurage, P., De Mol, J., & Van der Linden, M. (2015). Is dysfunctional use of the mobile phone a behavioural addiction? Confronting symptom-based versus process-based approaches. *Clinical Psychology & Psychotherapy*, *22*(5), 460–468. DOI: 10.1002/cpp.1910 PMID: 24947201

Bimber, B., Flanagin, A. J., & Stohl, C. (2015). Reconceptualizing collective action in the contemporary media environment. *Communication Theory*, *25*(4), 365–388. DOI: 10.1111/j.1468-2885.2005.tb00340.x

Binns, R. (2018). Fairness in machine learning: Lessons from political philosophy. *Proceedings of the 2018 Conference on Fairness, Accountability, and Transparency*, 149–159.

Bitkom Research. (2024). *Kinder- & Jugendstudie 2024*. https://www.bitkom.org/sites/main/files/2024-08/240806bitkom-chartskinderundjugend2024.pdf

Blakemore, E. (2022, Apr 11). *How photos became a weapon in Stalin's great purge*. History.com. https://www.history.com/news/josef-stalin-great-purge-photo-retouching

Blakeslee, S. (2004) The CRAAP test, *LOEX Quarterly: 31*(3), 6-7. https://commons.emich.edu/loexquarterly/vol31/iss3/4

Blasi, V. (1977). The checking value in First Amendment theory. *American Bar Foundation Research Journal. American Bar Foundation*, *1977*(3), 521–649. DOI: 10.1111/j.1747-4469.1977.tb01008.x

Bloomfield, B. P. (2020). *The Question of Artificial Intelligence. Philosophical and Sociological Perspectives*. Routledge.

Boccia Artieri, G. (2006). Farsi media. Consumo e media-mondo: tra identità, esperienza e forme espressive. In E. Di Nallo, R. Paltrinieri, *Con sumo, Prospettive di analisi del consumo nella società globale*. FrancoAngeli.

Boccia Artieri, G. (2012). *Stati di connessione. Pubblici, cittadini e consumatori nella (Social) Network Society*. Franco Angeli.

Boccia Artieri, G., Colombo, F., & Gili, G. (2022). *Comunicare. Persone, relazioni, media*. Laterza.

Bodensteiner, C. A. (1995). Predicting Public and Media Attention Span for Social Issues. *Public Relations Quarterly*, *40*(2).

Bollinger, L. C. (1988). *The tolerant society*. Oxford University Press.

Bowles, M. D. (1996). US technological enthusiasm and British technological skepticism in the age of the analog brain. *IEEE Annals of the History of Computing*, *18*(4), 5–15. DOI: 10.1109/85.539911

Boyd, D. (2014). *It's Complicated. The social life of networked teens*. Yale University Press.

Boyd, D. M., & Ellison, N. B. (2007). Social network sites: Definition, history, and scholarship. *Journal of Computer-Mediated Communication*, *13*(1), 210–230. DOI: 10.1111/j.1083-6101.2007.00393.x

Bozkurt, A., Xiao, J., Farrow, R., Bai, J. Y., Nerantzi, C., Moore, S., & Asino, T. I. (Eds.). (2024). The manifesto for teaching and learning in a time of generative AI: A critical collective stance to better navigate the future. *Open Praxis, 16*(4), 487-513.

Brandtzaeg, P. B., & Følstad, A. (2017). Trust and distrust in online fact-checking services. *Communications of the ACM*, *60*(9), 65–71. DOI: 10.1145/3122803

Breed, W. (1955). Newspaper 'opinion leaders' and processes of standardization. *The Journalism Quarterly*, *32*(3), 277–328. DOI: 10.1177/107769905503200302

Breuer, A., & Farooq, M. (2012). Online political participation: The impact of social media on political mobilization in the Middle East. *Journal of Communication*, *62*(5), 870–888. DOI: 10.1111/j.1460-2466.2012.01663.x

Brickhouse, Th. C., & Nicholas, D. Smith.(2010, 2 Jan.) "Socratic Teaching and Socratic Method." In Harvey Siegel (ed.), *The Oxford Handbook of Philosophy of Education*, Oxford Handbooks (2009; online edn, Oxford Academic.

Briot, J.-P., & Pachet, F. (2020). Deep learning for music generation: Challenges and directions. *Neural Computing & Applications*, *32*(4), 981–993. DOI: 10.1007/s00521-018-3813-6

Broadcasting Yearbook. (1980). Broadcasting Publications, Inc.

Brooks, A., Warner, L., Hammons, J., & Chesnut, M. (2019). *GEARUP*. Northern Kentucky University. https://www.nku.edu/qep.html

Brown, J. D., Bybee, C. R., Wearden, S. T., & Straughan, D. M. (1987). Invisible power: Newspaper news sources and the limits of diversity. *The Journalism Quarterly*, *64*(1), 45–54. DOI: 10.1177/107769908706400106

Brown, R., Smith, T., & Davis, L. (2021). The psychological impact of victimization through social aggression. *The Journal of Social Psychology*, *161*(3), 345–360. DOI: 10.1080/00224545.2020.1765234

Bruns, A. (2019). *Are filter bubbles real?* Polity Press. https://ebookcentral.proquest.com/lib/kxp/detail.action?docID=5887595

Buckingham, D. (1993). *The development of television literacy: talk, text and context* (Doctoral dissertation, Institute of Education, University of London).

Buckingham, D., Banaji, S., Carr, D., Cranmer, S., & Willett, R. (2005). The media literacy of children and young people: A review of the research literature.

Buckingham, D. (2003). Media Education: Literacy, Learning and Contemporary Culture. *Polity*.

Buckingham, D. (2003). *Media education: Literacy, learning, and contemporary culture*. Polity Press.

Buckingham, D. (2007). Digital media literacies: Rethinking media education in the age of the internet. *Research in Comparative and International Education*, *2*(1), 43–55. DOI: 10.2304/rcie.2007.2.1.43

Bump, P. (2025, Jan 18). *Baby boomers*. Encyclopedia Britannica. https://www.britannica.com/topic/baby-boomers

Bunton, K., Connery, T., Kanihan, S., Neuzil, D. M., & Nimmer, D. (1999). *Writing across the media*. Bedford/St. Martin's.

Burke, B. R. (1995). *A shifting nature of understanding: Media coverage of environmentalism during the early 1990s*. [Unpublished dissertation]. Purdue University, West Lafayette, Indiana, United States.

Burke, B.R. (1974). Assorted Class Notebooks [Personal collection].

Burke, B. R., & Machkasova, E. (2020). Critical media, information, and digital literacy: Increasing understanding of machine learning through an interdisciplinary undergraduate course. *Irish Communication Review*, *17*(1), 1.

Burrell, J. (2016). How the machine 'thinks': Understanding opacity in machine learning algorithms. *Big Data & Society*, *3*(1), 2053951715622512. DOI: 10.1177/2053951715622512

Busch, K. (2016). Polar bears or people? Exploring ways in which teachers frame climate change in the classroom. *International Journal of Science Education. Part B. Communication and Public Engagement*, *6*(2), 137–165. DOI: 10.1080/21548455.2015.1027320

Bute, S. (2014). The role of social media in mobilizing people for riots and revolutions: Four case studies in India. In *Public Administration and Information Technology* (Vol. 13). DOI: 10.1007/978-3-319-04666-2_19

Butler, H. A., & Halpern, D. F. (2020). Critical thinking impacts our everyday lives. In Sternberg, R. J., & Halpern, D. F. (Eds.), *Critical thinking in psychology* (pp. 152–172). Cambridge University Press. DOI: 10.1017/9781108684354.008

Buttigieg, P. (2024). *A conversation with U.S. secretary of transportation Pete Buttigieg*. [video] Institute of Politics Harvard Kennedy School YouTube. Retrieved March 11, 2025 from https://www.youtube.com/watch?v=qiV7xv24KDI

Calmbach, M., Flaig, B. B., Gaber, R., Gensheimer, T., Möller-Slawinski, H., Schleer, C., & Wisniewski, N. (2024). *Wie ticken Jugendliche? 2024: Lebenswelten von Jugendlichen im Alter von 14 bis 17 Jahren in Deutschland. Schriftenreihe / Bundeszentrale für Politische Bildung: Band 11133*. Bundeszentrale für politische Bildung. https://www.bpb.de/system/files/dokument_pdf/u18_SINUS-Jugendstudie_Wie-ticken-Jugendliche_2024_Print_24-06-07_Sperrfrist_12.06.24_12.00.pdf

Calo, R., & Citron, D. K. (2021). The automated administrative state: A crisis of legitimacy. *Emory Law Journal*, *70*, 797.

Campbell, R. (1997). *Media and culture: An introduction to mass communication*. St. Martin's Press.

Campbell, R., Martin, C. R., & Fabos, B. (2016). *Media essentials: A brief introduction* (3rd ed.). Bedford/ St. Martins.

Campus Library, University of Washington Bothell and Cascadia College. (2020, Oct 26). *News: Fake news, Misinformation, & disinformation*. https://guides.lib.uw.edu/c.php?g=345925&p=7772376

Capatina, A., Kachour, M., Lichy, J., Micu, A., Micu, A.-E., & Codignola, F. (2020). Matching the future capabilities of an artificial intelligence-based software for social media marketing with potential users' expectations. *Technological Forecasting and Social Change*, *151*, 119794. DOI: 10.1016/j.techfore.2019.119794

Capraro, V., & Celadin, T. (2023). "I Think This News Is Accurate": Endorsing Accuracy Decreases the Sharing of Fake News and Increases the Sharing of Real News. *Personality and Social Psychology Bulletin*, *49*(12), 1635–1645. DOI: 10.1177/01461672221117691 PMID: 35993352

Carter, E. L. (2017). "Not to disclose information sources": Journalistic privilege under Article 19 of ICCPR. *Communication Law and Policy*, *22*(4), 399–426. DOI: 10.1080/10811680.2017.1364912

Carter, E. L., Larsen, A. R., & Lambert, E. (2024, Oct). The anti-marketplace of ideas and the right to news literacy. *Communication Law and Policy*, *29*(4), 205–236. DOI: 10.1080/10811680.2025.2511045

Carter, E. L., & Westenskow, R. (2020). Freedom of journalism in international human rights law. *Communication Law and Policy*, *25*(2), 113–143. DOI: 10.1080/10811680.2020.1735188

Cascone, K. (2000). The Aesthetics of Failure: "Post-Digital" Tendencies in Contemporary Computer Music. *Computer Music Journal*, *24*(4), 12–18. DOI: 10.1162/014892600559489

Cash, S. J., & Schwab-Reese, L. (2020). When adolescent offline risks behaviors go online. In *Technology and Adolescent Health: In Schools and Beyond*. DOI: 10.1016/B978-0-12-817319-0.00003-7

Castaldo, M., Frasca, P., Venturini, T., & Gargiulo, F. (2024). Fake views removal and popularity on YouTube. *Scientific Reports*, *14*(1), 15443. DOI: 10.1038/s41598-024-63649-w PMID: 38965242

Castells, M. (1996). *The Rise of the Network Society: The Information Age: Economy, Society, and Culture*. Wiley.

Castells, M. (2000). Materials for an exploratory theory of the network society1. *The British Journal of Sociology*, *51*(1), 5–24. DOI: 10.1111/j.1468-4446.2000.00005.x

Castells, M. (2001). *The Internet Galaxy: Reflections on the Internet*. Oxford University Press. DOI: 10.1007/978-3-322-89613-1

Castells, M. (2010). Globalisation, networking, urbanisation: Reflections on the spatial dynamics of the information age. *Urban Studies (Edinburgh, Scotland)*, *47*(13), 2737–2745. DOI: 10.1177/0042098010377365

Caufield, M. (2019, Jun 19). SIFT: The four moves. *Hapgood*. https://hapgood.us/2019/06/19/sift-the-four-moves/

Chaka, C. (2020). Skills, competencies and literacies attributed to 4IR/Industry 4.0: Scoping review. *IFLA Journal*, *46*(4), 369–399. DOI: 10.1177/0340035219896376

Chaka, C. (2023). Detecting AI content in responses generated by ChatGPT, YouChat, and Chatsonic: The case of five AI content detection tools. *Journal of Applied Learning and Teaching*, *6*(2), 94–104.

Chandhok, G. A., & Nithya, V. (2019). Short-lived content, a social media platform it's purpose, perspective of generation z. *International Journal of Scientific and Technology Research*, *8*(12), 761–768.

Chandiwala, J., Agrawal, S., & Agarwal, S. (2022). Descriptive and Comparative Analysis of YouTube Trending Videos. In *Lecture Notes in Electrical Engineering* (Vol. 939). DOI: 10.1007/978-981-19-4364-5_61

Chandler, P., & Sweller, J. (1991). Cognitive load theory and the format of instruction. *Cognition and Instruction*, *8*(4), 293–332. DOI: 10.1207/s1532690xci0804_2

Chau, C. (2010). YouTube as a participatory culture. *New Directions for Youth Development*, *2010*(128), 65–74. DOI: 10.1002/yd.376 PMID: 21240954

Chen, A., & Chen, D. O. (2023). Accuracy of chatbots in citing journal articles. *JAMA Network Open*, *6*(8), e2327647–e2327647. DOI: 10.1001/jamanetworkopen.2023.27647 PMID: 37552482

Chen, C. W.-Y. (2020). Learning through participation: A case study on the affordances of making YouTube tutorial videos. *The JALT CALL Journal*, *16*(1), 51–67. DOI: 10.29140/jaltcall.v16n1.259

Cheng, X., Liu, J., & Dale, C. (2013). Understanding the characteristics of internet short video sharing: A youtube-based measurement study. *IEEE Transactions on Multimedia*, *15*(5), 1184–1194. DOI: 10.1109/TMM.2013.2265531

Cheng, Z., Shao, B., & Zhang, Y. (2022). Effect of Product Presentation Videos on Consumers' Purchase Intention: The Role of Perceived Diagnosticity, Mental Imagery, and Product Rating. *Frontiers in Psychology*, *13*, 812579. Advance online publication. DOI: 10.3389/fpsyg.2022.812579 PMID: 35250742

Chen, L., Zhou, Y., & Chiu, D. M. (2015). Analysis and detection of fake views in online video services. *ACM Transactions on Multimedia Computing Communications and Applications, 11*(2), 1–20. DOI: 10.1145/2700290

Chen, O., Paas, F., & Sweller, J. (2023). A Cognitive Load Theory Approach to Defining and Measuring Task Complexity Through Element Interactivity. *Educational Psychology Review, 35*(2), 1–18. DOI: 10.1007/s10648-023-09782-w

Chernikoff, S. (2024, May 18). The average age of first-time mothers continues to rise. *USA Today*, https://www.usatoday.com/story/news/health/2024/05/18/graphics-show-changing-trend-average-age-parents/73707908007/

Che, X., Ip, B., & Lin, L. (2015). A Survey of Current YouTube Video Characteristics. *IEEE MultiMedia, 22*(2), 56–63. DOI: 10.1109/MMUL.2015.34

Chhachhar, A. R., Chachar, A. A., & Arbab, N. F. (2022). Usage of YouTube for Academic Purpose Among University Students in Time of COVID-19. *International Journal of Media and Information Literacy, 7*(1), 38–47. DOI: 10.13187/ijmil.2022.1.38

Chintalapati, N., & Daruri, V. S. K. (2017). Examining the use of YouTube as a Learning Resource in higher education: Scale development and validation of TAM model. *Telematics and Informatics, 34*(6), 853–860. DOI: 10.1016/j.tele.2016.08.008

Cho, H., Cannon, J., Lopez, R., & Li, W. (2024). Social media literacy: A conceptual framework. *New Media & Society, 26*(2), 941–960. DOI: 10.1177/14614448211068530 PMID: 38328341

Chomsky, N. (1970). *Aspekte der Syntax-Theorie* (1st ed.). *Sammlung Akademie-Verlag / Sprache Series: v.6*. Walter de Gruyter GmbH. https://ebookcentral.proquest.com/lib/kxp/detail.action?docID=31605869

Chornoby, J., Florence, T., Linkenhoker, A., Meier, M., Simeone, M., Wray, M., & Napoli, P. M. (2023). *Media literacy as media policy: An assessment of state-level legislative activity* [Paper presentation]. Law and Policy Division of the Association for Education in Journalism & Mass Communication Conference.

Christian, S. E. (2023). *Everyday media literacy: an analog guide for your digital life*. Routledge. DOI: 10.4324/9781003247029

Chuai, Y., & Zhao, J. (2022). Anger can make fake news viral online. *Frontiers in Physics (Lausanne), 10*, 970174. DOI: 10.3389/fphy.2022.970174

Cinnamon, J. (2017). Social injustice in surveillance capitalism. *Surveillance & Society, 15*(5), 609–625. DOI: 10.24908/ss.v15i5.6433

Cismariu, L., Ciurel, D. L., & Hosu, I. (2019). Generation Z and Social Media. *Proceedings of the International Conference on Virtual Learning*, 367–373.

Citron, D. K., & Wittes, B. (2017). The Internet will not break: Denying bad Samaritans § 230 immunity. *Fordham Law Review*, *86*, 401.

Clarke, C. (2009). *Storytelling for grantseekers: A guide to creative nonprofit fundraising* (2nd ed.). Jossey-Bass.

Colditz, J. B., Woods, M. S., & Primack, B. A. (2018). Adolescents seeking online health information: Topics, approaches, and challenges. In *Technology and Adolescent Mental Health*. DOI: 10.1007/978-3-319-69638-6_2

Colohan, A., Freir, T., & Finlay, D. (2016). Optical wavelength ratiometric monitoring system for data centre CWDM applications. *Proceedings - 2016 51st International Universities Power Engineering Conference, UPEC 2016, 2017-Janua*, 1–7. DOI: 10.1109/UPEC.2016.8113984

Committee on Economic. Social and Cultural Rights. (1999). *General comment no. 13: The right to education.* UN Office of the High Commissioner for Human Rights. https://www.refworld.org/legal/general/cescr/1999/en/37937

Committee on the Rights of the Child. (2021). *General comment no. 25 on children's rights in relation to the digital environment*. United Nations Office of the High Commissioner for Human Rights. https://www.ohchr.org/en/documents/general-comments-and-recommendations/general-comment-no-25-2021-childrens-rights-relation

Considine, D. (2002). Media literacy: National developments and international origins. *The Journal of Popular Film and Television*, *30*(1), 7–15. DOI: 10.1080/01956050209605554

Coole, D. (2014). Der neue Materialismus und Politik der Materialisierung. In Witzgall, S., & Stakemeier, K. (Eds.), *Schriftenreihe des cx centrum für Interdisziplinäre Studien der Akademie der Bildenden Künste München. Macht des Materials - Politik der Materialität* (1st ed., pp. 29–46). Diaphanes.

Cooper, J. (Ed.). (1997). *Plato: Complete Works*. Hackett.

Cotter, K., & Reisdorf, B. C. (2020). Algorithmic knowledge gaps: A new horizon of (digital) inequality. *International Journal of Communication*, *14*, 21.

Couldry, N., & Mejias, U. A. (2019). Data Colonialism: Rethinking Big Data's Relation to the Contemporary Subject. *Television & New Media*, *20*(4), 336–349. DOI: 10.1177/1527476418796632

Coulter, M., & Bensinger, G. (2023). Alphabet shares dive after Google AI chatbot Bard flubs answer in ad. *Reuters.* https://www.reuters.com/technology/google-ai-chatbot-bard-offers-inaccurate-information-company-ad-2023-02-08

Cox, A. (2024). Algorithmic literacy, AI literacy and responsible generative AI literacy. *Journal of Web Librarianship, 18*(3), 93–110. DOI: 10.1080/19322909.2024.2395341

Cubeddu, F., & Scocco, M. (2024). Online Hate Speech as a Form of Cyberviolence: Communication Practices, Social Perception and Vulnerabilities in the Experience of Young People. In Gualda, E. (Ed.), *Teorias de la conspiraòn y discursos de odio en linea en la Sociedad de las plataformas. Comparación de pautas en las narrativas y redes sociales sobre COVID-19, inmigrantes, refugiados, estudios de género y personas LGTBIQ+* (pp. 221–235). Dykinson. DOI: 10.14679/2761

Culnan, M. J., & Williams, C. C. (2009). How ethics can enhance organizational privacy: Lessons from the ChoicePoint and TJX data breaches. *Management Information Systems Quarterly, 33*(4), 673–687. DOI: 10.2307/20650322

Cybersecurity and Infrastructure Security Agency (CISA). (2021). *Tactics of disinformation.* https://www.cisa.gov/sites/default/files/publications/tactics-of-disinformation_508.pdf

D'Angelo, S., Marcus, R., & Ngabonzima, E. (2022). Teaching and learning for life skills development: Insights from Rwanda's 12+ programme for adolescent girls: Special Issue Youth & Adolescent Skills Development: Preparing young people for diverse global challenges. *Development Policy Review, 40*(S2), e12622. DOI: 10.1111/dpr.12622

da Silva, A. H. B., & Gómez, Á. H. (2024). What's Behind the 'Likes'? – Development of Self-Image in Young YouTubers | O que está por trás dos "likes"? – Desenvolvimento da autoimagem em jovens youtubers. *Rotura: Journal of Communication, Culture and Arts, 4*(1), 64–79. DOI: 10.34623/qa6g-hn70

Dakhel, A. M. (2024). Generative AI for software development: A family of studies on code generation. In *Generative AI for Effective Software Development* (pp. 151–172). Springer Nature Switzerland. DOI: 10.1007/978-3-031-55642-5_7

Damota, M. D. (2019). The effect of social media on society. *New Media and Mass Communication, 78*, 12–17. DOI: 10.7176/NMMC

Dani, E. (2015). The HY-DE model: An interdisciplinary attempt to deal with the phenomenon of hyperattention. *6th International Multi-Conference on Complexity, Informatics and Cybernetics, IMCIC 2015 and 6th International Conference on Society and Information Technologies, ICSIT 2015 - Proceedings, 2*, 211–216.

Daniel, M., Maulik, P. K., Kallakuri, S., Kaur, A., Devarapalli, S., Mukherjee, A., Bhattacharya, A., Billot, L., Thornicroft, G., Praveen, D., Patel, A., & Peiris, D. (2021). An integrated community and primary healthcare worker intervention to reduce stigma and improve management of common mental disorders in rural India: Protocol for the SMART Mental Health programme. *Trials*, *22*(1), 179. DOI: 10.1186/s13063-021-05136-5 PMID: 33653406

Danks, D., & London, A. J. (2017, Aug). Algorithmic bias in autonomous systems. *IJCAI (United States)*, *17*, 4691–4697.

Das, A. (2018). Role of Mass Media in Fostering Values Among Students, JETIR August 2018, Volume 5, Issue 8 www.jetir.org (ISSN-2349-5162).

Data, I. B. M., & Team, A. I. (2023, Oct 16). Shedding light on AI bias with real world examples. *IBM*. https://www.ibm.com/think/topics/shedding-light-on-ai-bias-with-real-world-example

Dave, T., Athaluri, S. A., & Singh, S. (2023). ChatGPT in medicine: An overview of its applications, advantages, limitations, future prospects, and ethical considerations. *Frontiers in Artificial Intelligence*, *6*, 1169595–1169595. DOI: 10.3389/frai.2023.1169595 PMID: 37215063

Davison, W. (1983). The third-person effect in communication. *Public Opinion Quarterly*, *47*(1), 1–15. DOI: 10.1086/268763

Dawood, Y. (2020). Protecting elections from disinformation: A multifaceted public–private approach to social media and democratic speech. *Ohio State Technology Law Journal*, *16*, 639–668.

De Mendonça, R. R., de Brito, D. F., Rosa, F. de F., dos Reis, J. C., & Bonacin, R. (2020). A framework for detecting intentions of criminal acts in social media: A case study on Twitter. *Information (Basel)*, *11*(3), 154. DOI: 10.3390/info11030154

de Sousa Santos, B. (2009). *Una Epistemología del Sur. La reinvención del conocimiento y la emancipación social*. Clacso/Siglo XXI Editores.

DeFleur, M. L., & Ball-Rokeach, S. (1989). *Theories of mass communication* (5th ed.). Longman.

del Pilar Gutiérrez Arenas, M., García, A. R., & Reifs Ruíz, R. M. (2022a). Generation Z wants to be a youtuber and/or influencer. Factors that determine this trend | A Geração Z quer ser um youtuber e/ou influenciador. Factores que determinam esta tendência | La generación Z desea ser youtuber y/o influencer. Factores que determ. *Icono14, 20*(2). DOI: 10.7195/ri14.v20i2.1882

Delgado, R., & Stefancic, J. (2017). *Critical race theory: An introduction*. NYU Press.

Delic, H., & Bećirović, S. (2016). Socratic Method as an Approach to Teaching. *Evropejskij Issledovatel, 111*(10), 511–517. DOI: 10.13187/er.2016.111.511

de-Lima-Santos, M. F., & Ceron, W. (2021). Artificial intelligence in news media: current perceptions and future outlook. *Journalism and media, 3*(1), 13-26. DOI: 10.3390/journalmedia3010002

Dell'Acqua, F., McFowland, E., Mollick, E. R., Lifshitz-Assaf, H., Kellogg, K., Rajendran, S., Krayer, L., Candelon, F., & Lakhani, K. R. (2023). Navigating the jagged technological frontier: Field experimental evidence of the effects of AI on knowledge worker productivity and quality. *Harvard Business School Technology & Operations Mgt. Unit Working Paper* (24-013). DOI: 10.2139/ssrn.4573321

Dennis, P. M. (1998). Chills and thrills: Does radio harm our children? The controversy over program violence during the age of radio. *Journal of the History of the Behavioral Sciences, 34*(1), 33–50. DOI: 10.1002/(SICI)1520-6696(199824)34:1<33::AID-JHBS3>3.0.CO;2-K PMID: 9487691

Desai-Stephens, A. (2022). The Infrastructure of Engagement: Musical Aesthetics and the Rise of YouTube in India. *Twentieth-Century Music, 19*(3), 444–471. DOI: 10.1017/S1478572222000299

Dessler, A. (2016). *Introduction to modern climate change* (2nd ed.). Cambridge University Press.

Dewey, J. (1997). *Democracy and Education*. Free Press.

Dezuanni, M. (2019). Children's minecraft multiliteracy practices and learning through peer pedagogies. In *Multiliteracies and Early Years Innovation*. Perspectives from Finland and Beyond., DOI: 10.4324/9780429432668-11

DG RTD (European Commission Directorate-General for Research and Innovation). (2024). *ERA Industrial Technologies Roadmap on Human-Centric Research and Innovation for the Manufacturing Sector.* Publications Office of the European Union. https://data.europa.eu/doi/10.2777/0266

Dinev, T., & Hart, P. (2006). An extended privacy calculus model for e-commerce transactions. *Information Systems Research, 17*(1), 61–80. DOI: 10.1287/isre.1060.0080

Dittrich, P.-J. (2017). *Populismus im Netz: Im europäischen Vergleich liegt die AfD zurück.* Jacques Delors Institut – Berlin. https://www.hertie-school.org/fileadmin/user_upload/20170917_PopulismusWahleninDeutschland_Dittrich.pdf

DNE-TN2 (2024). Intelligence artificielle et éducation: apports de la recherche et enjeux pour les politiques publiques: édition trilingue 2024. *Éducation, numérique et recherche*. DOI: 10.58079/vq06

Dolata, U., & Schrape, J. F. (2016). Masses, crowds, communities, movements: Collective action in the internet age. *Social Movement Studies*, *15*(1), 1–18. DOI: 10.1080/14742837.2015.1055722

Doll, J., Petersen, B., & Bode, C. (2017). Skeptical but adapting: What Midwestern farmers say about climate change. *Weather, Climate, and Society*, *9*(4), 739–751. DOI: 10.1175/WCAS-D-16-0110.1

Donath, J., & Boyd, D. (2004). Public Displays of Connection. *BT Technology Journal*, *22*(4), 71–82. DOI: 10.1023/B:BTTJ.0000047585.06264.cc

Doni, T. (2015). *Dalla Media Education alla New Media Education. Cinema e dintorni*. Rassegna CNOS.

Donovan, J., Friedberg, B., & McCormick, K. (2023). *The Media Manipulation Casebook*. https://mediamanipulation.org/

Downey, M. (2003). *Effective coaching: Lessons from the coaches' coach* (2nd ed.). Texere.

Dureja, V., & Tanwar, S. (2024). Detection of False Information on Social Media. *2024 11th International Conference on Reliability, Infocom Technologies and Optimization (Trends and Future Directions), ICRITO 2024*. DOI: 10.1109/ICRITO61523.2024.10522238

Durkheim, E. (1922). *Éducation et sociologie*. PUF.

Dussel, I., & Trujillo Reyes, B. F. (2018). ¿Nuevas formas de enseñar y aprender? Las posibilidades en conflicto de las tecnologías digitales en la escuela. [– IISUE – UNAM.]. *Perfiles Educativos*, *XL*(159), 201. DOI: 10.22201/iisue.24486167e.2018.Especial.59182

Dutta, S. K., & Manna, S. (2024a). Role of youtube and instagram advertising in attracting gen-z consumers in delhi-ncr. In *Consumer Experience and Decision-Making in the Metaverse*. DOI: 10.4018/979-8-3693-4167-4.ch012

Dutta, H. S., Jobanputra, M., Negi, H., & Chakraborty, T. (2021). Detecting and Analyzing Collusive Entities on YouTube. *ACM Transactions on Intelligent Systems and Technology*, *12*(5), 1–28. DOI: 10.1145/3477300

Dyer, K. D., & Hall, R. E. (2018). Effect of critical thinking education on epistemically unwarranted beliefs in college students. *Research in Higher Education, 60*(3), 293–314. DOI: 10.1007/s11162-018-9513-3

Ecker, U. K. H., Lewandowsky, S., Cook, J., Schmid, P., Fazio, L. K., Brashier, N., Kendeou, P., Vraga, E. K., & Amazeen, M. A. (2022). The psychological drivers of misinformation belief and its resistance to correction. *Nature Reviews Psychology, 1*(1), 13–29. DOI: 10.1038/s44159-021-00006-y

Edelman. (2021). Edelman Trust Barometer 2021. https://www.edelman.com/trust/2021-trust-barometer

Eilperin, J., & Dennis, B. (2017, Mar 14). How James Inhofe is upending the nation's energy and environmental policies. *Washington Post.* https://www.washingtonpost.com/national/health-science/how-james-inhofe-is-upending-the-nations-energy-and-environmental-policies/2017/03/14/2bebdbfa-081c-11e7-a15f-a58d4a988474_story.html

Eisenberg, M., & Berkowitz, R. (1990). *Information problem-solving: The Big Six Skills approach to library & information skills instruction. Information management, policy, and services.* Ablex Pub. Corp. http://www.loc.gov/catdir/enhancements/fy1511/90022681-b.html

Eisenegger, M. (2021). Dritter, digitaler Strukturwandel der Öffentlichkeit als Folge der Plattformisierung. In Eisenegger, M., Prinzing, M., Ettinger, P., & Blum, R. (Eds.), *Digitaler Strukturwandel der Öffentlichkeit* (pp. 17–39). Springer Fachmedien Wiesbaden. DOI: 10.1007/978-3-658-32133-8_2

Elkins, Z. (2019, Feb 26). Ask a scientist: Are we ever 100 percent sure? *Columbia Daily Tribune.* https://www.columbiatribune.com/story/lifestyle/family/2019/02/26/ask-scientist-are-we-ever/5830985007/

Ellison, M., Pollock, G., & Grimm, R. (2020). Young people's orientations towards contemporary politics: Trust, representation and participation. *Zeitschrift für Erziehungswissenschaft, 23*(6), 1201–1226. DOI: 10.1007/s11618-020-00984-4

Ellison, N. B., Steinfield, C., & Lampe, C. (2007). The benefits of Facebook "friends": Social capital and college students' use of online social network sites. *Journal of Computer-Mediated Communication, 12*(4), 1143–1168. DOI: 10.1111/j.1083-6101.2007.00367.x

Elmer, T., Mepham, K., & Stadtfeld, C. (2020). Students under lockdown: Comparisons of students' social networks and mental health before and during the COVID-19 crisis in Switzerland. *PLoS One*, *15*(7), e0236337. DOI: 10.1371/journal.pone.0236337 PMID: 32702065

Emmer, M. (2017). Soziale Medien in der politischen Kommunikation. In Schmidt, J.-H., & Taddicken, M. (Eds.), *Handbuch soziale Medien* (pp. 81–100). Springer VS. DOI: 10.1007/978-3-658-03765-9_5

Ename, A. A. et al. (2022). A Study on Positive and Negative Effects of Social Media on Society, IJARCCE, International Journal of Advanced Research in Computer and Communication Engineering, ISSN (O) 2278-1021, ISSN (P) 2319-5940, ISO 3297:2007, Vol. 11, Issue 5, May 2022, DOI: .DOI: 10.17148/IJARCCE.2022.115161

Ennis, R. H., & Millman, J. (1971). Manual for Cornell Critical Thinking Test, Level X, and Cornell Critical Thinking Test, Level Z. Critical Thinking Project, University of Illinois.

Ennis, R. H. (1987). A taxonomy of critical thinking dispositions and abilities. In Baron, J., & Sternberg, R. J. (Eds.), *Teaching thinking skills: Theory and practice* (pp. 9–26). W.H. Freeman and Company.

Ennis, R. H. (1991). Critical thinking: A streamlined conception. *Teaching Philosophy*, *14*(1), 5–24. DOI: 10.5840/teachphil19911412

Ennis, R. H., Millman, J., & Tomko, T. N. (1985). *Cornell Critical Thinking Tests Level X & Level Z: Manual* (3rd ed.). Midwest Publications.

Entman, R. (1991). Framing U.S. coverage of international news: Contrasts in narratives of the KAL and Iran Air incidents. *Journal of Communication*, *41*(4), 6–27. DOI: 10.1111/j.1460-2466.1991.tb02328.x

European Center for Populism Studies. (n.d.). *Climate change denial*. https://www.populismstudies.org/Vocabulary/climate-change-denial/

European Commission High-Level Expert Group on AI. (2019). *Ethics Guidelines for Trustworthy AI*. https://ec.europa.eu/newsroom/dae/document.cfm?doc_id=60419

European Commission. *(2019). Communication From The Commission To The European Parliament, The Council, The European Economic And Social Committee And The Committee Of The Regions – Building Trust in Human-Centric Artificial Intelligence*. COM(2019) 168 final. https://eur-lex.europa.eu/legal-content/EN/TXT/PDF/?uri=CELEX:52019DC0168

European Commission. (2021). *Laying down harmonised rules on artificial intelligence (Artificial Intelligence Act) and amending certain Union legislative acts.* (Document 52021PC0206). EUR-Lex. https://eur-lex.europa.eu/legal-content/EN/TXT/?uri=celex:52021PC0206

European Commission. (2021). *Proposal for a Regulation of the European Parliament and of the Council laying down harmonised rules on Artificial Intelligence (Artificial Intelligence Act) and amending certain Union legislative acts.* COM/2021/206 final. https://eur-lex.europa.eu/legal-content/EN/TXT/?uri=celex:52021PC0206

European Commission. (2024). Horizon Europe Work Programme 2023-2025: Widening participation and strengthening the European Research Area. In *Research And Innovation: European Commission*. https://ec.europa.eu/info/funding-tenders/opportunities/docs/2021-2027/horizon/wp-call/2023-2024/wp-11-widening-participation-and-strengthening-the-european-research-area_horizon-2023-2024_en.pdf

European Union. (2018). *Directive (EU) 2018/1808 of the European Parliament and of the Council of 14 November 2018 amending Directive 2010/13/EU on the coordination of certain provisions laid down by law, regulation or administrative action in Member States concerning the provision of audiovisual media services (Audiovisual Media Services Directive) in view of changing market realities* (Publication No. 32018L1808). EUR-Lex. https://eur-lex.europa.eu/eli/dir/2018/1808/oj

European Union. (2024). *Regulation (EU) 2024/1689 of the European Parliament and of the Council of 13 June 2024, laying down harmonised rules on artificial intelligence and amending various regulations and directives (Artificial Intelligence Act).* Official Journal of the European Union. https://eur-lex.europa.eu/legal-content/EN/TXT/PDF/?uri=OJ:L_202401689 European External Action Service. (n.d.). *Learn*. EU vs Disinfo. https://euvsdisinfo.eu/learn/

Facione, P. (1990). Critical thinking: A statement of expert consensus for purposes of educational assessment and instruction. *Research findings and recommendations* (p. 315).

Facione, P. A. (1990c). *The California Critical Thinking Skills Test--College Level. Technical Report #3. Gender, ethnicity, major, CT self-esteem, and the CCTST.* ERIC Document ED326584.

Facione, P. A. (1990b). *California Critical Thinking Skills Test, CCTST – Form A.* The California Academic Press.

Facione, P. A. (2015). *Critical thinking: What it is and why it counts*. Insight Assessment.

Fadjar, A., Hartini, S., & Astuti, S. W. (2022). Instagram Usage Behavior: Does It Aim to Look More Attractive? *Quality - Access to Success*, *23*(189), 67–73. DOI: 10.47750/QAS/23.189.09

Faragó, L., Krekó, P., & Orosz, G. (2023). Hungarian, lazy, and biased: The role of analytic thinking and partisanship in fake news discernment on a Hungarian representative sample. *Scientific Reports*, *13*(1), 178. Advance online publication. DOI: 10.1038/s41598-022-26724-8 PMID: 36604448

Farooq, K. et. al. (2021). The Study on the Role of Social Media in Social Change in Society, International Journal of Innovation, Creativity, and Change, Volume 15, Issue 2.

Fastrez, P., Lacelle, N., Bihl, J., Gladu, E., Delamotte, E., Delarue-Breton, C., Ronveaux, C., & Sutter Widmer, D. (2022). The Media Literacy of Teenagers: An international study of Competence in Information Search and Multimodal Production. *Educare (San José)*, (1), 71–104. DOI: 10.24834/educare.2022.1.4

Fazil, A. W., (2024). Exploring the Role of social media in Bridging Gaps and Facilitating Global Communication, Studies in Media, Journalism, and Communications Journal, www.al-kindipublisher.com/index.php/smjc, SMJCDOI: DOI: 10.32996/smjc

Fazio, L. K., Brashier, N. M., Payne, B. K., & Marsh, E. J. (2015). Knowledge does not protect against illusory truth. *Journal of Experimental Psychology. General*, *144*(5), 993–1002. DOI: 10.1037/xge0000098 PMID: 26301795

FCC. US government (2022 Sep). *The Public and Broadcasting*. Federal Communications Commission. https://www.fcc.gov/media/radio/public-and-broadcasting#ACT

Feierabend, Sabine, Rathgeb, Thomas, Gerigk, Yvonne, & Glöckler, S. (2024). *JIM-Studie 2024: Jugend, Information, Medien. Basisuntersuchung zum Medienumgang 12- bis 19-Jähriger in Deutschland*. https://mpfs.de/app/uploads/2024/11/JIM_2024_PDF_barrierearm.pdf

Feldman, L., & Hart, P. (2018). Broadening exposure to climate change news? How framing and political orientation interact to influence selective exposure. *Journal of Communication*, *68*(3), 503–524. DOI: 10.1093/joc/jqy011

Ferrara, E. (2024). The butterfly effect in artificial intelligence systems: Implications for AI bias and fairness. *Machine Learning with Applications*, *15*, 15. DOI: 10.1016/j.mlwa.2024.100525

Feuerriegel, S., Hartmann, J., Janiesch, C., & Zschech, P. (2024). Generative AI. *Business & Information Systems Engineering, 66*(1), 111–126. DOI: 10.1007/s12599-023-00834-7

Finland Toolbox. *Media literacy and education in Finland.* Retrieved March 11, 2025 from toolbox.finland.fi

Fjeld, J., Achten, N., Hilligoss, H., Nagy, A., & Srikumar, M. (2020). Principled artificial intelligence: Mapping consensus in ethical and rights-based approaches to principles for AI. *Berkman Klein Center Research Publication.* https://papers.ssrn.com/sol3/papers.cfm?abstract_id=3518482

Flauzino, K. D. L., Pimentel, M. D. G. C., Batistoni, S. S. T., Zaine, I., Vieira, L. O. B., Rodrigues, K. R. D. H., & Cachioni, M. (2020). Digital Literacy for Older Adults: Perceptions about teaching-learning. *Educação e Realidade, 45*, e104913. DOI: 10.1590/2175-6236104913

Floridi, L., & Cowls, J. (2019). *A unified framework of five principles for AI in society. Harvard Data Science Review.Hanington, B., & Martin, B. (2022). The Pocket Universal Methods of Design, Revised and Expanded: 125 ways to Research Complex Problems, Develop Innovative Ideas, and Design Effective Solutions.* Rockport Publishers.

Forsdale, L. (1955). *Multi-media Literacy. Better Broadcasts Newsletter, 8(4).* American Council for Better Broadcasts.

Fowler, M. (2003). Patterns. *IEEE Software, 20*(2), 56–57. DOI: 10.1109/MS.2003.1184168 PMID: 12628886

Fraser, P., & Wardle, J. (Eds.). (2013). *Current Perspectives in Media Education: beyond the Manifesto.* Palgrave McMillan. DOI: 10.1057/9781137300218

Frattolillo, F. (2020). A watermarking protocol based on blockchain. *Applied Sciences (Basel, Switzerland), 10*(21), 7746. DOI: 10.3390/app10217746

Frau-Meigs, D. (2024). Algorithm Literacy as a Subset of Media and Information Literacy: Competences and Design Considerations. *Digital, 4*(2), 512–528. DOI: 10.3390/digital4020026

Freire, P. (1998). *Pedagogy of Freedom: Ethics, Democracy, and Civic Courage.* Rowman & Littlefield Publishers.

Freire, P. (2005). *Pedagogy of the Oppressed.* The Continuum Publishing Company.

Friesem, Y., Raman, U., Kanižaj, I., & Choi, G. Y. (2023). *The Routledge Handbook of Media Education Futures Post-Pandemic.* Routledge.

Frizzo, G. B. (2024). *Digital Media and Early Child Development. Theoretical and Empirical Issues*. Springer. DOI: 10.1007/978-3-031-69224-6

Fryer, W. (2024). Conspiracy & culture wars. https://medialiteracy.wesfryer.com/concw

Fu, A. (2023, Nov 16). *US lost more than two local newspapers a week this year, new Medill report finds*. Poynter Institute. https://www.poynter.org/business-work/2023/2023-news-deserts-report-penny-abernathy-medill/

Fui-Hoon Nah, F., Zheng, R., Cai, J., Siau, K., & Chen, L. (2023). Generative AI and ChatGPT: Applications, challenges, and AI-human collaboration. *Journal of Information Technology Case and Application Research, 25*(3), 277–304. DOI: 10.1080/15228053.2023.2233814

Furedi, F. (2016). Moral panic and reading: Early elite anxieties about the media effect. *Cultural Sociology, 10*(4), 523–537. DOI: 10.1177/1749975515626953

Gabaree, S. (2022). A metacognitive approach to reduce the spread of online misinformation. *The Journal of Media Literacy*. https://ic4ml.org/journal-article/a-metacognitive-approach-to-reduce-the-spread-of-online-misinformation/

Gajanayake, G. M. H. C., & Sandanayake, T. C. (2020). Trending pattern identification of youtube gaming channels using sentiment analysis. *20th International Conference on Advances in ICT for Emerging Regions, ICTer 2020 - Proceedings*, 149–154. DOI: 10.1109/ICTer51097.2020.9325476

Galant, R. (2012, Jun 5). *The most trusted man in America*. https://www.cnn.com/2012/06/05/opinion/brinkley-walter-cronkite/index.html

Gálik, S. (2017). Influence of cyberspace on changes in contemporary education. *Communication Today, 8*(1), 30–38.

Gangwal, A., & Lavecchia, A. (2024). Unlocking the potential of generative AI in drug discovery. *Drug Discovery Today, 29*(6), 103992. DOI: 10.1016/j.drudis.2024.103992 PMID: 38663579

Gans, H. J. (1979). *Deciding what's news: A study of CBS Evening News, NBC Nightly News, Newsweek and Time*. Random House.

Gapski, H. (2001). *Medienkompetenz: Eine Bestandsaufnahme und Vorüberlegungen zu einem systemtheoretischen Rahmenkonzept*. Diss. Westdt. Verl.

Gapski, H., & Gräßer, L. (2007). Medienkompetenz im Web 2.0 – Lebensqualität als Zielperspektive. In L. Gräßer & M. Pohlschmidt (Eds.), *Schriftenreihe Medienkompetenz des Landes Nordrhein-Westfalen: Vol. 7. Praxis Web 2.0: Potenziale für die Entwicklung von Medienkompetenz* (pp. 11–34). kopaed.

García, A. R., Arenas, M. P. G., & Moreno, M. G. (2023). Children want to be celebrities. Is it compatible with school engagement? | Los menores desean ser celebrities. ¿Es compatible con el compromiso escolar? *Revista Complutense de Educacion, 34*(4), 755–767. DOI: 10.5209/rced.80039

Gataullina, L. N., Tuktarova, G. M., Nezhmetdinova, F. T., & Fassakhova, G. R. (2024). Socialization of rural youth issues in the development of agricultural industry and society. *BIO Web of Conferences, 103*. DOI: 10.1051/bioconf/202410300068

Gemkow, J. (2023). Polarisierung durch oder auf soziale(n) Medien? In Institut für Demokratie und Gesellschaft (Ed.), *Wissen schafft Demokratie. Schwerpunkt Netzkulturen und Plattformpolitiken* (pp. 44–57).

Genner, S., & Süss, D. (2017). Socialization as media effect. *The International Encyclopedia of Media Effects, 1*(15), 1-16.

Gentzel, P. (2015). *Praxistheorie und Mediatisierung: Grundlagen, Perspektiven und eine Kulturgeschichte der Mobilkommunikation*. Springer VS. https://gbv.eblib.com/patron/FullRecord.aspx?p=1998476 DOI: 10.1007/978-3-658-08994-8

Gentzkow, M. (2018). *Media and artificial intelligence*. Toulouse Network for Information Technology Whitepaper.

Gerbner, G., & Gross, L. (1976). Living with television: The violence profile. *Journal of Communication, 26*(2), 172–199. DOI: 10.1111/j.1460-2466.1976.tb01397.x PMID: 932235

Gerhardt, M. (2024). *1980s television*. History of American Pop Culture https://www.explorepopculture.com/unit-6-1980s/1980s-television

Gerodimos, R. (n.d.). Journalism students as global citizens and mediators. *Journalism Education, 1*, 70–86. https://journalism-education.org/wp-content/uploads/2012/04/1-1-Global-Citizens.pdf

Gerris, J. R. M., & Grundmann, M. (2002). Reziprozität, Qualität von Familienbeziehungen und die intergenerationale Transmission von Beziehungskompetenz. *ZSE: Zeitschrift für Soziologie der Erziehung und Sozialisation, 22.* (ZSE: Zeitschrift für Soziologie der Erziehung und Sozialisation 22 (2002) 1, S. 3-24). DOI: 10.25656/01:8925

Gibney, A., & Kirby, L. (Executive Producers). (2017). *Water & power: A California heist* [Documentary]. Jigsaw Productions.

Gil de Zúñiga, H., Jung, N., & Valenzuela, S. (2012). Social media use for news and individuals' social capital, civic engagement, and political participation. *Journal of Computer-Mediated Communication, 17*(3), 319–336. DOI: 10.1111/j.1083-6101.2012.01574.x

Gillani, N., Eynon, R., Chiabaut, C., & Finkel, K. (2023). Unpacking the 'Black Box' of AI in Education. *Journal of Educational Technology & Society, 26*(1), 99–111.

Gitlin, T. (1980). Making democracy safe for America. *Columbia Journalism Review, 18*(6), 53.

Glaser, R. (1984). Education and thinking: The role of knowledge. *The American Psychologist, 39*(2), 93–104. DOI: 10.1037/0003-066X.39.2.93

Goad, A., & Homes, O. (2022). Bridging the digital divide: an evaluation of existing elderly digital literacy education.

Godwin, R. C., DeBerry, J. J., Wagener, B. M., Berkowitz, D. E., & Melvin, R. L. (2024). Grant drafting support with guided Generative AI software. *SoftwareX, 27*, 101784. DOI: 10.1016/j.softx.2024.101784

Goldberg, D. (2018). Responding to "fake news": Is there an alternative to law and regulation? *Southwestern Law Review, 47*, 417–447.

Goldfarb, A., & Tucker, C. (2011). Privacy regulation and online advertising. *Management Science, 57*(1), 57–71. DOI: 10.1287/mnsc.1100.1246

Goldstein, S. (2020). *Informed societies: Why information literacy matters for citizenship, participation and democracy*. Facet Publishing.

González Arévalo, B. (2013). [Cyberbullying at school]. | Cyberbullying en el colegio. *Revista de Enfermeria (Barcelona, Spain), 36*(10), 16–21. PMID: 24354128

Gonzalez, A., & Shulz, D. (2017). Helping truth with its boots: Accreditation as an antidote to fake news. *Yale Law Forum, 127*, 315–336.

Gonzalez-Mohino, M., Rodriguez-Domenech, M. Á., Callejas-Albiñana, A. I., & Castillo-Canalejo, A. (2023). Empowering Critical Thinking: The Role of Digital Tools in Citizen Participation. *Journal of New Approaches in Educational Research, 12*(2), 258–275. DOI: 10.7821/naer.2023.7.1385

González-pérez, L. I., & Ramírez-montoya, M. S. (2022). Components of education 4.0 in 21st century skills frameworks: Systematic review. *Sustainability (Basel), 14*(3), 1493. DOI: 10.3390/su14031493

Google. (2023). Bard [Large Language Model]. https://bard.google.com

Google. (2025). What is artificial general intelligence? *Google*. https://cloud.google.com/discover/what-is-artificial-general-intelligence

Gottfried, J., & Grieco, E. (2018) *Younger Americans Are Better than Older Americans at Telling Factual News Statements from Opinions*. Pew Research Center. https://www.pewresearch.org/fact-tank/2018/10/23/younger-americans-are-better-than-older-americans-at-telling-factual-news-statements-from-opinions/

Gran, A.-B., Booth, P., & Bucher, T. (2021). To be or not to be algorithm aware: A question of a new digital divide? *Information Communication and Society, 24*(12), 1779–1796. DOI: 10.1080/1369118X.2020.1736124

Greenhow, C. (2011). Online social networks and learning. *On the Horizon, 19*(1), 4–12. DOI: 10.1108/10748121111107663

Greenhow, C., & Lewin, C. (2016). Social media and education: Reconceptualizing the boundaries of learning. *Learning, Media and Technology, 41*(1), 1–6. DOI: 10.1080/17439884.2015.1064954

Greitemeyer, T., & Sagioglou, C. (2016). Subjective well-being and social media use: Do personality traits moderate the relationship between social media use and subjective well-being? *Social Media + Society, 2*(3), 1–9. DOI: 10.1177/2056305116665859

Groeben, N. (2002a). Anforderungen an die theoretische Konzeptualisierung von Medienkompetenz. In Groeben, N., & Hurrelmann, B. (Eds.), *Medienkompetenz: Voraussetzungen, Dimensionen, Funktionen* (pp. 11–22). Juventa-Verl.

Groshek, J., & Engelbert, J. (2013). A Cross-National Comparison of Populist Political Movements and Media Uses in the United States and the Netherlands. *New Media & Society, 15*(2), 183–202. DOI: 10.1177/1461444812450685

Groshek, J., & Vogts, T. (2025). *Misinformation Finds Them: Hybrid Media and Radicalization in Rural America*. Peter Lang Publishing.

Grundmann, M. (2006). *Sozialisation: Skizze einer allgemeinen Theorie. UTB Soziologie* (Vol. 2783). UVK Verl.-Ges. DOI: 10.36198/9783838527833

Grundmann, M. (2023). Sozialisation als Beziehungspraxis. Sozialkonstruktive Dynamiken und Gestaltungsmöglichkeiten in Kindheit und Jugend. In Scheid, C., Silkenbeumer, M., Zizek, B., & Zizek, L. (Eds.), *Rekonstruktive Sozialisationsforschung. Sozialisationstheorie und -forschung revisited* (pp. 27–41). Springer Fachmedien Wiesbaden., DOI: 10.1007/978-3-658-36002-3_2

Grundmann, M., & Wernberger, A. (2015). Familie und Sozialisation. In *Handbuch Familiensoziologie* (pp. 413–435). Springer VS., DOI: 10.1007/978-3-658-02276-1_14

Gué - Martini. R. (2020). Educomunicación: ¿Contracampo o intersección? In I. Aguded; A. Vizcaìno Verdù (Eds.). *Redes sociales y ciudadanía: hacia un mundo ciberconectado y empoderado.* Grupo Comunicar Ediciones (pp. 677-685).

Guess, A. M., Lerner, M., Lyons, B., Montgomery, J. M., Nyhan, B., Reifler, J., & Sircar, N. (2020). A digital media literacy intervention increases discernment between mainstream and false news in the United States and India. *Proceedings of the National Academy of Sciences of the United States of America, 117*(27), 15536–15545. , D. F. (1998). Teaching critical thinking for transfer across domains: Dispositions, skills, structure training, and metacognitive monitoring. *American Psychologist, 53*(4), 449–455. DOI: 10.1073/pnas.1920498117

Guèvremont, V., & Brin, C. (2024). *Intelligence artificielle, culture et médias.* Éthique, IA et société – OBVIA.

Guilherme Goulart Righetto, G. G. (2021). Imbecilization in the disinformation society: What can information literacy do about it? *Investigación Bibliotecológica, 35*(87), 33–55. DOI: 10.22201/iibi.24488321xe.2021.87.58310

Gulf News report,(2023, Jul 18) https://gulfnews.com,

Guo, Y., Li, Y., & Ito, N. (2014). How do different internet use functions affect bridging and bonding social capital? an empirical study of the chinese international students in japan. *International Journal of Cyber Society and Education, 7*(1), 71–88. DOI: 10.7903/ijcse.1074

Gurchiek, K. (2024, Feb 20). Employers want new grads with Ai experience, knowledge. *SHRM*. https://www.shrm.org/topics-tools/news/technology/employers-want-new-grads-with-ai-experience--knowledge

H., R. B., Buddayya, R., & Gujjarappa, N. L. (2019). Benefits of videos in youtube for the undergraduate students in engineering and technology in India. *Webology, 16*(2), 57–71.

Habermas, J., & Luhmann, N. (1971). Theorie der Gesellschaft oder Sozialtechnologie: Was leistet die Systemforschung? (1. Aufl.). *Theorie Theorie-Diskussion*. Suhrkamp.

Habermas, J. (2022). *Ein neuer Strukturwandel der Öffentlichkeit und die deliberative Politik* (1st ed.). Suhrkamp.

Haliti-Sylaj, T., & Sadiku, A. (2024). Impact of Short Reels on Attention Span and Academic Performance of Undergraduate Students. *Eurasian Journal of Applied Linguistics*, *10*(3), 60–68. DOI: 10.32601/ejal.10306

Hall, S. (1980). Encoding/decoding. In *Culture, Media, Language. S.* Hall, D. Hobson, A. Lowe, A. and P. Willis (Eds.), *Culture, Media, Language* (pp.128-138). Hutchinson Press.

Hallaq, T. (2016). Evaluating online media literacy in higher education: Validity and reliability of the digital online media literacy assessment (DOMLA). *The Journal of Media Literacy Education*, *8*(1), 62. DOI: 10.23860/jmle-8-1-5

Hallin, D. C. (1985). The American news media: A critical theory perspective. *Critical Theory and Public Life*, *121*, 146.

Hall, S. (1980). Encoding/decoding. In Hall, S., Hobson, D., Lowe, A., & Willis, P. (Eds.), *Culture, Media* (pp. 128–139). Language.

Halpern, D. F. (2014). *Thought and knowledge: An introduction to critical thinking* (5th ed.). Psychology Press.

Hameed, S., & Mathur, M. (2020). Generation Z in India: Digital Natives and Makers of Change. In *The New Generation Z in Asia: Dynamics, Differences, Digitalization*. DOI: 10.1108/978-1-80043-220-820201010

Hameleers, M., Brosius, A., & de Vreese, C. H. (2022). Whom to trust? Media exposure patterns of citizens with perceptions of misinformation and disinformation related to the news media. *European Journal of Communication*, *37*(3), 3. DOI: 10.1177/02673231211072667

Hameleers, M., & van der Meer, T. G. L. A. (2020). Misinformation and polarization in a high-choice media environment: How effective are political fact-checkers? *Communication Research*, *47*(2), 227–250. DOI: 10.1177/0093650218819671

Hamm, M. S., & Spaaij, R. (2017). *The age of lone wolf terrorism*. Columbia University Press., DOI: 10.7312/hamm18174

Hampton, K., & Wellman, B. (2003). Neighboring in Netville: How the Internet Supports Community and Social Capital in a Wired Suburb. *City & Community*, *2*(4), 277–311. DOI: 10.1046/j.1535-6841.2003.00057.x

Han, J., Cha, M., & Lee, W. (2020). Anger contributes to the spread of COVID-19 misinformation. *Harvard Kennedy School Misinformation Review*. DOI: 10.37016/mr-2020-39

Hargittai, E. (2005). Survey measures of web-oriented digital literacy. *Social Science Computer Review, 23*(3), 371–379. https://ssc.sagepub.com/content/23/3/371.short. DOI: 10.1177/0894439305275911

Harjani, T., Roozenbeek, J., Biddlestone, M., van der Linden, S., Stuart, A., Iwahara, M., Piri, B., Xu, R., Goldberg, B., Graham, M. (2022). A practical guide to prebunking misinformation.

Harris, T. (2017, Apr). *How a handful of tech companies control billions of minds every day*. [Video]. TED Conferences. https://www.ted.com/talks/tristan_harris_how_a_handful_of_tech_companies_control_billions_of_minds_every_day

Hasebrink, U., Lampert, C., & Thiel, K. (2019). *Online-Erfahrungen von 9- bis 17-Jährigen: Ergebnisse der EU Kids Online-Befragung in Deutschland 2019. eukidsonline.net*. Verlag Hans-Bredow-Institut. https://epub.sub.uni-hamburg.de/epub/volltexte/2022/132004/

Hattikar, A. A., & Bagi, J. S. (2024). The Influence of social media on Education, International Journal of Innovative Science and Research Technology, Volume 9, Issue 8, August – 2024, ISSN No: -2456-2165, https://doi.org/, International Journal of Innovative Science and Research Technology, Volume 9, Issue 8, August – 2024, ISSN No: -2456-2165, https://doi.org/,DOI: 10.38124/ijisrt/IJISRT

Haythornthwaite, C. (2002). Strong, Weak, and Latent Ties and the Impact of New Media. *The Information Society, 18*(5), 385–401. DOI: 10.1080/01972240290108195

Head, A., Wihbey, J., Metaxas, P., MacMillan, M., & Cohen, D. (2018). *How students engage with news: Five takeaways for educators, journalists, and librarians*. Project Information Literacy. https://eric.ed.gov/?id=ED591129

Heikkila, M. (2023, Feb 22). How OpenAI is trying to make ChatGPT safer and less biased. *MIT Technology Review*, www.technologyreview.com/2023/02/21/1068893/how-openai-is-trying-to-make-chatgpt-safer-and-less-biased/

Hellsten, L. M., Crespi, I., Hendry, B., & Fermani, A. (2021). Extending the Current teorization on Cyberbullying: Importance of Including Socio-Psychological Perspectives. *Italian Journal of Sociology of Education, 13*(3), 85–110.

Henry, N. B. (1954). *Mass Media and Education. Fifty-Third Yearbook of NSSE (National Society For The Study Of Education), Part II*. University of Chicago Press.

Hepp, A. (2016). Kommunikations- und Medienwissenschaft in datengetriebenen Zeiten. *Publizistik, 61*(3), 225–246. DOI: 10.1007/s11616-016-0263-y

Hepp, A. (2018). Von der Mediatisierung zur tiefgreifenden Mediatisierung. In Reichertz, J., & Bettmann, R. (Eds.), *Kommunikation – Medien – Konstruktion* (pp. 27–45). Springer Fachmedien Wiesbaden., DOI: 10.1007/978-3-658-21204-9_2

Hepp, A., Berg, M., & Roitsch, C. (2014). *Mediatisierte Welten der Vergemeinschaftung*. Springer Fachmedien Wiesbaden., DOI: 10.1007/978-3-658-02425-3

Higdon, J. (2020). *The anatomy of fake news: A critical news literacy education*. Routledge.

Hinduja, S., & Patchin, J. W. (2010). Bullying, cyberbullying, and suicide. *Archives of Suicide Research, 14*(3), 206–221. DOI: 10.1080/13811118.2010.494133 PMID: 20658375

Hitchcock, D. (2024). Critical thinking. In Zalta, E. N., & Nodelman, U. (Eds.), *The Stanford encyclopedia of philosophy* (Summer 2024 Edition)., https://plato.stanford.edu/archives/sum2024/entries/critical-thinking/

Hobbs, R. (2010). *Digital and Media Literacy: A Plan of Action. A White Paper on the Digital and Media Literacy Recommendations of the Knight Commission on the Information Needs of Communities in a Democracy*. Aspen Institute. 1 Dupont Circle NW Suite 700, Washington, DC 20036.

Hobbs, R. (2019). Media literacy foundations. *The international encyclopedia of media literacy*, 1-19.

Hobbs, R. (2021). *Gallery of grandparents of media literacy*. Grandparents of Media Literacy. https://grandparentsofmedialiteracy.com/

Hobbs, R. (2025, Apr 27). How Media Literacy Education for Adults Advances Active Listening & Intellectual Humility. American Educational Research Association Annual Conference. Denver. https://aera25-aera.ipostersessions.com/default.aspx?s=85-AA-15-20-82-7B-5D-E2-EA-64-C6-4D-F3-53-7C-6C

Hobbs, R. (1998). The seven great debates in the media literacy movement. *Journal of Communication, 48*(1), 6–32. DOI: 10.1111/j.1460-2466.1998.tb02734.x

Hobbs, R. (2007). *Reading the media: Media literacy in high school English*. Teachers College Press.

Hobbs, R. (2008). Debates and challenges facing new literacies in the 21st century. *International Handbook of Children, Media and Culture. Sage (Atlanta, Ga.)*, 431–447.

Hobbs, R. (2010). *Digital and media literacy: A plan of action*. Aspen Institute.

Hobbs, R. (2011). *Digital and Media Literacy: Connecting Culture and Classroom*. Corwin.

Hobbs, R. (2017). *Media literacy in the digital age*. Wiley-Blackwell.

Hobbs, R. (2021). *Media literacy in action: Questioning the media*. Rowman & Littlefield.

Hobbs, R. (2024). *Media Literacy in Action: Questioning the Media*. Rowman & Littlefield.

Hobbs, R., & Frost, R. (2021). *Mind over media: Propaganda education for a digital age*. W.W. Norton & Hobbs, R., & Frost, R. (2003). Measuring the acquisition of media-literacy skills. [Company.]. *Reading Research Quarterly*, *38*(3), 330–355. DOI: 10.1598/RRQ.38.3.2

Hobbs, R., & Jensen, A. (2009). The Past, Present, and Future of Media Literacy Education. *The Journal of Media Literacy Education*, *1*, 1–11. DOI: 10.23860/jmle-1-1-1

Hodges, C., & Ocak, C. (2023, Aug 30). Integrating generative AI into higher education: Considerations. *Educause Review*. https://er.educause.edu/articles/2023/8/integrating-generative-ai-into-higher-education-considerations

Hodge, S. D.Jr. (2021). Don't always believe what you see: Shallowfake and deepfake media has altered the perception of reality. *Hofstra Law Review*, *50*, 51.

Hoechsmann, M., Kumaran, B., & McKee, M. (2024, Jan). *What conspiracy? Media education in/and the mirror world* [Video]. Media Education Lab webinar. https://youtu.be/xyKSST3CRP0?si=jKbkU2GBnVOhjnZP

Hoechsmann, M., & Poyntz, S. (2012). *Media literacies: A critical introduction*. Blackwell Publishing. DOI: 10.1002/9781444344158

Hoes, E., Aitken, B., Zhang, J., Gackowski, T., & Wojcieszak, M. (2024). Prominent misinformation interventions reduce misperceptions but increase skepticism. *Nature Human Behaviour*, *8*(11), 1545–1553. DOI: 10.1038/s41562-024-01884-x PMID: 38858544

Hoffmann, D. (2018). Kinder, Jugend und Medien. In Lange, A., Reiter, H., Schutter, S., & Steiner, C. (Eds.), *Handbuch Kindheits- und Jugendsoziologie* (pp. 681–692). Springer Fachmedien Wiesbaden., DOI: 10.1007/978-3-658-04207-3_59

Holt, T. J., & Bossler, A. M. (2014). An assessment of the current state of cybercrime scholarship. *Deviant Behavior*, *35*(1), 20–40. DOI: 10.1080/01639625.2013.822209

Hopkins, W. W. (1996). The Supreme Court defines the marketplace of ideas. *Journalism & Mass Communication Quarterly*, *73*(1), 40–52. DOI: 10.1177/107769909607300105

Horn, S., & Veermans, K. (2019). Critical thinking efficacy and transfer skills defend against 'fake news' at an international school in Finland. *Journal of Research in International Education*, *18*(1), 23–41. DOI: 10.1177/1475240919830003

Hossain, M., Leminen, S., & Westerlund, M. (2018). A systematic review of living lab literature. *Journal of Cleaner Production*, *213*, 976–988. DOI: 10.1016/j.jclepro.2018.12.257

Howard, P. N., & Hussain, M. M. (2013). *Democracy's fourth wave? Digital media and the Arab Spring*. Oxford University Press. DOI: 10.1093/acprof:oso/9780199936953.001.0001

Howenstine, E. (1987). Environmental reporting: Shift from 1970 to 1982. *The Journalism Quarterly*, *64*(4), 842–846. DOI: 10.1177/107769908706400425

Howe, P., Mildenberger, M., Marlon, J., & Leiserowitz, A. (2015). Geographic variation in opinions on climate change at state and local scales in the USA. *Nature Climate Change*, *5*(6), 596–603. DOI: 10.1038/nclimate2583

Hugger, K.-U. (2014). Digitale Jugendkulturen. In Hugger, K.-U. (Ed.), *Digitale Jugendkulturen* (pp. 11–28). Springer Fachmedien Wiesbaden., DOI: 10.1007/978-3-531-19070-9_1

Hulbert, D. (2023). Tree-of-thought prompting to boost ChatGPT's reasoning. *GitHub*. DOI: 10.5281/zenodo.10323452

Human Rights Committee. (2011). *General comment no. 34 on Article 19: Freedoms of opinion and expression*. United Nations Office of the High Commissioner for Human Rights. https://www.ohchr.org/en/documents/general-comments-and-recommendations/general-comment-no34-article-19-freedoms-opinion-and

Hurrelmann, K., & Bauer, U. (2015). *Einführung in die Sozialisationstheorie: Das Modell der produktiven Realitätsverarbeitung* (9th ed.). Beltz Verlag.

Hussin, A. A. (2018). Education 4.0 made simple: Ideas for teaching. *International Journal of Education and Literacy Studies*, *6*(3), 92–98. DOI: 10.7575/aiac.ijels.v.6n.3p.92

Hwang, H., & Kim, K.-O. (2015). Social media as a tool for social movements: The effect of social media use and social capital on intention to participate in social movements. *International Journal of Consumer Studies*, *39*(5), 478–488. DOI: 10.1111/ijcs.12221

IBM. (n.d.). What is an AI model? *IBM.com.* https://www.ibm.com/topics/ai-model

Ibrahim, Y. (n.d.). *The new risk communities: Social networking sites and risk.* University of Brighton.

Idso, C., Carter, R., & Singer, F. (2016). *Why scientists disagree about global warming: The NIPCC report on scientific consensus* (2nd ed.). The Heartland Institute.

Ilangovan, A., Beswick, P. R., & Sarojini, B. (2021). The Impact of YouTube Personalization Algorithm on User-Generated Content Creation in India. *Proceedings of the 2021 2nd International Conference on Communication, Computing and Industry 4.0, C2I4 2021*. DOI: 10.1109/C2I454156.2021.9689393

Intergovernmental Panel on Climate Change. (2020). *About the IPCC.* https://www.ipcc.ch/about/

Ito, M., Horst, H. A., Bittanti, M., Boyd, D., Herr-Stephenson, B., Lange, P. G., & Robinson, L. (2009). *Living and learning with new media: Summary of findings from the Digital Youth Project.* MIT Press. DOI: 10.7551/mitpress/8519.001.0001

Ivanov, D. (2023). The industry 5.0 framework: Viability-based integration of the resilience, sustainability, and human-centricity perspectives. *International Journal of Production Research*, *61*(5), 1683–1695. DOI: 10.1080/00207543.2022.2118892

Iyengar, S., & Massey, D. (2018). Scientific communication in a post-truth society. *Proceedings of the National Academy of Sciences of the United States of America*, *116*(16), 7656–7661. DOI: 10.1073/pnas.1805868115 PMID: 30478050

Jackson, M. C. (2021). Artificial intelligence & algorithmic bias: The issues with technology reflecting history & humans. *Journal of Business & Technology Law.*, *16*(2), 299–316.

Jaffar, B. A., Riaz, S., & Mushtaq, A. (2019). Living in a moment: Impact of TicTok on influencing younger generation into micro-fame. *Journal of Content. Community and Communication*, *10*(5), 187–194. DOI: 10.31620/JCCC.12.19/19

Jaiswal, A., Porwal, P., Singh, A., Kumari, P., Bhalla, P., & Sachdeva, N. (2023). Empirical Analysis of Depression Detection Using Deep Learning on Twitter. In *Lecture Notes in Networks and Systems* (Vol. 787). LNNS., DOI: 10.1007/978-981-99-6550-2_23

Jandura, O., Wendelin, M., Adolf, M., & Wimmer, J. (Eds.). (2017). *Medien - Kultur - Kommunikation. Zwischen Integration und Diversifikation: Medien und gesellschaftlicher Zusammenhalt im digitalen Zeitalter.* Springer VS. DOI: 10.1007/978-3-658-15031-0

Jang, Y.-T., & Chiang, I.-T. (2024). Incorporating desire and persistence into understanding Gen Z learners' continuance intention toward using Youtube for learning in digital learning context. *Education and Information Technologies*, *29*(8), 10043–10068. DOI: 10.1007/s10639-023-12202-9

Jarren, O. (2017). Strukturwandel der Öffentlichkeit unter digitalen Bedingungen. *Frankfurter Hefte*, (9), 46–50.

Jarzyna, C. L. (2021). Parasocial Interaction, the COVID-19 Quarantine, and Digital Age Media. *Human Arenas*, *4*(3), 413–429. DOI: 10.1007/s42087-020-00156-0

Jebara, T. (2004). Generative versus discriminative learning. In Jabara, T. (Ed.), *Machine Learning. The International Series in Engineering and Computer Science. 755*. Springer., DOI: 10.1007/978-1-4419-9011-2_2

Jeong, M., Bae, R. E., & Kim, H. K. (2023). Psychological mechanisms of misinformation endorsement. *Journal of Health Psychology*, *28*(2), 179–196.

Jiao, W., Chang, A., Ho, M., Lu, Q., Liu, M. T., & Schulz, P. J. (2023). Predicting and Empowering Health for Generation Z by Comparing Health Information Seeking and Digital Health Literacy: Cross-Sectional Questionnaire Study. *Journal of Medical Internet Research*, *25*, e47595. Advance online publication. DOI: 10.2196/47595 PMID: 37902832

Jin, C.-H. (2015). The role of Facebook users' self-systems in generating social relationships and social capital effects. *New Media & Society*, *17*(4), 501–519. DOI: 10.1177/1461444813506977

Johnson, M. (2023). Defamation in the digital age: Legal and ethical implications. [https]. *Communication Law and Policy*, *28*(2), 89–110.

Jolls, T., & Wilson, C. (2014). The core concepts: Fundamental to media literacy yesterday, today and tomorrow. *The Journal of Media Literacy Education*, *6*(2), 68–78. DOI: 10.23860/jmle-6-2-6

Jones-Jang, S.M., Mortensen & T., Liu, J. (2021). Does Media Literacy Help Identification of Fake News? Information Literacy Helps, but Other Literacies Don't. *American Behavioral Scientist. 65(*2), 371-388. DOI: 10.1177/0002764219869406

Journalist's Resource. (2013, Aug 28). *The decline of big media, 1980s-2000s: Key lessons and trends.* Journalist's resource. https://journalistsresource.org/media/covering-america-journalism-professor-christopher-daly/

Joyce, K., & Cruz, T. M. (2024). A Sociology of Artificial Intelligence: Inequalities, Power, and Data Justice. *Socius: Sociological Research for a Dynamic World, 10*, 23780231241275393. DOI: 10.1177/23780231241275393

Joyce, K., Smith-Doerr, L., Alegria, S., Bell, S., Cruz, T. M., Hoffman, S. G., Noble, S., & Shestakofsky, B. (2021). Toward a Sociology of Artificial Intelligence: A Call for Research on Inequalities and Structural Change. *Socius: Sociological Research for a Dynamic World, 7*, 2378023121999581. DOI: 10.1177/2378023121999581

Jung, A. K., Stieglitz, S., Kissmer, T., Mirbabaie, M., & Kroll, T. (2022). Click me…! The influence of clickbait on user engagement in social media and the role of digital nudging. *PLoS One*, *17*(6), e0266743. DOI: 10.1371/journal.pone.0266743 PMID: 35767538

Kahan, D. M. (2013). Ideology, motivated reasoning, and cognitive reflection. *Judgment and Decision Making*, *8*(4), 407–424. DOI: 10.1017/S1930297500005271

Kalemi (2024). Publer, https: publer.io/blog/social-media-challenges

Kammerl, R., & Kramer, M. (2016). The changing media environment and its impact on socialization processes in families. *Studies in Communication Sciences*, *16*(1), 21–27. DOI: 10.1016/j.scoms.2016.04.004

Kanchan, S., & Gaidhane, A. (2023). *Social media and Its Impact on Public Health: A Narrative*. Cureus, Open Access Review Article Review., DOI: 10.7759/cureus.33737

Kang, M., & Kang, M. (2022). Daily Behavior of Generation Z Using a Smart Phone App for Content Recommendation based on Context Awareness. *Archives of Design Research, 35*(1), 277–295. DOI: 10.15187/adr.2022.02.35.1.277

Kapantai, E., Christopoulou, A., Berberidis, C., & Peristeras, V. (2021). A systematic literature review on disinformation: Toward a unified taxonomical framework. *New Media & Society*, *23*(5), 1301–1326. DOI: 10.1177/1461444820959296

Kaplan, A. M., & Haenlein, M. (2010). Users of the world, unite! The challenges and opportunities of social media. *Business Horizons*, *53*(1), 59–68. DOI: 10.1016/j.bushor.2009.09.003

Kaplún, M. (1998). *Una pedagogía de la comunicación*. Ediciones de la Torre.

Karim, F., Oyewande, A. A., Abdalla, L. F., Ehsanullah, R. C., & Khan, S. (2020). Social media use and its connection to mental26 mental health outcomes: A systematic review. *Frontiers in Psychiatry, 11*, 573326. DOI: 10.3389/fpsyt.202sexuality2020.573326://

Kariya, R., & Vidani, J. (2024). The Positive Aspects of Social media Use: Examining Social Support and Mental health Benefits, Journal of Advanced Research in Economics and Business Management, Volume 7, Print Issue 1 - 2024, Pg. No. 37-43

Kasneci, E., Sessler, K., Küchemann, S., Bannert, M., Dementieva, D., Fischer, F., Gasser, U., Groh, G., Günnemann, S., Hüllermeier, E., Krusche, S., Kutyniok, G., Michaeli, T., Nerdel, C., Pfeffer, J., Poquet, O., Sailer, M., Schmidt, A., Seidel, T., & Kasneci, G. (2023). ChatGPT for good? on opportunities and challenges of large language models for education. *Learning and Individual Differences, 103*, 102274. DOI: 10.1016/j.lindif.2023.102274

Kellems, R. O., Steinburg, M., Bahr, D., & Hansen, B. D. (2024). Using Video Modeling Via iPads to Teach Multiplication to Struggling Learners. *Journal of Special Education Technology, 39*(1), 67–78. DOI: 10.1177/01626434231180584

Kellner, D., & Share, J. (2007). Critical Media Literacy, Democracy, and the Reconstruction of Education. In Macedo, D., & Steinberg, S. R. (Eds.), *Media Literacy: A Reader* (pp. 3–23). Peter Lang Publishing.

Kellner, D., & Share, J. (2007). Critical media literacy: Crucial policy choices for a twenty-first-century democracy. *Policy Futures in Education, 5*(1), 59–69. DOI: 10.2304/pfie.2007.5.1.59

Kelly, K., & Donohew, L. (1999). Media and primary socialization theory. *Substance Use & Misuse, 34*(7), 1033–1045. DOI: 10.3109/10826089909039395 PMID: 10359221

Kemper, J. (2023). Glitch, the Post-digital Aesthetic of Failure and Twenty-First-Century Media. *European Journal of Cultural Studies, 26*(1), 47–63. DOI: 10.1177/13675494211060537

Kendall, A., & McDougall, J. (2012). Critical media literacy after the media. [Alfabetización mediática crítica en la postmodernidad]. Comunicar. *Revista Científica de Comunicación y Educación, 19*(38), 21–29. DOI: 10.3916/C38-2012-02-02

Kertysova, K. (2018). Artificial Intelligence and Disinformation. *Security And Human Rights, 29*(1–4), 55–81. DOI: 10.1163/18750230-02901005

Kessler, M. (2020). A text analysis and gatekeepers' perspectives of a promotional genre: Understanding the rhetoric of Fulbright grant statements. *English for Specific Purposes, 60*, 182–192. DOI: 10.1016/j.esp.2020.07.003

Khalaf, A. M., Alubied, A. A., Khalaf, A. M., & Rifaey, A. A. (2023). An Impact of social media on the Mental health of Adolescents and Young adults. *Systematic Reviews*. DOI: 10.7759/cureus.42990 PMID: 37671234

Kilbourne, J., & Jhally, S. (Director). (1979). *Killing us softly: Advertising's image of women* [motion picture]. Media Education Foundation.

Kim, D. (2025). Selling Otherness on YouTube: Digital inter-Asian Orientalism and YouTube monetization system. *International Journal of Cultural Studies, 28*(1), 39–55. DOI: 10.1177/13678779241240780

Kim, S., & Kim, H.-C. (2021). The benefits of youtube in learning english as a second language: A qualitative investigation of korean freshman students' experiences and perspectives in the U.S. *Sustainability (Basel), 13*(13), 7365. Advance online publication. DOI: 10.3390/su13137365

Kim, T. W., & Mejia, S. (2019). From Artificial Intelligence to Artificial Wisdom: What Socrates Teaches Us. *Computer, 52*(10), 70–74. DOI: 10.1109/MC.2019.2929723

Kingsley, S., Sinha, P., Wang, C., Eslami, M., & Hong, J. I. (2022). 'give Everybody [.] a Little Bit More Equity': Content Creator Perspectives and Responses to the Algorithmic Demonetization of Content Associated with Disadvantaged Groups. *Proceedings of the ACM on Human-Computer Interaction, 6*(CSCW2). DOI: 10.1145/3555149

Klausen, J. (2015). Tweeting the Jihad: Social media networks of Western foreign fighters in Syria and Iraq. *Studies in Conflict and Terrorism, 38*(1), 1–22. DOI: 10.1080/1057610X.2014.974948

Klein, N. (2024). *Doppelganger: A trip into the mirror world*. Random House.

Koc, M., & Barut, E. (2016). Development and validation of New Media Literacy Scale (NMLS) for university students. *Computers in Human Behavior, 63*, 834–843. DOI: 10.1016/j.chb.2016.06.035

Koltay, T. (2011). The media and the literacies: Media literacy, information literacy, digital literacy. *Media Culture & Society, 33*(2), 211–221. DOI: 10.1177/0163443710393382

Koppel, L., Robertson, C. E., Doell, K. C., Javeed, A. M., Rasmussen, J., Rathje, S., Vlasceanu, M., & Van Bavel, J. J. (2023). Individual-level solutions may support system-level change if they are internalized as part of one's social identity. *Behavioral and Brain Sciences*, *46*, e165. Advance online publication. DOI: 10.1017/S0140525X2300105X PMID: 37646255

Koutsantoni, D. (2009). Persuading sponsors and securing funding: Rhetorical patterns in grant proposals. *Academic Writing: At the Interface of Corpus and Discourse,* 37–57.

Kovach, B., & Rosenstiel, T. (2001). *The elements of journalism: What newspeople should know and the public should expect.* Three Rivers Press.

Kowalski, R. M., Giumetti, G. W., Schroeder, A. N., & Lattanner, M. R. (2014). Bullying in the digital age: A critical review and meta-analysis of cyberbullying research among youth. *Psychological Bulletin*, *140*(4), 1073–1137. DOI: 10.1037/a0035618 PMID: 24512111

Kozyreva, A., Lewandowsky, S., & Hertwig, R. (2020). Citizens versus the internet: Confronting digital challenges with cognitive tools. *Psychological Science in the Public Interest*, *21*(3), 103–156. DOI: 10.1177/1529100620946707 PMID: 33325331

Kozyreva, A., Lorenz-Spreen, P., Herzog, S. M., Ecker, U. K. H., Lewandowsky, S., Hertwig, R., Ali, A., Bak-Coleman, J., Barzilai, S., Basol, M., Berinsky, A. J., Betsch, C., Cook, J., Fazio, L. K., Geers, M., Guess, A. M., Huang, H., Larreguy, H., Maertens, R., & Wineburg, S. (2024). Toolbox of individual-level interventions against online misinformation. *Nature Human Behaviour*, *8*(6), 1044–1052. DOI: 10.1038/s41562-024-01881-0 PMID: 38740990

Kreps, S., McCain, R. M., & Brundage, M. (2022). All the news that's fit to fabricate: AI-generated text as a tool of media misinformation. *Journal of Experimental Political Science*, *9*(1), 104–117. DOI: 10.1017/XPS.2020.37

Kross, E., Verduyn, P., Demiralp, E., Park, J., Lee, D. S., Lin, N., Shablack, H., Jonides, J., & Ybarra, O. (2013). Facebook use predicts declines in subjective well-being in young adults. *PLoS One*, *8*(8), e69841. DOI: 10.1371/journal.pone.0069841 PMID: 23967061

Kruger, S., Walper, S., & Rauschenbach, T. (Eds.). (2021). *Aufwachsen in Deutschland 2019: Alltagswelten von Kindern, Jugendlichen und Familien: AID:A 2019.* wbv. https://elibrary.utb.de/doi/book/10.3278/9783763966325

Kruger, J., & Dunning, D. (1999). Unskilled and unaware of it: How difficulties in recognizing one's own incompetence lead to inflated self-assessments. *Journal of Personality and Social Psychology*, *77*(6), 1121–1134. DOI: 10.1037/0022-3514.77.6.1121 PMID: 10626367

Ksiazek, T. B. (2018). Commenting on the News. *Journalism Studies*, *19*(5), 650–673. DOI: 10.1080/1461670X.2016.1209977

Kubey, R., & Baker, F. (1999). Has media literacy found a curricular foothold. *Education Week*, *19*(9), 38.

Kübler, H.-D. (2001). Neue Medien – neues Lernen? Perspektiven und Bedingungen des Lernens mit „Neuen Medien". In K.-D. Felsmann (Ed.), *Neue Medien - neues Lernen? Erweiterte Dokumentation 2000; Buckower Mediengespräche (4)* (pp. 17–36). kopaed.

Kuchhal, D., & Li, F. (2022). A View into YouTube View Fraud. *WWW 2022 - Proceedings of the ACM Web Conference 2022*, 555–563. DOI: 10.1145/3485447.3512216

Ku, K. Y. L., & Ho, I. T. (2010). Dispositional factors predicting Chinese students' critical thinking performance. *Personality and Individual Differences*, *48*(1), 54–58. DOI: 10.1016/j.paid.2009.08.015

Kumar, P., & Mathew, A. O. (2023). EXAMINING CUSTOMER SATISFACTION AND BRAND LOYALTY OF GENERATION Z CUSTOMERS IN OTT MEDIA SERVICES. *Proceedings of the International Conferences on E-Society 2023, ES 2023 and Mobile Learning 2023, ML 2023*, 235–242.

Kumar, L., & Singh, D. K. (2023). A comprehensive survey on generative adversarial networks used for synthesizing multimedia content. *Multimedia Tools and Applications*, *82*(26), 40585–40624. DOI: 10.1007/s11042-023-15138-x

Kumar, L., & Singh, D. K. (2024). A novel aspect of automatic vlog content creation using generative modeling approaches. *Digital Signal Processing*, *148*, 104462. DOI: 10.1016/j.dsp.2024.104462

Kumar, L., & Singh, D. K. (2024). Diversified realistic face image generation GAN for human subjects in multimedia content creation. *Computer Animation and Virtual Worlds*, *35*(2), e2232. DOI: 10.1002/cav.2232

Kumar, L., Singh, D. K., & Ansari, M. A. (2024). Role of video content generation in education systems using generative AI. In *Integrating Generative AI in Education to Achieve Sustainable Development Goals* (pp. 354–368). IGI Global. DOI: 10.4018/979-8-3693-2440-0.ch019

Kumkar, N. C. (2022). *Alternative Fakten: Zur Praxis der kommunikativen Erkenntnisverweigerung* (Originalausgabe). Suhrkamp Verlag. https://www.content-select.com/index.php?id=bib_view&ean=9783518774731

Kurtz, T. (2010). Der Kompetenzbegriff in der Soziologie. In *Soziologie der Kompetenz* (pp. 7–25). VS Verlag für Sozialwissenschaften., DOI: 10.1007/978-3-531-91951-5_1

Kuss, D. J., & Griffiths, M. D. (2017). Social networking sites and addiction: Ten lessons learned. *International Journal of Environmental Research and Public Health, 14*(3), 3–11. DOI: 10.3390/ijerph14030311 PMID: 28304359

Kwek, A., Peh, L., Tan, J., & Lee, J. X. (2023). Distractions, analytical thinking and falling for fake news: A survey of psychological factors. *Humanities & Social Sciences Communications, 10*(1), 319. DOI: 10.1057/s41599-023-01813-9 PMID: 37333884

Landry, N., & Fastrez, P. (2023). *Media Literacy and Media Education Research Methods: A Handbook*. Routledge.

Lange, P. G. (2021). Conceptualizing communities of truth on YouTube. *Explorations in Media Ecology, 20*(1), 33–54. DOI: 10.1386/eme_00071_1

Lantian, A., Bagneux, V., Delouvée, S., & Gauvrit, N. (2021). Maybe a free thinker but not a critical one: High conspiracy belief is associated with low critical thinking ability. *Applied Cognitive Psychology, 35*(3), 674–684. DOI: 10.1002/acp.3790

Laughey, D. (2010). *Key themes in media theory*. Open University Press.

Lázaro-Cantabrana, J. L., Gisbert-Cervera, M., & Silva-Quiroz, J. E. (2018). Una rúbrica para evaluar la competencia digital del profesor universitario en el contexto latinoamericano. *Edutec. Revista Electrónica de Tecnología Educativa*, (63), 1–14.

LeAnne Basinger, K., Alvarado, D., Ortega, A. V., Hartless, D. G., Lahijanian, B., & Alvarado, M. M. (2021). Creating ACTIVE Learning in an Online Environment. *ASEE Annual Conference and Exposition, Conference Proceedings*. DOI: 10.18260/1-2--36870

Lee, C. S., Yeo, R. Q. Y., Zhang, S., Goh, D. H.-L., Ang, R. P., & Ng, B. (2023). Gen Z Transitions to University: A Preliminary Study on Everyday Information-Seeking Practices. In *Lecture Notes in Computer Science (including subseries Lecture Notes in Artificial Intelligence and Lecture Notes in Bioinformatics): Vol. 14457 LNCS*. DOI: 10.1007/978-981-99-8085-7_23

Leedom, F. (2024, Feb 29). "Building media literacy into school curriculums worldwide". News Decoder. https://news-decoder.com/building-media-literacy-into-school-curriculums-worldwide/

Lee, H., & Kim, S. (2022). Social media and reputational harm: The role of online slander. *Cyberpsychology, Behavior, and Social Networking*, *25*(4), 201–209. DOI: 10.1089/cyber.2021.0156

Lee, S. H. (2014). Digital literacy education for the development of digital literacy. [IJDLDC]. *International Journal of Digital Literacy and Digital Competence*, *5*(3), 29–43. DOI: 10.4018/ijdldc.2014070103

Lee, T., Markowitz, E., Howe, P., Ko, C., & Leiserowitz, A. (2015). Predictors of public climate change awareness and risk perception around the world. *Nature Climate Change*, *5*(11), 1014–1020. DOI: 10.1038/nclimate2728

Le, N. (2019). How do Technology-Enhanced learning tools support critical thinking? *Frontiers in Education*, *4*(126), 126. DOI: 10.3389/feduc.2019.00126

Lester, P.M. (1996). "Digital hegemony: The clash between words and pictures". Speech given during the "Spring Forum" at Middle Tennessee State University, Murfreesboro, Tennessee, reprinted in the Instructor's Manual for Harris and Lester's *Visual Journalism* (2001).

Levenson, J. C., Shensa, A., Sidani, J. E., Colditz, J. B., & Primack, B. A. (2016). The association between social media use and sleep disturbance among young adults. *Preventive Medicine*, *85*, 36–41. DOI: 10.1016/j.ypmed.2016.01.001 PMID: 26791323

Levi, L. (2020). Media literacy beyond the national security frame. *Utah Law Review*, *2020*(4), 941–985.

Lewandowsky, S., Ecker, U. K. H., Seifert, C. M., Schwarz, N., & Cook, J. (2012). Misinformation and its correction: Continued influence and successful debiasing. *Psychological Science in the Public Interest*, *13*(3), 106–131. DOI: 10.1177/1529100612451018 PMID: 26173286

Lewis, J., & Cushion, S. (2009). The thirst to be first: An analysis of breaking news stories and their impact on the quality of 24-hour news coverage in the UK. *Journalism Practice*, *3*(3), 304–318. DOI: 10.1080/17512780902798737

Lewis, P., Perez, E., Piktus, A., Petroni, F., Karpukhin, V., Goyal, N., Küttler, H., Lewis, M., Yih, W.-t., Rocktäschel, T., Riedel, S., & Kiela, D. (2020). Retrieval-augmented generation for knowledge-intensive NLP tasks. *arXiv*. https://arxiv.org/abs/2005.11401.

Li, A. (2024). The Effects of social media on Mental Health: A Study of Young Adults in the United States, *Proceedings of the 2nd International Conference on Interdisciplinary Humanities and Communication Studies*, DOI: DOI: 10.54254/2753-7064/27/20232070

Liebert, R., Sprafkin, J., & Davidson, E. (1982). *The early window: Effects of television on children and youth* (2nd ed.). Pergamon.

Lin, L., Gupta, N., Zhang, Y., Ren, H., Liu, C. H., Ding, F., . . . Hu, S. (2024). Detecting multimedia generated by large AI models: A survey. *arXiv preprint arXiv:2402.00045*. DOI: 10.36227/techrxiv.170723324.44685515/v1

Lin, B.-H., Chung, Y.-J., Cheng, H.-Y., Yen, Y.-T., Li, C.-C., & Cherng, F.-Y. (2024). Understanding the Effects of Short-Form Videos on Sustained Attention. *Conference on Human Factors in Computing Systems - Proceedings*. DOI: 10.1145/3613905.3651018

Lippmann, W. (2020). *Liberty and the news* (p. 47). mediastudies. Press.

Liu, Z. (2023). Cultural bias in large language models: A comprehensive analysis and mitigation strategies. *Journal of Transcultural Communication*, *3*(2), 224–244. DOI: 10.1515/jtc-2023-0019

Livingstone, S. (2005). Media literacy – challenges ahead. London: LSE Research Online. http://eprints.lse.ac.uk/archive/00000551

Livingstone, S. (2004). Media literacy and the challenge of new information and communication technologies. *Communication Review*, *7*(1), 3–15. DOI: 10.1080/10714420490280152

Livingstone, S. (2004). What is media literacy? *Intermedia*, *32*(3), 18–20.

Livingstone, S., & Blum-Ross, A. (2020). *Parenting for a Digital Future: How Hopes and Fears about Technology Shape Children's Lives*. Academic., DOI: 10.1093/oso/9780190874698.001.0001

Livingstone, S., & Haddon, L. (Eds.). (2009). *Kids online: Opportunities and risks for children*. Policy Press.

Loader, B. D., & Mercea, D. (2011). Networking democracy? Social media innovations and participatory politics. *Information Communication and Society*, *14*(6), 757–769. DOI: 10.1080/1369118X.2011.592648

Long, D., & Magerko, B. (2020). What is AI literacy: Competencies and design considerations. *Proceedings of the 2020 CHI conference on human factors in computing systems*. Association for Computing Machinery. https://dl.acm.org/doi/10.1145/3313831.3376727

Lowe, R., & Leike, J. (2022). Aligning language models to follow instructions. OpenAI. https://openai.com/research/instruction-following

Lowe, D., Galhotra, B., & Ahuja, Y. (2019). Unfurling the latest patterns of entertainment consumption by indian audience: A twitter sentiment analysis. *International Journal of Recent Technology and Engineering*, *7*(6), 135–139.

Lu, C., Hu, B., Bao, M. M., Wang, C., Bi, C., & Ju, X. D. (2024). Can Media Literacy Intervention Improve Fake News Credibility Assessment? A Meta-Analysis. *Cyberpsychology, Behavior, and Social Networking*, *27*(4), 240–252. DOI: 10.1089/cyber.2023.0324 PMID: 38484319

Lucchi, N. (2024). ChatGPT: A case study on copyright challenges for generative artificial intelligence systems. *European Journal of Risk Regulation*, *15*(3), 602–624. DOI: 10.1017/err.2023.59

Lull, J. (2002). Superculture for the communication age. In *Culture in the Communication Age* (pp. 142–174). Routledge. DOI: 10.4324/9780203136188-11

Lupton, D. (2016). Digital risk society. In Burgess, A., Alemanno, A., & Zinn, J. (Eds.), *The Routledge handbook of risk studies* (pp. 301–309). Routledge.

Lutzke, L., Drummond, C., Slovic, P., & Árvai, J. (2019). Priming critical thinking: Simple interventions limit the influence of fake news about climate change on Facebook. *Global Environmental Change*, *58*, 101964. DOI: 10.1016/j.gloenvcha.2019.101964

Machete, P., & Turpin, M. (2020). The use of critical thinking to identify fake news: A systematic literature review. In Hattingh, M., Matthee, M., Smuts, H., Pappas, I., Dwivedi, Y. K., & Mäntymäki, M. (Eds.), Lecture Notes in Computer Science: Vol. 12067. *Responsible design, implementation and use of information and communication technology* (pp. 268–286). Springer., DOI: 10.1007/978-3-030-45002-1_20

Mahrt, M. (2019). *Beyond Filter Bubbles and Echo Chambers: The Integrative Potential of the Internet*. Habilitationsschrift (Digital Communication Research 5). https://www.ssoar.info/ssoar/bitstream/handle/document/61606/ssoar-2019-mahrt-Beyond_Filter_Bubbles_and_Echo.pdf?sequence=1&isAllowed=y&lnkname=ssoar-2019-mahrt-Beyond_Filter_Bubbles_and_Echo.pdf DOI: 10.17174/dcr.v5.0

Main, P. (2022, Jan 17). *Cognitive Load Theory: A teacher's guide*. Retrieved from https://www.structural-learning.com/post/cognitive-load-theory-a-teachers-guide

Malhotra, S., Sharma, K., & Dogra, S. (2021). Introduction: Inhabiting Cyberspace in India: Theory, Perspectives, and Challenges. In *Inhabiting Cyberspace in India: Theory, Perspectives, and Challenges*. DOI: 10.1007/978-981-15-9934-7_1

Malhotra, S. (2022). The Youtube Companion to Film Education. *Studies in Media and Communication*, *10*(2), 320–334. DOI: 10.11114/smc.v10i2.5748

Malik, A. R., Pratiwi, Y., Andajani, K., Numertayasa, I. W., Suharti, S., & Marzuki, A. D. (2023). Exploring artificial intelligence in academic essay: Higher education student's perspective. *International Journal of Educational Research Open*, *5*, 5. DOI: 10.1016/j.ijedro.2023.100296

Malik, H. M., Lepinkäinen, N., Alvesalo-Kuusi, A., & Viljanen, M. (2022). Social harms in an algorithmic context, *Justice. Power and Resistance*, *5*(3), 193–207. DOI: 10.1332/OYUA8095

Manca, S., & Ranieri, M. (2016). Facebook and the others. Potentials and obstacles of social media for teaching in higher education. *Computers & Education*, *95*, 216–230. DOI: 10.1016/j.compedu.2016.01.012

Mangold, W. G., & Faulds, D. J. (2009). Social media: The new hybrid element of the promotion mix. *Business Horizons*, *52*(4), 357–365. DOI: 10.1016/j.bushor.2009.03.002

Marcos-Vílchez, J. M., Sánchez-Martín, M., & Muñiz-Velázquez, J. A. (2024). Effectiveness of training actions aimed at improving critical thinking in the face of disinformation: A systematic review protocol. *Thinking Skills and Creativity*, *51*, 101474. DOI: 10.1016/j.tsc.2024.101474

Margolin, D. B., Hannak, A., & Weber, I. (2017). Political fact-checking on Twitter: When do corrections have an effect? *Political Communication*, *35*(2), 196–219. DOI: 10.1080/10584609.2017.1334018

Markowitz, D. M. (2019). What words are worth: National Science Foundation grant abstracts indicate award funding. *Journal of Language and Social Psychology*, *38*(3), 264–282. DOI: 10.1177/0261927X18824859

Martel, C., Pennycook, G., & Rand, D. G. (2020). Reliance on emotion promotes belief in fake news. *Cognitive Research: Principles and Implications*, *5*(1), 47. DOI: 10.1186/s41235-020-00252-3 PMID: 33026546

Martel, C., & Rand, D. G. (2024). Fact-checker warning labels are effective even for those who distrust fact-checkers. *Nature Human Behaviour*, *8*(11), 1957–1967. DOI: 10.1038/s41562-024-01973-x PMID: 39223352

Martínez-Sanz, R. (2021). Communication of minor influencers: Measuring their impact in the medium term | La comunicación de los influencers menores de edad: Medición de su impacto en el medio plazo. *Observatorio (OBS*)*, *15*(3), 22–36. DOI: 10.15847/obsOBS15320211739

Martin-Kerry, J., McLean, J., Hopkins, T., Morgan, A., Dunn, L., Walton, R., Golder, S., Allison, T., Cooper, D., Wohland, P., & Prady, S. L. (2023). Characterizing asset-based studies in public health: Development of a framework. *Health Promotion International*, *38*(2). DOI: 10.1093/heapro/daad015 PMID: 36932994

Ma, S. Q., & Leung, L. (2019). The Impacts of Personality Traits, Use Intensity and Features Use of LinkedIn on Bridging Social Capital. *Applied Research in Quality of Life*, *14*(4), 1059–1078. DOI: 10.1007/s11482-018-9635-y

Masterman, L. (1989). *Media Awareness Education: Eighteen Basic Principles.* https://www.medialit.org/reading-room/media-awareness-education-eighteen - basic-principles

Masterman, L. (1985). *Teaching the Media.* Routledge., DOI: 10.4324/9780203359051

Mateus, J. C., Andrada, P., & Quiroz, M. T. (Eds.). (2019). *Media Education in Latin America.* Routledge. DOI: 10.4324/9780429244469

Matos, A. P. M., Vieira, C. C., Amado, J., Pessoa, T., & Martins, M. J. D. (2018). Cyberbullying in Portuguese Schools: Prevalence and Characteristics. *Journal of School Violence*, *17*(1), 123–137. DOI: 10.1080/15388220.2016.1263796

Matveeva, N., Moosally, M., & Willerton, R. (2017). Plain language in the twenty-first century: Introduction to the special issue on plain language. *IEEE Transactions on Professional Communication*, *60*(4), 336–342. DOI: 10.1109/TPC.2017.2759619

Mau, S. (2017). *Das metrische Wir: Über die Quantifizierung des Sozialen* (Erste Auflage, Originalausgabe). *Sonderdruck edition suhrkamp.* Suhrkamp.

Maulik, P. K., Devarapalli, S., Kallakuri, S., Bhattacharya, A., Peiris, D., & Patel, A. (2020). The systematic medical appraisal referral and treatment mental health project: Quasi-experimental study to evaluate a technology-enabled mental health services delivery model implemented in Rural India. *Journal of Medical Internet Research*, *22*(2), e15553. DOI: 10.2196/15553 PMID: 32130125

Maynard, A. D. (2020). How to Succeed as an Academic on YouTube. *Frontiers in Communication*, *5*, 572181. Advance online publication. DOI: 10.3389/fcomm.2020.572181

McCammon, S. (2021, Jan 30). *Combating Misinformation When A Loved One Is Caught In A Web Of Conspiracies*. National Public Radio. https://www.wabe.org/combating-misinformation-when-a-loved-one-is-caught-in-a-web-of-conspiracies/

McCombs, M. (2005). A look at agenda-setting: Past, present and future. *Journalism Studies*, *6*(4), 543–557. DOI: 10.1080/14616700500250438

McCombs, M. E., & Shaw, D. L. (1993). The evolution of agenda-setting research: Twenty-five years in the marketplace of ideas. *Journal of Communication*, *43*(2), 58–67. DOI: 10.1111/j.1460-2466.1993.tb01262.x

McCombs, M., & Shaw, D. (1972). The agenda-setting function of mass media. *Public Opinion Quarterly*, *36*(2), 176–187. https://www.jstor.org/stable/2747787. DOI: 10.1086/267990

McKay, S., & Tenove, C. (2020). Disinformation as a Threat to Deliberative Democracy. *Political Research Quarterly*, *74*(3), 703–717. DOI: 10.1177/1065912920938143

McLuhan, M. (1994). *Understanding media (original work published in 1964)*. MIT Press. Medialiteracynow.org.

McLuhan, M. (1964). *Understanding Media: The Extensions of Man*. Gingko Press.

McLuhan, M. (1964/2002). *Understanding media: The extensions of man*. MIT Press.

McRoberts, S., Bonsignore, E., Peyton, T., & Yarosh, S. (2016). 'Do it for the viewers!' Audience engagement behaviors of young YouTubers. *Proceedings of IDC 2016 - The 15th International Conference on Interaction Design and Children*, 334–343. DOI: 10.1145/2930674.2930676

Mediawijs. (2023, 16 May). What is the Media Literacy Competency Model? https://www.mediawijs.be/en/competentiemodel

Medienanstalten, D. (2023). *Mediengewichtungsstudie 2023-II*. https://www.die-medienanstalten.de/forschung/mediengewichtungsstudie/

Medienpädagogischer Forschungsverbund Südwest. (2024). *JIM 2024: Jugend, Information, Medien Basisuntersuchung zum Medienumgang 12- bis 19-Jähriger in Deutschland*. https://mpfs.de/app/uploads/2024/11/JIM_2024_PDF_barrierearm.pdf

Mehta, S. (2020). Localization, diversification and heterogeneity: Understanding the linguistic and cultural logics of Indian new media. *International Journal of Cultural Studies, 23*(1), 102–120. DOI: 10.1177/1367877919880304

Meiklejohn, A. (1961). The First Amendment is an absolute. *The Supreme Court Review, 1961*, 245–266. DOI: 10.1086/scr.1961.3108719

Mellman, L., Williams, M. K., & Slykhuis, D. A. (2021). Using generation Z's learning approaches to create meaningful online learning. In *Handbook of Research on Transforming Teachers' Online Pedagogical Reasoning for Engaging K-12 Students in Virtual Learning*. DOI: 10.4018/978-1-7998-7222-1.ch008

Merica, D. (2024, Aug 13). *Classes across the country help seniors interact with a world altered by AI.* AP News. https://apnews.com/article/seniors-artificial-intelligence-deepfake-education-classes-bc30958c273af7c79bfe77d321617738

Messaris, P. (1994). *Visual literacy: image, mind, and Reality.* Westview Press, Inc.

Messaris, P. (1998). Visual aspects of media literacy. *Journal of Communication, 48*(1), 70–81. DOI: 10.1111/j.1460-2466.1998.tb02738.x

Miao, F., & Holmes, W. (2023). *Guidance for generative AI in education and research.* UNESCO. https://unesdoc.unesco.org/ark:/48223/pf0000386693

Microsoft. (2023). Introduction to prompt engineering. *Microsoft Azure AI Services.* https://learn.microsoft.com/en-us/azure/cognitive-services/openai/concepts/prompt-engineering

Mill, J. S. (2002). *The basic writings of John Stuart Mill.* Penguin Random House.

Mirsky, Y., & Lee, W. (2021). The creation and detection of deepfakes: A survey. *ACM Computing Surveys, 54*(1), 1–41. DOI: 10.1145/3425780

Misnevs, B. (2023). Socratic Method for Prompt Engineering – New Teching Desing. *STEP into the FUTURE, 18*(2), 10–11.

Mohammad, W. (2020). Traditional media versus social media: challenges and opportunities, Technium Vol. 4, No. 10, pp. 145-160, ISSN: 2668-778X, Marwan Al-Quran International Media Cultural Work (M.A), Hochschule Darmstadt, University of Applied Sciences.

Mölders, M. (2023). Das umgelenkte Publikum? In Muhle, F., Sutter, T., & Wehner, J. (Eds.), *Das sichtbare Publikum?* (pp. 145–166). Springer Fachmedien Wiesbaden., DOI: 10.1007/978-3-658-41172-5_6

Moran, M. (2010). The reasonable person: A conceptual biography in comparative perspective. *Lewis & Clark Law Review*, *14*, 1233–1283.

Moravec, V., Hynek, N., Skare, M., Gavurova, B., & Polishchuk, V. (2025). Algorithmic personalization: A study of knowledge gaps and digital media literacy. *Humanities & Social Sciences Communications*, *12*(341), 341. DOI: 10.1057/s41599-025-04593-6

Morris, L. (2017). Moving beyond critical thinking to critical dialogue. *Innovative Higher Education*, *42*(5-6), 377–378. DOI: 10.1007/s10755-017-9413-z

Morrison, D. R. (Ed.). (2011). *The Cambridge companion to Socrates*. Cambridge University Press.

Moser, H. (2010). *Einführung in die Medienpädagogik: Aufwachsen im Medienzeitalter* (5., durchgesehene und erweiterte Auflage). *Lehrbuch*. VS Verlag für Sozialwissenschaften.

Mosier, K. E. (2022). Deconstructing the art of grantsmanship: The roles of the storyteller, grant writer, typesetter, proofreader, accountant and reviewer. *The Journal of Research Administration*, *53*(1), 93–121.

Moss, S. (2022). The Prevalence of Artificial Intelligence, Surveillance Capitalism, Disinformation, and Biased Algorithms Amplify the Need for Critical Skills Applied to Media. *International Council For Media Literacy: Bridging Academia to Action* (online journal). https://ic4ml.org/journal-article/the-prevalence-of-artificial-intelligence-surveillance-capitalism-disinformation-and-biased-algorithms-amplify-the-need-for-critical-skills-applied-to-media/

Mubarak, F., & Suomi, R. (2022). Elderly forgotten? Digital exclusion in the information age and the rising grey digital divide. *Inquiry : a Journal of Medical Care Organization, Provision and Financing*, *59*, 00469580221096272. DOI: 10.1177/00469580221096272 PMID: 35471138

Mundt, M., Ross, K., & Burnett, C. M. (2018). Scaling social movements through social media: The case of Black Lives Matter. *Social Media + Society*, *4*(4), 1–12. DOI: 10.1177/2056305118807911

Mura, G., & Diamantini, D. (2013). Cyberbullying among colombian students: An exploratory investigation | El ciberacoso entre los estudiantes de colombia: Una investigación exploratoria. *European Journal of Investigation in Health, Psychology and Education*, *3*(3), 249–256. DOI: 10.3390/ejihpe3030022

Murero, M. (2023). Coordinated inauthentic behavior: An innovative manipulation tactic to amplify COVID-19 anti-vaccine communication outreach via social media. *Frontiers in Sociology*, *8*, 1141416. DOI: 10.3389/fsoc.2023.1141416 PMID: 37006634

Mylrea, M. (2025). The generative AI weapon of mass destruction: Evolving disinformation threats, vulnerabilities, and mitigation frameworks. In *Interdependent Human-Machine Teams* (pp. 315–347). Academic Press. DOI: 10.1016/B978-0-443-29246-0.00007-9

Nabhan, S., & Habók, A. (2025). The digital literacy academic writing scale: Exploratory factor analysis. *SAGE Open*, *15*(1), 21582440241311709. DOI: 10.1177/21582440241311709

Nadaraja, R., & Yazdanifard, R. (n.d.). *Social media marketing: Advantages and disadvantages. Center of Southern New Hampshire University (SNHU).* Help College of Arts and Technology.

Nair, P (2015). Study on Social Justice to Women Through Judicial Activism in India, Deeksha, Bi-annual Journal of Social Work, Volume 13, Number 01, February, 2015, ISSN-2250-3919, pp. 63-76.

Na, S. H., Cho, S., & Shin, S. (2023). Evolving Bots: The New Generation of Comment Bots and their Underlying Scam Campaigns in YouTube. *Proceedings of the ACM SIGCOMM Internet Measurement Conference, IMC*, 297–312. DOI: 10.1145/3618257.3624822

Naslund, J. A., & Aschbrenner, K. A. (2019). Risks to privacy with use of social media: Understanding the views of social media users with serious mental illness. *Psychiatric Services (Washington, D.C.)*, *70*(7), 561–566. DOI: 10.1176/appi.ps.201800520 PMID: 30947635

Naslund, J. A., Aschbrenner, K. A., Marsch, L. A., & Bartels, S. J. (2016). The future of mental health care: Peer-to-peer support and social media. *Epidemiology and Psychiatric Sciences*, *25*(2), 113–122. DOI: 10.1017/S2045796015001067 PMID: 26744309

National Aeronautics and Space Administration. (n.d.-a). *Scientific consensus.* https://science.nasa.gov/climate-change/scientific-consensus/

National Aeronautics and Space Administration. (n.d.-b). *What's in a name? Global warming vs. climate change.* https://gpm.nasa.gov/education/articles/whats-name-global-warming-vs-climate-change

National Association for Media Literacy Education. (2024). *State of media literacy education report 2024*. https://namle.org/state-of-media-literacy-report-2024/

National Association of Media Literacy Educators. *Resources: Media literacy defined*. namle.org.

Neenan, M. (2008). Using Socratic questioning in coaching. *Journal of Rational-Emotive & Cognitive-Behavior Therapy*, *27*(4), 249–264. DOI: 10.1007/s10942-007-0076-z

Neilsberg Research. (2025, Feb 22). *United States population by age - 2025 update*. Neilsberg. https://www.neilsberg.com/insights/united-states-population-by-age/

Neumann, P. (2013). Radikalisierung, Deradikalisierung und Extremismus. *Bundeszentrale Für Politische Bildung*. https://www.bpb.de/shop/zeitschriften/apuz/164918/radikalisierung-deradikalisierung-und-extremismus/?utm_source=chatgpt.com

Neuwirth, R. J. (2024). The global institutional governance of AI: A four-dimensional perspective. *International Journal of Digital Law and Governance*, *1*(1), 113–153. DOI: 10.1515/ijdlg-2024-0004

New York Times Co. v. Sullivan, 376 U.S. 254 (1964).

Newell, J. (2007). Revisiting Schramm's Radiotown: Media displacement and saturation. *Journal of Radio Studies*, *14*(1), 3–19. DOI: 10.1080/10955040701301722

Nickerson, R. S. (1998). Confirmation bias: A ubiquitous phenomenon in many guises. *Review of General Psychology*, *2*(2), 175–220. DOI: 10.1037/1089-2680.2.2.175

NIH National Institutes of Health. (2023). The use of generative artificial intelligence technologies is prohibited for the NIH peer review process. *nih.gov*, NOT-OD-23-149. https://grants.nih.gov/grants/guide/notice-files/NOT-OD-23-149.html

NIH National Institutes of Health. (2024). Communicating research intent and value in NIH applications. *nih.gov*, https://grants.nih.gov/grants-process/write-application/general-grant-writing-tips/communicating-research-intent-and-value-in-nih-applications

North Carolina State University Libraries. (2009, Jul 13). *Anatomy of a scholarly article*. https://www.lib.ncsu.edu/tutorials/scholarly-articles/

Nossek, H., & Adoni, H. (2001). The New Media Consumers: Media Convergence and the Displacement Effect. *Communications*, *26*(1).

Notley, T., Hourigan, A., & Thomson, T. J. (2025). *Addressing everyday experiences with misinformation* [Conference presentation]. Media Education Forum (online conference).

Notley, T., Chambers, S., Park, S., & Dezuanni, M. (2021). *Adult media literacy in Australia: Attitudes, experiences and needs. Research Report*. Western Sydney University.

Noy, S., & Zhang, W. (2023). Experimental evidence on the productivity effects of generative artificial intelligence. *Science*, *381*(6654), 187–192. DOI: 10.1126/science.adh2586 PMID: 37440646

NSF National Science Foundation. (2023). Notice to research community: use of generative artificial intelligence technology in the NSF merit review process. *nsf. gov*. https://www.nsf.gov/news/notice-to-the-research-community-on-ai

Nugraha, A. P., (2024). The Impact of Social Media on Social Interaction and Self Identity in Indonesian Society, P-ISSN: 2827-9832, E-ISSN: 2828-335x, http://ijsr .internationaljournallabs.com/index.php/ijsr, DOI: . v3i9.2254, LicenseCC BY-SA 4.0DOI: 10.55324/josr

Nunan, D., & Di Domenico, M. (2019). Older Consumers, Digital Marketing, and Public Policy: A Review and Research Agenda. *Journal of Public Policy & Marketing*, *38*(4), 469–483. DOI: 10.1177/0743915619858939

Nussbaum, M. C. (2010). The liberal arts are not elitist. *The Chronicle of Higher Education*, 28.

Nyhan, B., & Reifler, J. (2010). When corrections fail: The persistence of political misperceptions. *Political Behavior*, *32*(2), 303–330. https://www.jstor.org/stable/40587320. DOI: 10.1007/s11109-010-9112-2

O'Mahony, C., Brassil, M., Murphy, G., & Linehan, C. (2023). The efficacy of interventions in reducing belief in conspiracy theories: A systematic review. *PLoS One*, *18*(4), e0280902. DOI: 10.1371/journal.pone.0280902 PMID: 37018172

O'Neil, C. (2017). *Weapons of math destruction*. Penguin Books.

Odgers, C. L., & Jensen, M. R. (2020). Annual research review: Adolescent mental health in the digital age: Facts, fears, and future directions. *Journal of Child Psychology and Psychiatry, and Allied Disciplines*, *61*(3), 336–348. DOI: 10.1111/jcpp.13190 PMID: 31951670

Oeldorf-Hirsch, A., & Neubaum, G. (2025). What do we know about algorithmic literacy? The status quo and a research agenda for a growing field. *New Media & Society, 27*(2), 681–701. DOI: 10.1177/14614448231182662

Okumus, E. (2024). *Media Society Relationships in the Context of Politics*. University Journal of Social Sciences Institute., DOI: 10.30794/pausbed.1430267

Olson, D. R. (1974). Media and symbols: The forms of expression, communication, and education. In Olson, D. R. (Ed.), *The 73rd Yearbook of the NSSE*. part 1 (pp. 1–24). National Society for the Study of Education.

Olumide, A. O., Adams, P., & Amodu, O. K. (2016). Prevalence and correlates of the perpetration of cyberbullying among in-school adolescents in Oyo State, Nigeria. *International Journal of Adolescent Medicine and Health, 28*(2), 183–191. DOI: 10.1515/ijamh-2015-0009 PMID: 26251981

Omar, A. S., & Ondimu, K. O. (2024). The Impact of Social Media on Society: A Systematic Literature Review, The International Journal of Engineering and Science (IJES), Volume 3, Issue 6, ISSN (e): 2319-1813

Open, A. I. (2022, Nov 30). *Introducing ChatGPT*. https://openai.com/index/chatgpt/

Open, A. I. (2023). Prompt engineering. *OpenAI.com*. https://platform.openai.com/docs/guides/prompt-engineering

Open, A. I. (2025). ChatGPT (Mar 14 version) [GPT-4]. https://chat.openai.com/chat

Orben, A., & Przybylski, A. K. (2019). Screens, teens, and psychological well-being: Evidence from three time-use diary studies. *Psychological Science, 30*(5), 682–696. DOI: 10.1177/0956797619830329 PMID: 30939250

Oremus, W. (2024, Dec 4). *Outraged? You're more likely to share misinformation, study finds*. Washington Post. https://www.washingtonpost.com/politics/2024/12/04/foreign-disinfo-2024-election-outrage-science-study/?itid=hp_latest-from-the-post_p003_f007

Overholser, J. C. (1993a). Elements of the Socratic method: I. Systematic questioning. *Psychotherapy (Chicago, Ill.), 30*(1), 67–74. DOI: 10.1037/0033-3204.30.1.67

Overholser, J. C., & Beale, E. (2023). The art and science behind Socratic questioning and guided discovery: A research review. *Psychotherapy Research, 33*(7), 946–956. DOI: 10.1080/10503307.2023.2183154 PMID: 36878221

Padesky, C. A. (1993, Sep). Socratic questioning: Changing minds or guiding discovery? Invited keynote address presented at the 1993 European Congress of Behaviour and Cognitive Therapies, London.

Palmer, E., & Fisch, S. M. (2001). The Beginnings of Sesame Street Research. In Fisch, S. M., & Truglio, R. T. (Eds.), *G" is for growing:Thirty years of research on children and Sesame Street* (pp. 3–24). Lawrence Erlbaum Publishers.

Pandit, S. (2020). Mapping the mechanics of truth: Fake news and suburban young adult news consumers in India. In *Information Nightmare*. Fake News, Manipulation and Post-Truth Politics in the Digital Age.

Pariser, E. (2011). *The filter bubble: What the internet is hiding from you.* Penguin Press.

Pariser, E. (2011). *The filter bubble: What the Internet is hiding from you.* Viking/ Penguin Press.

Park, J., & Chun, J. (2020). How does watching YouTube fashion content impact perception of appearance: A phenomenological study of Korean women in Generation Z. *Humanities & Social Sciences Communications*, *7*(1), 161. DOI: 10.1057/ s41599-020-00652-2

Park, S., Lee, J. Y., Notley, T., & Dezuanni, M. (2023). Exploring the relationship between media literacy, online interaction, and civic engagement. *The Information Society*, *39*(4), 250–261. DOI: 10.1080/01972243.2023.2211055

Parry, D. A., Davidson, B. I., Sewall, C. J., Fisher, J. T., Mieczkowski, H., & Quintana, D. S. (2021). A systematic review and meta-analysis of discrepancies between logged and self-reported digital media use. *Nature Human Behaviour*, *5*(11), 1535–1547. DOI: 10.1038/s41562-021-01117-5 PMID: 34002052

Pasquale, F. (2015). *The black box society: The secret algorithms that control money and information.* Harvard University Press. DOI: 10.4159/harvard.9780674736061

Patrikakis, C. Z., & Hurlburt, G. F. (2025). Could artificial intelligence write, review, edit, and produce this column? *IT Professional, 27*(1), 4–10. DOI: 10.1109/ MITP.2025.3530597

Pattier, D. (2024). Communication and Emerging Teaching Models: A Study on Youtubers Teachers | Comunicación y Modelos Docentes Emergentes: un Estudio sobre los Profesores Youtubers. *Multidisciplinary Journal of Educational Research*, *14*(1), 1–16. DOI: 10.17583/remie.9887

Paul, R. W., & Elder, L. (2006). *The Thinker's Guide to The Art of Socratic Questioning*. Foundation for Critical Thinking.

Paul, R., & Elder, L. (2020). *Fact over fake: A critical thinker's guide to media bias and political propaganda*. Rowman & Littlefield.

Paus-Hasebrink, I. (2017). Praxeologische (Medien-)Sozialisationsforschung. In D. Hoffmann, F. Krotz, & W. Reißmann (Eds.), *SpringerLink Bücher. Mediatisierung und Mediensozialisation: Prozesse - Räume - Praktiken.* Springer Fachmedien Wiesbaden.

Pavlik, J. V. (2023). Collaborating with ChatGPT: Considering the implications of generative artificial intelligence for journalism and media education. *Journalism & Mass Communication Educator, 78*(1), 84–93. DOI: 10.1177/10776958221149577

Pelaez, A. L., Diaz, H. L., Servos, C. M., & Castillo de Mesa, J. (Eds.). (2021). Digital Social Work: Challenges, Trends and Best Practices. *Journal of Sociology and Social Welfare, XLVIII*(3).

Pelly, S. (2013, Sep 2). *"Evening News" marks golden anniversary of 30-minute broadcast.* CBS News https://www.cbsnews.com/news/evening-news-marks-golden -anniversary-of-30-minute-broadcast/

Pennycook, G., & Rand, D. G. (2019). Lazy, not biased: Susceptibility to partisan fake news is better explained by lack of reasoning than by motivated reasoning. *Cognition, 188*, 39–50. DOI: 10.1016/j.cognition.2018.06.011 PMID: 29935897

Pennycook, G., & Rand, D. G. (2021). The Psychology of Fake News. *Trends in Cognitive Sciences, 25*(5), 388–402. DOI: 10.1016/j.tics.2021.02.007 PMID: 33736957

Perrin, A., & Anderson, M. (2019). Social media usage: Trends and implications. Pew Research Center. https://www.pewresearch.org/wp-content/uploads/2019/02/ Social-Media-Update-2019-FINAL.pdf

Peterson, J., & Densley, J. (2017). Cyber violence: What do we know and where do we go from here? *Aggression and Violent Behavior, 34*, 193–200. DOI: 10.1016/j. avb.2017.01.012

Picarella, L. (2025). Processi educativi e comunicativi orientati alla giustizia sociale in America Latina. In E. Mangone, E. Martini & A. Volterrani (a cura di), *Società frammentata e traiettorie educative. Disuguaglianze, giustizia sociale e intelligenza artificiale* (pp. 21-44). Mimesis.

Picarella, L. (2024a). Critical education between social justice and dialogic cultural action. *The Lab's Quarterly*, XXVI(2), 65-89. DOI: https://doi.org/DOI: 10.13131/ unipi/z182-yb80

Picarella, L. (2024b). Critical Education and Digital Media: A Binomial for the Exercising of Human Rights. *REVIEW OF HUMAN RIGHTS, 10*(1), 86–114. DOI: 10.35994/rhr.v10i1.272

PlainLanguage.gov. (2011). *Federal Plain Language Guidelines.* U. S. General Services Administration. https://www.plainlanguage.gov/media/FederalPLGuidelines.pdf

Plotnikova, M. V., Zavhorodnia, V. M., Degtyarez, S. I., & Polyakova, L. G. (2021). The role of decisions by the European Court of Human Rights in shaping the content of new media literacy education. *International Journal of Media and Information Literacy*, *6*(2), 376–386.

Poell, T., Nieborg, D. B., & Duffy, B. E. (2021). *Platforms and cultural production*. Wiley.

Pollay, R. W. (1986). The distorted mirror: Reflections on the unintended consequences of advertising. *Journal of Marketing*, *50*(2), 18–36. DOI: 10.1177/002224298605000202

Pope Francis. (2024). *Artificial Intelligence and the Wisdom of the Heart: Towards a Fully Human Communication. Message for the 58th World Day of Social Communications*. https://www.vatican.va/content/francesco/en/messages/communications/documents/20240124-messaggio-comunicazioni-sociali.html

Postman, N. (1985). *Amusing ourselves to death: Public discourse in the age of show business*. Penguin.

Potter, J. (1998). *Media literacy*. Sage Publications, Inc.

Potter, W. J. (2004). *Theory of Media Literacy: A Cognitive Approach*. SAGE Publications, Inc., DOI: 10.4135/9781483328881

Potter, W. J. (2010). The state of Media Literacy. *Journal of Broadcasting & Electronic Media*, *54*(4), 675–696. DOI: 10.1080/08838151.2011.521462

Potter, W. J. (2022). Analysis of definitions of media literacy. *The Journal of Media Literacy Education*, *14*(2), 27–43. DOI: 10.23860/JMLE-2022-14-2-3

Pöttinger, I. (1997). *Lernziel Medienkompetenz: Theoretische Grundlagen und praktische Evaluation anhand eines Hörspielprojekts*. Diss. kopaed.

Prachi, S. Deepa, & Manju. (2024). Exploring Regression Models for Youtube Views Prediction with Interpretable Insights. *2024 IEEE 9th International Conference for Convergence in Technology, I2CT 2024*. DOI: 10.1109/I2CT61223.2024.10544146

Pratschke, B. M. (2024). *Generative AI and education*. Springer. DOI: 10.1007/978-3-031-67991-9

Prelog, L., & Bakic-Tomic, L. (2020). The perception of the fake news phenomenon on the internet by members of generation Z. *2020 43rd International Convention on Information, Communication and Electronic Technology, MIPRO 2020 - Proceedings*, 452–455. DOI: 10.23919/MIPRO48935.2020.9245169

Prensky, M. (2001, Sep). Digital Natives, Digital Immigrants Part 1. *On the Horizon, 9*(5), 1–6. https://revistas.ucm.es/index.php/ESMP/article/view/58020. DOI: 10.1108/10748120110424816

Price v. *Time, Inc.*, 416 F.3d 1327, 1335–43 (11th Cir. 2005).

Price, S. (2005, Nov). *Learning to read: Working toward a practical model of media literacy*. Paper presented at the annual convention of the National Communication Association, Boston, MA.

Price, S. (2006, Apr). *Images of horror: Exploring the visual memory of 9-11*. Paper presented at the bi-annual conference on Visual Communication: Rhetorics and Technology, Rochester, NY.

Price, S. (2009, Nov). *Media literacy as a foundation for teaching television production*. Discussion Panel at the annual convention of the National Communication Association, Chicago, IL.

Primack, B. A., Feinberg, M. E., & Hollon, C. J. (2021). Social media use and mental health among young adults: A longitudinal study. *Computers in Human Behavior, 114*, 106526. DOI: 10.1016/j.chb.2020.106526

Primack, B. A., Shensa, A., Sidani, J. E., Whaite, E. O., Lin, L. Y., Rosen, D., Colditz, J. B., Radovic, A., & Miller, E. (2017). Social media use and perceived social isolation among young adults in the U.S. *American Journal of Preventive Medicine, 53*(1), 1–8. DOI: 10.1016/j.amepre.2017.01.010 PMID: 28279545

Prinz, K. D. (2025). Managing the legal risks of artificial intelligence on intellectual property and confidential information. *Consulting Psychology Journal, 77*(2), 169–179. DOI: 10.1037/cpb0000287

Przybylski, A. K., Murayama, K., DeHaan, C. R., & Gladwell, V. (2013). Motivational, emotional, and behavioral correlates of fear of missing out. *Computers in Human Behavior, 29*(4), 1841–1848. DOI: 10.1016/j.chb.2013.02.014

Qian, K., & Jain, S. (2024). Digital Content Creation: An Analysis of the Impact of Recommendation Systems. *Management Science, 70*(12), 8668–8684. DOI: 10.1287/mnsc.2022.03655

Quent, M., Salheiser, A., & Weber, D. (2020). Gesellschaftlicher Zusammenhalt im Blätterwald: Auswertung und kritische Einordnung der Begriffsverwendung in Zeitungsartikeln (2014–2019). In Deitelhoff, N., Groh-Samberg, O., & Middell, M. (Eds.), *Gesellschaftlicher Zusammenhalt: Ein interdisziplinärer Dialog* (pp. 73–88). Campus.

Ragnedda, M. (2017). *The third digital divide: A Weberian approach to digital inequalities*. Routledge. DOI: 10.4324/9781315606002

Rahaman, V. et al. (2024). Perspective Chapter: Social media through Digital Humanities – Why Not Educate the Non-Engineering Students Intech Open, License CC BY 3.0, DOI: DOI: 10.5772/intechopen.1006346

Raji, T. A., Udorah, D. C., & Akinpelu, A. M. (2025). *Digitalisation of Yorùbá Culture in YouTube Children's Performances*. English Academy Review., DOI: 10.1080/10131752.2025.2466885

Raju, R., Qbrien, B., & Kalaiselvi, R. (2018). Detection and Prevention of Copywriting Multimedia Contents in Youtube Using Multi-Keyword Ranking Algorithm. *7th IEEE International Conference on Computation of Power, Energy, Information and Communication, ICCPEIC 2018*, 197–202. DOI: 10.1109/ICCPEIC.2018.8525154

Rampazzo Gambarato, R., & Heuman, J. (2024). *Streaming Media and Cultural Memory in a Postdigital Society*. Taylor & Francis. DOI: 10.4324/9781032690872

Rasi-Heikkinen, P. (2025), *Promoting Older People's ML* [Conference session]. Media Education Forum, Online conference.

Rasi-Heikkinen, P., & Luksua, T. (2023). Increasing seniors' resilience against mis- and disinformation. Benchmarking report of training and materials provided for seniors in Europe. https://www.wearesum.eu/wp-content/uploads/SUM_D2.1_Updated-Benchmarking-report.pdf

Rasi, P., Vuojärvi, H., & Rivinen, S. (2021). Promoting media literacy among older people: A systematic review. *Adult Education Quarterly*, *71*(1), 37–54. DOI: 10.1177/0741713620923755

Reddy, P., Sharma, B., & Chaudhary, K. (2020). Digital literacy: A review of literature. [IJT]. *International Journal of Technoethics*, *11*(2), 65–94. DOI: 10.4018/IJT.20200701.oa1

Reid, D., & Weigle, P. (2014). Social media use among adolescents: Benefits and risks. *Adolescent Psychiatry (Hilversum, Netherlands)*, *4*(2), 73–80. DOI: 10.2174/221067660402140709115810

Reinemann, C., Nienierza, A., Fawzi, N., Riesmeyer, C., & Neumann, K. (2019). *Jugend - Medien - Extremismus*. Springer Fachmedien Wiesbaden., DOI: 10.1007/978-3-658-23729-5

Ren, Q. (2024). Advertising and Content Creation on Digital Content Platforms. *Marketing Science*, *43*(4), 734–750. DOI: 10.1287/mksc.2022.0387

Reynolds, L., & McDonell, K. (2021). Prompt programming for large language models: Beyond the few-shot paradigm. In *Extended abstracts of the 2021 CHI conference on human factors in computing systems* (pp. 1–7). DOI: 10.1145/3411763.3451760

Reyns, B. W., & Henson, B. (2016). The thief of time? An examination of the relationship between social media use and cybercrime victimization. Computers in Human Behavior, 65, 194–200. DOI: 10.1016/j.chb.2016.08.028

Richards, D. A. J. (1974). Free speech and obscenity law: Toward a moral theory of the First Amendment. *University of Pennsylvania Law Review*, *123*(1), 45–91. DOI: 10.2307/3311577

Rinehart, A., & Kung, E. (2022). Artificial Intelligence in Local News. *A survey of US newsrooms' AI readiness.*

Rivoltella, P. C., & Rossi, P. G. (2019). *Il corpo e la macchina. Tecnologia, cultura, educazione*. Morcelliana.

Roberts, D. F., & Foehr, U. G. (2010, Apr). *Youth: Trends in Media Use*. CYC Net. https://cyc-net.org/cyc-online/cyconline-apr2010-roberts.html

Rogers, C. (Producer). (2016). *Climate hustle* [Documentary]. Fathom Events.

Roodt, S., Harry, N., & Mwapwele, S. (2017). The effect of using youtube in the classroom for student engagement of the net generation on an information systems course. In *Communications in Computer and Information Science* (Vol. 730). DOI: 10.1007/978-3-319-69670-6_4

Roozenbeek, J., Culloty, E., & Suiter, J. (2023). Countering misinformation: Evidence, knowledge gaps, and implications of current interventions. *European Psychologist*, *28*(3), 189–205. DOI: 10.1027/1016-9040/a000492

Roozenbeek, J., van der Linden, S., Goldberg, B., Rathje, S., & Lewandowsky, S. (2022). Psychological inoculation improves resilience against misinformation on social media. *Science Advances*, *8*(34), eabo6254. Advance online publication. DOI: 10.1126/sciadv.abo6254 PMID: 36001675

Ropek, L. (2024, Dec 6). *Billionaire owner of LA Times plans to use AI-powered 'bias meter' on news.* Gizmodo. https://gizmodo.com/the-la-times-billionaire-owner-plans-to-use-an-ai-powered-bias-meter-on-editorials-2000535126

Roumeliotis, K. I., & Tselikas, N. D. (2023). ChatGPT and open-ai models: A preliminary review. *Future Internet, 15*(6), 192. DOI: 10.3390/fi15060192

Roy, D. R., Sinha, S. K., & Veenadhari, S. (2022). Big Data Analytics Based Recommender System for Tele-Communication Industry. *PDGC 2022 - 2022 7th International Conference on Parallel, Distributed and Grid Computing*, 525–530. DOI: 10.1109/PDGC56933.2022.10053201

Rubin, A. M. (1998). Media literacy. *Journal of Communication, 48*(1), 3–4. DOI: 10.1111/j.1460-2466.1998.tb02732.x

Ru, K. C., & Tang, R. (2025). Promoting AI literacy through U.S. academic libraries: An analysis of LibGuides from ARL and Oberlin group libraries using the EDUCAUSE AI literacy framework. *Information Research, 30*(i), 847–865.

Rybiński, K. (2025). Automation of grant application writing with the use of Chatgpt. *Scientific Papers of Silesian University of Technology., 2025*(216), 493–515. DOI: 10.29119/1641-3466.2025.216.30

Sabar (2024). The Impact of Social Media on Mental Health of Young Adults: A Literature Review, Information Management and Business Review (ISSN 2220-3796), Vol. 16, No. 3S(a), pp. 447-460

Sadiku, M. N. O. (2021). Artificial intelligence in social media. *International Journal of Scientific Advances, 2*(1), 15–20.

Sajuria, J., van Heerde-Hudson, J., Hudson, D., Dasandi, N., & Theocharis, Y. (2015). Tweeting Alone? An Analysis of Bridging and Bonding Social Capital in Online Networks. *American Politics Research, 43*(4), 708–738. DOI: 10.1177/1532673X14557942

Salib, S., de la Garza, K., & Kapadia, A. M. (2024). Asset framing: A tool for enhanced equity in feedback and assessment. *Medical Science Educator, 34*(5), 1189–1192. DOI: 10.1007/s40670-024-02094-w PMID: 39450041

Salinas Navarro, D. E., Vilalta-Perdomo, E., Michel-Villarreal, R., & Montesinos, L. (2024). Designing experiential learning activities with generative artificial intelligence tools for authentic assessment. *Interactive Technology and Smart Education, 21*(4), 708–734. DOI: 10.1108/ITSE-12-2023-0236

Salzano, D., & Battista, D. (2023). Social network e generazione Z: Tra empowerment e rischi educativi. *Q-TIMES WEBMAGAZINE, 1*, 47–59.

Salzano, D., Scognamiglio, I., & Battista, D. (2023). La rispazializzazione digitale nelle aree interne del Sud Italia= Digital respazialization in the inland areas of Southern Italy. *H-ermes. Journal of Communication, 24*, 51–72.

Sambhanthan, A., Thelijjagoda, S., Good, A., & Scupola, A. (2020). Virtual community based destination marketing with youtube: Investigation of a typology. In *Destination Management and Marketing* (Vol. 2–2). Breakthroughs in Research and Practice., DOI: 10.4018/978-1-7998-2469-5.ch065

Sangeorzan, I., Andriopoulou, P., & Livanou, M. (2019). Exploring the experiences of people vlogging about severe mental illness on YouTube: An interpretative phenomenological analysis. *Journal of Affective Disorders, 246*, 422–428. DOI: 10.1016/j.jad.2018.12.119 PMID: 30599364

Saridakis, G., Benson, V., Ezingeard, J. N., & Tennakoon, H. (2016). Individual information security, user behaviour and cyber victimisation: An empirical study of social networking users. *Technological Forecasting and Social Change, 102*, 320–330. DOI: 10.1016/j.techfore.2015.08.012

Sartori, R., Tommasi, F., Ceschi, A., Falser, M., Genero, S., & Belotto, S. (2022). Enhancing critical thinking skills and media literacy in initial vocational education and training via self-nudging: The contribution of the NERDVET project. *Frontiers in Psychology, 13*, 935673. DOI: 10.3389/fpsyg.2022.935673 PMID: 35992484

Schechter, S., & Bacher, W. (1909). Gamaliel I. In *Jewish encyclopedia*. https://www.jewishencyclopedia.com/articles/6494-gamaliel-i

Schemer, C., Wirth, W., Wettstein, M., Müller, P., Schulz, A., & Wirz, D. (2018). Wirkung populistischer Kommunikation. Populismus in den Medien, Wirkungen und deren Randbedingungen. *Communicatio Socialis, 51*(2), 118–130. DOI: 10.5771/0010-3497-2018-2-118

Scherr, A. (2009). *Jugendsoziologie: Einführung in Grundlagen und Theorien* (9., erw. und umfassend überarb. Aufl.). *Lehrbuch*. VS, Verl. für Sozialwiss.

Schiefner-Rohs, M. (2012). *Kritische Informations- und Medienkompetenz: Theoretisch-konzeptionelle Herleitung und empirische Betrachtungen am Beispiel der Lehrerausbildung*. Diss. Waxmann.

Schorb, B. (1997). Medienkompetenz durch Medienpädagogik. In Wessler, H. (Ed.), *Perspektiven der Medienkritik: Die gesellschaftliche Auseinandersetzung mit öffentlicher Kommunikation in der Mediengesellschaft; Dieter Roß zum 60. Geburtstag* (pp. 275–285). Westdt. Verl. DOI: 10.1007/978-3-322-85097-3_27

Schuurman, D., De Marez, L., & Ballon, P. (2016). The impact of living lab methodology on open innovation contributions and outcomes. *Technology Innovation Management Review*, *6*(1), 7–16. DOI: 10.22215/timreview/956

Schwarz, G. (2005). Overview: What is Media Literacy, who Cares, and Why? *Teachers College Record*, *107*(13), 5–17. DOI: 10.1177/016146810810701301

SCONUL. (2011). *The SCONUL Seven Pillars of Information Literacy. Core Model for Higher Education.* https://www.sconul.ac.uk/sites/default/files/documents/coremodel.pdf

Scott, K. (2022). I Do Not Think It Means What You Think It Means: Artificial Intelligence, Cognitive Work & Scale. *Daedalus*, *151*(2), 75–84. DOI: 10.1162/daed_a_01901

Scott, L. M. (1994). Images in Advertising: The Need for a Theory of Visual Rhetoric. *The Journal of Consumer Research*, *21*(2), 252–273. DOI: 10.1086/209396

Scott, M. (2014). *Media and development.* Zed Books. DOI: 10.5040/9781350221314

SDG16NOW. (n.d.). *Target 16.10.* https://sdg16now.org/report/target16-10/

Seckel, E., Stephens, B. Y., & Rodriguez, F. (2024). Ten simple rules to leverage large language models for getting grants. *PLoS Computational Biology*, *20*(3), e1011863–e1011863. DOI: 10.1371/journal.pcbi.1011863 PMID: 38427611

Seeger, M., & Sellnow, T. L. (2016). *Narratives of crisis: Telling stories of ruin and renewal* (Vol. 19). Stanford University Press.

Seeley, J. S., Wickens, C. M., Vingilis-Jaremko, L., Fleiter, J., Yildirim-Yenier, Z., Grushka, D. H., & Vingilis, E. (2019). Street racing, stunt driving and ghost riding YouTube videos: A descriptive content analysis. *Transportation Research Part F: Traffic Psychology and Behaviour*, *63*, 283–294. DOI: 10.1016/j.trf.2019.04.012

Selke, S. (2014). *Lifelogging: Wie die digitale Selbstvermessung unsere Gesellschaft verändert.* Econ.

Selwyn, N. (2012). Social media in higher education. *The Europa World of Learning*, *62*(1), 1–10. DOI: 10.4324/9781857436211

Selwyn, N., & Stirling, E. (2016). Social media and education: Now the dust has settled. *Learning, Media and Technology, 41*(1), 1–5. DOI: 10.1080/17439884.2015.1115769

Severin, W. J., & Tankard, J. W. (2001). *Communication theories: Origins, methods, and uses in the mass media*. Longman.

Seymoens, T., Van Audenhove, L., Van Den Broeck, W., & Mariën, I. (2020). Data literacy on the road: Setting up a large-scale data literacy initiative in the DataBuzz project. *The Journal of Media Literacy Education, 12*(3), 102–119. DOI: 10.23860/JMLE-2020-12-3-9

Shalevska, E. (2024). The future of political discourse: AI and media literacy education. *Journal of Legal and Political Education, 1*(1), 50–61. DOI: 10.47305/JLPE2411050sh

Shamim, M. I. (2024). How social media is Reshaping Society: A Look at Connection, Communication, and Change, Non-Human Journal, Vol. 1, No. 2; April; 2024.

Shanahan, E. A., Reinhold, A. M., Raile, E. D., Poole, G. C., Ready, R. C., Izurieta, C., McEvoy, J., Bergmann, N. T., & King, H. (2019). Characters matter: How narratives shape affective responses to risk communication. *PLoS One, 14*(12), e0225968. DOI: 10.1371/journal.pone.0225968 PMID: 31815957

Shao, Z., Zhao, R., Yuan, S., Ding, M., & Wang, Y. (2022). Tracing the evolution of AI in the past decade and forecasting the emerging trends. *Expert Systems with Applications, 209*, 118221. DOI: 10.1016/j.eswa.2022.118221

Sheets, P., Bos, L., & Boomgaarden, H. G. (2016). Media Cues and Citizen Support for Right-Wing Populist Parties. *International Journal of Public Opinion Research, 28*(3), 307–330. DOI: 10.1093/ijpor/edv014

Shensa, A., Sidani, J. E., Dew, M. A., Escobar-Viera, C. G., & Primack, B. A. (2018). Social media use and depression and anxiety symptoms: A cluster analysis. *American Journal of Health Behavior, 42*(2), 116–128. DOI: 10.5993/AJHB.42.2.11 PMID: 29458520

Shin, N., & Ahn, H. (2015). Factors Affecting Adolescents' Involvement in Cyberbullying: What Divides the 20% from the 80%? *Cyberpsychology, Behavior, and Social Networking, 18*(7), 393–399. DOI: 10.1089/cyber.2014.0362 PMID: 26167838

Shirky, C. (2011). The political power of social media: Technology, the public sphere, and political change. *Foreign Affairs, 90*(1), 28–41. https://www.foreignaffairs.com/articles/2010-12-20/political-power-social-media

Shi, W.-Q., Cheng, F., Zhan, H.-Y., Liu, J., Zhou, Y.-P., & Gu, Z.-H. (2021). Influence of Short Video on Apparel Consumers' Purchase Intention | . [Natural Science Edition]. *Journal of Beijing Institute of Clothing Technology*, *41*(1), 67–72.

Siemens, G. (2005). Connectivism: A learning theory for the digital age. *International Journal of Instructional Technology and Distance Learning*, *2*(1).

Silverblatt, A. (1995). *Medial literacy: Keys to interpreting media messages*. Praeger Publishers.

Size, R. (2020). Publishing fake news for profit should be prosecuted as wire fraud. *Santa Clara Law Review*, *60*, 29–99.

Skovsgaard, M., & Andersen, K. (2020). Conceptualizing news avoidance: Towards a shared understanding of different forms of news avoidance. *Journalism Studies*, *21*(6), 768–782.

Smahel, D., Machackova, H., Mascheroni, G., Dedkova, L., Staksrud, E., Ólafsson, K., Livingstone, S., & Hasebrink, U. (2020). *EU Kids Online 2020: Survey results from 19 countries*. London School of Economics and Political Science.

Smith, A., & Anderson, M. (2018). Social media use in 2018. Pew Research Center. https://www.pewresearch.org/internet/2018/03/01/social-media-use-in-2018/

Smith, D., Leonis, T., & Anandavalli, S. (2021). Belonging and loneliness in cyberspace: Impacts of social media on adolescents' well-being. *Australian Journal of Psychology*, *73*(1), 12–23. DOI: 10.1080/00049530.2021.1898914

Smith, J., & Jones, K. (2019). Humiliation and intimidation in interpersonal conflicts. *Journal of Interpersonal Violence*, *34*(5), 987–1005. DOI: 10.1177/0886260516645573

Soni, P.. (2024). *Deciphering the Psychological Implications of social media, In book: Mindful Media: Mental Health Challenges in the Digital AgePublisher*. Blue Rose Publishers.

Sparks, G. G. (2015). *Media effects research: A basic overview* (5th ed.). Thomson/ Wadsworth Press.

Spikes, M. A., & Calvert, K. (2024, Dec 11). *Media Literacy Education for Adult Audiences: Exploring ChatGPT and Conversational AI*. Programming Librarian - ALA. [Webinar] https://events.callacademy.org/event/media-literacy-education-adult-audiences-exploring-chatgpt-and-conversational-8698

Staender, A., Humprecht, E., Esser, F., Morosoli, S., & Van Aelst, P. (2021). Is sensationalist disinformation more effective? Three facilitating factors at the national, individual, and situational level. *Digital Journalism (Abingdon, England)*, *10*(6), 976–996. DOI: 10.1080/21670811.2021.1966315

Stanford History Education Group. (2019). *Evaluating information: The need for critical thinking*. Stanford University.

Steinberg, C. S. (1980). *TV facts*. Facts on File, Inc.

Stein, L., & Prewett, A. (2009). Media literacy education in the social studies: Teacher perceptions and curricular challenges. *Teacher Education Quarterly*, *36*(1), 131–148.

Stiftung, B. (2025). *Bridge-building instead of polarization: How algorithms can improve digital discourse*. https://bridging.reframetech.de/

Stoll, J. (2024, Nov 9). *Breakdown of cord cutters in the U.S. 2022, by age*. Statistica. https://www.statista.com/statistics/782564/usa-cord-cutter-distribution-by-age/

Stroud, N. J., Scacco, J. M., Muddiman, A., & Curry, A. L. (2015). Changing Deliberative Norms on News Organizations' Facebook Sites. *Journal of Computer-Mediated Communication*, *20*(2), 188–203. DOI: 10.1111/jcc4.12104

Student Press Law Center. (2024). *Legal considerations of artificial intelligence for student journalists*. SPLC. https://splc.org/ai/

Subramanian, K. R. (2018). Myth and mystery of shrinking attention span. *International Journal of Trend in Research and Development*, *5*(3), 1–6.

Su, J., Ng, D. T. K., & Chu, S. K. W. (2023). Artificial intelligence (AI) literacy in early childhood education: The challenges and opportunities. *Computers and Education: Artificial Intelligence*, *4*, 100124. DOI: 10.1016/j.caeai.2023.100124

Sullivan, A. (2009, Sep 26). *The daily dish: The ethics of photo cropping*. The Atlantic. https://www.theatlantic.com/daily-dish/archive/2009/09/the-ethics-of-photo-cropping/196090/

Sundie, J. M., Kenrick, D. T., Griskevicius, V., Tybur, J. M., Vohs, K. D., & Beal, D. J. (2011). Peacocks, Porsches, and Thorstein Veblen: Conspicuous Consumption as a Sexual Signaling System. *Journal of Personality and Social Psychology*, *100*(4), 664–680. DOI: 10.1037/a0021669 PMID: 21038972

Sunkad, G. (2023). The Impact of Social media on Society, International Journal of Social health, https://ijsh.ph/index.php/rp Volume 2, Number 10, October 2023, E-ISSN: 2984-7079.

Sunstein, C. R. (2021). *Liars: Falsehoods and free speech in an age of deception.* Oxford University Press.van Raemdonck, N., & Meyer, T. (2022). Why disinformation is here to stay: A socio-technical analysis of disinformation as a hybrid threat. In Lonardo, L. (Ed.), *Addressing hybrid threats: European law and policies*. Edward Elgar Publishing.

Suryandari, R. T., & Jeon, S. (2016). Consumers' Conspicuousness and its Underlying Traits. In *Developments in Marketing Science: Proceedings of the Academy of Marketing Science*. DOI: 10.1007/978-3-319-24148-7_52

Swami, V., Voracek, M., Stieger, S., Tran, U., & Furnham, A. (2014). Analytic thinking reduces belief in conspiracy theories. *Cognition, 133*(3), 572–585. DOI: 10.1016/j.cognition.2014.08.006 PMID: 25217762

Sweller, J. (1994). Cognitive load theory, learning difficulty, and instructional design. *Learning and Instruction, 4*(4), 295–312. DOI: 10.1016/0959-4752(94)90003-5

Swire, B., Ecker, U. K. H., & Lewandowsky, S. (2017). The role of familiarity in correcting inaccurate information. *Journal of Experimental Psychology. Learning, Memory, and Cognition, 43*(12), 1948–1961. DOI: 10.1037/xlm0000422 PMID: 28504531

Szymkowiak, A., Melović, B., Dabić, M., Jeganathan, K., & Kundi, G. S. (2021). Information technology and Gen Z: The role of teachers, the internet, and technology in the education of young people. *Technology in Society, 65*, 101565. DOI: 10.1016/j.techsoc.2021.101565

Tacheva, J., & Ramasubramanian, S. (2023). AI Empire: Unraveling the interlocking systems of oppression in generative AI's global order. *Big Data & Society, 10*(2), 20539517231219241. Advance online publication. DOI: 10.1177/20539517231219241

Tartari, E. (2015). Benefits and risks of children and adolescents using social media. *European Scientific Journal, 11*(13), 321–332. https://eujournal.org/index.php/esj/article/view/5650

Task Force FGZ-Datenzentrum. (2022). *Gefährdeter Zusammenhalt? Polarisierungs- und Spaltungstendenzen in Deutschland: ausgewählte Ergebnisse der FGZ-Pilotstudie 2020.* SOCIUM; Forschungsinstitut Gesellschaftlicher Zusammenhalt. https://doi.org/DOI: 10.26092/elib/1739*

Taylor & Francis Author Services. (n.d.). *Understanding the peer review process.* https://authorservices.taylorandfrancis.com/publishing-your-research/peer-review/

Taylor, P., & Miller, R. (2018). Social conflicts and group dynamics in the digital era. *The Sociological Review*, *47*(2), 123–140. DOI: 10.1080/00380253.2018.1436942

Ted. (2011, May 1). *Beware online "filter bubbles" | Eli Pariser* [Video]. YouTube. https://www.youtube.com/watch?v=B8ofWFx525s

Teichert, J. (2025). Loper Bright and the ebbing tide of the administrative state. *Utah Bar Journal*, *38*(2), 19–26.

Tess, P. A. (2013). The role of social media in higher education classes (real and virtual)—A literature review. *Computers in Human Behavior*, *29*(5), A60–A68. DOI: 10.1016/j.chb.2012.12.032

Thalmann, M., Souza, A. S., & Oberauer, K. (2019). How does chunking help working memory? *Journal of Experimental Psychology. Learning, Memory, and Cognition*, *45*(1), 37–55. DOI: 10.1037/xlm0000578 PMID: 29698045

The Brookings Institution. (2016). *Disrupting ISIS Recruitment Online*, Washington D.C. https://www.brookings.edu/wp-content/uploads/2016/09/20160907_disrupting_isis_transcript.pdf

The New Testament of Our Lord and Saviour Jesus Christ, King James Version. Acts 5. (2013). Intellectual Reserve, Inc. https://www.churchofjesuschrist.org/study/scriptures/nt/acts/5?lang=eng

Theodoridis, P. K., & Gkikas, D. C. (2019). How artificial intelligence affects digital marketing. In *Strategic Innovative Marketing and Tourism: 7th ICSIMAT, Athenian Riviera, Greece, 2018* (pp. [pages if known]). Springer International Publishing. DOI: 10.1007/978-3-030-12453-3_151

Theunert, H. (1999). Medienkompetenz: Eine pädagogische und altersspezifisch zu fassende Handlungsdimension. In F. Schell, E. Stolzenburg, & H. Theunert (Eds.), *Medienkompetenz: Grundlagen und pädagogisches Handeln* (pp. 50–59). kopaed.

Thoman, E., & Jolls, T. (2004). Media literacy—A national priority for a changing world. *The American Behavioral Scientist*, *48*(1), 18–29. DOI: 10.1177/0002764204267246

Tiernan, P., Costello, E., Donlon, E., Parysz, M., & Scriney, M. (2023). Information and Media Literacy in the Age of AI: Options for the Future. *Education Sciences*, *13*(9), 906. DOI: 10.3390/educsci13090906

Tilley, C. L. (2012). Seducing the innocent: Fredric Wertham and the falsifications that helped condemn comics. *Information & Culture*, *47*(4), 383–413. DOI: 10.1353/lac.2012.0024

Timung, B., (2024). *The influence of social media on learning behaviors: A social science perspective, Intercontinental Social Science Journal 6(1), 2024*. Pierre Online Publications Ltd., DOI: 10.62583/rjzw8r96

Tirocchi, S. (2013). *Sociologie della Media education. Giovani e media al tempo dei nativi digitali*. FrancoAngeli.

Tokunaga, R. S. (2010). Following you home from school: A critical review and synthesis of research on cyberbullying victimization. *Computers in Human Behavior*, *26*(3), 277–287. DOI: 10.1016/j.chb.2009.11.014

Torres-Toukoumidis, Á., Santín-Picoita, F. G., & Henríquez Mendoza, E. (2024). Inteligencia Artificial y Educomunicación. In A. Torres-Toukoumidis, T. León-Alberca, (coords.), *ComunicAI. La revolución de la Inteligencia Artificial en la Comunicación*. Comunicación Social Ediciones y Publicaciones.

Toth, M., Mertens, F., & Rodrigues Makiuchi, M. F. (2012). Novos espaços de participação social no contexto do desenvolvimento sustentável: As contribuições da Educomunicação. *Ambiente & Sociedade*, *15*(2), 113–132. DOI: 10.1590/S1414-753X2012000200007

Totlani, K. (2023). The evolution of generative AI: Implications for the media and film industry. *International Journal for Research in Applied Science and Engineering Technology*, *11*(10), 973–980. DOI: 10.22214/ijraset.2023.56140

Traberg, C. S., Harjani, T., Basol, M., Biddlestone, M., Maertens, R., Roozenbeek, J., & van der Linden, S. (2023). Prebunking Against Misinformation in the Modern Digital Age. In Purnat, T. D. (Ed.), *et al., Managing Infodemics in the 21st Century: Addressing New Public Health Challenges in the Information Ecosystem* (pp. 99–111). Springer. DOI: 10.1007/978-3-031-27789-4_8

Treumann, K. P., Meister, D. M., Sander, U., Burkatzki, E., Hagedorn, J., Kämmerer, M., Strotmann, M., & Wegener, C. (2007). *Medienhandeln Jugendlicher: Mediennutzung und Medienkompetenz. Bielefelder Medienkompetenzmodell*. VS Verlag., DOI: 10.1007/978-3-531-90509-9

Troy, G. (2005). *Morning in America: how Ronald Reagan invented the 1980s*. Princeton University Press.

Tsamados, A., Aggarwal, N., Cowls, J., Morley, J., Roberts, H., Taddeo, M., & Floridi, L. (2021). The ethics of algorithms: key problems and solutions. *Ethics, governance, and policies in artificial intelligence*, 97-123.

Tucker, L., & Sherwood, L. (2019). *Understanding climate change*. National Science Teachers Association. https://static.nsta.org/pdfs/202002BookBeatFactOrPhony.pdf

Tufekci, Z. (2015) Algorithmic harms beyond Facebook and Google: emergent challenges of computational agency. *Colorado Technology Law Journal*, (13) 203. https:// ctlj.colorado.edu/wp-content/uploads/2015/08/Tufekci-final.pdf

Tufekci, Z. (2017). *Twitter and tear gas: The power and fragility of networked protest*. Yale University Press.

Tully, M., Maksi, A., Ashley, S., Vraga, E. K., & Craft, S. (2022). Defining and conceptualizing news literacy. *Journalism*, *23*(8), 1589–1606. DOI: 10.1177/14648849211005888

Tulodziecki, G. (1998). Entwicklung von Medienkompetenz als Erziehungs- und Bildungsaufgabe. *Pädagogische Rundschau*, *52*(6), 693–709.

Turning (2024). The impact of social media on modern society, https://medium .comTwenge, J. M., Joiner, T. E., Rogers, M. L., & Martin, G. N. (2019). Increases in depressive symptoms, suicide-related outcomes, and suicide rates among U.S. adolescents after 2010 and links to increased new media screen time. Clinical Psychological Science, 6(1), 3–17. DOI: 10.1177/2167702617723376

Tuten, T. L., & Solomon, M. R. (2017). *Social media marketing* (3rd ed.). Sage Publications.

Tutton, M. (2018, Oct 15). Donald Trump: Climate "will change back again." *CNN Politics*. https://www.cnn.com/2018/10/15/politics/trump-climate-change-60 -minutes/index.html

Twenge, J. M. (2017). *Igen: Why today's super-connected kids are growing up less rebellious, more tolerant, less happy-and completely unprepared for adulthood*: *(and what this means for the rest of us)* (First Atria Paperback edition). Atria Paperback.

Twenge, J. M., & Campbell, W. K. (2019). Media use is linked to lower psychological well-being: Evidence from three datasets. *The Psychiatric Quarterly*, *90*(2), 311–331. DOI: 10.1007/s11126-019-09630-7 PMID: 30859387

Twenge, J. M., Haidt, J., Joiner, T. E., & Campbell, W. K. (2020). Underestimating digital media harm. *Nature Human Behaviour*, *4*(4), 346–348. DOI: 10.1038/ s41562-020-0839-4 PMID: 32303719

U.S. Copyright Office. (2023). Copyright registration guidance: Works containing material generated by artificial intelligence. *Federal Register*. https://www.copyright .gov/ai/ai_policy_guidance.pdf

Udry, J., & Barber, S. J. (2024). The illusory truth effect: A review of how repetition increases belief in misinformation. *Current Opinion in Psychology*, *56*, 101736. DOI: 10.1016/j.copsyc.2023.101736 PMID: 38113667

UNESCO. (1978/79). Mass Media Declaration. *Journal of Communication*, *29*(2), 190–191.

UNESCO. (2007). *Paris agenda or 12 recommendations for media education. Paris Conference*. UNESCO. http://www.ifap.ru/pr/2007/070625ba.pdf

UNESCO. (2021a). *Media and information literate citizens: think critically, click wisely!* UNESCO. https://www.unesco.org/mil4teachers/en/curriculum

UNESCO. (2021b). *IA et éducation: Guide pour les décideurs politiques*. UNESCO. https://unesdoc.unesco.org/ark:/48223/pf0000380006

UNESCO. (2024). *Operational Guidelines Constructing UNESCO Media and Information Literacy Cities*. UNESCO. https://unesdoc.unesco.org/ark:/48223/pf0000391748

UNESCO. (2024/25). *Media and Information Literacy Course for Adult Educators launched* https://www.uil.unesco.org/en/articles/media-and-information-literacy-course-adult-educators-launched

Union of Concerned Scientists. (2007, Jul 16). *Smoke, mirrors, & hot air: How ExxonMobil uses Big Tobacco's tactics to "manufacture uncertainty" on climate science*. https://www.ucs.org/resources/smoke-mirrors-hot-air

United Nations Children's Fund. (n.d.) *Frequently asked questions on the Convention on the Rights of the Child*. UNICEF. https://www.unicef.org/child-rights-convention/frequently-asked-questions

United Nations Educational, Scientific and Cultural Organization. (2023, Mar 22). *Imminent risk of a global water crisis, warns the UN World Water Development Report 2023*. https://www.unesco.org/en/articles/imminent-risk-global-water-crisis-warns-un-world-water-development-report-2023

United Nations Educational, Scientific, and Cultural Organization. (1982). *Grunwald declaration on media education*. https://milobs.pt/wp-content/uploads/2018/06/The-Grünwald-Declaration-on-Media-Education.pdf

United Nations Educational, Scientific, and Cultural Organization. (2018). UNESCO launches Observatory of Killed Journalists, tracking actions to punish crimes against media practitioners. https://www.unesco.org/en/articles/unesco-launches-observatory-killed-journalists-tracking-actions-taken-punish-crimes-against-media

United Nations Educational, Scientific, and Cultural Organization. (n.d.). *Unpacking sustainable development goal 4 education 2030.* https://www.gcedclearinghouse.org/sites/default/files/resources/190257eng.pdf

United Nations General Assembly. (1976). *International covenant on economic, social and cultural rights.* Office of the High Commissioner for Human Rights. https://www.ohchr.org/sites/default/files/cescr.pdf

United Nations General Assembly. (1989). *Convention on the Rights of the Child.* General Assembly Resolution 44/25. https://www.ohchr.org/en/instruments-mechanisms/instruments/convention-rights-child

United Nations. (n.d.) *Water scarcity.* https://www.unwater.org/water-facts/scarcity/

United Nations. (n.d.). *Goal 16.* Department of Economic and Social Affairs: Sustainable Development. https://sdgs.un.org/goals/goal16

United Nations. Climate Change. (2015, Jan 21). *President Obama: Climate change greatest threat to future generations.* https://unfccc.int/news/president-obama-climate-change-greatest-threat-to-future-generations

United States Agency for International Development. (2021). *Disinformation primer.* https://www.usaid.gov/sites/default/files/2023-01/Disinformation-Primer.pdf

University Corporation for Atmospheric Research. (2009). *Earth science literacy principles: The big ideas and supporting concepts of earth science.* https://scied.ucar.edu/sites/default/files/2021-10/earth_science_literacy_brochure.pdf

University of Utah Electrical and Computer Engineering. (n.d.). *Summarizing, analyzing, synthesizing.* https://www.ece.utah.edu/wp-content/uploads/2012/10/Summary-Analysis-Synthesis-Definitions.pdf

Valenzuela, S., Park, N., & Kee, K. F. (2009). Is There Social Capital in a Social Network Site? Facebook Use and College Students' Life Satisfaction, Trust, and Participation. *Journal of Computer-Mediated Communication, 14*(4), 875–901. DOI: 10.1111/j.1083-6101.2009.01474.x

Valkenburg, P. M., & Peter, J. (2013). The differential susceptibility to media effects model. *Journal of Communication, 63*(2), 221–243. DOI: 10.1111/jcom.12024

Valpadasu, H., Chakri, P., Harshitha, P., & Tarun, P. (2023). Machine Learning based Spam Comments Detection on YouTube. *Proceedings of the 7th International Conference on Intelligent Computing and Control Systems, ICICCS 2023*, 1234–1239. DOI: 10.1109/ICICCS56967.2023.10142608

Valtonen, T., Tedre, M., Mäkitalo, K., & Vartiainen, H. (2019). Media Literacy Education in the Age of Machine Learning. *The Journal of Media Literacy Education, 11*(2), 20–36. DOI: 10.23860/JMLE-2019-11-2-2

Van Audenhove, L., Vermeire, L., Van den Broeck, W., & Demeulenaere, A. (2024). Data literacy in the new EU DigComp 2.2 framework: How DigComp defines competences on artificial intelligence, internet of things and data. *Information and Learning Science, 125*(5/6), 406–436. DOI: 10.1108/ILS-06-2023-0072

Van Buggenhout, N., Van den Broeck, W., & Jennes, I. (2018). The Island Approach (TIA): a suited projective technique for evaluating a bevy of attributes. In *Research and Innovation Conference Proceedings 2018* (Vol. 2018, pp. 496-521). ENoLL - European Network of Living Labs. DOI: 10.5281/zenodo.1434994

van den Besselaar, P., & Mom, C. (2022). The effect of writing style on success in grant applications. *Journal of Informetrics, 16*(1), 101257. DOI: 10.1016/j.joi.2022.101257

Van Der Merwe, P. (2014). How could life orientation teachers in secondary schools make use of the proposed digital media literacy program for teaching and learning? *International Journal of Pedagogy and Curriculum, 20*(2), 89–109. DOI: 10.18848/2327-7963/CGP/v20i02/48961

Van Dijck, J., Poell, T., & De Waal, M. (2018). *The platform society: Public values in a connective world.* Oxford University Press. DOI: 10.1093/oso/9780190889760.001.0001

van Nooijen, C. C., de Koning, B. B., Bramer, W. M., Isahakyan, A., Asoodar, M., Kok, E., van Merrienboer, J. J., & Paas, F. (2024). A Cognitive Load Theory Approach to Understanding Expert Scaffolding of Visual Problem-Solving Tasks: A Scoping Review. *Educational Psychology Review, 36*(1), 12. DOI: 10.1007/s10648-024-09848-3

Van Peer, W. (1988). Reading, culture and modern mass media. *Journal of Information Science, 14*(5), 305–309. DOI: 10.1177/016555158801400508

Varona, M. N., Muela, A., & Machimbarrena, J. M. (2022). Problematic use or addiction? A scoping review on conceptual and operational definitions of negative social networking sites use in adolescents. *Addictive Behaviors, 134*, 107400. DOI: 10.1016/j.addbeh.2022.107400 PMID: 35820296

Vaswani, A., Shazeer, N., Parmar, N., Uszkoreit, J., Jones, L., Gomez, A. N., & Polosukhin, I. (2017). Attention is all you need. *Advances in Neural Information Processing Systems, 30*. DOI: 10.48550/arXiv.1706.03762

Vasylchyshyna et al. (2024). Social media as a factor in the transformation of public administration, justice and legality, Multidiscip. Rev. (2024), Published Online: June 12, 2024, DOI: 10.31893/multirev.2024spe039

Vaughan v. Menlove, 132 Eng. Rep. 490 (Court of Common Pleas 1837).

Većkalov, B., Gligorić, V., & Petrović, M. B. (2024). No evidence that priming analytic thinking reduces belief in conspiracy theories: A registered report of high-powered direct replications of Study 2 and Study 4 from Swami, Voracek, Stieger, Tran, and Furnham (2014). *Journal of Experimental Social Psychology, 110*, 104549. DOI: 10.1016/j.jesp.2023.104549

Villi, M. (2019). News fatigue and emotional drivers in the age of information overload. *Journalism Studies, 20*(8), 1123–1139.

Vogel, E. A., Rose, J. P., Roberts, L. R., & Eckles, K. (2014). Social comparison, social media, and self-esteem. *Psychology of Popular Media Culture, 3*(4), 206–222. DOI: 10.1037/ppm0000047

Vollbrecht, R. (1999). Medienkompetenz als kommunikative Kompetenz. *Rückbesinnung und Neufassung des Konzepts.*, (43), 13–18.

Vosoughi, S., Roy, D., & Aral, S. (2018). The spread of true and false news online. *Science, 359*(6380), 1146–1151. DOI: 10.1126/science.aap9559 PMID: 29590045

Waldron, J. (2012). *The harm in hate speech*. Harvard University Press. DOI: 10.4159/harvard.9780674065086

Walker, M., & Gottfried, J. (2019). Republicans far more likely than Democrats to say fact-checkers tend to favor one side. *Pew Research Center.* https://www.pewresearch.org/short-reads/2019/06/27/republicans-far-more-likely-than-democrats-to-say-fact-checkers-tend-to-favor-one-side/

Walsh, L. C., Regan, A., Okabe-Miyamoto, K., & Lyubomirsky, S. (2024). Does putting down your smartphone make you happier? the effects of restricting digital media on well-being. *PLoS ONE, 19*. DOI: 10.1371/journal.pone.0306910

Walsh, J. A., & Sattes, E. D. (2011). *Thinking through quality questioning: Deepening student engagement* (1st ed.). Corwin.

Wang, H., Liu, Y., Han, Z., & Wu, J. (2020, Jun). Extension of media literacy from the perspective of artificial intelligence and implementation strategies of artificial intelligence courses in junior high schools. In *2020 International Conference on Artificial Intelligence and Education (ICAIE)* (pp. 63-66). IEEE. DOI: 10.1109/ICAIE50891.2020.00022

Wang, Y., McKee, M., Torbica, A., & Stuckler, D. (2019). Systematic literature review on the spread of health-related misinformation on social media. *Social Science & Medicine, 240*, 112552. DOI: 10.1016/j.socscimed.2019.112552 PMID: 31561111

Wardle, C., & Derakhshan, H. (2017). *Information disorder: Toward an interdisciplinary framework for research and policy making*. Council of Europe Report. https://rm.coe.int/information-disorder-toward-an-interdisciplinary-framework-for-research/1680765e2b

Wartella, E. A., & Jennings, N. (2000). Children and computers: New technology. Old concerns. *The Future of Children, 10*(2), 31–43. DOI: 10.2307/1602688 PMID: 11255707

Wartella, E., & Reeves, B. (1985). Historical Trends in Research on Children and the Media: 1900–1960. *Journal of Communication, 35*(2), 118–133. DOI: 10.1111/j.1460-2466.1985.tb02238.x

Webster, J. G., & Ksiazek, T. B. (2012). The Dynamics of Audience Fragmentation: Public Attention in an Age of Digital Media. *Journal of Communication, 62*(1), 39–56. DOI: 10.1111/j.1460-2466.2011.01616.x

Weeks, B. E., Ardèvol-Abreu, A., & Gil de Zúñiga, H. (2017). Online influence? Social media use, opinion leadership, and political persuasion. *International Journal of Public Opinion Research, 29*(2), 214–239.

Weerasinghe, K., & Wijethunga, C. (2022). Child Influencers in the Creator Economy – The Good, the Bad and the Ugly. *ACIS 2022 - Australasian Conference on Information Systems, Proceedings.*

Weichert, S. A. (2008). Krisen als Medienereignisse: Zur Ritualisierung mediatisierter Kommunikation im Fernsehen. In Winter, C., Hepp, A., & Krotz, F. (Eds.), *Medien - Kultur - Kommunikation. Theorien der Kommunikations- und Medienwissenschaft: Grundlegende Diskussion, Forschungsfelder und Theorieentwicklungen* (pp. 311–328). VS Verl. für Sozialwissenschaften. DOI: 10.1007/978-3-531-90778-9_16

Weimann, G. (2016). *Terrorism in cyberspace: The next generation*. Woodrow Wilson Center Press., DOI: 10.7312/weim17172

Wei, X., Kumar, N., & Zhang, H. (2025). Addressing bias in generative AI: Challenges and research opportunities in information management. *Information & Management, 62*(2), 62. DOI: 10.1016/j.im.2025.104103

Wenger-Trayner, É., McDermott, R. A., & Snyder, W. (2010). *Cultivating communities of practice: A guide to managing knowledge* [Nachdr.]. Harvard Business School Press.

Wertham, F. (1954). V The Curse or the Comic Books: The value patterns and effects of comic books. *Religious Education (Chicago, Ill.)*, *49*(6), 394–406. DOI: 10.1080/0034408540490605

Westerlund, M., Leminen, S., & Habib, C. (2018). Key Constructs and a Definition of Living Labs as Innovation Platforms. *Technology Innovation Management Review*, *8*(12), 51–62. DOI: 10.22215/timreview/1205

Wettstein, M. (2019). YouTube and the rising trend of indigenous folk dance: The case of the sakela dance of the Rai in Nepal and their diaspora. In *Media*. Indigeneity and Nation in South Asia., DOI: 10.4324/9780429424649-12

White & Case. (2025). *The global dash to regulate AI.* AI Watch: Global regulatory tracker—United States. https://www.whitecase.com/insight-our-thinking/ai-watch-global-regulatory-tracker

White, J., Fu, Q., Hays, S., Sandborn, M., Olea, C., Gilbert, H., Elnashar, A., Spencer-Smith, J., & Schmidt, D. C. (2023). A prompt pattern catalog to enhance prompt engineering with ChatGPT. arXiv. https://doi.org//arXiv.2302.11382DOI: 10.48550

Willerton, R. (2015). *Plain language and ethical action.* ATTW/Routledge. DOI: 10.4324/9781315796956

Williams, J. (2018). *Stand out of our light: Freedom and resistance in the attention economy*. Cambridge University Press. DOI: 10.1017/9781108453004

Wineburg, S., Breakstone, J., McGrew, S., Smith, M. D., & Ortega, T. (2022). Lateral reading on the open internet: A district-wide field study in high school government classes. *Journal of Educational Psychology*, *114*(5), 893–909. DOI: 10.1037/edu0000740

Wineburg, S., & McGrew, S. (2017, Oct 6). Lateral reading: Reading less and learning more when evaluating digital information. *SSRN*, *121*. DOI: 10.2139/ssrn.3048994

Winstone, L., Mars, B., Haworth, C. M. A., & Kidger, J. (2021). Social media use and social connectedness among adolescents in the United Kingdom: A qualitative exploration of displacement and stimulation. *BMC Public Health*, *21*(1), 1736. DOI: 10.1186/s12889-021-11802-9 PMID: 34560872

Winter, C. [Charlie], Neumann, P., Meleagrou-Hitchens, A., Ranstorp, M., Vidino, L., & Fürst, J. (2020). Online Extremism: Research Trends in Internet Activism, Radicalization, and Counter-Strategies. *International Journal of Conflict and Violence (IJCV), 14*(2), 1–20. DOI: 10.4119/ijcv-3809

Wissing, C., & Häseler-Bestmann, S. (2022). Engagement im Digitalen Raum. Ein interdisziplinärer Blick auf Chancen und Risiken. In Bush, A., & Birke, J. (Eds.), *Nachhaltigkeit und Social Media* (pp. 17–35). Springer Fachmedien Wiesbaden., DOI: 10.1007/978-3-658-35660-6_2

Wojcik, S., Hilgard, S., Judd, N., Mocanu, D., Ragain, S., Hunzaker, M. B. F., Coleman, K., & Baxter, J. (2022, October 27). *Birdwatch: Crowd Wisdom and Bridging Algorithms can Inform Understanding and Reduce the Spread of Misinformation.* http://arxiv.org/pdf/2210.15723

Woods, H. C., & Scott, H. (2016). #Sleepyteens: Social media use in adolescence is associated with poor sleep quality, anxiety, depression, and low self-esteem. *Journal of Adolescence*, *51*(1), 41–49. DOI: 10.1016/j.adolescence.2016.05.008 PMID: 27294324

Worth, K. (2018, Mar 23). Mailings to teachers highlight a political fight over climate change in the classroom. *PBS Frontline.* https://www.pbs.org/wgbh/frontline/article/mailings-to-teachers-highlight-a-political-fight-over-climate-change-in-the-classroom/

Wright, M. R. (2009). *Introducing Greek Philosophy.* Routledge. DOI: 10.1017/UPO9781844654390

Wu, J. (2011). Improving the writing of research papers: IMRAD and beyond. *Landscape Ecology*, *26*(10), 1345–1349. DOI: 10.1007/s10980-011-9674-3

Wuyckens, G., Landry, N., & Fastrez, P. (2022). Untangling media literacy, information literacy, and digital literacy: A systematic meta-review of core concepts in media education. *The Journal of Media Literacy Education*, *14*(1), 168–182. DOI: 10.23860/JMLE-2022-14-1-12

Xu, T. (2024). From recorded to AI-generated instructional videos: A comparison of learning performance and experience. *British Journal of Educational Technology.*

Yigit, M. F., & Tarman, B. (2013). The Impact of Social Media on Globalization, Democratization, and Participative Citizenship, Journal of Social Science Education, JSSE 2013, Volume 12, ISSN-1618-5293.

Younger, I., Goldsmith, M., & Sonenshein, D. A. (2000). *Principles of evidence.* Anderson Publishing Co.

Youyou, W., Kosinski, M., & Stillwell, D. (2015). Computer-based personality judgments are more accurate than those made by humans. *Proceedings of the National Academy of Sciences of the United States of America*, *112*(4), 1036–1040. DOI: 10.1073/pnas.1418680112 PMID: 25583507

Yue, M., Jong, M. S. Y., & Dai, Y. (2022). Pedagogical design of K-12 artificial intelligence education: A systematic review. *Sustainability (Basel), 14*(23), 15620. DOI: 10.3390/su142315620

Yuvaraja, N., & Perumandla, S. (2023). Financial knowledge and online payment decisions of Generation Z consumers: An empirical study using SEM approach. *International Journal of Process Management and Benchmarking, 15*(2), 198–217. DOI: 10.1504/IJPMB.2023.133153

Zabel, I. (2017). *The teacher-friendly guide to climate change*. Paleontological Research Institution.

Zettl, H. (1998). Contextual media aesthetics as the basis for media literacy. *Journal of Communication, 48*(1), 81–95. DOI: 10.1111/j.1460-2466.1998.tb02739.x

Zettl, H. (2016). *Sight, sound, motion* (8th ed.). Wadsworth.

Zhang, H. (2022). Contextual Factors behind Audience Engagement Behaviours of YouTube Vloggers: A Case Study. *9th European Conference on Social Media, ECSM 2022*, 284–287. DOI: 10.34190/ecsm.9.1.105

Zhang, Y., & Gosline, R. (2023). Human favoritism, not AI aversion: People's perceptions (and bias) toward Generative AI, human experts, and human–GAI collaboration in persuasive content generation. *Judgment and Decision Making, 18*, e41. DOI: 10.1017/jdm.2023.37

Zhao, L., Liang, C., & Gu, D. (2021). Mobile Social Media Use and Trailing Parents' Life Satisfaction: Social Capital and Social Integration Perspective. *International Journal of Aging & Human Development, 92*(3), 383–405. DOI: 10.1177/0091415020905549 PMID: 32098476

Zhitomirsky-Geffet, M., & Blau, M. (2016). Cross-generational analysis of predictive factors of addictive behavior in smartphone usage. *Computers in Human Behavior, 64*, 682–693. DOI: 10.1016/j.chb.2016.07.061

Ziegele, M., & Heinbach, D. (2021). *Hallo liebe Community! Konstruktive Online-Debatten fördern durch bestärkende Moderation*. www.medienanstalt-nrw.de/fileadmin/user_upload/NeueWebsite_0120/Zum_Nachlesen/WhitePaper_HalloLiebeCommunity_DIGITAL_210518.pdf

Ziemer, C. T., & Rothmund, T. (2024). Psychological underpinnings of misinformation countermeasures: A systematic scoping review. *Journal of Media Psychology, 36*(6), 397–409. DOI: 10.1027/1864-1105/a000407

Zlateva, P. (2024). A conceptual framework for solving ethical issues in generative artificial intelligence. In *Electronics, Communications and Networks* (pp. 110–119). IOS Press. DOI: 10.3233/FAIA231182

Zollo, F., Bessi, A., Del Vicario, M., Scala, A., Caldarelli, G., Shekhtman, L., Havlin, S., & Quattrociocchi, W. (2017). Debunking in a world of tribes. *PLoS One*, *12*(7), e0181821. DOI: 10.1371/journal.pone.0181821 PMID: 28742163

About the Contributors

Tom Hallaq is a media literacy researcher and documentary filmmaker. He is the creator of the Digital Online Media Literacy Assessment (DOMLA), a self-assessment tool employed globally to gauge media literacy among students from middle school to university levels. He currently serves as an associate professor on the faculty of the A.Q. Miller School of Media and Communication at Kansas State University. Dr. Hallaq's professional background includes extensive experience in live television production and direction. He began his career as a key member of the startup news team for KSTU Fox 13 in Salt Lake City, UT. Additionally, he has worked as a News Operations Manager for WDEF-TV, CBS, in Chattanooga, TN, and for KNDU-TV, NBC, in Kennewick, WA. As an award-winning documentary filmmaker, Dr. Hallaq focuses on issues affecting Kansans. His 2016 documentary, Slow & Low: The story of the Kansas ag. pilot, highlights the lives of agricultural pilots, formerly known as crop dusters, and received multiple awards, including a Telly Award and an Aegis Award. In 2021, he collaborated with the late Dr. Ian Punnett to produce *The Empty Breadbasket: When the Land That Feeds the Nation Cannot Feed Itself*, a documentary that explores food access challenges in rural Kansas and celebrates community-driven solutions. This work earned a Silver Telly Award. Dr. Hallaq holds a Bachelor of Arts (B.A.) in Communications from Brigham Young University, a Master of Education (M.Ed.) in Instructional Media and Technology from Eastern Washington University and a Doctor of Education (Ed.D.) in Educational Leadership with a focus on Instructional Methods and Design from Idaho State University where he was also on the faculty as an Assistant Professor. Theoretically speaking, Dr. Hallaq is a constructivist, promoting the idea that learning is most effective when concepts are applied to real-life situations to build new knowledge. His research and creative interests encompass media literacy, media accessibility, and documentary storytelling.

Jacob Groshek has a long list of research, teaching, and industry appointments, which currently include Executive Director of the newly-formed Institute for Representation in Society and Media, the Chair of Emerging Media at Kansas State University, and as President of Metro Boston NFL Flag Football. He is also affiliated faculty with the Department of Communication and Arts at Roskilde University (Denmark) and served as Associate Director of the Center for Mobile Communication Studies at Boston University. In addition, he has also been a leading Digital Experience Management consultant at the International Data Corporation and member of the faculty at Boston University (tenured), the Toulouse School of Economics (France), the University of Melbourne (Australia), and Erasmus University (The Netherlands). He earned his Ph.D. in media research at Indiana University Bloomington, where he specialized in applied analytics for international, political, and health communication networks and advanced econometric methods. Topically, his areas of expertise now address online and mobile media technologies as their use may relate to sociopolitical and behavioral health change at the macro (i.e., national) and micro (as in individual) levels. His work also includes analyses of sports and media marketing content along with user influence in social media campaigns that drive engagement, participation, and revenue. Put simply, He puts his academic research to the test everyday with media marketing analytics efforts that build programs and drive millions in ongoing, annual revenue across industry verticals. His research makes it easy deploy and engage a blend of interpretive as well as relatively advanced AI-driven statistical tools for network analysis, forecasting, and explaining where and how the use of media has shaped public opinion and global events, in particular as it relates to political and health decision making.

***

Prasanth A. P. Assistant Professor, Dept. of Commerce and Management, School of Arts, Humanities & Commerce, Kochi | Research Supervisor, Dept. of Commerce and Management, School of Arts, Humanities & Commerce, Kochi Qualification: B.Ed., MCom, NET-JRF, Ph.D Research Interest: Entrepreneurship Development, Tourism, Financial Management, Human Resource Management & Green Marketing I currently serve as an Assistant Professor at the Department of Commerce and Management, School of Arts, Humanities & Commerce, Amrita Vishwa Vidyapeetham, Kochi. I am also a member of the Board of Studies for Commerce and BBA programs and guide five Ph.D. candidates at Amrita Vishwa Vidyapeetham in areas including Entrepreneurship Development, Tourism, Green Banking, and Green Marketing. I earned my Ph.D. in Commerce from M.G. University, Kottayam, Kerala. My academic background includes a Master's in Commerce from the University of Calicut and a Bachelor of Education from M.G. University. I have 14 years of teaching experience and four years of research experience. I have delivered invited talks on various topics, including Entrepreneurship Development, Tourism, SPSS, Jamovi, APA refe

Mohd. Aquib Ansari received a B.E. degree in Information Technology from SATI, Vidisha, in 2014. He completed his M.Tech. in Information Technology at MITS, Gwalior 2017. He received his Ph.D. degree from MNNIT Allahabad, Prayagraj, India, in 2022. Currently, he is working as an assistant professor at SCSET, Bennett University, Greater Noida, India. He has published more than 28 research papers in various International Journals and Conferences. His research interests include Computer Vision and Image Processing, Block Chain Technologies, Artificial Intelligence and Machine Learning.

Neelendra Badal is presently working as Director in REC Bijnor and also working as Professor in KNIT Sultanpur in the CSE department. He has completed his bachelor of engineering from BIET Jhansi in 1997. And he completed his master of engineering from MITS Gwalior in 2001. And he completed his PHD from MNNIT Allahabad in 2009. He has published nearly 50 papers in reputated journals in India and abroad. He attended many national and international conferences and publish qualitative paper which is improve the qualitative education of the computer science. His interesting research area are Image and Video processing, Distributed system, big data, data mining, data ware housing and networking. He is also guiding several U.G., P.G and Ph.D. as a domain expert.

Nicklas Bang Bådum, Senior Project Manager and Team Leader. MSc in International Business and Politics. Nicklas is team leader for 'Digitalisation and AI' and has more than 10 years of experience in planning, coordinating and executing national and international engagement processes on highly complex topics and is also an experienced facilitator. He specialises in the areas of AI, new technology, research and innovation, and data security and privacy.

Barbara Ruth Burke is an Associate Professor at the University of Minnesota Morris. Her research explores online community building, and the reciprocal nature of media messages and ideas about identity. Burke earned her MA in Telecommunication Arts from the University of Michigan, and her MA and PhD in American Studies from Purdue University. Burke has worked in mass media, taught at Ivy Tech Community College (Indiana), and has been a Guest Instructor at the University of Iceland, and a Fulbright Scholar at Vidzeme University of Applied Sciences, in Latvia. OCRID 0000-0002-9906-448X

Edward L. Carter is a journalist, lawyer and Brigham Young University professor of communications. He has authored dozens of academic journal articles on media law and related topics. He has taught at BYU since 2004. Carter completed Fulbright Grants in Colombia and Chile. He enjoys traveling internationally with students. He has represented journalists and others in state and federal courts. He holds degrees from BYU, Northwestern University, the University of Edinburgh and Oxford University.

Ron Cole pays rigorous attention to emerging technologies, ensuring an integration of technological solutions into the grant writing framework. He works in professional writing and communication. His activities include assisting nonprofit organizations in the southwestern Ohio region with developing proposals and other aspects of the grant process. He has been the primary grant writer for awarded proposals totaling millions of dollars from grantors including the Federal Government, public foundations, and regional entities. He is also an instructor of scientific and technical writing at the University of Cincinnati.

Francesca Cubeddu, is a research fellow at the Institute for Research on Population and Social Policies (IRPPS) of the National Research Council (CNR). She is a lecturer at the University of Salerno and the Higher Institute of Religious Sciences (Bologna) of the Theological Faculty of Emilia-Romagna. Recent publications include: Culture, Communication, Resilience. La società tra rischi, crisi ed emergenze, Paolo Loffredo Editore (Naples), 2024.

Edward De Vooght, PhD is a senior researcher at Artevelde University of Applied Sciences with expertise in Critical Thinking with a background in Communication Sciences. His work focuses primarily on how interventions and media products shape critical attitudes in young citizens to increase the democratic public sphere.

Aline Duelen is a PhD Candidate researching the engagement of vulnerable citizens in participatory research for new technology development.

Panos Kapetanakis has studied philosophy and psychology, and holds a PhD in Philosophy from the University of Edinburgh. He has worked as a Researcher on Visual Argumentation, Archelogos Projects (University of Edinburgh) for over a decade. He is currently a researcher at NCSR Demokritos.

Adam J. Kuban is a professor in the School of Journalism & Strategic Communication and an affiliate faculty member of the Honors College at Ball State University. Before his arrival in Indiana, he attained both Bachelor and Master of

Science degrees from Iowa State University. The former included a double major in meteorology and journalism and mass communication and the latter in journalism and mass communication. His Ph.D. comes from the Department of Communication at the University of Utah. He has taught for 20 years as the solo instructor of record for an array of media-oriented courses such as News Reporting, Writing, & Editing; Multimedia Storytelling; Mass Communication Theory; Career Readiness & Freelance; Fundamentals of Sports Content Creation; and Leadership & Media. In that time, he has earned teaching awards from Iowa State (in 2007), from Utah (in 2010) and from Ball State (in 2015 and in 2021).

Lalit Kumar is working as an Assistant Professor in Acharya Narendra Deva University of Agriculture and Technology, Ayodhya in Computer Science and Engineering department. He has two years of academic experience. He is currently working in the application domains of Image and Video generation. He is also guiding several U.G. and P.G as a domain expert. Her research interests include Artificial Intelligence, Computer Vision and Generative AI.

Lauren Maher's extensive experience securing grants and contracts for emergency management and human services initiatives enriches the textbook with valuable tactics for persuading grant-making organizations. Maher has worked in emergency management in public and private sectors since 2005. Starting as a technical writer for the Texas A&M University's National Emergency Response and Rescue Training Center, she became Chief of Staff for the Texas Division of Emergency Management before transitioning to the private non-profit sector. She has led proposal teams and been the primary proposal writer for awarded state and federal grants, cooperative agreements, and contracts for emergency management and health and human services programs.

Arvind Mewada is an accomplished academic and researcher in the field of Computer Science and Engineering. He serves as an Assistant Professor at the School of Computer Science Engineering and Technology at Bennett University. With a strong background in advanced computing technologies, he has contributed significantly to research and education. Dr. Mewada recently submitted his Ph.D. thesis at MNNIT Allahabad in 2023, showcasing his expertise in the domain. His work focuses on emerging areas in computer science, and he is dedicated to fostering innovation and knowledge among students and researchers.

Eirini Papachristou holds a degree in Psychology from the University of Athens and is currently pursuing postgraduate training as a psychotherapist (arts and play-based approaches). Has also worked as an assistant researcher at NCSR

Demokritos, contributing to various projects, including those funded by HORIZON and ERC programs.

Ioannis Elissaios Paparrigopoulos holds a BA in History and Philosophy of Science from the National and Kapodistrian University of Athens, a Master's degree in International Relations from Goldsmiths University of London and an MLitt degree in Transnational, Global and Spatial History from the University of St. Andrews. His main research interests revolve around the digital humanities, AI & disinformation, as well as historical mapmaking and cartography. He is currently working as a research assistant in the Institute of Informatics and Telecommunications (ITT) at the National Center for Scientific Research "Demokritos".

Lucia Picarella, PhD. is an Associate Professor of Sociology of Culture and Communication at the Social Sciences Department of University of Foggia (Italy). From 2013 to January 2025, she was Senior Researcher and Full Professor at the Law Faculty of the Universidad Católica de Colombia (Bogotá, Colombia). From 2008 to 2013, she was Adjunct Professor at the Faculty of Political Science of the University of Salerno (Italy). Her main research interests: communication processes and new digital technologies, culture and critical education, edu-communication.

Ike Picone is Associate Professor Media and Journalism Studies at the Department of Communication Sciences at the Vrije Universiteit Brussel (VUB). He heads the News: Uses, Strategies & Engagements research unit of research group imec-SMIT, VUB (Studies on Media, Innovation and Technology). His research is situated at the crossroads of Journalism Studies and Audience Research. The common thread within his research is the study of evolutions in news use. More concretely, he is interested in how news users constitute different news repertoires, and how these news repertoires are socially constructed. He combines this with the study of specific participatory practices, conceptualised as small acts of engagements. He mostly takes an ethnographic approach to news use, exploring also new methodological pathways to news uses such as data donations and user tracking, while looking at quantitative surveys such as the Digital News Report.

Stephen Price, Jr. is a Professor at the University of Central Missouri and has worked in the media industry for almost 30 years. He started out in Sports Radio, but has since produced TV News, Commercials, Music Videos, Corporate Videos, and Documentary Films. He was the President of the Missouri Broadcast Educators Association for 6 years, and has been the Chair of the Production Aesthetics and Criticism Division of the national BEA organization. He's been teaching for over 20 years across four different Universities, with classes that cover every type of video production, including Scriptwriting, Cinematography, Video Editing, Documentary Film Production, and Corporate and Freelance Production.

Rich Rice is Professor of English at Texas Tech University where he researches grant and proposal writing, service-learning, intercultural communication, and rhetoric. He teaches writing for nonprofits, for businesses and organizations, and for scholars and academic programs. He also serves as TTU Director of the Center for Global Communication. See https://richrice.com.

Iranna Ronad, having completed his Master's in Social Work, makes significant contributions to social work education. As an academic with over a decade of experience in teaching and research, Ronad brings invaluable insights and practical experience from his prior work as a social worker and counselor in the development sector. He shares this expertise with his students, enriching their learning. Additionally, he is a dedicated academic writer with 30 publications to his credit. Ronad's passion lies in counseling, professional social work, and social development. He significantly contributes to the theoretical and practical facets of social work education by actively mentoring students at the graduate and postgraduate levels, fostering a dynamic learning environment.

Wendy Van den Broeck is Associate Professor in communication sciences at Vrije Universiteit Brussel. She is head of the Media, Marketing and User Experience unit and senior researcher within the imec-smit research group. Her main research expertise is in the domain of personalised and immersive media. She also has an interest in research methodology and focuses mainly on living lab research and user research methods to foster media innovation.

Index

A

B

C

D

N

P

R

S

T

U

Y

www.ingramcontent.com/pod-product-compliance
Ingram Content Group UK Ltd.
Pitfield, Milton Keynes, MK11 3LW, UK
UKHW050843101026
15624UKWH00018B/470

9 798337 308722